Betty Comden
and Adolph Green

Betty Comden and Adolph Green attend a reading of one of their musicals in the 1970s. Photograph courtesy of The Billy Rose Theatre Collection, The New York Public Library for the Performing Arts, Astor, Lenox and Tilden Foundations.

CONTENTS

Photographs	ix
Preface and Acknowledgments	xi
Biography of Betty Comden and Adolph Green	1
Chronology	45
Stage Musicals for Which Comden and Green Wrote Both the Book and the Lyrics	51
A Revue for Which Comden and Green Wrote Both the Sketches and the Lyrics	91
Stage Musicals for Which Comden and Green Wrote the Lyrics Only	95
Stage Musicals for Which Comden and Green Wrote the Book Only	121
Musicals and Revues for Which Comden and Green Contributed Lyrics	133
Retrospections of Stage Musicals	143
Films for Which Comden and Green Wrote the Screenplay and/or the Lyrics	149
Comden and Green as Performers	199
Other Performances by Comden and Green Both on Stage and in Films	205

Radio Programs Presented by The Revuers	211
Television Appearances of Comden and Green	215
Comden and Green Musicals Presented on Television	223
Discography	227
Bibliography	253
Appendix: Awards, Nominations, and Honors	271
Index	277

Betty Comden and Adolph Green
A Bio-Bibliography

Alice M. Robinson

Bio-Bibliographies in the Performing Arts, Number 45

Greenwood Press
Westport, Connecticut • London

Library of Congress Cataloging-in-Publication Data

Robinson, Alice M.
  Betty Comden and Adolph Green : a bio-bibliography / Alice M. Robinson.
    p. cm.—(Bio-bibliographies in the performing arts, ISSN 0892-5550 ; no. 45)
  Includes bibliographical references and index.
  Discography: p.
  ISBN 0-313-27659-5 (alk. paper)
  1. Comden, Betty—Bibliography. 2. Green, Adolph—Bibliography.
  3. Comden, Betty. 4. Green, Adolph. 5. Librettists—United States—Biography.   I. Title. II. Series.
ML134.5.C66R6   1994
782.1'4'0922—dc20
  [B]   93-21050

British Library Cataloguing in Publication Data is available.

Copyright © 1994 by Alice M. Robinson

All rights reserved. No portion of this book may be reproduced, by any process or technique, without the express written consent of the publisher.

Library of Congress Catalog Card Number: 93-21050
ISBN: 0-313-27659-5
ISSN: 0892-5550

First published in 1994

Greenwood Press, 88 Post Road West, Westport, CT 06881
An imprint of Greenwood Publishing Group, Inc.

Printed in the United States of America

The paper used in this book complies with the Permanent Paper Standard issued by the National Information Standards Organization (Z39.48-1984).

P

> In order to keep this title in print and available to the academic community, this edition was produced using digital reprint technology in a relatively short print run. This would not have been attainable using traditional methods. Although the cover has been changed from its original appearance, the text remains the same and all materials and methods used still conform to the highest book-making standards.

In memory of my husband,

James Eugene Robinson

PHOTOGRAPHS

1.	The Revuers: Judy Tuvim (Holliday), Betty Comden, Alvin Hammer, John Frank, and Adolph Green	7
2.	Betty Comden, Adolph Green, Leonard Bernstein, and Jerome Robbins writing *On the Town*, 1944	12
3.	Betty Comden as Claire, the anthropologist, and Adolph Green, as Ozzie, one of the three sailors, in the museum scene in *On the Town*, 1944	13
4.	Betty Comden and Adolph Green in their 1958 production of *A Party With Betty Comden and Adolph Green*	25
5.	Phyllis Newman and Adolph Green at the time of their wedding in 1960	27
6.	In 1960 Betty Comden, Adolph Green, and Leonard Bernstein get together to record *On The Town*, which had not been recorded by the original cast in 1944	32
7.	Betty Comden and her husband, Steven Kyle, on their 25th wedding anniversary, 1967	36
8.	Betty Comden at the time of the first production of *A Party With Betty Comden and Adolph Green*, 1958	197
9.	Adolph Green at the time of the first production of *A Party With Betty Comden and Adolph Green*, 1958	198

PREFACE AND ACKNOWLEDGMENTS

This is the story of Betty Comden and Adolph Green--playwrights, lyricists, screenwriters, performers--who for over fifty years have collaborated on skits, musicals, revues, and films. As a team they occupy a unique place in stage and screen history. They have worked together since 1938 and neither of them has written a lyric, a libretto, or a screenplay without the other. In their contracts they are treated as one person, and one is seldom mentioned without the other. Comden and Green are magical words on Broadway.

On December 6, 1991, Betty Comden and Adolph Green were given America's highest tribute for those in the performing arts when they received the Kennedy Center Award for Lifetime Achievement in the Performing Arts. Former and present performers in Comden and Green musicals and films were there to pay tribute to them. Keith Carradine and the chorus of *The Will Rogers Follies*, currently running on Broadway, Gene Kelly, film star of *On the Town* and *Singin' in the Rain*, Lauren Bacall of the Broadway musical *Applause*, Carol Burnett of *Fade Out--Fade In*, and Phyllis Newman of *Subways Are For Sleeping* were all present to attest to their contributions to musical theatre. Mike Nichols, performer and director, introduced scenes from their films and called the work from their partnership of fifty years "a legacy of joy."

In the 1930s Betty Comden and Adolph Green were young and ambitious would-be actors, who, when they could not get jobs in the professional theatre, created their own theatre act in a cellar club in Greenwich Village. With three other frustrated actors they began to write and perform their own material. Known as The Revuers, the five clever young people worked together for nearly five years. Upon the promise of an appearance in a film, four of them went to Hollywood. But the scenes they did ended up on the cutting room floor. Only Judy Tuvim (later Judy Holliday) was given a film contract. Betty and Adolph returned, dejected, to New York. The two of them continued with their clever, satirical Revuers act at the Blue Angel. There they were sought out by an old friend, Leonard Bernstein, to write the book for a musical inspired by Bernstein and Jerome Robbins' ballet *Fancy Free*. The result was *On the Town* (1944). *On the Town* was an immediate success and today is considered a classic. Since then Comden and Green have collaborated on sixteen musicals or revues for Broadway. For some they have written both the book and the lyrics, for others just the lyrics, and for two just the book. A second trip to Hollywood in the late 1940s was more successful than the first and resulted in their writing the screenplay or the lyrics for ten films. They always returned to New York between films to write for the theatre. They have contributed lyrics to other musicals and have even performed on Broadway themselves in *A Party With Betty Comden and Adolph Green* (1958 and 1977).

Betty Comden and Adolph Green have had a remarkable collaboration that has lasted for nearly fifty-five years. The number of successful musicals and films that they have written is astounding. Underlying the usual humor and optimism of their shows, is a brilliant intelligence and a sure knowledge of their craft. Their stories revolve around well-developed characters, and the songs come directly from those characters. Though Comden and Green are at their best writing humorous and satiric songs, they also have written beautiful love songs and songs of loneliness and sadness, as in one of their most popular songs, written for their friend, Judy Holliday, in *Bells Are Ringing* (1956), "The Party's Over."

"We write with humor about basically serious things," Betty Comden has said. "We like to think we're expressing something of ourselves, something of what we feel is important in the world today. At the same time, we try to help audiences feel the way they should when they leave the theatre--that is, glad to be alive. That windows have been opened, fresh air has been let in, and they're leaving as happy people" ("Betty Comden and Adolph Green," in Al Kasha and Joel Hirschhorn, *Notes on Broadway*, p. 73).

THE FORMAT OF THIS BOOK

This book is intended as a complete reference to the career of Betty Comden and Adolph Green. The book begins with a biography and a chronology that serves as a summary of the major events of their lives and their career. After that there are six sections on their works for the Broadway theatre. The first of these is a detailed account of the musicals for which they wrote both the book and the lyrics. The second section is about their only Broadway revue, *Two on the Aisle* (1951). The third section is about the musicals for which they wrote only the lyrics, and the fourth is about the musicals for which they wrote only the book. The fifth section gives a brief review of the musicals for which Comden and Green contributed additional lyrics. All of these stage musicals are numbered S01, S02, etc. The sixth section summarizes the retrospections of their stage musicals, numbered R01, R02, etc. Following these six sections, there is a section giving detailed information about all of the films for which they wrote either or both the screenplay and the lyrics. The films are numbered F01, F02, etc. An additional section of the book discusses Comden and Green as performers and includes an account of their *A Party With Betty Comden and Adolph Green* (1958 and 1977) and some of the recent acting they have been doing both on the stage and in films. These performances are numbered P01, P02, etc.

These more detailed sections are followed by a listing of Comden and Green's appearances on radio numbered RA01, RA02, etc. There follows a listing of their television appearances and their musicals which have been shown on television. These are numbered T01, T02, etc. There is also a discography which lists the record albums that have been made of their musicals and films. These are numbered D01, D02, etc. These listings are followed by a bibliography and an appendix that gives the awards and nominations that Comden and Green and their works have received. Finally, there is a very detailed index listing names, musical, film, and song titles, theatres, reviews, awards, etc.

ACKNOWLEDGMENTS

I should like to thank Ms. Comden and Mr. Green who have read the manuscript for this book. They have corrected some errors that had previously been published, and they have suggested some additions of their own. I should like to acknowledge two biographies of Judy Holliday, which were very useful in providing information about The Revuers: *Judy Holliday* by Will Holtzman (1982) and *Judy Holliday, An Intimate Life Story* by Gary Carey (1982). Also, for more personal information about Betty Comden and Adolph Green, I am indebted to biographies of Leonard Bernstein and to Phyllis Newman's autobiography, *Just in Time*. I should like to thank Robert Petza of Baltimore for his interest and cooperation. Mr. Petza is a collector of record albums and has in his possession nearly every album that has been made of both the performances by Comden and Green themselves and the original cast recordings of their musicals. He has gladly shared these records with me. Brad Bennett of Los Angeles, also a record collector, has helped me to list some of the more obscure recordings. I should also like to thank Mr. Milton Terry Cobb and Ms. Elizabeth Hutton for their help in explaining to me the intricacies of my new computer.

Betty Comden and Adolph Green

BIOGRAPHY OF
BETTY COMDEN AND ADOLPH GREEN

Adolph Green was born in the Bronx, New York, on December 2, 1914. His parents were Daniel and Helen (Weiss) Green. The family was of Hungarian descent. Adolph had two brothers. One was to become an engineer and the other a doctor. Even in grammar school Adolph wrote poetry and acted in plays at school and at summer camps. He loved music, and he and his friends frequently attended musical concerts. Though he was not really musically trained, he had a phenomenal musical memory.

Adolph attended DeWitt Clinton High School and graduated from there in 1934. He began attending some college classes but dropped out after only a few days. He did not find what he wanted to learn. His heart was in the theatre. He began looking for work as an actor. To support himself he took various jobs in New York City. For a while he was a runner on Wall Street. He also worked for a carpet company, measuring rooms for new carpeting. At night he worked with little theatre groups.

Betty Comden was born Betty Cohen in Brooklyn, New York, on May 3, 1917. Her parents were Leo and Rebecca (Sadvoransky) Cohen. Her father was a lawyer and her mother an English teacher. Betty had piano lessons as a child. From the age of eight she was taken to the opera.

When Betty was eleven years old she was cast as Rebecca in a seventh-grade dramatization of Sir Walter Scott's *Ivanhoe*. Her school was the Brooklyn Ethical Culture School located in two old Brooklyn mansions on Prospect Park West. The dramatization had been made by the class, who, under the direction of their teacher, Miss Della A. Stebbins, had read and re-read the novel. They had found the story line, examined the characters, and broken the book into sections for dramatizing. They had learned how to turn prose into dialogue and how to construct scenes. It was Betty's first experience with dramatic structure and also with collaboration. For *Ivanhoe* she worked with twelve partners. Putting things into dramatic form was much in favor as a means of teaching at the Ethical Culture School, and Betty Comden was one child who greatly profited from the experience. For years she had been "dressing up" in her mother's discarded clothes and parading around the house as a character other than herself, but the performance of *Ivanhoe* in a library near the school brought Betty her first triumph as an "actress." The families, friends, faculty, and students who witnessed the performance were enthusiastic, and Betty experienced that wonderful feeling of being loved by the audience (Betty Comden, "So Eat Your Heart Out, Elizabeth Taylor," *New York Times*, March 31, 1985).

Betty Comden went to Erasmus Hall High School where she continued to write, but rather than participate in the high school plays she began to hang out at the Clay Club in Greenwich Village. After graduating from high school, Betty attended New York University. She majored in drama and took some education courses so that she might be able to teach drama in high school. However, she did not complete her required education courses. She graduated with a Bachelor of Science degree in drama in 1938.

Upon graduation, Betty began acting in theatre groups. In the summer of 1938 she worked with the Studio Players who were performing at Guild Hall in East Hampton. She appeared in their first play of the season, *The Warrior's Husband*, playing Pomposia. The next week she played Irene Hibbard in *First Lady*. A reviewer for the *Hampton Star* wrote that she had "an exciting power and a command of her role that must far exceed her years of experience." The reviewer called her "an all around actress, with unusual talent" (August 11, 1938). Later in the summer she played Miss Prism in *The Importance of Being Earnest* and took the leading role of Julie in Ferenc Molnar's *Liliom*. Betty also dabbled in sculpture at this time and even exhibited and sold some of her work. But her real love was the theatre. At last she did get a small part in a subway-circuit production of *Having Wonderful Time*, a play that had been a Broadway hit during the 1937-1938 season.

In the summer of 1937 Adolph Green was asked to play the Pirate King in a production of *The Pirates of Penzance* at a boys' summer camp, Camp Onata, near Pittsfield, Massachusetts. That summer Camp Onata had hired a young Harvard music student as the music counselor for the camp. The young student was Leonard Bernstein. He had decided to do a Gilbert and Sullivan operetta for the camp. Friends of Bernstein told him about Adolph Green. They told him that Adolph was not only an actor but also had a vast knowledge of music and could sing nearly any work in the concert repertoire. When Adolph arrived at the camp, Bernstein could hardly wait to play a practical joke on him. He sat down at the piano and mentioned a Shostakovich prelude. Green asked, "Which one?" "This one," Bernstein replied and played a series of dissonances. Green said that he could not place any such Shostakovich prelude. Bernstein was delighted. He had tried the trick before, and everyone else had "recognized" the music. From then on Leonard Bernstein and Adolph Green were the best of friends (John Briggs, *Leonard Bernstein*, p. 35).

Leonard Bernstein and Adolph were entranced with each other's sense of humor and knowledge of music. Bernstein's younger brother, Burton, has written that Adolph, though he had no formal musical training, was "capable of performing--a capella and with every orchestral instrument outrageously imitated--just about any symphonic work, classical or modern, down to its last cymbal crash" (Burton Bernstein, *Family Matters*, p. 126).

The Bernstein family had a large red brick house in Newton, Massachusetts, and a red-shingled cottage in Sharon. Green was occasionally invited to visit the cottage in Sharon. There, Lenny and Adolph would sit around for hours quizzing each other on musical trivia, or inventing musical parodies. Sam Bernstein, Lenny's father, was a businessman who did not understand his son's interest in music. He would pace the house asking his wife, "Who is that nut? I want him out of my house!" Later, both Sam Bernstein and his wife Jennie were to have a genuine affection for Adolph (Burton Bernstein, *Family Matters*, p. 126).

After playing the Pirate King, Adolph returned to New York. Unable to find a theatre job, he joined with a group of other young hopefuls, which later included Betty Comden, to do short plays and scenes and songs in a loft. The group was called Six and Company. In the summer of 1938, while Betty was performing in East Hampton, a few of the Six and Company actors took a short job at a summer camp near the Massachusetts border. In the late 1930s the American economy was still recovering from the Depression, and many people who could not afford to rent a cottage or a hotel room for a summer vacation went to a summer camp. There were many summer camps in the Catskill Mountains or the Berkshires where New Yorkers went to get away from the heat of the city.

The "light entertainment" that the young people from Six and Company provided consisted of some songs, two short non-royalty plays, and a few comedy routines "borrowed" from popular radio shows. Adolph performed and also kept the variety show together. He was energetic and funny on stage. He has described himself at this time. "I was fat and wildly unattractive. I was memorably odd-looking. My clothes were shreddy and ill-fitting. I was matted. But I was terribly polite and terribly shy--except on stage" (quoted by Gary Carey in *Judy Holliday, An Intimate Life Story*, p. 21).

One night during the summer of 1938, there was a shy seventeen year old New York girl named Judy Tuvim in the audience. She was with her mother. Judy was attracted to the clever young Adolph Green, and she stayed after the show to talk with him. She was interested in the theatre and thought that she would some day like to write for the stage or possibly direct. Adolph Green asked Judy Tuvim if she would like to join the group while she was at the camp. Judy was much too shy to act, but she volunteered to help the group with lights or properties. The shy seventeen year old girl found the slightly older, clever Adolph Green, who talked a blue streak, fascinating. When her two weeks were up, Judy and Adolph exchanged telephone numbers and promised to keep in touch.

The next September Judy Tuvim was walking in Greenwich Village in New York. She had on a new white dress, and suddenly it started to rain. Seeking some cover from the rain, she retreated down a stairway. Looking around she discovered that the steps led to a dark basement room that looked like a dive where no nice girl would enter. While she hesitated in the doorway, a short, slight man came over to the door to greet her. This was Max Gordon, the proprietor of the Village Vanguard. He saw that Judy was hesitant to come in . He invited her to come have a cup of coffee and wait for the rain to stop. Judy did venture into the place. The Village Vanguard at 178 Seventh Avenue South in Greenwich Village had been opened by Max Gordon in 1934 in a basement room that had formerly been a speak-easy. The room was dark with some rickety tables and chairs scattered about. At this time, Gordon did not have a liquor license. He served coffee and sodas and people brought their own bottles. The place was frequented by some Village poets who often recited their poetry or that of other poets. Most famous of the poets who frequented the Village Vanguard was Maxwell Bodenheim. On this September afternoon Judy had coffee and talked with Max Gordon, who sat at the table with her. Judy said to Max Gordon that he needed a show for the Vanguard. When he inquired what she meant, she said, "Oh, songs and skits." She said that she knew someone who had such a show. When Max Gordon agreed to let her friends bring their act to the Vanguard for a trial performance, she ran out and called Adolph Green.

Adolph was excited and on the next Sunday evening he and a few from Six and Company performed. The poets whose own readings had been displaced by the show were hostile and so were their followers. Things did not go well for the young actors, and the other Six and Company members did not want to continue at the Village Vanguard. Adolph recruited Alvin Hammer to go with him the next Sunday evening. Al Hammer was about Adolph's age and came from a similar background. He had worked days as a shipping clerk in the garment district so that he could perform at night in little theatre groups. He had acted with the Youth Theatre, worked at the New Theatre School, and recently had been performing monologues at women's clubs, fraternal organizations, and neighborhood nightclubs in Brooklyn, Queens, the Bronx, and on Long Island. He received ten dollars a night for his monologues.

Before his next appearance, Adolph ran into Betty Comden standing in line waiting to audition for *The Boys from Syracuse*. He was just leaving the audition. Betty and Adolph had first met through a mutual friend when Betty was at New York University. Then they had known each other through Six and Company. Betty, tall and dark-haired, seemed cool and reserved, but she had a sly humor that could match that of Adolph Green. She also could play the piano and sing. Betty Comden suggested that John Frank be asked to join the group. John Frank was a friend she had known at New York University and had then met again in Brooklyn when both of them were trying to get parts in plays with the Brattleboro Players. John had worked his way through college by singing with a group called the Peasants' Quartette. He played the piano and the mandolin and guitar.

There were now three men, Adolph, Al Hammer, and John Frank, and one woman, Betty Comden. The four decided they needed another woman--one who was not so aristocratic looking as Betty, preferably a blond. They turned to Judy Tuvim. She insisted that she would help them with lights and props, but she did not want to perform. But there seemed to be no one else, so at last Judy agreed to join the group.

Now the five needed a name. Max Gordon suggested "Judy and the Kids," but Judy objected because their act was a cooperative one. For a few weeks they called themselves "The Vanguarders," but then one of them came up with the name, "The Revuers."

The Village Vanguard was in a long, triangular-shaped basement space. The ceiling was low, and the walls were covered with travel posters and photographs from magazines. The Revuers made a stage by hanging up a length of cheesecloth at one end of the room. Their dressing room was the areaway leading to the ladies' powder room.

The group started out playing one show a week. Their number of shows gradually increased, but their pay did not. They were each paid five dollars a night. They knew they needed new material, but they could not afford to pay royalties. They decided they would have to write their own material. They began to meet in the afternoons to write their new skits and songs. They would meet at a diner on Sixth Avenue and Eighth Street, or often at Judy's mother's flat on 75th Street. They would "brainstorm," each throwing out ideas for subjects to be developed. Betty, using a yellow pad and a pencil, would jot down any possible ideas that she or the others would throw out. When a subject appealed to them, they would improvise on it. They worked cooperatively, and it was later impossible for them to know who had contributed what to their sketches and songs.

At first The Revuers thought they had to have new material every week. While they were performing one week they were writing and rehearsing the next week's show in the afternoons.

The winter of 1938-1939 was one of the coldest on record for New York City. The heat in the Village Vanguard was almost non-existent. So during that winter they began their shows dressed in heavy winter hats and coats. They entered their make-shift stage in a line, each one walking backwards, looking apprehensively at the audience over his shoulder. After they warmed up to their performance they could remove their coats. Because of the terrible winter, the audience at the Village Vanguard was small. One night The Revuers outnumbered the four members of the audience. The Revuers later said that the turning point came one night when a group of men wandered into the place and laughed long and loudly at the sketches and musical numbers. After the show the men asked to meet the cast. One of the men said, "We'll tell everybody in the Erie freight yard about you" (Kyle Crichton, "Musical Express," *Colliers*, November 25, 1939, p. 19, ff). From then on the attendance seemed to pick up.

When people in the audience began calling for old numbers, The Revuers realized that they did not need new material each week. They began to put their best old numbers into one show and run it for a month.

One night Betty and Adolph arrived and found a crowd of people outside the Village Vanguard. Betty called Max Gordon from a telephone across the street to ask what was going on. They couldn't get in. "Come to the back door. I'll let you in," Max Gordon responded. "It's that write-up Dick Manson did in the *New York Post* yesterday" (Max Gordon, *Live at the Village Vanguard*, p. 35).

Dick Manson, drama critic for the *New York Post*, heard through the grapevine about five "kids" doing some wild material at some basement club in the Village. He decided to see for himself. Next day he wrote: "They knocked me out! The freshest, funniest, brightest, most original material I have ever seen in a nightclub." After describing some of the acts, Manson concluded his review by saying, "so run, don't walk, if you want a night you'll always remember" (*Live at the Village Vanguard*, pp. 36-37). A lot of people followed his advice.

In the spring of 1939, with his business booming, Max Gordon was able to afford a liquor license. The only place for the bar was on stage. So The Revuers and the waiters carried on a running battle over the space on the stage--the waiters trying to rush in with orders to be filled before the show started.

That summer of 1939, Adolph's friend, Leonard Bernstein, came to New York. He had graduated from Harvard in the spring. His father wanted Leonard to join the family business selling beauty supplies, but he did allow Lenny one last fling, a summer in New York City. He gave him only a small amount of money and thought that when the money ran out Lenny would come back to accept an executive position in the Samuel Bernstein Hair Company.

The first person Lenny got in touch with in New York was Adolph Green. Green offered him a bed in his Greenwich Village apartment. Lenny attended parties with Green and frequently ended up at the piano, enchanting his listeners with his serious music. Often he would suddenly shift to a popular song like "Alexander's Ragtime Band." One evening, after one of these parties, Betty Comden went home and awakened her mother to tell her, "I met a real genius." Harold Clurman, founder of the Group Theatre in New York, was another person who recognized Bernstein's potential from these informal performances. "Lenny," he would say, "is hopelessly fated for success" (David Ewen, *Leonard Bernstein*, pp. 32, 33).

When The Revuers were asked to record one of their sketches, "The Girl with the Two Left Feet," Lenny accompanied them and earned a welcome twenty-five dollars (Burton Bernstein, *Family Matters*, p. 135).

When the summer ended Bernstein went back to Massachusetts, but shortly after that he returned to New York to see the conductor, Dimitri Mitropoulos, whom he had met while he was a student at Harvard. Mitropoulos insisted that Bernstein should commit himself to music. He suggested that Leonard enter the Curtis Institute in Philadelphia to study conducting. That was what Bernstein did.

The Revuers were now performing two shows five nights a week. They had four different shows--each a miniature musical revue centered around a theme. On the fifth night they presented a potpourri of all of their sketches. Otis Ferguson, writing in August 1939 in *The New Republic*, bemoaned the lack of good comedy during the year. "The only thing to break away from Olsen and Johnson, Behrman and Coward, Rose and Reinhardt ... is a little amateurish affair playing in an underground lower Seventh Avenue cancer pit known as the Vanguard. ... It is a group of five calling themselves The Revuers, playing a cabaret act on a packing-box stage before a six-foot home-made backdrop, managing to be lyrical-satirical-pastoral-tragical most of their time, which is two-a-day except Sunday and Monday." Ferguson also wrote that the shows are sometimes a little ragged and the performers haven't had the "knockabout drilling of a Fields or a Durante," but "collectively--conceiving, working out, presenting their material--they have a conception of stage ends and means that you could shop around for all year without matching" ("Vanguard Underground," *The New Republic*, August 30, 1939, p. 104.)

The Revuers' satire was good-natured and was inspired mainly by the entertainment pages of the newspapers. They made fun of movies, radio, and Broadway; but, since they were in love with all three, their ridicule was affectionate. One of their most popular early sketches was a meeting of the Joan Crawford fan club. The members of the club have gathered to praise Miss Crawford, but they are interrupted by one member who has become a Sonja Henie fan. This skit was written while Joan Crawford was appearing in *Ice Follies of 1939*. The critics had compared the film unfavorably with those of Sonja Henie. Another skit was a parody of the Mickey Rooney-Andy Hardy comedies. Al Hammer played Mickey Rooney as Andy Hardy, and he kept mugging and upstaging all of the other actors until at last they tied him to a chair and gagged him with a napkin.

One later sketch was a series of variations on the potion scene from *Tristan and Isolde*. First it was given as a typical Metropolitan Opera production. Adolph played Tristan and Betty, padded and with horns on her helmet, played Isolde. Then the scene was done in a sophisticated style as Noel Coward might have written it. The scene was next presented with Betty and Adolph in Clifford Odets trench coats acting in the naturalistic Group Theatre style, and then as a Maxwell Anderson poetic play (described by Gary Carey in *Judy Holliday*, pp. 33-34).

In August 1939 The Revuers went to the Westport Country Playhouse where they shared the bill with a young dancer named Gene Kelly. Earlier in the year, Kelly had appeared in a little revue, *One for the Money*, devised by Nancy Hamilton with some fresh tunes by Morgan Lewis. The revue with its talented and youthful cast was seen by Johnny Haggott, the stage manager of the Theatre Guild, who asked Kelly to choreograph a season of three shows for the Westport Country Playhouse. In the final show of the season, Kelly appeared as master of ceremonies and introduced The Revuers. Their show was "The Magazine Page." Each section of the show was represented by a page in a magazine, and as the show progressed the pages turned. During the evening Gene Kelly also did a series of satirical take-offs on how various types of dancers would negotiate a tap routine--a ballet dancer, a "flash" dancer, a "personality" girl. Adolph Green later said that "everything that Gene was, or was later to become, was already there in a nugget in that act" (Clive

The Revuers: Judy Tuvim (Holliday), Betty Comden, Alvin Hammer, John Frank, and Adolph Green. Photograph courtesy of The Museum of the City of New York, The Theatre Collection.

Hirschhorn, *Gene Kelly*, p. 64). Ten years later, Betty and Adolph were to work with Gene Kelly in Hollywood.

In November 1939, The Revuers received an offer to perform in the Rainbow Room, a sophisticated club on the top floor of Rockefeller Plaza. There were many night spots in New York in the late 1930s. There were the Persian Room in the Plaza Hotel and the Starlight Room at the Waldorf. There were ice shows at the Iridium Room in the St. Regis Hotel. There was a Gay Nineties Revue at Billy Rose's Diamond Horseshoe. There were black entertainers at the Kit Kat Club. The large Rainbow Room was one of the newest and most elegant of the clubs, but it had had difficulty in building a regular clientele. The club had tried novelty acts, dancers, puppets, and even a table tennis exhibition. The Revuers had made a guest appearance there in the spring. Then they were booked in as the opening attraction for the 1939 fall season. They were promised $250 a week for three weeks. They were to share the bill with Jack Cole and his Balinese Dancers.

On their opening night at the Rainbow Room, nothing seemed to work for The Revuers. They did spoofs of Joan Crawford, Queen Victoria, Noel Coward, Oscar Wilde, Broadway, and Hollywood. They even tried their new sketch on the New York World's Fair that was being held at Flushing Meadows. In this sketch each of The Revuers depicted one of New York City's landmarks. Adolph was Grant's Tomb, Betty was Cleopatra's Needle, Judy Tuvim was the Statue of Liberty, Al Hammer was Rockefeller Center, and John Frank was the Empire State Building. These landmarks castigate the tourists for attending the World's Fair instead of visiting them.

The Rainbow patrons proved to be conservative and a little bit stuffy. The Revuers prided themselves on "deflating the pompous," and here the pompous evidently could see little humor in their skits. What had worked in the small, dark Village Vanguard did not succeed when brought out into the bright, open spaces of the Rainbow Room. The reviews of their show were respectable, but Adolph said of their performance, "We bombed!"

The reputation of The Revuers had by now reached the world of radio. After their appearances at the Rainbow Room, they were asked to appear on a local radio show sponsored by Consolidated Edison. They did much the same material they had done at the Rainbow Room, and they received a good write-up in *Variety*. Then NBC Radio wanted them for a weekly network spot at $250 a week for 25 weeks. The Revuers wrote and performed a new half-hour show every week. On Tuesday evenings at 9:30 p.m., the announcer introduced them: "Yes, here are The Revuers ... five clever youngsters who write and perform their own material ... original lyrics, original music" (quoted by Holtzman in *Judy Holliday*, p. 69). For their NBC Radio series they took a different theme for satirizing each week. They also had some guest singers on their shows. One of these singers was the young Dinah Shore. (See RA01-RA20.)

The Revuers' next venture was into recording. Musicraft was producing a series of records entitled *Night Life in New York*. The Revuers recorded two of their skits. One was "The Joan Crawford Fan Club," and the other was "The Girl with Two Left Feet," in which Judy played Maryrose Rosemary, a squeaky-voiced ingenue. The record had a piano accompaniment by Leonard Bernstein. The album was released, but did not make much of an impact. (See D30.)

In October 1940 The Revuers were asked to perform at Radio City Music Hall between the showings of the film, *Escape*, which starred Norma Shearer and Robert Taylor. They performed five times a day for three weeks. Here they did their

Tin Pan Alley number in which they satirized five types of popular songs.

One day while The Revuers were appearing at Radio City Music Hall, Adolph did not show up for their performances. Fortunately, the other four were able to carry on. Late in the day Adolph arrived, very happy but a little bit woozy. He had married Elizabeth Reitel at City Hall. The newlyweds had run into some friends at the Algonquin Hotel and had had several drinks to celebrate the wedding.

At the end of 1940, The Revuers returned to the Village Vanguard. Max Gordon had renovated the club. The Revuers now had two little cubicles for dressing rooms, and they came through a slightly worn velvet curtain rather than the cheesecloth that had been their first backdrop. However, in spite of the warm reception given them at the Vanguard, The Revuers--especially Betty and Adolph--were disappointed. They seemed to be right back where they had started.

Nineteen forty-one was a depressing period for The Revuers. They had hired a booking agent, and the agent booked them in supper clubs and roadhouses in cities across the country as far west as St. Louis. Then a promising opportunity came their way. The lyricist, Irving Caesar, who had written songs for *Pins and Needles of 1922*, *No, No, Nanette*, and *The George White Scandals of 1931*, was doing a new musical called *My Dear Public*. Caesar had written such popular songs as "Swanee," "My Mammy," "Tea for Two," and "I Want To Be Happy." *My Dear Public* was about an actress who tries to get her wealthy husband to back a musical that will star her as a sultry harem queen. The play consisted mainly of auditions and rehearsals for the fictional musical. Irving Caesar was wanting various acts for the auditions. The five members of The Revuers were cast as separate characters who performed as a Greenwich Village comedy act. They were promised $400 a week and were asked to write their own material. On March 1, 1942, they went to New Haven for the tryouts. The reviews of the show were not good, but The Revuers were singled out for a commendation by the critic for *Variety*. Their sketch was a spoof of Shubert operettas and was called "The Baroness Bazooka." After five days in New Haven, the company went to Boston. There the critic for the *Boston Post* called The Revuers' act "a corking good burlesque of the cornier kind of operettas" (quoted by Carey in *Judy Holliday*, p. 49). *My Dear Public* then went to Philadelphia where it opened to terrible reviews. The next day a closing notice was posted. The show did open six months later in New York with a new cast. It ran for 55 performances.

Leonard Bernstein by this time had completed his conducting training at the Curtis Institute and he had glowing recommendations, but he was unable to get a job that would pay him enough to live on. Since he had little else to do, he began to hang out with the cast of *My Dear Public*. When the cast gathered after rehearsals, Bernstein invariably took over the piano and played and sang. Irving Caesar, the author of the show, thought Bernstein had some similarities to George Gershwin and promised him a job. The next fall in New York Bernstein ran into Irving Caesar who did get him a job making piano arrangements for a music publishing company. It was his first steady job in music. He made twenty-five dollars a week plus a twenty-five dollar advance on royalties for what he might write. A year later, Artur Rodzinski was appointed conductor of the New York Philharmonic, and in 1943 he made Bernstein his assistant. On November 14, 1943, the guest conductor for the symphony, Bruno Walter, was ill and Rodzinski, because of snow, was not able to get to New York from his Stockbridge farm. Bernstein, at the age of twenty-five, was going to have to conduct the symphony. That was Bernstein's chance, and he took advantage of it. The next day he was famous, not only in New York, but all across the country because the performance had been broadcast on radio.

In the meantime, The Revuers, having failed in their attempt at performing in musical comedy, went back to the nightclub circuit. This time they played the more elite clubs--like Cafe Society both Uptown and Downtown. They had a long and successful engagement at the Blue Angel, a cabaret that Max Gordon had recently opened on East 56th Street. Then they went on the road again. One of their engagements was at the prestigious Blackstone Hotel in Chicago. However, only two days after opening in Chicago, they had to cancel their performances. John Frank had developed a drinking problem and needed professional help. The Revuers returned to New York where they drew up a severance agreement.

On January 4, 1942, Betty Comden had married Siegfried Schutzman, a young man whom she had dated since 1938. He was an artist who was soon to become a sergeant in the Army Engineers connected with the Information and Educational Division. He later changed his name to Steven Kyle. Betty and Steven were later to have two children, Susanna, born in 1949, had the distinction of having a musical number written in honor of her birth. It was called "Anniversary for Susanna Kyle" and was written by Leonard Bernstein. Alan Kyle was born four years later, in 1953.

About this time The Revuers were contacted by Kurt Frings, a Hollywood agent, who told them he could get them a spot in a film version of the radio show, *Duffy's Tavern*. Adolph and Betty had both been fascinated by the movies. In fact, Adolph was such a motion picture fan that he could rattle off the casts of nearly any film that had ever been made. Betty's new husband was now in the army, so late in the summer of 1943 Betty, Adolph, Judy, and Al Hammer took the train to Los Angeles. Helen Tuvim, Judy's mother, accompanied them. The train trip across the country took five days. The weather was hot and the air cooling system on the train was inefficient. Betty and Judy read and played cards. Al Hammer slept, and Adolph worked crossword puzzles to pass the time. Adolph was the only one who remained optimistic during the long journey.

When they arrived in Los Angeles, the five of them checked into the Roosevelt Hotel until they could find an apartment. Much to their dismay, they found that the film they were to be in had been canceled. (*Duffy's Tavern*, a loosely held-together revue style, all-star picture, was later made and released by Paramount Pictures in September of 1945.) The Revuers did manage to get an engagement at the Trocadero. They found an apartment above a realtor's office on Wilshire Boulevard not far from the La Brea tar pits. The apartment was only partially furnished. In one room there was a bed. In the other bedrooms there were only cots and collapsible cardboard closets. From their "terrace" The Revuers could look out on traffic-clogged Wilshire Boulevard. Because their apartment was some distance from the Trocadero, they had to buy a car (Carey, *Judy Holliday*, p. 55).

The Los Angeles critics gave The Revuers' debut at the Trocadero sensational reviews. Only a few days after their opening, agents began coming to offer Judy Tuvim contracts. The other performers received no such offers. Judy put off the agents because she did not want to accept a contract unless the others were included. Finally she talked with Betty, Adolph, and Al about the situation. Betty and Adolph were sad at the thought of breaking up the act, but they did tell her she should accept a contract. At last Judy signed with Twentieth Century-Fox with the assurance from the company that she would first appear as one of The Revuers. If the first screen appearance was a success, the other members of the group would also be placed under contract. So The Revuers made their first film. It was called *Greenwich Village* and starred Vivian Blaine and Don Ameche. The Revuers worked on the film for eight weeks. They did two of their nightclub sketches. One was the spoof of the Shubert operettas. When the film was edited, both sketches were cut and all that could be seen of any of The Revuers was a brief moment when Betty Comden, playing a hat check girl, handed Don Ameche his hat. Twentieth Century-Fox did not pick up its option for The Revuers. Judy Tuvim, however, did remain in Hollywood under contract to Twentieth Century-Fox. Her name was changed to Judy Holliday.

Both Betty and Adolph were infatuated with the movies and would have liked to have been able to get work in Hollywood, but the possibility seemed very slim. Betty left for New York to join her soldier husband who was on leave there. After Steve Kyle's furlough was ended, Betty was about to return to Hollywood when she received a call from Adolph. He said he was coming East to visit his mother who was ill. He asked Betty to wait in New York and they would return to Hollywood together. Betty got to thinking about how miserable Adolph would be feeling when he returned to New York. They were now totally unemployed. She decided to meet him at Grand Central Station. Adolph walked up the long ramp at the New York station carrying his heavy suitcase. When he arrived at the exit, there was Betty carrying a sign that read "The Adolph Green Fan Club." Betty and Adolph later used a similar scene in the film they wrote for Fred Astaire, *The Band Wagon*.

In New York, Betty and Adolph contacted Max Gordon about performing, along with Al Hammer, at the Blue Angel. He agreed. They called Al asking him to join them, but he was getting small parts in films and thought The Revuers were finished. Max Gordon agreed to book just the two, Betty and Adolph, at the Blue Angel.

One night while they were playing at the Blue Angel, their friend Leonard Bernstein came by between their shows. He had Paul Feigay and Oliver Smith with him. These two men, inspired by the success of the ballet, *Fancy Free*, which Jerome Robbins and Leonard Bernstein had presented with the Ballet Theatre, were interested in co-producing a musical comedy. It was Jerome Robbins, a dancer with the Ballet Theatre, who had had the idea for the ballet. Leonard Bernstein had been recommended to him as a composer who could write jazz. The twenty-five minute ballet about three sailors on leave in New York had premiered at the Metropolitan Opera House on April 18, 1944, and had been an instant success. Oliver Smith, who had designed the set for the ballet, and Paul Feigay decided they would like to produce a musical. Thus the visit from the three men to the Blue Angel to talk with Betty and Adolph about writing the script and the lyrics for the musical. Betty and Adolph were enthusiastic about writing a musical.

Betty and Adolph and Bernstein began talking through their ideas for the musical. Over the summer Betty and Adolph wrote the libretto and the lyrics and Bernstein wrote the music. They called the new musical *On the Town*. Betty and Adolph wrote clever parts for themselves in *On The Town*. They had to audition for the roles, but they did get to play them. Betty was Claire, the anthropologist, and Adolph was one of the three sailors, Ozzie, who fascinates Claire because he looks so much like her concept of pre-historic man.

Oliver Smith and Paul Feigay, the producers, took the show to the Theatre Guild, but it was turned down. Then they took it to George Abbott the great director of comedies and musicals. George Abbott had seen the ballet, *Fancy Free*, and he admired the work of Leonard Bernstein and Jerome Robbins, but he had never

Betty Comden, Adolph Green, Leonard Bernstein, and Jerome Robbins writing *On the Town*, 1944. Photograph courtesy of Betty Comden.

Betty Comden as Claire, the anthropologist, and Adolph Green, as Ozzie, one of the three sailors, in the museum scene in *On the Town*, 1944. Photograph courtesy of Betty Comden.

heard of Betty Comden and Adolph Green. He took the play to read while riding on the train out of New York. He was so excited by the story and the lyrics that he wanted to jump off the train to tell the young authors how much he liked it. This, of course, thrilled Comden and Green when he told them. Abbott agreed to direct the musical. As soon as it was known that Abbott would direct, there was no difficulty in raising funds for the show. He was the only "veteran" connected with the musical. Betty, Adolph, Leonard Bernstein, and Jerome Robbins, the choreographer, were all in their twenties, and for them it was their first Broadway musical. *On the Town* opened at the Adelphi Theatre in New York on December 28, 1944. "Fresh" was the term most often used by the critics to describe the musical. The integration into the story of the dancing and the singing was also commented on, and most of the critics praised the book of the new, young writing team, Comden and Green. (For details about *On the Town* see S01.)

Bernstein's music for *On the Town* was outstanding, but the conductor, Serge Koussevitzky, one of Bernstein's mentors, berated him for wasting his time with show tunes. However, Koussevitzky was going to have a hard time trying to mold Bernstein into the European style of conductor. Bernstein spent his evenings, not with the intellectual and cultural figures in American and international society, but with Betty and Adolph. He had even conducted the whole symphony orchestra accompanying Comden and Green singing "Mabel, Mabel" in Tschaikovsky's Fourth Symphony.

After the success of *On the Town*, Betty and Adolph did not waste time. They immediately started writing another musical. This time it was an original story about the 1920s. Once again Oliver Smith and Paul Feigay were the producers, George Abbott was the director, and Jerome Robbins the choreographer; but Leonard Bernstein with whom Betty and Adolph had worked so well was not available. Morton Gould wrote the music for the Comden and Green lyrics. The musical was *Billion Dollar Baby*, which opened at the Alvin Theatre on December 21, 1945. The story was about Maribelle Jones, played by Joan McCracken, who works her way up in the world during the fabulous 1920s only to marry a millionaire whose fortune is lost in the Stock Market Crash of 1929. In *Billion Dollar Baby* the witty Comden and Green satirized the Miss America pageant, marathon dances, speakeasies, movie idols, gangsters, and millionaires. Some of the critics referred to Maribelle Jones as a female Pal Joey, but the play was only moderately successful. It ran for 220 performances. (For details about the musical see S02.)

Betty Comden and Adolph Green now had two Broadway musicals behind them, but they were still interested in Hollywood. They had asked their agents to try to get a studio contract for them. Nevertheless, they were surprised when they received an offer from Metro-Goldwyn-Mayer to come to Hollywood to work with producer Arthur Freed. This time when they arrived in Hollywood they were graciously received by Arthur Freed and his associate producer, Roger Edens. Freed revealed to them that he wanted them to write a screenplay for a film based on the Broadway musical of college life, *Good News*. *Good News* had been one of the best of Broadway's 1920s musicals. It had opened in 1927 and had been written by Ray Henderson, Lew Brown, and B. G. DeSylva. This team wrote six popular stage musicals between 1927 and 1932. Metro-Goldwyn-Mayer had acquired the rights to *Good News* in 1929 and had made it into a film in 1930. Now Freed wanted a new version. Comden and Green were not at first enthusiastic about a college musical. They tried to give the story some relevance to the late 1940s by having an old graduate of the school come back to visit his son who was studying under the G. I. Bill of Rights. Arthur Freed did not want that, so Betty and Adolph had to stick to the outline of the original story. They wrote an entirely new screenplay but used most of the songs from the original script. They did change the subject that the football hero was flunking from astronomy to French, and thus were able to write their clever song, "The French Lesson," with music by Roger Edens. They also wrote some extra lyrics for some of the songs. *Good News* starred June Allyson and Peter Lawford. Joan McCracken, who had played Maribelle Jones in *Billion Dollar Baby*, was brought from New York to play the comedy role of Babe Doolittle. Comden and Green's new version of *Good News* proved to be one of the best of all of the college musicals produced at this time. (See F01 for details about the film.) Their first film completed, Betty and Adolph returned to New York.

During rehearsals for *On the Town*, Adolph, whose first marriage had ended in divorce, met Allyn McLerie, a young actress who was a bit player and understudy in the musical. When Sono Osato, who played the original Miss Turnstiles, Ivy, left the cast, Allyn McLerie was promoted to that leading role. She was only eighteen at the time. Adolph married Allyn before Comden and Green's next musical, *Bonanza Bound!*, was produced. *Bonanza Bound!* was in rehearsal in 1947 when the film *Good News* was presented as the Christmas holiday attraction at Radio City Music Hall.

Bonanza Bound! is about the gold rush in Alaska. Betty and Adolph wrote one of the leading roles, Leonardo Da Vinci, for Adolph. Eustasia, the villain's daughter who falls in love with Leonardo, was played by Adolph's new wife. Paul Feigay, Oliver Smith, and Herman Levin produced *Bonanza Bound!* The music was written by Saul Chaplin, a well-known composer who had written many hit songs with Sammy Cahn. Betty and Adolph had first met him when The Revuers were playing at the Trocadero in Hollywood.

Bonanza Bound! was given a pre-Broadway tryout at the Sam S. Shubert Theatre in Philadelphia. It opened there on December 26, 1947, and closed there on January 8, 1948. It did not get to Broadway. The plot of *Bonanza Bound!* is melodramatic, even including the heroine who is threatened by the villain. Evidently, the musical was played straight. Had it been played as a burlesque of melodrama as Comden and Green probably intended it, it might have been more successful. (See S03 for details about the musical.)

With their failed musical behind them, Comden and Green returned to Hollywood and the Freed Unit at Metro-Goldwyn-Mayer to write an original screenplay for Judy Garland and Fred Astaire. Garland and Astaire had starred in the film, *Easter Parade*, in 1948. The film had been a great success, and Freed wanted another picture that would bring them together again. Comden and Green jumped at the chance to write for Fred Astaire. Adolph had been a fan of Astaire for many years, having first seen him and his sister Adele in 1931 in the Broadway revue, *The Band Wagon*. Comden and Green's story for the new film was about a husband and wife acting and dancing team. They danced beautifully together but frequently had disagreements off stage. After they had written their story, Betty and Adolph read the script to Fred Astaire and Judy Garland. Being performers themselves, Betty and Adolph were always able to put across their material. After their reading of the script, Judy Garland commented to Fred Astaire, "If we can only do as well as they did, we're O.K." (Michael Freedland, *Fred Astaire*, p. 198). Astaire and Garland liked the script. Harry Warren was to write the music and Ira Gershwin the lyrics.

The cast began rehearsals, but it was soon evident that Judy Garland was not well enough emotionally to do the picture. Freed suggested that she be replaced by Ginger Rogers. Astaire was delighted with the prospect of working with Ginger again. He and Ginger Rogers had made nine pictures together during the 1930s. Their last picture had been *The Story of Irene and Vernon Castle*, made in 1939. Since Judy Garland and Ginger Rogers were very different in style, several songs that had been written for Judy had to be dropped. The film was titled *The Barkleys of Broadway* and was one of the top films of 1949. It was nominated for a Screenwriters Guild Award. (See F02 for details about the film.)

Also in 1949, Comden and Green were asked by Arthur Freed to work once again with Roger Edens to write some of the songs for a Gene Kelly film, *Take Me Out To the Ball Game*. When they first went to Hollywood, Betty and Adolph, the New Yorkers, knew few people there except Gene Kelly, whom they had worked with ten years earlier at the Westport Country Playhouse. Kelly had first gone to Hollywood in 1941. After serving in the war, Kelly returned, and he and his wife Betsy bought a big house on North Rodeo Drive. The Kellys held "open house" nearly every Saturday and Sunday evening. At about 7:00 o'clock friends would begin dropping in. Sometimes there were as many as fifty people who would arrive, help themselves to an assortment of food set out on the dining room table, and spend the evening. After the food and the drinks, the guests would often gather around the piano where musicians and performers like Johnny Green, Frank Sinatra, Phil Silvers, Lennie Hayton, or Leonard Bernstein would start to play. Judy Garland, Lena Horne, Roger Edens, Noel Coward, Nancy Walker, and Peter Lawford would frequently sing or perform. Betty and Adolph would also sing or do some of their Revuers routines. At these informal evening get-togethers, Betty and Adolph made many long-time friends. André Previn later wrote of these evenings: "I think I can honestly say that I have never met so many extraordinary people in one room, on so many occasions in my life ... the prerequisite was talent" (Clive Hirshhorn, *Gene Kelly*, p. 147). Previn later dropped out of the group because of the competitiveness of the performers. He came to feel that many of the guests tried to show how clever they were.

Gene Kelly and his friend and assistant, Stanley Donen, had written the story for *Take Me Out to the Ball Game*. It was to star Kelly and Frank Sinatra. Freed had asked George Wells to write the screenplay and Harry Warren and Ralph Blane to write the score. Freed wanted Judy Garland to be the female owner of the baseball team. But Judy Garland was not well enough to do the film, so Esther Williams was cast as K. C. Higgins. This meant changing the screenplay. The old script was abandoned and a new screenplay was written by Harry Tugend. The songs by Harry Warren and Ralph Blane were also discarded. This was when Comden and Green were brought in to write the lyrics. They contributed the lyrics for four songs. One was a lovely ballad, "The Right Girl for Me," sung by Frank Sinatra. The other three were humorous--"Yes, Indeedy," sung by Kelly and Sinatra, "It's Fate, Baby, It's Fate," sung by Betty Garrett and Sinatra, and "O'Brien to Ryan to Goldberg," sung by the three baseball pals played and danced by Kelly, Sinatra, and Jules Munshin. *Take Me Out To the Ball Game* was released in 1949 and was well received by the audiences. (See F03 for details about the film.)

Comden and Green's biggest success of 1949 was the film made from their musical *On the Town*. Arthur Freed had convinced Louis B. Mayer of Metro-Goldwyn-Mayer to buy the rights to the stage show even before it was presented on Broadway. This is thought to be the first time that the film rights to a Broadway musical were sold before the show had proved itself in New York. Metro-Goldwyn-Mayer had held the rights for five years. At last in 1949 Mayer gave Freed permission to go ahead with the film. Arthur Freed had not liked the Leonard Bernstein score for *On the Town*. He considered Bernstein's music too avant-garde for a general audience. Comden and Green hesitated. They loved Bernstein's music for the show. However, they were under contract to Metro-Goldwyn-Mayer. Freed negotiated a contract with Bernstein allowing him to interpolate new music into the film.

Gene Kelly and Stanley Donen were to co-direct the film. They chose as the three sailors, the same three who had been friends in *Take Me Out To the Ball Game*, Gene Kelly, Frank Sinatra, and Jules Munshin. This casting made it necessary for Comden and Green to change their original concept of the three sailors. In the stage musical, the men are naive and rather helpless in the big city of New York. Comden and Green had known Gene Kelly for many years. They knew that the story had to be adapted to fit this new cast. They wrote the first half of the screenplay in New York and then went to Hollywood to complete the writing. Working closely with Kelly and Stanley Donen, they adapted the story to fit the personalities and the talents of the new cast. Only four of Bernstein's original musical numbers were used in the film. Comden and Green worked with Roger Edens to write eight new songs.

The filming of *On the Town* was a very happy experience. The members of the Freed Unit involved in the film became almost like a repertory company. Betty and Adolph, Gene Kelly, Stanley Donen, Jeannie Coyne, Kay Thompson, Roger Edens, Conrad Salinger, and Johnny Green would often eat lunch together in the Metro-Goldwyn-Mayer commissary. Adolph has said they were "the laughingest bunch of people in Hollywood." He said "it was a disgrace. We were so loud and raucous and behaved as if we owned the place, that a lot of people could not stand us, or the private jokes we had at their expense" (Clive Hirschhorn, *Gene Kelly*, p. 160).

On the Town premiered at Radio City Music Hall on December 30, 1949. *On the Town* won for Comden and Green a Screenwriters Guild Award. (See F04 for details about the film.)

Betty and Adolph had returned to New York after writing the screenplay for *On the Town*, but in May of 1950 they received an urgent call from Metro-Goldwyn-Mayer asking them to come to Hollywood to work once again with the Freed Unit. After they arrived in Hollywood, Arthur Freed, who always called Betty and Adolph "the kids," informed them that he wanted them to write an original screenplay called *Singin' in the Rain*. It was to use some of the songs that he and Nacio Herb Brown had written nearly twenty years before. At first Comden and Green objected to using lyrics that they had not written. However, they did begin to look through the stacks of songs by Freed and Brown. Among the songs were some very familiar ones like "Broadway Melody," "You Were Meant for Me," and "Singin' in the Rain." The problem was to come up with an idea for a story that some of these songs could fit into. Betty and Adolph sat in their little cubby-hole of an office at Metro-Goldwyn Mayer and looked at each other. At last the idea came to them to write a story that took place at the time when the songs were written, which was between 1929 and 1931. This was the transition period in Hollywood when the studios were changing from the silent films to the use of sound. Comden and Green felt very comfortable with this period because they were both amateur authorities on the silent films and the early talkies. They knew the stories connected with that period, like that of John Gilbert, the reigning king of the silent movies, whose career was finished after one talking picture in which he improvised his own love scene by repeating "I love you, I love you, I love you," as he had always done in the silent movies.

With this decision made, Comden and Green began to come up with their story. They wanted their hero to survive the advent of sound in the film, so they thought he should be someone who had had song and dance experience in vaudeville. Of course they wanted their good friend Gene Kelly to play the role. At this time Kelly was filming *An American in Paris* and was so much in demand that Comden and Green did not dare approach him until their screenplay was completed. But at the moment, they were stuck. They had three possible opening scenes, but could not choose which one and did not seem to be able to progress from there with the story. At this time when they were most depressed and nearly ready to admit defeat, Betty's husband, Steven Kyle, arrived from New York. Betty and Adolph read the three possible opening scenes to him and he asked, "Why not use all three?" This is what they did. They used them all: the premiere of the silent film, the interview with the star, the shots of the silent movie, the star's escape from his fans and his meeting with the girl. From then on the writing of the screenplay seemed to flow more easily.

When the script was finished, they gave Gene Kelly a copy to read. He and his directing partner, Stanley Donen, both read it and were delighted with it. Kelly had now finished filming *An American in Paris*, and he agreed not only to star in the film but also to co-direct along with Donen. Comden and Green and Kelly and Donen started meeting and going over the screenplay, camera shot by camera shot. Comden and Green have written that the success of the film and its continued popularity has much to do with the "four-way mental radar" they had with Kelly and Donen. (Comden and Green wrote about their experiences in writing *Singin' in the Rain* in the Introduction to the published script, 1972.) Before leaving Hollywood, Comden and Green wrote the clever lyric of tongue twisters, "Moses Supposes," which is the only song used in the film that was not written by Freed and Brown.

The filming of *Singin' in the Rain* was completed in late November 1951. It opened at Radio City Music Hall on March 27, 1952, and won for Comden and Green their second Screenwriters Guild Award. The film has maintained its popularity and was recently voted by international film critics the third best film ever made (Neil Sinyard, *Classic Movies*, p. 51). (For details of the film see F05.)

While *Singin' in the Rain* was being filmed, Comden and Green were in New York using their comic and satirical skills to write sketches and songs for America's great comedian, Bert Lahr, and for singer, Dolores Gray. *Two on the Aisle*, after previews in Philadelphia, opened in New York at the Mark Hellinger Theatre on July 19, 1951. Audiences and critics were glad to welcome back to New York one of the funniest men in the world. Veteran of many Broadway musicals and revues, Lahr is best remembered today as the Cowardly Lion in the film, *The Wizard of Oz*. Dolores Gray, an American, had had her first big success in London playing Annie Oakley in *Annie Get Your Gun*. With a powerful voice and great versatility both as singer and comedienne, Dolores Gray held her own in *Two on the Aisle*. Comden and Green wrote most of the skits and all of the lyrics for the revue. In writing *Two on the Aisle*, Comden and Green collaborated for the first time with the composer, Jule Styne. (For additional information see S09.)

Arthur Freed's successes with *An American in Paris* and *Singin' in the Rain* inspired him to try to acquire another collection of songs to use as the basis for a new musical film. Freed was a friend of Howard Dietz, who at this time was vice-president of Loew's Inc. Dietz, a lyricist, had worked with Arthur Schwartz, a musician, in writing the songs for some popular Broadway revues of the 1920s and early 1930s. Freed had often told Dietz that some day he would do a picture using some of his songs. Now seemed to be the time. He called Betty and Adolph to ask them to provide an original screenplay. They arrived in Hollywood in February 1952. Others who had been called in to work on the project were Vincente Minnelli, who was to direct, Roger Edens, Fred Astaire, Michael Kidd, a dancer and choreographer, and Oliver Smith, the Broadway scene designer who had also co-produced Comden and Green's early musicals. Freed was tentatively calling the new musical film "I Love Louisa," which was the name of one of the songs in the popular Schwartz-Dietz revue, *The Band Wagon*. This 1931 Broadway revue had starred Fred and Adele Astaire and had had one of the best scores of any of the revues of the time.

Betty and Adolph were delighted to be working again with Fred Astaire, but it took them several weeks to come up with an idea for the story. They began to visualize a character somewhat like Astaire himself--someone who had been a star but whose popularity had waned. Then in looking through the Schwartz-Dietz scores again, they came upon the song, "By Myself," from the 1937 show called *Between the Devil*. This made them think of the time when Adolph returned to New York after the very unsuccessful first trip to Hollywood and was greeted by Betty carrying an "Adolph Green Fan Club" sign. This recollection gave Comden and Green the start for their story.

The hero of their story would be Tony Hunter (Fred Astaire), an aging film star who has been invited by his friends, a married writing team, to come to New York to do a Broadway musical. Their first scene would be his arrival all alone in New York where the writers, Lester and Lily Marton, would meet him carrying a "fan club" sign. Astaire liked the idea. Working with Freed, Minnelli, and Astaire himself, Comden and Green were now able to finish the screenplay. Their rather mad writing team, the Martons, was based on themselves. The film was re-named *The Band Wagon*, and was finished in January 1953. It was shown in July of 1953 at Radio City Music Hall. *The Band Wagon* received an Academy Award nomination. (For details about the film see F06.)

Before *The Band Wagon* was released in July of 1953, Comden and Green had already had another hit on Broadway. On January 19, 1953, *Wonderful Town* opened in New Haven and then went on to Boston and Philadelphia, where it was held over for an extra week because of the demand for tickets. When it opened at the Winter Garden Theatre in New York on February 25, 1953, all of the New York critics gave it rave reviews. *Wonderful Town* was a musical based on the 1940 play, *My Sister Eileen*, by Joseph Fields and Jerome Chodorov. The play had been based on Ruth McKenney's stories about herself and her beautiful sister and their adventures in New York in the 1930s. *My Sister Eileen* had been made into a film in 1942 and had starred Rosalind Russell as Ruth. Robert Fryer decided to produce a musical version of the play. He asked the authors, Fields and Chodorov, to adapt the play and he asked George Abbott to direct. Rosalind Russell was engaged to play Ruth once again. Some music was written by Leroy Anderson with words by Arnold Horwitt, but the total musical score for the play seemed to be going nowhere. A rehearsal date was set, but there was still no score. Then George Abbott asked Comden and Green to work with Leonard Bernstein to write the music and lyrics. Koussevitzky, who had objected to Bernstein's writing for Broadway, had died in 1951, so Bernstein now felt free to use some of his time writing for musical comedies. Betty and Adolph hesitated because for the first time they would not be writing both the book and the lyrics. However, their desire to work once again with their friend Bernstein and with the director George Abbott made them decide to do it. Also, they liked the play and they knew Rosalind Russell. They had only five weeks to write the entire score.

One thing that helped Comden and Green and Leonard Bernstein was their knowledge of the music of the 1930s--the big band sound of Benny Goodman, the Eddie Duchin vamp, and the sounds of "swing." Bernstein used all of these sounds in his music for the show. Comden and Green matched him with clever as well as romantic and sentimental lyrics. The plot of the play was strong and the characters well drawn. Comden and Green and Bernstein's songs captured the mood of the play and the age, defined the characters, advanced the plot, and added considerably to the gaiety of the story. *Wonderful Town* won a Tony Award for Outstanding Musical of the year, and Rosalind Russell won as Outstanding Musical Actress. Betty Comden and Adolph Green won a Donaldson Award for their lyrics. *Wonderful Town* played 559 performances in New York. (For details about the musical see S10.)

During rehearsals for *Wonderful Town*, Allyn McLerie, Adolph's wife, met the leading man, George Gaynes. After the show opened, she divorced Adolph and married Gaynes.

Taking a train to the Coast for their next film assignment, Betty and Adolph used the time to think of an idea for a new musical for Broadway. One of their ideas was an *On the Town* revisited, the three sailors' having a reunion ten years later. However, they decided to change the sailors to soldiers. In Hollywood they mentioned the idea to Gene Kelly who immediately wanted the idea for his next film. Betty and Adolph outlined the story for Arthur Freed. He was enthusiastic and hired them to write both the screenplay and the lyrics for the film. He suggested André Previn for the composer. Previn had done the accompaniment for the film, *Invitation to the Dance*, but this was to be his first chance to compose songs for a film. Previn later said, "Betty and Adolph initiated me into the mysteries of how to construct a musical. They pointed out the fact that the songs must be inevitable instead of the way they were inserted in other producers' films" (Hugh Fordin, *The World of Entertainment*, p. 433).

Gene Kelly wanted to use Frank Sinatra and Jules Munshin once again for the other two buddies. Frank Sinatra had just made a big comeback in the films. He had been cast in a serious supporting role in *From Here to Eternity*, and on March 25, 1954, he had won an Oscar for the role. Betty and Adolph had attended a party at Frank's apartment that night after the Academy Award ceremony. Sinatra turned down the role in the new film. He did not want to go back to musical comedy (Kitty Kelley, *His Way*, p. 217). Jules Munshin was not available. Michael Kidd, the choreographer, was under contract to Metro-Goldwyn-Mayer and was chosen for one of the men while the dancer, Dan Dailey, was cast as the third. Kelly had three dancers to work with for the film. Comden and Green's screenplay was about three buddies, who, when they get out of the army after World War II, agree to meet again in ten years. The film shows that meeting. Though the film has much humor and satire, it is really about the disillusionment of the three men. None has lived up to his dreams. *It's Always Fair Weather* began filming in October 1954. It opened at Radio City Music Hall on September 15, 1955. Though most of the critics liked *It's Always Fair Weather*, it did not have the appeal for the general public that *On the Town* and *Singin' in the Rain* had. Comden and Green were nominated for both an Academy Award and a Screenwriters Guild Award for their screenplay. (For details about the film see F07.)

While writing the screenplay for *It's Always Fair Weather*, Comden and Green were called in, along with Jule Styne, to help out the ailing musical version of *Peter Pan* starring Mary Martin. When Jerome Robbins decided to direct and choreograph a new production of *Peter Pan* with Mary Martin as Peter and Cyril Ritchard as Captain Hook, he had planned to use only a few incidental songs by composer Mark ("Moose") Charlap and lyricist Carolyn Leigh. However, the show began to develop into a full scale musical. *Peter Pan* first played in Los Angeles and San Francisco, and the producers could see that it would not make it on Broadway. Robbins asked Styne and Comden and Green for help. According to Jule Styne, he asked Comden and Green to go to San Francisco with him to try to help--not to re-write but to give some advice. Carolyn Leigh was very bitter and did not even want to meet with them, but Styne convinced "Moose" Charlap that he and Comden and Green had more experience and could improve the show. So in one week, from Monday through Friday, the Styne, Comden and Green team wrote eight songs. Not all of them were used. Among those that were used were "Never, Never Land," "O! My Mysterious Lady," and the very clever song sung by Captain Hook called "Captain Hook's Waltz." "I Gotta Crow" and "I Won't Grow Up" were written by Charlap and Leigh ("Jule Styne," in *Notes on Broadway* by Al Kasha and Joel Hirschhorn, pp. 295-296).

Peter Pan opened at the Winter Garden Theatre on Broadway on October 20, 1954, for a limited engagement before being given a live telecast. There were to be three television versions of *Peter Pan*. The third one was taped and made available on video. This version of *Peter Pan* continues to be shown on television and in homes across the country. (See S17 and see T43, T44, and T46 for details about the television versions.)

In 1955 Betty and Adolph missed out on an exciting project. Jerome Robbins and Leonard Bernstein were working together once again on a musical for Broadway. It was about rival gangs in New York City. Robbins and Bernstein needed a lyricist for the show, and their first choice was, of course, Comden and Green. Because they were busy in Hollywood at the time, Betty and Adolph had to turn down the offer. The young Stephen Sondheim was eventually hired to work with Bernstein in writing the lyrics for *West Side Story*.

Nearly a year earlier when Comden and Green were on the West Coast, they had talked with their good friend Judy Holliday about a Broadway musical for Judy. It had been Adolph who had helped Judy to get her first Broadway role. She had returned from Hollywood after an unsuccessful career there just before *On the Town* had opened in New York. She went to the opening night of the new show *On the Town* and was one of the first backstage to congratulate Betty and Adolph and Leonard Bernstein. Seeing how successful her friends were, she was feeling discouraged with her own career. A few days later she met Adolph for lunch and he took her to see Herman Shumlin, a director, who had seen Betty, Adolph, and Judy perform at the Village Vanguard. Adolph knew that Shumlin was directing a play, *Kiss Them For Me*, and that he had not yet cast one of the parts. Shumlin took one look at Judy and offered her the part. It was her first play, and, though the play was not very successful, Judy received good notices. Then in 1946 Judy was cast as Billie Dawn in *Born Yesterday*, winning a Tony Award. In 1950 she played the same part in the film version and won an Academy Award for her role. Unfortunately, her long association with the part had given her a reputation as the "dumb blonde" with the squeaky voice. Betty and Adolph knew that Judy Holliday was intelligent as well as being very talented. They wanted to write a role for her that would show off her talents.

In May 1956 Betty and Adolph were in Hollywood and Judy was filming *Full of Life* there. They presented her with the first draft of *Bells Are Ringing*. The story was an original one. The idea had come to them while they were looking through a telephone book where they saw an advertisement for an answering service. Judy was to play Ella Peterson, a switchboard operator who works for an answering service and takes a personal interest in her customers. Judy consented to do the show, and the three of them agreed that this was a good time to do it. Jerome Robbins was to direct, and the Theatre Guild agreed to produce the show. Jule Styne was signed to do the music. Judy had sung with The Revuers but she had never sung on the Broadway stage. Jule Styne later said, "She was a wonderful actress, so I figured, let her acting ability and the mere fact that she's Judy Holliday make up fifty percent of whatever we write" ("Jule Styne," *Notes on Broadway*, p. 289). He wrote music that fitted the character of Ella Peterson and that Judy could sing.

Bells Are Ringing opened at the Sam S. Shubert Theatre in New York on November 29, 1956, and ran for over two years--924 performances. For her role in the musical, Judy won a 1957 Tony Award. (See S04 for details about the musical.)

Nineteen fifty-eight was a very busy year for Comden and Green. They wrote the lyrics for a play with music, wrote a screenplay, and performed their own material both on and off Broadway. *Say, Darling* was first a novel written by Richard Bissell, a writer from Iowa. It was an account by Mr. Bissell of his experience adapting an earlier novel, *7 1/2 Cents*, into a Broadway musical called *The Pajama Game*. He pictured himself as the naive Mid-Westerner trying to hold his own against the sophisticated and egotistical New York backers, producers, directors, song writers, and actors connected with a Broadway musical. With his wife, Marian Bissell, and Abe Burrows, Bissell adapted his novel, *Say, Darling*, for the stage. Comden and Green and Jule Styne were brought in to add musical numbers. The resulting *Say, Darling* cannot be called a musical because it has no orchestra and no production numbers. It shows the auditions and the rehearsals for the stage show called *The Girl From Indiana*. Comden and Green and Styne were asked to provide some very bad musical numbers that the musical director for *The Girl from Indiana* wrote and also a few well-written numbers that helped to carry the story line of *Say, Darling*. They managed to create both the bad and the good, but *Say, Darling* received mixed reviews from the critics. It opened at the ANTA Theatre on April 3, 1958, and played 332 performances. (For details see S11.)

All of the screenplays that Comden and Green had written had been for the Freed Unit at Metro-Goldwyn-Mayer, but in 1958 they were asked by Warner Bros. to write a screenplay for the popular Broadway play, *Auntie Mame*, by Jerome Lawrence and Robert E. Lee. *Auntie Mame* was also the name of the 1955 best-selling novel by Patrick Dennis about his eccentric but exuberant aunt who had reared him after his own parents had died. Morton DaCosta had directed the play and was asked to direct the film version. Rosalind Russell had played Mame Dennis on Broadway for 639 performances and now consented to play the role on film. Three touring companies were still traveling across the country with the play when the film was released. *Auntie Mame* was the first film Morton DaCosta had directed.

Working with him, Comden and Green made few changes in the story line, and the resulting film was little changed from the play, except for the many outdoor scenes. Mame Dennis was such a favorite character for the American public, that the film, which opened at Radio City Music Hall on December 4, 1958, became one of the top money-makers of 1959. (For details of the film see F08.)

Betty and Adolph had always considered themselves performers. They had started writing their own material when they were performing as The Revuers only because they could not afford to pay royalties on someone else's material. Since writing *On the Town* in 1944 they had been so much in demand as writers that they had had little chance to act and sing themselves. Their chance to get on stage again came in 1958. By accident, they ran into an old friend, Gus Schirmer, Jr., who managed the Cherry Lane Theatre in Greenwich Village. He told them that he was starting a series called "Monday Nights at Nine," and he asked them if they would like to make a Monday night appearance in a program of some of the material that they had written. At first, Betty and Adolph were reluctant. They had started out in the Village and were not sure that they wanted to return there. However, they did like to perform, and, though they had not acted publicly since *On the Town*, they had been performing in their friends' living rooms for years. Betty's husband, Steve, encouraged them to accept the offer. They agreed to play two Monday nights, November 10 and 17, 1958.

Betty and Adolph began choosing material. They decided to use some of their old numbers from The Revuers and also songs from *On the Town, Bonanza Bound!, Two on the Aisle, Peter Pan, Wonderful Town, Bells Are Ringing*, and from the film, *Good News*, for which they had written "The French Lesson."

On November 10 they performed before an enthusiastic audience. In fact, they were such a success that Armina Marshall and Lawrence Langner of the Theatre Guild asked them if they would like to move uptown for a regular run. Betty and Adolph thought that the Langners must be kidding, but they were not. They played a few more Monday nights at Cherry Lane and then they moved the show exactly as it was to the Golden Theatre uptown. They opened there on December 23, 1958, to rave reviews from all seven New York critics.

A Party With Betty Comden and Adolph Green was presented very simply. Comden and Green appeared before a screen of gray, purple, and green set against a backdrop that changed color with the lights. They were accompanied by Peter Howard at the piano. They played 38 performances, and then, because of previous commitments, had to close the show. They promised to return in the spring. They did return in April for 44 more performances. Comden and Green's performance at the Cherry Lane Theatre brought them an "Obie" Award for best Off Broadway musical. (For more details see P01.)

While performing *A Party With Betty Comden and Adolph Green*, Betty and Adolph were also writing the screenplay for *Bells Are Ringing*. It was this commitment that had made them reluctantly give up their performance. Arthur Freed had bought the screen rights to *Bells Are Ringing* while the show was still playing on Broadway. As early as January 1958 he announced that Metro-Goldwyn-Mayer would make the film, to be adapted for the screen by Comden and Green and to star Judy Holliday. When Comden and Green signed the contract they were performing in *A Party* and they wanted to do most of the writing in New York. They were not only to adapt the script but also add some new songs. Because they were enjoying their performing so much, Comden and Green suggested that the adaptation be made by someone else. Judy Holliday insisted that no one but her friends write the screenplay.

    Bells Are Ringing had been so well written for the stage that it proved to be very difficult to change to the medium of film. The filming date was postponed several times. Rehearsals finally started on August 15, 1959, and shooting on October 6. Vincente Minnelli was the director. The rehearsal and filming experience was not a happy one. Judy thought the screenplay was not very cinematic, and she frequently disagreed with Minnelli. She thought she knew the character better than he did. Judy's health was very fragile at this time and she was difficult to work with. However, it was her characterization of Ella Peterson that held the film together and made it so popular with movie audiences. *Bells Are Ringing* opened at the Radio City Music Hall on June 23, 1960. The screenplay won for Comden and Green their third Screenwriters Guild Award. Unfortunately, *Bells Are Ringing* was Judy Holliday's last film. She died of cancer on June 7, 1965. (For additional details about the film see F09.)

    In 1956 when Comden and Green and Jule Styne were casting the stage show, *Bells Are Ringing*, they were holding auditions for Judy Holliday's understudy. One of the young singers auditioning was a pretty brunette called Phyllis Newman. She had done some performing as a child, and then as an adult had understudied the female comic lead dancer in *Wish You Were Here* and had appeared in some television shows. At the auditions for Judy's understudy, she sang and read a scene with the stage manager. Then three people came down the aisle of the theatre. They were Jule Styne and Comden and Green. They complimented her and told her that she had the part. This was her first meeting with Adolph Green.

    Adolph was a good friend of both Judy Holliday and the leading man, Sydney Chaplin, the son of Charlie Chaplin. Adolph was around the theatre a lot while *Bells Are Ringing* was rehearsing and playing. Phyllis Newman was attracted to Adolph, but she was also intimidated by "his age, his reputation as an intellectual, his success, and, most of all, by his mind-boggling eccentricity" (Phyllis Newman, *Just in Time*, p. 66). Nevertheless, she began to sit on the back steps of the theatre so that when Adolph entered the stage door he would be sure to see her. In her autobiography, Phyllis has described Adolph as "smallish, slender, dark-skinned with a funny nose and teeth that have a life of their own. He doesn't resemble anyone else. He always looks suspicious and guilty, as though he has just done something he shouldn't have. He rarely looks you straight in the eye. He seems to be hiding something, but I have never found out what it is" (Phyllis Newman, *Just in Time*, p. 65).

    After passing Phyllis on the steps many times, Adolph at last asked her for a date. Phyllis was terrified, but somehow she did manage to get through that first date at Sardi's where they sat at a table next to the writers, Ruth Gordon and Garson Kanin. During the year that Phyllis understudied Judy Holliday, Adolph courted her "warily." She was impressed with his talented and famous friends. One night be brought Lauren Bacall with him, and one night he took Phyllis to Carnegie Hall to hear the New York Philharmonic which his good friend, Leonard Bernstein, was conducting. They sat in a box with Bernstein's wife, Felicia. Phyllis felt awkward and gauche beside the elegant Felicia. After the concert they went backstage to Bernstein's dressing room and then across the street to the Bernstein's apartment. Felicia Bernstein was to become a good friend to Phyllis, just as Leonard continued to be Adolph's special friend.

    After a year, Phyllis left *Bells Are Ringing* and took the part of Jane in the

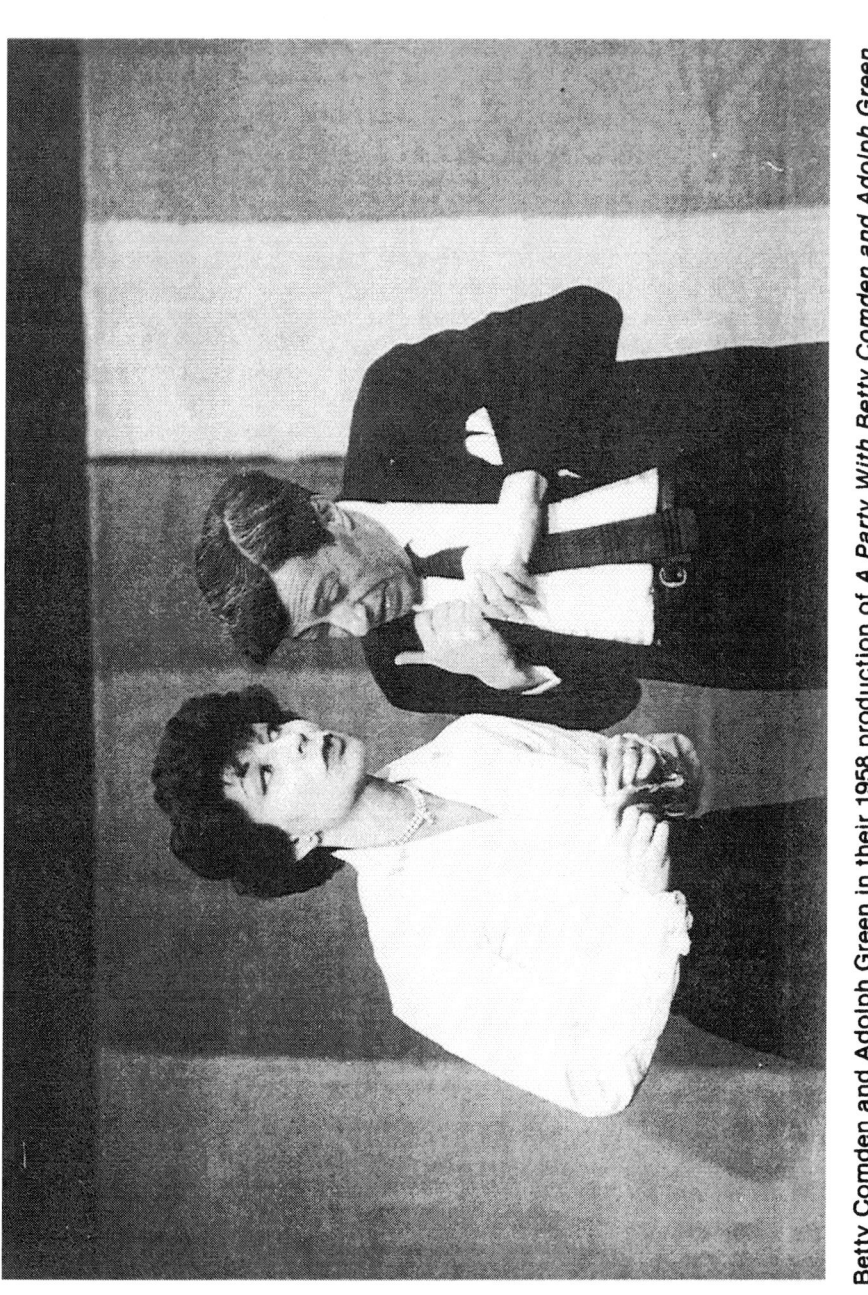

Betty Comden and Adolph Green in their 1958 production of *A Party With Betty Comden and Adolph Green*. Photograph courtesy of Betty Comden.

musical version of *Pride and Prejudice* called *First Impressions* with a book by Abe Burrows. Adolph came to visit Phyllis in Philadelphia, where the show was trying out before going to Broadway. The show opened in New York at the Alvin Theatre on March 19, 1959. It was not very successful, playing only 84 performances.

In her attempt to create a 19th century character for *First Impressions*, Phyllis had read the novels of Jane Austen and other books of the period and had become fascinated with Great Britain. She decided to go to London and Paris that summer of 1959. Another enticement was that Adolph was going to be in Europe. Sydney Chaplin had asked him to go to Switzerland with him to visit his famous father. Phyllis and Adolph made very vague plans about possibly meeting in Europe.

After a few days in London, Phyllis went to Paris where Adolph and Sydney were staying before going on to Switzerland. When Phyllis called Adolph he was a little evasive. She discovered that he was seeing an ex-girl friend who also was in Paris. Phyllis joined Adolph and his friends for dinner several times. One evening, Sydney Chaplin asked Phyllis if she would like to join him and Adolph in visiting his "old man" and Oona and the children. Who could resist that invitation? The three of them went off to Vevey, Switzerland.

Charlie Chaplin was now a stocky, white-haired man, but he was still the inimitable performer. Phyllis could see that Adolph was completely fascinated by Chaplin. She began to realize that her competition for Adolph was not another girl but his "family" of "geniuses and artistic visionaries" (Phyllis Newman, *Just in Time*, p. 84). This family consisted of Betty Comden, Leonard Bernstein, Judy Holliday, and Sydney Chaplin. They had their family jokes and family history, and their own language. At the Chaplins' home, Adolph sat entranced while Charlie recalled his experiences. Adolph was able to hum every note of Chaplin's movie scores. He could recall any film title or bit of film business that Charlie could mention.

Phyllis left Switzerland for Cannes and then went on to Rome. Adolph joined her in Rome where he had another group of friends. Phyllis wanted to sightsee in Rome and not sit around reminiscing with Adolph and his friends. Even when Adolph took her to see the Colosseum, he was talking about a vaudeville routine or telling her about some experience with Betty or Lenny. At last, Phyllis, in exasperation, told Adolph to stop talking and to leave her. He did leave, but later he apologized and joined her in Venice. He tried to enjoy sightseeing and not keep going back to the past. Adolph left for New York, and Phyllis returned a short time later, confused about their relationship.

A few weeks after her return to the United States, Phyllis went with a girl friend to the Westport Playhouse in Connecticut to see Adolph and Betty perform in *A Party With Betty Comden and Adolph Green*. She thought they were wonderful, and it was this night that made her decide she really was in love with Adolph. They now began to see each other regularly.

A short time later, Phyllis took a part in an English adaptation of a French play by Marcel Ayme called *Moonbirds*. After previewing in Philadelphia, the show opened at the Cort Theatre in New York on October 9, 1959. The opening night of the play was a very nerve-wracking experience for Phyllis because her parents were to met Adolph for the first time. Though the play was not a success, the meeting between the Newmans and Adolph was, and Phyllis and Adolph began to plan their wedding.

Adolph and Phyllis were married at a Sunday night wedding in Adolph's apartment on January 31, 1960. Phyllis's sister, Mrs. Elliott Porte, was the matron

Phyllis Newman and Adolph Green at the time of their wedding in 1960. Photograph courtesy of Adolph Green.

of honor, and Adolph's brother, William, was the best man. Just as the wedding was about to begin, Adolph realized that he had forgotten to hire a musician to play "Here Comes the Bride." However, one of the guests was the composer, Jule Styne, who sat down to play the song for the bride to make her entrance. A reception was held at the Sheraton East (the former Ambassador Hotel). Phyllis was much impressed by Adolph's many friends who happened to be celebrities and who attended the reception--the Bernsteins, Abe Burrows, Ray Bolger, George Abbott, Lauren Bacall, the Lawrence Langners, Moss Hart and his wife Kitty Carlisle, Phil Silvers and his wife, Betty Comden and her husband Steven Kyle, Sydney Chaplin, Henry Fonda and his wife, Arlene Frances, Mike Nichols, and Arthur Laurents. The wedding pictures were taken by the famous photographer, Richard Avedon. Phyllis and Adolph danced the first dance to the tune of "Lucky to Be Me" from *On the Town* (*Just in Time*, p. 94). Adolph Green and Phyllis Newman later had two children. Adam Green was born in 1961 and Amanda was born in 1964.

On Adolph Green's wedding day, January 31, 1960, CBS Television aired a television spectacular called *The Fabulous Fifties*. It was a two hour show celebrating the decade. Comden and Green appeared on the show, along with Julie Andrews, Shelly Berman, Henry Fonda, Jackie Gleason, Rex Harrison, Elaine May, Mike Nichols, Suzy Parker, and Eric Sevareid. Leland Hayward was the producer (Les Spindle, *Julie Andrews*, p. 86). (See T14.)

In 1960 Betty and Adolph wrote the lyrics for another Broadway musical. In 1955 Garson Kanin had written a novella called *Do Re Mi*. He adapted the story for the stage, and Comden and Green and Jule Styne were asked to write the songs for it. *Do Re Mi* was about a loser named Hubert Cram who had always wanted to be somebody. Not content with an ordinary job, he always had his head filled with great plans that would make him successful or wealthy or both. His great plans usually failed, and this is what happens in the play when he decides to go into the jukebox and record business. The role of Hubie Cram was played by Phil Silvers, who at this time was well known to television viewers as Sergeant Bilko. His wife was played by the popular comedienne, Nancy Walker.

After tryouts in Philadelphia and Boston, *Do Re Mi* opened at the St. James Theatre on December 26, 1960. It received favorable reviews from most of the New York critics and ran for 400 performances. Comden and Green and Jule Styne had a hit song with "Make Someone Happy," and Comden and Green contributed very clever lyrics to "It's Legitimate" and "What's New at the Zoo?" On October 22, 1961, the first three scenes from the play were shown on the Ed Sullivan Show on CBS television. (See T47.) The play also had a successful run in London with a British cast. (For details about the musical, see S12.)

In 1961 Comden and Green wrote both the book and the lyrics for another Broadway musical, *Subways Are For Sleeping*. The story was based on a book with the same title that had been written in 1957 by Edmund G. Love. Mr. Love had met and talked with men who had dropped out of the main stream and were living a minimal existence in New York. His book contained vignettes describing the lives of some of these men. From these vignettes, Comden and Green wrote the story of Tom Bailey who had once been a businessman, but after the failure of his business had decided to live an "independent" life, not worrying about making money. He earns a dollar and a half a day walking a wealthy couple's dog, and he sets up his "office" in Grand Central Station every day where he dispenses information and advice to other vagrants. Angie McKay, a magazine writer, has been given the assignment of writing an article about these men and meets Tom Bailey. An unlikely romance develops between them.

Both Adolph and Betty thought that Phyllis Newman would be wonderful in the role of Martha Vail, a young former Southern beauty contestant, who has come to New York to become an actress and singer. Martha has run out of money to pay for her hotel room. In order not to be ejected onto the street, she dresses in a towel which she threatens to drop every time the landlord asks for the rent. Phyllis wanted very much to be in a Broadway play again. She had just taken time out from her career to have the Greens' first child, Adam. She auditioned for the role, but David Merrick, the producer, was hesitant about casting her. She was called back twice. The third time she was told to wear a towel and a blond wig for the audition. She did get the part and sang one of the funniest songs in the show, "I Was a Shoo-In" about what she did for the talent section in her beauty queen contest. At the tryout in Philadelphia, Phyllis got a spontaneous ovation from the audience after the song. The scenes with Martha Vail and her boyfriend, played by Orson Bean, were much more interesting than the scenes between Tom Bailey and Angie McKay. While the play was still in Philadelphia, Betty and Adolph did some fast re-writing to try to make the main plot line more enjoyable for the audience.

Subways Are For Sleeping opened at the St. James Theatre in New York on December 27, 1961. The musical received only two favorable reviews from the critics and closed after 205 performances. For her performance as Martha Vale, Phyllis Newman won a Tony Award for Best Featured Performer in a Musical. (For details about the musical, see S05.)

In 1963 Adolph sang the "Tschaikovsky" number in a recording of selections from the musical play, *Lady in the Dark*. *Lady in the Dark*, with a book by Moss Hart, music by Kurt Weill, and lyrics by Ira Gershwin, had originally been presented in 1941 at the Alvin Theatre in New York. It had starred Gertrude Lawrence and had the young Danny Kaye playing the role of the ringmaster. In the recording made by Columbia Records in 1963, the Gertrude Lawrence role was sung by Risë Stevens, and Adolph Green sang the Danny Kaye role. The "Tschaikovsky" number so cleverly sung by Adolph is an explosive, fast-paced, humorous song listing the names of some forty-nine Russian composers. The song was based upon a poem called "The Music Hour" that Ira Gershwin had written for *Life* magazine in 1924 under the pseudonym of Arthur Francis. (See D55.)

On April 19, 1964, both Betty and Adolph sang in a memorial concert for Marc Blitzstein. Blitzstein, a long time friend of Leonard Bernstein, had been killed in Martinique in January of 1964. The memorial was held at Philharmonic Hall and consisted of individual songs by Blitzstein, excerpts from *Regina*, a musical version of Lillian Hellman's play, *The Little Foxes*, for which Blitzstein wrote the lyrics, and also Blitzstein's best and most well-known work, *The Cradle Will Rock*. *The Cradle Will Rock* had made history on Broadway in 1937. It had been written under the sponsorship of the Federal Theatre Project, a branch of the Works Progress Administration, which provided employment for the jobless during the Depression. John Houseman was the producer and Orson Welles the director. Three days before the scheduled production of the musical play, it was canceled. When Houseman and Welles appealed the ruling, President Roosevelt himself called the director of the Federal Theatre Project to say the show must not go on. Blitzstein's libretto leaned much too far to the left, making heroes of steelworkers and blackguards of capitalists. Since the play was sponsored by a Federal agency, it would seem to be expressing the government's point of view. On the night of the scheduled performance, Houseman, Welles, Jean Rosenthal, the lighting designer, and the actors led the assembled audience in a march up Sixth Avenue to the Venice Theatre. There the show was given. Blitzstein himself played the piano and the singers sang from their seats in the house. At the memorial concert for Blitzstein in 1964, Leonard Bernstein played the piano and the cast was seated in tiers of seats behind him. Several members of the original cast were there. Betty Comden sang the important role of Mrs. Mister. Adolph Green was also in the cast.

In May of 1964 Comden and Green had a new film released and a new Broadway production opening. The film was *What a Way To Go!* starring Shirley MacLaine. This time the screenplay was written for Twentieth Century-Fox. It was based on a story by Gwen Davis and was about Louisa May Foster and her extremely bad luck with husbands. All Louisa wanted was a simple life with a husband and children, but each husband she married made enormous amounts of money and then died. After this had happened four times, Louisa, feeling guilty with so much money, tried to give the money to the government. Everyone thought that she was crazy and advised her to see a psychiatrist. As she talks to the psychiatrist, Louisa tells of her four husbands. Her life with each husband reminded her of a type of movie--the jerky silent movies, the sexy French films, the glamorous Hollywood movies of the 1930s, and the song and dance films directed by Busby Berkeley. The story had a clever and original idea and the film was laden with stars. Dick Van Dyke, Paul Newman, Robert Mitchum, and Gene Kelly were the four husbands, and Dean Martin was the fifth husband with whom she at last found happiness. Most of the critics did not like the film, but it was the top box office success for Twentieth Century-Fox in 1964. (See F10 for more details about the film.)

On May 26, 1964, a new Comden and Green musical starring Carol Burnett opened at the Mark Hellinger Theatre in New York. The show was *Fade Out--Fade In*. Carol Burnett was at the height of her career. She had wanted to be in Broadway musicals, but she made her reputation first on television on the Garry Moore Show and on specials on CBS Television. Then in 1959 she did get her chance to appear on Broadway, playing Princess Winifred in *Once Upon a Mattress*. Carol Burnett liked Comden and Green's story about a movie usherette who is mistakenly chosen to go to Hollywood to star in a film. *Fade Out--Fade In* made hilarious fun of movie moguls and their "yes" men, of egotistical stars, of unbelievable plots, and of "fake" shots staged for the cameras. Comden and Green's satire was, as always, kindly and affectionate. Carol Burnett was very funny as the angular Hope Springfield who becomes a star. The show received favorable reviews from the New York critics, and it looked as if the musical would have a long run. It was not long into the run of the show when Carol began to miss performances. In July 1964 film star, Betty Hutton, took over Carol's role for a week. After the play had run for 199 nights, Carol withdrew from the cast claiming back and neck injuries from the sudden braking of a taxi in which she was riding. The whiplash had aggravated an old injury. Without its star, the show had to close. The producers filed legal action. At last Carol returned, and the show reopened on February 15, 1965, but it played for only 72 performances. Then Carol announced that she was pregnant and would have to leave the show. *Fade Out--Fade In* closed. Carol Burnett had missed 60 out of 271 performances. The show lost more than five hundred thousand dollars (George Carpozi, Jr., *The Carol Burnett Story*, p. 146). (For more information about the musical, see S06.)

In 1964 Comden and Green worked for six months with Leonard Bernstein and Jerome Robbins trying to write a musical version of Thornton Wilder's *The Skin of Our Teeth*. Leland Hayward, the producer, had scheduled a Broadway premiere for September, but an announcement was made on January 4, 1965, saying that the project had to be canceled due to other commitments (Sam Zolotow, "Skin of Our Teeth Musical Dropped," *New York Times*, January 5, 1965).

On June 28, 1965, a retrospective of some of Leonard Bernstein's music for the theatre was presented Off Broadway at the Theatre de Lys. The musical program was called *Leonard Bernstein's Theatre Songs* and was presented by three singers. Songs with lyrics by Comden and Green that were included were "I Feel Like I'm Not Out of Bed Yet" and "Some Other Time" from *On the Town* and "A Quiet Girl" and "It's Love" from *Wonderful Town*. (For more information about this revue, see R01.)

In 1967 Comden and Green wrote the script and lyrics and Jule Styne wrote the music for an original television musical called *I'm Getting Married*. Anne Bancroft played a young American lady about to be married. The only other cast member was Dick Shawn as the man she is to marry. Comden and Green tried to make the hour long play fit the medium of television by concentrating on just the two characters "acting and reacting to each other" (Quoted from Betty Comden and Adolph Green, "He Says 'I Do,' She Says 'I Do'," *New York Times*, March 12, 1967). (See T48.)

While writing *I'm Getting Married*, Comden and Green were also writing the lyrics for *Hallelujah, Baby!*, which opened at the Martin Beck Theatre on April 26, 1967. *Hallelujah, Baby!* had a book by Arthur Laurents and won the 1968 Tony Award for Best Musical of the year. Comden and Green and Jule Styne won the Tony Award for Best Score and Best Lyrics. Leslie Uggams, the young star of the musical, received an Outer Circle Award for her performance and was selected the Most Promising New Broadway Actress in the poll conducted by *Variety*. Yet the play ran for only 293 performances. The musical told the history of black Americans' struggle for equality by showing scenes from the end of the 19th century, the 1920s, the 1930s, the 1940s, and the 1950s. The leading characters in each scene were the same people, who remained the same age throughout all of those decades. It was a clever idea, but the critics thought the story was filled with racial clichés. Only one of the New York reviewers gave the show an entirely favorable review. Most of the critics did like Leslie Uggams who played Georgina, who goes from a domestic in the first scene to a popular night club singer in the last. (See S13 for more details about the musical.)

During the summer of 1967 Adolph went to Israel with Leonard Bernstein, who had been asked to conduct the Israel Philharmonic in a concert on the top of Mt. Scopus to commemorate the reuniting of Jerusalem after the Six-Day War. For years Bernstein had worked with the Israel Philharmonic Orchestra, but this was a special occasion. An audience of fourteen-hundred people had gathered in the amphitheatre and some one hundred and ten musicians were on the stage. The violin soloist was Isaac Stern. Adolph has written about the experience of listening to the concert and seeing his good friend of thirty years conducting on this important occasion. "The great bond between Lenny and myself is music," he wrote. Over the years since they had first met, Adolph and Lenny had "hummed, screamed, and bellowed our way through thousands of pieces--each one an important part of our common bond, music." Adolph became aware as he listened to the concert that day that all who had gathered on Mt. Scopus had done so to celebrate their "faith in the victory of light over darkness" (Adolph Green, "The Day

In 1960 Betty Comden, Adolph Green, and Leonard Bernstein get together to record *On the Town*, which had not been recorded by the original cast in 1944. Photograph courtesy of Betty Comden.

They Made Music on Mt. Scopus," *New York Times*, August 6, 1967).

After the concert, Bernstein was joining his family at a villa in Ansedonia, a small town at the foot of Mount Argentario in Italy, for a rest from his busy schedule. Adolph visited the family there for a few days. That summer Betty Comden and her husband Steven Kyle were vacationing in the area and also stopped by to visit the Bernsteins for a few days. While the Kyles were visiting, Charlie Chaplin and his wife Oona and two of their daughters came for dinner. The evening proved to be a Chaplin-Bernstein festival of "high-powered storytelling, music-making, and mad cutting-up," as John Gruen wrote in his book, *The Private World of Leonard Bernstein* (page 31). Chaplin was at this time 78 years old. Bernstein asked him to play some of the music from his old movies. Then Bernstein took over the piano and Chaplin got up and was suddenly transformed into the young Chaplin of the films. Bernstein then played a mock Italian opera and Chaplin sang an aria in mock-Italian. All at once Betty Comden joined Chaplin and the two of them sang a frenzied duet.

Also during the summer of 1967, the Greens bought a big, rambling house in East Hampton on Long Island. The house had been built in the early part of the century and was approached by means of a long dirt road lined on either side by enormous trees. It made a cool retreat from the summer heat of New York City. Two years later Adolph and Phyllis volunteered their big house as a setting for the wedding of Phyllis's niece. Just before the scheduled time for the wedding, while guests were still arriving, the house caught fire. The wedding was eventually held on the lawn, but the house was destroyed. The next year the Greens had to spend the summer in a small, compact prefabricated house set up in front of the burned out shell. They later built another summer home there. Betty Comden and Steven Kyle also began to spend their summers on Long Island, at first renting a house.

In 1967 Comden and Green's song, "I Said Good Morning," was published as *Good Morning, Good Night*, a children's book with illustrations by Simeon Shimm. The song had music by André Previn. Betty and Adolph had written the song for the film, *It's Always Fair Weather*, but it had not been used. Then Betty and Adolph had used the song as their opening number for their 1958 performance of *A Party With Betty Comden and Adolph Green*. The children's book was published by Holt, Rinehart and Winston. Also in 1967 Betty Comden was elected one of the council members for the Dramatists Guild.

Comden and Green had not had a really successful Broadway musical for some years. Then in 1970 they at last had a big hit. It was *Applause*, starring Lauren Bacall. Comden and Green wrote the book for *Applause*. The music was by Charles Strouse and the lyrics by Lee Adams. *Applause* was based on the popular motion picture, *All About Eve*, which had starred Bette Davis and Anne Baxter. The original story about an aging Broadway star had been written by Mary Orr.

Lauren Bacall had made her reputation as a sultry-voiced actress in films. In 1965, after the death of her husband, Humphrey Bogart, and her marriage to Jason Robards, she had moved back to New York and to the theatre. She played in *Cactus Flower* for two years, and she felt that the stage was really her home. Then she received an offer to do the musical adaptation of *All About Eve*. The first writer for the adaptation had to be replaced, and Bacall was asked by the producers about using Comden and Green to write the book. Bacall had always thought it bad to mix friendship and work, so she hesitated because both Betty and Adolph were very good friends. However, as she wrote, "they were so smart and funny, and talented" that she agreed (Lauren Bacall, *By Myself*, p. 353). Both Betty and Adolph called Bacall to see how she felt about their working together. They all agreed to work through the director, Ron Field. Their collaboration worked out very well.

Lauren Bacall was now 45 years old. She had never been in a musical before. She spent three months taking singing and dancing lessons before the actual rehearsals for the play began. Comden and Green did not have the movie rights. They worked from the original story. They changed some characters, but they did keep the basic story line of the film. The book that they wrote was a solid one with well-defined characters. They built up the character of the star, Margo Channing, to fit the personality of Lauren Bacall. They also added scenes to help develop the character of Eve Harrington, the young actress who tries to take away both Margo's role in the play and her fiancé.

Applause opened at the Palace Theatre on March 30, 1970. The critics were enthusiastic, and the musical won the Tony Award for Best Musical, with Betty and Adolph and Charles Strouse and Lee Adams all winning Tony Awards. Lauren Bacall won as Best Actress in a Musical. The show continued to play to capacity houses even after Bacall left New York for the road tour. *Applause* was given 840 performances on Broadway, closing on May 27, 1972. (See S15 for more details about the musical.)

In 1971 a revival of *On the Town* was given on Broadway, but it was not very successful. Ron Field, who had so successfully directed *Applause*, directed and choreographed *On the Town*. However, in spite of its outstanding cast, which included Phyllis Newman as Claire and Bernadette Peters as Hildy, this production was not successful. The revival ran for only 53 performances.

Betty and Adolph were able to perform once again in 1971. They appeared on January 11 in the second in a monthly series called *Lyrics and Lyricists* at the Young Men's and Young Women's Hebrew Association's Kaufman Auditorium. Also they presented a new version of *A Party With Betty Comden and Adolph Green* at the Julliard School of Music.

In 1974 Comden and Green and Jule Styne contributed some new songs to *Lorelei*, a revised version of the 1949 musical, *Gentlemen Prefer Blondes*. Carol Channing had been touring in *Lorelei* for eleven months and finally brought it to New York, opening at the Palace Theatre on January 27. (See S18 for more information about the musical.)

In 1975 Comden and Green had the idea to present once again some of the music of Leonard Bernstein. They wrote a musical entertainment called *By Bernstein*. This revue presented songs that had been written for Broadway shows but had not been used. *By Bernstein* opened at the Chelsea Theatre Center on November 23, 1975, and closed on December 7, after 17 performances and 40 previews. Lyricists represented were Comden and Green, Bernstein, John Latouche, Jerry Leiber, and Stephen Sondheim. (See R02 for more details about this revue.)

Also in 1975 Comden and Green contributed some lyrics to *Straws in the Wind*, a musical that did not reach Broadway. (For more details about the musical, see S19.)

On May 1976 Betty and Adolph were in the cast of a spectacular tribute to George Abbott. It was called *George Abbott ... A Celebration* and was sponsored by the Friends of the Theatre and Music Collection of the Museum of the City of New York. The celebration honored Abbott's 63 years as a Broadway producer, director, playwright, and actor.

On February 10, 1977, Betty and Adolph were back on the boards again performing *A Party With Betty Comden and Adolph Green* at the Morosco Theatre. Their program included some new songs as well as some of the same material they had used in 1958. This presentation was more relaxed with more information included between the musical numbers. The critics once again were struck by Comden and Green's wit and intelligence and their professionalism as performers. This 1977 version of *A Party* ran for 92 performances following four previews. It closed on April 30. (See P01 for information about this 1977 version of *A Party*.)

In 1978 Comden and Green had another hit on Broadway. They wrote both the book and the lyrics for *On the Twentieth Century*. Cy Coleman wrote the music. The musical was based on a play, *Twentieth Century*, that had been written in 1932 by Ben Hecht and Charles MacArthur. Hecht and MacArthur had adapted an earlier play written by Bruce Millholland called *Napoleon on Broadway*. Comden and Green kept the period of the 1930s and let the two flamboyant characters of the play-- Oscar Jaffee, an impresario-director, and Lily Garland, a Hollywood actress--dictate the style they would use for their adaptation. Working with Cy Coleman and Harold Prince, the director, they developed a comic opera style for both the words and the music. Robin Wagner, the scene designer, created a wonderful Art Deco train that could be viewed from the outside as well as reveal its elegant interior rooms.

On the Twentieth Century previewed in Boston and then opened at the St. James Theatre on February 20, 1978. It ran for 449 performances on Broadway and then began an extended tour of the country. *On the Twentieth Century* won five Tony Awards. Comden and Green won two awards--one for Best Book and one, with Cy Coleman, for Best Score of a Broadway Musical. John Cullum won for his outstanding performance of Oscar Jaffee, the impresario, and Kevin Kline won for his performance in a featured role. Robin Wagner won for his ingenious scenic design. In January of 1979, Betty Comden played the role of Letitia Primrose, the religious fanatic. She took over the role for a week while Imogene Coca was on vacation. The musical had a successful run in London. (See S07 for details about the musical.)

While *On the Twentieth Century* was still playing, Imogene Coca was honored by the governor of the state, by the mayor, and other politicians and theatre people for her fifty years in show business. Miss Coca was most famous to American audiences for her television series with Sid Caesar, *Your Show of Shows*, which had brought her zany comedy into American living rooms. The celebration was part of the "I Love New York" publicity campaign to bring visitors to the city. It was held on January 15, 1979. The entertainment was provided by Comden and Green and Cy Coleman. Comden and Green sang some songs from their musicals with updated lyrics that satirized the New York of 1979.

Also in 1979, Phyllis Newman, working with playwright, Arthur Laurents, wrote a one woman show for herself called *The Madwoman of Central Park West*. The show is a humorous look at a wealthy New York woman who is torn between coping with her husband and two children and resuming her show business career. The show included many songs, both old and new. Comden and Green and Leonard Bernstein wrote the opening song for the show, "Up, Up, Up," which is about how much self-approval this character needed to begin another day. *The Madwoman of Central Park West* opened at the 22 Steps Theatre on June 13, 1979, and ran for 85 performances. The show was later produced on television for Mobil Showcase Network's *Summershow*. (For more details about this one-woman show, see S21.)

Betty Comden and her husband, Steven Kyle, on their 25th wedding anniversary, 1967. Photograph courtesy of Betty Comden.

In October of 1979 Betty Comden's husband, Steven Kyle, died of acute pancreatitis. After having served in World War II, Mr. Kyle, an artist, had returned to New York City where he opened Americraft, a store for decorative accessories, some of which he himself designed. He had closed the store when he retired in 1970. Mr. Kyle was a tall, handsome man, quiet, but with a wonderful sense of humor. He took being married to a famous playwright with great serenity. He was always interested in Betty's work, as she was in his. Betty said of him, "He was an enormous help to me in my work. We used him as a sounding board. He was very important to me in that part of my life" (Obituary, *New York Times*, October 18, 1979).

On March 17, 1980, Comden and Green were installed into the Songwriters' Hall of Fame. The next year they were elected to the Theatre Hall of Fame. They were inducted on April 5 in "A Tribute to Broadway" at the Uris Theatre. A group of drama critics and editors make the selection of those to be taken into the Theatre Hall of Fame. To be eligible for membership a person must have had a career spanning at least twenty-five years on Broadway and more than five major credits. Members' names appear on the walls of the Uris Theatre lobby. Comden and Green's frequent collaborator, Jule Styne, was inducted at the same time.

In February of 1982 Betty Comden, who had been contending with poor vision for some time, underwent a successful corneal transplant on her right eye. She went to Pittsburgh for the operation, but she soon returned to New York to join with Adolph in teaching master classes in writing musical comedies for New York University's Tisch School of the Arts. Some of the classes were held in her own living room on East 59th Street. New York University started its two year program in the writing of musicals in 1981, and the first graduating class received their Master of Fine Arts degrees in the spring of 1983. Comden and Green were part of the visiting faculty helping to teach the classes. The major part of the class time in the program is devoted to workshops in which the students, working in teams, write scenes and, eventually, full musicals under the supervision of the master teachers like Comden and Green.

In 1982 Comden and Green had to divide their time between teaching and auditioning for their newest musical, *A Doll's Life*. They had been working for nearly two years on the book. They had had the idea of continuing the story of Henrik Ibsen's Nora after she leaves her husband and children at the end of the play, *A Doll's House*. For them it meant attempting something more serious than most of their writing had been. For Betty especially the idea seemed an interesting one. She had had a home and family as well as a career, but she knew that many women even today live only in the shadow of their husbands. It seemed a challenging idea to try to visualize what a woman like Nora could do to make her way on her own in the 1870s. Comden and Green talked with Harold Prince, who was going to direct the show. He liked the idea, but when he started working with them he wanted to "free the script from realism" and suggested setting the story within a modern day rehearsal of *A Doll's House*. He advised using the modern cast members as a chorus, and he also wanted to use dancers to symbolize the three stages in a woman's life to add "abstraction" to the musical (Carol Ilson, *Harold Prince*, p. 323).

The *A Doll's Life* cast and crew went to Los Angeles for final technical rehearsals and previews. The musical opened there at the Ahmanson Theatre on June 15, 1982. The reviews were not good. Some minor changes were made, but the musical lost money every week for ten weeks. Extra money was raised to keep the show going and to bring it back to New York. After 18 previews in New York, *A Doll's Life* opened at the Mark Hellinger Theatre on September 23, 1982. The reviews were devastating, and the show closed after five performances. In spite of its early closing, *A Doll's Life* was nominated for Tony Awards for Best Book and Best Score of a Musical. Those awards, however, were won by *Cats*. (See S08 for more details about the musical.)

In December of 1982, Betty and Adolph's old friend, Gene Kelly, was honored at the Kennedy Center. Along with Lillian Gish, Benny Goodman, Eugene Ormandy, and George Abbott, he was given an award for a Lifetime Achievement in the Performing Arts. In celebrating the life of Gene Kelly, a film clip of his famous rain number from Comden and Green's film, *Singin' in the Rain*, was shown. Then Donald O'Connor, Cyd Charisse, Betty, and Adolph did a take-off on the "Singin' in the Rain" number, dancing and singing "Take Kelly's face. He has charm! He has grace!" (Clive Hirschhorn, *Gene Kelly*, p. 277).

The failure of *A Doll's Life* was a great disappointment to Comden and Green, but it did not stop them from continuing their many activities. Adolph, who, as a young man, had wanted so much to be in motion pictures, now was getting acting roles in them. In 1980 he had appeared in *Simon*, which starred Alan Arkin. Adolph appeared as a guru in a commune. He was very funny and received good notices by the critics. (See P03.) In 1982 he was in *My Favorite Year*, produced by Metro-Goldwyn-Mayer-United Artists and starring Peter O'Toole. O'Toole played the role of an aging film star, Alan Swann, who is invited to appear as a guest artist on a live television show. Adolph played Leo Silver, the producer of the television show. (See P04.)

In 1984 Betty and Adolph were both in the film, *Garbo Talks*, produced by United Artists. Sidney Lumet, the director, wanted Betty to play the role of Garbo because he thought she looked like her. Betty was in only a few scenes; however, the entire film was about the search for the elusive Garbo. (See P07.)

Betty also was acting in New York. In December 1983 she appeared at Playwrights Horizon Theatre Off Broadway in Wendy Wasserstein's new comedy, *Isn't It Romantic?* Betty played Tasha Blumberg, the Jewish mother of the young woman who aspires to be a writer. Betty said that she accepted the role because "it seemed like a good way to shake oneself up. It's good to do something new every 40 years" (Carol Lawrence, "Broadway," *New York Times*, January 6, 1984). (See P05.)

In the fall of 1984 Adolph and his wife, Phyllis Newman, and their daughter, Amanda, presented two one act plays written by Murray Schisgal as a benefit performance for a new theatre to be built at Trinity School. Amanda had been a student there before going away to college. The two plays were presented under the title, *The New Yorkers*. Adolph and Amanda were in the first play and Adolph and Phyllis in the second. (See P06.)

In 1984 Comden and Green contributed one of the lyrics used in *Diamonds*, a revue about baseball. *Diamonds* was presented at the Off Broadway Circle in the Square Downtown Theatre, opening on November 23 and closing after 122 performances. (See S22 for more details about the musical.)

In 1985 Comden and Green's *A Party With Betty Comden and Adolph Green* was presented on cable television. (See T37.) Also during 1985 Adolph went to Budapest for the filming of *Lily in Love*, starring Christopher Plummer and Maggie Smith. He was delighted to get to go to Budapest because his family had come from Hungary. In fact, Adolph had spoken Hungarian before he spoke English.

Since Betty and Adolph were used to working together every day, Adolph made it a condition of his contract that the film company would fly Betty there and pay for her hotel room so that the Comden and Green team could continue working during the three weeks that the filming took. (See P08.)

In 1985 Comden and Green had another musical on Broadway. This time it was a stage version of their popular film, *Singin' in the Rain*. Maurice Rosenfield, a lawyer from Chicago, had persuaded Metro-Goldwyn-Mayer-United Artists to license the worldwide stage rights to *Singin' in the Rain* to him. Rosenfield and his wife wanted to try out their concept of the stage musical in London before doing it in New York. They licensed Harold Fielding to stage a production there. He hired Tommy Steele, a popular British song and dance man, to direct and act the Gene Kelly role of Don Lockwood in the musical. The stage musical opened in London in 1983 and ran for 894 performances. However, the Rosenfields were not happy with Tommy Steele's "Cockney" version of Don Lockwood and thought that it would not be suitable for an American audience.

In 1984 the Rosenfields saw *Nine Sinatra Songs*, directed by the choreographer, Twyla Tharp, and decided to ask her to direct the American stage version of *Singin' in the Rain*. She had never directed a Broadway musical. Comden and Green agreed to do the book for the musical, though they knew it would be very difficult to adapt the film story for the stage. The Rosenfields and Twyla Tharp really did not want to change the story to fit the stage. They wanted to reproduce the film on the stage and would not let Comden and Green make changes. There were many difficulties with the show, and the opening was postponed several times. After 38 previews, *Singin' in the Rain* opened on July 2, 1985, at the Gershwin Theatre. The critics were unanimous in their negative reviews. The producers seriously considered closing the show, but then they decided to try to keep the show open. They poured money into publicity, and the cast members took cuts in their salaries. They did keep the show running for 367 performances. It was unfortunate that Comden and Green were not allowed to adapt the show for the stage. (See S16 for details about the musical.)

On September 8 and 9, 1985, Betty Comden, Adolph Green, Phyllis Newman, George Hearn, Lee Remick, Mandy Patinkin, Barbara Cook, Carol Burnett, Elaine Stritch, and Lilianne Montevecchi sang and performed a concert version of Stephen Sondheim's *Follies* in Avery Fisher Hall at Lincoln Center. They were accompanied by the Philharmonic orchestra. The more humorous songs were sung by Carol Burnett, Elaine Stritch, and Betty and Adolph, who played Emily and Theodore Whitman and sang "Rain on the Roof." Each night the audience of over three thousand stood and cheered when the concert was over. It was a thrilling experience for the performers. (See P09.) This concert version of *Follies* was being recorded for an RCA album. (See D52.) It was also filmed as part of the Public Broadcasting Service's Great Performances and was later released as a video.

In 1986 a production of *On the Town* was a highlight of the 19th annual American Theatre Festival at Long Island University's C. W. Post Campus. On April 12, Comden and Green were special guest speakers before the matinee performance of the musical. That same evening they performed their newest version of *A Party* at the Suffolk YM-YWHA in Commack. In the last few years they had presented *A Party* in Canada, California, Florida, Texas, and Illinois. In this new version they included one of their more recent songs, "Learn to Be Lonely," from *A Doll's Life*.

The nostalgic looking back at the great musicals of the '40s, '50s, and '60s continued in 1988 when Jerome Robbins began to try to reconstruct some of the dance numbers he had choreographed for Broadway shows. In 1943 Jerome Robbins, then a dancer with the Ballet Theatre, had worked with Leonard Bernstein to present a twenty-five minute ballet called *Fancy Free*. The ballet had provided the inspiration for Comden and Green and Bernstein and Robbins' first Broadway musical, *On the Town*. After twenty years of choreographing for Broadway musicals, Robbins began to devote himself exclusively to the ballet. In 1988, at the age of 70, he decided to try to recreate some of his greatest dances. His new production was *Jerome Robbins' Broadway*. For it he called in Comden and Green, as well as many other former collaborators and dancers, to help him re-construct his original choreography. Before the days of video-tape most Broadway shows were not recorded and the movement and dance of the performance was lost. Included in *Jerome Robbins' Broadway* were ballets and songs from *On the Town, Billion Dollar Baby, A Funny Thing Happened on the Way to the Forum, High Button Shoes, West Side Story, The King and I, Gypsy, Peter Pan, Miss Liberty, Call Me Madam*, and *Fiddler on the Roof*. Using a cast of sixty-two dancers, *Jerome Robbins' Broadway* opened at the Imperial Theatre on February 26, 1989, and played for 634 performances and 55 previews. The musical won the Tony Award for Best Musical, and Jerome Robbins won a Tony for Best Direction. *Jerome Robbins' Broadway* left the critics wondering why the new shows on Broadway do not have the kind of dancing these shows of the '40s, '50s, and '60s had. A national tour of the show was begun in May 1991 (For more information about the revue, see R03.)

In 1988 Adolph was one of about one hundred famous people who told their favorite jokes in *Funny*, an 81 minute documentary produced, directed, and photographed by Bran Ferren. Among those performing besides Green were Dick Cavett, Fred Ebb, Eli Wallach, Anne Jackson, and Alan King. (See P13.) In 1989 Adolph Green had a leading role in the film, *I Want To Go Home*. Green played Joey Wellman, a cartoonist who goes to Paris to attend an exhibition of comic strip art and to visit his daughter who is attending classes at the Sorbonne. *I Want To Go Home* was filmed in Paris. (See P12.)

In 1989 Betty Comden had her turn in performing in a film. It was *Slaves of New York*, based on Tama Janowitz's short stories about various denizens of the downtown art scene. James Ivory adapted the material and directed the film which starred Bernadette Peters. Famous comediennes like Betty Comden and Tammy Grimes made brief appearances in the picture. The film was released by Tri-Star Pictures. (See P14.)

In 1990 Adolph sang the role of Dr. Pangloss in a new recording of Leonard Bernstein's *Candide*. *Candide*, based on Voltaire's story, was originally called a comic operetta. It had a book by Lillian Hellman, a score by Bernstein, and lyrics credited to Richard Wilbur, John Latouche, and Dorothy Parker. It was really a political comment on the McCarthy hearings of the 1950s. It opened on December 1, 1956, and was not very successful, running fewer than eighty performances. In 1973 Harold Prince directed a revival of *Candide* with a new book written by Hugh Wheeler. It played first in Brooklyn's Chelsea Theatre and then moved to the Broadway Theatre, where it ran for 740 performances. In 1982 there was a New York City Opera "opera house" version and in 1988 a Scottish Opera production. The new recording by Deutsche Grammophon is called the "final revised version, 1989" and is a concert version with narration replacing dialogue. The London

Symphony Orchestra is conducted by Leonard Bernstein and uses the London Symphony Chorus with guest singers Jerry Hadley as Candide, June Anderson as Cunegonde, Adolph Green as Dr. Pangloss and Martin, and Christi Ludwig as the Old Lady. The recording was released in 1991. (See D50.) On October 14, 1990, Leonard Bernstein had died of cardiac arrest brought on by lung failure.

Even while acting in motion pictures and giving occasional performances of *A Party*, Comden and Green were also writing the lyrics for a Broadway musical. On March 18, 1991, during a work session for the new musical, Betty slipped and fell. She broke her kneecap. From her bed the next day, she declared that Adolph and she would still perform at a benefit for Long Island Stage scheduled for the next Saturday. "I just don't want to lie here," she said. "I'll perform in a wheel chair, and Adolph will dance around me, as usual" ("Chronicle," *New York Times Metropolitan*, March 20, 1991).

The new musical was *The Will Rogers Follies*, which opened at the legendary Palace Theatre on May 1, 1991. The Palace, built in 1913, had been a famous vaudeville house. After the days of vaudeville, the Palace became a legitimate theatre. Just prior to the opening of *The Will Rogers Follies* the theatre had undergone another renovation. So the opening of May 1 was not only the opening of a new show but also a grand opening for the old, beloved theatre. The musical, with a book by Peter Stone, told the story of Will Rogers' life as Florenz Ziegfeld might have depicted it in one of his elaborate *Follies*.

The combination of the simple story of the down-to-earth cowboy-philosopher and the elaborate production numbers of a Ziegfeld *Follies* was a strange one that brought a few negative reviews from some of the critics. However, the audiences liked the show, which played on Broadway for 982 performances. As of this writing, the road company is still touring. Much of the credit for the success of the show must go to the director-choreographer, Tommy Tune, to the appealing performance of Keith Carradine as Will Rogers, to the scenic design by Tony Walton, and to the songs by Cy Coleman and Comden and Green. *The Will Rogers Follies* won six Tony Awards. The show itself won as Best Musical. Comden and Green and Cy Coleman won a Tony for Best Score. Tommy Tune won for both direction and choreography. Willa Kim won for her costume designs and Jules Fisher for his lighting. *The Will Rogers Follies* also won the Drama Desk Award for Outstanding Musical. Comden and Green won a Grammy Award for their lyrics for *The Will Rogers Follies* record album. (See S14 and D39.)

Also in 1991 Comden and Green contributed the lyrics for a song, "Mamushka," with music by Marc Shaiman to the film, *The Addams Family*. Based on Charles Addams' macabre *New Yorker* pen-and-ink drawings, the film was released by Paramount Pictures in November of 1991. (See D42.)

On May 29, 1991, Comden and Green were presented the Johnny Mercer Award for Lifetime Achievement at the Songwriters Hall of Fame's annual induction ceremonies at the New York Hilton. The presentation was made by their friend and collaborator, Jule Styne. On December 8, 1991, Comden and Green were presented the Kennedy Center Honors for Lifetime Achievement in the Performing Arts. Among those paying tribute to their work were Gene Kelly, Lauren Bacall, and Carol Burnett. Adolph's wife and daughter sang one of Comden and Green's songs. The two hour program was presented on CBS Television on December 26, 1991.

In July of 1992 Betty and Adolph went to London to narrate a concert version of their very first musical, *On the Town*, which had originally been given in

1944. The music for the concert version was provided by the London Symphony Orchestra. Guest singers included British opera stars and the American musical comedy actress, Tyne Daly. The concert version was given twice at the Barbican Theatre and was recorded for PBS television. The television program and the recording have not yet been released.

The night after their performances at the Barbican Theatre, Betty and Adolph presented their *A Party With Betty Comden and Adolph Green* for the first time in London.

On October 9 and 10, 1992, Betty and Adolph performed *A Party With Betty Comden and Adolph Green* at the Kennedy Center. For this latest version of their on-going "party," they included a song from their newest musical, *The Will Rogers Follies*. They were accompanied by Paul Trueblood at the piano. Mr. Trueblood began his association with Betty and Adolph when they presented their *A Party* on Broadway in 1977.

Betty and Adolph were once again at the Kennedy Center in December of 1992 when the Kennedy Center Award for Lifetime Achievement in the Performing Arts was presented to their friend, Paul Taylor. Betty spoke the words of appreciation for the work of Paul Taylor. Betty and Adolph knew the famous dancer and choreographer primarily through their work with him on a benefit for the Paul Taylor Dance Company, when they presented a satire on America called "From Sea to Shining Sea."

Betty and Adolph have no intention of resting on their laurels. Now, in 1993, they are beginning work on a new musical. It is just in the planning stages, and they will not give out any hints about the subject.

Betty Comden and Adolph Green have always been very generous in donating their time and their talents to help raise money for good causes. Among the many charitable and cultural organizations they have helped are the Federation for Jewish Charities, the National Conference for Christians and Jews, the New York Public Library for the Performing Arts at Lincoln Center, Carnegie Hall, and the New York Philharmonic Orchestra.

Both Betty and Adolph serve on the Council for the Dramatists Guild. The Council meets once a month to decide on policies for the Guild, to oversee production contracts, and to sponsor educational programs.

Betty Comden lives in an East Side townhouse located between Park and Lexington Avenues. In her den framed playbills blend with the early American flavor of the room. Betty lives alone. Her son, Alan, died in 1990. Her daughter, Susanna, who has always been extremely fond of animals, has a boarding and walking service for dogs. Adolph Green lives with his wife on the West Side of Central Park. Their daughter, Amanda, is continuing her career as an actress, and their son, Adam, is a writer. Adolph and Phyllis spend much of each summer at their summer home in East Hampton on Long Island. For years Betty and her husband rented a summer place on Long Island, but recently Betty has bought a house in Bridgehampton, Long Island, where she spends much of the summer.

Since 1939 the team of Comden and Green has been working together. They started writing their own material because they could not afford to pay royalties. At first there were five of them, but by 1943 there were only the two--two talented, energetic young people who have kept writing and performing for nearly fifty-five years. Neither one has ever worked with anyone else. It is indeed a remarkable collaboration.

Betty Comden and Adolph Green at first seem an unlikely pair. Betty is poised, dignified. She appears calm and seems always to have herself under control. Adolph, on the other hand, is restless, always moving. No room seems big enough to contain him. Betty has a mind that combines the ability to organize with a brilliant imagination. She has, according to her partner, a "ready-at-hand, well-digested fund of erudition, a dazzling sense of humor, and a concise wit--sharp, but never unkind." Betty says of Adolph that he has done a "stupendous amount of reading and every bit of it has been stored away for easy reference." But she adds that his mind is "not merely encyclopedic. It is also filled with crazy, unpredictable humor and imagination." (The quotations are from the cover of the original cast record album of Comden and Green's first Broadway performance of *A Party With Betty Comden and Adolph Green*, Capitol Records.)

Betty and Adolph meet every day, usually in Betty's apartment. They get together at about one o'clock and map out the day's work while they eat a sandwich and drink coffee. Then they begin to create. Betty types their ideas on her portable typewriter--as she had written in pencil on a yellow pad many years before when they were The Revuers. When they have a show rehearsing, they hover in the wings or in the front rows of the theatre. Betty begins to move her head, sometimes even to hum, while the songs are being rehearsed. Adolph finds it difficult to stay still. He sings, snaps his fingers, shuffles his feet, and sometimes does a few dance steps to the music. When they whisper together about the show, their minds seem to merge together into one (Arthur and Barbara Gelb "'On the Town' With Comden and Green," *New York Times*, December 11, 1960).

After fifty years of collaboration, Comden and Green speak almost as one person. One of them starts a sentence and the other finishes it. They seldom, if ever, disagree about their work. Their only disagreement is over time. Betty is always punctual and Adolph is frequently late. This minor disagreement is not going to disrupt their fifty years of collaboration. They are still meeting, still planning for their next big project. Betty worries about Adolph because he reads while he walks, weaving through New York traffic. Of their collaboration she says, "If I am ever without Adolph, it will simply be because he has been run over by a truck." Adolph says, "Alone, nothing. Together, a household word, a legend, Romulus and Remus, Damon and Pythias, Loeb and Leopold--Mr. Words and Miss Words" (original cast album, *A Party*, Capitol Records).

The work of Comden and Green seems to shine brightest when they write about New York, their home town, or about the love of their life, show business. They take delight in creating "egotistical, larger-than-life characters who are likable in spite of themselves, and who they cut lovingly down to human size" (Sheryl Flatow, "On the Town" in *Stagebill*, October 1992, for their Kennedy Center performance of *A Party*). There are Don Lockwood, the actor in *Singin' in the Rain*; Jeffrey Cordova, the director in *The Band Wagon*; Oscar Jaffee, the director in *On the Twentieth Century*; and Margo Channing, the actress in *Applause*. But there are also the lonely characters in a large city--Gabey, the sailor searching for Miss Turnstiles in *On the Town*; Tony Hunter, the has-been actor and dancer in *The Band Wagon*; and Ella Peterson, the wistful telephone operator in *Bells Are Ringing*. With unfailing humor and affection, Comden and Green have vividly depicted life in the big city.

Behind these characters and their emotions there is a sure structure to the musicals and films that Comden and Green have created. "The more structure you have, the better off you are, and the more tightly the songs and the plot will mesh," Adolph Green has said ("Betty Comden and Adolph Green," in Al Kasha and Joel

Hirschhorn, *Notes on Broadway*, p. 66). This knowledge of their craft, along with the unfailing humor and affection they have for their characters, helps to explain the many awards and honors that Comden and Green have won and also the respect accorded them by their peers and the public. Because their musicals are so filled with wit and seem to flow so easily, some critics have thought that the process of creation has been an easy one for Comden and Green. Adolph says the process is "agony." He describes their method for getting an idea: "Just read, think, kick around things, meet every day and stare at each other and say no to something for a year, then suddenly say, 'Let's try it'" (*Notes on Broadway*, p. 67).

It is almost impossible to summarize a production career that has been so rich and engrossing as that of Betty Comden and Adolph Green. Paul Kresh once wrote in a profile of the pair in *Stereo Review*: "If the names of Comden and Green were removed from the record, great blank stretches would be left in the history of the Broadway musical. We would lose some of the happiest interludes on Hollywood celluloid as well, and without the words they supplied, many of the country's cleverest songs would wind up as mere fodder for Muzak" (Quoted by Didier C. Deutsch in his notes for the newly released record album, *The Comden and Green Songbook*. See D51).

CHRONOLOGY

December 2, 1914	Adolph Green is born in the Bronx, New York
May 3, 1917	Betty Cohen is born in Brooklyn, New York
1937	Betty receives her Bachelor of Science degree from New York University
1937	Betty and Adolph work with a group called "Six and Company"
1937-1938	Betty appears with the Studio Players in East Hampton
1938	Betty has small role in *Having Wonderful Time* and tours the subway circuit
1938	Adolph, Betty, Judy Tuvim, Alvin Hammer, and John Frank form "The Revuers" and perform at the Village Vanguard
1939	The Revuers perform at the Rainbow Room in the RCA Building
1940	The Revuers play Radio City Music Hall
1940	Adolph marries Elizabeth Reitel
1940	The Revuers present a weekly radio program on NBC
1941	The Revuers return to the Village Vanguard
1942	The Revuers play in *My Dear Public* out of town
January 4, 1942	Betty marries Steven Kyle
1942	The Revuers go on tour
1943	The Revuers play at the Blue Angel

1943	The Revuers go to Hollywood, but the film is canceled
1943	The Revuers perform at the Trocadero in Los Angeles
1944	The Revuers perform in the film, *Greenwich Village*, but the sketches are cut out
1944	Betty and Adolph return to New York
1944	Betty and Adolph perform at the Blue Angel
1944	Betty and Adolph are asked by Leonard Bernstein to write the book and lyrics for a musical
December 28, 1944	*On the Town* opens to good reviews
December 21, 1945	*Billion Dollar Baby* opens to mixed reviews
1947	Adolph marries Allyn McLerie
1947	*Good News*, Betty and Adolph's first film, is released
December 26, 1947	*Bonanza Bound!* previews in Philadelphia. It closes out of town.
1949	Susanna Kyle is born
1949	*The Barkleys of Broadway* is released
1949	*Take Me Out to the Ball Game* is released
1949	The film version of *On The Town* is released
1951	Adolph and Allyn McLerie are divorced
July 19, 1951	The revue, *Two on the Aisle*, opens to good reviews
1952	*Singin' in the Rain* is released
1953	*The Band Wagon* is released
1953	Alan Kyle is born
February 25, 1953	*Wonderful Town* opens to rave reviews
October 20, 1954	*Peter Pan* opens in New York
1955	*It's Always Fair Weather* is released
November 29, 1956	*Bells Are Ringing* opens to favorable reviews

1958	*Auntie Mame* is released
April 12, 1958	*Say, Darling* opens to mostly unfavorable reviews
November 10 & 17, 1958	Betty and Adolph appear Off Broadway in *A Party With Betty Comden and Adolph Green*
December 23, 1958	*A Party* opens on Broadway for a limited run
May 18, 1959	Betty and Adolph return to Broadway with *A Party*
Summer 1959	Adolph goes to Europe with Sydney Chaplin. He visits Charlie Chaplin in Switzerland
1960	*Bells Are Ringing* is released
1960	Betty makes a recording of songs from *Treasure Girl* and *Chee-Chee* on a record called "Remember These"
January 31, 1960	Adolph marries Phyllis Newman
December 26, 1960	*Do Re Mi* opens to good reviews
1961	Adam Green is born
October 22, 1961	Betty and Adolph appear in *The Fabulous Fifties* on television
December 27, 1961	*Subways Are for Sleeping* opens to mixed reviews
1963	Adolph sings the Danny Kaye role for a recording of *Lady in the Dark*
1964	Amanda Green is born
1964	*What a Way To Go!* is released
April 19, 1964	Betty and Adolph appear in a memorial concert for Marc Blitzstein
May 26, 1964	*Fade Out--Fade In* opens to favorable reviews
June 28, 1965	*Leonard Bernstein's Theatre Songs* plays Off Broadway
1967	The song, "*I Said Good Morning*," is published as a children's book, *Good Morning, Good Night*, by Holt, Rinehart and Winston
March 1967	*I'm Getting Married* is presented on Stage 67 on ABC Television

April 26, 1967	*Hallelujah, Baby!* opens to mixed reviews
Summer 1967	Adolph goes to Europe with Leonard Bernstein. Betty and Steven Kyle also are in Europe
Summer 1967	The Greens buy a house in East Hampton
March 30, 1970	*Applause* opens to rave reviews
1971	Betty and Adolph appear in the "*Lyrics and Lyricists*" series
January 27, 1974	*Lorelei* opens in New York
November 23, 1975	*By Bernstein* opens Off Broadway
May 1976	Betty and Adolph appear in a tribute to George Abbott
February 10, 1977	Betty and Adolph present a new version of *A Party* on Broadway
February 19, 1978	*On the Twentieth Century* opens to good reviews
1979	Adolph appears in the film, *Simon*
January 15, 1979	Betty and Adolph perform at a program celebrating Imogene Coca's 50 years in show business
January 16-22, 1979	Betty plays comedy role in *On the Twentieth Century* while Imogene Coca is on vacation
June 13, 1979	*The Madwoman of Central Park West* opens Off Broadway
October 17, 1979	Betty's husband, Steven Kyle, dies
March 17, 1980	Betty and Adolph are installed in the Songwriters' Hall of Fame
April 5, 1981	Betty and Adolph are inducted into the Theatre Hall of Fame
1982	Betty and Adolph conduct master classes in musical comedy writing for New York University
1982	Adolph appears in the film, *My Favorite Year*
September 23, 1982	*A Doll's Life* opens and closes after five performances

December 1982	Betty and Adolph pay tribute to Gene Kelly at the Kennedy Center
December 15, 1983	Betty appears Off Broadway in *Isn't It Romantic?*
1984	Adolph and Betty both appear in the film, *Garbo Talks*
November 23, 1984	*Diamonds* opens Off Broadway
1985	*A Party* is presented on cable television
1985	Adolph appears in the film *Lily in Love*
July 2, 1985	*Singin' in the Rain* opens to poor reviews
September 8 & 9, 1985	Betty and Adolph appear in a concert version of Stephen Sondheim's *Follies*
April 1986	Betty and Adolph speak before a revival of *On the Town* at Long Island University
1988	Adolph appears in the documentary, *Funny*
1989	Adolph appears in the film *I Want To Go Home*
1989	Betty appears in the film *Slaves of New York*
February 26, 1989	*Jerome Robbins' Broadway* opens to rave reviews
1990	Betty and Steven Kyle's son dies
October 14, 1990	Betty and Adolph's good friend, Leonard Bernstein, dies
May 1, 1991	*The Will Rogers Follies* opens to good reviews
May 29, 1991	Betty and Adolph are presented the Johnny Mercer Award for Lifetime Achievement by the Songwriters' Hall of Fame
1991	Betty and Adolph contribute lyrics for the song, "Mamushka" in the film, *The Addams Family*
1991	Adolph sings the role of Dr. Pangloss in a new recording of Leonard Bernstein's *Candide*
December 8, 1991	Betty and Adolph receive the Kennedy Center Award for Lifetime Achievement in the Performing Arts
July 1992	Betty and Adolph narrate a concert version of *On The Town* in London.

July 1992	Betty and Adolph perform *A Party* in London
October 9 & 10, 1992	Betty and Adolph perform *A Party* at the Kennedy Center
December 8, 1992	Betty pays tribute to Paul Taylor, one of the honorees at the Kennedy Center Honors for Lifetime Achievement in the Performing Arts

STAGE MUSICALS FOR WHICH COMDEN AND GREEN WROTE BOTH THE BOOK AND THE LYRICS

S01 *ON THE TOWN* (1944)

Adelphi Theatre, New York City; Opened December 28, 1994
463 Performances

Credits
Based on an idea by Jerome Robbins

Book	Betty Comden
	Adolph Green
Lyrics	Betty Comden
	Adolph Green
Music	Leonard Bernstein
Director	George Abbott
Choreographer	Jerome Robbins
Designer	Oliver Smith
Costumes	Alvin Colt
Musical Director	Max Goberman
Producers	Oliver Smith
	Paul Feigay

Cast

Workman	Marten Sameth
2nd Workman	Frank Milton
3rd Workman	Herbert Greene
Ozzie	Adolph Green
Chip	Chris Alexander
Sailor	Lyle Clark
Gabey	John Battles
Andy	Frank Westbrook
Tom	Richard D'Arcy
Flossie	Florence MacMichael
Flossie's Friend	Marion Kohler
Bill Poster	Larry Bolton
Little Old Lady	Maxine Arnold
Policeman	Lonny Jackson
S. Uperman	Milton Taubman
Hildy	Nancy Walker

52 Comden and Green

Policeman	Roger Treat
Figment	Remo Bufano
Claire	Betty Comden
High School Girl	Nellie Fisher
Sailor in Blue	Richard D'Arcy
Maude P. Dilly	Susan Steell
Ivy	Sono Osato
Lucy Schmeeler	Alice Pearce
Pitkin	Robert Chisholm
Master of Ceremonies	Frank Milton
Singer	Frances Cassard
Waiter	Herbert Greene
Spanish Singer	Jeanne Gordon
The Great Lover	Ray Harrison
Conductor	Herbert Greene
Bimmy	Robert Lorenz

Synopsis

The play opens before six o'clock in the morning at the Brooklyn Navy Yard. Workmen are coming to work. When the six o'clock whistle sounds, three young sailors, Gabey, Chip, and Ozzie, come from their ship. They have a twenty-four hour shore leave and are eager to see all they can of New York. They are also hoping to pick up some girls. They sing "New York, New York."

The three sailors take the subway. On the train they see a poster with a picture of the new "Miss Turnstiles for the Month," one Miss Ivy Smith. Gabey takes one look at Ivy Smith and decides that she is the girl for him. In spite of the impossibility of finding this one girl among the thousands of girls in New York, Gabey decides to search for her. The other two sailors want to help him. They take down the poster and run off the train, followed by an irate elderly woman shouting "Vandals!"

The three sailors read the information about Ivy and decide to follow the clues given on the poster. Ivy is studying singing and ballet at Carnegie Hall. Gabey will go there. She is studying painting at the museum. Ozzie will go there. Chip will investigate through the people in charge of the subway. They agree to meet at Nedicks in Times Square at eleven o'clock that night. While Chip is consulting his guide book, an aggressive taxi-driver, Hildy, offers to give him a ride. He agrees to let her give him a quick tour of New York, but she wants to take him to her place. Ozzie goes to the Museum of Natural History looking for Ivy. While standing by a statue of a Pithycanthropics erectus whom he resembles, he is suddenly confronted by Claire, an anthropologist, who wants to take his picture and his measurements. When Ozzie asks Claire for a date, she tells him she is engaged to Judge Pitkin W. Bridgework, who advised her to study anthropology so that she could learn to know men objectively and get them out of her system. However, the cure has not been complete, and Claire grabs Ozzie and gives him a passionate kiss. Clair and Ozzie sing "Carried Away."

Gabey goes to Carnegie Hall. There he accidentally stumbles into a music studio where Ivy Smith is taking singing lessons from Madame Maude P. Dilly. He makes a date with Ivy for eleven o'clock that night at Nedicks on Times Square. Claire takes Ozzie to her apartment where her "understanding" fiancé is glad to meet him. Hildy takes Chip to her apartment. There he meets Hildy's roommate,

Lucy Schmeeler, who stayed home from work because she is suffering from a terrible cold. Chip and Hildy talk Lucy into leaving them alone.

Gabey arrives at Times Square early, but then walks around watching the people. When Ivy does arrive and before Gabey sees her, she is convinced by Madame Dilly that she must not miss her job at Coney Island because she owes Madame Dilly fifty dollars for her lessons. Ivy leaves to go to work. When Gabey comes back to Nedicks she is not there. Chip and Ozzie arrive with their new girl friends, each pretending to be Ivy Smith. Madame Dilly tells Gabey that Ivy regrets that she can't meet him. She is going to a party. The two couples want to go to some night clubs, and Hildy calls her roommate, Lucy Schmeeler, to ask her to come be Gabey's date.

The three sailors, Hildy, and Claire go to two different night clubs. They leave each club just as Judge Pitkin W. Bridgework, Claire's fiancé, arrives and just before Lucy Schmeeler catches up with them. At the third nightclub, Gabey sees Madame Dilly, who tells him that Ivy is at Coney Island, the playground of the rich. They all start for Coney Island, leaving the Judge to take care of the sneezing Lucy. While riding the subway train, Gabey has a dream, danced in a ballet, about himself and Ivy at a beautiful, imaginary Coney Island. At the real Coney Island the sailors and their girls find Ivy dressed in a Turkish costume and doing a cooch dance in a cheap show. Ivy explains to Gabey, and, as he reaches for her, he accidentally pulls off her skirt, causing the police to threaten to arrest her for indecent exposure. Pitkin and Lucy arrive and Pitkin insists that all six young people be arrested. The three sailors are escorted back to their ship by the police.

The final scene of the play takes place just before six o'clock in the morning at the Brooklyn Navy Yard. Gabey, Chip, and Ozzie are brought in by the policemen. Just before they board the ship they hear their names called, and the three girls are there. They explain that Judge Pitkin W. Bridgework "understood" and let them go. They throw themselves into the arms of the sailors. The six o'clock whistle blows, and as Gabey, Chip, and Ozzie go reluctantly back to the ship, three other young sailors come from the ship singing "New York, New York."

The Play's History

In 1943, Jerome Robbins, a dancer with the Ballet Theatre Company, had an idea for a ballet about three sailors on shore leave. Leonard Bernstein was recommended to Robbins as a composer who could write jazz. Robbins contacted Bernstein and the two wrote the ballet, *Fancy Free*, a twenty-five minute ballet about three sailors on shore leave in New York. In a bar the three sailors treat two girls to beer and entertain them with solo dances, fight over them, lose them, and pursue another girl.

The first performance of *Fancy Free* by the Ballet Theatre at the Metropolitan Opera House with Leonard Bernstein conducting was on April 18, 1944. The demand for tickets was so great that the Ballet Theatre season was extended two weeks beyond its scheduled closing. Instead of seven performances of the ballet, there were nineteen. Altogether, *Fancy Free* was danced 161 times during its first season. The following season the Ballet Theatre took *Fancy Free* on tour. It was considered the finest ballet on an American theme, and it became the signature piece for the Ballet Theatre. Columbia made a recording of the music.

Shortly after the success of the ballet, Oliver Smith, the designer for the ballet, suggested to Bernstein and Robbins that they do a full length musical. Paul Feigay, who was a long time friend of Betty and Adolph and who greatly admired their work with The Revuers, suggested that they write the book and the lyrics. Smith and Feigay decided to work together to try to produce the musical. Bernstein and Smith went with the idea to the Blue Angel, where Betty Comden and Adolph Green were performing. Betty Comden and Adolph Green were enthusiastic about the idea and were very eager to try writing a book for the musical. That summer of 1944 Leonard Bernstein needed an operation for a deviated septum in his nose, and Adolph Green had been told to have his tonsils removed. The former roommates decided to have their surgery at the same time and in the same hospital and to share a room. There, with Betty Comden joining them, they began work on the musical. The plot that evolved was very different from that used for the ballet. In *Fancy Free* the three sailors are competitive, but in the new story the three sailors are supportive of each other. When Gabey falls in love with the picture of Miss Turnstiles, his two friends try to help him find her. Bernstein wrote the music to fit the new story. He did not use any of the music that he had written for *Fancy Free*.

Oliver Smith took the new show to the Theatre Guild, but Lawrence Langner was not interested. Elia Kazan, the director, turned the show down. Then the producers brought the show to George Abbott, the man famous for his directing of many musicals and comedies. He was already a legend in the theatre. Abbott had seen *Fancy Free*, and he was enthusiastic about the work of Bernstein and Robbins. However, he had never heard of Betty Comden and Adolph Green. He read the script for the new show while riding on a train, and could hardly wait to get off the train to call the young authors to express the joy he found in reading their work.

Abbott quickly established his control. Comden and Green had written the story as a flashback. Their script opened in a night court where all of the characters have been taken. The judge demands that each person tell the story of the evening that ended in their being hauled into court. Comden and Green thought that this scene helped to give the show form and shape. Abbott insisted that the prologue, be cut. He told the young authors that they did not need it. Though at first they were angry, Comden and Green soon realized that Abbott was right. Abbott also cut some of the musical numbers and divided one long ballet in half in order to insert a scene in the middle of it. The young authors and musician discovered that the master director knew what he was doing.

George Abbott's reputation as a director was so great that as soon as he agreed to direct the show, the money for its production was over-subscribed. Metro-Goldwyn-Mayer film studios made a pre-production deal with the producers. It was reportedly the first time the film rights to a musical were sold before the stage production was given.

On the Town opened at the Adelphi Theatre on West Forty-fourth Street on December 28, 1944. It was competing with *Oklahoma!*, *Bloomer Girl*, *Mexican Hayride*, and *Follow the Girls*. *On the Town*, in its original production, ran for 463 performances, closing on February 6, 1946.

An inferior production of *On the Town* was started on a national tour, but it played only a few cities. *On the Town* was made into a popular film starring Gene Kelly. The film premiered at Radio City Music Hall on December 8, 1949. (See F04.) The stage musical was first presented on the West Coast in arena style by the Gallery Stage on Santa Monica Boulevard in Los Angeles during the 1951-1952 season. An Off Broadway revival at the Carnegie Hall Playhouse in the 1958-1959 season was not successful, lasting only eight nights. London at last saw a production of the musical in 1963, opening on May 30 at the Prince of Wales Theatre. The London production was directed and choreographed by Joe Layton and received mostly favorable reviews. It ran for 53 performances.

A 1971 revival of *On the Town* in New York was not successful. Ron Field directed and choreographed the show, but the whole spirit of the revival was strained. This revival lasted only 65 performances. By the 1980s, however, *On the Town* was considered a classic. In 1981 there was a symposium on the musical which Betty Comden and Adolph Green attended. The symposium was reviewed in *The Dramatists Guild Quarterly* (Vol. 18, no. 2, Summer 1981, pp. 11-24). The musical has been successfully produced in regional theatres throughout the country. One recent production was at Arena Stage in Washington, D.C.

The first recording of some of the songs from *On the Town*, using some of the original cast members, was made by Decca in 1950. Another studio recording using some of the original cast was made by Columbia. (See D21 and D22.)

Reviews

"Fresh" was the term most frequently used by the critics for the original production of *On the Town*. The critic for *Time* magazine called it "one of the freshest, liveliest, most engaging musicals in many years" (January 8, 1945, pp. 67-68). Louis Kronenberger of *PM* called the musical "one of the freshest, gayest, liveliest musicals I have ever seen" (December 29, 1944). Lewis Nichols of the *New York Times* wrote: "There can be no mistake about it: *On the Town* is the freshest and most engaging musical show to come this way since the golden days of *Oklahoma!*. Everything about it is right. It is fast and it is gay, it takes neither itself nor the world too seriously, it has wit. Its dances are well placed, its players are a pleasure to see, and its music and backgrounds are both fitting and excellent. *On the Town* even has a literate book, which for once instead of stopping the action dead speeds it merrily on its way" (December 29, 1944). The critic for *The Nation* wrote that the musical has "charm and freshness and the gaiety generated when a group of amateur professionals put their heads together" (January 13, 1945, p. 48).

Most of the critics liked Comden and Green's book. Louis Kronenberger called *On the Town* "the best musical comedy book since *Pal Joey*" (*PM*, December 29, 1944). The critic for the *Christian Science Monitor* was complimentary about the book, and the reviewer for *The Nation* called the book "satisfactory, not least because it is free of the senseless complications in which most musical-comedy books get entangled" (January 13, 1945, p. 48). The reviewer for *Saturday Review* commented that the book "has room in it for sharp satire of the people, the manners, and the night clubs of that helluva town which it describes New York as being--yet even while its spirit is gay, this gaiety is the more intelligently observed because beneath it one feels the present's poignancy for those in the service whose hours of carefree pleasure are numbered" (February 17, 1945). However, Howard Barnes of the New York *Herald Tribune* concluded that George Abbott's "shrewd direction" had made much of "scant material" (December 29, 1944).

Most of the critics were also enthusiastic about the music. John Mason Brown wrote that "Mr. Bernstein is no Tin Pan Alley tunesmith. ...His music does not stop at being either lively or lovely, although it can be both. It is adventurous, written in an idiom uncommon along Broadway, and as fresh in its feeling as is the production as a whole" (*Saturday Review*, February 17, 1945).

Commentary

When Comden and Green started writing their book for *On the Town*, they wanted to make their characters three dimensional, especially the three young sailors with their feeling of being in a strange, large city and wanting to crowd everything into twenty-four hours. Working with Leonard Bernstein and Jerome Robbins, they tried to make the music and the ballet spring naturally from the story. "Integration" was the term they used. In 1944 modern ballet was still considered avant-garde by Broadway. Agnes de Mille had used the ballet in *Oklahoma!* In *On the Town*, Robbins made the point that dance in musical comedy could be a part of the story, not stopping the story but advancing it. The narration was extended through dance. In the late 1950s choreographers like Robbins were to become directors.

"New York, New York" was the most popular song from the show. Nancy Walker as the taxi driver, Hildy, made a show-stopper out of the humorous songs, "Come Up to My Place" and "I Can Cook, Too." Betty Comden, as Claire the anthropologist, and Adolph Green sang another comic song, "Carried Away." "Lonely Town" and "Lucky to Be Me" were beautiful ballads sung by John Battles, who played Gabey. "Some Other Time," sung by Claire, Hildy, Ozzie, and Chip, was a poignant reminder that the war was on and time was limited.

*****

S02   *BILLION DOLLAR BABY* (1945)

Alvin Theatre, New York City; Opened December 21, 1945
220 Performances

Credits

Book and Lyrics	Betty Comden
	Adolph Green
Music	Morton Gould
Director	George Abbott
Choreographer	Jerome Robbins
Designer	Oliver Smith
Costumes	Irene Sharaff
Musical Director	Max Goberman
General Manager	Charles Harris
Producers	Paul Feigay
	Oliver Smith

Cast

Ma Jones	Emily Ross
Pa Jones	William David
Esme	Shirley Van
Janet	Maria Harriton
1st Neighbor	Edward Hodge
2nd Neighbor	Howard Lenters
3rd Neighbor	Douglas Deane
Champ Watson	Danny Daniels
Photographer	Anthony Reed

Reporter	Allan Gilbert
Maribelle Jones	Joan McCracken
1st Newsboy	Douglas Jones
2nd Newsboy	Richard Thomas
Gawky Girl	Helen Gallagher
Mother	Beverly Hosier
Master of Ceremonies	Richard Sanford
Miss Texas	Althea Elder
Miss California	Virginia Gorski
Miss Florida	Peggy Ellis
Miss Oklahoma	Beth Shea
Miss Virginia	Beverly Hosier
Miss Indiana	Joan Mann
Miss Louisiana	Future Fulton
Miss Massachusetts	Doris Hollingsworth
Miss Vermont	Thelma Stevens
Miss South Dakota	Lyn Gammon
Miss Kentucky	Betty Saunders
Georgia Motley	Mitzi Green
Dream Heroes	Jim Mitchell
	Fred Hearne
	Bill Skipper
Violin Player	Tony Gardell
Jerry Bonanza	Don De Leo
Cop	Arthur Partington
Three Flappers	Virginia Gorski
	Helen Gallagher
	Lorraine Todd
Rich Girl	Joan Mann
Playboy	Fred Hearne
A Timid Girl	Ann Hutchinson
Good Time Charlie	Bill Skipper
Collegiates	Virginia Poe
	Douglas Deane
Younger Generation	Bill Sumner
	Maria Harriton
Older Generation	Jacqueline Dodge
	Joe Landis
Two Gangsters	Lucas Aco
	Allan Waine
Two Bootleggers	Anthony Reed
	Allan Gilbert
Dapper Welch	David Burns
Rocky Barton	William Tabbert
Cigarette Girl	Jeri Archer
Waiter	David Thomas
M. M. Montague	Robert Chisholm
Marathon M. C.	Allan Gilbert

Chorines: Joan Mann, Lorraine Todd, Virginia Gorski, Virginia Poe, Helen Gallagher, Maria Harriton

Comic	Douglas Deane
Danny	Tony Gardell
J. C. Creasy	Horace Cooper
Art Leffenbush	Eddie Hodge
Rodney Gender	Richard Sanford
Watchman	Robert Edwin
Rocky (who dances)	James Mitchell
Policeman	Howard Lenters

Synopsis

Billion Dollar Baby, A Musical Play of the Terrific Twenties opens in a living room on Staten Island. Mr. and Mrs. Jones are listening to the radio. The time is 1928 and the announcer promises prosperity ahead. Maribelle, the beautiful daughter of Mr. and Mrs. Jones, has just won the title of Miss New York and is now eligible to enter the Miss America contest in Atlantic City. The neighbors come by to wish her well, the photographers come to take her picture, and her boy friend Champ comes to say goodbye. We are now transported to Atlantic City. The elaborate floats parade across the stage, and then we see the final stages of the Miss America contest. The special guest for the evening is Miss Georgia Motley, the hostess of a not too reputable night club. She has been drinking and is hardly able to stand when she is asked to speak. Her advice to the girls is to quit the contest and put away their money. She is hustled off the stage. The contestants parade before the judges and the audience. After each parade of contestants, some of the girls are eliminated. Finally, only Miss Texas and Miss New York remain. Miss Texas wins, and Maribelle does not accept defeat graciously.

Back in her home on Staten Island, Maribelle is very depressed because she did not win the contest. Champ comes by to ask Maribelle to meet him on the Staten Island ferry tonight. He works on the ferry as it goes back and forth across the river. What he really wants to do is enter the big dance marathon contest that is being held in Florida. Maribelle consents to join Champ on the ferry for the evening. After Champ leaves and her folks go to the movies, Maribelle, feeling very discontented, yearns for the "high Life." She sings "Dreams Come True" and dreams of herself dancing with the great movie lovers.

On the ferry that night, Maribelle wants Champ to take her into New York to "do the town." But Champ has to work and he has no money. Maribelle, feeling very frustrated, meets Jerry Bonanza, a cheap gangster, whose card reads "Beverages Delivered Discreetly." He wants to take Maribelle to an elegant night club, but she insists she wants to go to Chez Georgia. Jerry Bonanza takes her to the speakeasy Chez Georgia which Georgia Motley runs. At Chez Georgia Maribelle meets Georgia and her boy friend, Dapper Welch. Jerry Bonanza is called into the back room and shot. Dapper, the night club owner, is attracted to the beautiful Maribelle. At this moment the fabulously wealthy M. M. Montague comes in to tell Georgia that his wife has consented to a divorce and he wants to marry her. Georgia is tempted and sings "There I'd Be" as she visualizes how she would live if she had all of Montague's money. But still she refuses his offer of marriage. Dapper Welch takes Maribelle home.

Dapper Welch has promised Maribelle that he can get her into the Jollities, a song and dance team of girls. He sends his body guard, Rocky, to bring her to his elegant apartment. She agrees to go, leaving Champ still wanting her to go with him to enter the dance marathon. When Maribelle leaves, Champ takes Esme as his dancing partner and starts for Florida.

Rocky takes Maribelle to Dapper's apartment, but he, too, has fallen in love with the beautiful Maribelle. Dapper tries to make love to Maribelle but is interrupted by Ma Jones, Maribelle's mother. She has brought her suitcases and her cooking utensils and proceeds to move in, promising Dapper a beautiful home-cooked dinner. A few days later, Dapper has a grand party in honor of Maribelle, who has just made her debut in the Jollities. He announces that he is going to marry Maribelle.

Backstage in the theatre where the Jollities perform, Ma Jones insists that Maribelle marry Dapper. Maribelle is in love with Rocky and agrees to run away with him rather than marry Dapper. Dapper tries to stop the young lovers, but Rocky shoots him. Rocky, in turn, is shot by the gangsters.

Ma Jones now sends Maribelle to Florida to join Champ at the dance marathon. When Maribelle arrives at the Palmo Plaza Hotel in Florida, she sees the wealthy M. M. Montague and his men. Maribelle manages to attract the attention of the men and tells them she is a friend of Georgia. But when Georgia enters, Maribelle tells her she has come to see her fiancé, Champ. Montague has placed a large bet on Champ. They all go in to watch the marathon. It is now the one-hundred and forty-third day, and many of the dancers have been eliminated. Champ and Esme are exhausted and Esme wants to quit. Champ sees Maribelle, and, with renewed vigor, he grabs Esme, twirls her about and wins the contest. He is carried out on a stretcher. Georgia insists that he be taken to her room. Maribelle, using this as an excuse, implies to M. M. Montague that Georgia is unfaithful to him. Montague sings "Faithless" and turns to Maribelle.

A few weeks later, Rocky shows up at Maribelle's room in the hotel. He was not killed as she thought. However, the police are after him for Dapper's murder. Rocky is sure of Maribelle's love, but in a ballet Maribelle visualizes what life with Rocky would be like. She tells the police where he is. A policeman comes after Rocky and he rushes out.

In the final scene of the play we are in the church where M. M. Montague and Maribelle are to be married. Two of Montague's men warn him about the stock market, but he brushes them aside. The wedding guests arrive and the wedding is performed in pantomime. From the street we hear the newsboys cry, "Panic on Wall Street," and "M. M. Montague wiped out." Maribelle, in her joy at being fabulously wealthy, throws diamond jewelry to the girls in her wedding party. Montague frantically tries to retrieve the jewelry. Maribelle, not understanding the situation, begins to dance the Charleston with her guests.

The Play's History

Billion Dollar Baby opened at the Alvin Theatre on December 21, 1945. Once again Paul Feigay and Oliver Smith were the producers, but Leonard Bernstein was not available for the music. Morton Gould supplied the music. The show ran for 220 performances, closing on June 29, 1946. The story by Betty Comden and Adolph Green was original.

The published libretto is not available, but there is a copy in the New York Public Library Performing Arts Research Center at Lincoln Center. The sheet music was published by the Chappell Music Company. There is no original cast recording of the musical; however, some of the songs have been recorded. (See D07 and D19.)

Donaldson Awards were won by George Abbott, the director, and Jerome Robbins, the choreographer. Joan McCracken also won a Donaldson Award as a supporting actress and dancer.

Reviews

Of the New York critics two gave rave reviews and two were generally favorable. John Chapman of the *Daily News* gave an unqualified good review of the show. He called the musical "engaging" and even better than *On the Town*. He summed it up by calling it "an evening of song and dance which is swift and smart" (December 22, 1945). Some other reviewers thought the subject of the Twenties was a good idea that did not succeed. Louis Kronenberger of *PM* wrote that the show "can never make up its mind whether to burlesque an era or to catch its real quality of melodrama." He said that there was not enough burlesque to "make for sustained fun," and thus the book became "hard and cold" (December 23, 1945). Howard Barnes of the *Herald Tribune* called *Billion Dollar Baby* "a brashly satirical and bountiful musical show," but stated that the satire and musical romance "jar rather harshly" at times (December 22, 1945). Burton Roscoe of the *New York World Telegram* called the first act "fast moving, clever, rhythmical, broadly satirical, and diverting," but he felt that in the second act the authors became fatigued and "satiric inspiration lags" and the comedy "gives up the ghost altogether" (December 22, 1945). Ward Morehouse of the *Sun* called *Billion Dollar Baby* "a ragged musical play" that "flounders frequently," though it "has pace and a lot of vitality" (December 22, 1945).

Comden and Green's book was called "thin" and "weak in comedy and sparse in lyrics" by Burton Roscoe and "a stumbling yarn" by Howard Barnes. Kronenberger thought the book "a liability" and called some scenes "feeble" and much of the verbal humor "forced."

Ben Rosenberg of the *New York Post* thought Joan McCracken was worthy of better material. Several of the critics mentioned *Pal Joey*. Kronenberger thought Comden and Green had tried too hard to "make a Pal Josie of their heroine." But he did think Comden and Green's comic sense showed forth in the first act finale which spoofed a big production number of the 1920s by having the show girls imitate birds and in the clever song, "Speaking of Pals" (*PM*, December 23, 1945).

Most of the critics praised the choreography of Jerome Robbins and called the production numbers well integrated into the story. The costumes of Irene Sharaff were praised by Howard Barnes as "a brilliant burlesque of fashion designing" (*Herald Tribune*, December 22, 1945).

Commentary

The "Terrific Twenties" would seem to be an ideal subject for the witty satire of Comden and Green. The Miss America pageant, the marathon dances, the speakeasies, the movie idols, the lineup of dancing girls, the gangsters, and the pre-Wall Street Crash millionaires are all depicted in this story of the rise of a beautiful girl who tries to make her dreams of an exciting life come true. Some of the critics called the social-climbing heroine a female Pal Joey. Maribelle is a ruthless girl determined to marry a billionaire. The role of Maribelle was played by the very talented Joan McCracken. At the beginning of the play we identify with the beautiful Maribelle and her foolish dreams of dancing with the great movie stars of the time. We appreciate her desire to experience some of the excitement of the

1920s, but as she heartlessly drops one boy friend after another in her climb up the ladder to what she thinks is to be a fabulously wealthy marriage, we no longer cheer her on.

The satire of the play and the mood of "burlesqued nostalgia" (Wolcott Gibbs, *The New Yorker*, January 5, 1946) for the good old days before the crash are undermined by some sentimental love songs and the long moralistic ballet in which Maribelle visualizes the humiliating end for a girl who takes up with a gun-toting gangster. Lewis Nichols of the *New York Times* wrote that "often the book sounds as though neither Miss Comden nor Mr. Green had his heart in it" (December 22, 1945).

*****

S03   *BONANZA BOUND!* (1947)

Pre-Broadway tryout, Sam S. Shubert Theatre, Philadelphia;
Opened December 26, 1947; Closed January 8, 1948

Credits

Book and Lyrics	Betty Comden
	Adolph Green
Music	Saul Chaplin
Staged by	Charles Friedman
Choreography	Jack Cole
Designer	Oliver Smith
Costumes	Irene Sharaff
Lighting	Peggy Clark
Musical Director	Lehman Engel
Orchestrations	Philip Lang
Producers	Herman Levin
	Paul Feigay
	Oliver Smith

Cast

Chokkilok	Sidney Melton
Chokkilok's Wife	Tina Prescott
First Prospector	Ted Thurston
Waldo Cruikshank	George Coulouris
Hunk	Ben Miller
Larsen	Robert Penn
Peter Fleet	Hal Hackett
Second Prospector	John Mooney
Third Prospector	Johnny Silver
Clarabelle	Vici Raaf
Leonardo Da Vinci	Adolph Green
Toodles Da Vinci	Betty Lou Barto
Belinda Da Vinci	Carol Raye
Eustasia (Cruikshank's Daughter)	Allyn McLerie
Mrs. Cornelia Van Rensselaer	Zamah Cunningham

Digby	Sydney Arnold
Croupiers	Sven Holst
	Ken Foley
Prospectors: Remi Martel, Robert Evans, John Ward, Hugh Ellsworth	
Gambling Dancer	Gwen Verdun
First Siren	Myra Lynn
Second Siren	Pat Horne
Third Siren	Mary Statz
White Foxes	Richard Reed
	Wayne Lamb
Sea Lion	Paul Godkin

Synopsis

An eskimo, Chokkilok, and his wife sit in front of their shack in the frozen North. A man rushes in shouting that he has discovered gold. First by twos and threes, then by the dozens, people hurry in on their way to the gold fields. An opportunist, Waldo Cruikshank, stops and, seeing all the people, decides there is no need to go on to the gold fields; he will build a city right here. He confides to Peter Fleet, a young man who has read all of the stories and poems about the far North, that there is gold right here. The story spreads from person to person, people start to build, and suddenly there is "Cruikshank Town."

It is nearly a year later, and we are in the lobby and office of Cruikshank Palace. People are coming in with bags of gold to exchange for supplies. Cruikshank is weighing the gold and selling supplies at enormous prices. He is assisted by Hunk, who marvels at the success of the new town started because Cruikshank said there was a Bonanza lode right here. Young Peter Fleet, bedraggled and weary, comes in for supplies. He has found no gold. Cruikshank offers him a job mopping the floor in return for fifty dollars for supplies. As he is mopping the floor, the vaudeville team hired by Cruikshank to entertain the miners, enters. The team consists of Leonardo Da Vinci and his two sisters, Belinda and Toodles, a twelve year old. Eustasia, Cruikshank's daughter, is immediately attracted to Leonardo. Cruikshank himself is entranced with the beautiful Belinda, as is Peter, in spite of the fact that she is an actress.

That night a crowd is gathered in the bar at the Palace to see the vaudeville act. Cruikshank, at his front table, has brought a piece of jewelry to give Belinda. Before the act starts, Mrs. Cornelia Van Rensselaer and her butler, Digby, arrive with plans to search for gold. Mrs. Van Rensselaer wants Cruikshank to finance her efforts. He agrees to do so because he is very interested in getting himself and his daughter Eustasia into high society in the big city back East. The Da Vincis present their act, but the night's entertainment is interrupted by Peter who brings in Chokkilok who has just caught a fish with a gold nugget in its mouth. Everyone rushes out to search for the Bonanza lode.

The Da Vincis, having completed their weeks of performing in Cruikshank Town, are planning to leave. However, Cruikshank has insisted that Belinda come for their check. He has had a table set for two and placed in his den. Belinda wisely brings Leonardo with her to collect the pay, but Cruikshank sends Leonardo and Eustasia to have fun gambling in the casino. Peter bursts in saying he has found gold, but it proves to be fool's gold. Peter sees the table set for two and calls Belinda a hussy. Hunk pushes Peter out the door and Belinda follows. Cruikshank, determined to keep Belinda, gets his poker cards.

In the gambling casino, Leonardo has refrained from gambling, but when Cruikshank comes he convinces Leonardo to play poker with him. At first Leonardo wins, but then his luck turns, thanks to Cruikshank's marked cards, and suddenly Leonardo finds himself $65,000 in debt to Cruikshank. Cruikshank says that the vaudeville act must stay for twelve years to pay off the debt. Peter volunteers to help the Da Vincis try to find the Bonanza lode so they can pay Cruikshank.

It is two days later. The three dejected Da Vincis have found no gold, but they have found a cave where they can get warm. Eustasia brings a sled full of food. Peter apologizes to Belinda for calling her a hussy. He says that the snow is about to melt and Chokkilok will steal a boat and help them escape on the river as the snow melts. Their plans are thwarted, however, when Cruikshank comes in with a reinforcement of burly men to take Belinda and Eustasia back to the town. Belinda, in order to save the others, pretends that she is pleased to go with Cruikshank.

There is a grand party at the Palace. The party has been arranged by Mrs. Van Rensselaer. She, Cruikshank, and Eustasia receive the guests as they arrive. All of the men must give up their guns. Peter, Toodles, and Leonardo come to the party disguised as the Brothers Karamasov. Belinda has a plan for them to get the guns from the safe in Cruikshank's office. She tries to keep Cruikshank's attention while they sneak into the office. They do get the guns but are quickly disarmed by the miners. A great free-for-all follows. The Da Vincis and Peter, with the help of Mrs. Van Rensselaer, escape from the Palace. Cruikshank, realizing that they will head for the cave, orders the cave to be blown up. Then he realizes that Eustasia has gone to the cave with them. In the cave Peter and Belinda pledge their love for each other, and Peter plants his flag to claim Belinda as his own. Cruikshank runs in to get Eustasia out before the bomb explodes, but she will not leave. Cruikshank must tell them of the bomb. Peter grabs the bomb and throws it at Cruikshank. There is a great explosion. One wall of the cave is blown away, and when the smoke clears, we can see that a vein of gold has been revealed right where Peter has staked his claim. Cruikshank has disappeared with the explosion.

Now that the lode has been discovered and belongs to Peter, the other people begin leaving Cruikshank Town. As people are departing, Cruikshank comes in much tattered. Gradually the town is dismantled, leaving only Chokkilok singing "Happy All Alone."

The Play's History

Bonanza Bound! was produced by Herman Levin, Paul Feigay, and Oliver Smith. The music was by Saul Chaplin, a friend whom Comden and Green met when The Revuers were playing at the Trocadero in Hollywood. Saul Chaplin had written many popular songs with Sammy Cahn. Adolph Green played one of the major roles in the play, Leonardo Da Vinci, the leader of a vaudeville act. The musical was given a pre-Broadway tryout at the Sam S. Shubert Theatre in Philadelphia on December 26, 1947. It closed in Philadelphia on January 8, 1948, and was never produced on Broadway.

The libretto has not been published, but a manuscript copy and a program for the Philadelphia production are in the Museum of the City of New York. The sheet music was published by the Crawford Music Corporation. An original Philadelphia cast recording with an unnamed label (LP-508/JJA-19764) is not available. However, some of the songs have been recorded. (See D08 and D09.)

Reviews

There are few reviews of *Bonanza Bound!* Edwin H. Schloss of the Philadelphia *Evening Bulletin* called the book "dull" and the lyrics "ailing" (December 27, 1947). The critic of *Variety* noted that the melodramatic story was presented straight and thus was just "silly, unbelievable burlesque, without humor, flavor or entertainment." He thought that if it had been presented in a "tongue-in-cheek fashion," it might have had some merit. Of the complicated and melodramatic plot he commented that the only thing missing was Eliza crossing the ice and that Cruikshank "could have doubled for Simon Legree" (December 27, 1947).

Commentary

The plot of *Bonanza Bound!* is definitely melodramatic, with the beautiful heroine, Belinda, threatened by the villain, Cruikshank. Evidently, the play was presented straight and thus, without satire or burlesque, it was merely a rather dull melodrama. The setting in the far North is unusual. There are some clever scenes that should have been funny, like the grand party given by Cruikshank. There are some clever songs. For example, in the bar the entire cast sings "Fill 'er Up," while they drink the liquor down. The villainous Cruikshank sings "Misunderstood" about himself, justifying his behavior. Eustasia sings "Inspiration" to Leonardo telling him that she will be his inspiration. She sings that Beethoven could not have written the "Fifth" without the inspiration of his wife and Rimsky-Korsakov could never have written his "Flight of the Bumblebee" without female inspiration. This gave Adolph Green as Leonardo, the chance to do his solo performance of the bumblebee. This had been one of the popular numbers that he had done while one of The Revuers. This song was later sung by Comden and Green in their revue, *A Party With Betty Comden and Adolph Green*. The humor and satire intended by Comden and Green in *Bonanza Bound!* evidently did not come across in the production.

*****

S04   *BELLS ARE RINGING* (1956)

Sam S. Shubert Theatre, New York City; Opened November 29, 1956; 924 Performances

Credits

Book and Lyrics	Betty Comden
	Adolph Green
Music	Jule Styne
Director	Jerome Robbins
Choreographer	Jerome Robbins
Designer	Raoul Pène DuBois
Costumes	Raoul Pène DuBois
Musical Director	Milton Rosenstock
Orchestrations	Robert Russell Bennett
Vocal Arrangements and Direction	Herbert Greene
	Buster Davis
Dance Arrangements	John Morris
Lighting	Peggy Clark
Producer	Theatre Guild

Cast

Sue Summers	Jean Stapleton
Gwynne Smith	Pat Wilkes
Ella Peterson	Judy Holliday
Carl	Peter Gennaro
Inspector Barnes	Dort Clark
Francis	Jack Weston
Sandor	Eddie Lawrence
Jeff Moss	Sydney Chaplin
Larry Hastings	George S. Irving
Telephone Man	Eddie Heim
Ludwig Smiley	Frank Milton
Charles Bessemer	Frank Green
Dr. Kitchell	Bernie West
Blake Barton	Frank Aletter
Another Actor	Frank Green
Clerk	Tom O'Steen
Olga	Norma Doggett
Henchman from Corvello Mob	John Perkins
Other Henchman	Kasimir Kokich
Carol	Ellen Ray
Paul Arnold	Steve Roland
Michelle	Michelle Reiner
Master of Ceremonies	Eddie Heim
Singer at Nightclub	Frank Green
Waiter	Ed Thompson
Maitre d'Hotel	David McDaniel
Police Officer	Gordon Woodburn
Madame Grimaldi	Donna Sanders
Mrs. Mallet	Jeannine Masterson

Dancers: Norma Doggett, Phyllis Dorne, Patti Karr, Barbara Newman, Nancy Perkins, Marsha Rivers, Beryl Towbin, Anne Wallace, Doria Avila, Frank Derbas, Don Emmons, Eddie Heim, Kasimir Kokich, Tom O'Steen, Willy Summer, Ben Vargas, Billy Wilson

Singers: Pam Abbott, Joanne Birks, Urylee Leonardos, Jeannine Masterson, Michelle Reiner, Donna Sanders, Frank Green, Marc Leon, David McDaniel, Paul Michael, Julian Patrick, Steve Roland, Ed Thompson, Gordon Woodburn

Synopsis

The play opens with a musical number called "Bells Are Ringing." Eight girls are on stage waiting for telephone calls. They are advised by an announcer not to miss calls anymore but to call Susanswerphone, whose operators will answer their phones and inform them of calls and messages.

The first scene shows the office of Susanswerphone. Susanswerphone is owned by Sue Summers who has hired her cousin, Ella Peterson, and another girl, Gwynne Smith, as her assistants. Sue Summers and Gwynne Smith are impersonal when they talk to customers, but Ella Peterson is interested in each of the customers and becomes personally involved with the problems of each caller.

Among her customers is an opera singer called Madame Grimaldi to whom Ella has given a recipe for mustard plaster to help clear the cold in her chest. Inspector Barnes and his assistant Francis overhear Ella talking to Madame Grimaldi and become suspicious, thinking that Susanswerphone may be a front for a "dating" service and that the Madame is no opera singer. They decide to keep Susanswerphone under surveillance.

J. Sandor Prantz, a con man who is Sue Summers' boy friend, has talked her into combining his Titanic Record Company, which is really a front for a booking operation, with Susanswerphone. In a disreputable-looking alley Sandor explains to his fellow con men the system which they will use for placing bets on the horses. They will call Susanswerphone to leave orders for records. Each composer's name means a particular race track. For example, Debussy stands for Del Mar and Humperdinck means Hollywood.

One of Ella's customers is Jeff Moss, a playwright who no longer has a collaborator and who seems to find it impossible to write without a partner. Ella has fallen in love with Jeff because of his nice voice. She uses an older woman's voice with him, and he calls her "Mom" and frequently seeks her advice. Jeff's producer calls Susanswerphone to leave a message for Jeff that he must have the outline for his new play, *The Midas Touch*, in the producer's office the next day at noon. When Jeff does not answer his phone to get this important message, Ella decides to go to his apartment to be sure he gets the producer's ultimatum. She is followed out onto the street by the suspicious Inspector Barnes.

Ella finds Jeff asleep in his apartment. He has disconnected the phone. Ella connects the phone and is crawling out on her hands and knees when Jeff wakes. Jeff is not only amazed to find a strange young woman in his apartment but he is also surprised that Ella seems to know so much about him. She does not tell him that she is "Mom" at Susanswerphone, but gives her name as Melisande Scott. Ella convinces Jeff that he can write the outline and scene for his new play before the deadline. Jeff does write the outline, and when he takes it to the producer the next day the producer likes it. Jeff's producer tells him to go to his cabin for a week to try to finish the script. Ella meets Jeff after he has talked with the producer. They are both jubilant. They get on a crowded subway train and Ella notices that no one looks at anyone else. She says "Hello" to a particularly dour-looking man, who responds with a big smile and "Hello." The "Hello" is contagious as each person speaks to another person. The song, "Hello, Hello There!" follows.

Among Ella's Susanswerphone customers are Dr. Kitchell, a dentist who composes songs, and Blake Barton, an actor, who thinks the only way to get an acting job is to talk and dress like Marlon Brando. Since Sue has warned Ella not to interfere in her customers' lives, Ella, rather than calling Dr. Kitchell and Blake Barton to give them some advice, decides to visit them out of sight of Sue. She wants to tell Dr. Kitchell about an audition for new song writers, and she wants to tell Blake Barton that he needs to buy a Brooks Brothers suit and talk like a civilized man if he wants to be cast in a play.

When Ella returns to Susanswerphone after visiting her two customers, she discovers that the answering service is swamped with calls for records, in this case Beethoven's Tenth Symphony. Carl, the delivery boy, is knowledgable about music and he tells Ella that Beethoven wrote only nine symphonies. Ella changes all of the orders to Beethoven's Ninth. Jeff calls to talk to "Mom," and Ella hears a woman's voice. She dashes out to Jeff's apartment where she pretends to be Jeff's secretary and runs out the other girl. Ella and Jeff end the first act in each other's arms.

Jeff has asked Ella to go out with him, and at the beginning of Act II, Ella is dressed in Madame Grimaldi's *La Traviata* ball gown. All of Ella's friends know how important this date is for her and try to help her. Carl tells her she should know how to do the Cha Cha and offers to teach her. Ella is still dancing the Cha Cha when she meets Jeff in the park. Jeff tells Ella that his producer liked the script he wrote and has invited the two of them to a party in celebration. Before going to the party, Jeff and Ella dance in the park and Jeff sings "Just in Time." At the party, Jeff leaves Ella for a few minutes to confer with his producer. Ella feels very much out of place at this party in the producer's penthouse apartment. All of the elegant people there seem to be trying to outdo each other in name-dropping. When Jeff returns from his conference, he has told the producer about Ella and her uncanny intuition about people. Ella realizes that Jeff is in love with Melisande Scott and not with her. Left alone again, she sings "The Party's Over," leaves Jeff a note, and slips out of the apartment.

Jeff cannot understand what has happened to Ella. He looks everywhere for her. At last he goes to the Pyramid Club, and there he happens to meet Dr. Kitchell, whose song has just been sung, and Bruce Barton, who has landed an acting job. As the men talk, they realize that it was the same girl who helped each of them. They exchange telephone numbers so that they can keep in touch if one of them finds Ella. Later that night Jeff calls the two men. Each call is answered by Susanswerphone. Jeff now knows where Ella works.

Ella has returned to Susanswerphone. She says that she does not know who she is and she has decided to go back to her former job. She sings "I'm Goin' Back to the Bonjour Tristesse Brassiere Company." Before Ella can leave, Sandor comes in with his henchmen. He wants to know who changed the orders for the records. He must pay back the money the men who bet on the horses lost. He demands all of Sue's money. At this moment Inspector Barnes, still suspicious about Susanswerphone, comes in. Ella congratulates him for breaking up an illegal bookie operation. Though much surprised, Barnes does arrest Sandor and takes him off to prison. Ella is trying to leave, but Sue insists she stay at the switchboard until she returns. Left alone in the office, Ella hears Jeff's voice and tries to disguise herself as a little old lady. Jeff is not fooled by her disguise and tells her that she has so much love to give that he would like for her to give it to him. The play ends with all of Ella's customers coming in to thank her for what she has done for them.

The Play's History

Bells Are Ringing opened on Broadway on November 29, 1956, at the Sam S. Shubert Theatre. It was presented by the Theatre Guild. The show ran for over two years, closing in mid-December 1958 after 924 performances. The musical starred Judy Holliday and was written especially for her by her friends, Betty Comden and Adolph Green. Judy Holliday, under her real name of Judy Tuvim, had performed with them in their satirical comedy group called The Revuers. The musical was an outstanding box office success. For her role in the play Judy Holliday won an Antoinette Perry (Tony) Award in 1957 beating out Julie Andrews in *My Fair Lady*. Sydney Chaplin also received a Tony Award as Outstanding Supporting or Featured Musical Actor.

The cast recording was made by Columbia Records. (See D05.) Stratford Music Corporation and Chapell and Co., Inc., published the score. The musical, without Judy Holliday, was produced in London in 1957. The libretto was published in book form by Random House in 1957. The book, music, and orchestrations for the musical are available from Tams-Witmark Music Library.

The film version of *Bells Are Ringing* was released by Metro-Goldwyn-Mayer in 1960. It starred Judy Holliday. The film was adapted by Betty Comden and Adolph Green and was directed by Vincente Minnelli. (See F09.)

Reviews

John McClain of the *Journal American* called *Bells Are Ringing* "a big, brilliant success, the best original book show in recent memory." He praised the "intelligent scripting" of Comden and Green, "the engaging music of Jule Styne," and "the swift and sure direction of Jerome Robbins." "Miss Holliday is only sensational," he wrote (November 30, 1956).

Walter Kerr of the *Herald Tribune* also praised the performance of Judy Holliday and wrote: "the quality that most distinguishes *Bells Are Ringing* is its homey, comfortable, old-shoe belief in its attractive people and its wide-eyed love story" (November 30, 1956). Richard Watts, Jr., of the *Post* wrote that "the outstanding virtue of both *Bells Are Ringing* and its star is a warm-hearted friendliness that is wonderfully endearing" (November 30, 1956).

Brooks Atkinson of the *New York Times* thought *Bells Are Ringing* reverted to the kind of "labored plot complication and manipulation that we knew before *Oklahoma!* drove hackneyed musical comedy out of business" (November 30, 1956). Henry Hewes, writing in the *Saturday Review of Literature*, called *Bells Are Ringing* an example "of a good idea gone wrong." "Rewarding numbers are interspersed with dull stretches of more-or-less unimportant story material." The songs of Comden and Green he thought pleasant with a distinguishing satirical edge, but the production he thought lacked "sparkle" and lacked faith in a good fundamental emotional situation (December 29, 1956, p. 25).

The reviewer for *Time* called *Bells Are Ringing* "a very likeable show." "Holliday can look engagingly blank or beguilingly large-eyed, can be daft, sly, small-girl, strong-minded, touching," he wrote. He thought that the love story "bulks much too large for wit to keep pace with sentiment, for the Comden-Green book to display the usual fresh, crisp Comden-Greenness." However, he called Jerome Robbins' staging "brisk," the Comden-Green lyrics "sprightly," and the Jule Styne tunes "often schmalzy and now and then rousing" (December 10, 1956, p. 70).

Harold Clurman, writing in *The Nation*, credited Judy Holliday with a "wholly winning performance" that reflected "the lovable spirit which constitutes the surprising gift of Betty Comden and Adolph Green." "Comden and Green," he wrote "are frequently crude and gauche. Yet once in a while they can burst into a crazy improvisation which replaces judgment with the bubbling enthusiasm of kids." Comden and Green "just can't get over the exhilaration of not being grown up" (December 15, 1956, pp. 526, 527).

Commentary

Bells Are Ringing was written by Betty Comden and Adolph Green for their good friend, Judy Holliday, whom they had known as Judy Tuvim one of the original five Revuers. Judy Holliday, after her success in the Broadway production and then in the film of *Born Yesterday*, was at this time famous as Billy Dawn, the dumb blond with the squeaky voice. Comden and Green wanted to give her a role that would change the dumb blond image and show her real warmth and intelligence. Ella Peterson, the role they created for her, is described in the script as "Pretty, warm, sympathetic ... with a quick mind and a vivid imagination." Judy Holliday had never sung or danced on the stage before. In the two years that the musical was being planned and written, she took singing lessons, and in the play she raised her voice "quite confidently and triumphantly," as one critic said. Another critic commented that with her "buoyancy of spirit" she did not need a good singing voice. One critic commented on Judy Holliday's "nimble" feet when she danced the Cha Cha with the talented Peter Gennaro.

The role created by Comden and Green gave Judy Holliday ample opportunities to use her many talents. Her performance was called "wonderful," "memorable," "touching," and she herself was called an "adroit performer," and an "inimitable personality." However, as Judy Holliday herself said, it was Comden and Green who created the likable character of Ella for her to play. The idea for the play was a clever and an original one.

Jule Styne's score included romantic ballads, a burlesque waltz, a sizzling Cha Cha, soliloquies, and light hearted comedy tunes. Most popular of the songs were "Just in Time" and "The Party's Over." Clever production numbers included "Hello, Hello There!," sung in the subway train, and "It's a Simple Little System" with its jaunty and witty lyrics. "I'm Goin' Back to the Bonjour Tristesse Brassiere Company" was added as an "eleven o'clock number" shortly before the play opened. Judy Holliday's singing of it made it a show-stopper.

*****

S05 *SUBWAYS ARE FOR SLEEPING* (1961)

St. James Theatre, New York City; Opened December 27, 1961;
205 Performances

Credits
Suggested by the book by Edmund G. Love
Book and Lyrics	Betty Comden
	Adolph Green
Music	Jule Styne
Director, Choreographer	Michael Kidd
Settings and Lighting	Will Steven Armstrong
Costumes	Freddie Wittop
Musical Director	Milton Rosenstock
Orchestrations	Philip J. Lang
Associate Choreographer	Marc Breaux
Dance Music Arranger	Peter Howard
Production Supervisor	Neil Hartly
Producer	David Merrick

Cast
The Sleepers	Gene Varrone, Cy Young, Bob Gorman, John Sharpe
Myra Blake	Grayson Hall
Angela McKay	Carol Lawrence
Tom Bailey	Sydney Chaplin
Station Guard	Robert Howard
J. Edward Sykes	Joe Hill

Bill	Anthony Saverino
Harry Shelby	Eugene R. Wood
Gus Holt	Cy Young
Charlie Smith	Orson Bean
Jack	Gene Varrone
A Drunk	Jim Weiss
Max Hillman	Gene Varrone
Martha Vail	Phyllis Newman
Mr. Pitman	Gordon Connell
A Delivery Boy	Michael Bennett
Lancelot Zuckerman	Horase
Freddie	Bob Gorman
Mac, a Caretaker	John Sharpe
Social Worker	Joe Hill
Photographer	John Sharpe
The Models	Sari Clymas
	Diane Ball
Teenagers	John Sharpe
	Michael Bennett
Jack Flint	Lawrence Pool
Lt. Pilsudski	Robert Howard
Mary Tompkins	Dean Taliaferro
Joe, the museum guard	Anthony Saverino
Relief Doorman	Robert Howard
Mr. Barney	Joe Hill

Singers: Helen Baisley, Vicki Belmonte, Bob Gorman, Stokely Gray, Joe Hill, Robert Howard, Jeannine Michael, Bruce Payton, Anthony Saverino, Joan Sheller, Ruth Shepard.

Dancers: Diane Ball, Carlos Bas, Michael Bennett, Pepe de Chazza, Sari Clymas, Joel Craig, Robert Evans, Ted Forlow, Valerie Harper, Reby Howells, Gene Kelton, Victoria Mansfield, Wendy Nickerson, Larry Roquemore, Sandra Roveta, Ron Stratton, Dean Taliaferro, Jim Weiss.

Synopsis

Act I begins early one winter morning on a deserted Manhattan street. An alarm clock rings and four nattily dressed characters enter from behind a board fence around a construction project and from an open manhole. They sing the joys of the carefree life. Tom Bailey enters and joins them in their exuberant declarations of independence. It seems that their only problem is finding a free place to sleep, but they rejoice in not being part of the world of dull, "solid folk."

In the second scene of the play we are in the executive offices of *Madame* magazine. Angie McKay has been planning a European vacation. Her boss, Myra Blake, reminds her that she must complete her story of the well-dressed drifters before she leaves. Preliminary research has revealed that the man to contact about this special breed of New York bums is Tom Bailey, whose office is a bench at Grand Central Station. From his office Tom Bailey acts as a one-man employment agency, finding other drifters jobs and sleeping quarters, for a small fee, of course. Tom himself exists on the one dollar and a half per day he makes walking a wealthy couple's dog. Angie reluctantly cancels her Bon Voyage dinner and agrees to complete her story before going to Europe.

It is the morning rush hour at Grand Central Station. Men and women with their newspapers and briefcases are running in all directions to get their trains that will take them to their dull eight-to-five jobs. In the midst of this confusion, Tom Bailey saunters in carrying a newspaper and an attaché case. He takes his usual place on the bench he has made his office. One of his first customers of the day is Charlie Smith, a likable sponger who survives mainly on dinner invitations from former school friends. He tells Tom that he is on his way to another friend's hotel room to borrow a dinner jacket for a Bon Voyage dinner for some magazine writer. After Charlie leaves, Angie, pretending to be a stranded girl from out of town looking for a place to spend the night, comes in to get advice from Tom. Tom gives her some valuable advice about how to avoid detection by the police while in waiting rooms. Tom tells Angie that his reward for living as he does is that he is responsible for no one but himself.

In the corridor of the rather shabby hotel, the Brunswick Arms, Charlie Smith tells his friend Max that he won't be needing the dinner jacket because the Bon Voyage dinner has been canceled. Max, who is very shy, asks Charlie if he will go knock on the door of a girl he sees nearly every night across the court and tell her that Max would like to meet her. Charlie does go to Martha Vail's room. He finds her dressed in a bath towel. She dresses in a towel so she won't be put out on the street by the manager. Martha, a former Miss Watermelon, Miss Cotton Blossom, and Miss Southern Comfort, came from Mississippi to New York expecting to make it big as an actress. Martha Vail did not conquer New York, and now she exists by making dates with men who come to her room. She orders food to be served in her room and passes the bill to the gentlemen. She is eleven-hundred dollars behind on her rent and tells the landlord that she is "sick." Martha tells Charlie that she has written a one-woman nightclub sketch with which she hopes to break into show business. She sings "I Was a Shoo-In" for Charlie, saying if just given the chance she would be a "shoo-in" again as she was in Mississippi. Charlie gives her his last five dollars to pay for the food she has ordered, and he volunteers to help her pay her debt to the hotel as well.

Angie has found Tom and his unusual philosophy strangely fascinating. He and a group of commuters give Angie intricate "Subway Directions" for sleeping on the subway trains. The heat has now been turned off in Martha's hotel room. Her one concession to the cold is the addition of black gloves to her single piece outfit, the towel. Martha and Charlie, at opposite sides of the stage, sing a duet in which they discuss on the telephone Martha's situation and the problem of her rent money.

Tom takes Angie to the Metropolitan Museum to demonstrate for her how one can get some sleep in one of the museum's empty mummy cases. Tom tells Angie that until a few years ago he was considered a financial genius. He financed many projects on credit and on checks, but one day one of his checks bounced and he was thrown in jail. He finds it safer and more fun to stay away from big business.

To make some extra money, Tom has taken a job as a Community Chest Santa Claus. As he and other drifters dressed as Santas gather to begin their Christmas fund collecting, Tom gives a stirring "call to arms," modeled on Shakespeare's King Henry V's speech to his soldiers before the battle of Agincourt. He sings "Be a Santa" and works all of the Santas into a frenzied holiday spirit that ends in a joyous Cossack-like dance. Angie joins Tom at his post beside a pasteboard chimney set up in Rockefeller Plaza. She is recognized by a magazine photographer who stops to congratulate her on one of her recent articles. Angie is forced to admit to Tom that she has been trying to get information from him for the new article she is writing. Understandably, Tom's exuberant Christmas spirit deserts him and he is very angry with Angie.

As the second act opens, Angie is sitting alone on a bench on a subway platform. Charlie recognizes her from seeing her picture in the paper and sits down to talk to her. Angie tells Charlie that she is not going to follow through with her article on Tom and she is not going to return to the magazine. When she tells Charlie that the magazine is offering a reward for information about her whereabouts, Charlie sees the chance to get some money to pay Martha's hotel bill.

Tom now regrets his anger and, as he and the other Santas are turning in their collections, he tries to describe for them what Angie looks like. He sings the beautiful ballad, "How Can You Describe a Face?" Charlie goes to Martha's hotel room to tell her that he has found a way to pay her rent, and that now he can show her off to the world. He sings "I Just Can't Wait," which describes how eager he is to see her with clothes on. When Martha and Charlie begin to realize that Angie and Tom are in love, they decide that they must forego the reward money.

Tom and Angie are united again and pay a visit to the French Wing of the Metropolitan Museum. They sing the joyful song, "Comes Once in a Lifetime," which advocates taking life one day at a time. When Tom goes to perform his daily chore of walking the dog, he is told by the hotel doorman that the dog has been shipped off to Florida to be with his owners. Now Tom's daily one dollar and a half income is gone. At this moment he realizes that he cannot even buy Angie breakfast. Now he really feels like a "bum." In the parking lot outside the hotel, Tom is talked into starting a coffee service for his fellow "subway sleepers," and they concoct a coffee machine out of scraps of plumbing and a discarded bathtub. Just then Martha, fully dressed, walks into the parking lot. Charlie is delighted to see her in a dress, and she explains that a sympathetic hotel detective from her hometown in Mississippi paid her bill. Tom decides he does not want to enter the business world again. He will join Angie in writing a book about his experiences. He gives the new coffee business to Charlie and Martha.

The Play's History

Subways Are for Sleeping opened at the St. James Theatre in New York on December 27, 1961, after tryouts in Philadelphia and Boston. The source for Comden and Green's book was the 1957 book of vignettes about New York City's people who have dropped out of the main stream and are living a minimal existence on the street, *Subways Are for Sleeping*, by Edmund G. Love. Jule Styne had bought the rights to *Subways Are for Sleeping* and then brought it to Comden and Green asking them to write the book for a musical based on the stories. Comden and Green, perhaps sensing the difficulty of making a plot for a musical out of the ten unconnected stories, insisted that they wanted to write only the lyrics. At first Ketti Frings agreed to write the book, but in January of 1960 she bowed out of the project. Arthur Laurents and Abe Burrows could not be talked into writing the book, so at last Comden and Green agreed to do the book as well as the lyrics. David Merrick, who had produced *Do Re Mi* just the year before, agreed to produce the show and hired Michael Kidd to direct and choreograph. In Comden and Green's original version, Angie is the personal secretary to an advertising executive. She is scheduled to marry her boss and takes some shots in preparation for her honeymoon trip. Groggy from the shots, she wanders into the subway where she meets Tom Bailey, a dropout from society. Tom falls in love with her and tries to help her start a new life while at the same time trying to keep her fiancé from finding her.

When *Subways Are for Sleeping* started tryouts in Philadelphia, the audience was more interested in the comedy sub-plot than in the story of Angie and Tom. Comden and Green did some fast re-writing. They eliminated the fiancé and made Angie a writer for a magazine. She is given an assignment to write a feature story about the well-dressed bums who inhabit the subways. She pretends to be one of these and meets Tom on the subway.

When the musical opened in New York on February 19, 1978, it received only two favorable reviews. David Merrick, the producer, sensing that the musical was only mediocre, had a quote advertisement ready for the newspapers. In the telephone directory he found people with the same names as the New York theatre critics and "helped" them write fantastic reviews of the play. Only the *Herald Tribune* was fooled by the advertisement and ran it. That and the publicity that followed helped keep *Subways Are for Sleeping* running for 205 performances. It closed on June 23, 1962. Phyllis Newman won a Tony Award as best Musical Actress in a Featured or Supporting Role, and Orson Bean was nominated for an award as a Featured or Supporting Musical Actor.

The original cast recording was made by Columbia Records. (See D34 and D35.) The sheet music was published by Stratford Music Corporation/Chappell. The libretto, music, and orchestrations for the musical are available from Tams-Witmark Music Library.

Reviews

Robert Coleman of the *New York Mirror*, called the show "no masterpiece," but he thought it had "enough heart and speed to make an evening at the St. James highly enjoyable." He praised Michael Kidd's staging and "choreographic invention and irresistible showmanship." He thought that Comden and Green's lyrics advanced the action and had "a humorous glint" (December 28, 1961).

Richard Watts, Jr., of the *New York Post* said that there was "an agreeable freshness of material" in *Subways Are for Sleeping* and that "the spirit is bright and the manner likable." He called the lyrics "deft" and the songs "tuneful." Betty Comden and Adolph Green have, he wrote, "added their sly touches of incidental comedy that keep popping up with comforting regularity." He does mention "trouble" with the book that leaves the story seeming "unfinished" (December 28, 1961).

Howard Taubman of the *New York Times* called the book "dull and vapid" and thought that "its characters barely breathe" (December 28, 1961). John McClain of the *Journal American* called the musical "disappointing," due to the fact that it was "based on a feeble idea." In spite of the talents of Betty Comden and Adolph Green, he wrote, "there is nothing highly hilarious or entertaining or remotely believable in this hoked-up kingdom of vagrants who infest the city." He praised the music of Jule Styne, calling it "gay, haunting, slick and singable" (December 28, 1961).

Walter Kerr of the *New York Herald Tribune* called the musical "a noble try," but "the moving spirit is limp, and the love story hasn't enough get-up-and-go to tide us past the uncoordinated whimsy." Kerr called Betty Comden and Adolph Green "sophisticates, alive and alert when they are free to be wry, knowing, engagingly impertinent," but he thought their sentimental material in the show was at odds with their "instincts" (December 28, 1961).

John Chapman of the *Daily News* also thought that Comden and Green had had "a tussle" with the plot and the show ended up as "just noisy, energetic, and good-natured" (December 28, 1961). Norman Nadel called the play book "thin" and the show "light entertainment, but without distinction" (*New York World Telegram*, December 28, 1961). The critic for *Time* magazine called the book "flat" (January 8, 1962), and the critic for *Newsweek* called the libretto "limp," but he did think Comden and Green's lyrics "jaunty" and Stynes's music "engaging" (January 8, 1962).

Commentary

Edmund G. Love had met an habitué of the Bowery who preferred to sleep on subway trains, ferry boats, and in railway stations rather than in Bowery "hotels." Love wrote about the man in an article published in *The New Yorker*. His acquaintance with this man led to his meeting other men who had no permanent home. Love wrote a series of articles and finally a book which consisted of vignettes about these drifters. Comden and Green seem to have had difficulty in weaving these characters into a story. The love story between Tom and Angie is not very believable, and no one really seems to believe in the main thesis of the musical that it is fun to sleep in a subway or a museum. The ending of the show reaffirms the idea of making money. The plot has a whimsical, sentimental quality that does not fit Comden and Green's usual impertinent and satirical style.

Evidently, in production, only Orson Bean in the role of Charlie Smith managed to get the quality of satire and buffoonery which the entire play should have had. Comden and Green's sparkling wit shines through in some very clever songs and production numbers. Martha's account of her success as a Southern beauty queen is hilariously told in the song, "I Was a Shoo-In," and Charlie's song in which he imagines seeing his girl friend in clothes, "I Just Can't Wait," is very funny. "Swing Your Projects," in which Tom tells of his success in the business world, is also a very cleverly worded song. The first act ends with the big, jaunty production number in which an unlikely assortment of vagrants dressed as Santa Clauses sing and dance to "Be a Santa." There are also the beautiful ballad, "How Can You Describe a Face?" and two joyous love songs, "Comes Once in a Lifetime" and "What Is This Feeling in the Air?"

*****

S06   *FADE OUT–FADE IN* (1964)

Mark Hellinger Theatre, New York City; Opened May 26, 1964;
271 Performances

Credits

Book and Lyrics	Betty Comden
	Adolph Green
Music	Jule Styne
Director	George Abbott

Book and Lyrics 75

Dances and Musical Numbers	Ernest Flatt
Settings and Lighting	William Eckart
	Jean Eckart
Costumes	Donald Brooks
Musical Director	John Berkman
Orchestrations	Ralph Burns
	Ray Ellis
Vocal Arrangements	Buster Davis
Dance Music Arrangements	Richard De Benedictis
Production Co-ordinator	Dorothy Dicker
Production Assistant	Joe Regan
Producers	Lester Osterman
	Jule Styne

Cast

Pops	Frank Tweddell
Autograph Kids	Roger Allan Raby
	Charlene Mehl
Helga Sixtrees	Alice Glenn
Roscoe	Bob Neukum
Billy Vespers	Paul Michael
Byron Prong	Jack Cassidy
Lyman	John Dorrin
Hope Springfield	Carol Burnett
Rex	Barney Johnston
Chauffeur	John Richardson
Girl	Trish Dwelley
Cowboy Extra	David Cryer
Gangster Extra	Gene Varrone
Ralph Governor	Mitchell Jason
Rudolph Governor	Dick Patterson
George Governor	Paul Eichel
Frank Governor	John Dorrin
Harold Governor	Gene Varrone
Arnold Governor	David Cryer
Waiters:	Richard Frisch, Roger Allan Raby, Steve Elmore
Publicity Men	Dean Doss
	Barney Johnston
Convicts:	Gene Kelton, John Richardson, Bill Starr, Jerry Gotham
Myra May Melrose	Virginia Payne
Seamstress	Diane Arnold
Custer Corkley	Dan Resin
Max Welch	Richard Frisch
Lou Williams	Tiger Haynes
Dora Dailey	Aileen Poe
Lionel Z. Governor	Lou Jacobi
Dr. Anton Traurig	Reuben Singer
Gloria Currie	Judy Cassmore
Madame Barrymore	Penny Egelston

Lead Dancer	Don Crichton

Singing Ensemble: Terri Baker, Dell Brownlee, Trish Dwelley, Carolyn Kemp, Bobbi Lange, Mari Nettum, David Cryer, John Dorrin, Dean Doss, Paul Eichel, Steve Elmore, Richard Frisch, Barney Johnston, Roger Allan Raby, Gene Varrone

Dancing Ensemble: Virginia Allen, Diane Arnold, Lynne Broadbent, Diana Eden, Alice Glenn, Charlene Mehl, Judy Newman, Jodi Perselle, Carolsue Shaer, Pat Sigris, Jerry Gotham, Gene Kelton, John Richardson, Buddy Spencer, Bill Starr, Ron Tassone, Michael Toles

Synopsis

The scene is glamorous Hollywood in the mid-1930s. In front of the FFF Studio we witness the arrival of a new hopeful starlet, the awkward Hope Springfield, who, much to her own surprise, was picked out of a line of usherettes at the Strand Theatre in New York by none other than the great movie mogel, L. Z. Governor. Later, in the executive dining room, Hope is introduced to the six vice-presidents of FFF Studios, all nephews of L. Z. Governor. Only Rudolph Governor is brave enough to state that Hope is not his uncle's usual type. L. Z. usually picks "floozies," and Hope is a wholesome girl, he says. Hope also meets her handsome leading man, Byron Prong, who is not eager to work with this unlikely starlet. When the nephews learn that their uncle will be in Europe for the next month, panic sets in, for the studio is to begin filming *The Fiddler and the Fighter* and Hope is to play the Fiddler, a violinist who falls in love with a boxer. Ralph Governor decides he will direct the film, but only one scene has been written. The script writer, Max Welch, has not been able to come up with the story. When the cast and crew begin to film the one scene, Hope, who as an usherette has seen hundreds of films, begins to visualize and describe what the story must be that could provide such a scene. The screenwriter gladly writes down her outline and the filming continues.

L. Z. Governor has been delayed in Vienna because he is under the care of a psychiatrist. The psychiatrist discovers that L. Z. cannot say the number "four" because he senses that his fourth nephew, Ralph, is trying to take over his own position in the company. By the time L. Z. returns to Hollywood, the picture is finished and the nephews proudly prepare to show the film to their uncle. As they start the film, L. Z., in a fury, stops it. Hope Springfield was not the girl he picked, he says. He orders her out, fires Ralph, and demands that the film be burned. He puts Rudolph in charge of production because he was the only one who realized that Hope was not his uncle's type. L. Z. had counted the girls in the line of usherettes, but since he could not say "four" the number was off. He meant to pick gorgeous Gloria Currie, and now he sends for her and insists that the film be made again with Gloria as the violinist.

Though Gloria is a terrible actress, L. Z. is crazy about his new curvaceous star whom he has renamed Lila Tremaine. Hope, having been thrown out of the studio, has had difficulty finding a job and finally is reduced to dressing like Shirley Temple and wearing a sandwich-board advertising the Kiddie Kareer School that promises to make a star out of any cute little child. She sings "There's Always One Step Further Down You Can Go." Rudolph sees Hope as she walks about in her sandwich-board. He tells her that he loves her and gives her a job disguised as a male extra in the film, *The Fiddler and the Fighter*. The film with Gloria in it is at last finished, and Rudolph tries to tell L. Z. how terrible Gloria is, but he will not listen.

When the new movie is to be previewed, Rudolph substitutes the film that starred Hope. He did not burn it as ordered by L. Z. L. Z. sees the original movie and is impressed with Hope Springfield. He admits that he has been wrong. After the premiere, Hope is mobbed by movie fans.

In the final scene of the play, an audience has gathered in front of Grauman's Chinese Theatre where Hope, as Lila Tremaine, is to be immortalized in the cement in front of the theatre. A wooden frame of cement is brought on and Hope, swathed in yards of fur, steps to the microphone to introduce herself as "Mrs. Rudolph Governor." She removes the furs and in her gold dress kneels down to keep for posterity her famous smile. Smiling broadly, she puts her face in the cement. The crowd freezes as they realize that the cement has set and Hope cannot get her face out. Rudolph and L. Z. try desperately to pull her out of the cement as the curtain falls.

The Play's History

Fade Out--Fade In, starring Carol Burnett, opened at the Mark Hellinger Theatre on May 26, 1964. Five of the New York theatre critics gave it favorable reviews. The show closed on November 14, 1964, after 199 performances. It reopened at the same theatre on February 15, 1965, for 72 performances, closing on April 17, 1965. The total number of performances was 271. Carol Burnett had asked Jule Styne to write a show for her. Styne asked Comden and Green to write the book and the lyrics. They came up with the idea for the story. The show was originally titled A Girl to Remember.

During its opening week at the Mark Hellinger Theatre, Fade Out--Fade In set a record for the largest weekly gross ever taken in at that box office. Carol Burnett was the star and was at the time America's premiere television comedienne, so her many fans came to see the show. Early in the run Burnett began to miss performances--twenty-six in the first twenty-five weeks. In November she left the show for treatment of back and neck injuries which she had received when a taxi she was riding in suddenly braked. The producers filed legal action against Burnett. They then entered into negotiations and closed the show.

While the show was closed, Comden and Green tried to improve the libretto. They and Jule Styne added two new songs, "A Girl to Remember," which replaced "Lila Tremaine," and "Notice Me." Two other songs, "The Thirties" and "Go Home Train," were cut. Jack Cassidy, who played the matinee idol, dropped out of the cast and was replaced by Dick Shawn. For thirteen weeks the idle company collected their paychecks. When the show re-opened, it was at an additional cost of $100,000. The show ran for only seventy-two more performances. Burnett announced that she was pregnant and, without its star, the show was forced to close (Cecil Smith and Glenn Litton, Musical Comedy in America, p. 260). For his role as the egotistical leading man, Byron Prong, Jack Cassidy was nominated for a Tony Award as a Featured or Supporting Actor.

An original cast recording was made by ABC Records. (See D14.) The sheet music was published by Stratford Music/Chappell and Company. The libretto was published by Random House in 1965. Rights to production of the play are available through the Tams-Witmark Music Library.

Reviews

The New York critics' reviews of Fade Out--Fade In were mostly favorable. John Chapman of the Daily News was enthusiastic, calling it "a real World's Fair musical, with something in it for everybody and everything in it for somebody." He wrote that he "never stopped enjoying it." "Betty Comden and Adolph Green...have written about the old Hollywood with affection and haven't pretended to be superior or satirical" (May 27, 1964).

John McClain of the *Journal American* thought that it would be a smash hit. "Comden and Green have developed enough bright situations and laugh lines to make everybody happy." He especially liked Carol Burnett and concluded that *Fade Out--Fade In* was "a generally joyous if not distinguished big musical" (May 27, 1964).

Howard Taubman of the *New York Times* wrote: "Like some of the gaudy film spectacles of the thirties that it lampoons, *Fade Out--Fade In* is big, lavish, colorful, and sporadically diverting." He thought the play had been paced "so swiftly and robustly by George Abbott that it gives the impression of spinning happily and imaginatively without cease." However, he added, "much of the material in the book by Betty Comden and Adolph Green is old hat. It hasn't been fresh since *Once in a Lifetime*" (May 27, 1964).

Walter Kerr of the *Herald Tribune* couldn't see why he couldn't like it. "Everything workable, everything swift, and I never could persuade myself that any of it was necessary" (May 27, 1964). Richard Watts, Jr., of the *New York Post* thought the play had "enough enthusiastic relish and sheer gusto to make it entertaining." Though he thought the musical did not have much of a story, he did think that Comden and Green had "enlivened it with incidental moments of their witty deftness" (May 27, 1964).

Harold Clurman of *The Nation* called the story "hackneyed," but it had "a little folksy nostalgia for the legendary glamour of the bad old days of Hollywood's prosperity, which, combined with a slightly mocking enthusiasm characteristic of Comden-Green, relieves the story of any oppressive gush or of an even more oppressive condescension" (June 15, 1964). Other magazine reviewers were less complimentary. The critic for *Newsweek* thought the book "continually gets in its own way" and called the characters "caricatures" (June 8, 1964). Henry Hewes of *The Saturday Review of Literature* thought there was "nothing particularly fresh or remarkable about the new musical, *Fade Out--Fade In*, except Carol Burnett..." He thought the songs by Comden and Green and Styne merely "passable" (June 20, 1964). The reviewer for *Time* wrote that the "show goes down for the long, long count of boredom" (June 6, 1964).

Commentary

In the film, *Singin' in the Rain*, Comden and Green had satirized the Hollywood of the 1920s when the "talkies" were first introduced. They themselves had had experience in the movie business. In *Fade Out--Fade In* they satirize the early 1930s Busby Berkeley days in Hollywood. They picture the all-powerful but artistically ignorant movie mogul, the vice-presidents who are all relatives and "yes" men, the beautiful starlet who cannot speak or act, the handsome leading man who will make love to whichever female star is in the ascendancy, the gossip columnist, the adoring fans, and the former stars reduced to bit parts. Here Comden and Green make hilarious fun of the unbelievable plots and the filming without a script. They satirize the elaborate production numbers and the "faking" of scenes that is possible in the movies. Comden and Green's satire is not biting but is mixed with nostalgia and affection.

The production of *Fade Out--Fade In* owed much to the able direction of George Abbott and the wonderful clowning of Carol Burnett. However, it was Comden and Green who provided some very funny scenes like the one in which the awkward Hope Springfield is being mistakenly costumed for the wrong show. She is outfitted in a very brief costume ornamented with great ropes of beads. Since she is embarrassed in this revealing costume she borrows a man's jacket to put on top. With the ropes of beads hanging from the sleeves of the jacket, she sings one of Comden and Green's cleverly rhyming songs, "Call Me Savage."

In another funny scene, Hope, as the "fiddler" in the movie that the studio is making, is supposed to play the violin. When she protests that she cannot play the violin she is told to put her hands behind her, and two arms come around her to hold and play the instrument that is tucked under her chin.

Other clever songs by Comden and Green are "Fear," sung by the vice-presidents and nephews of the movie mogul, and Hope's song about her past, "The Usher from the Mezzanine." Comden and Green also make delicious fun of popular love songs in the terrible "My Heart Is Like a Violin," sung by Byron Prong. Prong, who always carries a mirror about with him, also sings "My Fortune Is My Face" as he looks lovingly at his own reflection in the mirror. In clever, rhyming songs, Comden and Green are at their best.

*****

S07   *ON THE TWENTIETH CENTURY* (1978)

St. James Theatre, New York City; Opened February 19, 1978.
460 Performances

Credits
Based on plays by Ben Hecht, Charles MacArthur, and Bruce Millholland
Book and Lyrics   Betty Comden
                                                  Adolph Green
Music   Cy Coleman
Director   Harold Prince
Designer   Robin Wagner
Costumes   Florence Klotz
Lighting   Ken Billington
Musical Director   Paul Gemignani
Orchestrations   Hershy Kay
Musical Numbers Staged By   Larry Fuller
Producers: The Producers Circle 2, Inc.: Robert Fryer, Mary Lea Johnson,
              James Cresson, Martin Richards, Joseph Harris, Ira Bernstein

Cast
Priest   Ken Hilliard
Bishop   Charles Rule
Stage Manager   Ray Gill
Joan   Maris Clement
Wardrobe Mistress   Carol Lurie
Actor   Hal Norman
Owen O'Malley   George Coe

Oliver Webb	Dean Dittman
Porter	Keith Davis
Porter	Quitman Fludd, III
Porter	Ray Stephens
Porter	Joseph Wise
Congressman Lockwood	Rufus Smith
Conductor Flanagan	Tom Batten
Train Secretary Rogers	Stanley Simmonds
Letitia Primrose	Imogene Coca
Redcap	Mel Johnson, Jr.
Anita	Carol Lugenbeal
Oscar Jaffee	John Cullum
Max Jacobs	George Lee Andrews
Imelda	Willi Burke
Maxwell Finch	David Horwitz
Mildred Plotka/Lily Garland	Madeline Kahn
Otto Von Bismark	Sal Mistretta
Bruce Granit	Kevin Kline
Agnes	Judy Kaye
Fanny	Peggy Cooper
Hospital Attendants	Sal Mistretta
	Carol Lurie
Dr. Johnson	Willi Burke

Singers: Susan Cella, Maris Clement, Peggy Cooper, Karen Gibson, Carol Lurie, Melanie Vaughan, Ray Gill, Ken Hilliard, David Horwitz, Craig Lucas, Sal Mistretta, Hal Norman, Charles Rule, David Vogel.

Swing Singers: Linda Poser, Gerald Teijelo

Synopsis

It is Chicago in the early 1930s. On stage are part of a cathedral, a priest, a bishop, and a stake surrounded by piled-up faggots. Tied to the stake is Joan of Arc. It is the middle of the last act of a play called *The French Girl*. As the executioner lifts the torch to light the faggots, the stage manager steps out and stops the show. The last member of the audience has just left the theatre, and it is another commercial failure for the flamboyant impresario-director, Oscar Jaffee. The angered actors try to find Jaffee to demand their back pay, but Jaffee successfully evades them by staying inside a full suit of armor. He slips a note to his press agent, Owen O'Malley, and his business manager, Oliver Webb, to get him Drawing Room A on the Twentieth Century and to meet him there tomorrow.

The scene changes to show the Twentieth Century train at the station in Chicago. The passengers sing a paean of praise to the magnificent train that travels between New York and Chicago in sixteen hours. Suddenly we are inside the train. On stage are the Observation Car and Drawing Room A. By threatening to expose a congressman who is traveling with an attractive secretary, Owen and Oliver have managed to get Drawing Room A for Oscar Jaffee. Jaffee himself makes a rather ignominious entrance into the Observation Car by crawling through the window after the train has started. After pulling their boss through the window, Owen and Oliver remind him that he is two hundred and fifty thousand dollars in debt and by going back to New York he is only going home to bankruptcy. Oscar proudly sings "I Rise Again!" He tells Owen and Oliver that Lily Garland is getting on the train at the next stop. She is booked into Drawing Room B. He will get her to star in his next play. When the men question him, Oscar admits that he has not yet talked with Lily Garland and he has no play, but those, he assures them, are mere details. Lily Garland is now a famous movie star who has won an Academy Award, but Oscar remembers when he first met her. In a flashback we see Oscar Jaffee auditioning an older actress, who has had to hire a substitute pianist to play for her. The pianist, who rushes in late for the audition, is a rather plain young girl named Mildred Plotka. When the actress cannot sing the audition song, Mildred sings it for her. Oscar talks Mildred into taking the part. He gives her the name, Lily Garland, and hands her the script for his play about the little French street-singer, Veronique. As Lily Garland sings "Veronique" we see her become a star. Oscar comes out of his remembrance of his first meeting with Lily Garland and prepares to meet her again.

At the train's first stop, Lily Garland makes a grand entrance, surrounded by reporters and photographers. She is accompanied by Bruce Granit, her co-star. Now on stage we see the Observation Car, Drawing Room A, and Drawing Room B. In the Observation Car, all is confusion because someone has been putting stickers that read "Repent for the time is at hand" on everyone and everything. After everyone has left the car we see that it is Miss Letitia Primrose who is putting up the stickers and singing "Repent." When Oscar sees the stickers he has an inspiration--he will star Lily Garland as Mary Magdelene in a religious play. Now he has something to offer her. He sets Owen writing press releases for the new play that will star Lily Garland. While Owen is writing in the Observation Car, Letitia Primrose begins to talk to him. She tells him that her company, Primrose Restoria Pills, has made so much money that they don't know what to do with it all.

Oscar has made his first visit to Lily, reminding her of their "private world" that they once had. Bruce Granit becomes very jealous, and Lily throws him out. Oscar tells Lily that she has sold out to Hollywood and has gone stale as an actress. Lily insists that she is doing very well without Oscar and tells him that she knows he is broke. When Oscar goes back to Drawing Room A, he discovers that Owen and Oliver have met Letitia Primrose, who just might be interested in investing in a religious play.

As the second act opens we see Owen, Oliver, and Oscar all beaming at Letitia Primrose as she writes a check for two hundred thousand dollars. They sing happily, "Five Zeros." They are interrupted by a message that Lily wants to see Oscar. Thinking that Lily has been touched by seeing him again, Oscar rushes to her room. She presents him with a check for thirty-five dollars with the promise of a check every week to help him out of his financial difficulties. Oscar shows her the check for two hundred thousand dollars and tells her of the magnificent part of the Magdelene. Lily at once visualizes herself in the role and begins to expand on the story. Oscar introduces Letitia Primrose to Lily, and he, Oliver, Owen, and Letitia all urge Lily to sign the contract to star in the play, while Bruce Granit urges her not to sign it. At last she does sign on the condition that after a year on the stage she will star in the movie which will be produced in her own studio, thanks to the generosity of Letitia.

In the Observation Car, Flanagan and two officers from the Benzinger Clinic are looking for Mrs. Primrose. She climbed the fence and escaped from the institution. Flanagan tells Oliver that the woman is a "nut." Gradually, the news spreads among the passengers, and a big production number follows as everyone looks for Letitia. We see Letitia spread-eagled on the front of the train and then we see her on the observation platform at the end of the train. She waves as the train disappears. Oscar and Lily lament their lost money. Just then the Hollywood director, Max Jacobs, gets on the train. He has a new play script for Lily. She reads the play, but she still thinks of the grand role of the Magdelene.

In the Observation Car, Owen and Oliver are quite drunk. Oscar comes in. He has a revolver. He has decided he does not want to live. He sings "The Legacy," in which he lists his theatrical memorabilia he is leaving to Owen and Oliver. They don't really believe he will shoot himself, but after he leaves they hear a shot. Oscar runs in followed by Letitia. She tried to take the gun away from him, and Oscar thinks he has been shot. When the doctor can find nothing wrong with him, Oscar decides to play a little trick. He has Lily brought in. He pretends to be dying and urges her to sign the contract for him. She signs. When Max Jacobs comes in, Oscar jumps up, triumphantly waving the contract. Lily tells him she wasn't taken in, just look at her signature. She has signed "Peter Rabbit." While still calling each other names, Oscar and Lily begin to laugh and then jump into each other's arms.

The Play's History

On the Twentieth Century was based on the 1932 play, Twentieth Century, by Ben Hecht and Charles MacArthur, which, in turn, had been derived from an earlier play called Napoleon on Broadway by Bruce Millholland. Millholland had sent the script to the producer, Jed Harris, who agreed to do it if Hecht and MacArthur would re-work it. Twentieth Century received rave reviews but ran only 152 performances. In 1934 the Hecht-MacArthur play was made into a famous movie with John Barrymore and Carole Lombard. Comden and Green could not use anything from the film because the rights were held by Columbia Pictures.

On the Twentieth Century began a four week out-of-town tryout at Boston's Colonial Theatre on January 7, 1978. The Variety critic, F. Snyder, thought the show had all of the ingredients of a Broadway hit. He did suggest some cuts and some simplification of the elaborate physical production. The musical opened on Broadway on February 19, 1978, at the St. James Theatre. It ran for 460 performances, closing on March 18, 1979, before beginning a national tour that included San Francisco, Los Angeles, and other major cities. On the Twentieth Century won five Tony Awards. John Cullum won for Outstanding Performance in a Broadway Musical. Kevin Kline was given an award as an actor in a featured role. Cy Coleman, Betty Comden, and Adolph Green were honored for Best Score of a Broadway Musical, and Comden and Green also won for Best Book for a musical. Robin Wagner was awarded a Tony for his outstanding scenic design. Madeline Kahn and Imogene Coca were both nominated for awards, as was Harold Prince for his direction. The musical itself was nominated for a Tony Award, but lost to Ain't Misbehavin'.

There was a major change in the cast during the Broadway run. Shortly after the opening, Madeline Kahn began to miss performances. Her understudy, Judy Kaye, who was cast as Lily's maid, substituted nine times in the role of Lily. Judy Kaye was such a success that Madeline Kahn was invited to leave the show. Kahn played her last performance on April 24, 1978, and Judy Kaye took over the role. Late in the run, Betty Comden took the role of Letitia Primrose for one week from January 16 through January 22, 1979, while Imogene Coca was on vacation.

A national company toured the show in 1979 with Judy Kaye and Imogene Coca from the Broadway cast and Rock Hudson as Oscar. *On the Twentieth Century* had a successful run in London starring Keith Mitchell and Julia McKenzie. The London Company, directed by Peter Coe, opened on March 19, 1980, and ran for 165 performances. In 1985 the off-off Broadway York Theatre Company presented a cleverly scaled-down production of the show, proving that the book and music could succeed without the elaborate staging. Another touring production was undertaken in the 1986-1987 season with Kaye and Coca once again playing their roles and with Frank Gorshin as Oscar.

The original New York cast recording was made by Columbia Records. The musical has recently been re-issued on compact disc. (See D26.) The libretto, music, and orchestrations are available from Tams-Witmark Music Library.

Reviews

The reviews of *On the Twentieth Century* were mixed. Clive Barnes of the *New York Post* called it "enchantment put on wheels and sent rolling." Though he thought the idea not a very good one, he concluded that "the musical works like a fantasy. It works because of its style, or rather its comprehension of style at all levels." He called the music "a lovely score" which "runs a gorgeous gamut from Jacques Brel to Menotti." He thought that Comden and Green had shaped the plays upon which it was based "into a perfect musical entity." Of Comden and Green's lyrics he said that they don't have the poetry of Stephen Sondheim, "but they do have a marvelous gift for the expectedly right rhyme, a feel for verbal tension within a phrase, and also a sense for the traditional formalities of show business that goes so neatly with Coleman's music" (February 20, 1978).

Douglas Watt of the *Daily News* complimented both the book and the "well-fashioned lyrics," but thought the score "overly ambitious" (February 20, 1978). Richard Eder of the *New York Times* called the play "funny, elegant and totally cheerful" with "an exuberance, a bubbly confidence in its own life." He thought the book was "a unique marriage of civilized wit and wild humor ... closely blended with a strong score by Cy Coleman and the inspired scenic design of Robin Wagner" (February 20, 1978).

Howard Kissel of *Women's Wear Daily* remarked that the production of the play was so "stunning" that one could easily not notice that the material itself was "thin." The virtue of Comden and Green's lyrics, he wrote, "is that they are eminently actable." He thought the musical a "marvelously stylish show" (February 21, 1978).

John Beaufort of *The Christian Science Monitor* called the musical a "stunning example of Broadway craftsmanship and technology at work." He called it "a glossy and glittering spectacular," but he concluded that Lily and Oscar "wind up as caricatures with scarcely a shred of romantic appeal" (February 23, 1978).

Harold Clurman, writing in *The Nation*, called *On the Twentieth Century* "a triumph of a certain professionalism and Chutzpah. I ascribe this to Adolph Green's ebullient nature disciplined by Betty Comden's decorous wit" (March 11, 1978). Martin Gottfried of *The Saturday Review of Literature* praised Comden and Green's lyrics. "Their words for Coleman's tricky and witty music are technically immaculate, appropriate in sense, and genuinely clever in a modern, offbeat way." He also refers to the "fresh and quirky humor in the Comden and Green script" (April 15, 1978).

On the other hand, Edwin Wilson of the *Wall Street Journal* thought the creators of the musical did not know what to do with the 1930s story in the 1970s. "The result is a melange that is part musical comedy, part operetta, part parody and part pure bombast" (February 22, 1978). T. E. Kalem of *Time* thought the plot line of the musical "monorail thin" and said that Harold Prince had "taken refuge in camp and stylistic cartoonery" (March 6, 1978). Stanley Kauffmann of *The New Republic* thought the musical filled with "the desperate bustle of the very weary and the imaginatively bankrupt." Of John Callum he wrote, "He cannot act, he has no charm, sex, or color ... He has no comic sense and no ability to move" (March 18, 1978). And Dean Valentine of the *New Leader* thought no one seemed to care about the Lily-Oscar love affair--"certainly not writers and lyricists Betty Comden and Adolph Green. They were counting on the audience's apparently insatiable hunger to believe that there were good old days--not on character or innovation--to carry the day." His conclusion was that "tedious acting aggravates a tedious conception" (March 27, 1978).

Commentary

When Betty Comden and Adolph Green decided to adapt the 1932 Ben Hecht-Charles MacArthur play, *The Twentieth Century*, they were faced with the difficult question of style. The Hecht-MacArthur play is steeped in the 1930s cynicism of H. L. Mencken. Cynicism is not Comden and Green's style. They may be satirical but they are kindly and up-beat, not cynical. Also, the farcical elements of the play were just right for the 1930s when Broadway had its madcap farces and the films were doing screwball comedies. Comden and Green did not want to write a 1930s musical, but also they did not want to write a musical with a contemporary sound. Finally they found their style in the leading characters themselves. Oscar Jaffee and Lily Garland were "larger than life, extravagant, egomaniacal giants of the theatre. They were characters who cut a wide swath through their own and everyone else's lives," Comden and Green wrote in an article in the *New York Times* (Comden and Green, "Head of Steam for the old Twentieth Century," *New York Times*, February 19, 1978). Working with Cy Coleman, they experimented with music and songs that were flamboyant, almost operatic. For this they needed big voices, and therefore chose John Collum, who has a big voice, and Madeline Kahn, who had had operatic training. The critics were divided on these two actors. Some thought John Cullum, though fine vocally, was not physically adept in the exaggerated farcical movement required. Madeline Kahn was not able to sustain the largeness of the part. She frequently missed performances, and after eleven weeks she was replaced by Judy Kaye, who took over in April of 1978. Harold Prince, the director, thought the show would have been more successful if Judy Kaye had been used from the beginning (Carol Ilson, *Harold Prince*, p. 254).

Harold Prince was best known at this time for his sophisticated, sardonic collaborations with Stephen Sondheim. He was interested in doing something that was up-beat and he was challenged by the farcical style, eager to know if he could make audiences "laugh at Marx Brothers routines in trains" ("Harold Prince," *Newsday*, February 3, 1980, quoted by Carol Ilson in *Harold Prince*, p. 259). Most of the critics applauded the style and Prince's direction.

In adapting the play, Comden and Green built up the character of Lily Garland so that she could hold her own with the flamboyant Oscar. They also gave her more tenderness and emotion so that the love story could be more believable. Two of Comden and Green's changes from the original play proved to be very successful. The Hecht-MacArthur play had two actors from the Oberammergau Passion Play on the train. Comden and Green eliminated these characters but added the woman religious fanatic to give Oscar the inspiration for a religious play.

The role was played by the wildly comic Imogene Coca. Comden and Green also created an entirely new character in Bruce Granit, a young leading man who is Lily's newest love. Kevin Kline made the role one of the best parts of the musical.

Comden and Green created some very funny songs for the musical. During the song, "Mine," Oscar looks in a mirror on one side of the door between the two drawing rooms while Bruce Granit looks in a mirror on the other side of the door. They are both preparing themselves to meet with Lily Garland. Oscar admires his own "flashing wit" and "brilliant brain," while Bruce Granit sings of his own "flashing eyes" and "brutal thighs." Other clever songs are "Five Zeros," which refers to the check for two-hundred thousand dollars Oscar and his partners think they are getting from Letitia Primrose, and "The Legacy," in which Oscar lists his strange assortment of theatrical properties and memorabilia that he will leave to Owen and Oliver.

For many of the reviewers, the hit of the musical was set designer Robin Wagner's gleaming, Art Deco re-creation of the famous Twentieth Century train. His ingenious design allowed us to see both the train's silvery exterior and its elegant interior rooms.

*****

S08   *A DOLL'S LIFE* (1982)

Mark Hellinger Theatre, New York City; Opened September 23, 1982;
5 Performances

Credits
Book and Lyrics	Betsy Comden
	Adolph Green
Music	Larry Grossman
Director	Harold Prince
Choreography	Larry Fuller
Musical Director	Paul Gemignani
Orchestrations	Bill Byers
Designers	Timothy O'Brien
	Tazeena Firth
Costumes	Florence Klotz
Lighting	Ken Billington

Producers: James M. Nederlander, Sidney L. Shlenker, Warner Theatre Productions, Joseph Harris, Mary Lea, Johnson, Martin Richards, Robert Fryer, Harold Prince

Cast
Nora	Betsy Joslyn
Actor, Torvald, and Johan	George Hearn
Otto	Peter Gallagher
Eric	Edmund Lyndeck
Astrid	Barbara Lang
Audition Singer, Selma, and Jacqueline	Penny Orloff
Conductor, Gustafson, Escamillo, Audition Singer, Loki, and Mr. Zetterling	Norman A. Large

Stage Hand, Dr. Berg, Audition Singer, and Ambassador	David Vosburgh
Stage Manager, Hamsun, Petersen, Warden, and Nilson	Michael Vita
Dowager	Diane Armistead
Musician and Mr. Kloster	Gordon Bovinet
Camilla Forrester	Willi Burke
Assistant Stage Manager and Helga	Patti Cohenour
Prison Guards	John Corsaut
	David Cale Johnson
Helmer's Maid and Waitress	Carol Lurie
Musician and Waiter	Larry Small
Waiter, Audition Singer, and Muller	Paul Straney
Maid and the Widow	Olga Talyn
Ivar	Jim Wagg
Emmy	Kimberly Stern
Bob	David Seaman
Woman in White	Lisa Peters
Woman in Red	Teri Gill
Woman in Black	Patricia Parker
Man in Black	David Evans

Synopsis

    A Doll's Life opens with a rehearsal of the last scene of Henrik Ibsen's play, *A Doll's House*. When Betsy, the actress playing Nora, tells Torvald that she is leaving him, the director of the play stops the rehearsal. He tells Betsy that she is not realizing the significance of the lines. She is playing a modern woman and not a woman of 1879. She has not put herself into the time period when a woman had very few options if she left her husband. This makes Betsy begin to transport herself back in time. While Betsy and the cast sing, we are transported back to 1879. Nora boards a train and is seated alone in a compartment. A young man carrying a violin case enters. It is Otto Bernick. Nora realizes that she has left home without any money and must try to get the young man to pay for her ticket. Nora speaks flirtatiously to the man and then realizes that she is using the same old tricks she used with Torvald. Otto Bernick does pay for her ticket.

    In Christiania, Nora at last finds work as a waitress. On New Year's Eve she waits on four wealthy men who are celebrating together. Two of the men are Johan, a lawyer, and Eric Didrickson, an industrialist. The men, who are slightly drunk, insist that Nora drink with them. The manager of the cafe does not like this and fires Nora. Nora sings "Letter to the Children," explaining to her children why she has left them. Outside of the cafe she meets Otto Bernick, the musician, again. He says that he might be able to get her a job backstage at the opera and invites her to celebrate New Year's Eve with him. She goes to his rooming house where they talk and Otto begs her to stay with him. She does. Otto does get Nora a job in the wardrobe department at the opera. While helping the diva, Astrid Klemnacht, Nora tells her about the opera Otto has written and asks if she will listen to some of it. Astrid is not interested, but Nora runs into Johan, the lawyer, a friend of Astrid's lover, Eric, the industrialist. Nora asks Johan to mention the opera to Astrid and to stress the wonderful role in it for her. Johan does convince Astrid to listen to the opera. Astrid hosts a reception after the regular performance of the opera that is playing. Otto and his singers present portions of his opera. Astrid is attracted to the young musician, Otto, and agrees to meet with him to talk over the opera. But when Astrid discovers that Nora is so intimately involved with Otto, she cancels the plans to meet with Otto. In their room later that night, Otto blames Nora for Astrid's refusal to talk with him about the opera. The words of Torvald come back to Nora. Otto receives a letter from Astrid saying that she liked the music and that she will subsidize the work. Otto, like Torvald, now forgives Nora. But Nora has realized that Otto does not consider her an equal partner and she leaves him. She now decides that she must not depend on a man. She has only herself. She sings "Learn to Be Lonely."

The only job that Nora can find now is in a fish cannery. Here the girls work sixteen hours a day in a cold, wet room. Nora, in what spare time she has, is reading books borrowed from the University. When the overseer tells the girls that they will now have to work seven days a week instead of six, Nora objects and is taken to jail as a troublemaker. In prison, Nora sings one of her letters to her children, telling them that she has been studying the law, and that the law is wrong. Johan gets Nora out of prison. He takes her to hear Otto's opera which is now playing. At the opera Johan introduces Nora to Eric Didrickson, who is the industrialist who owns the fish cannery where Nora works. Nora tells Eric of the terrible working conditions in the cannery. He says that he will make changes in the working conditions if she will come home with him. She insists that he reduce the number of hours of work per day to eight. They argue and at last compromise on eleven hours a day. During the arguing they have discovered that they are very attracted to each other, and Nora agrees to go home with Eric.

The second act reveals Nora in Eric's home exulting in the luxury of the bedroom and in the passionate love that Eric has given her. She has discovered her body which she had been taught to pretend wasn't there. Eric sees some of the books on investing which she has been reading. He forbids her to read such books. But Eric is too late. She has already learned about investing and has been using some of the jewels he has given her to get money for her investments. Eric tells Nora to learn the names of his business friends who are coming for billiards and supper this evening. She is to act as his hostess. That evening, Nora, looking lovely in black velvet, talks with and flatters the men who have come to Eric's house. Johan is one of the guests and Otto, the musician, is acting as a waiter. Astrid has now dropped Otto as her lover. Nora gambles with some of the men and discovers the joy of winning financially. As the men go in for a cold supper, Eric tells Nora to go to bed. He will not see her until the next day. The next morning Nora comes to Eric's bedroom to take him his breakfast. She is surprised to see a young woman leaving his room. Nora is heartbroken. She scolds Eric for bringing another woman into her house. Eric reminds her that it is his house and she is merely one of his possessions. Nora gets her hat and coat and leaves Eric's house.

Nora has discovered that the young woman, Jacqueline, who was Eric's guest for the night, sells perfume in her father's shop. The father wishes to sell the shop, and Nora and Jacqueline decide to go into business together. Nora must call on her lawyer friend, Johan, to sign the papers in order for her to buy the business. A woman cannot own a business in her own name. Over the next year Nora's business succeeds and she buys more shops. She and Johan are now living together, and he asks her to marry him. It is nearly Christmas, and Nora wants to visit her children. She decides to return to her home on Christmas Day to see the children. She does go back to Torvald's house and discovers that Torvald has let the children read her letters. Torvald has heard of her business success but wonders if there have been men along the way. She says yes, there have been men, but only one man saw her as a person and not "a doormat or a pet." She explains how she has changed and challenges Torvald to talk with her as an equal. After some hesitation, Torvald says, "Sit down, Nora ...we must talk."

The Play's History

A Doll's Life was to play in Los Angeles for twelve weeks before opening in New York. After the cast arrived in Los Angeles they had a week of technical rehearsals and four previews. On June 15, 1982, the musical opened at the Ahmanson Theatre. The local reviews were mostly negative; however, one favorable review in Daily Variety gave the cast and production team hope for the show. For five weeks Harold Prince, the director, and the company made minor changes. Then Prince left for a vacation at his home in Majorca. The show continued to lose money at a reputed average of $140,000 a week. By the end of ten weeks the show had incurred an additional one million dollars in costs. The producers had little difficulty in raising the extra million dollars. However, the Los Angeles run was cut by two weeks in order to avoid extra expenses. On September 8 previews began in New York. The preview audiences were sympathetic, but when the show opened, after eighteen previews, on September 23, 1982, at the Mark Hellinger Theatre, the reviews were terrible. The play ran for only five performances.

In spite of the early closing of the musical, Betty Comden and Adolph Green were nominated for a Tony Award for the Best Book and Comden and Green and Larry Grossman were nominated for Tony Awards for Best Score of a Musical. Cats won those awards. George Hearn was also nominated for Best Performance in a Musical. The award went to Tommy Tune. Peter Gallagher was given the Annual Theater World Award for outstanding new talent.

The libretto of A Doll's Life was published by Samuel French in 1983. The sheet music was published by Fiddleback/Bettdolph/Manor Lane/Valendo. The musical was recorded by CBS Special Products. (See D13.) There is a videotaped performance available in the New York Public Library Billy Rose Collection at Lincoln Center.

Reviews

The most complimentary review of A Doll's Life by a New York critic was that of Howard Kissel in Women's Wear Daily. "Betty Comden and Adolph Green have made an admirable, sometimes witty, invariably intelligent attempt to chart Nora's course through the meager options women faced in late 19th century Norway," he wrote. However, he did comment that "very few scenes take place in such a way that characters relate directly to one another. More often than not if they are talking to each other they are also making asides to the audience; if they aren't, any number of peripheral people around them are" (September 24, 1982).

Most of the critics were devastating in their reviews. Douglas Watt of the Daily News titled the play "A Doll's Lifelessness" and called the musical "ponderous." "The authors, director, etc., and cast all seem hopelessly adrift all the long evening," he wrote. "While the book is impossible, Comden and Green's lyrics are characteristically well-turned, though often pointless in their jumble of a book" (September 24, 1982).

Frank Rich of the New York Times wrote, "The season is still young, but it's not likely to produce a more perplexing curiosity than A Doll's Life, the dour musical that opened at the Mark Hellinger last night." He goes on to say that the show "collapses in its prologue and then skids into a toboggan slide from which there is no return." "It doesn't take long to see that things are wildly out of control," he writes. With all of the flashbacks of Act One and the three different time frames of Act Two, Mr. Rich states that he and the audience have no idea where they are. Nora is merely a symbol, "propelled through a series of agitprop consciousness-raising crises," he writes. He calls Harold Prince's direction "fluid," but criticizes him for using staging devices he has used before--like the bridge from which the chorus comments on the action, as did the chorus in *Sweeney Todd* (September 24, 1982).

John Simon of *New York Magazine* called Comden and Green's book "presumptuous and execrable" and their lyrics "scarcely better." "The whole thing is awash with watered-down Pirandello," he wrote, criticizing the commenting chorus and the dance ensemble of three women and one man who "punctuate the ends of many scenes with something between dancing and posturing, though much closer to the latter." Simon criticizes the music, the design, the lights, and, especially, the actress who plays Nora. "Nora is mugged by Betsy Joslyn, who is too cute by half for even the macaroon-munching Nora, much less the liberated woman." She has "a smug face that mostly smiles and smiles, like a happy dishpan in a Brillo commercial" (October 4, 1982, pp. 91-92).

Brendan Gill of *The New Yorker* best summed up the disappointment that critics and audiences felt about the life of Nora after she left her husband and children: "Having possessed the intelligence to perceive her stultification as a twittering little lark of a wife and mother, she owed it to herself not merely to make a place for herself in the world but to become a superior human being. Surely, then, instead of being content to beat--or attempt to beat--men at their own dirty games, she would seek to outwit and surpass them, as Shaw's Ibsenesque women were later to do. Oddly, Betty Comden and Adolph Green ... abandoned Ibsen's gallant, questing Nora in favor of a Nora who was in part an unscrupulous sexual bully and in part a ninny, and who therefore bore an unlucky resemblance to the heroine of some nineteenth century French melodrama by Scribe" (October 4, 1982, p. 122).

Commentary

Why was *A Doll's Life* such a failure? Harold Prince thought that one reason was that it was about the place of women and that the musical pointed out that not enough change had been made over the past hundred years (from an interview with Prince in 1983 quoted by Carol Ilson in *Harold Prince*, p. 323).

Betty Comden and Adolph Green had had the idea of continuing the story of Nora after she leaves her husband and children. They consulted with Prince who encouraged their idea. For two years Comden and Green worked on the script. Betty Comden felt especially close to the idea. She commented that she herself had had both a home and family and a career. Her husband was "a totally enlightened man interested in what I did and a supporter of Adolph and me. But the fact that I had that wonderful thing didn't mean I wasn't aware of what it's like for others" (*New York Times*, September 19, 1982). For both Betty Comden and Adolph Green the show represented a venture into more serious subject matter.

When Harold Prince worked with the script, he tried to "free it from realism." The "show lacked the poetry that abstraction brings," he wrote (Jeremy Gerard, "Hal Prince and the Poetry of Abstraction," *Los Angeles Times*, June 13, 1982). Prince conceived the idea of setting the story within the context of a modern-day rehearsal of *A Doll's House*. The cast members not in the scene being depicted could, he suggested, become a commenting and questioning chorus. However, this device seemed to interrupt rather than help the play progress from scene to scene. Prince's attempt at "abstraction" also included four dancers. There were three women--one in white, one in red, and one in black--representing three stages in a woman's life. The fourth dancer was a man in black who danced with the women. The dancers appeared at the end of certain scenes, further confusing the plot. The dancers were patterned after the painting, "The Dance of Life," by Edvard Munch, a contemporary of Ibsen. In fact, Prince's visual concept of the play was much influenced by the paintings of Munch. Thus the set by Timothy O'Brien and Tazeena Firth is dominated by dark expressionist swirls, dimly lit. The changes in the time frame and the unexplained symbolism of the dancers contributed to the over-all confusion of the play. The critics used the terms, "perplexing," "a concept gone adrift," "an idea gone askew," and "a strange concoction."

Some of the critics commented on what a good idea it was to construct a story about Nora's life after she left her home. *A Doll's House* ends with a very serious Nora finally facing her situation and resolving to discover for herself who she is, what she believes in, and what capabilities she has as a person. Comden and Green tried to show Nora's learning how to make a living for herself, acquiring social consciousness, learning to enjoy sex, and learning to make money through investments. But the serious Nora who leaves her husband and children at the end of Ibsen's play did not appear in *A Doll's Life*. As Richard Gilman wrote in *The Nation*, Comden and Green have turned Nora into "a silly, flirtatious creature having *fun* and *adventure* in her life of freedom and at the same time mouthing feminist jargon" (October 16, 1982).

A REVUE FOR WHICH COMDEN AND GREEN WROTE BOTH THE SKETCHES AND THE LYRICS

S09 *TWO ON THE AISLE* (1951)

Mark Hellinger Theatre, New York City; Opened July 19, 1951; 281 performances

Credits

Lyrics and Sketches	Betty Comden
	Adolph Green
Additional Sketch	Nat Hiken
	William Friedberg
Music	Jule Styne
Director	Abe Burrows
Musical Numbers Staged by	Ted Cappy
Settings and Lighting	Howard Bay
Costumes	Joan Personette
Ochestrations	Philip Lang
Dance Music Arranged by	Genevieve Pitot
Vocal Arrangements	Herbert Greene
Orchestra Directed by	Herbert Greene
Producer	Arthur Lesser

Cast

Bert Lahr
Dolores Gray
Elliott Reid
Colette Marchand
J. C. McCord
Kathryne Mylroie
Stanley Prager
Robert Gallagher
Larry Laurence
Alan LeRoy
Richard Gray

Singers: Marion Lauer, Leila Martin, Beverly McFadden, Leslie Parry, Peggy Reiss, Carol Sawyer, Joanne Spiller, Julie Williams, John Allen, Arthur Arney, Fred Bryan, Buford Jasper, Walter Kelvin, John Raye, Arthur Rubin

Dancers: Jeannett Aquilina, Margery Beddow, Betty Buday, Gloria Danyl, Dorothy Etheridge, Doris Goodwin, Vera Lee, Jane Mason, Bob Emmett, Jerry Fries, John Kelly, Paul Lyday, Victor Reilley, Frank Reynolds

Showgirls: Gregg Evans, Rosemary Kittelton, Dell Parker, Mira Stefan, Jeanne Tyler, Charlotte Van Lein

Synopsis

Two on the Aisle contained some very clever sketches and lyrics written by Comden and Green. The first was a short skit and the song, "Hold Me, Hold Me, Hold Me (Hold Me Tight)", sung by Dolores Gray. This was followed by the sketch, "Highlights from the World of Sports," which featured Bert Lahr as a slightly boozy, over-the-hill baseball player who says all of the wrong things on a children's radio program. After a dance, "Here She Comes Now," an East River Hoe Down, Dolores Gray sang "There Never Was a Baby Like My Baby." In the next sketch, "Space Brigade," Lahr was Captain Universe, the heroic leader of a space ship that has landed on Venus. Dolores Gray then sang Comden and Green's very clever song, "If You Hadn't, But You Did," and Lahr sang "The Clown," in which he laments always being cast as a clown instead of getting to play a great lover like Valentino or Queen Victoria as she was portrayed by Helen Hayes.

Also in the first act was "Here's What You Said," a one man skit written and performed by Elliott Reid. It was a take-off on the Kefauver committee hearings, and Reid imitated all of the voices. The skit had originally been performed on television.

As the finale of the first act, Bert Lahr and Dolores Gray played two vaudevillians. The sketch shows what might happen if show business took over the Metropolitan Opera. Lahr as Siegfried and Dolores Gray as Brunnhilde in a Wagnerian opera sing "Catch Our Act at the Met.".

One of the outstanding sketches in the second act was written by Nat Hiken and William Friedberg. It was called "Schneider's Miracle." Lahr played a member of the Sanitation Corps who picks up litter with a sharp-pointed stick in Central Park. He is a veteran of the Sanitation Corps and has been proud to be its top man for years. Suddenly, his position is threatened by an ambitious young man who is determined to collect more bags of litter than anyone else. Lahr takes the challenge and wildly fills his litter bag with pieces of paper including some one hundred dollar bills that have been accidentally scattered about. In this skit Lahr was able to project not only the humor but also the pathos of the man whose job and position is in danger.

Also in the second act Dolores Gray sang "Give a Little, Get a Little" and "How Will He Know?" The second act included an elaborate dance choreographed by Ruthanna Boris called "Dog Show." The dancers played Russian Wolfhounds, Cocker Spaniels, Dalmatians, a Pekinese, a French Poodle, and the dogs' trainers. Colette Marchand, the featured dancer of *Two on the Aisle*, danced the role of the French Poodle.

The Play's History

After a preview in Philadelphia, which opened on June 18, 1951, the revue, *Two on the Aisle,* opened at the Mark Hellinger Theatre in New York on July 19, 1951. It ran until March 15, 1952, for a total of 281 performances. The revue was produced by Arthur Lesser and starred the great American comic, Bert Lahr, and the singer and comedienne, Dolores Gray. Jule Styne provided the music. This was the first time Comden and Green had worked with Styne. During the 1930s and 1940s Styne had written many successful movie songs. In 1944, with lyricist Sammy Cahn, he supplied the songs for *Glad to See You*, a musical that never reached Broadway, but in 1947 his *High Button Shoes*, again with Cahn, and starring Phil Silvers, played for two and a half years. Then in 1949, working with lyricist Leo Robin, he produced the score for Anita Loos's story of the 1920s, *Gentlemen Prefer Blondes*, which catapulted Carol Channing to stardom.

The original cast album of *Two on the Aisle* was released by Decca Records. It contains only orchestrations and songs from the revue, not the sketches. (See D37.)

Reviews

Most of the New York critics rejoiced in the return to Broadway of the great Bert Lahr, a "true performer" and a "genuine clown," as Brooks Atkinson called him in his *New York Times* review. He described Lahr: "He looks funny. He has a wide mouth, a long upper lip, a bulbous nose, eyes too small for so big a face and set so close to the nose that they look startled, as if he could not control the mad things that are happening around him. He radiates a kind of genial though lunatic good nature. His voice has range, volume, and color." Mr. Atkinson says that there is "an element of basic emotion in his comedy," and he sites the sketch, "*Schneider's Miracle*," which "Mr. Lahr manages to make dramatic by the casual pathos of his acting" (July 29, 1951). In an earlier review, Mr. Atkinson wrote: "Betty Comden and Adolph Green have written the pithiest material any revue has had in these parts for a long time" and "Miss Comden and Mr. Green are the right litterateurs for Mr. Lahr's comic antics. He wraps that creased mug and those startled eyes around their impish sketches and lets loose that madman's ululation that has delighted America for years" (July 20, 1951).

Otis L. Guernsey, Jr., writing in the *Herald Tribune* was not so enthusiastic about the material, calling the greater part of it "mechanical stuff, sold with more energy than is present in the material." "Almost all the sketches have a good basic joke to act out," he wrote, "but they trail off to damp finishes instead of building" (July 20, 1951).

Ward Morehouse of the *New York World Telegram* called *Two on the Aisle* a "lively and funny revue" with "several good songs and some amusing sketches" (July 20, 1951). John Chapman of the *Daily News* called some of the sketches "pretty funny" and mentioned especially Lahr as Captain Universe and as Siegfried in Wagnerian opera. He also liked "*Schneider's Miracle*" and Elliott Reid's imitation of the members of the Kefauver committee (July 20, 1951).

Richard Watts, Jr., of the *New York Post* wrote that the show "is filled with good comic ideas and has pace, tunefulness, and vigor." He thought the ballets "not very impressive" (July 20, 1951). Robert Coleman of the *Daily Mirror* thought that Jule Styne and Betty Comden and Adolph Green provided Bert Lahr and Dolores Gray "with just the songs and sketches they need to show to best advantage." He predicted *Two on the Aisle* would be a "sure-fire hit" (July 20, 1951).

The magazine reviewers also were generally favorable. In the *Commonweal* Walter Kerr wrote that he found much of the material funny "and thus Lahr can use calm geniality and assurance and not try to wring laughs out of pallid material." "The sketches almost always have good ideas and they almost always capture the basic, logical humor inherent in the ideas. If Comden and Green stop somewhere short of perfection as sketch-writers, it is in their failure to produce that zany and unpredictable absurdity which reduces the audience to a state of collapse almost by the force of its illogic" (August 3, 1951, pp. 405-406).

The reviewer for *Time* commented that "sketch writers Comden and Green have really satiric minds, and at their best are very funny." However, he thought the music "too thin," the dances "dullish," and the production numbers "mostly colorless" (July 30, 1951, p. 47). The reviewer for the *New Yorker* was not complimentary about Comden and Green and Styne's songs and sketches, saying "they do not give Mr. Lahr a chance to do much more than radiate good will." He thought Elliott Reid's skit on the Kefauver Committee was the high point of the evening (July 28, 1951, p. 48).

Commentary

The musical and satirical revue was what Comden and Green had written and performed in their Revuers days. So they were in their element in writing *Two on the Aisle* for such professional performers as Bert Lahr and Dolores Gray. They satirized old baseball heroes, the outer space films, and opera singers. One of Comden and Green's specialties is clever wording and rhyming in their lyrics, and "If You Hadn't, But You Did," sung by Dolores Gray, is one of their best of this kind of humorous song. Comden and Green were later to include it in their own revue, *A Party With Betty Comden and Adolph Green*.

Two on the Aisle was Comden and Green's first collaboration with Jule Styne. It was a successful teaming, and they were to work together for seven future musicals. Betty Comden later said that they loved Styne's enthusiasm and that "he was great, great fun to work with" (quoted by Al Kasha and Joel Hirschhorn in *Notes on Broadway*, p. 68).

STAGE MUSICALS FOR WHICH COMDEN AND GREEN WROTE THE LYRICS ONLY

S10   *WONDERFUL TOWN* (1953)

Winter Garden Theatre, New York City; Opened February 25, 1953; 559 performances

Credits
Based on the play *My Sister Eileen* by Joseph Fields and Jerome Chodorov and the stories by Ruth McKenney

Book	Joseph Fields
	Jerome Chodorov
Music	Leonard Bernstein
Lyrics	Betty Comden
	Adolph Green
Director	George Abbott
Dances and Musical Numbers	Donald Saddler
Sets and Costumes	Raoul Pène DuBois
Miss Russell's Clothes	Main Bocher
Lighting	Peggy Clark
Musical Direction and Vocal Arrangements	Lehman Engel
Orchestrations	Don Walker
Producer	Robert Fryer

Cast

Guide	Warren Galjour
Appopolous	Henry Lascoe
Lonigan	Walter Kelvin
Helen	Michele Burke
Wreck	Jordan Bentley
Violet	Dody Goodman
Valenti	Ted Beniades
Eileen	Edith Adams
Ruth	Rosalind Russell
A Strange Man	Nathaniel Frey
Drunks	Lee Papell
	Delbert Anderson
Robert Baker	George Gaynes
Associate Editors	Warren Galjour
	Albert Linville
Mrs. Wade	Isabella Hoopes

Frank Lippencott	Chris Alexander
Chef	Nathaniel Frey
Waiter	Delbert Anderson
Delivery Boy	Alvin Beam
Chick Clark	Dort Clark
Shore Patrolman	Lee Papell
First Cadet	David Lober
Second Cadet	Ray Dorian

Policemen: Lee Papell, Albert Linville, Delbert Anderson, Chris Robinson, Nathaniel Frey, Warren Galjour, Robert Kole
Ruth's Escort   Chris Robinson

Greenwich Villagers: Jean Eliot, Carol Cole, Marta Becket, Maxine Berke, Helena Seroy, Geraldine Delaney, Margaret Cuddy, Dody Goodman, Ed Balin, Alvin Beam, Ray Dorian, Edward Heim, Joe Layton, David Lober, Victor Moreno, William Weslow, Pat Johnson, Evelyn Page, Libi Staiger, Patty Wilkes, Helen Rice, Delbert Anderson, Warren Galjour, Ray Kirchner, Robert Kole, Lee Papell, Chris Robinson.

Synopsis

Wonderful Town opens with a raucous musical number as a guide shows visitors around Christopher Street in Greenwich Village. Two newcomers to the Village are Ruth and Eileen Sherwood, sisters come to seek fame or at least a job in New York City. Ruth is a would-be writer and Eileen has aspirations for the stage. At the moment they are exhausted and they are talked into renting a run-down basement apartment from Mr. Appopolous. When they begin to move in they realize what a mistake they have made. A large window at sidewalk level makes them feel they are almost living on the street. Not only that, but they discover workmen are blasting for the new subway right below their apartment. Unhappy and homesick, the girls, with their arms around each other, sing "Ohio," wondering why they ever left home.

The next day the girls begin their assault on the big city. Over the first few days the wide-eyed and beautiful Eileen meets many young men who are eager to do things for her. Ruth has made no impression on any men, young or old. She sings in a show-stopping number "One Hundred Easy Ways to Lose a Man."

Ruth finally gets an appointment to see Bob Baker at his office at the *Manhatter*. She leaves her manuscripts with him. After she leaves, Bob Baker sits down to read her short stories, and as he reads her improbable plots they are acted out by Ruth in his imagination.

Eileen invites Frank Lippencott and Chick Clark, two of the young men she has met, for dinner. Frank brings her a box of chocolates from the drugstore where he works, and she sings the lovely ballad "A Little Bit in Love." When Bob Baker comes by to see Ruth to talk with her about her stories, Eileen also invites him for dinner. When the three men and two girls assemble before dinner, they try awkwardly to converse. The result is an hilarious musical number called "Conversation Piece" in which each person in turn tries to talk about something that will be of interest to the others. Each attempt fails and the conversation stops in an embarrassing pause, which is satirized by the music. When Bob Baker gets to talk with Ruth about her stories, he tells her that she has talent but she should write about something that she knows. She is very offended and runs off. Chick, in an attempt to get Eileen alone, sends Ruth off to the Navy Yard to get a story for his newspaper. Ruth, not knowing that the interview is a hoax, goes to the Navy Yard where a ship from Brazil has just docked. When she tries to interview the young cadets, they cannot understand English. They want her to teach them the Conga. She teaches them the dance, but then she cannot get away from them. They follow her home, and Ruth and Eileen nearly cause an international incident. In fact, Eileen is arrested.

Act Two begins in the police station where Eileen has been taken. It is the next morning and Eileen has charmed all of the Irish cops, who insist that she must be Irish also. The morning newspapers have a front page story about Eileen and the Brazilian Navy. When all is explained, Eileen is allowed to leave the police station. Ruth gets a job advertising Valenti's restaurant. She wears a sign that lights up. Her patter that she gives about the restaurant turns into a big production number with the Villagers called "Swing!" Ruth has written a story about her experience with the Brazilian Navy. Bob Baker likes the story and shows it to his editor, but the editor does not like the story and Bob loses his job over his insistence that the story be used.

Since Ruth and Eileen have not been able to pay their rent, they are about to be thrown out of their apartment. But just then Valenti, the owner of the restaurant, comes in and says that he has seen the publicity about Eileen and the navy in the paper. He wants to hire her as a singer in his nightclub, the Vortex. In a scene outside of the Vortex, Eileen tells Bob Baker that he lost his job over Ruth and that he is in love with her. She sings "It's Love" and he joins in. Within the Village Vortex Ruth tries to calm the nervous Eileen before she is to sing for the nightclub for the first time. Chick, who had sent Ruth to the Navy Yard, comes into the nightclub with good news. He has a job for Ruth on his newspaper. Eileen also tells Ruth that Bob Baker is in love with her. The time has come for Eileen to make her debut as a singer. She is so nervous that she insists that Ruth join her. The play ends with the hilarious duet, "The Wrong Note Rag," that Ruth and Eileen had sung back in Ohio.

The Play's History

Wonderful Town was an adaptation of the 1940 play, *My Sister Eileen*, by Joseph Fields and Jerome Chodorov, which had been based on the stories by Ruth McKenney. *My Sister Eileen* proved very popular and ran on Broadway for 865 performances. In 1942 Columbia Pictures made a film version of *My Sister Eileen* starring Rosalind Russell and Janet Blair. The film musical, also called *My Sister Eileen*, opened at Radio City Music Hall while the play was still running at the Martin Beck Theatre.

Several producers had expressed an interest in doing a musical version of *My Sister Eileen*, but their projects fell through. In June of 1952 Robert Fryer, who had produced *A Tree Grows in Brooklyn* in 1951, decided to go ahead with the musical. He asked the original authors of the play, Joseph Fields and Jerome Chodorov, to do the book. George Abbott was to direct. The original plan was for Frank Loesser or Irving Berlin to do the score, but then some music was written by Leroy Anderson with lyrics by Arnold Horwitt, who had been a collaborator on the lyrics for Beatrice Lillie's *Inside U.S.A.* Evidently, things were not going well, and Leonard Bernstein and Comden and Green were brought in. They had five weeks to do the score and the lyrics.

On January 19, 1953, *Wonderful Town* opened in New Haven to rave reviews. After a few changes, the show went into the Sam S. Shubert Theatre in Boston, where the production set a house record in its first week of previews. The show moved to the Forrest Theater in Philadelphia. It was scheduled to stay two weeks, but because of the demand for tickets, remained for a third week. *Wonderful Town* opened in New York at the Winter Garden Theatre on February 25, 1953, to rave reviews by all of the New York critics. It played 559 performances.

Wonderful Town won a Tony Award for Outstanding Musical of the year and Rosalind Russell was given a Tony as Outstanding Musical Actress. Tony Awards were also presented to Joseph Fields and Jerome Chodorov (librettists), Donald Saddler (choreographer), Robert Fryer (producer), Raoul Pène DuBois (scenic designer), and Lehman Engel (musical director). Leonard Bernstein's score won for him the Tony, the Donaldson Award, and the Drama Critics Circle Award. Donaldson Awards were also won by Betty Comden and Adolph Green, Joseph Fields and Jerome Chodorov, Rosalind Russell, Edith Adams, George Abbott, and Raoul Pène DuBois. *Wonderful Town* also won the New York Drama Critics Circle Award.

After *Wonderful Town*'s spectacular opening and excellent reviews, Decca could not keep up with the demand for the original cast recording. (See D40.) During the long run of the show, Rosalind Russell was replaced by Carol Channing. It was Carol Channing who toured with the show. *Wonderful Town* with Rosalind Russell was televised after the Broadway show closed. Columbia recorded this television version. (See D41 and T45.)

Wonderful Town was produced at City Center in 1958 with Nancy Walker as Ruth and Jo Sullivan as Eileen. When the United States sent two musicals to play at the Brussels World's Fair in 1959, *Wonderful Town* was chosen along with *Carousel*. The musical was again revived at City Center in 1963 with Kay Ballard as Ruth and Jacqueline McKeever as Eileen. Howard Taubman headlined his review in the *New York Times* "Wonderful Town Still Has Its Bounce" (February 15, 1963).

Columbia Pictures, which had produced *My Sister Eileen*, wanted to make a film of *Wonderful Town*, but had difficulty getting the rights to the script and the score. They did a different musical version. Judy Holliday was to be in it but dropped out. The film had Betty Garrett as Ruth, Janet Leigh as Eileen, and Jack Lemmon as a publishing executive. The film lacked the vigor, the pace, and the integration of plot and music that had made the stage musical such a success.

Reviews

The New York critics were unanimous in their raves for *Wonderful Town*. Brooks Atkinson of the *New York Times* called it "the most uproarious and original musical carnival we have had since *Guys and Dolls* appeared in this neighborhood." Bernstein has written a "bright and witty score in a variety of modern styles," and Comden and Green "have written some extraordinarily inventive lyrics in a style as unhackneyed as the music," he wrote (February 26, 1953). A short time later he wrote of Comden and Green that "their fresh and pertinent lyrics, with a little acid mixed into them, are post-graduate work" (March 8, 1953).

John McClain of the *Journal American* called *Wonderful Town* the "best song and dance offering of the season to date" (February 26, 1953). John Chapman of the *Daily News* called *Wonderful Town* "one of the gayest, smartest shows of recent times." He also complimented Bernstein by saying that there "hasn't been any one around like Bernstein since George Gershwin for jauntiness, tricky and intriguing modulations and graceful swoops into simple and pleasant melody." The songs and music fit the show, he wrote, and the score is a "record of and an intelligent comment upon the musical fads of two decades ago" (February 26, 1953).

Robert Coleman of the *Daily Mirror* wrote that Betty Comden and Adolph Green "have penned superior lyrics to Leonard Bernstein's sensational score." They were "as fast afoot as Man-O'-War, as gay and giddy as a Mardi Gras, plus a dish of persuasive sentiment." "The songs and dances ... speed the action and move the story forward" (February 26, 1953).

Walter F. Kerr of the *Herald Tribune* catalogued the number of times Rosalind Russell stopped the show with the wonderful words and music. The first time was with "One Hundred Easy Ways to Lose a Man," which was not only a clever song but also a good characterization of the intelligent Ruth who could not bring herself to bat her eyes at the men. The second number that stopped the show was the Conga number when Ruth sang and danced with the Brazilian navy. The third was "Swing!" another big production number, and the fourth was the ending number, "The Wrong Note Rag," sung by Ruth and Eileen (February 26, 1953).

Richard Watts, Jr., of the *New York Post* called the musical "delightful entertainment, gay, bright, vital, alert, and engaging" with "intelligent amusing lyrics" (February 26, 1953).

The magazine reviewers joined the chorus of enthusiastic critics. Henry Hewes of the *Saturday Review* called *Wonderful Town* "the most competent, original, and adult musical comedy to reach this dreary metropolis in a long, long time" (March 14, 1953, p. 36). The critic for *Theatre Arts* called the play, "an electric delight, fresh, humorous, tuneful." Bernstein "has contributed songs both witty and tender, with lyrics by Betty Comden and Adolph Green that are not only independently alive but that beautifully further the story and stage action" (May 1953, p. 16).

Wolcott Gibbs of *The New Yorker* called Comden and Green's lyrics "ingenious and also admirably suited to the mood of the play" (March 7, 1953, p. 59). Harold Clurman of *The Nation* called *Wonderful Town* a "masterpiece." "The piece has a unified texture; it is a complete thing. The songs define the situations, tell the story--as do the dances." He wrote that Comden and Green had "not lost the ungainly, improvisatory, hard-hitting enthusiasm" of their old Village Vanguard days. "They are still inspired amateurs--thank God!" (March 14, 1953, p. 232).

Commentary

When George Abbott asked Comden and Green if they would be interested in doing the lyrics for *Wonderful Town*, they said yes if they could get a composer. They at once called Bernstein, who agreed to work with them. Leonard Bernstein had been away from Broadway since they had all done *On the Town* together. Comden and Green liked the warm and funny play, *My Sister Eileen*. However, working with a play that had been so well-loved did pose problems. The biggest problem, however, was that they had only five weeks in which to write the entire score and the lyrics. The play took place in the 1930s, and when Comden, Green, and Bernstein first started to work they thought the play seemed dated. Then Bernstein began to think about the Thirties and the excitement of the people just coming out of the Depression. For Bernstein the Thirties meant the big-band sound of Benny Goodman, the characteristic Eddy Duchin vamp, and the age of "swing." All of these Thirties musical sounds were incorporated into *Wonderful Town*. Betty

100   Comden and Green

Comden and Adolph Green have written that they and Leonard Bernstein "seem to think alike, and the resultant creative shorthand allows us to work fast and furiously with lots of fights and with great joy" (Betty Comden and Adolph Green, "My Sister Eileen Goes on the Town with Songs," *Theatre Arts*, August 1953, p. 21).

The book, written by Fields and Chodorov with the help of George Abbott, was a strong one with likable and well-developed characters. The great success of the musical was largely due to the way in which Comden, Green, and Bernstein managed to retain the story and the characters and write the music and lyrics so that they captured the mood of the play, helped to define the characters and the age, and at the same time advanced the plot and added to the gaiety of the story. The result was an extremely well integrated and joyous musical.

One clever addition to the original play was the enactment of Ruth's highly romantic stories that she submitted to Bob Baker of the *Madhatter*. These sketches were a contribution of Comden and Green. The music and lyrics were extremely varied. There was the homesick lament of Ruth and Eileen in "Ohio" and the Irish lilt in "My Darlin' Eileen" sung by the Irish policemen. There were three beautiful love songs, "A Quiet Girl," "A Little Bit in Love," and "It's Love." There were the spirited opening number, "Christopher Street" and the big production number "Swing!" by Ruth and the Villagers. Ruth had the clever "One Hundred Easy Ways to Lose a Man," and Ruth, Eileen, and their dinner guests had the very funny "Conversation Piece." All of these numbers seemed to fit perfectly into the story.

*****

S11   *SAY, DARLING* (1958)
Anta Theatre, New York City; Opened April 12, 1958;
333 performances

Credits
Book	Richard Bissell
	Abe Burrows
	Marian Bissell
Songs	Betty Comden
	Adolph Green
	Jule Styne
Director	Abe Burrows
Designer	Oliver Smith
Costumes	Alvin Colt
Lighting	Peggy Clark
Dances	Matt Mattox
At the Pianos	Colin Romoff
	Peter Howard
Producers	Jule Styne
	Lester Osterman
Associate Producer	George Gilbert

Cast
Mr. Schneider	Gordon B. Clarke
Frankie Jordan	Constance Ford

Jack Jordan	David Wayne
Photographer	Jack Naughton
Pilot Roy Peters	Jack Manning
Ted Snow	Robert Morse
June, the Secretary	Eileen Letchworth
Schatzie Harris	Horace McMahon
Richard Hackett	Jerome Cowan
Irene Lovelle	Vivian Blaine
Rudy Lorraine	Johnny Desmond
Sidemen	Wendell Marshall
	Peter Howard
Charlie Williams	Robert Downing
Maurice, a Pianist	Colin Romoff
Arlene McKee	Wana Allison
Jennifer Stevenson	Jean Mattox
Earl Jorgeson	Elliott Gould
Cheryl Merrill	Virginia Martin
Accompanist	Peter Howard
Sammy Miles	Steve Condos
Rex Dexter	Mitchell Gregg
Boris Reschevsky	Matt Mattox
Waiter	Jack Naughton
Morty Krebs	Walter Klavun
Tatiana	Jean Mattox
Joyce	Kelly Leigh

Kids in the Show: Wana Allison, Marcella Dodge, Barbara Hoyt, Kelly Leigh, Julie Marlowe, Jean Mattox, Carolyn Morris, Elliott Gould, Charles Morrell, Richard Tone, Calvin von Reinhold

Synopsis

Say, Darling opens with a scene at a small airport in Iowa. Jack Jordan is preparing to leave on a plane for New York City. His wife Frankie is there to see him off. Jack has taken three days off work to go to New York to meet with a producer who is interested in having him convert his novel, Paddlewheeling, into a play. In the second scene we are in the office of Ted Snow, a young producer, and his co-producer and director, Richard Hackett. They and Schatzie Harris, their publicity man, are waiting for Jack to arrive. When Jack arrives he is surprised to learn that the producers want him to write a musical, not a play. Also, they have changed the title of the play to The Girl from Indiana, in spite of the fact that the novel is about Jack's great uncle in Wisconsin. The producers have engaged the popular recording star of the jukebox crowd, Rudy Lorraine, to write the music. Jack has never heard of Rudy Lorraine and is not impressed by his top hit, "Chief of Love," which they play for him. Jack is astounded to learn that making the novel into a musical will take at least six months and he will have to move his family to New York. Irene Lovell, a glamorous actress and singer, comes by the office to inform the producers that she is interested in playing the leading female role, Rosie.

Jack moves Frankie and the children to a house in Stamford and begins writing the musical. At the producers' office, arguments arise over Irene Lovell. Rudy insists he does not want her in the show. He used to be married to her. The producers insist that she should be given a chance to audition. Rudy has turned the character of Rosie into a fortune teller so he can use a new song he has written called "I Know What a Person's Gonna Do Before He Does It." The producers want to begin the show with a corn husking bee. Though Jack objects, Rudy begins a song for the husking bee.

In the second act the producers are holding auditions. Each girl auditioning begins to sing "I Could Have Danced All Night" and is quickly stopped. Irene sings Rudy's number, "Chief of Love," and is hired. At a first meeting of the cast in a rehearsal hall, Rudy plays some of the music for the show. He has written "Say, Darling" for the scene when Orville, the river boat captain proposes to Rosie. He has also written "The Carnival Song," a song for Rosie, who has now become a carnival girl selling patent medicine.

All of the evenings of work for Jack have left Frankie alone with the children in their house in Stamford. They have also thrown Jack and Irene Lovell together. One of the nights when he calls Frankie to tell her he has to work, she hangs up the phone saying, "I hate show business," and decides to go back to Iowa. On this particular evening Jack goes to Irene's apartment for a drink. Under the influence of too many drinks he tells Irene that he loves her. When the others come by Irene's apartment for a drink and Jack takes this additional drink, he passes out. Rudy, Irene's former husband, is among those dropping by. He and Irene find themselves in each other's arms. They leave a note on the sleeping Jack and go out for dinner.

Act Three takes place in a hotel suite in New Haven where the musical has just been given its first tryout performance. The show was a flop, and the producers and backers all have different ideas about what it needs to be successful. Each of the contributors to the show puts the blame on everyone else's contribution. At last, Jack interrupts them to tell them that he has made all of the changes that they wanted and now the show hardly resembles his original story. He needs to go back to the original and re-write. Rudy, the ego-maniac, suddenly loses his confidence and says he has no new ideas for songs. Jack insists that he and Rudy go to his now empty house in Stamford and re-write the book and the songs.

After forty-eight hours of work, Jack and Rudy return to New York with a re-worked script and some new songs. A few hours with the director and the show begins to take shape. Rehearsals are begun again. One of the major changes is the ending. Jack has decided that his Uncle Orville would never leave the river, and Rudy has written "The River Song" for the ending. While the cast is rehearsing "The River Song," Frankie comes in to be re-united with Jack.

The last scene of *Say, Darling* takes place at Idlewild Airport. Jack is waiting for a plane to Los Angeles. A producer in Hollywood wants to make a movie of his play based on the book about the musical he wrote. Frankie is seeing him off.

The Play's History

Say, Darling, a play with music, opened at the ANTA Theatre on April 12, 1958. It ran for 333 performances, closing on January 17, 1959. It was revived at the City Center on February 25, 1959, with a new cast except for Robert Morse who continued in his role of the producer.

In 1953 Richard Bissell, a writer from Iowa, had written a novel about a Middle Western pajama factory, *7 1/2 Cents*, that became something of a best seller. Working with George Abbott, Bissell then turned the novel into the popular musical, *The Pajama Game*, which ran on Broadway for 1,063 performances. Bissell then wrote another novel, *Say, Darling*, about his experiences in New York working with a Broadway producer, director, and composer to convert his novel *7 1/2 Cents* into *The Pajama Game*. *Say, Darling*, the play with music, is an adaptation of that novel. Bissell was assisted by his wife, Marian Bissell, and Abe Burrows in turning the novel into a play. The play combines the idea of his first novel, *A Stretch on the River*, with his experiences of converting a novel into a Broadway musical.

The original cast recording of *Say, Darling* was made by RCA Victor. (See D31.) The book and music are available from Tams-Witmark Music Library.

Reviews

Say, Darling received from the New York critics four rave or favorable reviews, two mixed reviews, and one unfavorable review. Richard Watts, Jr., of the *New York Post*, called *Say, Darling* "a delightful entertainment, gay, charming, humorous and warmhearted." He thought it "an enormously engaging and likable show" (April 4, 1958). Robert Coleman of the *Daily Mirror* called the show "jet-propelled japery from a sophisticated tap." He called Comden and Green and Jule Styne's songs "easy on the ears" and yet making "satiric points" (April 4, 1958).

John McClain of the *New York Journal American* called *Say, Darling* "a big, fat smash" with "enormous style and humor and lilt." It is, he wrote "a delightful evening's entertainment." The charm of the musical, he thought, came from its "intimacy." There are no big production numbers in the show, and thus "the engaging songs by Betty Comden and Adolph Green and Jule Styne emerge informally from the plot, with only piano accompaniments" (April 4, 1958).

Walter Kerr of the *New York Herald Tribune* called the show "smart, sassy and wonderfully funny." He did warn the audiences not to wear themselves out looking for a plot, and he thought there were small lapses here and there. But he adds that there is always "another Betty Comden and Adolph Green lyric (sometimes purposely grisly, sometimes simply pleasant) to pick you up again" (April 4, 1958).

Brooks Atkinson of the *New York Times* was more critical. He thought the show "a show-business cartoon in a tired vein." "Although the surface is bright and agile and the acting vivacious, the point of view is mechanical," he wrote. "Everything is wonderfully facetious," he wrote, but there was nothing "touching" about the play, and he was left with a feeling of having "wasted an evening" (April 13, 1958). His first impression of the show had been even harsher: "This is hardly more than a clever college show. It is a higgledy-piggledy yarn composed of snappy gags and enlivened here and there with songs written by Comden and Green and Styne" (April 4, 1958).

Most of the magazine reviewers of *Say, Darling* were not very enthusiastic. Henry Hewes of the *Saturday Review of Literature* called it "a new departure in theatrical entertainment. It accepts most of the benefits of being a musical comedy, hardly any of the responsibilities. It wants the privilege of getting away with no strong plot or dramatic situation, but instead of furnishing bright production numbers, it offers us cut-down rehearsals and auditions of songs which don't have to be very good because the play is about a musical in which the songs are not supposed to be very good" (April 19, 1958).

The reviewer for *Newsweek* called the plot a "patchwork." "In between illogical lapses and lunacies, the collaborators keep their dialogue bright and Betty Comden and Adolph Green and Jule Styne supply nine songs that are variously atrocious and attractive, as the action requires" (April 14, 1958). Wolcott Gibbs of the *New Yorker* also commented on the songs. The plot, he wrote, "permits the introduction of perfectly horrible songs, for satiric purposes, and of quite good ones, which by contrast, often sound wonderful" (April 12, 1958).

All critics were enthusiastic about the hilarious portrayal by Robert Morse of the producer, Ted Snow. Henry Hewes of the *Saturday Review of Literature* described this boy producer (some thought he was based on a young Harold Prince) as speaking "in unfinished, pretentious sentences using body-english to steer them away from any clear meaning or arguable logic" (April 19, 1958).

Commentary

Say, Darling is a difficult show to categorize. It is halfway between a musical and a play with music. The story is about the making of a musical, but the show itself does not have an orchestra or a real production number. The music is played on two onstage pianos.

Say, Darling satirizes those people who produce, direct, write the music, and star in Broadway musicals. The authors (Richard Bissell, Abe Burrows, and Marian Bissell) take the point of view of the "innocent" author from Iowa, Jack Jordan, who is pitted against the self-centered Broadway professionals. As Richard Hayes of *Commonweal* wrote, the humor of *Say, Darling* comes from the contrast between the "cartoons of theatre sophistication and corn-fed naiveté" (July 4, 1958).

Say, Darling has little plot, and what plot there is is a tired and mechanical one. There are more clichés about show business than genuine insights. Comden and Green and Jule Styne were put in the awkward position of having to write terrible songs for the poor musical that resulted from the collaboration of Jack Jordan and Rudy Lorraine, the popular but not very talented star of the juke boxes. Perhaps the funniest of these was "Doom," a satire of the kind of song composers often inflict upon musicals. One clever song was "The Carnival Song." Rudy Lorraine had insisted that the heroine of the play within the play be a carnival girl because he had written a carnival song he wanted to use. In the song she is selling patent medicine. Here Comden and Green are able to write some very clever words for this absurd "pitch" to sell the medicine.

Comden and Green and Jule Styne did get to write two pleasant love songs, "Try to Love Me Just As I Am" and "Dance, Dance Only With Me." The best of their songs was a jubilee tune written for the climax of the play within the play, "The River Song" or "Something's Always Happening on the River." For Brooks Atkinson of the *New York Times*, however, the best musical number of the evening was the old evangelistic song, "Let the Lower Lights Be Burning." "It was simple and sincere in the thick of an avalanche of glibness," he wrote (April 4, 1958).

*****

S12   *DO RE MI* (1960)

St. James Theatre, New York City; Opened December 26, 1960; 400 performances

Credits
Book   Garson Kanin
Lyrics   Betty Comden
                                            Adolph Green

Music	Jule Styne
Director	Garson Kanin
Choreography	Marc Breaux
	Deedee Wood
Designer	Boris Aronson
Costumes	Irene Sharaff
Musical Direction	Lehman Engel
Orchestrations	Luther Henderson
Vocal Arrangements and Direction	Buster Davis
Dance Arrangements	David Baker
Producer	David Merrick

Cast

The Casa Girls:	Marilyn Allwyn, Diane Ball, Sandra Devlin, Regina Groves, Nancy Van Rhein, Carol Stevens, Dean Taliaferro
The Dance Team:	Patti Karr
	Ray Kirchner
Kay Cram	Nancy Walker
Hubert Cram	Phil Silvers
A Waiter	Frank Derbas
John Henry Wheeler	John Reardon
The Swingers	Betty Kent
	Donna Sanders
	Suzanne Shaw
The Headwaiter	Marc Jordan
Fatso O'Rear	George Mathews
Skin Demopoulos	George Givot
Brains Berman	David Burns
Thelma Berman	Marilyn Child
The Interviewer	David Gold
The Photographer	Stuart Hodes
Wheeler's Secretaries	Carol Stevens
	Dean Taliaferro
James Russell Lowell, IV	Chad Block
The Sumo Student	Ray Kirchner
Tilda Mullen	Nancy Dussault
Wolfie	Al Nesor
Marsha	Carolyn Ragaini
Lou	Steve Roland
Gretchen	Betty Kent
The Recording Engineer	Albert Linville
The Maitre D'	Bob McClure
The Animal Girls:	Marilyn Allwyn, Diane Ball, Sandra Devlin, Regina Groves, Patti Karr, Nancy Van Rhein, Carol Stevens, Dean Taliaferro
Moe Shtarker	Al Lewis
The Commentators	Bob McClure
	Allan Stevenson
Senator Rogers	Albert Linville
Senator Redfield	Edward Grace
The Chief Counsel	Steve Roland

Fatso's Lawyer   Marc Jordan
Brains's Lawyer   Pat Tolson
The Public: Marilyn Allwyn, Doria Avila, Diane Ball, Frank Derbas, Sandra Devlin, David Gold, Edward Grace, Regina Groves, Stuart Hodes, Curtis Hood, Daniel Jasinski, Marc Jordan, Patti Karr, Betty Kent, Ray Kirchner, Barbara Lang, Josephine Lang, Bob McClure, Ken Malone, Jim Marley, James Moore, Dawn Nickerson, Ed Pfeiffer, Carolyn Ragaini, Steve Roland, Donna Sanders, Suzanne Shaw, Carol Stevens, Liza Stuart, Dean Taliaferro, Pat Tolson, Nancy Van Rhein, Richard Young.

Synopsis

At the Casacabana in New York City, Kay Cram sits alone at a table waiting for her husband, Hubie. It is their tenth wedding anniversary. She sings "Waiting, Waiting." She is accustomed to waiting for Hubie. She knows that Hubie did not have to work late at the office because he doesn't have an office. She knows that he is out there somewhere making a deal because Hubie does not want an ordinary job. He wants something big. When Hubie does arrive, sure enough, he has had a brilliant idea. He will go into the juke box and record business and make a fortune. Just then John Henry Wheeler, a young tycoon in the juke box and record business, comes in to hear his recording stars, the Swingers, sing "All You Need is a Quarter."

Later that night in their bedroom, while they are getting ready for bed, Kay tries to convince Hubie just to take a job and be content, but he thinks about Wheeler and he says,"If he, why not me?" He thinks about the old days of the real slot machines in New York and nostalgically begins to recall the three men he worked with before the slots were made illegal. There were Fatso O'Rear, Skin Demopoulos, and Brains Berman. Hubie gets dressed again and goes out to try to find the three men. Hubie visits Fatso in his ice cream parlor where the young people are dancing to "All You Need is a Quarter." He convinces Fatso to join him in his new project by singing "It's Legitimate." Fatso and Hubie visit Skin at the race track and Brains at his chicken farm. The men all join in singing "It's Legitimate." The men open an office called Music Enterprise Associates.

Contrasting with the rather make-shift Music Enterprise Associates office is the grand office of John Henry Wheeler, where Wheeler is being interviewed about his new competition in the jukebox business. Wheeler is not concerned because, as he says confidently, he knows about love, and it is love that sells records. However, after the reporter leaves, Wheeler sings "I Know About Love," in which he confesses he hasn't really experienced it.

The scene changes to a pancake parlor in Greenwich Village where James Russell Lowell, IV, the proprietor, is practicing his Karate attacks. Standing at the pancake grill is Tilda Mullen singing a haunting folk song. Hubie comes in to check if they have a juke box. He is followed by his three partners, who tell James Russell Lowell, IV, that from now on he will be getting his music from them. Hubie tries to keep the men from violence, but Brains steps up and prepares to throw a punch at Lowell. Suddenly Lowell leaps into the air emitting a blood-curdling scream. Brains is stunned and slowly collapses.

The new juke box business is not doing well. They still owe for the boxes and the records. Hubie comes up with another one of his brilliant ideas. They will record a hit song. The four partners and Kay hold auditions for a new singer. Those who audition are terrible singers, and the three other men blame Hubie for the fix they are in. Hubie has another idea. He rushes to the pancake parlor, where he asks Tilda to sing the folk song she was singing when he was there before. Tilda sings "Cry Like the Wind." Hubie thinks he has found his talent, but Tilda doubts if anyone would pay to hear her sing. Hubie sings "Ambition," recounting to her all that she could have if her song is a success. At last he convinces Tilda to record the song. In a juke box montage we see and hear the popularity of the song grow. Suddenly Tilda is a big star.

In a recording studio, Kay and Hubie wait for Tilda to appear to make another recording. Hubie now thinks he has at last made it big. Hubie's partners arrive for the recording session. Then, unexpectedly, John Henry Wheeler and the Swingers come in. They thought they had the studio at this time. When Tilda enters, she and Wheeler see each other and suddenly a rocket explodes and bits of fire rain down. Tilda and Wheeler sing "Fireworks." Hubie, who is now the big producer and musician, conducts the band for Tilda and the Animal Girls as they sing "What's New at the Zoo?" Instantly, the girls are singing "What's New at the Zoo?" as an encore at the Imperial Room. After the floor show at the Imperial Room, there is dancing and John Henry Wheeler dances with Tilda. The three partners get very upset when they see their star singer dancing with their competitor. They want to start a fight, but Hubie convinces them to let him handle the problem. He goes to Wheeler and sings "The Late, Late Show," in which he tells Wheeler about the old gangster movies on the Late, Late Show. For the three men he pretends to be talking to Wheeler in the style of the gangsters threatening their victims. Wheeler does not get the point and once again dances with Tilda. Brains comes over to fight with Wheeler, but before he can hit him James Russell Lowell, IV, leaps into the air with his ear-splitting scream, and Brains keels over in a faint.

Act Two opens in Hubie and Kay's bedroom. Hubie cannot sleep because he is afraid that the three partners are going to get violent over Wheeler's romancing Tilda. Kay tells Hubie that Wheeler is famous for his feminine conquests. She will let Tilda know of Wheeler's reputation. Hubie is pacified and says he doesn't know why Kay ever married him. Kay sings "Adventure." Being married to Hubie has certainly been an adventure. After Kay has shown Tilda some clippings about Wheeler's amorous affairs, Tilda confronts Wheeler with them and tells him she cannot believe he is sincere when he says he loves her. Wheeler sings "Make Someone Happy." Tilda at last joins him in singing the song and they embrace.

All is not well with Music Enterprise Associates. Tilda has married Wheeler. Fatso has wired for an enforcer from the old days, a big man with little brains, Moe Shtarker. Shtarker arrives and, over Hubie's objections, the three partners agree to pay Shtarker's men to break up Wheeler's juke boxes. Kay tries to get Hubie to walk out on the business. When he refuses, she resolves to leave him. In a series of pantomimed scenes we see the juke box violence as Shtarker's men break up Wheeler's juke boxes. Shtarker's men are rounded up by the police. Newspaper headlines are projected, reading "Senate to Investigate Juke Box War" and "Seek Mr. Big of Juke Box Rackets." In the final scene of the play the Senators are investigating the juke box war. After three weeks of investigation they have still not uncovered the Mr. Big of the juke box racket; but, in this scene, singing their stories, the three partners point to Hubie as the man who started the whole thing. Now the spotlight is on Hubie, and the crowd sings "He's a V.I.P." Hubie at last has made it big. At the hearing he is asked to tell his story. In the song, "All of My Life," Hubie confesses that he thought the American dream was to wait for your big break, but now he admits he is a loser. The hearing ends. The crowd leaves and Hubie is left alone. Then a welcome voice is heard singing "Take a Job." It is Kay. She rushes to Hubie and they embrace and then dance to the music of "Make Someone Happy."

The Play's History

Do Re Mi, after tryouts in Philadelphia and Boston, opened at the St. James Theatre on December 26, 1960. It played 400 performances, closing on January 13, 1962. The book for the musical was adapted by Garson Kanin from his 1955 novella.

Phil Silvers was one of the top comedians of the time. He had played 727 performances as Harrison Floy in High Button Shoes, which had opened on Broadway on October 9, 1947. Then he had had enormous success as Sergeant Bilko on television.

In 1961 Do Re Mi was nominated for a Tony Award as best musical. It lost to Bye Bye Birdie. Nancy Walker, Phil Silvers, and Nancy Dussault were all nominated for Tony Awards, as was Garson Kanin for his direction of the musical.

On October 22, 1961, CBS Television offered a half hour of music and comedy from Do Re Mi on the Ed Sullivan Show. (See T47.) The first three scenes of the musical were shown. These scenes included three songs: "Waiting, Waiting," "Take a Job," and "It's Legitimate." The musical was later presented in London, where it ran for 170 performances. The role of Hubie was played by Max Bygraves.

The original cast recording was made by RCA Victor. (See D10, D11, and D12.) The book and music is available from Tams-Witmark Music Library.

Reviews

Do Re Mi opened on December 26, 1960, to favorable reviews by all of the New York critics except two. John Chapman of the Daily News called it "a great big razzle-dazzle of a musical" (December 27, 1960). Walter Kerr of the Herald Tribune called it "a musical for people who haven't been going to musicals lately." "You know what it is?" he asks, and then answers himself,"It's fun. Silly fun, loud fun, fast fun, old-fashioned fun, inconsequential fun, grand fun..." (December 27, 1960).

John McClain of the Journal American called the musical "a brassy and bountiful blockbuster." "This is a sure hit," he wrote, and "could better be called 'Dough Re Mi'" (December 27, 1960). Howard Taubman of the New York Times was generally favorable, but he did point out that though the show was fast and loud it was only "occasionally funny." "Often it makes speed and a high quotient of decibels do for entertainment," he wrote. "A team of expensive talent has turned out some lively songs, set them in motion in feverishly paced production numbers and has managed to overcome, at least part of the time, the cheapness of a machine-made book." Though he felt Garson Kanin's book uninspired, he did think that Betty Comden and Adolph Green had written "sprightly lyrics," and Jule Styne had contributed "some attractive as well as some ear-shattering tunes" (December 27, 1960).

Robert Coleman of the New York Mirror wrote that "Styne and Comden and Green have penned several ditties that are going to keep the nation's juke boxes running hot." He especially liked the songs "I Know About Love," "Fireworks," "Cry Like the Wind," and "What's New at the Zoo?" (December 27, 1960). John McClain of the New York Journal American also liked the last two songs mentioned as well as "The Late, Late Show," "Make Someone Happy," "Adventure," and "All of My Life" (December 27, 1960).

Frank Aston of the *World Telegram and Sun* wrote the one most negative review calling the play "an extravagant disaster" (December 27, 1960). The *New York Times* critic, writing a week or so after the opening, noted that *Do Re Mi* was "saved by the imagination of some of the songs and production numbers and by the personal gifts of its chief performers" (January 8, 1961).

Most of the magazine critics also praised *Do Re Mi*. The *Newsweek* critic called it "fast, funny, and immensely likable" (January 9, 1961). Harold Clurman of *The Nation* called it "the best musical of the season," and wrote "there is, very strikingly, the zany ebullience of the Betty Comden and Adolph Green lyrics" (January 14, 1961). However, John McCarten of the *New Yorker* could find little to like about the show. When the pretty singing girls are not present "the show flattens out like a shot-down blimp," he wrote. "The music by Jule Styne, is strident; the book, by Garson Kanin, is a bore; and the lyrics, by Betty Comden and Adolph Green, are for the most part labored" (January 14, 1961).

Nearly all of the critics complimented the direction by Garson Kanin, the set design by Boris Aronson, and the comic acting by Phil Silvers and Nancy Walker.

Commentary

Do Re Mi, in spite of its star, Phil Silvers, and the favorable reviews, was something of a disappointment. The idea for the plot seemed a clever one, but the story often recalled to playgoers the extremely popular *Guys and Dolls*, and the comparison was not a favorable one. Louis Kronenberger wrote in his *The Best Plays of 1960-1961* that the story was not "raffish enough," and "made vice as insipid as virtue." In fact, he concluded that the book was "a bore" and that the music, perhaps to compensate for the dullness of the book, "seemed fiendishly loud and the dancing fiendishly frenzied" (pp. 25, 26).

One of the best things about the musical was the songs. The critics picked out for praise nearly all of the songs. One of the most popular was "Cry Like the Wind," with its hypnotic rhythm written in the style of a coffeehouse folk song. "Make Someone Happy" was a beautiful love song that was to become a standard. Among the best of the humorous songs with characteristic clever rhyming by Comden and Green were "It's Legitimate," "Adventure," and "What's New at the Zoo?"

*****

S13   *HALLELUJAH, BABY!* (1967)

Martin Beck Theatre, New York City; Opened April 26, 1967; 293 performances

Credits

Book	Arthur Laurents
Lyrics	Betty Comden
	Adolph Green
Music	Jule Styne
Director	Burt Shevelove
Dances and Musical Numbers	Kevin Carlisle

110 Comden and Green

Designers	William Eckart
	Jean Eckart
Costumes	Irene Sharaff
Lighting	Tharon Musser
Musical Direction and Vocal Arrangements	Buster Davis
Orchestrations	Peter Matz
Dance Orchestrations	Luther Henderson
Producers	Albert W. Selden
	Hal James
	Jane C. Nusbaum
	Harry Rigby
Associate Producer	Joe Linhart

Cast

Georgina	Leslie Uggams
Momma	Lillian Hayman
Clem	Robert Hooks
Provers	Clifford Allen
	Garrett Morris
	Kenneth Scott
	Alan Weeks
Harvey	Allen Case
Captain Yankee	Justin McDonough
Calhoun	Lou Angel
Mary	Barbara Sharma
Mister Charles	Frank Hamilton
Mrs. Charles	Marilyn Cooper
Tip and Tap	Winston DeWitt Hemsley
	Alan Weeks
Cuties	Hope Clarke
	Sandra Lein
	Saundra McPherson
Prince	Bud Vest
Princess	Carol Flemming
Sugar Daddy	Darrell Notara
Bouncer	Chad Block
Mistress	Marilyn Cooper
Master	Darrell Cooper
Director	Alan Peterson
Ethel	Marilyn Cooper
Official	Chad Block
Brenda	Ann Rachel
Timmy	Frank Hamilton
G.I.'s	Winston DeWitt Hemsley
	Kenneth Scott
	Alan Weeks
	Clifford Allen
Bus Driver	Lou Angel
Dorothy	Marilyn Cooper
Maid	Hope Clarke

Lyrics 111

Ensemble: Clifford Allen, Barbara Andrews, Lou Angel, Chad Block, Hope Clarke, Norma Donaldson, Carol Flemming, Nat Gales, Maria Hero, Lee Hooper, Alan Johnson, Sandra Lein, Justin McDonough, Saundra McPherson, Garrett Morris, Darrell Notara, Paul Reid Roman, Suzanne Rogers, Kenneth Scott, Ella Thompson, Bud Vest

Synopsis

When the curtain rises, the stage is filled with multi-colored umbrellas. Downstage center one of the umbrellas lifts to reveal Georgina, a black girl, who explains to the audience that tonight the play will cover from the turn of the century to the present, but that through all of that time she will remain the same age-- twenty-five.

The first scene takes place near the end of the nineteenth century. Georgina and her mother are maids in the white man's big house. Georgina is tired of mopping other people's floors and wants to quit her job. Her boy friend, Clem, a Pullman porter, has taken their money to put a down payment on a house for them, but he didn't have enough money and was drawn into a poker game. He won the game but lost the money to a white policeman who kept taking a slice of the money. Clem promises Georgina that he is going to get her a house. Harvey, a white man carrying a banjo, hears Georgina singing as she works and offers her a small role in a play about the War Between the States if she can learn to play the banjo. She is cast as a black kitchen slave and has one line in which she excitedly tells her mistress, Miss Betty Lou, that Ft. Sumpter has been fired on. The cast of the play goes on to another town without Georgina, but she has now caught stage fever and tells her mother they are moving where there are more chances for her.

The second time period is the Nineteen Twenties. The scene is a nightclub for white patrons. There are black tap dancers and a chorus line of black women. Georgina is a member of the chorus. Harvey is the manager of the club, and Clem is a waiter. Mary, the actress who played Miss Betty Lou, is in the audience with a prince and princess from Europe. Mary introduces Georgina to the prince and princess, who ask her to sit down with them. Georgina must tell them that she is not allowed to sit in the night club. A fight breaks out between the black performers and waiters and the white bouncer. Clem and Georgina are both fired. Harvey is outraged and protests their firing but manages only to get himself fired too. Georgina and her mother go back to work in a white family's kitchen. Clem once again becomes a Pullman porter. Shortly after, the stock market crashes and the white family must dismiss Georgina and her mother.

The third period takes place during the Depression in the Nineteen Thirties. Harvey and Clem meet again in a breadline. A young white couple come in on a scavenger hunt. They need "One Forgotten Man" and "One Negro." Harvey and Clem go with them on the promise of a dinner. Georgina is working in the Federal Theatre production of *The Haitian Macbeth*. Georgina and her actress friend, Mary, play two of the witches. As they rehearse, an official comes in to say that the show is being closed by Federal order for "subversive activity with intent to overthrow the duly elected government of the people." Georgina and her mother cannot find jobs as maids this time and are reduced to living in an empty restaurant. Clem has decided to join the Communist Party. Mary comes into the deserted restaurant to tell Georgina that she has arranged for them to audition for a play that is going to tour Hawaii. At that moment, Georgina's mother reports that the Japanese have bombed Pearl Harbor. Georgina dejectedly sings "Being Good Isn't Good Enough."

The Second Act begins with the Nineteen Forties. Mary and Georgina are in a USO show. Clem is a sergeant in the army. Harvey is a second lieutenant. As they prepare for the show, Georgina discovers that there are to be two shows--one for a white audience and one for a black audience. She quits the show because of this.

The next scene takes place in the Nineteen Fifties. Georgina is making her debut as a singer in a nightclub. Harvey, as the Master of Ceremonies, introduces her. Her reputation as a singer grows. She poses for a photograph for her new record album. Clem, too, poses for a photograph. He has gained notoriety as the leader of a protest march and as a speaker on civil rights. He wants Georgina to marry him and join him in his protest marches. Harvey also is in love with Georgina. Georgina, now a popular night club entertainer, is invited to a party in her honor given by the prince and princess. When the white guests take her mother for a maid, Georgina leaves the party with her mother, deciding that she wants to get arrested in a Freedom march.

The last scene takes place in the Sixties. Georgina now has a house of her own. She and Clem still cannot agree about marriage, but they sing that someday they will get together.

The Play's History

Hallelujah, Baby! opened at the Martin Beck Theatre on April 26, 1967, and closed on January 13, 1968, after 293 performances. *Hallelujah, Baby!* won the 1968 Tony Award for Best Musical of the Year. Jule Styne, Betty Comden, and Adolph Green won Tony Awards for Best Score and Best Lyrics. Lillian Hayman, who played Georgina's mother, also won a Tony Award as Best Supporting Actress in a Musical Play. Leslie Uggams and Robert Hooks were both nominated for Tony Awards for their leading roles, as were Burt Shevelove for his direction, Kevin Carlisle for his choreography, and Irene Sharaff for her costume design. Leslie Uggams received an Outer Circle Award for 1966-1967 for her performance. She was also nominated, though she did not win, as Best Female Lead by the New York Drama Critics in *Variety*'s Poll. She was selected as the Most Promising New Broadway Actress in this poll. Allen Case was nominated as Most Promising New Broadway Actor. Nominations were also made for William and Jean Eckart for their scene design, Irene Sharaff for her costumes, Jule Styne for his music, and Betty Comden and Adolph Green for their lyrics.

A published libretto for *Hallelujah, Baby!* is not available; however, there is a copy of the script in the New York Public Library at Lincoln Center. The sheet music was published by Stratford/Chappell, and the original cast recording was made by Columbia Records. (See D16.)

Reviews

From the daily New York critics, *Hallelujah, Baby!* received only one entirely favorable review. John Chapman of the *Daily News* called the show "a completely professional--and stunning piece of show business." "It has the best score Jule Styne has written, a really original libretto by Arthur Laurents, and splendidly polished lyrics by Betty Comden and Adolph Green." Chapman wrote, "It has been a long time since I have seen as finely, as carefully wrought a musical as *Hallelujah, Baby!*" (April 27, 1967). Richard P. Cooke of the *Wall Street Journal* thought the musical "a real show-biz evening, even though we don't learn much about the racial problem" (April 28, 1967).

Though most of the critics liked the star, Leslie Uggams, they did not like the book. "The combination of the story, songs, and dances is rarely stimulating or very imaginative, always seems to be promising more than it is able to fulfill, lags somewhat fitfully, and, in the second half, threatens almost to the end to give up the battle," wrote Richard Watts, Jr., of the *New York Post* (April 27, 1967). Martin Gottfried of *Women's Wear Daily* wrote, "The work was doomed to be episodic and static, as shallow theatrically as is its less than superficial study of the Negro in America." He put part of the blame on the director, Burt Shevelove. This was his first experience in the staging of a musical and did not seem to know what to do with his actors. "The result is everybody is wandering off in separate directions," he wrote (April 27, 1967). Norman Nadel of the *World Journal Tribune* wrote: "What it amounts to as entertainment is one stereotype of the musical stage after another" (April 27, 1967).

Walter Kerr of the *New York Times* wrote two reviews of *Hallelujah, Baby!* He liked Leslie Uggam's song, "Talking to Yourself," but he said the show also seemed to be talking to itself. It "can't really be talking to Negroes, who have long ceased to think of themselves as perennial patsies who need to be escorted by loving, liberal white hands across streets to near-safety. And it can't very well be talking to white liberals, either, not at this late date ..." He concluded that the musical put together by Laurents, Styne, Comden, and Green "with the best intentions in the world is a course in Civics One when everyone in the world has already got to Civics Six." Of the music he wrote, "Mr. Styne has inhaled a real breeze from the thirties for a down-the-scale trill called "Another Day," he has written a straightforward ballad ("Not Mine") that liberal Allen Case can sing with earnestness and genuine energy, he has drummed out a beat for the title song that lets Miss Uggams and confreres tear up the floor. Miss Comden and Mr. Green have kept the words lively enough here, too" (April 27, 1967).

The magazine critics, except for Priscilla L. Buckley of the *National Review*, who called the show "a blockbuster" (September 5, 1967), were scathing in their comments on *Hallelujah, Baby!* Lowell D. Streiker of *Christian Century* wondered how such a professional team of collaborators could produce "the flattest, sourest dish on the current Broadway menu" (August 30, 1967). The critic for *Time* called the show "a petrified forest of liberal and sentimental clichés" (May 5, 1967). Richard Gilman of *Newsweek* wrote that "every cliché of interracial attitudes, every form of condescension, every trick of patronization, every comfortably masochistic white liberal attitude is relentlessly exploited" (May 6, 1967).

Commentary

Though the idea of telling the history of black America's struggle for equality seemed a good one, the result was a disappointment. The book was, of necessity, episodic; and the characters became personifications. Arthur Laurents' idealized version of black history was at best naive, and the critics thought the attitude outdated and the book filled with stereotypes and clichés. The music and lyrics also did not seem quite up to the standard of Jule Styne, Betty Comden, and Adolph Green. Some of the songs did momentarily lift the tone of the play. "My Own Morning" and "Talking to Yourself," both sung by Leslie Uggams, expressed the dreams of Georgina. "Smile, Smile" was a satirical look at the way the blacks had to put on a happy face for the white people they worked for, and "Being Good Isn't Good Enough" expressed their frustration. Cecil Smith and Glenn Litton wrote in *Musical Comedy in America*: "The submerged rage and open, raw despair of blues, jazz, gospel, and spirituals were missing from a score that was strictly Tin Pan Alley" (p. 261).

*****

S14   *THE WILL ROGERS FOLLIES, A LIFE IN REVUE* (1991)

Palace Theatre, New York City; Opened May 1, 1991;
Closed September 1993

Credits
Inspired by the words of Will and Betty Rogers
Book	Peter Stone
Music Composer and Arranger	Cy Coleman
Lyrics	Betty Comden
	Adolph Green
Director and Choreographer	Tommy Tune
Designer	Tony Walton
Costumes	Willa Kim
Lighting	Jules Fisher
Sound	Peter Fitzgerald
Production Design	Wendall K. Harrington
Wig Design	Howard Leonard
Orchestrations	Billy Byers
Musical Direction	Eric Stern
Associate Director	Phillip Oesterman
Associate Choreographer	Jeff Calhoun

Producers: Pierre Cossette, Martin Richards, Sam Crothers, James M. Nederlander, Stewart F. Lane, Max Weitzenhoffer, Japan Satellite Broadcasting, Inc.

Cast
Ziegfeld's Favorite	Cady Huffman
Indian of the Dawn	Jerry Mitchell
Indian Sun Goddess	Jillana Urbina
Will Rogers	Keith Carradine
Unicyclist	Vince Bruce
Wiley Post	Paul Ukena, Jr.
Clem Rogers	Dick Latessa

Will's Sisters: Roxane Barlow, Maria Calabrese, Colleen Dunn, Dana Moore, Wendy Waring, Leigh Zimmerman

Betty Blake	Dee Hoty

The Wild West Show: Bonnie Brackney, Tom Brackney with B.A., Cocoa, Gigi, Rusty, Trixie, and Zee

Betty's Sisters: Roxane Barlow, Maria Calabrese, Colleen Dunn, Dana Moore, Wendy Waring, Leigh Zimmerman

Will Rogers, Jr.	Rick Faugno
Mary Rogers	Tammy Minoff

James Rogers	Lance Robinson
Freddy Rogers	Gregory Scott Carter
The Roper	Vince Bruce
The Will Rogers Wranglers:	John Ganun, Troy Britton Johnson, Jerry Mitchell, Jason Opsahl
The New Ziegfeld Girls:	Roxane Barlow, Maria Calabrese, Ganine Derleth, Rebecca Downing, Colleen Dunn, Sally Mae Dunn, Toni Georgiana, Eileen Grace, Luba Gregus, Tonia Lynn, Dana Moore, Aimee Turner, Jillana Urbina, Wendy Waring, Christina Youngman, Leigh Zimmerman
The Voice of Mr. Ziegfeld	Gregory Peck

Synopsis

The Will Rogers Follies opens with a big Ziegfeld Follies chorus number, "Will-a-Mania," at the end of which Will Rogers descends from the flies on a rope. Will explains to the audience that he, a boy from Oogalah, Oklahoma, who can't do much but swing a rope, has become a Ziegfeld star and that Mr. Ziegfeld is going to let him tell his life story in this particular Ziegfeld Follies. To give us a taste of the Old West of Oklahoma, Will and the Will Rogers Wranglers sing and dance "Give a Man Enough Rope."

In a series of flashback scenes we begin to get the story of the life of Will Rogers. His father, Clem, is delighted to discover that after having six girls he at last has a boy. He and Will's six sisters sing "It's a Boy." When Will is a young boy, his father tells him of his Indian ancestry. Will is not very interested in school, and as a young man he decides to go to Argentina. Before going to Argentina, he orders some long underwear from the mail order catalogue. He goes to the local post office to see if his long underwear has arrived, and there he meets Betty Blake, a young lady newly arrived from "back East." She works in the post office, and she knows at once when she sees him that this is "Clem Rogers' no good son, Will," that she has heard so much about. It is love at first sight. When Will decides he wants to ask Betty to marry him, Ziegfeld, whose voice can be heard from the back of the house, insists that Will and Betty should have a more romantic place than Oklahoma for Will's proposal. Ziegfeld orders the stage manager to get the "moon" set. Betty perches upon the crescent moon to sing "My Unknown Someone." Then Will asks her to marry him as soon as he gets back from Argentina.

While Will is away in Argentina he joins a touring variety show doing his rope twirling act. Betty waits at home until she finds out that he is coming to St. Louis with his show to appear at the St. Louis Exposition. She meets him there and urges him to come back home to run his farm, but Will is now scheduled to play in vaudeville across the United States. Will and Betty are married, but they cannot have the big wedding scene until the end of the act--the way Ziegfeld always ended his first act. Betty joins Will on his vaudeville tour, and over the years they have three boys and a girl. The whole family now travels the vaudeville circuit. Will has added talking and philosophizing to his roping act, and gradually he works his way from the small to "the Big Time." Betty urges him once again to take the family back to the Oklahoma farm. This time Will says that he will, but just then he receives an invitation from Florenz Ziegfeld to join the *Follies* in New York. Betty tells him he can't reject such an offer. So Will appears in the *Follies*. He has a friend, Wiley

Post, who sits in a box at the theatre and urges Will to come flying in his airplane with him. The first act of *The Will Rogers Follies* ends with the big spectacular *Follies* wedding of Will and Betty.

Act Two opens with a reprise of "Give a Man Enough Rope." Will's fame has spread. He now makes films, writes a newspaper column, and has a radio show. He is asked to run for President by both the Republicans and the Democrats. With his money Will has built a large house on his Hollywood Ranch. Betty and the children enjoy the Hollywood Ranch, but Will is now so well known as a public speaker that he is gone most of the time. Betty sings "No Man Left for Me." Will returns home and gives Betty the presents he has brought her. There follows a parade of elaborately costumed Follies girls, each wearing a dress more beautiful than the last. This parade glorifying the American girl was a feature of the *Ziegfeld Follies*. However, this time the parade of beautiful girls is stopped by the stage hands who come in to take the costumes. The girls must wrap themselves in plain pieces of cloth. The stock market crash has taken the opulence out of the 1920s.

The Depression follows, and Will is concerned about the country. President Hoover has asked Will to talk to the nation by radio after he gives his Presidential address. Will wonders what he can say to the people who are out of work and don't have enough food. He does give his talk on radio, speaking with compassion about the people. It seems to him unfair that in this country "ten men could buy the world and ten million can't buy enough to eat." He urges the people who have enough to share it with those who don't.

Once again Will's friend, Wiley Post, urges him to go flying with him. This time he wants to fly to Alaska. Will agrees to go. Projections show the newspaper headlines about the airplane crash that killed both Will Rogers and Wiley Post. Over pictures of Americans in the 1930s, a chorus of voices tell of the effect this tragedy had on the nation. Betty sadly sings "Without You." Then once again Will descends on the rope from the flies and he and the chorus sing the finale, "Never Met a Man I Didn't Like."

The Play's History

After previews in April, *The Will Rogers Follies: A Life in Revue* opened at the newly refurbished Palace Theatre in New York on May 1, 1991. The show closed in September 1993 after 982 performances. As of this writing, the road company is still touring.

The Palace Theatre was a famous vaudeville house built in 1913. To "play the Palace" was the dream of every vaudevillian. With the advent of movies vaudeville began to decline, and in 1932 the Palace became a four-a-day theatre with live performances interspersed with newsreels and cartoons. In 1965 the theatre was renovated as a legitimate house. In 1987 the interior of the Palace was granted Landmark status, and when *La Cage Aux Folles* completed its long run there, the theatre was closed again for renovations. New lighting and sound systems were installed as well as new heating and cooling systems. The decorative plaster work was restored; new carpeting was installed and the seats re-cushioned and recovered. *The Will Rogers Follies* was the first show in the refurbished theatre and thus has restored to the old theatre variety entertainment, for which the Palace was most famous.

The Will Rogers Follies, in spite of some negative reviews by the New York critics, built a solid box office and went on to win six Tony Awards--as best musical, best score (music by Cy Coleman, lyrics by Betty Comden and Adolph Green), best costumes (Willa Kim), and best lighting (Jules Fisher). Tommy Tune won a Tony for direction and for choreography. Keith Carradine was nominated as best actor in a musical, as were Dee Hoty as best actress and Cady Hoffman as best featured actress. Peter Stone was nominated for best book of a musical and Tony Walton was nominated for his scenic design. Tommy Tune, for the second year in a row, won the *Astaire Award* as the top choreographer of the Broadway season. *The Will Rogers Follies* also won three Drama Desk Awards--for outstanding musical, for music (Cy Coleman tied with William Finn for *Falsettoland*), and for choreography (Tommy Tune).

The original cast recording of The Will Rogers Follies was made on compact disc by Columbia Records. (See D39.) The recording won a Grammy Award.

The Will Rogers Follies provoked two controversies. Feminists were angered by the large billboards outside the theatre. The billboards showed the Follies showgirls dressed in skin tight cowhide branded with Will Rogers' initials and being roped by him. More serious were the allegations of racial discrimination raised during and after the show's initial casting process. A formal request from Performers Against Racism on the Theatrical Stage caused the New York City Commission on Human Rights to investigate the charge. The casting policy was changed and minority performers were auditioned and hired for the musical.

Reviews

The reviews for *The Will Rogers Follies* were mixed. Frank Rich of the *New York Times* was especially devastating. He titled his review "The Two Personalities of *Will Rogers Follies*." He wrote: "Will Rogers never met a man he didn't like. Tommy Tune never met a costume he didn't like. Just how these two great but antithetical American archetypes--the humble cowboy philosopher, the top-hatted impresario of glitz--came to be roped together in a multi-million-dollar Broadway extravaganza is the real drama of *The Will Rogers Follies*, the most disjointed musical of this or any other season." When Will Rogers is on stage, he writes, the musical "is a drippingly pious testimonial to a somewhat remote American legend," but when Mr. Tune "gets his chance to grab the production reins, suddenly Will is shunted aside so the high-flying director and choreographer ... can bring on the girls, the boys, the dog tricks, and a Technicolor parade of Willa Kim costumes and Tony Walton sets." Mr. Rich thinks that the two "personalities" of the musical "fight each other all evening, until finally the book wins and *The Will Rogers Follies* crashlands with a whopping thud a good half act or so before Rogers has his fatal airplane crash in Alaska." Mr. Rich faulted Peter Stone's book for being "longer on exposition than humor." He wrote that the musical never decides what it is making jokes about. He thought that Will Rogers' Depression era speech championing the poor seemed hypocritical in the midst of this lavishly expensive production (May 2, 1991).

Howard Kissel of the *Daily News* was not so negative as Frank Rich. He titled his review "*Follies*: a Tribute to Rogers and Heart." He thought Cy Coleman's music "more relaxed and engaging than his frenetic *City of Angels*. He called Betty Comden and Adolph Green's lyrics "simple and attractive." He felt that Peter Stone's book draws "interesting historical parallels," but that the "gag-oriented dialogue grows tiresome." "Will Rogers sets out to show you a good time and it does," he writes. He called the show "gorgeous to look at, winningly performed" and said that it "is the homegrown musical Broadway has been awaiting a long time" (May 2, 1991).

Writing a week later in the *Daily News*, Douglas Watt called *The Will Rogers Follies* "the right show at the right time at the right place." He thought it "a synthesis of the old and the new" and thought it "an astutely balanced musical intertwining highlights of the career of the famous cowpoke-philosopher and Ziegfeld star with stunning configurations by the New Ziegfeld Girls." He found "the characteristic energy" in the Coleman score and "the familiar deftness and fluency in the Comden-Green lyrics." However, he thought only three of the lyrics of more than "marginal interest." These were the ballad, "My Big Mistake," sung by Dee Hoty, "Never Met a Man I Didn't Like," and "Look Around," an ecological solo sung by Keith Carradine while he accompanied himself on the guitar (May 10, 1991).

Edwin Wilson of the *Wall Street Journal* called the show "riddled with contradictions," "a goulash." "There are marvelous moments--the dance routines, several songs, the dog act. But none of the parts go together. It's like a covered-dish supper where everyone brought desserts and no one thought to bring a main course" (May 8, 1991).

Jan Stuart of *New York Newsday* summarized her impression of the play: "At its best, the fractured chronology generates some good-natured chuckles. At its worst, it feels still born. The archness mostly manages to trumpet the sidestepped clichés and mute the unaddressed issues" (May 2, 1991).

David Patrick Stearns of *USA Today* called *The Will Rogers Follies* "a breezy, stylish, utterly heavenly biography of the Oklahoma-born humorist told in the style of the Ziegfeld Follies." He thought Cy Coleman, Betty Comden, and Adolph Green responded to Peter Stone's "ticklish libretto with sweet, infectious songs" (May 2, 1991).

John Beaufort of the *Christian Science Monitor* wrote: "Peter Stone wrote the funny, smartly paced book. Cy Coleman composed a score that mingles themes and periods with easy nonchalance. The Betty Comden-Adolph Green lyrics are also amusingly attuned to the now and the then." He thought the show was "an entertainment to be enjoyed and even treasured" (May 16, 1991).

Jack Kroll of *Newsweek* called the show "the nicest, most agreeable musical on Broadway." He thought the format "so retro it's positively daring. They call it *A Life in Revue*, which works out to be a kind of 'This Is Your Life' with songs and showgirls. These Broadway veterans, gambling that audiences are starved for simplicity, sweetness, and sex, have supplied all that, but it's not quite enough." He thought that if the character of Rogers had been "handled with as much punch and theatricality as Tommy Tune's dance numbers, *The Will Rogers Follies* could have gone beyond nice and headed straight for great" (May 13, 1991, p. 68).

Commentary

The idea of the musical was to tell the story of Will Rogers' life in terms of a Ziegfeld Follies. It is based on the actual fact that the down-to-earth cowboy-philosopher, Will Rogers, was a headliner in a series of Florenz Ziegfeld's opulent *Follies* in the 1920s. Still, the 1991 combining of the story of Will Rogers' life and the *Ziegfeld Follies* resulted in a strange mixture of styles and content. On the one hand was the home-spun philosophy of Will Rogers and the simple story of his love and marriage, and on the other hand the extravagant, flashy musical numbers of the Follies.

Keith Carradine made a very appealing Will Rogers, playing with easy, natural charm. He seemed a misfit among the glittering lights and elaborate costumes, as surely the real Will Rogers must have appeared in the *Follies* he starred in. Tommy Tune has perfected the use of ensemble in the musicals he choreographs. From the first novelty number of *The Will Rogers Follies* when the girls sit on the steps slapping their ropes in rhythm, the chorus emerges as an element of the musical that is as important as the book or the music and lyrics.

The scene design by Tony Walton (with ideas from Tommy Tune) is outstanding. Will Rogers was famous for his rope tricks, and Walton has used rope to outline the proscenium arch and the other portals that frame the acting area. He has also used rope to make some of the properties. Characteristic of Ziegfeld's staging were the stairs, usually located center stage. Walton has used stairs that can shrink into themselves and thus open up the stage for production numbers. When extended, the stairs span the entire width of the proscenium and look as if they go on forever as line after line of the chorus come down them. They have been imaginatively lighted by Jules Fisher. Willa Kim's 200 bright and glittering costumes also contribute to the spectacular appearance of *The Will Rogers Follies*.

Among the songs written by Betty Comden, Adolph Green, and Cy Coleman perhaps the one that most easily remains in the mind is "Will-a-Mania," the opening song. They have also written several lovely ballads for Betty Rogers, especially "My Big Mistake." Characteristic of the clever songs that Comden and Green are most famous for is "Never Met a Man I Didn't Like," expressing Will Roger's philosophy. This song makes a very moving ending to the show.

STAGE MUSICALS FOR WHICH COMDEN AND GREEN WROTE THE BOOK ONLY

S15 *APPLAUSE* (1970)

Palace Theatre, New York City; Opened March 30, 1970; 840 performances

Credits
Based on the film *All About Eve* and the original story by Mary Orr

Book	Betty Comden
	Adolph Green
Music	Charles Strouse
Lyrics	Lee Adams
Director and Choreographer	Ron Field
Designer	Robert Randolph
Costumes	Ray Aghayan
Lighting	Tharon Musser
Musical Direction and Vocal Arrangements	Donald Pippin
Orchestrations	Philip J. Lang

Producers: Joseph Kipness, Lawrence Kasha, Nederlander Productions, George M. Steinbrenner, III

Cast

Tony Announcer	John Anania
Tony Host	Alan King
Margo Channing	Lauren Bacall
Eve Harrington	Penny Fuller
Howard Benedict	Robert Mandan
Bert	Tom Urich
Buzz Richards	Brandon Maggart
Bill Sampson	Len Cariou
Duane Fox	Lee Roy Reams
Karen Richards	Ann Williams
Bartender	Jerry Wyatt
Peter	John Anania
Bob	Howard Kahl
Piano Player	Orrin Reiley
Stan Harding	Ray Becker
Danny	Bill Allsbrook

Bonnie	Bonnie Franklin
Carol	Carol Petri
Joey	Mike Misita
Musicians	Gene Kelton
	Nat Horne
	David Anderson
TV Director	Orrin Reiley
Autograph Seeker	Carol Petri

Singers: Laurie Franks, Ernestine Jackson, Sheilah Rae, Jeannette Seibert, Henrietta Valor, Howard Kahl, Orrin Reiley, Jerry Wyatt

Dancers: Renee Baughman, Joan Bell, Debi Carpenter, Patti D'Beck, Marily D'Honau, Marybeth Kurdock, Carol Petri, Bill Allsbrook, David Anderson, John Cashman, Jon Daenen, Nikolas Dante, Gene Foote, Gene Kelton, Nat Horne, Mike Misita, Ed Nolfi, Sammy Williams

Synopsis

Applause opens on a Tony Awards night. The program is being telecast and there are monitors on either side of the proscenium. The host for the television show introduces Margo Channing, a stage and film star and a two-time Tony Award winner. She is to present the award for best actress in a starring role in a straight play. She announces the nominees, a page gives her an envelope, and she reads the winner--Eve Harrington. A spotlight hits Eve who rushes on to the stage to make her acceptance speech and to thank those who have helped her. Over her effusive speech we can hear, on tape, Margo's voice comparing the glamorous Eve on stage now with the quiet, mouselike creature she was a year and a half ago when Margo first met her. The rest of the play tells the story of Eve's rise to fame.

After the opening night of her show, *The Friendly Arrangement*, Margo Channing is in her dressing room receiving congratulations from the producer, the playwright, the director, and many friends and members of the first night audience. Karen, the playwright's wife, asks Margo if she can bring in a girl who has seen every preview of the show for three weeks and who idolizes Margo. Margo consents, and Karen brings in Eve Harrington, a mousy and bedraggled girl wearing an old raincoat. Eve tells the story about herself, her young husband's death in Vietnam, and how seeing Margo on the stage saved her life. Even Margo cannot resist this, and she invites Eve to stay a while. Bill Sampson, the director of the play and Margo's lover, is off to direct a play in Rome, much against Margo's wishes. After Bill leaves, Margo decides she does not want to go to the cast party where they will wait for the reviews of the play. She asks her hairdresser, Duane, to take her and Eve out for the rest of the evening. As she sings, "I feel groggy and weary ... But alive!" the scene changes to a bar in Greenwich Village, where Margo is greeted with great enthusiasm. Still later that night, Margo, Duane, and Eve go to Margo's apartment. There they receive the news that the reviews of the play have been terrific and Margo has been called "glowing," "brilliant," and "incandescent." When Duane leaves, Eve, on the pretext of fixing a "hometown toddy" for Margo, stays the night.

In the next scene, which takes place four months later in Margo's dressing room, we see that Eve has now made herself indispensable to Margo. She even advises Margo not to insist on taking a week off from the play to join Bill Sampson in Rome because it is Christmas week and the audiences will be expecting to see Margo and not an understudy. Howard, the producer of the show, thanks Eve for taking his side, and invites her out for a drink. Margo's dressing room is suddenly changed to a bar and restaurant where Howard and Eve go for a drink. Eve subtly criticizes Margo's understudy to Howard and he asks her if she would like to read for the part. Eve coolly says that she is happy back stage. At this point the "gypsies," the boys and girls who are the dancers in the shows on Broadway and who frequent this bar, begin to sing and dance to "Applause." They are led by an energetic dancer named Bonnie.

Gradually, Eve has begun to run Margo's life, even writing and telephoning Bill in Rome. Margo is delighted when she learns that Bill is coming home. She promises him a party when he arrives. The party for Bill proves to be a disaster. Margo has at last realized that Eve is trying to take her place, even with Bill. She and Bill have a fight over Eve. Buzz Richards, the playwright, and his wife Karen urge Eve to audition for the role as understudy to Margo. Margo overhears this and is very angry. The guests know Margo when she is angry and a little drunk. They sing, "Fasten Your Seat Belts."

Act One ends with a surreptitious audition for Eve carried on behind Margo's back. The producer and the playwright are ecstatic about Eve's audition, but Margo walks in just as it is over and believes Bill has coached Eve. She is very jealous.

The second act opens at Buzz and Karen's Connecticut home. Karen, after plotting with Eve, has invited Margo to spend the weekend with them. When Buzz tries to take Margo to the train so she can get to the theatre for the play in the evening, his car runs out of gas. Karen has drained the tank. A telephone call to the theatre reveals that Eve was at the theatre early and will play the part. In the next scene we see Eve's dressing room after the play. Eve has been a big success, and everyone is congratulating her. When Bill stops by to compliment her, Eve tells him how much he has helped her and makes a not very subtle play for him. Bill deftly steps out of her embrace saying it is not good to press too hard either on stage or off. After he leaves, Howard the producer comes in and Eve, now confident of herself, tells him she does not want to be just an understudy--she wants a part of her own. Howard says that something like that might be arranged. He takes Eve to the bar where the gypsies hang out. There Eve is interviewed by a reporter.

The next day Margo has seen the paper which printed Eve's interview. Eve has lamented the fact that mature actresses often are so self-deluded as to keep playing younger roles to the detriment of the play. Margo realizes the remark is aimed at her. When Bill comes by to cheer Margo up, she suggests that they get married. But Bill says that she is already married to being a star. Late that night Eve enters backstage. She is there to meet the playwright, Buzz, who is now infatuated with her and adapting his new play for her. He tells her they will no longer have to meet like this because he has arranged for an apartment where they can meet from now on. When Buzz leaves, Eve is startled by the arrival of Howard. He has been doing some research on Eve and has discovered that the story she told about her husband's having been killed in Vietnam was a lie. Her husband is still alive. He also realizes now how she has used the stage manager, the reporter, himself, and now Buzz to make her climb to the top. She tries to tell him that she really loves Buzz, but Howard says she is his until he tires of her. He is the one who can get her what she wants. He tells her to go to meet him at his place in an hour.

It is a week later and Margo is in her dressing room. She has discovered that Eve is to get the part that she thought was to be hers in Buzz's new play. Karen comes in. She now realizes that Buzz has been unfaithful to her. She confesses to Margo that she drained the gas tank so Eve could take Margo's role. Margo tells Karen to go home and wait. Buzz will come back, she says, because he is only a stepping stone for Eve. Margo also realizes that there is something greater than being a star and that is "being to your man what a woman should be." She sings "Something Greater." As she goes out on the empty stage she sees Bill, who joins her in singing the song.

The Play's History

Applause was based on the motion picture *All About Eve*, which starred Bette Davis and Anne Baxter, and upon the original story by Mary Orr. When the musical played in Baltimore before the Broadway opening, the critics liked Lauren Bacall but not the production. The problem was that Bacall's performance was so strong that in order to make the plot believable, the producers needed to recast several roles, particularly, that of Eve. Penny Fuller was brought in during the road tryouts to portray Eve. By the time *Applause* opened in New York at the Palace Theatre on March 30, 1970, all production problems had been worked out. The critics were enthusiastic, and *Applause* played to capacity houses and earned back its investment of $725,000 in less than a year. It won the Tony Award as best musical of the season. Betty Comden and Adolph Green received Tony Awards for the book, and Charles Strouse and Lee Adams for the Score. Tony Awards were also given to Ron Field as Best Director and Choreographer and to Lauren Bacall as Best Actress in a Musical. Bacall also won the *Variety* poll of Drama Critics as the Best Female in a Musical. The Outer Circle cited Bonnie Franklin, the leader of the dancers, for her outstanding performance. *Theatre World* included Len Cariou and Bonnie Franklin in its annual list of promising new actors.

When Lauren Bacall was ready to leave the New York company for a vacation before starting a long road tour, the producers announced that Rita Hayworth, the motion picture actress and dancer, would replace Bacall as Margo Channing. However, Miss Hayworth withdrew from the assignment saying she did not have enough time to prepare for the role. The producers then chose Anne Baxter, who had played Eve in the film version, to play Margo. In the fall of 1971 Lauren Bacall started the road tour of the show, which drew capacity houses across the country. On May 1, 1972, Arlene Dahl took over the role of Margo Channing on Broadway. All together, *Applause* was given 840 performances on Broadway, closing on May 27, 1972. During the long run, Penny Fuller was replaced by Janice Lynde.

Applause was presented in London, opening on November 16, 1972, and ran for 384 performances. The musical was given on CBS Television on March 15, 1973. (See T49.)

The book for *Applause* was published by Random House in 1971. The original cast album was made by ABC Records. (See D01.)

Reviews

Clive Barnes of the *New York Times* called the book for *Applause* "among the best in years." He was glad that Comden and Green had kept the cynicism of the original screen play. "This is a musical play that is bright, witty, direct, and nicely punchy," he wrote. "The whole show is sharp and fun--everyone's idealized version of what show business ought to be" (March 31, 1970). Walter Kerr of the *New York Times* also praised Comden and Green for not softening "the cat-eat-cat implications of Mary Orr's original short story or the screenplay that celebrated it." He wrote that "*Applause* has a libretto that plays like a solid play; it's fun, ample, straight-forward, hard-headed, and could probably do without its music if it had to." He called *Applause* "a meticulously thought-out, serenely developed entertainment that has all the song-and-dance fun it wants to without ever for a moment thinning out the believable behavior of its wayward, wicked, winning people" (April 5, 1970).

John J. O'Connor of the *Wall Street Journal* wrote that the writers "have admirably maintained the brittle, brassy qualities of the original, whipping up beautifully the glamor, foolishness and even insanity of off-stage life in the New York theatre" (April 1, 1970). Martin Gottfried of *Women's Wear Daily* commented that Lauren Bacall had all the material to work with that an actress could want. However, Gottfried thought the book "the weakest part of the show." He called Comden and Green's style of satire "out-dated" and said the show was neither "funny nor perceptive" and "never as thrilling as it thinks it is." Gottfried did admit that the show was "a glittering super-professional splash of musical theatre" (March 3l, 1970).

The critics were not enthusiastic about the music. Clive Barnes called it "second rate" (*New York Times*, March 31, 1970). Stanley Kauffmann called the work of Charles Strouse and Lee Adams not as good as in *Bye Bye Birdie* and *Superman* (*The New Republic*, May 23, 1970). John J. O'Connor thought the score sometimes was "merely competent, though more often it's first-rate" (*The Wall Street Journal*, April 1, 1970).

All of the critics were in agreement on Lauren Bacall. "Marvelous," "sensational" were terms used by Martin Gottfried (*Women's Wear Daily*, March 31, 1970). Richard Watts thought Bacall played "with sparkling, biting humor and splendid authority" (*New York Post*, March 31, 1970). Henry Hewes of *The Saturday Review* thought that Bacall was "pouring maximum energy, concentration, and honesty" into a role that seemed to be "exploring her own personal and professional situation" (April 18, 1970).

All of the critics agreed that *Applause* was very "professional" and exemplified "show business at its best" (John Chapman, *Daily News*, March 31, 1970). Brendan Gill of *The New Yorker* described it as "a model Broadway musical--it comes on strong and coarse and bold and false and funny and eye-bedazzling and ear-deafening, and it never for a moment slackens its fierce, breakneck pace; like some merry, many-colored juggernaut, it hurls itself through two acts of songs, dances, wisecracks, and schmalz without the least sign of tiring, or of fearing to tire us" (April 11, 1970).

Commentary

Betty Comden and Adolph Green did not have the rights to the movie version of the story, *All About Eve*. They made some changes in the characters and in the original story. They built up the character of Margo, trying to make her fit the charismatic Lauren Bacall. Also, they omitted the acid-tongued critic, Addison Dewett, played in the film by George Sanders. The wise-cracking maid played by Thelma Ritter in the film became Margo's faithful hairdresser, Duane. In the motion picture, the final scene showed Eve in her dressing room with a young, aspiring actress trying to ingratiate herself, just as Eve had done with Margo. Comden and Green substituted two scenes in which Eve is rejected. In the first scene Bill evades her embrace and walks out on her. At most performances the audiences applauded

126 Comden and Green

Eve's rejection. In the second scene Eve tells the producer with whom she has been having an affair that she is in love with the playwright. The producer slaps her and orders her to pack her clothes and go to his apartment because she is his as long as he wants her. Comden and Green also provided a happy ending with marriage plans for Margo and Bill, after Margo realizes that there is something greater than being a star. Comden and Green also updated the story with new dialogue that made the musical seem as modern as any of the current shows on Broadway.

Applause opened the same year, 1970, as Stephen Sondheim's more experimental "concept" musical, *Company*. *Company* had only one set, no chorus, and virtually no costume changes. *Applause*, on the other hand, had many set and costume changes. It was a traditional backstage glamor musical which included familiar scenes like an opening-night celebration, the Tony Awards ceremony, and the backstage friction between performers. *Applause* had a good book with more fully developed major characters than most musicals. The critics were unanimous in their praise for Lauren Bacall in the role of Margo Channing. Brendan Gill of *The New Yorker* called her "tall, tigerishly restless, blazing with energy and humor" (April 11, 1970). Penny Fuller also received acclaim as Eve Harrington.

Most critics agreed that the music was not outstanding. Smith and Litton in their book, *Musical Comedy in America* wrote that Strouse and Adams "paired clipped phrases with lopsided, insistent rhythms, which lunged, fell back, flashed a compulsive smile, and plunged onward" (Cecil Smith and Glenn Litton, *Musical Comedy in America*, p. 267). Clive Barnes of the *New York Times* described the music as having a kind of "here-we-go-round again" sound to it (March 31, 1970). There were several big production numbers that included energetic dancing by the "gypsies."

*****

S16   *SINGIN' IN THE RAIN* (1985)

Gershwin Theatre, New York City; Opened July 2, 1985;
367 performances

Credits
Based on the Metro-Goldwyn-Mayer film
Screenplay and Adaptation   Betty Comden
                                             Adolph Green
Songs   Nacio Herb Brown
                                             Arthur Freed
Director and Choreographer   Twyla Tharp
Original Choreography in Film   Gene Kelly
                                             Stanley Donen
Scene Design   Santo Loquasto
Costumes   Ann Roth
Lighting   Jennifer Tipton
Sound   Sound Associates
Film Sequences   Gordon Willis
Music Supervision-Arrangements   Stanley Lebowsky
Music Director   Robert Billig

Ochestrations	Larry Wilcox
Associate Producer	Eugene V. Wolsk
Producers	Maurice Rosenfield
	Lois F. Rosenfield
	Cindy Prizker

Cast

Dora Bailey	Melinda Gilb
Cosmo Brown	Peter Slutsker
Lina Lamont	Faye Grant
Don Lockwood	Don Correia
R. F. Simpson	Hansford Rowe
Roscoe Dexter	Richard Fancy
Rod	Robert Radford
Kathy Selden	Mary D'Arcy
Sid Phillips	Martin Van Treuren
Phoebe Dinsmore	Jacque Dean
Diction Coach	Austin Colyer
Sound Engineer	John Spalla
Ticket Taker	Martin Van Treuren
A Warner Brother	Austin Colyer
Zelda Zanders	Mary Ann Kellogg

Cast in film sequences *The Royal Rascal*: Philippe, Pierre (Don Lockwood)-Don Correia; Jeanette, Yvonne (Lina Lamont)-Faye Grant; Enemies of the King ("Talking Picture Demonstration")-Ray Benson, Craig Frawley, Gene Sager, Martin Van Treuren; Man on Screen ("The Dueling Cavalier," "The Dancing Cavalier")-John Spalla; Lady in Waiting-Cynthia Thole; Ladies of the Court-Diane Duncan, Alison Mann, Barbara Moroz; Manservant-Gene Sager; Villain-Martin Van Treuren.

Ensemble: Ray Benson, Richard Colton, Austin Colyer, Jacque Dean, Diane Duncan, Yvonne Dutton, Craig Frawley, Mark Frawley, Melinda Gilb, Katie Glasner, Barbara Hoon, David-Michael Johnson, Mary Ann Kellogg, Raymond Kurshals, Alison Mann, Barbara Moroz, Kevin O'Day, Robert Radford, Tom Rawe, Gene Sager, John Spalla, Amy Spencer, Cynthia Thole, Martin Van Treuren, Shelley Washington, Laurie Williamson.

Swing Performers: David Askler, Cheri Butcher, Brad Moranz, Christina Saffran.

Synopsis

The first act of the stage musical, *Singin' in the Rain*, followed very closely the story line of the film. (See the synopsis of the film (F05) for the basic story.) There were a few differences, however. In the opening scene in front of Grauman's Chinese Theatre at the premiere of *The Royal Rascal* when Don Lockwood is interviewed by the gossip columnist, it was not so easy to show on stage all of the flashbacks of Don's early life. So Don's and Cosmo's previous "performing experience" is shown in one scene that took place ten years earlier in a vaudeville theatre in Altoona, Pennsylvania, where they sang and danced "Fit as a Fiddle." There were two numbers added to the first act that were not in the film. After

Cosmo's song and clowning in "Make 'Em Laugh," Cosmo and six stage hands danced "Hub Bub," a slapstick precision drill with music by Stanley Lebowsky. Another change was made in the love scene in the empty studio when Don is trying to tell Kathy that he loves her. In the film Don and Kathy sing and dance to "You Were Meant for Me." In the stage version Kathy sings "You Stepped Out of a Dream" (lyric by Gus Kahn), and Don and Kathy sing "You Are My Lucky Star," a song used only in the final scene of the film. The first act ends with the "Singin' in the Rain" number.

Since the major part of the story is told in the first act of the stage version, most of the second act is made up of production numbers. First there are numbers supposedly being filmed in the Warner Bros. Studio. These are "Wedding of the Painted Doll," "Rag Doll," "Temptation," "Takin' Miss Mary to the Ball" (lyric by Edward Heymann), and "Love Is Where You Find It" (lyric by Gus Kahn). In a return to Monumental Pictures we see Kathy recording "Would You?" Then there is another series of production numbers; supposedly, these are scenes being filmed at Monumental as part of *The Dancing Cavalier*. These include "Broadway Rhythm," followed by "Blue Prelude" (music by Al Bishop and lyric by Gordon Jenkins). This elaborate number has members of the French court, Apache dancers, French peasants, and many other characters. At last the stage production of *Singin' in the Rain* ends with the premiere of *The Dancing Cavalier* and reprises "Would You?" "You Are My Lucky Star," and "Singin' in the Rain."

The Play's History

Singin' in the Rain opened July 2, 1985, at the Gershwin Theatre and closed May 18, 1986, after 367 performances and 38 previews.

Maurice Rosenfield, a lawyer from Chicago, had persuaded Metro-Goldwyn-Mayer-United Artists to license the worldwide stage rights to *Singin' in the Rain* to him in 1981. Rosenfield and his wife Lois wanted to try out their concept of the stage musical in London. They licensed Harold Fielding to stage a production there. Fielding hired the popular British song-and-dance man, Tommy Steele, to direct and play the leading role. Tommy Steele's Don Lockwood became a "sort of Cockney homage to Douglas Fairbanks, Sr." (Susan Churcher, "Still Kicking: Miracle on 51st Street, *New York Magazine*, October 14, 1985, p. 43). The Rosenfields thought this version would not play on Broadway. Therefore, the New York version was very different from the London version, which premiered in London on July 1, 1983, and went on to become the longest running musical in the history of the London Palladium, running for 894 performances. The musical was revived in London in 1989 with Tommy Steele once again heading the cast.

In 1984 the Rosenfields were in New York and went to the Brooklyn Academy of Music to see a production of *Nine Sinatra Songs* directed by choreographer Twyla Tharp. The Rosenfields were fascinated by Tharp's work and asked her to direct *Singin' in the Rain*. Tharp had experimented with adding scenery, lighting, and finally speaking to her dances, but she had never directed a Broadway play and had little regard for Broadway. She seemed to prefer film and television to stage work. However, she thought doing *Singin' in the Rain* would be a challenge. She wanted to do the musical like a movie, with the audience as the camera.

After warning the Rosenfields that it would be very difficult to adapt the story for the stage, Betty Comden and Adolph Green agreed to try to re-write the screenplay. The Rosenfields and Twyla Tharp did not really want to change the script from one medium to another, but rather wanted to reproduce the movie on stage. Evidently, Twyla Tharp would not let Comden and Green make changes and, according to the author of a long article about the difficulties of *Singin' in the Rain*, "banished" them from rehearsals. Maurice Rosenfield said, "I really didn't think that a book was terribly important. It's just a device to get from scene to scene" (Susan Churcher, "Still Kicking: Miracle on 51st Street," *New York Magazine*, October 14, 1985, p. 44).

Twyla Tharp insisted on using eleven dancers from her troupe in the show. There was some friction between them and the Broadway actors. Tharp's style of directing was disconcerting to many of the actors. Previews for the show began in May but did not go well. John Allen, a longtime colleague of director George Abbott, was brought in as a book writer. After a week he quit and was replaced by Sean Kelly. When Kelly tried to restructure the script, he was dismissed. Opening night for the play was postponed. Jerome Robbins and Mike Nichols, friends of Twyla Tharp, attended several previews and gave her notes. Finally, an experienced director, Albert Marre, who had directed *Man of LaMancha*, was hired. The opening night was postponed again, giving Marre two weeks to flesh out and direct the narrative scenes. Marre insisted that his name not be listed in the credits. Marre packed most of the story into the first act, ending the act with the "Singin' in the Rain" number. This left the original dance numbers added by Tharp to make up most of the second act. Though entertaining in themselves, there was hardly any narrative to hold them together or to explain their relevance to the story.

On opening night the audience rose to their feet at the end of the show, but the New York theatre critics were devastating. The producers considered closing the show after that one opening night, but then they decided to put up an additional one million dollars to try to keep the show running. The producers cut salaries and used most of the additional money for advertising on television. The actors appeared on television, gave interviews to the newspapers, and even staged a rain dance in Times Square. Gradually, they built up an audience and kept the show running for 367 performances.

Singin' in the Rain was nominated for a Tony Award for Best Book of a Musical, but Rupert Holmes's *The Mystery of Edwin Drood* won the award. Don Correia was nominated for Best Leading Actor in a Musical, but George Rose won for his role in *Edwin Drood*. Faye Grant, who played Lina Lamont, was chosen the 1986 Theatre World Award winner for Outstanding New Talent and *Best Plays* named her as one of the Best Actresses in a Secondary Role. *Singin' in the Rain* did win a Drama Desk Award for Special Effects. The rain effect had been staged by Showtech.

Reviews

Frank Rich of the *New York Times* wrote that "the rain is wonderful ... but the rain can take us only so far." "Transposed to the stage in realistic terms," he wrote, "the fantasy evaporates even as the rain pours down." Mr. Rich faults the director, Twyla Tharp, for making no attempt to find "theatrical equivalents to film techniques," and using, for example, blackouts instead of giving the show "any sense of cinematic continuity and mobility" (July 3, 1985).

Edwin Wilson of the *Wall Street Journal* wrote that the difficulty with *Singin' in the Rain* was not the "direction" but the "conception." "Successful musicals have been based on many things: novels, short stories, Shakespeare, and films. In each case, though, a creative vision informs the work, and the original material has been transformed into something wholly belonging to the stage." He asks, "Why spend $5 million to duplicate on the stage almost line for line and scene for scene a definitive film musical?" (July 10, 1985).

Douglas Watt of the *Daily News* headlined his review "Singin' Down the Drain." "Though it is splashy and in living color, *Singin' in the Rain* ... is a pallid imitation of the celebrated Gene Kelly, Debbie Reynolds, Donald O'Connor movie ..." "The show falls to pieces in the second half with a long-winded mish-mash of song-and-dance routines" (July 3, 1985).

Clive Barnes of the *New York Post* called *Singin' in the Rain* "a strange fish of a show." He called the book "bright, literate, and fun," but he asked, "Why try to place on stage what is already--by almost general consent--the most successful movie musical ever created?" He thought that "when Miss Tharp is reviving the movie's original choreography she does pretty well ... on her own she is surprisingly disastrous. She recycles Busby Berkeley, Jerome Robbins; she introduces a comic dancing horse reminiscent of the one in the Massine/Picasso ballet *Parade*; she even at one point seems to recycle some of her own dances from the movie *Amadeus*" (July 3, 1985).

Brendan Gill of the *New Yorker* thought that "the rain falling from the fly loft of the Gershwin serves only to bring to mind the incomparable original (the film)." The present version, he wrote, gives us more dancing than the book of the show requires, "and one's overriding impression is that of energetic incoherence." Even the songs, he thought, "make up a jumble of seemingly unrelated odds and ends" (July 15, 1985).

Arlene Croce, writing a week later in the *New Yorker,* noted that the stage version "has no irony--not even the irony with which Comden and Green originally viewed the scene they wrote about." She said, "Tharp has made a pretty, cozy, childish show." She did think it deserved to be noticed (July 22, 1985, p. 79).

Jack Kroll of *Newsweek* wrote that "Tharp's inventiveness is restricted to a few production numbers that sometimes erupt into her unique kinetic wit but sometimes founder in ill-advised devices such as roller skates." Broadway needs the new blood of an artist like Twyla Tharp, he wrote, "but it needs her own ideas, her own energy, her own sensibility. Why hire Picasso to copy Matisse?" (July 15, 1985, p. 73).

Commentary

The credits for the stage version of *Singin' in the Rain* say: "Based on the Metro-Goldwyn-Mayer film; screenplay and adaptation by Betty Comden and Adolph Green." However, Comden and Green were evidently not really allowed by the director, Twyla Tharp, to adapt the film for the stage. This was unfortunate because they, of all people, are familiar with both stage and film and know that the two media are not the same. Both the inexperienced director and the producers merely wanted to imitate the film and put it on the stage. Thus there really was no adaptation--no "book" for the stage musical. The producer had even said that a book was "only a device to get from scene to scene." The result was that many of the scenes with dialogue that worked in intimate filmed close-up shots sounded sketchy and insipid on the large stage of the Gershwin Theatre. Even some of the dances and songs that filled the movie screen were lost on the stage. Also, for the film, the role of Don Lockwood was tailored specifically for the personality and the talent of Gene Kelly. Comden and Green were personal friends of Gene Kelly and had known him for a long time. Comden and Green, Kelly, and Stanley Donen worked over each scene together. The Broadway dancers were expected, not so much to create the characters of the script, but to imitate the real actors of the film. This imitation was what most of the critics objected to. They asked why the director and the producers wanted to duplicate when one could just watch the film to see the original.

Because of the lack of a book, the stage musical, especially the second act, was almost like a revue with one production number after another. In the second act there was very little continuity. Also lacking was the good-natured satire of the film.

MUSICALS AND REVUES FOR WHICH COMDEN AND GREEN CONTRIBUTED LYRICS

S17 *PETER PAN* (1954)

Winter Garden Theatre, New York City; Opened October 20, 1954; 149 performances

Credits
Musical version of the play by James M. Barrie

Music	Mark Charlap
Lyrics	Carolyn Leigh
Additional Music	Jule Styne
Additional Lyrics	Betty Comden
	Adolph Green
Incidental Music	Trude Rittman
	Elmer Bernstein
Director	Jerome Robbins
Designer	Peter Larkin
Costumes	Motley
Lighting	Peggy Clark
Technical Direction	Richard Rodda
Orchestral Arrangements	Albert Sendrey
Producers	Edwin Lester's production presented by Richard Halliday

Cast

Wendy	Kathy Nolan
John	Robert Harrington
Liza	Heller Halliday
Michael	Joseph Stafford
Nana	Norman Shelly
Mrs. Darling	Margalo Gillmore
Mr. Darling	Cyril Ritchard
Peter Pan	Mary Martin
Lion	Richard Wyatt
Kangaroo	Don Lurio
Ostrich	Joan Tewkesbury

134 Comden and Green

Slightly	David Bean
Tootles	Ian Tucker
Curly	Stanley Stenner
Nibs	Paris Theodore
Crocodile	Norman Shelly
First Twin	Alan Sutherland
Second Twin	Darryl Duran
Captain Hook	Cyril Ritchard
Smee	Joe E. Marks
Tiger Lily	Sondra Lee
Cecco	Robert Tucker
Noodler	Frank Lindsay
Jukes	William Burke
Starkey	Robert Vanselow
Mullins	James White
Wendy Grown-Up	Sallie Brophy
Jane	Kathy Nolan
Voice of Tinker Bell	Jaye Rubanoff

Pirates: Robert Tucker, Frank Lindsay, Frank Marasco, James White, William Burke, Chester Fisher, John Newton, Arthur Tookoian, Robert Vanselow, Richard Winter

Indians: Robert Banas, Don Lurio, Robert Piper, William Summer, Richard Wyatt, Linda Dangcil, Lisa Lang, Suzanne Luckey, Joan Tewkesbury

History and Commentary

The story of *Peter Pan* has been a favorite with children and adults since James M. Barrie's play was first produced in England in 1904. The next year the winsome and beloved Maude Adams brought Barrie's delightful hero to life on the American stage. In 1954 producer Leland Hayward and choreographer Jerome Robbins decided to do a new version of the story starring Mary Martin and Cyril Ritchard. Only four years before there had been a production starring Jean Arthur and Boris Karloff. That production had acquired four songs by Leonard Bernstein. The Jerome Robbins production was originally mounted for Edwin Lester's West Coast circuit and was not intended to be a full scale musical. There were only a few songs with music by Mark ("Moose") Charlap and lyrics by Carolyn Leigh. The show opened in San Francisco, but something was not right. Jule Styne and Betty Comden and Adolph Green were in Hollywood working on the film, *It's Always Fair Weather*, when they received a call from Jerome Robbins asking for help. Jule Styne has said in an interview that he said to Comden and Green, "Let's go up and help them. Let's not re-write. Let's give them our advice" ("Jule Styne," *Notes on Broadway*, Al Kasha and Joel Hirschhorn, p. 295). When the three of them arrived in San Francisco, Carolyn Leigh did not want to talk with them, but Styne convinced "Moose" Charlap that he and Comden and Green had more experience and could help the show.

Styne and Comden and Green had only a week to prove to Jerome Robbins and Mary Martin that they could make the musical better. The first thing they decided was that the show needed a theme. It needed a song that expressed Barrie's play, something "enchanting" that would set the stage for "Never, Never

Land." So they wrote a song with that title to set the mood for the fantasy ("Conversations With Comden and Green and Guare," *Dramatists Guild Quarterly*, Autumn 1986). Styne thought it strange that the two stars of the show had no song together. He knew that Mary Martin had a beautiful coloratura voice, so he and Comden and Green wrote "O! My Mysterious Lady," in which Peter (Mary Martin), singing in a high voice, leads Captain Hook about the stage looking for the "mysterious lady." Another Comden and Green and Styne contribution to the show was "Captain Hook's Waltz," a mock-macabre song which Cyril Ritchard sang with an effete lisp, describing himself as "the swiniest swine" in the world. Other songs by the three were "Wendy" sung by Peter and the Lost Boys, "Ugg-A-Wugg" sung by Peter, Tiger Lily, the Indians, the Lost Boys, and the Darling children, and "Distant Melody" sung by Wendy.

Peter Pan, with the new songs, opened at the Winter Garden Theatre in New York on October 20, 1954. Three of the New York critics gave the show rave reviews, and the other four critics gave very favorable reviews. The musical ran for 149 performances. The run had to be cut short because of a previously scheduled live telecast. Mary Martin won the 1955 Tony Award as Outstanding Musical Actress and Cyril Ritchard won the Tony Award for Outstanding Supporting Actor. They both won Donaldson Awards. Richard Rodda won a Tony Award as Outstanding Stage Technician.

Brooks Atkinson of the *New York Times* thought the show a little "overproduced" and thought the music sounded as if it "had come out of Tin Pan Alley tune factories." However, he thought the cast "impeccable" and the direction of Jerome Robbins inventive and delightful. Of Mary Martin's Peter Pan, he wrote: "*Peter Pan* may have been a proper Victorian originally. He is a healthy, fun-loving American now" (October 21, 1954).

Richard Watts, Jr., of the *New York Post* thought that "the note of Broadway musical comedy was a pleasant antidote to some of the saccharinity of the original text" (October 21, 1954).

William Hawkins of the *World Telegram and Sun* thought the production had "the unfettered inventiveness of a crowd of kids making up games as they go along" (October 21, 1954).

An original cast recording of the musical was made by RCA Victor. (See D29.) *Peter Pan* was given three colorcasts on NBC Television. The first was in 1955. Mary Martin won an Emmy Award for this performance. Another colorcast was given in 1956. A third colorcast was presented in 1960. This third production had most of the original cast except for the children. The children used in the first performances had now grown too big for their roles, and a new cast of children had to be used. This third production was videotaped, and that tape has kept alive the image of Mary Martin as Peter Pan for another generation of American children. (See T43, T44, and T46.)

The musical stage version of *Peter Pan* was produced once again on Broadway in 1979 with Sandy Duncan as Peter. On December 11, 1991, a new production starring Cathy Rigby opened on Broadway.

*****

S18   *LORELEI* (1974)

Palace Theatre, New York City; Opened January 27, 1974;
320 performances

Credits
Based on the musical, *Gentlemen Prefer Blondes*, adapted from Anita Loos's collection of stories

Original Book	Anita Loos
	Joseph Fields
Original Music	Jule Styne
Original Lyrics	Leo Robin
New Book	Kenny Solms
	Gail Parent
New Music	Jule Styne
New Lyrics	Betty Comden
	Adolph Green
Director	Robert Moore
Choreography	Ernest O. Flatt
Designer	John Conklin
Costumes	Alvin Colt
Miss Channing's Costumes	Ray Aghayan
	Bob Mackie
Lighting	John Gleason
Orchestrations	Philip J. Lang
	Don Walker
Vocal Arrangements	Hugh Martin
	Buster Davis
Dance Music Arrangements	Jay Thompson
Producers	Les Guber
	Shelly Gross

Cast

Lorelei Lee	Carol Channing
Henry Spofford	Lee Roy Reams
Mrs. Ella Spofford	Dody Goodman
Lord Francis Beekman	Jack Fletcher
Lady Phyllis Beekman	Jean Bruno
Josephus Gage	Brandon Maggart
Dorothy Shaw	Tamara Long
Gus Esmond	Peter Palmer
Bartender; Pierre; Announcer	Ray Cox
Frank	Steve Short
George; Engineer	Bob Daley
Charles; Master of Ceremonies	Robert Riker
Robert Lemanteur	Bob Fitch
Louis Lemanteur	Ian Tucker
Lobster	Brenda Holmes

Caviar	Linda McClure
Pheasant	Aniko Farrell
Salade	Marie Halton
Dessert	Carol Channing
Maitre D	Willard Beckham
Simone Duval	Sherrill Harper
Mr. Esmond	David Neuman

Bridesmaids: Aniko Farrell, Marie Halton, Sherrill Harper, Linda McClure

Ship's Personnel, Passengers, Tourists, Olympic Team Members, Waiters, Wedding Guests: Aniko Farrell, Joela Flood, Marie Halton, Marian Haraldson, Sherrill Harper, Brenda Holmes, Linda Lee MacArthur, Linda McClure, Susan Ohman, Gina Ramsel, Roxanna White, Willard Beckham, Ray Cox, Bob Daley, Bob Fitch, Gregg Harlan, Wayne Mattson; Jonathan Miele, Jeff Richards, Robert Riker, Rick Schneider, Steve Short, Don Swanson, Ian Tucker

History and Commentary

In 1973 Betty Comden and Adolph Green contributed four new songs to a sequel to the 1949 musical, *Gentlemen Prefer Blondes*. Jule Styne had written the music for the original musical which starred Carol Channing as Lorelei, the wide-eyed gold-digger. This 1949 musical had lyrics by Leo Robin and a book by Joseph Fields and Anita Loos that was based on the collection of stories about the 1920s by Anita Loos. *Gentlemen Prefer Blondes* opened on Broadway to rave reviews from seven of the New York critics. John Chapman of the *Daily News* called Carol Channing "the funniest female to hit the boards since Fanny Brice and Beatrice Lillie began knocking entire audiences out of their seats" (December 9, 1949). Channing played Lorelei Lee for over two years on Broadway and then toured with the show for another two years, making her songs,"Diamonds Are a Girl's Best Friend" and "A Little Girl from Little Rock," famous across the country. In spite of another great success as Dolly Gallagher Levi in *Hello, Dolly*, which she played for 1,273 performances, Carol Channing remained associated with her famous role of Lorelei Lee in *Gentlemen Prefer Blondes*.

In 1973 Channing began out of town tryouts of the sequel, *Lorelei, or Gentlemen Still Prefer Blondes*. Though the musical was called a sequel, it was really a new version of *Gentlemen Prefer Blondes*. The new book was by Kenny Solms and Gail Parent. Jule Styne provided new music and Comden and Green provided the lyrics for four new songs. Ten of the old songs, including "Gentlemen Prefer Blondes," "*Diamonds Are a Girl's Best Friend*," "A Little Girl from Little Rock," and "It's Delightful Down in Chile," were retained.

In *Lorelei*, Lorelei Lee Esmond looks back on her 1920s escapades from the viewpoint of the present. She is now the wealthy, widowed Mrs. Esmond who, in flashbacks, tells the story of her trip to Paris with her friend Dorothy. One of the new songs contributed by Comden and Green is "Looking Back," sung by Channing at the beginning of the show. "Miss Lorelei Lee" is a lively ensemble number somewhat similar to the popular song, "Hello, Dolly," from the musical of the same name. "Men" was called "an incisive feminist number" by Douglas Watt of the *Daily News* (January 28, 1974). It was sung by Channing to bring down the first act curtain. "I Won't Let You Get Away" is a dance duet number sung by a young man who has just discovered love.

138 Comden and Green

After eleven months of touring, *Lorelei* opened at the Palace Theatre on Broadway on January 27, 1974. It played 320 performances, closing on November 3, 1974. Carol Channing was nominated for a Tony Award as Best Actress in a Musical. Douglas Watt, of the *Daily News* called *Lorelei* a "40s musical with a 20s look" (January 28, 1974). Edwin Wilson of the *Wall Street Journal* called the musical "a revised but not revitalized edition of *Gentlemen Prefer Blondes*." It "needs freshness, creativity, and a new vision," he wrote (January 31, 1974). Martin Gottfried of *Women's Wear Daily* wrote that the show "has energy, polish, and style though its technique is sorely dated and its jokes are often flat." He called it "the first genuinely professional musical of the season" (January 28, 1974). The critics were glad to see Carol Channing back on Broadway.

There are two recordings of *Lorelei*--one a pre-Broadway recording and the other with the original Broadway cast (See D20).

*****

S19   ***STRAWS IN THE WIND*** (1975)

American Place Theatre, New York City; Opened February 21, 1975; 34 subscription performances. Not opened for review.

Credits
Sketches	Donald Barthelme, Marshall Brickman, Brock Bower, Peter Stone
Songs	Betty Comden, Adolph Green, Cy Coleman, Ira Gasman, Galt MacDermot, Billy Nichols, Stephen Schwartz
Director	Phyllis Newman
Designer	Peter Harvey
Costumes	Ruth Morley
Lighting	Roger Morgan
Producer	American Place Theatre

Cast
Tovah Feldshuh
Carol Jean Lewis
Brandon Maggart
Josh Mostel
George Pentecost

History and Commentary

Straws in the Wind was a revue directed by Adolph Green's wife, Phyllis Newman, and given a workshop production at The American Place Theatre on February 21, 1975. The American Place Theatre was founded at St. Clement's Church in 1964 as a theatre for living American writers. In 1971 the group moved to 111 West 46th Street where they have a space they can use for flexible staging. There is a seating capacity of 299. The American Place Theatre continues to try to provide a place for American writers who wish to write for the stage.

Straws in the Wind was called "A Theatrical Look Ahead" and consisted of skits and songs about the future. The pieces and songs included were by Donald

Barthelme, Marshall Brickman, Cy Coleman, Betty Comden, Adolph Green, Ira Gasman, Galt McDermot, Lenny Meyers, Billy Nichols, Stephen Schwartz, and Peter Stone. There were five performers. Cy Coleman and Comden and Green provided the opening musical number, the finale, and three other songs--"The Lost Word," "Goin' Home," and "Simplified Language." Two of these songs, "The Lost Word" and "Simplified Language," were included by Comden and Green in their 1977 production of *A Party With Betty Comden and Adolph Green* (See P0l). "The Lost Word" is a serious song about the difficulty people in the future may have in conveying their emotions. The "lost word" is "love." "Simplified Language" is a humorous song contemplating how words in the future may be "simplified" to denote both genders. Thus, instead of the words "boy" and "girl," why not just say "birl" to mean either gender. Both of these songs are on the recording of the 1977 version of *A Party With Betty Comden and Adolph Green*. (See D28.)

Since *Straws in the Wind* was given only a workshop production at The American Place Theatre, there are no newspaper reviews. However, Howard Kissel of *Women's Wear Daily*. in his review of *A Party*, calls "Simplified Language" a "marvelous song about nouns in a genderless future" (February 11, 1977).

*****

S20   *THE MADWOMAN OF CENTRAL PARK WEST* (1979)

22 Steps Theatre, New York City; Opened June 13, 1979;
85 performances

Credits
Book	Phyllis Newman
	Arthur Laurents
Music and Lyrics	Peter Allen, Leonard Bernstein, Jerry Bock, Martin Charnin, John Clifton, Betty Comden, Fred Ebb, Jack Feldman, Adolph Green, Sheldon Harnick, John Kander, Ed Kleban, Barry Manilow, Phyllis Newman, Joe Raposo, Mary Rodgers, Carol Bayer Sager, Stephen Sondheim, Bruce Sussman
Director	Arthur Laurents
Designer	Phillip Jung
Costumes	Theoni V. Aldredge
Lighting	Ken Billington
Sound	Abe Jacob
Musical Director	Herbert Kaplan
Orchestrations	John Clifton
Special Orchestrations	Kirk Nurock
Producers	Gladys Rackmil, Fritz Holt, Barry M. Brown
Producers' Associate	Amos Abrams

Cast
Phyllis Newman

140 Comden and Green

History and Commentary

Betty Comden and Adolph Green and Leonard Bernstein contributed the opening number for *The Madwoman of Central Park West*, a one-woman show written by Phyllis Newman, Green's wife, and Arthur Laurents. *The Madwoman of Central Park West* is about a wealthy New York woman who is torn between caring for her husband and two children and resuming her singing and acting career. In fact, it is based on Phyllis Newman's own life.

The one-woman show has many musical numbers, both old and new. The opening song by Comden and Green and Bernstein is called "Up, Up, Up." Phyllis Newman describes it as "an unusual and brilliant" number that "accurately shows how much self-approval is needed to begin another day" (Phyllis Newman, *Just in Time*, p. 155).

The Madwoman of Central Park West opened June 13, 1979, at 22 Steps Theatre on Broadway. It was a revision of Newman's show, *My Mother Was a Fortune Teller*, which had been given at the Hudson Guild the year before. *The Madwoman* ran for 85 performances and received mixed reviews. Clive Barnes of the *New York Post* called the show "utterly delightful." "This new *Madwoman* is an idiotic charmer full of vitality, fun, fantasy, and guts," he wrote (June 14, 1979). Richard Eder of the *New York Times* wrote that "the unvarying quality of rueful kookiness becomes very tiresome after the first half hour or so" (June 14, 1979). Edwin Wilson of the *Wall Street Journal* applauded Newman's "personal honesty" (June 22, 1979), but other critics found the material so personal that it was "embarrassing" (*New York*, July 9, 1979, p. 95 and Brendan Gill, *The New Yorker*, June 25, 1979, p. 59).

The Madwoman of Central Park West was videotaped for television in March of 1980 and presented on the Mobil Showcase Network's *Summershow* on August 18, 1980. (See T50.) The videotape is available in the New York Public Library Billy Rose Theatre Collection at Lincoln Center.

*****

S21   *DIAMONDS* (1984)

Circle in the Square Downtown Theatre, New York City;
Opened November 23, 1984;
122 performances

Credits

Sketches	Bud Abbott, Ralph G. Allen, Roy Blount, Jr., Richard Camp, Jerry L. Crawford, Lou Costello, Lee Isenberg, Sean Kelly, Jim Wann, John Lahr, Arthur Masella, Harry Stein, John Weidman, Alan Zweibel
Music	Gerard Allessandrini, Craig Carnelia, Cy Coleman, Larry Grossman, John Kander, Doug Katsaros, Alan Menken, Jonathan Sheffer, Lynn Udall, Harry Von Tilzer, Jim Wann

Lyrics	Gerard Allessandrini, Howard Ashman, Craig Carnelia, Betty Comden, Fred Ebb, Ellen Fitzhugh, Adolph Green, Karl Kennett, Jack Norworth, Jim Wann, David Zippel
Director	Harold Prince
Choreography	Theodore Pappas
Designer	Tony Straiges
Costumes	Judith Dolan
Lighting	Ken Billington
Sound	Tom Morse
Musical Direction/Orchestrations	Paul Gemignani
Producers	Stephen G. Martin, Harold DeFelice, Louis W. Scheeder, Kenneth John Productions, Inc., in association with Frank Basile

Cast
Loni Ackerman
Susan Bigelow
Jackee Harry
Scott Holmes
Dick Latessa
Dwayne Markee
Wade Raley
Larry Riley
Nestor Serrano
Chip Zien
Bill McComb

History and Commentary

There were fourteen authors, eleven composers, and eleven lyricists who contributed to the Off Broadway production of *Diamonds*, a revue in two acts directed by Harold Prince. The unifying theme of the revue was baseball.

The revue opened at the Circle in the Square Downtown Theatre on November 23, 1984. It ran for 122 performances, closing on March 31, 1985. The contribution of Comden and Green and Cy Coleman was small. Frank Rich of the *New York Times* wrote: "Should you blink, you'll miss the sole (though twice used) contribution by Cy Coleman, Betty Comden, and Adolph Green--a roughly six-note-long song fragment for popcorn vendors" (December 17, 1984).

Most of the reviews of *Diamonds* were negative. Clive Barnes of the *New York Post* titled his review "And It's I, 2, 3, and You're Out." To Harold Prince he wrote: "You struck out. And no one was even pitching! And certainly no one got to first base. It was a fiasco of the smallest, dullest kind" (December 17, 1984). Frank Rich of the *New York Times* called *Diamonds* "a minor league affair" (December 17, 1984). However, Douglas Watt of the *Daily News* wrote that the revue "runs up a good score" (December 17, 1984), and John Beaufort of the *Christian Science Monitor* wrote: "This good-natured celebration of the American national pastime aims to please all comers and scores handily in the process" (December 28, 1984).

RETROSPECTIONS OF STAGE MUSICALS

R01   *LEONARD BERNSTEIN'S THEATRE SONGS* (1965)

Theatre De Lys, New York City; Opened June 28, 1965;
88 performances

Credits
Conception of the Idea	Will Holt
Music	Leonard Bernstein
Lyrics	Leonard Bernstein, Betty Comden, Adolph Green, Lillian Hellman, Stephen Sondheim, Richard Wilbur
Director	Will Holt
Lighting	Jules Fisher
Orchestrations	Fred Werner
Producers	Judith Rutherford, Marechal Productions, Inc., Josephine Forrestal Productions, Inc., and Seymour Litvinoff, by arrangement with Lucille Lortel Productions, Inc.

Cast
Trude Adams
Don Francks
Micki Grant

History and Commentary
   Leonard Bernstein's Theatre Songs opened at the Theatre de Lys, Off Broadway, on June 28, 1965. It ran until September 12, 1965. Called a "musical entertainment," it was, as Lewis Funke of the *New York Times* wrote, "a tribute as well as a reminder of some of the splendid contributions the versatile composer and orchestra leader has made to the library of the musical theatre of our time" (June 29, 1965).
   Leonard Bernstein's Theatre Songs was conceived and directed by Will Holt. The staging was simple. In the background was a billboard covered with posters, and on stage right there was a traffic signal post with the green light facing the audience. There were three singers.

144 Comden and Green

In the first half of the program the selections were dramatized and held together with a combination commentary and biography of Bernstein. This first half was made up mainly of songs from *On the Town* and *Wonderful Town*, both with lyrics by Comden and Green. The songs used were "Christopher Street," "Conversation Piece," "The Wrong Note Rag," "What a Waste," "It's Love," "Ohio," and "A Quiet Girl" from *Wonderful Town* and "I Feel Like I'm Not Out of Bed Yet" and "New York, New York" from *On the Town*. Especially popular with the audience was "It's Love," sung in three different styles by the three performers. Trude Adams sang the song straight. Then Micki Grant sang it in imitation of Lena Horne. Last, Don Francks sang it as an hilarious take-off on the style of Elvis Presley. Two songs from *West Side Story*, with lyrics by Stephen Sondheim, and two songs from *Candide*, with lyrics by Richard Wilbur or Lillian Hellman, were also used in the first half of the program.

In the second half of the program, Will Holt abandoned the dramatization and grouped the songs together based on themes of love, marriage, reality, and human determination and hope. Most of the songs were from *West Side Story*, *Candide*, and *Trouble in Tahiti*, for which Bernstein wrote his own lyrics. The show concluded with "Some Other Time" from *On the Town*. This song laments that the time has gone by too quickly but advises that we "be glad for what we had." The audiences seemed to agree with the words of the song.

The critics were divided on their opinions of the show. Lewis Funke of the *New York Times* thought Will Holt had used a "graceful understated touch" and had used three "friendly, able, and attractive actor-singers" (June 29, 1965). Carter Harman of *Life* titled his review "Musical Show Minus the Show" and thought Bernstein's popular tunes required "more showmanship to put them across than Holt gives them" (July 30, 1965, p. 12). Theophilus Lewis of *America* would have preferred more tunes from *Wonderful Town* and *West Side Story*, but he concluded that "the spate of Bernstein's theatre songs is a delectable theatrical viand" (July 31, 1965, p. 122).

*****

R02　　　　　　　　　　*BY BERNSTEIN* (1975)

Westside Theatre, Chelsea Theatre Center, Brooklyn;
Opened November 23, 1975; 17 performances

Credits

Conception of the Idea	Betty Comden, Adolph Green, Michael Bawtree, Norman L. Berman and the Chelsea Theatre Center
Book	Betty Comden
	Adolph Green
Music	Leonard Bernstein
Lyrics	Leonard Bernstein, Betty Comden, Adolph Green, John Latouche, Jerry Lieber, Stephen Sondheim
Director	Michael Bawtree
Scenery and Costumes	Lawrence King
	Michael H. Yeargan

Lighting   Marc B. Weiss
Vocal Arrangements and Musical Direction   Clay Fullum
Orchestrations   Thomas Pierson

Cast
Jack Bittner
Margery Cohen
Jim Corti
Ed Dixon
Patricia Elliott
Kurt Peterson
Janie Sell

History and Commentary

By Bernstein, which was presented at the Chelsea Theatre Center in Brooklyn, took another approach. Betty Comden and Adolph Green, along with Michael Bawtree, Norman L. Berman, and the Chelsea Theatre Center, conceived the idea of using theatre songs that had been written by Bernstein for Broadway but had been dropped from the shows before they opened. Comden and Green wrote *By Bernstein*, and Michael Bawtree directed the show.

By Bernstein opened November 23, 1975, in the upstairs Westside Theatre at the Chelsea Theatre Center in Brooklyn and closed on December 7, 1975, after 17 performances and 40 previews. Most of the songs had lyrics by Comden and Green, but there were also songs with lyrics by Stephen Sondheim, Bernstein himself, John Latouche, and Jerry Leiber. The songs with lyrics by Comden and Green included: "Welcome," "Gabey's Coming," "Lonely Me," "Say When," "I'm Afraid It's Love," "Another Love" (with Bernstein), "Dream With Me" (with Bernstein), "The Intermission's Great," "The Story of My Life," "Ain't Got No Tears Left" (with Bernstein), "Spring Will Come Again," and "Here Comes the Sun." The last two songs had been written for the proposed musical version of *The Skin of Our Teeth* which Comden, Green, and Bernstein had started but never completed.

The designers, Lawrence King and Michael H. Yeargan, transformed the entire auditorium into a night club with a bar and tables and chairs. There were seven singers, and the connecting script was narrated by the bartender, played by Jack Bittner.

The critics once again disagreed in their opinions of the show. Douglas Watt of the *Daily News* wrote: "It's a glittering but tired entertainment that Michael Bawtree has staged with a kind of arch desperation." He added: "In all but a couple of instances, it is abundantly clear why these numbers were left to languish" (November 24, 1975). On the other hand, Howard Kissel of *Women's Wear Daily* called the show "an enormously enjoyable evening of theatre." He especially liked the songs, "Another Love" and "Dream With Me," calling them "simply marvelous." He thought the song, "The Story of My Life," which had been dropped from *Wonderful Town*, "would have rounded out the character of Ruth" (November 24, 1975). John Beaufort of the *Christian Science Monitor* called the commentary written by Comden and Green "perky" (December 28, 1975), and Gina Mallet of *Time* wrote that the songs "brim with confidence and fun." "So does the patter," she added (December 15, 1974).

*****

146 Comden and Green

R03   *JEROME ROBBINS' BROADWAY* (1989)

Imperial Theatre, New York City; Opened February 26, 1989;
634 performances

Credits

Book and Songs	James M. Barrie, Irving Berlin, Leonard Bernstein, Jerry Bock, Sammy Cahn, Moose Charlap, Betty Comden, Larry Gelbart, Morton Gould, Adolph Green, Oscar Hammerstein II, Sheldon Harnik, Arthur Laurents, Carolyn Leigh, Stephen Longstreet, Hugh Martin, Jerome Robbins, Richard Rodgers, Burt Shevelove, Stephen Sondheim, Joseph Stein, Jule Styne
Director and Choreographer	Jerome Robbins
Co-Director	Grover Dale
Assistants to Choreographer	Cynthia Onrubia, Victor Castelli, Jerry Mitchell
Designer	Robin Wagner
Scenery	Boris Aronson, Jo Mielziner, Oliver Smith, Robin Wagner, Tony Walton
Supervising Costume Designer	Joseph G. Ausili
Costumes	Joseph Ausili, Alvin Colt, Raoul Pène DuBois, Irene Sharaff, Tony Walton, Miles White, Patricia Zipprodt
Lighting	Jennifer Tipton
Sound	Otts Munderlok
Musical Director	Paul Gemignani
Orchestrations	Sid Ramin

Cast

Jason Alexander
Richard Amaro
Dorothy Benham
Jim Borstelmann
Jeffrey Lee Broadhurst
Bill Burns
Christophe Caballero
Mindy Cartwright
Irene Cho
Jamie Cohen
Charlotte d'Amboise
Camille deGanon
Donna Di Meo
Donna Marie Elio
Mark Esposito
Susann Fletcher
Scott Fowler
Angelo H. Fraboni
Ramon Galindo
Michael Kubala
Robert LaFosse
Mary Ann Lamb
Jane Lanier
David Lanier
Andrea Leigh-Smith
David Lowenstein
Michael Lynch
Greta Martin
Joey McKneely
Julio Monge
Troy Myers
Maria Neenan
Jack Noseworthy
Steve Ochoa
Kelly Patterson
Luis Perez
Faith Prince
Stephen Reed

Nicholas Garr
Gregory Garrison
Michael Scott Gregory
Andrew Grose
Carolyn Goor
Sean Grant
Alexia Hess
Nancy Hess
Louise Hickey
Mark Hoebec
Eric A. Hoisington
Barbara Hoon
JoAnn M. Hunter
Scott Jovovich
Pamela Khoury
Susan Kikushi
Joe Konicki

James Rivera
Tom Robbins
George Russell
Greg Schanuel
Debbie Shapiro
Renee Stork
Mary Ellen Stuart
Linda Talcott
Leslie Trayer
Ellen Troy
Andi Tyler
Sergio Trujillo
Scott Wise
Elaine Wright
Barbara Yeager
Alice Yearsley

History and Commentary

As he approached his seventieth birthday, Jerome Robbins, who, along with Betty Comden and Adolph Green and Leonard Bernstein, had helped to create their first musical, *On the Town*, in 1944, began to plan a retrospective show of his twenty years as a choreographer and director on Broadway. Robbins had had the idea in the back of his head for nearly ten years, but he really began to work on the project in 1987. When his early work was done there was no such thing as videotape and there were few notations taken on the dances that were included in the Broadway shows; therefore, the original choreography was lost. With the help of former cast members and dancers, Robbins started out to recreate some of the outstanding dance numbers from his many shows. Comden and Green were among those who helped him to remember what those dances of the 1940s and 1950s were like.

It was a long and tedious but exhilarating project. At last, after 22 weeks of rehearsals and seven weeks of previews, *Jerome Robbins' Broadway* opened at the Imperial Theatre on February 26, 1989, and played for 634 performances, closing on September 1, 1990.

It was a joyous revival of some of the best numbers from the great musicals produced from 1944 to 1964. There were 62 performers and an orchestra of 28. The Comden and Green musicals represented in *Jerome Robbins' Broadway* were *On the Town*, *Billion Dollar Baby*, and *Peter Pan*. From *On the Town* were the songs and dances, "New York, New York," "Sailors on the Town," and "Ya Got Me." From *Billion Dollar Baby* was the "Charleston" dance. The song and dance from *Peter Pan* was "I'm Flying," which had lyrics by Carolyn Leigh. The show ended with "Some Other Time" and a reprise of "New York, New York" from *On the Town*. Other shows Robbins had choreographed that he included were *High Button Shoes*, *The King and I*, *West Side Story*, *Gypsy*, *A Funny Thing Happened on the Way to the Forum*, *Fiddler on the Roof*, *Look, Ma, I'm Dancin'!*, *Call Me Madam*, *Miss Liberty*, and *Funny Girl*.

Jerome Robbins' Broadway left the audiences and critics applauding and wondering why the current shows did not seem so good as these earlier musicals. However, there was some controversy over the eligibility of *Jerome Robbins'*

Broadway's being considered for the Tony Awards. Some critics said that the works were re-created and not original. Nevertheless, the show was not only nominated for an award, but did win the Tony Award for Best Musical, and Robbins himself won a Tony Award for Best Direction. Other Tony Awards were given for Best Leading Actor, Best Featured Actor, and Best Lighting. A national tour of *Jerome Robbins' Broadway* began in May 1991. An original cast recording was made of the musical. (See D19).

Most of the New York critics were ecstatic about the show. Clive Barnes of the *New York Post* titled his review "Old Gold, New Again" (February 27, 1989). Howard Kissel of the *Daily News* wrote: "I want this show to run and run and run to remind me that the greatness I imagined back then was indeed a reality" (February 27, 1989). In the *New York Times* review, Frank Rich wrote of the three sailors' numbers from *On the Town*: "What comes through is not an imitation of the original production but presumably an equivalent to the electricity with which the upstart creative team of Mr. Robbins, Leonard Bernstein, Betty Comden, and Adolph Green first took Broadway by storm" (February 27, 1989). Edwin Wilson of the *Wall Street Journal* wrote that in the "Charleston" number from *Billion Dollar Baby* Jerome Robbins "has cleverly exploited every cliché accumulated during the 1920s. The result is not just another Charleston number but a pastiche of character types and physical attitudes that is continually amusing" (February 28, 1989).

FILMS FOR WHICH COMDEN AND GREEN WROTE THE SCREENPLAY AND/OR THE LYRICS

F01 *GOOD NEWS*

(Metro-Goldwyn-Mayer; 1947; 83 minutes; color;
Video: Metro-Goldwyn-Mayer-United Artists)

Credits
Based on the musical comedy by Lawrence Schwab, Lew Brown, Frank Mandel, B. G. De Sylva, and Ray Henderson
Screenplay   Betty Comden
                                          Adolph Green
Songs   B. G. De Sylva, Lew Brown, Ray Henderson, Betty Comden,
             Adolph Green, Roger Edens, Hugh Martin, Ralph Blane
Director   Charles Walters
Musical Direction   Lennie Hayton
Vocal Arrangements   Kay Thompson
Art Directors   Cedric Gibbons
                                          Edward Carfagno
Set Decorations   Edwin B. Willis
                                          Paul B. Chamberlain
Women's Costumes   Helen Rose
Men's Costumes   Valles
Director of Photography   Charles Schoenbaum
Color   Technicolor
Color Director   Natalie Kalmus
Recording Director   Douglas Shearer
Film Editor   Albert Akst
Producer   Arthur Freed
Associate Producer   Roger Edens

Cast
Connie Lane   June Allyson
Tommy Marlowe   Peter Lawford
Pat McClellan   Patricia Marshall
Babe Doolittle   Joan McCracken
Danny   Mel Tormé
Peter Van Dyne, III   Robert Strickland
Bobby   Ray McDonald

Coach Johnson	Donald MacBride
Pooch	Tom Dugan
Professor Burton Kennyon	Clinton Sundberg
Beef	Lon Tindall
Cora, the Cook	Connie Gilchrist
Dean Griswold	Morris Ankrum
Flo	Georgia Lane
Mrs. Drexel	Jame Green

Synopsis

Good News opens with a chorus of college students enthusiastically singing and dancing "*Good News*" on the steps of one of the buildings at Tait College. Pat McClellan, a beautiful new student, has just registered for the year and is welcomed by the students. A scene in the locker room introduces us to the coaches and the Tait College football team. It is one week before the first game. Handsome ladies' man, Tommy Marlowe, is the star player. Big, strong Beef has let his love for vivacious Babe Doolittle affect his playing and is reprimanded by the coach. Bobby is an eager member of the team, but he is so small that he is seldom put into the game. As the players leave the locker room, Bobby asks Tommy if he has approached the new girl, Pat. Tommy says girls come to him. He advises Bobby in a song and dance to "Be a Ladies' Man."

At the sorority house we find the girls getting ready for a party. One of the girls, Connie Lane, is under the sink fixing the plumbing. The girls have come to depend on the practical Connie. Now they come to her with another problem. Pat McClellan has asked one of the girls to sew sequins on her dress, and the girls consider the slinky dress that she intends to wear to the party very inappropriate. When Connie speaks to Pat, she discovers that Pat is interested in knowing who is the wealthiest man on campus. Babe tells her it is Peter Van Dyne, III. At the party, when Pat comes down the stairs in her sequined dress, self-confident Tommy asks her to dance, but she sweeps past him to meet Peter Van Dyne, III. Pat sings "Lucky in Love," and they all join in. Connie, working in the kitchen, sings "Guess I'll never be lucky in love." Pat, who sprinkles her conversation with French words and phrases, impresses some of the students; but Connie, who is an assistant to the French teacher, Professor Burton Kennyon, remains unimpressed.

The next evening Connie is working at the college library when Tommy comes in. He wants a French dictionary to look up a word that Pat used to describe him. He tells Connie that he wants to study French and asks her who is the best French teacher. Connie tells him Professor Kennyon is the best. Then she proceeds to teach him some French words in the song "The French Lesson." As they leave the library, Tommy tells Connie that at first he felt sorry for her having to work and thus miss out on much of the fun at college. Connie sings "The Best Things in Life Are Free." Tommy kisses Connie, but then he says he wants to learn French in order to impress Pat.

Tommy faithfully attends the French class and then writes a speech in French. At the student hang-out, the local ice cream shop, Tommy tries out his speech on Pat and asks her to the prom. Pat turns him down. She is going with Peter Van Dyne. After Tommy leaves, Babe, who has overheard the conversation, says in a loud voice that Tommy is the heir to a big pickle fortune--a fortune greater even than that of the Van Dynes'. Then Babe sings "Pass That Peace Pipe" and leads the students in a vigorous dance.

The rejected Tommy asks Connie to the prom which is scheduled the night after the first football game. Connie is ecstatic. She has to work in the library during the game. Tommy makes a touchdown and leads his team to victory. After the game, Pat waits for Tommy and tells him she would like to go to the prom with him. He is delighted. He tries to call Connie to break their date, but the telephone at the sorority house is always busy so he cannot reach her until just before the prom. Connie is crushed.

Some weeks later, while the students are waiting for the mid-term examination grades to be posted, Pat hints that she and Tommy are going to announce their engagement at the party scheduled after the final game of the season. The grades are posted, and the football coach and the students discover that Tommy has flunked French. He will not be able to play in the big game. The coach begs Professor Kennyon to let Tommy take a make-up exam. He agrees, and then the students ask Connie to coach Tommy for the exam. She refuses but finally relents for the sake of the school. Working in the kitchen at the sorority house, Tommy, with Connie's help, crams for the exam. When they hear one of the boys, Danny, in the living room singing "The Best Things in Life Are Free," Connie and Tommy's affection for each other is re-kindled. Tommy deliberately flunks the make-up exam, answering the questions wildly. Connie realizes that it is because he does not want to have to announce his engagement to Pat after the game. Professor Kennyon passes Tommy in spite of his nonsensical paper.

Tommy plays in the big game, but he makes mistake after mistake until the coach takes him out of the game. Beef is hurt in the game and the coach is forced to send in little Bobby. Much to everyone's surprise Bobby makes a touchdown. In the meantime, Connie makes sure that Pat overhears her say that Tommy's father has lost his fortune. Pat sends a note to Tommy saying she cannot go through with the engagement. Tommy tells the coach that now he is ready to play. He makes the winning touchdown.

Connie is escorted to the dance that evening by Professor Kennyon. Tommy, thinking that Connie is still angry with him, starts to leave the dance to go home. He is stopped by the Professor and sent in to the waiting Connie. The film ends with the students singing and dancing "The Varsity Drag."

The Film's History

Good News was one of the best Broadway musical comedies of the 1920s. It opened on September 6, 1927, at the Forty-Sixth Street Theatre and played for 551 performances. *Good News* was the first of six successful musicals written between 1927 and 1932 by the De Sylva-Brown-Henderson team. Ray Henderson wrote the music; Lew Brown and B. G. De Sylva wrote the lyrics; and De Sylva and Lawrence Schwab wrote the book. *Good News* was a college musical. The strongest asset of the show was its songs--especially "Lucky in Love," "The Best Things in Life Are Free," "The Varsity Drag," and the title song.

Metro-Goldwyn-Mayer acquired the rights to *Good News* in 1929 and made it into a film in 1930 with some additional songs written for it by Nacio Herb Brown and Arthur Freed. The movie starred Bessie Love.

Though Betty Comden and Adolph Green had, by 1946, two successful Broadway musicals behind them, they were still interested in Hollywood. They had asked their agents, A. and S. Lyons, to try for a studio contract for them. Still, they were surprised when they suddenly received an offer from Metro-Goldwyn-Mayer. When they arrived in Hollywood, Comden and Green were warmly received by producer Arthur Freed and associate producer Roger Edens. However, they were somewhat taken aback to discover that they were to write a screenplay for a new version of *Good News*. Betty Comden wondered if they were considered "authorities" on the 1920s since their recent play, *Billion Dollar Baby*, was set in that decade. The 1930 film was not available, so they read the original script for the musical, *Good News*. After a meeting with Freed and Edens, it was decided that Comden and Green would write an entirely new screenplay retaining only the barest plot line but using most of the original songs. Comden and Green wanted to give some relevancy to the 1940s by having a former student come back to the college to visit his son who was studying on the GI Bill, but Freed did not want this. One plot change they did make was to have their hero failing not in astronomy, but in French. This gave Comden and Green the opportunity to write their clever song, "The French Lesson." Roger Edens supplied the music. Roger Edens, Ralph Blane, and Hugh Martin wrote the song, "Pass That Peace Pipe," for Joan McCracken, fresh from *Bloomer Girl* and *Billion Dollar Baby* on Broadway.

Good News was the first film directed by Charles Walters, who was to go on to direct *Easter Parade* and many other films. The film was first shown at the Radio City Music Hall on December 4, 1947. The original sound track was recorded by Metro-Goldwyn-Mayer. (See D15.)

After the successful revivals of *Irene* and *No, No, Nanette* on Broadway, *Good News*, the 1927 musical, was produced in New York in 1974. This version contained "The Varsity Drag" and "The Best Things in Life Are Free" from the original musical plus "Button Up Your Overcoat," "Life Is Just a Bowl of Cherries," "You're the Cream in My Coffee," "Together," and "Keep Your Sunnyside Up" gleaned from other shows of the 1920s.

Reviews

Bosley Crowther of the *New York Times* called *Good News* a "bright movie version" of the musical. "Curiously," he wrote, "Metro hasn't troubled to change matters very much, permitting the old plot to work out in a rigidly old-fashioned style." He thought the humor was "obviously inferior to the frequent interjections of dance." He also thought there were no "striking talents in the musical line...with the possible exception of Joan McCracken's." He liked the old tunes and felt that "the pleasures of reminiscence which the picture affords are worth-while" (December 5, 1947).

The critic for *Variety* was more enthusiastic, writing that the movie "has an infectious appeal that should click with all types of audiences." "Familiar complications are ably wrapped around music and dance ingredients by scripters Betty Comden and Adolph Green. The dialog (sic) is sprightly with some modernization from its 1920s origin, the fun clean and hearty as written. Walters' direction misses no bets in getting the most and the best from the excellent material," he wrote (December 3, 1947).

The critic for *Newsweek* wrote that the musical was "a Broadway smash back in 1927, and it is just as successful now as Metro-Goldwyn-Mayer brings it to the screen." Few of the many musicals like it "have offered such a varied and tuneful score," he concludes (December 15, 1947, p. 88).

The critic for *Time* wrote that "Betty Comden and Adolph Green, who wrote the screenplay, have loaded it with medium-accurate slang and period mannerisms and with smooth, medium-sophisticated comedy." He thought the film contained "more than enough good humor and tunefulness to make *Good News* a pleasure," but he did think that "those who made the picture ignored--or failed to understand--their opportunity to recapture the poignant flavor of a dead but well-remembered time" (December 22, 1947, pp. 79-80).

Commentary

In the 1940s college musical films were popular, and *Good News* was one of the best. Some critics consider it the definitive college musical film. Though the leading actors were not especially musically talented, they made their characters appealing, especially June Allyson, as the hard-working Connie Lane. The best singing voice belonged to a 1940s radio singer, Mel Tormé. Joan McCracken gave great energy to her production numbers. The old songs, like "Lucky in Love" and "The Best Things in Life Are Free," still have their appeal. Comden and Green's "The French Lesson" was clever, and the big production numbers, "Good News" and "The Varsity Drag," began and ended the film in a spirited manner. All of these assets tended to compensate for the rather trivial plot. The best thing about the film was its lack of pretension. It never tried too hard or pretended to be more than a pleasant, slightly nostalgic, and sentimental entertainment.

*****

F02   *THE BARKLEYS OF BROADWAY*

(Metro-Goldwyn-Mayer; 1949; 109 minutes; color; Video: Loew's, Inc.;)

Credits

Story and Screenplay	Betty Comden
	Adolph Green
Music	Harry Warren
Lyrics	Ira Gershwin
Director	Charles Walters
Musical Director	Lennie Hayton
Orchestrations	Conrad Salinger
Vocal Arrangements	Robert Tucker
Staging of Musical Numbers	Robert Alton
Art Directors	Cedric Gibbons
	Edward Carfagno
Set Decorations	Edwin B. Willis
	Arthur Krams
Miss Rogers' Costumes	Irene
Men's Costumes	Valles
Hair Styles	Sydney Guilaroff
Make-up	Jack Dawn
Director of Photography	Harry Stradling
Color	Technicolor
Color Director	Natalie Kalmus
Associate	Henri Jaffa
Special Effects	Warren Newcombe
"Shoes With Wings On" Direction	Hermes Pan
Dancing Shoes Effects	Irving Ries
Recording Director	Douglas Shearer

154   Comden and Green

Film Editor	Albert Akst
Producer	Arthur Freed
Associate Producer	Roger Edens

Cast

Josh Barkley	Fred Astaire
Dinah Barkley	Ginger Rogers
Ezra Millar	Oscar Levant
Mrs. Livingston Belney	Billie Burke
Shirlene May	Gale Robbins
Jacques Pierre Barredout	Jacques Francois
The Judge	George Zucco
Bert Felsher	Clinton Sundberg
Pamela Driscoll	Inez Cooper
Gloria Amboy	Carol Brewster
Larry	Wilson Wood
Blonde	Dee Turnell
Ladislaus Ladi	Hans Conried
Genevieve	Joyce Mathews
First Man	Roger Moore
Guest in Theatre Lobby	Bess Flowers

Synopsis

    As the film begins, the talented husband and wife dance team, Josh and Dinah Barkley, finish an opening night dance number before an appreciative audience. In the taxi ride to the opening night party, Josh comments that he thought Dinah could have been more emotional in one of the skits. Dinah is offended. At the party at Mrs. Livingston Belney's home, Dinah meets Jacques Barredout, a handsome young playwright, who tells her that her talent is wasted in comedy skits and dancing. He tells her that he was deeply moved by her emotion in one skit in particular--the very skit her husband had criticized. Jacques Barredout says that he has written a serious play about the young Sarah Bernhardt and she, Dinah, would be ideal for the role of Sarah. Dinah is very flattered and talks with him about the play which he is also directing.
    At their home that night Dinah tells Josh that Jacques told her she should be a serious actress. They argue and finally make up as Josh sings "You'd Be Hard to Replace." When Josh and Dinah get to the theatre the next day, they discover that Ezra and the director of their show are about to audition an attractive young chorus girl, Shirlene, for a possible understudy for Dinah. When Josh comments that Shirlene is "cute," Dinah is jealous, but she does accept Shirlene as her understudy. At the show that night we see one of their comic musical numbers, "My One and Only Highland Fling," done with a Scottish accent.
    On Sunday Josh and Dinah and their friend Ezra go to a party that Mrs. Belney is giving in honor of Jacques. The party is at her country estate, and while Josh and Ezra play golf, Dinah once again talks with Jacques and reads his play about the Young Sarah. She likes the play and Jacques insists that she is the one who should play Sarah. When Dinah tells Josh that she wants to be in the play, he is very angry. Dinah, determined to act in the play, leaves Josh.
    The dance duo has now broken up. We see one of Josh's solo numbers that he has inserted into the show. In "Shoes With Wings On" Josh plays a shoemaker

who dances with a number of animated shoes. Josh is unhappy without Dinah, and he sneaks into the back of the theatre where she is rehearsing the play. He sees that she is not doing well in the role, and Jacques seems unable to help her. Josh knows just how to help her realize the part. That evening, using a French accent in imitation of Jacques, he calls Dinah on the telephone and helps her to work out the scene. The next day Dinah astonishes Jacques and the rest of the cast with her new understanding of the role. Josh continues to direct Dinah by telephone while posing as Jacques.

Josh and Dinah had previously agreed to make an appearance at a hospital benefit show. Ezra has told each of them that the other is not going to appear at the benefit. They both show up, and the old magic is revived as they dance together again to "They Can't Take That Away From Me." Josh wants Dinah to come back to him, but she says she must show that she can stand on her own.

On the opening night of *The Young Sarah*, we see the final scene of the play. Sarah is auditioning for a place in a French acting company. We see the other actresses reciting their soliloquies from Shakespeare, and then Sarah begins hers. She stops and says she will instead recite the "Marseillaise." The judges are horrified, but after she starts they are entranced. Sarah is accepted.

After the play, Dinah receives many admirers backstage and many telegrams, but she does not hear from Josh. Then Josh, using his French accent, calls to congratulate her. While he is speaking, Jacques walks into her dressing room. She realizes that it must be Josh on the telephone. When Jacques tells her that he did not call her at home during rehearsals, Dinah realizes that it was Josh who helped her succeed in the play. She goes to their home to wait there for Josh. In the final scene of the film we see the dance team together, dancing to "Manhattan Downbeat."

The Film's History

In January 1948 Betty Comden and Adolph Green returned to Hollywood and to the Freed Unit at Metro-Goldwyn-Mayer to write an original screenplay for Judy Garland and Fred Astaire. *Easter Parade*, which starred Garland and Astaire, had been so successful that Freed wanted to put them together again. Both Betty Comden and Adolph Green had admired Astaire for years. Green had first seen him and his sister Adele in the 1931 Broadway musical revue, *The Band Wagon*. Comden and Green's story for the new film was about a successful husband and wife acting and dancing team whose career was occasionally disrupted by explosions of temper. Astaire and Garland liked the play. Freed talked to Harry Warren about writing the score, and Warren suggested Ira Gershwin as his lyricist. Astaire asked for the choreographer Hermes Pan to help him with the creation of the "Shoes With Wings On" dance number. The cast began rehearsing in June, but during the third week of rehearsals, Judy Garland began to miss rehearsals or to come for only a short time (as she had done in preparing for the film, *The Pirate*). Arthur Freed contacted her physician, who said that Judy could not get better emotionally if she kept working. Freed had to take her off the picture. He then considered Ginger Rogers for the part and talked with Astaire about it. Astaire was elated. He and Ginger Rogers had talked about getting together again. During the 1930s they had made nine pictures together. Their last picture together was *The Story of Irene and Vernon Castle* made in 1939. Since Ginger Rogers and Judy Garland were very different in their performing styles, changes had to be made in the script and especially in the score. Three songs written with Judy Garland in mind were dropped. Roger Edens came up with the idea of using the song, "They Can't Take That Away From Me," for the sake of nostalgia. The song had been written by George and Ira Gershwin for Astaire and Rogers in their 1937 film, *Shall We Dance?* One slight change in the plot was that the English playwright became a Frenchman and Jacques Francois was cast in the part.

The Barkleys of Broadway began shooting on August 8, 1948, and was completed on October 30, 1948. It was released on May 14, 1949. It was well received by the critics and the public. It was one of the top films at the box office in 1949 and was nominated for a Screenwriters Guild Award. The film received no Academy Awards at the 1949 Oscar ceremony, but Astaire was given a special Academy Award "for his unique artistry and his contributions to the technique of musical pictures." Ginger Rogers presented the award. The sound track for *The Barkleys of Broadway* was recorded by Metro-Goldwyn-Mayer. (See D04.)

Reviews

Bosley Crowther, writing in the *New York Times*, delighted in the bringing together again of Ginger Rogers and Fred Astaire. They had not made a film together for ten years, and this was to be their last. "No team," he wrote, "has ever been able to give light comedy the lilting, lovely style that these two can manage in a picture." He continues: "Miss Rogers and Mr. Astaire do a darling and debonaire job with the cleverly ornamented clichés of Betty Comden's and Adolph Green's script. They quarrel in a civilized fashion, with rich meaning in a shrug or a glance, and they snap barbed rejoinders at each other with beautifully supercilious smiles. Perhaps we forget, when they're together, what able comedians these two are. Their brilliantly calculated timing is not only applied to the dance...But, of course, it is in this department that they make the most dazzling displays. And when they unlimber their torsos, the movement is lyrical and clean." Crowther concludes his review by writing: "Charles Walters' fluid direction matches the talents of his stars, and the production, in fine Technicolor, is right out of Metro's top drawer" (May 5, 1949).

The critic for *Variety* thought the dialogue in the film "good," and he writes: "the cast is very competent in getting over the light material" (April 13, 1949, p. 11). The critic for *Newsweek* called *The Barkleys of Broadway* "a gay and stimulating offering much in their (Astaire and Rogers) old manner." "The dancing, of course, is out of Hollywood's top drawer" (May 2, 1949, p. 83).

The critic for *Time* called *The Barkleys of Broadway* "a light-hearted Technicolored reunion for Hollywood's best-known dance team." He noted a few slow spots in the film--the Scottish number and the piano solo by Oscar Levant--but other than those moments, he thought the show moved along "at a lively clip " (April 25, 1949, p. 96).

The *Theatre Arts* critic commented that "Miss Rogers appears to be delighted, even to the extent of dropping the deadpan expression that characterized her non-musical efforts ... and at the same time her comic gifts are more apparent than they used to be." "Fred Astaire, of course, is still the most ingratiating performer on stage or screen, still doing his dances ... as only he can do them." This critic called the book "the only disappointing part of *The Barkleys of Broadway*. "Done by two people who are capable of much better, Betty Comden and Adolph Green, it abounds in such lines as 'I'm sneezing and coughing like a Model T,' and totally lacks the sprightliness of some other Astaire-Rogers plots" (June 1949, p. 7).

Commentary

Critics who remembered the Astaire-Rogers RKO films of the 1930s, though glad for the reunion of the two dancers, could not accept *The Barkleys of Broadway* as quite the equal of those nine films. Those films, except the first, had been written especially for Astaire and Rogers. *The Barkleys of Broadway* had originally been written for Astaire and Judy Garland. When Garland was unable to do the film, some of the numbers that had been written with her in mind were dropped. However, there were few changes in the script made to fit Ginger Rogers. The new songs in *The Barkleys of Broadway* also suffer in comparison with those of the previous films, and they seem to have little emotional connection with the rather inconsequential plot. Many of the songs and dances are presented as part of the Barkleys' stage performances. *The Barkleys of Broadway* is, therefore, only an average musical with some excellent numbers rather than a film with the style and the quality of the classic Astaire-Rogers movies.

The high point of the film is Astaire's solo dance, "Shoes With Wings On," presented in the film as part of Josh's show after Dinah leaves him. Astaire devised this dance with choreographer Hermes Pan, who had worked with him on the dances in the RKO films. In this number Josh plays a worker in a shoe repair shop. After the customers have left, an empty pair of white shoes begins to dance on its own. Josh puts on the pair of shoes and begins dancing. On the sound track we hear Astaire singing "I've Got Shoes With Wings On." As he dances, more shoes begin to dance. At last, in an effort to stop the dancing shoes, Josh tries to shoot them with pistols. The dance ends when dozens of shoes fall on his head.

*****

F03 *TAKE ME OUT TO THE BALL GAME*

(Metro-Goldwyn-Mayer; 1949; 93 minutes; color;
Video: Metro-Goldwyn-Mayer-United Artists)

Credits

Based on a story by Gene Kelly and Stanley Donen

Screenplay	Harry Tugend
	George Wells
Music and Lyrics of some songs	Betty Comden
	Adolph Green
	Roger Edens
Director	Busby Berkeley
Musical Director	Adolph Deutsch
Vocal Arrangements	Robert Tucker
Staging of Musical Numbers	Gene Kelly
	Stanley Donen
Art Directors	Cedric Gibbons
	Daniel B. Cathcart
Set Decorations	Edwin B. Willis
	Henry W. Grace
Women's Costumes	Helen Rose
Men's Costumes	Valles
Hair Styles	Sydney Guilaroff

Make-up	Jack Dawn
Director of Photography	George Folsey
Color	Technicolor
Color Director	Natalie Kalmus
Associate	James Gooch
Special Effects	Warren Newcombe
Montage Sequence	Peter Ballbusch
Recording Director	Douglas Shearer
Film Editor	Blanche Sewell
Producer	Arthur Freed
Associate Producer	Roger Edens

Cast

Dennis Ryan	Frank Sinatra
K. C. Higgins	Esther Williams
Eddie O'Brien	Gene Kelly
Shirley Delwyn	Betty Garrett
Joe Lorgan	Edward Arnold
Nat Goldberg	Jules Munshin
Michael Gilhuly	Richard Lane
Slappy Burke	Tom Dugan
Salinka	Murray Alper
Nick Danford	Wilton Graff
Two Henchmen	Mack Gray
	Charles Regan
Steve	Saul Gross
Karl	Douglas Fowley
Dr. Winston	Eddie Parkes
Cop in Park	James Burke
Specialty	The Blackburn Twins
Senator Catcher	Gordon Jones

Synopsis

The time is 1908 when baseball was becoming America's favorite pastime. The members of the Wolves baseball team are gathering in Sarasota, Florida, to begin training for the season. Two favorite players have not yet arrived--Eddie O'Brien, the short stop, and Dennis Ryan, the second baseman. When a reporter inquires about them, the manager says they spend the off-season performing in vaudeville, but they will be there. We now see O'Brien and Ryan in a song and dance act in Pottstown, Illinois. They are singing "Take Me Out to the Ball Game." Then they rush to catch a train to Florida. O'Brien and Ryan, though best of friends, are very different. O'Brien is handsome and self-confident. He is very interested in girls and thinks he is a great "lady-killer." Ryan is small and skinny. He is shy and bashful around girls. When they arrive for spring training they are greeted with enthusiasm by the team. They sing "Yes, Indeedy," which tells of their adventures with the girls across the country.

The joy of the reunion of the manager and the players is short-lived. The manager receives word that the team has been left to a distant relative of the former owner. The new owner is K. C. Higgins from Providence, Rhode Island. The word is that the new owner intends to be an active participant in managing the team. The new owner turns out to be a very beautiful young lady named Katharine. O'Brien and Ryan are both attracted to her, and they are dismayed to discover that she knows a lot about baseball. In fact, she even corrects O'Brien's batting. Katharine joins the men in the dining room for dinner. After dinner O'Brien and Ryan are joined by their friend, the first baseman, Nat Goldberg, in singing and dancing "O'Brien to Ryan to Goldberg." Later in the evening, O'Brien asks Katharine for a date the next night, but she coolly fines him for breaking training rules by being up so late.

Now we see the team warming up for their first game. O'Brien, Ryan, and Goldberg perform their comedy routine with a huge bat and a soft ball that they do before every game, much to the delight of the fans. During the game, a fight breaks out between the teams. Ryan is knocked out. A girl in the stadium, Shirley Delwyn, has been watching Ryan, and when he is lying unconscious on the ground, she runs out and carries him back to the bleachers. The game resumes and Ryan is able to continue playing. When the game is over, Shirley waits for Ryan and chases him around the stadium singing "It's Fate, Baby, It's Fate."

On tour, the Wolves begin winning games until finally they head the league. On their return, Joe Lorgan gives a clam bake for the team. At the party, O'Brien, Ryan, and Goldberg lead a big production number, "Strictly U.S.A." During the party Shirley pursues Ryan until he finally discovers that she is the one for him. O'Brien pursues the still cool Katharine. Upon the request of the guests at the party, O'Brien sings and dances an Irish air, "The Hat My Dear Old Father Wore Upon St. Patrick's Day."

The next day O'Brien is approached by Joe Lorgan and his henchmen. The big final game of the season is coming up in a few weeks. Lorgan has bet heavily against the Wolves. He thinks that if he can get O'Brien out of the way, the Wolves will lose. He offers O'Brien a chance to sing and dance with a bevy of thirty beautiful girls in his new restaurant and nightclub that he is opening. O'Brien tells him he will do it right after the final game, but Lorgan insists he needs to start rehearsing with the girls right now. O'Brien cannot resist the offer and agrees to rehearse secretly at night.

Over the next few weeks O'Brien, after rehearsing late into the night, begins to make errors. The team loses game after game. Mr. Lorgan tells Katharine that O'Brien has been rehearsing at night, and she fires him. When the pennant play-off begins, O'Brien hires some little boys to chant "We want O'Brien." The chant grows, and finally O'Brien is put into the game. Shirley overhears Lorgan tell his men that O'Brien must not play today. She warns Ryan and tells him he must keep O'Brien out of the game. In the pre-game comedy act that O'Brien, Ryan, and Goldberg do, Ryan throws a real baseball at O'Brien and knocks him out. He is carried out to the locker room. Lorton sends his men, telling them to pretend to be doctors and to keep O'Brien unconscious. Without O'Brien, the Wolves are losing the game. Finally Shirley tells Katharine that the two men are not doctors. The two girls get the police. O'Brien wakes up to find Katharine kissing him. She tells him that Ryan used a real baseball to knock him out. He runs out on the field to get Ryan. Ryan has just hit a ball, and the manager tells O'Brien to hit another and then go after Ryan on the diamond. He does and both of them get to home plate, winning the game.

The film ends with O'Brien, Ryan, Katharine, and Shirley singing a reprise of "Strictly U.S.A."

The Film's History

In the summer of 1946 Gene Kelly proposed a baseball picture to Arthur Freed. Kelly had met Stanley Donen when Donen was a young dancer in the chorus of *Pal Joey*, which was Kelly's first big starring role on Broadway. When Kelly began staging the musical numbers for the film *Best Foot Forward*, he made Donen his assistant and also got him a role in the show. Donen began collaborating with Kelly on the musical numbers for *Anchors Aweigh*. So when Kelly was driving across the country to Hollywood in 1946 he asked Donen to join him. When they arrived at the film studio they handed Freed a synopsis of a story about baseball. It was to star Kelly and Frank Sinatra and Kathryn Grayson. Freed put George Wells to work writing a screen play from the outline, but he wanted to use Judy Garland instead of Kathryn Grayson. Harry Warren and Ralph Blane, who had just finished doing *Summer Holiday*, were asked to do the score.

It was soon obvious that Judy Garland was not able to make the picture. Esther Williams was cast as the new owner of the team. This threw off Wells's script, and Harry Tugend began writing a new screenplay. Warren and Blane's score also was abandoned. Betty Comden and Adolph Green and Roger Edens were asked to write new songs for the film.

Four of the songs used in *Take Me Out to the Ball Game* were written by Comden, Green, and Edens--"The Right Girl for Me," "O'Brien to Ryan to Goldberg," "Yes, Indeedy," and "It's Fate, Baby, It's Fate." One song, "Strictly U.S.A.," was written by Edens alone. "The Hat My Dear Old Father Wore Upon St. Patrick's Day" was written by Jean Schwartz and William Jerome. The title song was an old one written in 1908 by Harry Von Tilzer and Jack Norworth. Norworth was a popular song and dance man, who for a time--from 1908 until 1913--was the husband and partner of vaudeville and Ziegfeld Follies star, Nora Bayes. He later was the owner and star of the Norworth Theatre in New York.

Take Me Out to the Ball Game started shooting on July 28, 1948. Busby Berkeley directed the dialogue scenes and Kelly and Donen the musical numbers. The film was finished on October 26, 1948. It premiered at Loew's State in New York on March 9, 1949, and was released for general distribution on April 1, 1949. It was retitled *Everybody's Cheering* for foreign distribution. The sound track for *Take Me Out to the Ball Game* was released on record by Metro-Goldwyn-Mayer. (See D36.)

Reviews

Bosley Crowther of the *New York Times* wrote that movies about ballplayers have two strikes against them, but "the studio has simply made this picture a rowdy-dow musical show featuring Gene Kelly and Frank Sinatra--who, incidentally, play a little ball." "The only hits in this Ball Game are those which are danced and sung." He wrote: "For all its high spots, however, the show lacks consistent style and pace, and the stars are forced to clown and grimace much more than becomes their speed. Actually, the plotted humor is conspicuously bush-league stuff" (March 10, 1949).

Variety concluded that the film was short on story, but "has some amusing moments--and Gene Kelly." The critic thought the combination of talents was "worthy of better material," but he did note that "Busby Berkeley's direction keeps the pic at a breezy pace" (March 9, 1949).

The critic for *Time* called *Take Me Out to the Ball Game* "a lazy Technicolored cinemusical aimed squarely and accurately at the summer box office." However, he wrote that "Sinatra and Kelly get in a lot of pleasant, unpretentious hoofing and harmonizing" (March 28, 1949, pp. 98-101).

Commentary

The critics agreed that the musical numbers and dances were the highlights of *Take Me Out to the Ball Game*. The story was neither inventive nor especially intriguing. Freed had probably bought the story outline to accommodate Gene Kelly. One of the ideas was to re-unite Kelly and Frank Sinatra, who had been teamed together in the successful film *Anchors Aweigh*.

Of the songs used in *Take Me Out to the Ball Game*, four were written by Comden and Green and Roger Edens. "Yes, Indeedy" was a clever song sung by Ryan and O'Brien, in which they brag to the other members of the baseball team about all of the women they have left with broken hearts while they were on their vaudeville tour. "The Right Girl For Me" was the only romantic song in the film and the only one that gave Frank Sinatra a serious solo.

"O'Brien to Ryan to Goldberg" was a celebration of the three buddies' respective cultural heritages. It contained an Irish jig for O'Brien, a Scottish fling for Ryan, and a hora and Yiddish monologue for Goldberg. The energetic dance contained a face-forward slide on the restaurant floor by the three men and ended with a human pyramid on top of a table.

Another clever song by Comden and Green was "It's Fate, Baby, It's Fate," sung by Shirley (Betty Garrett) and Ryan. Shirley, having decided that Ryan is the man for her, chases him around the ball park and up into the stands. As he tries to get away from her, she at last picks up the skinny Ryan, throws him over her shoulder, and then catches him after he has slid down the slippery hand rail.

Roger Edens wrote the song, "Strictly U.S.A.," used for the big production number with the whole cast as they celebrate at the clam bake. This number is full of movement. The highlight of the film, however, is O'Brien's dance at the clam bake, "The Hat My Dear Old Father Wore Upon St. Patrick's Day," written by Jean Schwartz and William Jerome. Here Gene Kelly could really show off his versatility. He tap dances, jigs, marches, and struts. Suddenly, just before the climax, the sound track goes silent except for Kelly's whisper and the sound of distant bagpipes.

Though *Take Me Out to the Ball Game* had little plot, the musical numbers had the kind of vitality that was to characterize the three great Gene Kelly film musicals, *On the Town* (1949), *An American in Paris* (1951), and *Singin' in the Rain* (1952).

*****

F04   *ON THE TOWN*

(Metro-Goldwyn-Mayer; 1949; 98 minutes; color;
Video: Metro-Goldwyn-Mayer-United Artists)

Credits

Screenplay	Betty Comden
	Adolph Green
Music	Leonard Bernstein
	Roger Edens
Lyrics	Betty Comden

Directors	Adolph Green
	Gene Kelly
	Stanley Donen
Musical Director	Lennie Hayton
Orchestrations	Conrad Salinger
Vocal Arrangements	Saul Chaplin
Art Directors	Cedric Gibbons
	Jack Martin Smith
Set Decorations	Edwin B. Willis
Associate	Jack D. Moore
Costumes	Helen Rose
Hair Styles	Sydney Guilaroff
Make-up	Jack Dawn
Director of Photography	Harold Rosson
Color	Technicolor
Color Consultants	Henri Jaffa
	James Gooch
Special Effects	Warren Newcombe
Recording Supervisor	Douglas Shearer
Film Editor	Ralph E. Winters
Producer	Arthur Freed
Associate Producer	Roger Edens

Cast

Gabey	Gene Kelly
Chip	Frank Sinatra
Brunhilde Esterhazy	Betty Garrett
Claire Huddesen	Ann Miller
Ozzie	Jules Munshin
Ivy Smith	Vera-Ellen
Mme. Dilyovska	Florence Bates
Lucy Shmeeler	Alice Pearce
Professor	George Meader
Brooklyn Girl	Bea Benaderet
Waiter	Eugene Borden
Francois	Hans Conried
Dubbed Voice of a Sailor's Date	Judy Holliday

Synopsis

See the synopsis of the play for a detailed summary of the plot (S01). The film retains the basic story of three sailors on a twenty-four hour leave in New York. The film shows the same carefree delight of the sailors as in the original play. However, there are many changes. Only four of Leonard Bernstein's musical numbers have been kept--"I Feel Like I'm Not Out of Bed Yet," "New York, New York," "Come Up to My Place," and the music for the "Miss Turnstiles" dance. The music for Kelly's dance, "A Day in New York," was a new arrangement of themes from the show's ballet music. Bernstein's lovely song, "Lonely Town," has been omitted. New songs have been added with lyrics by Comden and Green and music by Roger Edens. One of the new songs is "Pre-Historic Man," sung by Claire (Ann Miller) before she goes into a tap dance number about pre-historic man. Another new song is "Main Street," sung by Gabey when he finds Ivy (Vera-Ellen) in the dance studio. Other new songs are "You're Awful," which Chip (Frank Sinatra) sings to Hildy (Garrett), and "We're Goin' on the Town," sung by the three sailors and the three girls when they meet on the top of the Empire State Building. When Gabey is feeling lonely after Ivy leaves him, the others sing "You Can Count on Me." A novelty number, "Pearl of the Persian Sea," is sung by the three sailors while dressed as ladies of the harem.

In the film, Ivy meets Gabey and the others on top of the Empire State Building early in the evening. Thus, she gets to join the others in the joyous singing and dancing there and at the first nightclub. She leaves to go to her job on Coney Island at 11:30. After Ivy leaves, Hildy calls Lucy, who joins the others at the nightclub. Gabey takes Lucy home and it is then that he sees the "A Day in New York" poster and imagines that he is dancing with Ivy. The role of Claire's fiancé has been eliminated.

The film has been well adapted to fit the talented cast. Gene Kelly adds his special dancing to the show. Vera-Ellen and Ann Miller are excellent dancers also, and dances have been added to use their talents.

The Film's History

Lily Messager, assistant to Louis B. Mayer, heard the score of *On the Town* in New York and prevailed upon Mayer of Metro-Goldwyn-Mayer to buy the rights to the stage show even before it was presented on Broadway. This is thought to be the first time that the film rights to a musical were sold before the stage production was given. It was not until five years later, however, that Arthur Freed was given permission by Mayer to go ahead with the film.

Freed had not liked the score for *On the Town*. Leonard Bernstein's music was still considered avant-garde, and Freed thought that the music for the film should be more easily accessible for a mass audience. Comden and Green had worked with Freed on *Good News* and *The Barkleys of Broadway*, for which they had written the screen plays, and on *Take Me Out to the Ball Game*, to which they had contributed some of the songs. When Freed asked them to write the screenplay and to write new songs with Roger Edens, they hesitated. They were good friends of Leonard Bernstein and did not want to change the score which they loved, but they were under contract to Metro-Goldwyn Mayer.

Gene Kelly and Stanley Donen, who had directed the musical numbers in *Take Me Out to the Ball Game*, were scheduled to co-direct this as their first musical film. They had already cast the roles of the three sailors. Gene Kelly was to play Gabey, Frank Sinatra was to be Chip, and Jules Munshin was to play Ozzie. It was the same three who had been pals in *Take Me Out to the Ball Game*, but this casting did change the original show. The three characters in the musical had been innocent sailors. As Comden said, "With Gene as the leading character and the star of the picture, the angle of the story had to be changed. He couldn't be a helpless, naive type. The whole structure of the story had to be changed to suit the people who were going to play the characters" (quoted by Hugh Fordin in *The World of Entertainment!*, p. 259).

Comden and Green wrote the first half of their screenplay in New York and then went to Hollywood to complete the screenplay and to write the new songs. The picture started shooting on March 28, 1949. Most of the scenes were shot in the studio, but on May 5 the six principals and the crew left for New York, where they remained until May 23. In that time they shot sequences in the Brooklyn Navy

Yard and covered New York from the Battery to the George Washington Bridge. After the cast and crew returned to Hollywood, there was still the problem of filming Kelly's ballet, "A Day in New York." Leonard Bernstein joined Kelly in California in June to work on this.

On the Town was completed on July 2, 1949, after forty-seven days of filming at a cost of $2,111,250. The picture was premiered at Radio City Music Hall on December 30, 1949. A seven block long line of 10,000 people waited to get in to see the film. The sound track of the film was released on record by Metro-Goldwyn-Mayer. (See D24.)

At the Academy Awards presentation on March 23, 1950, two Oscars were presented to Roger Edens and Lennie Hayton for the "Best Scoring of a Musical Film" for On the Town. Comden and Green received their first Screenwriters Guild Award for the film.

Reviews

Bosley Crowther of the New York Times wrote that "Gaiety, rhythm, humor and a good, wholesome dash of light romance have been artfully blended together in this bright Technicolored comedy." Even with the changes, he writes, "the over-all picture flits and frolics with the same carefree delight as did the popular original-- and with equal originality, too." Gene Kelly and Stanley Donen "have cleverly liberated action in the manner of the musical stage and they have engineered sizzling momentum by the smart employment of cinema techniques." "From the moment the picture opens ... the whole thing precipitately moves, with song, dance, comedy and romance ingeniously interwoven and performed" (December 9, 1949).

The reviewer for Variety wrote that "the pep, enthusiasm and apparent fun the makers of On the Town had in putting it together comes through to the audience and gives the picture its best asset." He goes on to say that "a bright, breezy touch predominates in the direction and performances" (December 7, 1949, p. 6).

The critic for Time magazine wrote: "By combining a fluid cinematic approach and slick Broadway professionalism, co-directors Gene Kelly and Stanley Donen have turned out a film so exuberant that it threatens at moments to bounce right off the screen" (January 2, 1950, pp. 63-64).

The critic for Newsweek called On the Town "a picture that achieves the rare virtue of being pure musical comedy instead of just another story with music tacked on" (December 19, 1949, p. 76). The reviewer for The New Republic called the picture "fast, tuneful, with moments of stylish dancing and with a comic sense which, if obvious, is too good-humored and unassuming to be resisted" (December 26, 1949, p. 23).

Commentary

Working closely with Gene Kelly and Stanley Donen, Betty Comden and Adolph Green rewrote the stage script to fit the personalities and the talents of the major players. They cut some of the show's ballets and stressed the camaraderie of the three men. The film has more sentiment and pathos than the stage play, but this is counterbalanced by the satire and the slapstick, giving the film both humor and humanity. In spite of the mad car chase, the men dressed up as cooch dancers, the joyous singing and dancing, the film is dominated by a feeling of sadness. There is the ever present awareness of time's running out. This is cleverly depicted by a time strip that runs across the bottom of the screen in the style of the

New York Times news billboard. The desperate attempt by the young people to have a good time, the finality of good-byes, and, most of all, the sad character of Lucy add to the humanity of the film. In the stage musical, Lucy is used for comedy. In the film, the situation of this unattractive girl who stands outside the group with no possibility of ever really finding the love she so desires, is treated sympathetically.

An interesting point that the film makes perhaps even more strongly than the play, is the inevitability of change. When Chip wants to see the sights in New York that he has been told about, he discovers that many of them are no longer there. The city is in constant change. Also, the three men are not aware of the change in women's roles in society that has taken place while they have been away at sea during the war. Hildy is a cab driver; Claire is a graduate student of anthropology; and Ivy works at night at Coney Island to pay for her dance instruction. These women are aggressive, knowledgable, and responsible.

The musical numbers in the film use every conceivable dance style from burlesque to classical ballet. The film is one of almost constant movement wonderfully integrated with the story, the characterizations, and the photography.

Today *On the Town* is considered a turning point in the history of the Hollywood musical. It was the first dance musical that moved dance, as well as the musical genre, out of the theatre and "captured it with and for film rather than on film" (Joseph Andrew Casper, *Stanley Donen*, p. 34). *On the Town* was the first film to abandon the chorus, to feature location shooting, and to use contemporary rhythms.

*****

F05 *SINGIN' IN THE RAIN*

(Metro-Goldwyn-Mayer; 1952; 103 minutes; color;
Video: Metro-Goldwyn-Mayer-United Artists)

Credits
Suggested by the song, "Singin' in the Rain," lyrics by Arthur Freed and music by Nacio Herb Brown

Story and Screenplay	Betty Comden
	Adolph Green
Music	Nacio Herb Brown
Lyrics	Arthur Freed
Directors	Gene Kelly
	Stanley Donen
Musical Director	Lennie Hayton
Orchestrations	Conrad Salinger
	Wally Heglin
	Skip Martin
Vocal Arrangements	Jeff Alexander
	(Roger Edens)
Musical Numbers Directors	Gene Kelly
	Stanley Donen
Assistants	Carol Haney
	Jeanne Coyne

Art Directors	Cedric Gibbons
	Randall Duell
Set Decorations	Edwin B. Willis
	Jacques Mapes
Costume Design	Walter Plunkett
Hair Styles	Sydney Guilaroff
Make-up	William Tuttle
Director of Photography	Harold Rosson
Color	Technicolor
Color Consultants	Henri Jaffa
	James Gooch
Special Effects	Warren Newcombe
	Irving G. Ries
Recording Supervisor	Douglas Shearer
Film Editor	Adrienne Fazan
Producer	Arthur Freed
Associate Producer	Roger Edens

Cast

Don Lockwood	Gene Kelly
Cosmo Brown	Donald O'Connor
Kathy Selden	Debbie Reynolds
Lina Lamont	Jean Hagen
R. F. Simpson	Millard Mitchell
Zelda Zanders	Rita Moreno
Roscoe Dexter	Douglas Fowley
Dancer	Cyd Charisse
Dora Bailey	Madge Blake
Rod	King Donovan
Phoebe Dinsmore	Kathleen Freeman
"Beautiful Girl" Singer	Jimmie Thompson
Girl Dancers	Patricia Denise
	Jeanne Coyne
Male Dancing Quartet:	Bill Chatham, Ernest Flatt, Don Hulbert, Robert Dayo
Kid	David Kasday
Man in Talking Motion Picture	Julius Tannen

Synopsis

The place is Hollywood and the time is 1927 at the peak of the silent movie era and just before the introduction of sound into the films. *Singin' in the Rain* opens outside of Grauman's Chinese Theatre with the grand premiere of a new silent movie called *The Royal Rascal*. The new film features those popular stars, Don Lockwood and Lina Lamont. Dora Bailey, a Hollywood gossip columnist, is gushing into a microphone describing each celebrity as he arrives. The police are holding back the adoring fans gathered to see their idols of the silent screen. The excitement peaks as the glamorous Lina Lamont and her co-star Don Lockwood get out of their limousine and walk toward the theatre. Dora Bailey stops them and asks Don to tell of his early life before his movie fame. Don tells of his childhood and youth with his good friend Cosmo Brown. As he describes his idealistic early childhood we see his life as it really was. Then as he describes his rigorous early training we see Don and Cosmo playing at an amateur hour contest and performing in a crude burlesque house. The two young men come to Hollywood where they are at last hired to play mood music for a film. Don volunteers to act as a stunt man, and finally comes to the attention of Mr. Simpson, the producer.

After Don's recitation about his background, we go inside the theatre to see the silent movie, *The Royal Rascal*. The time of the film is the period of the French Revolution. Don does many heroic deeds and then is united with the beautiful Lina. The film ends to much applause, and Don and Lina take bows in front of the curtain. Don does all of the talking before the audience. As they go backstage, Lina complains because Don would not let her talk. This is the first time that we have heard the terrible voice that comes from the lovely Lina.

As Don and Cosmo are driving to the cast party that night, they have a flat tire. When Don gets out of the car he is mobbed by young fans. He escapes by jumping onto a moving trolley car and then jumping into an open car driven by Kathy Seldon. Kathy does not recognize the film star, and when she learns that he is in the movies she is not impressed. She is going to be a real actress and not just a shadow on a screen. She drives Don by his house so he can change his torn clothes. She drives on to the party at Mr. Simpson's mansion.

When Don arrives at the party his confidence has been shaken by Kathy's remark that a movie actor is only a shadow and not flesh and blood. Mr. Simpson shows the cast a new invention that has just been developed--talking pictures. The cast laughs and says it is just a toy. Mr. Simpson says another company has made a talking picture called *The Jazz Singer*, but they are all convinced that such a picture will fail. Part of the entertainment for the evening is a large cake out of which jumps Kathy Seldon. She is one of the dancers sent by the Coconut Grove to sing and dance for the party. They sing "All I Do Is Dream of You." Lina catches Don talking with Kathy, and, since she thinks Don is her private property, she is angry. Don mockingly calls Kathy a "real" actress from the legitimate stage and Kathy throws a cake at him. He ducks and Lina gets the cake in her face. As Kathy runs out, Don tries to follow her, but she gets away.

The next scene takes place inside a giant silent movie studio. Several films are being shot at once. Cosmo has read in *Variety* that *The Jazz Singer* has been a great success. Don is very depressed because he cannot find Kathy and feels partly responsible for her having lost her job at the Coconut Grove. In order to try to cheer him up. Cosmo sings and dances a mad comedy number called "Make 'Em Laugh."

While Don is filming a love scene with Lina in his new picture, Mr. Simpson suddenly stops the filming. They are closing for a few weeks, he says, while they prepare to add sound to the film. The success of *The Jazz Singer* has forced all movies to become "talkies." In the meantime Kathy has found a job with the film company dancing and singing in an elaborate number called "Beautiful Girl." She comes to the attention of Mr. Simpson, who hires her for a speaking role just as Don comes to the set. Don wants to tell Kathy that he loves her, but he needs a romantic setting. He pulls her into an empty studio and turns on lights for moonlight and a fan for an evening breeze. He sings "You Were Meant for Me."

All of the silent film actors must now learn to speak. A diction coach, Phoebe Dinsmore, is trying to get Lina to make "round tones," but Lina cannot hear her own flat nasal voice. Another diction coach is working with Don. He is having Don repeat tongue twisters. One of these is "Moses supposes his toeses are roses, but Moses supposes erroneously." Cosmos has dropped by, and he and Don cannot resist singing and dancing to this absurd sentence.

A few weeks later Lina and Don are trying to film their love scene from *The Dueling Cavalier* for the first time with sound. Lina cannot be heard because she cannot remember to speak into the microphone which is hidden in a bush. The microphone is then put into a large corsage pinned to the front of Lina's dress. This time the microphone picks up her heart beat. Another try is made by pinning the corsage on the shoulder of Lina's dress. As the scene is being recorded, Mr. Simpson comes into the studio. He nearly trips on the microphone cord, and angrily he jerks the cord pulling Lina over backwards.

At the preview of the new "talking picture," we see the love scene as it was recorded. Everything has gone wrong. Only part of Lina's words are heard because she had moved her head from side to side. Don, rather than memorizing the flowery words of the script, has fallen back on his silent film technique of repeating "I love you, I love you, I love you." Then the sound and the picture go out of synchronization, and the audience laughs hysterically.

Later that night, Don, Cosmo, and Kathy have been having dinner at Don's house. Don says that his career is finished. Cosmo decides that Don should do a musical. *The Dueling Cavalier* should be made with music. He also has the idea that Kathy should speak and sing for Lina, whose voice has not improved, in spite of her speech lessons. Feeling much better, Don sees Kathy home. As he starts home himself, he dismisses the cab and dances in the rain, singing "Singin' in the Rain," expressing his exuberant feelings about being in love and solving his career problem as well.

At Simpson's office the next morning, Don and Cosmo present their idea to Mr. Simpson. He likes it, and they decide on the title *The Dancing Cavalier*. The filming begins. Kathy records her voice to be synchronized with Lina's lip movements. As the filming nears its end, Don describes to Mr. Simpson how the opening scenes (the only ones not yet filmed) will be. The film will begin in the present with a young actor arriving in New York. As he describes it, we see the opening numbers, "Broadway Melody" and "Broadway Rhythm," and a dance number by Don and a long-legged, sexy dancer (Cyd Charisse).

Lina has discovered that Kathy's voice is being used for hers and is very angry. She calls the newspapers and quotes Mr. Simpson as saying that Lina Lamont is the "greatest singing and dancing star" in films. When Simpson objects she reminds him that her contract says she has control over her publicity. She insists that Kathy go on being her voice but not be given a role in any picture.

At the premiere, *The Dancing Cavalier* is a big success, and the crowd calls for Don and Lina. This time Lina insists on talking, and the audience is confused when her voice does not match that in the film. They ask her to sing. She is terrified and insists that Kathy sing behind the curtain while she mouths the words. While she is miming the words, Cosmo, Don, and Mr. Simpson pull up the curtain to reveal Kathy. The audience laughs and Don announces that it was Kathy's voice used in the picture. He and Kathy sing "You Are My Lucky Star."

The Film's History

In May of 1950 Betty Comden and Adolph Green were urgently called to Hollywood by Metro-Goldwyn-Mayer to write an original story and screenplay. They were to work once again under the producer, Arthur Freed. After arriving in Hollywood they were informed by Mr. Freed that he wanted them to write a story and screenplay that would use some of the songs from the many that had been written two decades before by himself and Nacio Herb Brown. Freed had written the words and Brown the music. The musical was to be called "*Singin' in the Rain*." At first Comden and Green balked at the assignment. They thought that their contract specified that they themselves would write the lyrics for their own stories. However, in re-reading their contract they discovered that it did not state who would write the lyrics. Reluctantly, they began to listen to and to sing some of the songs. They discovered that many of the songs had been very popular--"Broadway Melody," "Broadway Rhythm," "You Were Meant for Me," and, of course, "Singin' in the Rain."

The problem Comden and Green faced was coming up with a story into which the songs could be integrated. Their first important decision was to write a story that took place at the time when the songs were originally written. Freed and Brown had written many of the songs for the earliest musical pictures between 1929 and 1931. Comden and Green felt very comfortable with that period because they were both amateur authorities on the silent films and the early talkies. They knew many stories of famous silent screen stars whose careers were wrecked when their voices did not match their images on the screen. Since they wanted their hero to survive the advent of talking pictures, they decided that they had better present him as someone who had had song and dance experience in vaudeville. Of course they wanted Gene Kelly, with whom they had worked in *On the Town*. But Kelly was involved in acting in *An American in Paris* and was in great demand.

At last Comden and Green's ideas began to mesh, and by the time they had finished the script, Kelly had finished filming *An American in Paris*. He liked the script, and he and his friend, Stanley Donen, agreed to direct. Gene Kelly and Stanley Donen worked very well with Comden and Green, going over the script with them for changes and re-writes. Comden and Green contributed one song to the musical, the clever "Moses Supposes" sung and danced by Kelly and Donald O'Connor.

Rehearsals started on April 12, 1951, and production started on June 18 and closed on November 21. *Singin' in the Rain* was previewed at the DeAnza Theatre, Riverside, on December 21 and at the Loew's 72nd Street Theatre in New York on March 11, 1952. It opened at the Radio City Music Hall on March 27, 1952. The picture cost $2,540,800. The original sound track was released on record by Metro-Goldwyn-Mayer. (See D32.)

The film won for Comden and Green the Screenwriters Guild Award. After a successful re-opening at Radio City Music Hall in 1975, the film has made the Best Ten List in a number of film publications. The American Film Institute voted *Singin' in the Rain* one of the best American films of all time. *Sight and Sound* magazine and other film magazines have named the film one of the ten best films, including international films. Neil Sinyard, in his recent book, *Classic Movies*, writes that a recent poll of international film critics voted *Singin' in the Rain* the third best film ever made (p. 51).

Reviews

After the opening of *Singin' in the Rain* at Radio City Music Hall on March 27, 1952, Bosley Crowther of the *New York Times* wrote: "Compounded generously of music, dance, color, spectacle, a riotous abundance of Gene Kelly, Jean Hagen, and Donald O'Connor on the screen, all elements in this rainbow program are carefully contrived and guaranteed to lift the dolors of winter and put you in a buttercup mood." Though he notes that there is little plot and the title has nothing to do with the story, Mr. Crowther says that that does not matter "for the nonsense is generally good and at times it reaches the level of first-class satiric burlesque." He gives as an example, the scene in which Lina Lamont is making her first acquaintance with the hidden microphone. "No funnier lampoon of film-making has yet swum within our ken than this brief but side-splitting revelation of the battle with the machine. And some of the musical numbers that kid the old musical clichés, such as fashion parades and pin-wheel chorus groups, are as mischievous as they come" (March 28, 1952).

The critic for *Variety* wrote that the musical "has pace, humor, and good spirits-a-plenty, in a breezy, good-natured spoof of the film industry itself." He commented that the film has more humor than in the usual musical, "mostly low comedy of high grade." "There's plenty of satire, but the slap-stick element predominates," he wrote (March 12, 1952, p. 6.).

The reviewer for *The Saturday Review of Literature* called *Singin' in the Rain* "a big, bouncy Technicolored show that has just about everything you could ask of a musical." "Its story, by Adolph Green and Betty Comden, is a sturdy and delightful spoof of the early talkies," he writes (April 12, 1952, p. 42).

Some of the critics were not so enthusiastic. The reviewer for *Newsweek* wrote that this time Gene Kelly "is handicapped by a sluggish yarn about a famous pair of screen lovers." "The only times the authors live up to expectations are when they compound broad slapstick with an occasional satiric nudge in the Hollywood ribs" (April 7, 1952). The critic for *Time* wrote that "the wordy book ... is a rather strenuous satire, without much warmth or wit" (April 21, 1952, p. 108).

Commentary

Singin' in the Rain has become a movie classic. It has often been called Hollywood's most enjoyable musical. It is also one of the most optimistic and charming. The film actually has little plot, and some of the musical numbers and dances have been inserted without any real connection with the story. However, those songs and dances are so lively and so wonderfully executed that we don't mind their lack of integration. Gene Kelly's solo dance on a rainy street singing the title number is often considered his best work. It is a spontaneous expression of happiness. The joy of being in love and also the thought that the movie can be saved makes his character, Don Lockwood, want to play and dance and sing like a child. Like a little boy he splashes in puddles and stands under a broken drainpipe letting the water pour over him. The dance is exhilarating and unpretentious. The camera movement and angling add to the fluidity of the number.

The big production number, the ballet "Broadway Melody-Broadway Rhythm," is one of the musical numbers inserted into the story with very little reason. Don Lockwood is describing the opening of the new film to the producer. His description dissolves into the dance showing the young hoofer's arrival in New York, his meeting with a femme fatale, his rise to fame, his meeting once again with the gambler's moll and her rejection of him. This fifteen minute number, though beautifully executed and photographed, is an interruption to the main story line of the film.

Comden and Green had started out as satirists in their first original scripts for The Revuers. In writing the screenplay for *Singin' in the Rain* they were in their element. The satire of the era is very funny--the posing, glamorous movie vamp, the gushing Hollywood gossip columnist, the fans so eager to see and worship those "shadows" of the silent screen, the diction teachers brought out from New York wanting to cash in on the new "talkies." Comden and Green's script reflects a real knowledge and an affection for the era it is satirizing. The memory of the giddy times in early Hollywood is a happy one for the collaborators, tinged with a yearning to return to and relive those earlier years. The production team carefully studied old photographs to recreate accurately the silent screen era. The clever, humorous script, the detail of the lavish production, the excellent cast, and the cheerful songs of Freed and Brown, all contribute to the enduring popularity of *Singin' in the Rain*.

*****

F06 *THE BAND WAGON*

Metro-Goldwyn-Mayer; 1953; 112 minutes; color;
Video: Metro-Goldwyn Mayer-United Artists)

Credits

Story and Screenplay	Betty Comden
	Adolph Green
Songs	Howard Dietz
	Arthur Schwartz
Director	Vincente Minnelli
Assistant Director	Jerry Thorpe
Musical Director	Adolph Deutsch
Orchestrations	Conrad Salinger
	Skip Martin
	Alexander Courage
Staging of Dances and Musical Numbers	Michael Kidd
Art Directors	Cedric Gibbons
	Preston Ames
Set Decorations	Edwin B. Willis
	Keogh Gleason
Design for Musical Numbers	Oliver Smith
Costumes	Mary Ann Nyberg
Hair Styles	Sydney Guilaroff
Make-up	William Tuttle
Director of Photography	Harry Jackson
Color	Technicolor
Color Consultants	Henri Jaffa
	Robert Brower
Special Effects	Warren Newcombe
Recording Supervisor	Douglas Shearer
Film Editor	Albert Akst
Producer	Arthur Freed
Associate Producer	Roger Edens

Cast

Tony Hunter	Fred Astaire
Gabrielle Gerard	Cyd Charisse

172 Comden and Green

Lester Marton	Oscar Levant
Lily Marton	Nanette Fabray
Jeffrey Cordova	Jack Buchanan
Paul Byrd	James Mitchell
Hal Benton	Robert Gist
Col. Tripp	Thurston Hall
Guest Star	Ava Gardner
Shoe Shine Boy	LeRoy Daniels
Troupe Members	Dee Trunell
	Jimmie Thompson
Girls in "Private Eye" Number	Dee Hartford
	Eden Hartford
	Julie Newmar
Man	Steve Forrest
Gushy Woman	Madge Blake
Tall Woman in Penny Arcade	Sue Casey
Specialty Dancer	Matt Mattox

Synopsis

The Band Wagon opens with an auction. Among the belongings of famous people to be auctioned are the hat and cane of Tony Hunter, a dancer whose popularity has now declined. In fact, no one at the auction will even make a bid on the hat and cane. In the next scene we see Tony Hunter on a train to New York. He has been asked by his friends, Lily and Lester Marton, to star in a light Broadway musical they have written for him. No one recognizes him on the train, and when he gets to New York there are photographers waiting to take pictures of Ava Gardner who has been on the train. The photographers recognize Tony but they don't take any pictures of him. He is feeling very much alone and sings "By Myself" as he goes into the train station. Then he hears someone call "Tony," and, looking around, he sees his zany friends, Lily and Lester Marton. They are carrying signs reading "The Tony Hunter Fan Club." The Martons are excited because they have just discovered that Jeffrey Cordova is going to direct their show. Tony has never heard of Jeffrey Cordova. They assure him that Jeffrey can do anything. He has directed and is starring in *Oedipus Rex* right now, and they are to meet with him tonight after the show. Tony wonders if he can direct a musical. Tony tells his friends to go on to dinner. He will meet them later. He wants to look around the old theatre district where he had played years before. He discovers that the New Amsterdam Theatre has become a cheap "grind" house, and Broadway has become a place for pinball machines and other forms of cheap entertainment. He is very depressed. He knows that one way to beat his depression is to get a "Shine on Your Shoes." He sings and dances this number, assisted by a shoe shine man.

After the Martons and Tony see *Oedipus Rex*, they go backstage to talk with Jeffrey Cordova. The Martons tell him the outline of their new script. Without reading the script, Jeffrey decides he would like to make it into a modern day Faust story. He himself will play the devil, he says. Tony tries to back out, saying he is a musical comedy actor. Jeffrey tells him whether it is Bill Shakespeare or Bill "Bojangles" Robinson, it is all entertainment. The four, Tony, Jeffrey, Lily, and Lester, sing "That's Entertainment."

As plans for the show begin, Jeffrey decides he wants the famous Gabrielle Gerard, a ballet dancer, to be the female star. In order to get her, he asks her boy friend, Paul Byrd, to do the choreography. Gabrielle and Paul have never done musical comedy. Tony, on the other hand, though he agrees that Gabrielle is "magnificent," says she is too tall for him. Besides, he cannot do ballet. When Gabrielle meets Tony she knows that he does not want her as his partner, and she thinks he is too old anyway. All protestations are swept away by Jeffrey.

Rehearsals for the show are begun. Tony finds that his dance numbers are being cut, and he feels that Gabrielle and Paul look down on him as just a song and dance man. He decides to leave the show. Gabrielle comes to Tony's apartment to apologize for the way she has been treating him. She starts to cry. Tony says they need to find out if they can dance together. They go to Central Park, where, in a quiet spot all by themselves, they begin to take a few tentative dance steps to the tune of "Dancing in the Dark." Gradually, they begin to move together. When they stop they both feel fulfilled as they realize that they can dance together.

The technical rehearsals for the show are a disaster. The complicated scenery and the magical effects overwhelm the play. The show, called *The Band Wagon*, opens out of town in New Haven. An excited New York crowd comes for the opening. At the end of the show, they leave, dejected. The show has been a complete failure. The chorus members gather in one of the hotel rooms. They are sad. Tony joins them. Then Gabrielle, and then the Martons. Suddenly, Tony says it is a shame to waste all of this talent. Lester and Lily get the idea to change the show and fill it with entertainment. Tony decides that he will direct the show. Even Jeffrey agrees to be in the new show. As the show moves from city to city, new acts and new musical and dance numbers are added. Gabrielle sings "New Sun in the Sky." Tony and Jeffrey do a top hat and cane dance, "I Guess I'll Have to Change My Plans," Lily Marton and the chorus sing "Louisiana Hayride," and Tony, Lily, and Jeff do "Triplets," a novelty number in which they are dressed in identical baby clothes. As the show travels from place to place, Tony realizes he is in love with Gabrielle.

At last the train brings them back to New York for the opening night there. On opening night we see their final number, a long ballet called "The Girl Hunt Ballet, A Murder Mystery in Jazz."

The show is a success in New York, but Tony is disappointed that no one has come back stage to see him after the show. He sings "By Myself" as he prepares to leave the theatre alone. When he leaves his dressing room, he discovers that the entire cast is waiting for him on the stage. Gabrielle tells him that they all want to thank him and that they have come to love him. She kisses him, and Tony is no longer alone.

The Film's History

The Band Wagon, presented on Broadway in 1931, contained one of the best scores ever written for a revue. The music was by Arthur Schwartz with lyrics by Howard Dietz. Among the songs in the show were "New Sun in the Sky," "I Love Louisa," and "Dancing in the Dark," all of which were to be used later in the film. *The Band Wagon*, the revue, starred Fred and Adele Astaire. It was Adele Astaire's last Broadway show. She left show business for marriage. Fred Astaire went on to do *The Gay Divorce* on Broadway and then went to Hollywood where he took a small role in the Joan Crawford, Clark Gable film, *Dancing Lady*, and then began the series of nine films that he did for RKO with Ginger Rogers. He was reunited with Rogers ten years later in Metro-Goldwyn-Mayer's *The Barkleys of Broadway* with the screenplay written by Betty Comden and Adolph Green, and then in 1948 he did *Easter Parade* for Metro-Goldwyn-Mayer.

Arthur Freed's recent successes with *An American in Paris* and *Singin' in the Rain* made him decide to acquire another song catalogue as the basis for a new musical film. By this time Howard Dietz was vice-president of Loew's, Inc. and a friend of Freed. Freed had frequently told Dietz that some day he would do a picture that would include his songs. He took *I Love Louisa* as the title for his new musical. He called in Vincente Minnelli, Betty Comden, Adolph Green, Roger Edens, Fred Astaire, Michael Kidd, a dancer and choreographer, and Oliver Smith, the Broadway scene designer and producer, and told them to use Schwartz and Dietz's songs and come up with a "terrific picture."

In February 1952 Comden and Green arrived at the studio to begin work on their original story and screenplay. After several agonizing weeks, they came up with a vague idea for a character much like Astaire himself. Then, in looking through the Schwartz-Dietz scores again, they came upon a song, "By Myself," from a 1937 book show called *Between the Devil*. They at once envisioned Astaire singing it as he walked up the ramp at Grand Central Station, returning from Hollywood to New York. This made Adolph Green remember when he returned to New York after a very unsuccessful first visit to Hollywood. He was, as he wrote, "an unemployed nightclub performer, broke, discouraged, and conspicuously unknown," carrying a heavy suitcase off the train. Suddenly, he saw Betty Comden carrying a large banner reading "The Adolph Green Fan Club" (Adolph Green, "The Magic of Fred Astaire," *American Film*, April 1981, p. 38). This scene Comden and Green were to use in the film as well as the song, "By Myself." Working with Freed, the director Vincente Minnelli, and Astaire himself, Comden and Green were able to come up with the story for the film--a story that is a part of the creative lives of all of them. The roles of Lily and Lester Marton, the writing team of *The Band Wagon*, are probably based upon Comden and Green themselves. The role of the director, Jeffrey Cordova, is based partly on José Ferrer who was at the time both directing and playing on Broadway. There is also a little bit of Orson Welles in the character. Comden and Green wanted to put into the film as much as they could of what really happens while putting on a musical. They based the story on some of their own experiences.

Comden and Green and Roger Edens made the final selection of the songs to be used in the picture. They came from six of Schwartz and Dietz's Broadway shows: *Three's a Crowd* (1923), *The Little Show* (1929), *The Band Wagon* (1931), *Flying Colors* (1932), *At Home Abroad* (1935), and *Between the Devil* (1937). Schwartz and Dietz also wrote an original song for the film, "That's Entertainment." Freed was not happy with the title, *I Love Louisa*, and wanted to change it to *The Band Wagon*. That title belonged to Twentieth Century-Fox who had acquired the rights to the Broadway revue, so Freed had to buy the rights to the title from the other film company.

Rehearsals for *The Band Wagon* started in April 1952 and production started in September. The film was finished on January 28, 1953. The final cost was $2,169,120. The picture was shown at Radio City Music Hall on July 9, 1953. *The Band Wagon* received an Academy Award nomination. The sound track of the film was released on record by Metro-Goldwyn-Mayer. (See DO3.)

Reviews

Bosley Crowther of the *New York Times* wrote of *The Band Wagon*: "That wonderful talent for satire which Betty Comden and Adolph Green possess and which was gleefully turned upon the movies in their script for last year's *Singin' in the Rain* is even more gleefully let loose upon the present-day musical stage in their book for Metro's *The Band Wagon*." He goes on to say that the script, combined with the talents of Fred Astaire, Jack Buchanan, and Cyd Charisse and the music of Schwartz and Dietz "delivers a show that respectfully bids for recognition as one of the best musical films ever made." "Take it from us," he writes, "it is a honey--a genial and comprehending snipe at the rampant egos of theatre people, their reckless excursions and alarums and all of the manifold headaches that accompany the production of a show. It is also, by chance, a very touching appreciation of the nature of Mr. Astaire" (July 9, 1953).

The critic for *Variety* called the film "a sure b.o. winner." "The musical numbers have been put together with the eye-catching lavishness expected of the MGM label," he wrote (July 8, 1953, p. 6).

The reviewer for *Newsweek* wrote that *The Band Wagon* "has a brisk and funny original script by Betty Comden and Adolph Green, and no connection with the old Broadway revue." "The whole production," he continues, "is rich with Technicolor and moves with sophisticated élan under the direction of Vincente Minnelli." He calls Astaire "a performer of incomparable stylistic finesse" (July 6, 1953, p. 48).

The reviewer for *The Saturday Review of Literature* also compliments Astaire, who, he writes, "gives the impression that he dances out of delight in pure movement, out of sheer love for music and for life." "A new story line by Betty Comden and Adolph Green has been added which turns it into a curiously personalized Astaire saga" (July 25, 1953, p. 28).

Jesse Zunser of *Cue* writes: "The picture's backstage story ... has been given a neat plot twist and reels of fresh ideas, brilliant production numbers, and original songs and dances." "*The Band Wagon*," he writes, "bounces along at a great rate--overflowing with mirth, melody and good humor" (July 11, 1953, p. 15). The reviewer for *Fortnight* was not so pleased. He called the story "weak but sometimes amusing" and the picture "worthwhile as a chance to renew acquaintance with Astaire, but a disappointment in general" (August 17, 1953, p. 30).

Commentary

Though *The Band Wagon* has a happy ending, it is really about loneliness and failure and the passing of time, unlikely themes for a Hollywood musical. It is in many ways a story about Fred Astaire himself and presented him with one of the most challenging roles of his career. Astaire was fifty-four, a man who had had a long and successful career, but who was now past his greatest popularity and old enough to be considering retirement or a new venture in his life. Betty Comden and Adolph Green were nervous about telling Astaire of the character they had created for the film, but Astaire liked the character of Tony Hunter immediately. Comden and Green built into the story many details that had to do with Astaire as well as Tony Hunter. For example, Astaire was of medium height and was concerned about dancing with Cyd Charisse, who was nearly as tall as he. Good humor is made of this in the film. Also, the age difference between Astaire and Charisse is written into the script. The story and the characters are ably developed in the songs and dances. In the story, Tony Hunter, alone and unnoticed by the reporters and photographers, quietly sings "By Myself" as he walks down the train platform in New York, thus assuring himself that he can face whatever is in store for him. He continues to cheer himself up by singing and dancing "Shine on Your Shoes." Later in the story the conflict between Tony, a song and dance man, and Gabrielle, a classically trained ballerina, is resolved in a dance.

Of the musical numbers added to the new show as it develops, one of the best is "I Guess I'll Have to Change My Plans," a simple and relaxed soft shoe routine danced by Astaire and the British actor, Jack Buchanan. The outstanding novelty number is "Triplets," a song and dance by Astaire, Buchanan, and Nanette Fabray dressed in identical baby clothes. False baby legs were attached to the actors' knees, and the triplets seemed to dance on their little baby feet. Nearly every Metro-Goldwyn-Mayer musical of the 1950s had a big ballet number near the end of the film. In *The Band Wagon* it was "The Girl Hunt Ballet, A Murder Mystery in Jazz," which parodies not only the elaborate ballets but also the Mickey Spillane thrillers that were so popular. Astaire plays Rod Riley, a hard-boiled detective, who encounters both a beautiful blonde and a curvaceous brunette, both women danced by Cyd Charisse. The long ballet is a very clever satire and is excellently danced and choreographed. It makes an exciting climax to the show within the film and to the film itself.

In *Singin' in the Rain* Betty Comden and Adolph Green had lovingly satirized the film industry. In *The Band Wagon* they satirize the New York professional theatre--the egocentric director, the temperamental stars, the elaborate scenery and stage effects, and even themselves as playwrights. Here again the satire is good-hearted and affectionate.

The Band Wagon is a stylish and elegant film, full of wit, satire, and outstanding musical numbers. The excellent cast, the direction of Vincente Minnelli, and the choreography of Michael Kidd combine to make the picture one of the best of its genre.

*****

F07   *IT'S ALWAYS FAIR WEATHER*

(Metro-Goldwyn-Mayer; 1955; 101 minutes; color;
Video: Metro-Goldwyn-Mayer-United Artists)

Credits
Story and Screenplay	Betty Comden
	Adolph Green
Music	André Previn
Lyrics	Betty Comden
	Adolph Green
Directors	Gene Kelly
	Stanley Donen
Assistant Director	Al Jennings
Music Arrangement, Conductor	André Previn
Vocal Supervision	Robert Tucker
	Jeff Alexander
Dances and Musical Numbers	Gene Kelly

	Stanley Donen
Art Directors	Cedric Gibbons
	Arthur Lonergan
Set Decorations	Edwin B. Willis
	Hugh Hunt
Costumes	Helen Rose
Hair Styles	Sydney Guilaroff
Make-up	William Tuttle
Director of Photography	Robert Bronner
Color	Eastman
Color Consultant	Alvord Eiseman
Special Effects	Warren Newcombe
	Irving G. Ries
Recording Supervisor	Wesley C. Miller
Film Editor	Adrienne Fazan
Producer	Arthur Freed

Cast

Ted Riley	Gene Kelly
Doug Hallerton	Dan Dailey
Jackie Leighton	Cyd Charisse
Madeline Bradbille	Dolores Gray
Angie Valentine	Michael Kidd
Tim	David Burns
Charles Z. Culloran	Jay C. Flippen
Kid Mariacchi	Steve Mitchell
Rocky Heldon	Hal March
Mr. Fielding	Paul Maxey
Mr. Trasker	Peter Leeds
Mr. Stamper	Alex Gerry
Mrs. Stamper	Madge Blake
Roy, TV Director	Wilson Wood
Mr. Grigman	Richard Simmons
Lady	Almira Sessions
Chef	Eugene Borden

Synopsis

Three G. I. buddies march happily out of the army at the end of World War II. They go to a favorite little bar in New York to have a farewell drink. There, one of the men, Ted Riley, finds a letter waiting for him. It is from his girl, who writes that while he has been overseas she has married. Ted is disconsolate and begins to drink. He goes from bar to bar followed by his two friends, Doug Hallerton and Angie Valentine. Late into the night they drink, and then they dance madly in the deserted streets, at one time each with one foot inserted into the handle of a garbage can lid. Eventually, they end up at the first bar, where it suddenly dawns on them that they must part. They swear eternal friendship and resolve to meet again at 12:00 o'clock the same day, October 11, in ten years, 1955, at the same bar. They tear a dollar bill into three pieces, each taking one piece. Then they go their separate ways.

In time collages we see how the ten years pass for each of the men. Angie gets married and has four children. He had always wanted to manage a very nice restaurant, but has had to be content with a hamburger joint. Doug had wanted to be a painter, but he gets married and climbs up in the world of commercial advertising. Ted, who had intended to go to law school, drinks and gambles and at last becomes a small time boxing manager. On the day his boxer is scheduled for a big fight, Ted sees the one-third of a dollar bill in his billfold and realizes that this is the day when his army friends had agreed to meet in 1955. He doubts that the other men will be there, but he decides to go to the bar.

Doug Hallerton is the first to arrive at the bar. He has flown in from Chicago. He looks old and tired. He calls his wife who is threatening to divorce him. Angie and Ted arrive, and, after a jubilant greeting, the three men have a drink at the bar. After the drink the men find that they have little to talk about. Doug takes them to a fancy restaurant, where their uncomfortable feelings with each other continue. As the camera zooms in on each man, he sings, unheard by the others, "I shouldn't have come," "I'd like to get lost," or "This thing's a bad dream," to the music of "The Blue Danube" being played softly in the background. Ted is distracted by a beautiful brunette who is sitting at the next table. Suddenly, the brunette sees her boss, Mr. Fielding, and rushes to him to talk about the television show that is to be broadcast today. Fielding recognizes Doug as one of the men from their Chicago advertising office. He introduces Doug and his friends to the brunette, Jackie Leighton, who is a television production coordinator. Mr. Fielding invites the men to come see the rehearsal for the television show. Ted, attracted to the beautiful Jackie, cleverly manages to ride with her in a cab to the television station. When he starts to put his arm around her, he is surprised to find himself suddenly grabbed and kissed. Jackie says that she has discovered that is a good way to get rid of amorous men. She says she scares men off by her intelligence, and to prove it she recites some scientific information and a quotation from Shakespeare. Ted asks her if she has ever heard of Kid Mariacchi, his boxer. She reels off statistics about the fighter. Ted invites her to visit the gym where his boxer will be training later in the afternoon.

At the television rehearsal for *Midnight with Madeline*, the hostess, Madeline, discovers that the guest for the show cannot come and she rejects the substitute who has been provided. She wants something that will be more emotional for her viewers. Jackie suggests the three men who have been having their ten year reunion. Madeline agrees and someone is assigned to each of the men to be sure he is there. The gimmick of the show is that the guest to be featured is picked out of the audience and does not know that he is to be chosen. Jackie is assigned to bring Ted.

Jackie goes to Stillman's, the gym where the fighters train, to find Ted. The fighters and the trainers are much impressed with the curvaceous Jackie. They sing "Stillman's Gym," a song very much like a college alma mater song, and Jackie joins them in a strenuous song and dance called "Baby, You Knock Me Out." When Ted arrives at the gym, he tells Jackie he has discovered that the big boss of organized crime, Charles Z. Culloran, has paid off his boxer to lose the fight. Jackie innocently asks if he has reported this to the boxing commission. This question begins to bother him because he has already changed his bets so he will not lose his money.

In the meantime, Fielding has invited Doug Hallerton to his home for dinner. Doug has been drinking steadily. He feels so disgusted with himself and his field of business that he deliberately insults Fielding and makes fun of the double-talk of the television advertising executives in a song called "Situation Wise and Saturation Wise." He dances about the room until he passes out.

Jackie and Ted go to the television studio for Jackie to do some last minute checking on details. Here Jackie tells Ted that she thinks his tough guy act is because he was disappointed in love once and ever since has been taking it out on the world and himself. Ted tells her that she is the big business woman because she is inhibited and afraid to love someone. They both admit that the unasked-for psychological analysis is correct. While Jackie is changing her clothes for the broadcast, Ted is pursued by Culloran's henchmen. He runs into a skating rink, borrows the jacket and cap of the attendant, and joins the skaters while the henchmen search for him. When they are gone, he, still on his skates, looks outside in the street. He is so happy now that he has discovered that Jackie really cares for him that he begins to skate down the street, much to the amazement of passersby. In his joy he begins to tap dance on his skates, to the song, "I Like Myself."

That night, the three friends all show up for the television show. They watch as the hostess gushes over the audience, advertizes Kleenright soap, and sings a big production number, "Thanks a Lot, But No Thanks." Then the spotlights search out the three friends and they are escorted on stage. Madeline asks them about their reunion, and Ted tells her it has been a terrible experience. The three "friends" no longer even like each other. He now realizes that he dislikes the others because he dislikes himself. At this point Culloran and his thugs come in and threaten Ted. Jackie, seeing what is happening, tells the cameraman to focus on Ted. He cleverly gets the gang boss to say on camera that he and his men fixed the fight. When the gangsters are told that they have just confessed on television, they start to fight with Ted. Doug and Angie jump in to help their friend, and a free-for-all fight follows. At last the cops come and arrest the gangsters.

Ted, Doug, and Angie, now pals again, go to their favorite bar for a final drink. Doug calls his wife to tell her he knows they are going to make it. Angie is happy to go back to his hamburger joint. When Jackie joins them, Doug and Angie know that from now on all will be right for Ted.

The Film's History

While taking a train to the West Coast to work on one of their films, Betty and Adolph used the time to think of an idea for a new musical for Broadway. They thought about a reunion of the three sailors from *On the Town*. Then they thought of changing the men to three soldiers. In Hollywood, they mentioned the idea to Gene Kelly, who immediately wanted the idea for his next movie. He was eager to direct a film again with his co-director, Stanley Donen. Betty and Adolph outlined their story for Arthur Freed He liked the idea and Comden and Green began their screenplay. This time they were to write the lyrics for the film as well as the screenplay. Roger Edens, who had provided the music for the songs they had written for previous films, was not available. Freed suggested André Previn, who had done the accompaniment for the film, *Invitation to the Dance*. This would be Previn's first chance to compose songs for a film.

Gene Kelly wanted to use Frank Sinatra and Jules Munshin again. They had played the other two sailors in the film, *On the Town*. However, Frank Sinatra, who had just had a big dramatic success in *From Here to Eternity*, did not want to go back into musical comedy, and Munshin was not available. Choreographer Michael Kidd was under contract to Metro-Goldwyn-Mayer, and Stanley Donen was eager to use him as an actor-dancer. The dancer, Dan Dailey, was chosen as the third buddy. Gene Kelly now had two other dancers to work with. Dolores Gray, the actress and singer who had starred with Bert Lahr in the revue, *Two on the Aisle*, on Broadway, was cast as the television hostess, and Cyd Charisse was chosen as the love interest for Gene Kelly.

It's Always Fair Weather started production on October 13, 1954, and closed on March 15, 1955. The good humor and camaraderie that had existed during the filming of *On the Town* did not materialize for *It's Always Fair Weather*. Kelly and Donen, who had worked so brilliantly together, were not getting along. This was to be their last picture together. While the screenplay was being written, Arthur Freed was elected president of the Screen Producers Guild (later called the Producers Guild of America). He took his new job seriously and spent much of his time in this new position. His guiding hand was much missed during the filming. The final cost for the film was $2,062,256. It opened at Radio City Music Hall on September 15, 1955. Betty Comden and Adolph Green were nominated for both an Academy Award and a Screenwriters Guild Award for their screenplay. Metro-Goldwyn-Mayer released the original soundtrack on record. (See D17.) Betty Comden and Adolph Green also made a recording of some of the songs in the film. (See D18.)

Reviews

Bosley Crowther, writing in the *New York Times* after the Radio City Music Hall opening of *It's Always Fair Weather*, wrote that Comden and Green have now made amends to Metro-Goldwyn-Mayer for satirizing the film industry in *Singin' in the Rain*. He says that in *It's Always Fair Weather* they are "spoofing the whiskers off TV." He writes: "Howling with derision at such idiocies of TV as singing and slobbering commercials, audience-participation shows, give-away plugs for mundane products, and the wise-talking agency boys, Miss Comden and Mr. Green fling some pretty sharp barbs in this bright film." Crowther goes on to say: "Tightness and cinematic cohesion are not the clearest virtues of this show, which is bright in a panoply of color and large in Cinema-Scope. The authors have let it ramble, and producer Arthur Freed and the directors, Mr. Kelly and Stanley Donen, have not seen fit to discourage their whims ..." He concludes, however, that "it doesn't matter much that it rambles. So much and so many clever things are happening, one after another, that it consistently entertains." Mr. Crowther thought the film a "winner" (September 15, 1955).

The reviewer for *Variety* called *It's Always Fair Weather* "topnotch musical satire of television, advertising agencies, and commercials." "Kelly and Stanley Donen ... give the proceedings the right tongue-in-cheek touch for sock results," he wrote, and Betty Comden and Adolph Green "have provided a number of hilarious sketches that fit neatly into the framework of the story." "André Previn's music ... in combination with the Comden and Green lyrics, is geared perfectly for integration into the film." He picked out as particularly good the luncheon at the "swank" restaurant where each man's thoughts are revealed, Kelly's roller-skating number, Dan Dailey's drunk scene, and Charisse's dance with the "gym crowd" (August 24, 1955, p. 6).

The critic for *Time* called *It's Always Fair Weather* "a sunny example of a Hollywood rarity--a song-and-dance movie with enough plot to justify its dialogue and enough needling satire to make some points." He concluded: "For its superb dancing, inventive musical numbers, witty spoofery of TV's overstuffed brass and mawkish product-hawking of such goodies as H2O Cola, as well as its spirited jabs and gibes at Madison Square Garden's crooks and pug-ugly environs, *Fair Weather* rates as one of the top contenders for the year's light-weight title" (September 5, 1955, p. 80).

Leo Rogow, writing in *The Saturday Review of Literature*, commented on the wide Cinema-Scope screen which "has been used in these musical numbers with a flexibility and intimacy not before seen in the wide-screen musicals." "*It's Always Fair Weather* has its problems," he wrote, "but it does have clever lyrics, inventive numbers, and Gene Kelly on skates" (September 3, 1955, p. 20).

Commentary

Betty Comden and Adolph Green had touched on sadness in their screenplay for *The Band Wagon*. In *It's Always Fair Weather*, in spite of the humor and the satire, the theme is the disillusion of our youthful dreams as we meet the realities of life. The three young soldiers have great plans for the future when they get out of the army. After ten years, no one has lived up to his dreams. The reunion of the three men is a sad one. They no longer have anything in common, and they discover they do not even like each other. Ted thinks Doug is a snob and Angie is a hick. The joy they found in each other while in the army is no longer there. The transitoriness of time and the fragility of friendship is another disillusion to face.

Comden and Green had satirized the film industry in *Singin' in the Rain* and the legitimate theatre in *The Band Wagon*. In *It's Always Fair Weather* they take on television. In the 1950s television was becoming a real threat to the other forms of entertainment. Many people were content to sit at home glued to the tube in the living room. Comden and Green's satire is not so affectionate this time. It is much stronger and harsher. The role of the television hostess, Madeline, with her desire to be loved by her audience, is played with great exaggeration by Dolores Gray. The singing commercials and the take-off on Ralph Edwards' *This Is Your Life* program are very funny.

Comden and Green's satire of the corporate business world is also strong and culminates in a nonsense song, "Situation Wise and Saturation Wise" that makes savage fun of the conversations of these high level businessmen.

Gene Kelly and Stanley Donen's wonderful use of the wide Cinemascope screen gives the film a very special look. At the beginning of the film we have a spoof of military marches, "March, March," sung by an off-screen male chorus, while on the screen is a war montage produced by dissolves and superimpositions of infantry lines, trenches, flags, explosions, and V. J. Day celebrations. Out of the montage come the three soldiers. Later, the same melody is used behind a civilian montage in a triple-split frame that shows the passage of the ten years in the lives of the three protagonists.

The use of the triple-split screen is used again at the luncheon at the elegant restaurant and for a number called "Once Upon a Time." Here the three men are in different locations, but each is thinking of the lost friendship. Their movements are identical but each is in a different frame.

There are several outstanding dance numbers in the film. One is Jackie's dance when she joins the managers and boxers at Stillman's gym in "Baby, You Knock Me Out." The dance is part ballet, part modern jazz, and part gymnastics. Unfortunately, it is the only dance for Cyd Charisse in the film. The best dance of all is Kelly's dance on skates. He has forgotten to leave the skates at the rink. Thinking about the fixed fight but especially thinking about Jackie, he floats out onto the street and glides around the corner. The curious passersby who follow him make him realize he is on skates. Singing "Why do I feel so good?" he begins to tap dance on his skates. It is a joyous realization of his new-found love, and the dance is almost equal to his marvelous dance in the rain in *Singin' in the Rain*.

Most of the critics liked *It's Always Fair Weather*, but the public response was only lukewarm. This was Stanley Donen's last picture at Metro-Goldwyn-Mayer.

*****

F08　　　　　　　　　　*AUNTIE MAME*

(Warner Bros.; 1958; 143 minutes; color; Video: Warner Bros.)

Credits
Based on the novel, *Auntie Mame*, by Patrick Dennis and the play, *Auntie Mame*, by Jerome Lawrence and Robert E. Lee

Screenplay	Betty Comden
	Adolph Green
Musical Score	Bronslau Kaper
Director	Morton DaCosta
Musical Director	Ray Heindorf
Art Direction	Malcolm Bert
Set Decoration	George James Hopkins
Costumes	Orry-Kelly
Cinematography	Harry Stradling
Color	Technicolor
Film Editor	William Ziegler
Producer	Morton DaCosta for Warner Bros.

Cast

Mame Dennis	Rosalind Russell
Beauregard Burnside	Forrest Tucker
Vera Charles	Coral Browne
Mr. Babcock	Fred Clark
Patrick Dennis (older)	Roger Smith
Patrick Dennis (younger)	Jan Handzlik
Lindsay Woolsey	Patric Knowles
Agnes Gooch	Peggy Cass
Gloria Upson	Joanna Barnes
Michael Dennis	Terry Kelman
Pegeen Ryan	Pippa Scott
Mrs. Upson	Lee Patrick
Mr. Upson	Willard Waterman
Brian O'Bannion	Robin Hughes
Norah Muldoon	Connie Gilchrist
Ito	Yuki Shimoda
Sally Cato	Brook Byron
Mrs. Burnside	Carol Veazie
Acacuis Page	Henry Brandon

Synopsis

The date is 1928. *Auntie Mame* begins with the reading of the will of Mame Dennis's brother. Though he is in excellent health and thinks it will not be necessary, in the unlikely event that he should die while his son is still a child he wishes to leave the care of his son, Patrick, to his sister, Mame, with a Mr. Babcock of the bank to oversee the finances of his care. Shortly after, a newspaper reports that Michael Dennis has dropped dead, and Patrick, aged ten, is taken by Norah Muldoon, the nurse, to live with his Auntie Mame.

Norah Muldoon and Patrick arrive at Mame's elaborate New York City apartment while Mame is having one of her parties. Among those attending are Mame's best friend, Vera Charles, an actress, who, when she attends one of Mame's parties, always drinks until she passes out and thus must spend the night. Though she was not expecting the boy until the next day, Mame greets him effusively and introduces him to her eccentric friends.

The next afternoon, while Vera is still "sleeping it off" and Mame is not yet ready to receive company, Mr. Babcock from the Nickerbocker Bank calls on Mame to arrange about a school for the boy. He thinks that he has talked Mame into a nice conservative boys' school, but a few days later he discovers that Mame has sent Patrick to a school run by a friend of hers, a very "progressive" teacher. Mr. Babcock is horrified when he visits the school and discovers that the teachers, the boys, and the girls are all nude. He insists that Patrick be sent to a more conventional school.

Mame's extravagant life style is brought to a sudden halt with the stock market crash. Mame must go to work. Vera offers her a small role in her current play. Mame, who has only a few lines at the end of the play, tries to make something of her part. She dresses in her usual flamboyant style and wears bracelets that jingle so loudly that little else can be heard on stage. When she greets the leading character, played by Vera, her bracelet gets caught in Vera's dress. Since she can't disentangle the bracelet, Mame is forced to walk beside Vera throughout the end of the play and even for the curtain calls. The audience thinks it is hilarious, but Vera says Mame has ruined her play. Thus Mame's acting career comes to an end.

Mame's next job is as a switchboard operator in an office. The intricacies of the switchboard are beyond Mame, and she loses her job. Next she gets a job as a saleswoman at Macy's. She is all right as long as her orders are to be delivered C.O.D., but she does not know how to make out a sales slip if someone wants to pay cash. Beauregard Burnside, a wealthy man from the South, comes in to get twenty-one pairs of skates for the children of his town. When Mame's supervisor discovers that Mame cannot make out a sales slip for the order, he fires her, in spite of Beauregard Burnside's protests. Mame goes despondently back to her apartment where Patrick is trying to decorate for Christmas. Mame, Patrick, Norah, and Ito, the houseboy, are giving each other Christmas presents, when Beauregard Burnside comes to the apartment. He felt responsible for Mame's being dismissed and has been searching for her. He takes them all out for dinner and insists that Mame must visit him at his plantation.

When Mame and Patrick arrive at Beauregard's plantation, Mame has already equipped herself with a new wardrobe and a Southern accent. Beauregard's dour mother and his friends resent his interest in a "Northerner" and plot to have Mame ride a dangerous horse in a fox hunt scheduled for the next day. Mame keeps her seat on the horse during a wild ride and even brings back the fox alive. Her costume had stuck to the saddle and kept her on the horse.

Mame marries Beauregard, and they go off on a two year round-the-world tour. They visit, among other places, Egypt and Paris, and then they climb the Matterhorn. Everywhere they go, Beauregard takes pictures. On the Matterhorn he takes a misstep while taking Mame's picture and is killed. The widowed Mame visits and re-visits the tourist spots she and Beauregard had enjoyed.

Finally, Mame returns to her apartment in New York. She finds Vera and a publishing friend, Lindsey Woolsey, there to surprise her. They have decided that she should write a book about her life and have hired a secretary and a ghost writer to help her. Mame enthusiastically begins her book. The secretary, Agnes Gooch, is a very unattractive and dowdy girl. The ghost writer, Brian O'Bannion, is an Irish poet and freeloader. Soon they are both living in Mame's apartment. When O'Bannion gets amorous toward her, Mame transforms Agnes into a more glamorous-looking person and sends her off with O'Bannion to a party.

By this time Patrick is a college student and has fallen in love with a girl from Connecticut, Gloria Upson. Gloria is from a family who are really "top-drawer," as she says, but Mame sees that she is shallow and bigoted. Upon the Upsons' insistence, Mame visits them in Connecticut and finds out that they have Patrick's life planned for him. They want her to go in with them to buy the property next door to them for Patrick and Gloria. This will help keep the area "restricted" to the "right kind" of people. Mame does not want Patrick to marry into this family. She invites the Upsons to come to a party at her apartment in New York.

Agnes Gooch, after her one night out with Brian O'Bannion, is now pregnant and Brian is nowhere to be found. Mame has taken Agnes in to live with her. She has also hired an attractive new secretary, Pegeen Ryan. In preparation for the party for the Upsons, Mame has her apartment completely redecorated with modern furniture and hanging mobiles. She invites her actress friend, Vera, her publisher, Lindsay Woolsey, and the "progressive" educator. Lindsay Woolsey brings along to the party several copies of Mame's book which is called *Live, Live, Live*. The conservative Upsons are somewhat unnerved by Mame's life style, but the final straw that sends them running from the apartment is the announcement by Lindsay that Mame intends to use the proceeds from her book to buy the property next door to the Upsons and build a home for homeless Jewish children. After the Upsons leave, Patrick thanks Mame for saving him from them. Anyway, he has found Pegeen Ryan very appealing.

In the last scene, which takes place about ten years later, Mame, now married to Lindsay, is going back to India. She wants to take Patrick and Pegeen's little boy with her. Patrick and Pegeen start to object, but they know it will do no good. Auntie Mame will have her way.

The Film's History

The story of Patrick Dennis's Auntie Mame has had a long history. First, there was the novel, *Auntie Mame*, published in 1955, that was on the best-seller lists for one hundred and twelve weeks. Then Jerome Lawrence and Robert E. Lee adapted the novel into a play which was directed by Morton DaCosta and starred Rosalind Russell. The play opened on Broadway at the Broadhurst Theatre on October 31, 1956, and played for 639 performances. Rosalind Russell was nominated for a Tony Award, and Peggy Cass won a Tony for her portrayal of Agnes Gooch. At the time the film was released in 1958 the play was still being toured about the country by three different companies, starring Constance Bennett, Sylvia Sidney, and Eve Arden in the role of Auntie Mame. Bea Lillie was playing the role in a production in London.

The film, *Auntie Mame*, with a screenplay by Betty Comden and Adolph Green, starred Rosalind Russell and was directed by Morton DaCosta. DaCosta had directed the play on Broadway, and this was his film directing debut. It was a faithful recording of the play with only a few minor changes. The film was made by Warner Bros. It opened at Radio City Music Hall on December 4, 1958, and was the top money-maker of 1959. Highlights from the film were put on record by Bronislau Kaper. (See D02.)

On May 24, 1966, a musical adaptation of the play opened on Broadway under the title, *Mame*. *Mame* was adapted by Lawrence and Lee from their own play and had a score by Jerry Herman. In cutting down and condensing scenes to allow time for musical numbers, Lawrence and Lee managed to develop the mutual affection between Mame and Patrick more fully than they had in the stage play. Also, Angela Lansbury's portrayal of Mame was less bizarre than Patrick Dennis's original characterization and more subdued than Rosalind Russell's. Miss Lansbury won a Tony Award for her portrayal of Mame, as did Frankie Michaels for his role as the young Patrick and Beatrice Arthur for her characterization of Mame's actress friend, Vera Charles. Angela Lansbury played Mame for two years. Janis Page, Sheila Smith, Jane Morgan, and Ann Miller followed her in the role. *Mame* finally closed in January 1970 after a total of 1,508 performances, making it one of Broadway's longest running shows.

The story of Auntie Mame was not yet over. The musical, *Mame*, was made into a film starring Lucille Ball. It was released in 1974 but was not successful.

Reviews

Bosley Crowther of the *New York Times* wrote of the film, *Auntie Mame*, that it "does sure enough generate gales of laughter as it sweeps across the screen." However, he thinks, like the stage play and like the character of Auntie Mame, "it is largely inflated with hot air--or a sort of intoxicating vapor or theatrical laughing-gas." "Most of its whirling, swirling action is in a succession of virtual skits, strung together in a loose chronological order that extends from the Prohibition era until the present." Nevertheless, he has to admit that "this picture of a tireless party-giver is a highly entertaining thing to see. And, because of the gags that gush from it, it is a constantly amusing thing to hear." It does have a "few glints of irony," he adds, and "the picture is every bit as potent, if not a good deal more so, than the play." "Actually," he writes, "the stage play was more like a movie script in its pile-up of pictorial business and its multiplicity of scenes ..." In the film, Betty Comden and Adolph Green and the director, Morton DaCosta, have "reveled in the greater physical range" (December 5, 1958).

The reviewer for *Variety* called *Auntie Mame* "a faithfully funny recording of the hit play, changed only in some small details to conform to motion picture mores." He called the film "a top screenplay job" (November 26, 1958, p. 6).

The critic for *Newsweek* wrote that "it is possible that two and a half hours of this breakneck foolery will prove a little monotonous to all but the most devoted Mamists." However, his final statement is: "Summing Up: One-woman hit" (December 15, 1958, pp. 113, 114).

Stanley Kauffmann of the *New Republic* was negative in his review. "The play has been filmed almost intact. It is hard to see what contribution screenwriters

Comden and Green have made besides legalizing Agnes Gooch's baby and inserting some unfunny mechanical furniture. Morton DaCosta repeats his Broadway staging--so closely, in fact, that the actors on the veranda of the Southern mansion look tidily lined up to avoid a falling curtain." He thinks that the film script, like the play, starts out as "high comedy growing out of credible characters; then, for fear of losing momentum, the writers start to pump in gags and gaggy situations. What starts out as glittering comedy descends through farce to circus." "But if you like Auntie Mame ... you will like the film," he concludes (January 19, 1959, p. 21).

Arthur Knight, writing in *The Saturday Review of Literature*, said that Morton DaCosta had "wisely stuck fairly close to his original stage business," but he thought the film editing was not good, making many of Rosalind Russell's actions and reactions seem to be "simply pasted in." "The line of her movement is broken by the need to simulate cinematic movement through editing." The result, he concluded, "is a disturbingly static picture." "*Auntie Mame* is still good fun, but the pace of the film never touches the wild frivolity of the stage version" (December 27, 1958, p. 21).

Commentary

Most of the humor of both the play and the film, *Auntie Mame*, is due to the flamboyant character of Mame herself, played with exuberance by Rosalind Russell. However, in the film Miss Russell also conveys a more serious side to the character and certainly shows the love and concern that she has for her nephew. The film medium makes it possible to show the outdoor scenes--the wild fox hunt and the places all over the world that Mame and Beauregard visit. As one critic points out, the film editing is occasionally abrupt, cutting quickly to a closeup of Mame to show her action or reaction. The film also resorts to gimmicks that seem forced, especially the suspended, mechanically operated furniture in Mame's apartment.

*****

F09   *BELLS ARE RINGING*

(Metro-Goldwyn-Mayer; 1960; 126 minutes; color;
Video: Metro-Goldwyn-Mayer/CBS)

Credits

Based on the musical, *Bells Are Ringing*, book and lyrics by Betty Comden and Adolph Green, music by Jule Styne, as presented on the stage by the Theatre Guild.

Screenplay	Betty Comden
	Adolph Green
Music	Jule Styne
Lyrics	Betty Comden
	Adolph Green
Director	Vincente Minnelli
Assistant Director	William McGarry
Music Arrangements, Conductor	André Previn
Orchestrations	Alexander Courage
	Pete King

Choreography	Charles O'Curran
Art Directors	George W. Davis
	Preston Ames
Set Decorations	Henry Grace
	Keogh Gleason
Costumes	Walter Plunkett
Hair Styles	Sydney Guilaroff
Make-up	William Tuttle
Director of Photography	Milton Krasner
Screen	Cinemascope
Color	Metrocolor
Color Consultant	Charles K. Hagedon
Special Effects	A. Arnold Gillespie
	Lee LeBlanc
Recording Supervisor	Franklin Milton
Photographic Lenses	Panavision
Film Editor	Adrienne Fazan
Producer	Arthur Freed

Cast

Ella Peterson	Judy Holliday
Jeffrey Moss	Dean Martin
Larry Hastings	Fred Clark
J. Otto Prantz	Eddie Foy, Jr.
Sue	Jean Stapleton
Gwynne	Ruth Storey
Inspector Barnes	Dort Clark
Blake Carton	Frank Gorshin
Francis	Ralph Roberts
Olga	Valerie Allen
Dr. Joe Kitchell	Bernie West
First Gangster	Steven Peck
Ella's Blind Date	Gerry Mulligan
M.C.	Hal Linden
Woman	Madge Blake
Nervous Man	Olan Soulé

Synopsis

The screenplay for *Bells Are Ringing* is basically the same as the script for the stage show. For a detailed description of the plot see the synopsis of the play (S04). One new scene has been added. Early in the story, the film shows Ella on a blind date. Her cousin and employer, Sue Summers, has insisted that Ella have a date with a young man whom she knows. Reluctantly, Ella goes for dinner with the man. Everything goes wrong, and then as Ella leaves the restaurant, the back of her dress brushes across a burning candle and catches on fire. She leaves the restaurant not realizing that she is ablaze in the rear. When she returns home she is trying to hide a big black hole in her dress. The scene is used to show that Ella's few dates are almost always disasters.

A few songs from the play are omitted and two new songs have been added. Omitted is Ella's "Is It a Crime?" which in the musical she sings to Inspector

Barnes. Also omitted are "Long Before I Knew You," sung by Jeffrey, and "Salzburg," sung by Sue and Otto. Added to the film are "Do It Yourself," sung by Jeffrey Moss, and "Better Than a Dream," a duet sung by Ella and Jeffrey when Ella visits him for the first time. This song had been added to the stage show a few months after the opening. The duet is really the thoughts of the two people, happy that they have found each other. The "Hello, Hello There!" song, sung on the subway in the play, is sung with a large crowd of people on the street in the film.

The Film's History

    Bells Are Ringing, the musical that Comden and Green had written for their good friend and fellow Revuer, Judy Holliday, opened in New York on November 29, 1956. Judy Holliday had attained stardom on Broadway in her role as Billy Dawn in *Born Yesterday*. When she recreated the role on film she won the Academy Award. After that she had made the films, *The Marrying Kind*, *It Should Happen to You*, and *The Solid Gold Cadillac*. Arthur Freed was quick to act to get the film rights to *Bells Are Ringing*. He announced his intention to make the film in January 1958 while the play was still playing to standing room only audiences in New York. He advertised that the film would be written by Comden and Green with music by Jule Styne and that it would star Judy Holliday. He paid $400,000 for the rights. He had to wait until the expiration of Holliday's contract, as well as for her approval of the screenplay.

    Comden and Green's contract stipulated that they would provide an unlimited number of new songs with Styne, as well as revising any existing lyrics. At the time the contract was signed Comden and Green were performing *A Party With Betty Comden and Adolph Green*. The revue had opened Off-Broadway and then moved to Broadway. They wanted to do the initial writing of the screenplay in the East so they could continue their show. Freed insisted that the first draft of the screenplay should be delivered to him by December 31, 1958. When Arthur Freed received the screenplay it contained 153 pages and there were no new songs. Comden and Green requested more time to do their show in New York. Freed granted them an extra two weeks to continue *A Party With Betty Comden and Adolph Green*, but he insisted that the script was much too long and needed to be re-written. Comden and Green agreed to report to the studio on January 26. The film was to go into production in February, but, since there was no script, the date was changed to June. Vincente Minnelli was hired to direct the show, his twelfth directorial job for Freed. Dean Martin was hired as co-star. Judy Holliday wanted to appear in the touring production of the musical which was to go to Washington, Los Angeles, and San Francisco. The tour to the West Coast would end on July 4. Betty Comden and Adolph Green sent their second script and four new songs, "To Love and to Lose," "Do It Yourself," "Better Than a Dream," and "My Guiding Star." Only two of these, "Do It Yourself" and "Better Than a Dream," were used in the film. Freed returned the script. It was still too long. Freed now decided to start rehearsals on August 15 with shooting to begin on October 6. Jean Stapleton, Bernie West, and Dort Clark from the Broadway cast were hired to recreate their roles on film. Hal Linden, who had taken over the Jeffrey Moss role on stage, was given a minor role. The music was to be adapted and conducted by André Previn.

    Bells Are Ringing, the stage musical, seemed to be a script that did not adapt well to the medium of film. Comden and Green had opened it up and added a few scenes, but it was still too long and had lost the quality that had made it so appealing on the stage. Judy Holliday objected to the script, saying it was not cinematic. She also objected to the casting of Dean Martin as Jeffrey Moss. When filming began there was tension between Holliday and Minnelli. She thought that she knew the play and the character of Ella Peterson better than anyone, but Minnelli would not take any of her suggestions. The tension continued during the entire filming period. Much of Judy Holliday's unhappiness was due to her fragile physical condition, but it was she and her wonderful characterization of Ella Peterson that held the film together. *Bells Are Ringing* opened at the Radio City Music Hall on June 23, 1960. It had cost $2,203,123. Betty Comden and Adolph Green received their third Screenwriters Guild Award for *Bells Are Ringing*. It was Judy Holliday's last screen appearance. She died of cancer on June 7, 1965. The *Bells Are Ringing* sound track was recorded by Capitol Records. (See D06.)

Reviews

Bosley Crowther of the *New York Times* writes that *Bells Are Ringing*, the film, was "hoisted bodily off the stage." He writes that it is a good thing that Judy Holliday is "neither shy nor stingy with her abundant performing skills, even though she's supposed to be a shrinking violet in the role she plays in the film. For this time, her usually glib script writers, Betty Comden and Adolph Green, ... have sort of shoved her forth and left her on her own. That is to say, the jangled romance they have prepared for her to play is a poor thing, made up of one slight gimmick and a lot of surrounding gags. What Miss Holliday does with the latter is the measure of the quality of the show." Mr. Crowther felt that *Bells Are Ringing* "owes more to Miss Holliday than it does to its authors, its director (Vincente Minnelli), or even to Alexander Graham Bell" (June 24, 1960).

The reviewer for *Variety* took the opposite point of view. "Few musicals," he wrote, "have been translated to the screen so effectively." He thought that *Bells Are Ringing* was ideally suited to the intimacy of the film medium. "Vincente Minnelli's graceful, imaginative direction puts spirit and snap into the musical sequences, warmth and humor into the straight passages and manages to knit it all together without any traces of awkwardness in transition." He called Jule Styne's score "bright" and Comden and Green's lyrics "smooth and workable, rarely intricate." He commented that Judy Holliday gives a "performance of remarkable variety and gusto" (June 8, 1960, p. 6).

The reviewer for *Time* wrote: "In this $3,000,000 Metrocolored musical based on her Broadway boff of 1956, Judy Holliday employs her limited vocal resources with showmanly style, supports them with a comic gift that is a major wonder of the entertainment world, and with some skillful assistance from Director Vincente Minnelli manages to jog and jazz and jigger a merely middling book and some fairly forgettable tunes into one of the year's liveliest and wittiest cinemusicals." "The beauty of Judy Holliday's talent lies not least in her meticulous control of it. She knows her type to a tee-hee, and she is never for an instant out of character" (June 20, 1960, p. 67).

The critic for *The New Yorker* wrote: "Except for a jolly performance by Judy Holliday, who can hold her own in any comic league, there isn't much to be said in favor of *Bells Are Ringing*." He wrote that the play had been "transposed almost intact to the screen" (July 9, 1960, p. 55). The *Newsweek* reviewer commented on the "special brand of breezy intelligence" of Betty Comden and Adolph Green and thought that the screenplay, the cast, the color, and Judy Holliday made "a superbly stylish show" (June 27, 1960, p. 92).

Commentary

Evidently, Comden and Green, enjoying performing again in *A Party With Betty Comden and Adolph Green*, were not very eager to make the screen adaptation of *Bells Are Ringing*. Arthur Freed thought that a new writer should be brought in, but Judy Holliday insisted that her friends make the adaptation. The play proved very difficult to change to fit the film medium, and thus the film is almost exactly like the stage musical. Dean Martin seemed merely to walk through his role and this did not help the romantic element. Judy Holliday, in spite of her unhappiness during the filming, tailored her performance to the intimacy of film. There was great variety in her character and she engaged the viewer. It was due to her that the film was popular with movie-goers.

*****

F10   *WHAT A WAY TO GO!*

(Twentieth Century-Fox; 1964; 111 minutes; color; Video: None)

Credits
Based on a story by Gwen Davis

Screenplay	Betty Comden
	Adolph Green
Music	Nelson Riddle
Lyrics for Songs: "*I Think That You and I Should Get Acquainted*" and "*Musical Extravaganza*"	Betty Comden
	Adolph Green
Music for Songs	Jule Styne
Director	J. Lee Thompson
Assistant Director	Fred R. Simpson
Orchestration	Arthur Morton
Choreography	Gene Kelly
Assistant to Mr. Kelly	Richard Humphrey
Dialogue Coach	Leon Charles
Art Directors	Jack Martin Smith
	Ted Haworth
Set Decorations	Walter M. Scott
	Stuart A. Reiss
Costumes for Miss MacLaine	Edith Head
Men's Wardrobe	Moss Mabry
Make-up	Ben Nye
Director of Photography	Leon Shamroy
Color	DeLuxe
Special Photographic Effects	L. B. Abbott
	Emil Kosa, Jr.
Sound	Bernard Freericks
	Elmer Raguse
Unit Production Manager	William Eckhardt
Film Editor	Marjorie Fowler
Producer	Arthur P. Jacobs

Cast

Louisa May Foster	Shirley MacLaine
Leonard Crawley	Dean Martin
Larry Flint	Paul Newman
Rod Anderson, Jr.	Robert Mitchum
Pinky Benson	Gene Kelly
Dr. Vincent Stephanson	Bob Cummings
Edgar Hopper	Dick Van Dyke
Painter	Reginald Gardiner
Mrs. Foster	Margaret Dumont
Tentino	Lou Nova
Baroness	Fifi D'Orsay
Rene	Maurice Marsac
Agent	Wally Vernon
Polly	Jane Wald
Hollywood Lawyer	Lenny Kent
Movie Executive	Sid Gould
Movie Executive's Girl	Paula Lauc
TV Announcer	Army Archerd
Movie Star	Tracy Butler
Mr. Foster	Anton Arnold
Crawleyville Lawyer	Burt Mustin
Geraldine Crawley at Age 4	Pamelyn Ferdin
Jonathan Crawley at Age 5	Jeff Fithian
Leonard Crawley at Age 7	Billy Corcoran
Doris	Helen F. Winston
Chester	Jack Greening
Lady Kensington	Queenie Leonard
Lord Kensington	Tom Conway
Girl on Plane	Barbara Bouchet
Mrs. Freeman	Marjorie Bennett
Lawyer	Milton Frome
Willard	Anthony Eustrel
French Lawyer	Marcel Hillaire
Neighbor	Eugene Borden
Ned	Chris Connelly

Additional Cast Members: Lynn Borden, Cleo Ronson, Pat O'Moore, Justin Smith

Synopsis

Louisa May Foster Hopper Flint Anderson Benson is first seen dressed in black coming down an impressive staircase followed by somber men, also in black, who are carrying a casket. One of the men trips on the stairs and the casket glides down the stairs and whirls around on the polished floor of the hall. The men try to catch up with the casket, but they also slide on the floor and fall over each other. It is a madcap scene which precedes the credits. Next we see the widowed Louisa in line at the office of the Internal Revenue Service. She tries to give a check for two-hundred and eleven million dollars to an astonished cashier. He refuses to take the check. Louisa goes from place to place trying to give the check to the government, finally visiting the President. No one will take her check. They all think she is crazy.

At last Louisa visits Dr. Stephanson, a psychiatrist. To him she begins to pour out her tale of sorrow. She tells him that every man whose life she has touched has died, and she feels guilty about being so wealthy. She tells of her childhood. At church the minister rails against money. On the wall of her home is the motto, "Money is the root of all evil." Yet when she grows up to be a young lady, her mother tries to force her to marry for money. Her mother insists that she should marry Leonard Crawley, the son of the owner of the biggest department store in her small home town. Upon her mother's insistence, she does go on a date with Leonard, though she dislikes his arrogant manner. While they are driving down the main street, they see Edgar Hopper walking along carrying a book and a fishing pole. Edgar owns a small store which he seldom opens. Leonard deliberately runs through a mudhole, splashing Edgar with mud. Edgar with good humor takes the splashing as an accident. He says he is going fishing and that if the fish are not biting he has his copy of Thoreau with him. Louisa is attracted to Edgar. The next day she looks up the works of Thoreau in the library, and then, seeing Edgar drifting lazily in a boat on the lake, she swims out to the boat. Edgar is surprised at Louisa's interest in him because he has no ambition. He swears he will never make good. Louisa marries Edgar. Their life, Louisa tells the psychiatrist, was like an old silent movie. We are transported to a jerky film with titles where we see Louisa and Edgar in their little shack of a home. Then we see the real house, which is indeed a shack with a leaky roof. Edgar lounges on a chair reading his book while Louisa tries to patch the ceiling of the room. Leonard Crawley looks in on them and taunts Edgar for letting his wife live in such a place. After Leonard leaves, Edgar goes to his store. He resolves to make money. He has a big sale of the goods in his store. The sale is a success and he buys more goods. He expands his store and buys more goods. He buys a grand house for himself and Louisa, but now he is never home and she is unhappy. At last he buys out the big Crawley's department store. He works harder and harder, always telling Louisa that "A little hard work never killed anyone." His store gets bigger and bigger. At last his hard work kills him. He leaves Louisa two million dollars.

Louisa, now a wealthy widow, takes a trip to Europe. She arrives all alone in Paris. Her taxicab driver, to whom she tries to speak French, reveals that he is Larry Flint, an American, and he is really an artist. He takes her to see his studio, where he has devised a new contraption that paints mechanically. The machine's long arms hold paint brushes and splash paint on canvas. The arms are moved by sound waves. Louisa falls in love with the artist and marries him. Their life together, she tells the psychiatrist, was like one of those "wicked" French movies. We see their sensual life together in their tiny apartment. Louisa enjoys keeping house in the apartment over Larry's studio. One day she gets the idea to try some good classical music to create the sound waves for his mechanical painting machine. The long arms of the machine begin to move to the music. Larry is astounded at the painting that is created. He takes it to sell in exchange for food, and the painting is seen by a wealthy man who wishes to buy it. Larry tries other classical music for his paintings, and suddenly he is an acclaimed artist. He holds an exhibition of his art, and the pseudo-critics and art patrons are ecstatic. The money begins to pour in, and Larry buys a large chateau. But now he is always at his studio, and Louisa is lonely. Larry's paintings become more and more valuable. But one day the long arms of the painting machine begin to fight with each other. Larry scolds them and tries to conduct them in accord with the music. The arms grab him and crush him to death. This time Louisa inherits four million dollars.

Louisa decides to go back to the United States. However, she misses her plane, and while she is standing watching the plane take off, Rod Anderson, Jr., the inheritor of a maple syrup empire, offers to take her in his private plane named Melissa. Louisa accepts his invitation. Afraid of the take-off, Louisa creeps into the cockpit where Rod Anderson is flying the plane. Gradually, the big executive relaxes and admits that it is nice to have someone to share all this with. Louisa and Rod are married in Rod's penthouse apartment in New York. Their life, Louisa tells the psychiatrist, was like "one of those glamorous Hollywood movies." We see their life together--long limousines, glamorous dresses for Louisa, parties, gushing society matrons. Rod Anderson neglects his business empire and then is angry when he discovers that his fortune has been tripled. He knows that someone has been running the business for him. He decides to liquidate all of his holdings and buy a farm. He and Louisa settle in to lead the simple life. Rod, in overalls, goes out that first morning to milk the cows. One cow he calls Melissa, but when he tries to milk her he discovers that Melissa is a bull. Though he apologizes, Melissa does not like that kind of treatment and kicks him. Rod Anderson dies leaving Louisa one hundred and fifty million dollars.

Louisa now resolves that she will live alone. She goes into a small restaurant for a cup of coffee. There she meets a small time entertainer, Pinky Benson, who invites her to see his act at the night club across the street. She goes to the third rate night club where Pinky, dressed as a clown with a red nose, performs a terrible song and dance act that no one in the night club pays any attention to. When Louisa asks him if he has ambitions for becoming a star, he says he wants only the simple life and does not want to get ahead. Louisa marries Pinky and they live on his small houseboat. Their life together, Louisa tells the psychiatrist, was like a big musical. Suddenly, the houseboat turns into a huge ship where Louisa and Pinky, along with a big cast, do a large production number on the deck. Pinky and Louisa are planning a party, and Pinky finds that he is too late to put on his clown makeup for his act. Louisa encourages him to sing and dance as himself. He does, and gradually the noisy night club becomes quiet. Pinky now becomes popular. He succeeds on Broadway and then goes to Hollywood. Louisa is unhappy because now she has lost him to his own fame. We see them now at the preview of his five and one half hour film, *Gleaming Lips*. It is a big success. Pinky and Louisa slip out the back way to avoid his adoring fans. Then Pinky has a feeling of remorse for not meeting his fans. He steps out and calls to his fans, who break through a fence to get to see him. They come at him and trample him to death. Louisa is now left with thirty million dollars.

As Louisa finishes telling her story to the psychiatrist, the IRS calls to say that they have discovered that her check is good and are willing to take it now. The psychiatrist faints. As Louisa is trying to bring him around, the janitor comes in. It is Leonard Crawley, the man Louisa's mother had wanted her to marry. He has lost all of his money and now leads a simple life. Louisa marries him and they live happily on a farm. They have four children, and at last Louisa is happy. Then one day when Leonard is plowing, oil begins to shoot up out of the plowed field. Louisa rushes out of the house. Tears flow down her cheeks when she thinks that they have struck it rich. Then two angry men drive up in a truck. Leonard's plow has punched a hole in an oil line. Louisa and Leonard and the children, all covered with oil, now begin to celebrate the simple life that they can go on living.

The Film's History

In 1964 when *What a Way To Go!* was released, the movie industry had changed. The major studios were giving way to the new independence of producers, directors, writers, and actors. By 1962, most major actors and directors had formed their own corporations. Deals were no longer made simply by putting together various people under contract. Each element of a project had to be individually assembled. Salaries had skyrocketed in a new era of super-stars and super-productions. In some cases, a percentage of the box-office gross income was demanded by the star, as was the case with Elizabeth Taylor in Twentieth Century-Fox's *Cleopatra*. Crew members, too, through their unions, were demanding higher wages. Studios could no longer afford fully staffed departments, so crews were assembled for individual films. The distribution of films had also changed. Audiences were dropping due to television and other entertainments. As the audiences shrunk, the prices for attending the movie theatres rose. All of these changes led to a reduction in the number of films produced by a film studio each year. Each film now became very important.

In 1962 Twentieth Century-Fox lost 39.8 million dollars after taxes, and in the three preceding years the company had lost an additional $48.5 million in feature film production. The studio had had to sell 260 of its 334 acres (John Gregory Dunne, *The Studio*, p. 6).

In 1962 Darryl Zanuck returned from France to take over Twentieth Century-Fox himself. He cut back in all departments of the studio and cut down on the number of new films begun. Stars were brought in to attract audiences. In 1964 Twentieth Century-Fox was overshadowed by its competitors, releasing only six rather undistinguished films. It was not until 1965 that Fox began to make money again and to make some really successful motion pictures, including *The Sound of Music* and *Those Magnificent Men in Their Flying Machines*.

What a Way To Go! was Twentieth Century-Fox's "major" product in 1964. It was the top-grossing film of the year, bringing in over six million dollars. It had also cost the most to produce--$3,750,000. The film was produced by Arthur P. Jacobs, a former press agent. It was his first picture. Jacobs was later to produce *Dr. Doolittle* with Rex Harrison, and in 1968 he produced *Planet of the Apes*, which became one of the biggest non-road show successes in Twentieth Century Fox's history.

In this his first venture into film production, Arthur P. Jacobs seemed to think that "bigger was better." He used a cast of seven top performers of the 1960s: Shirley MacLaine, Paul Newman, Robert Mitchum, Dean Martin, Gene Kelly, Bob Cummings, and Dick Van Dyke. Some of the cameo roles were played by veteran players like Margaret Dumont, who had been in many of the Marx Brothers' films, and Tom Conway, the former "Falcon" of the movies. He also filled the movie with huge sets and elaborate costumes. In the film Shirley MacLaine modeled seventy-two Edith Head dresses and wore jewelry valued at three and a half million dollars. The film score was recorded by Twentieth Century-Fox. (See D38.)

Reviews

Bosley Crowther of the *New York Times* was not pleased with *What a Way To Go!*, calling it an "odd lot of comic contrivance." "It may be a funny idea and some of the incidents by which it is revealed may have a certain sprightliness about them," he writes, "but the whole thing, alas, lacks wit and grace." He calls the film a "farrago of disjointed social satire, slapstick farce and sheer unadulterated nonsense carried to the nth degree." He thought the humor was at best the kind one might "encounter in a fairly well-done blackout skit." Of the four different romances and marriages, he says they "are all slight situations that are heavily overworked in the not very smart elaborations that Miss Comden and Mr. Green have given them." Mr. Crowther calls Shirley MacLaine's performance "showy but dull" and her scanty costumes "gaudy and tasteless." He thinks that the director, J. Lee Thompson, "has failed to coalesce a good film farce" (May 15, 1964).

The critic for *Variety* called the film a "big, gaudy comedy" that "telegraphs too many of its yoks and lacks consistent style, but has a powerhouse cast and enough laughs to indicate good box office response." This critic thinks that if the film had been "played and directed with more original wit and a sense of cinema style--it might have been a swinging classic." "Yet," he concludes, "there is much that hits the wild and wacky tone that Comden and Green intended." He thought that Gene Kelly gave "the most consistently stylish performance, followed by Newman" (April 1, 1964, p. 6).

Stanley Kauffmann, of the *New Republic*, thought that the humor "is like a long series of cartoons with captions omitted." He wrote that "every gag is either telegraphed or trite, sometimes both; and a good deal is reminiscent of previous Comden-Green opera." He gives as an example the four fantasy-satires of a stock type of movie (May 30, 1964, p. 26).

The critic for *Newsweek* concedes that the story may be "absolute nonsense," but "it is nonsense with style, with flair, and with appealing extravagance" (May 18, 1964, p. 100). Brendon Gill of *The New Yorker* calls the picture "a monotonously prolonged gag about sex and death." He thought the script "reads as if it had been written by a ninety-year-old necrophile but is, in fact, the handwork of Betty Comden and Adolph Green, who have been witty enough on other occasions" (May 16, 1964, p. 191).

The critic for *Time* wrote that *What a Way To Go!* "is five or six big, splashy movies rolled into none." The film, he writes, "sets out to satirize the very things it seems head over heels in love with: moom pitchers and the cult of success-money-success." He thought the film was "extravagantly overdrawn" (May 22, 1964, p. 104).

Commentary

In spite of bad reviews by most of the film critics, *What a Way to Go!* was a box office success, grossing six million dollars. Probably, the names of the stars in the cast were enough to bring many viewers to the movie houses. However, the film has not continued its success and is the only one of Comden and Green's screenplays not to be put on video for home viewers. In fact, it is difficult to find a print of the film for viewing today. (The Library of Congress does have a copy.)

The film had a clever and unusual idea, an outstanding cast, a large budget, and two knowledgable and experienced screenplay writers. The story with its "wacky" humor and its four love affairs, each a separate episode, is reminiscent of the satirical sketches that had made Comden and Green famous. Also, the reference by Louisa to each of her marriages as similar to a particular type of movie, gave Comden and Green the opportunity to satirize each of these types--the jerky silent movies, the sexy French films, the glamorous Hollywood movies of the 1930s, and the elaborate song and dance Busby Berkeley movies. Comden and Green had had a long love affair with the films and were knowledgable about the history of the motion picture industry. Their satire of the different styles is affectionate and adds to the humor of the story.

The question remains. What went wrong with the film? There are two main subjects in *What a Way To Go!*--death and money. It is difficult to make death and widowhood funny, and, for many people in American society, an over abundance of money does not seem a problem as it was for Louisa. For *What a Way To Go!* to be really successful, a consistent style of "wackiness" is necessary. This the film did not achieve, even with its super-star cast. Shirley MacLaine, in spite of her reputation for being somewhat "kookie" herself, did not seem to enter into the spirit of the play as it must have been envisioned by Comden and Green. Paul Newman and Gene Kelly perhaps most nearly achieved the exaggerated style the film needed. Also, the film was over-produced, especially in the extravagance of its costuming. During some of the episodes, Shirley MacLaine seemed called upon merely to model clothes. As the wife of the artist in Paris, she wore a succession of abbreviated dresses with slits up the sides. In the episode in which she is married to the wealthy businessman, she wore a series of extravagant and revealing evening dresses. Clothes, jewelry, and sets may help, but they do not make a motion picture.

Betty Comden at the time of the first production of *A Party With Betty Comden and Adolph Green*, 1958. Photograph courtesy of The Billy Rose Theatre Collection, The New York Public Library for the Performing Arts, Astor, Lenox and Tilden Foundations.

Adolph Green at the time of the first production of *A Party With Betty Comden and Adolph Green*, 1958. Photograph courtesy of The Billy Rose Theatre Collection, The New York Public Library for the Performing Arts, Astor, Lenox and Tilden Foundations.

COMDEN AND GREEN AS PERFORMERS

P01 *A PARTY WITH BETTY COMDEN AND ADOLPH GREEN*
(1958 and 1977)

Credits (1958 and 1977)
Sketches and Lyrics   Betty Comden
                                                     Adolph Green
Music: André Previn, Leonard Bernstein, Morton Gould, Roger
              Edens, Jule Styne, Saul Chaplin, Cy Coleman

Credits (1958)
At the Piano   Peter Howard
Decor and Lighting   Marvin Reiss
Producers: Theatre Guild by special arrangements
                                               with Town Productions
Associate Producer   Frank Perry

Credits (1977)
At the Piano   Paul Trueblood
Miss Comden's Gowns   Donald Brooks
Gowns Executed by   John Fitzpatrick
Lighting   Andrea Wilson
Technical Director   Mitch Miller
Production Assistant   Thomas Madigan
Producers   Arthur Cantor
                                                     Leonard Friedman

Cast
Betty Comden
Adolph Green

Synopsis (1958)
    The 1958 version of *A Party With Betty Comden and Adolph Green* began with the song, "I Said Good Morning," with music by André Previn. This song had been written for the film, *It's Always Fair Weather*, but was not used. This was followed by several sketches that had been written for The Revuers. There was one sketch that satirized the show-business argot of *Variety* and then a series of synopses of the plots of some great classic literary pieces as *The Reader's Digest*

might condense each into one sentence. These fast-spoken, humorous selections were followed by a take-off on a Shubert operetta called "*The Baroness Bazooka.*"

Comden and Green then introduced some songs from *On the Town* with music by Leonard Bernstein. These included "New York, New York," "Lonely Town," "Some Other Time," and the humorous song, "I Get Carried Away," which, as Claire and Ozzie, Betty and Adolph had sung in the original Broadway production of *On the Town*. The first act concluded with "The French Lesson," with music by Roger Edens from the film *Good News*.

The second act started once again with some spoken material from The Revuers, this time a satire of movie advertisements as they might be written for Radio City Music Hall, for an art theatre, and for an x-rated movie house. Two songs from the revue, *Two on the Aisle*, followed. They were the humorous "If You Hadn't, But You Did" and "Catch Our Act at the Met," both with music by Jule Styne. Comden and Green then sang "O! My Mysterious Lady" with music by Styne from *Peter Pan*. They then introduced the musical *Wonderful Town*, on which they had collaborated with Leonard Bernstein. From it Green sang "A Quiet Girl," and they both sang "The Wrong Note Rag." They then sang the humorous "Inspiration" from *Bonanza Bound!* with music by Saul Chaplin. "Inspiration" is about the influence of the woman behind the accomplishments of every man. Mrs. Rimsky-Korsakov's influence on her husband inspired him to write "The Flight of the Bumblebee," which gave Green his chance to sing the part of the bumblebee. This had been a favorite Revuers' number. Comden and Green concluded their program with songs from *Bells Are Ringing* with music by Jule Styne. These were "Just in Time" and "The Party's Over."

Synopsis (1977)

The 1977 version of *A Party With Betty Comden and Adolph Green* included many of the same numbers from The Revuers and the early musicals, but there were also some songs from the more recent musicals. Comden and Green started with "I Said Good Morning," as they had done in their 1958 version. This was followed by some of their Revuers sketches. First was the one sentence book summaries in "The Reader's Digest" skit. In "The Screen Writers" they try to think up scenarios for films. This was followed by "The Banshee Sisters," which is a song by the two sisters of a singing trio who are left after the one sister who sings the melody has gone off to get married. Once again they did the satire of the Shubert operettas, "The Baroness Bazooka."

The Revuers numbers were followed by three "songs with heart," as Betty called them, from *On the Town*. They sang a medley of "Lonely Town," "Lucky to Be Me," and "Some Other Time." Then they sang "Carried Away," from *On the Town*. Next, turning to their other show with music by Leonard Bernstein, *Wonderful Town*, Betty sang the show-stopping humorous song "One Hundred Easy Ways to Lose a Man" and together they sang a medley of "Ohio" and "The Wrong Note Rag."

In the second act, Comden and Green introduced some of their early songs with music by Jule Styne. Adolph sang "Capital Gains" from *Subways Are For Sleeping* and Betty sang "If You Hadn't, But You Did" from their revue, *Two on the Aisle*. They both sang "Catch Our Act at the Met" from *Two on the Aisle*. This was followed by "The French Lesson," with music by Roger Edens, that had been written for the film *Good News*.

Comden and Green included three songs from two musical shows that never reached Broadway. *Straws in the Wind* was a revue that was given a workshop production at the American Place Theatre in 1975. Adolph's wife, Phyllis Newman, was to direct the show and asked Comden and Green to write a few lyrics for it. Their lyrics had music by Cy Coleman. *Straws in the Wind* was a look into the future. From that show Betty sang "The Lost Word," a song about the difficulty of people to convey emotions. In this case "the lost word" was "love." Betty and Adolph also sang "Simplified Language" from *Straws in the Wind*. This is a clever song about the attempt to find a word that would do for both genders. Instead of "boy" and "girl," why not "birl?" The other song from an unsuccessful musical was "Inspiration" from *Bonanza Bound!* This had also been used in their 1958 "*Party*."

From *Peter Pan* Adolph sang "Captain Hook's Waltz," Betty sang "Never, Never Land," and together they sang " O! My Mysterious Lady." Comden and Green concluded their revue with a medley of three of their most popular songs: "Just in Time" from *Bells Are Ringing*, "Make Someone Happy" from *Do Re Mi*, and "The Party's Over" from *Bells Are Ringing*, all with music by Jule Styne.

As an encore, Betty and Adolph sang "Drink to Me Only With Thine Eyes" to the tune of Sousa's "Stars and Stripes Forever" and "The Marseillaise" to the tune of "Take Me Out to the Ball Game."

The Revue's History

Betty Comden and Adolph Green happened to run into an old friend, Gus Schirmer, Jr., who ran the Cherry Lane Theatre in Greenwich Village. He was planning a series at the theatre called "*Monday Nights at Nine*" and asked Comden and Green if they would like to do a Monday Night appearance in a program of their own material. Since they both liked to perform, they consented and scheduled two Monday appearances on November 10 and 17, 1958. They called their program *A Party With Betty Comden and Adolph Green*. The first night was such a success that Armina Marshall and Lawrence Langner of the Theatre Guild asked them if they would like to move the show uptown. After several more Monday Nights at the Cherry Lane, Comden and Green moved the show, just as it was, to the Golden Theatre. They opened there on December 23, 1958, to rave reviews by all seven of the New York critics.

At the same time they were performing in *A Party*, Comden and Green were also writing the screenplay for *Bells Are Ringing*. Arthur Freed of Metro-Goldwyn-Mayer wanted the completed screenplay. Comden and Green asked for an extension of time so that they could continue playing in *A Party*, but after six successful weeks, they had to cancel their "*Party*" to go to Hollywood to complete the screenplay and new lyrics for the film. They promised to return to New York in the spring. They did return to Broadway to continue the run, opening on May 18, 1959. Comden and Green's appearances at the Cherry Lane Theatre won for them an Obie Award for the Best Off Broadway Musical of the Year.

After their 1958-1959 Broadway run of *A Party*, Comden and Green continued to do various versions of their show at the Westport Country Playhouse in Westport, Connecticut (1959), at the Nyack-Tappen Zee Playhouse (1960), at the Julliard School of Music (1971), and at many other places. In 1976 Arthur Cantor, who was on the board of the Loeb Theatre Center at Harvard University, asked Comden and Green to perform there. After several requests from Mr. Cantor, they agreed to give four performances. To their surprise, they discovered that many college students at this time took film courses and had studied their screenplays for *Singin' in the Rain*, *The Band Wagon*, and some of their other films. The Harvard University students loved *A Party* and so did the Boston critics. Comden and Green took their show to Philadelphia, to Toronto, and finally back to the Loeb Theatre for another week. They were having so much fun performing, and the show was going so well, that they decided to take it once again to Broadway. Arthur Cantor and Leonard Friedman produced the show. It opened at the Morosco Theatre on February 10, 1977, once again to rave reviews. *A Party* moved to the Little Theatre on March 21, 1977, to continue its run. It closed on April 30, 1977, after 92 performances and four previews.

Capitol Records made an original cast recording of selections from the 1958 performance on Broadway, and Stet and Out Take Records made a recording of the complete 1977 performance. (See D27 and D28.) The show was presented on the "*Summershow*" on WNEW Television in 1980 and on the Arts and Entertainment Cable Network in 1985. (See T34 and T37.)

Reviews (1958)

After *A Party With Betty Comden and Adolph Green* was moved from the Cherry Lane Theatre to Broadway, Brooks Atkinson of the *New York Times* wrote: "What is good enough for Greenwich Village is good enough for West Forty-fifth Street, especially in the case of Betty Comden and Adolph Green ... In fact, they are good enough for just about any civilized corner of the world. For the songs and sketches they have recently been performing downtown are brilliant pieces of theatre, and Miss Comden and Mr. Green are ideal performers. They have the expertness of the professional although they have not lost the enthusiasm of the amateur." "What Al Hirschfield is to the satiric line and S. J. Perelman to the satiric word, they are to the satire of song and sketch." He concluded: "Two brilliant minds are at work on the follies and vulgarities of the world. They observe but they do not participate. For they have style, taste, and standards. They also have manners" (December 24, 1958).

John Chapman of the *Daily News* wrote: "They work very quietly, very easily. They have style without affecting stylishness, and a remarkable respect for what they have written." He also commented: "Every syllable they sing, be it nonsense or love stuff, is as clear as an infant's conscience" (December 31, 1958).

John McClain of the *New York Journal American* called the show "the biggest little show in town" (December 29, 1958). Richard Watts, Jr., of the *New York Post* called *A Party* "one of the most delightful evenings of the theatrical year," and he called Comden and Green "brilliant lyric writers ... and performers of great charm, skill, and humor" (December 29, 1958).

The critic for *Theatre Arts* recommended that Comden and Green in the future "spend at least half of their time behind footlights." "They sing and act," he wrote, "as jauntily as they create lyrics, librettos, and revue material. At midseason, this program of their own songs and sketches made several going enterprises among full-scale musical comedies (including one of their own making) seem impoverished indeed" (March 1959, p. 67).

Reviews (1977)

Clive Barnes wrote in the *New York Times* that Betty Comden and Adolph Green "are hams, and you have, have, have--and then really have--to love them." He calls them "fantastic performers" who sing "with a grace and zest. They also act out their songs with a special fervor." As writers, he says, they "have a manic dexterity with words, a gift for rhyme and an ear for reason. As performers they have this dazzling charm, which makes them the kind of people you would like to invite into your home." "Their command of intimacy, their ability to make a large theatre seem like a small living room, is truly remarkable." He concludes: "They are clearly having such a good time" (February 11, 1977).

Martin Gottfried of the *New York Post* noted that in *A Party* Comden and Green omitted songs from three of their musicals--*Say, Darling, Hallelujah, Baby!*, and *Fade Out--Fade In*. He thought they did not do good work for those shows and in his opinion the main reason was their working with Jule Styne. He thought that "their lyrics for Styne were heavyhanded when trying to be funny and contrived when in search of romance." He felt that the only exception to this was "The Party's Over" from *Bells Are Ringing*. He noted that in *A Party* "their cleverness and erudition are stimulating and not show-offy." He concluded his review by saying, "One can only hope they regain their sense of fun, their pleasure with verbal dexterity, for few contemporary lyricists can match their wit and honest intelligence" (February 11, 1977).

Gerald Clarke, writing in *Time* said of their performance: "These comic Prosperos can conjure up whole casts with a mere wink of the eye or shrug of the shoulder ... Rarely has so much wit and fun been packed into two hours. To cop a line from another song-writer, Cole Porter, what a swellegant, elegant party this is" (February 21, 1977, p. 57).

Commentary

When Betty Comden and Adolph Green wrote and performed in *On the Town*, they were in their twenties, and the critics commented on their youth and the "fresh" quality of the play. Over thirty years later when they performed in their own work, they had not lost this "freshness" and this joy in their writing and in their performing. As one critic commented, they combined the expertise of professional performers with the enthusiasm of amateurs.

It is very difficult for two people to "hold" an audience for an entire evening, but because of their versatility and their own pleasure in performing, Comden and Green were able to leave their audiences wanting more.

OTHER PERFORMANCES BY COMDEN AND GREEN BOTH ON STAGE AND IN FILMS

P02 *THE REVUERS* (1938-1944)

Betty Comden and Adolph Green, along with Judy Tuvim (Holliday), Alvin Hammer, and John Frank, began performing satirical sketches and songs at the Village Vanguard in 1938. They worked together at various night clubs, at Radio City Music Hall, and on radio. In 1943 four of them went to Los Angeles where they performed at the Trocadero. The group disbanded in 1944. Judy Tuvim and Alvin Hammer remained in Hollywood. Betty Comden and Adolph Green returned to New York. See pages 3-11 in the Biography.

P03 *ON THE TOWN* (1944)

Betty Comden played Claire the anthropologist and Adolph Green played Ozzie in their own first musical, *On the Town*. See S01 for details about the musical.

P04 *LYRICS AND LYRICISTS* (1971)

On January 10, 1971, Betty Comden and Adolph Green gave a reprise of their careers for one of the monthly series on *Lyrics and Lyricists* at the Young Men's-Women's Hebrew Association auditorium on 92nd Street in New York. They began with some of the songs and skits they had created for the Revuers and then, beginning with songs from *On the Town*, they progressed through the decades singing songs from their collaborations with Leonard Bernstein and Jule Styne. The program was similar to their *A Party With Betty Comden and Adolph Green*.

P05 *ON THE TWENTIETH CENTURY* (1979)

In January of 1979, toward the end of the Broadway run of *On the Twentieth Century*, Betty Comden took over the role of Letitia Primrose, the religious fanatic, while Imogene Coca was on vacation. Comden played the role from January 16 through January 22. Aside from her performances in *A Party With Betty Comden and Adolph Green*, Betty Comden had not appeared on Broadway since playing the role of Claire in *On the Town*. (See S07 for information about *On the Twentieth Century*.)

P06   *SIMON* (1980)

Adolph Green appeared in the film, *Simon*, an Orion release through Warner Brothers. *Simon* was produced by Martin Bregman and was written and directed by Marshall Brickman. The film was reviewed at the Directors Guild Theatre in Hollywood on February 19, 1980. Alan Arkin played a self-important but inept professor of psychology at Columbia University. The professor falls into the hands of a band of zany geniuses in a "think-tank" somewhere in Maine. The "thinkers" have become bored with thinking about practical and useful improvements for society and have become interested in outer space. They brainwash the professor into thinking he is an alien from some other planet. At last he escapes and is befriended by a commune of television-worshiping flower-children. Adolph Green plays the benign guru of the commune. Vincent Canby of the *New York Times* wrote that the guru was "impeccably played by Adolph Green in a manner that, at long last, defines for me the meaning of 'laid back.' Without half trying, Mr. Green ... radiates the lunatic cheerfulness that is the tone of *Simon* at its best" (March 16, 1980).

P07   *MY FAVORITE YEAR* (1982)

In 1982 Adolph Green appeared in the Metro-Goldwyn-Mayer film, *My Favorite Year*, which starred Peter O'Toole. The film was produced by Michael Guiskoff and directed by Richard Benjamin. The screenplay was by Norman Steinberg and Dennis Palumbo. The film was reviewed at the Metro-Goldwyn-Mayer Studios in Culver City on September 22, 1982. Peter O'Toole played Alan Swann, a movie idol, who is much given to drink and women. He is to appear on a live television show, and, in order to keep him sober for the occasion, the producers assign a junior script-writer, Benjy, (played by Mark Linn-Baker) to keep watch over him. Adolph Green played Leo Silver, a worried member of the television production staff.

P08   *ISN'T IT ROMANTIC?* (1984)

Betty Comden had been performing in *A Party With Betty Comden and Adolph Green*, but, aside from her one week as Letitia Primrose in *On the Twentieth Century* she had not acted in a dramatic role for nearly forty years. However, in 1984 she played a role in Wendy Wasserstein's play, *Isn't It Romantic?*, presented at Playwrights Horizons, Off Broadway. The play was directed by Gerald Gutierrez. In the play, thirty year old Janie Blumberg, an aspiring writer, finally frees herself from her domineering mother, Tasha Blumberg, played by Betty Comden. *Isn't It Romantic?* had originally been done at the Phoenix Theatre in 1981. Walter Kerr of the *New York Times* thought that the two young women, Janie and her friend Harriet, were well developed in the original version of the play but that their mothers were not. For the new version at Playwrights Horizons, he felt Wasserstein had rounded out the characters of the two mothers. Betty Comden, he wrote, was funny, but in the reworked version the audience was "instantly aware of a decidedly complicated woman behind Miss Comden's worried, ravishing smile" (February 26, 1984).

P09   *THE NEW YORKERS* (1984)

In the same year, Adolph Green took to the stage again. On September 12, 1984, he and his wife, Phyllis Newman, acted in two one act plays by Murray Schisgal as an opening production for the new 220 seat theatre, the Morse Center, at Manhattan's Trinity School on West 91st Street. The Green's daughter, Amanda, had graduated from the school in 1980. The two plays were *Pushcart Peddler*, a one act play that had been given some years earlier at the Ensemble Studio Theatre, and *Jealousy*, a new play written for the occasion. The two plays were given under the title, *The New Yorkers*, and were directed by William Maloney. Adolph Green was in both plays, acting with his daughter in the first play and with his wife in the second.

P10   *GARBO TALKS* (1984)

Also in 1984 both Betty Comden and Adolph Green were in *Garbo Talks*, a United Artists presentation of an Elliott Kastner production. The film was produced by Burtt Harris Kastner and directed by Sidney Lumet. The screenplay was written by Larry Grusin, and Cy Coleman provided the music. *Garbo Talks* starred Anne Bancroft as Estelle Rolfe, a woman who for years has been devoted to the films of Greta Garbo. When she realizes that she is dying, Estelle Rolfe's one wish is to meet the great actress. Her son Gilbert, played by Ron Silver, sets out to find the elusive Garbo. At last he sees her and, finally, is able to tell her about his mother. Garbo goes to visit Estelle in the hospital before she dies. Sidney Lumet, the director, wanted Betty to play Garbo because he and many others thought Betty resembled the famous actress. Adolph Green played a small role in a party scene. The film was reviewed on October 3, 1984.

P11   *LILY IN LOVE* (*JATSZANI KELL*) 1985

In 1985 Adolph Green was in the film, *Lily in Love*, a co-production with A Dialog Studio, Mafilm-Robert Halmi, Inc. The film was shot in Hungary and was directed by Koroly Makk. The screenplay was by Frank Cucci. The film starred Christopher Plummer and Maggie Smith as a husband and wife actor-writer team. Fritz is a famous Broadway actor whose wife has written a marvelous movie script. The script calls for a blond Italian. Fritz, with the help of his longtime agent, Jerry Silber (Adolph Green), and a make-up man, disguises himself in a blond wig and fakes an Italian accent. Fritz and his wife, Lily, fly to Budapest for the filming. They are accompanied by their friend, Jerry Silber. There are several very funny scenes involving the making of the film. The *New York Times* critic wrote that "Mr. Green is a delight as the implacable voice of reason" (April 19, 1985).

P12   Concert Version of *FOLLIES* (1985)

In 1985 both Betty Comden and Adolph Green appeared in a concert version of the musical, *Follies*. *Follies* had first been given as a fully produced musical in 1971. It had a book by James Goldman and music and lyrics by Stephen Sondheim. It was directed by Harold Prince and choreographed by Michael Bennett. The original Broadway cast album had been hastily assembled, and some songs were missing and others abridged. It was decided a new recording of the complete score needed to be made. The concert version was produced by Thomas Z. Shepard at Avery Fisher Hall at Lincoln Center. It was directed by Herbert Ross. The concert version was presented twice before a live audience on September 6 and 7, 1985. The New York Philharmonic Symphony Orchestra accompanied the concert, Paul Gemignani conducting. Narrative transitions were spoken by André Gregory. The occasion was a reunion of veterans of Sondheim musicals with the addition of other musical comedy performers. The audiences "simply erupted into pandemonium" when the stellar cast walked out on stage, and "the cheering went on and on," according to Frank Rich of the *New York Times* (September 9, 1985). In the cast were George Hearn, Lee Remick, Mandy Patinkin, Barbara Cook, Carol Burnett, Elaine Stritch, Liliane Montevecchi, Phyllis Newman, Betty Comden, Adolph Green, and others. Betty Comden and Adolph Green played the humorous couple, Emily and Theodore Whitman, and sang the song, "Rain on the Roof." The concert was recorded for an RCA Red Seal album. (See D52.) It was also filmed as a part of the Public Broadcasting Service's Great Performances Series. Frank Rich thought the concert was "as complete, gorgeously sung, and sumptuously played as Mr. Sondheim or his fans could wish" (*New York Times*, September 9, 1985).

P13   *FUNNY* (1988)

Adolph Green was one of the one hundred famous people who told their favorite jokes on Bran Ferren's 81 minute documentary film, *Funny*. The film was produced, directed, and photographed by Bran Ferren. Some others appearing in the film were Dick Cavett, Fred Ebb, Eli Wallach, Anne Jackson, and Alan King. The premiere was on August 13 at the John Drew Theatre at Guild Hall in East Hampton, New York. "The effect is good natured but a little numbing," wrote Vincent Canby of the *New York Times* (June 28, 1989).

P14   *SLAVES OF NEW YORK* (1989)

Betty Comden made a brief appearance in the 1989 film, *Slaves of New York*, which was based on Tama Janowitz's short stories about various denizens of the downtown art scene. Janowitz also wrote the screenplay. The film starred Bernadette Peters. It was directed by James Ivory and was released by Tri-Star Pictures. The film opened in New York at Cinema 1 on March 17, 1989. Betty Comden appeared as Mrs. Wheeler. Janet Maslin of the *New York Times* wrote that "the entire film feels like a series of jokes whose punch lines are missing." She thought the direction "surprisingly gimmicky at times" (March 17, 1989).

P15 *I WANT TO GO HOME* (1989)

Adolph Green appeared in the film, *I Want to Go Home*, which was co-produced by Films A2/La Sept and was filmed in Paris. Marin Karmitz produced the film and Alain Resnais directed. The screenplay was written by Jules Feiffer. Green played Joey Wellman, a cantankerous but likable American cartoonist, who travels to Paris accompanied by Lena Apthorp (Linda Lavin) to attend an exhibition of comic strip art in which his work is being shown. His real reason for going to Paris is to see his daughter, Elise (Laura Benson), who is taking some classes at the Sorbonne. Elise is infatuated with her professor, Christian Gauthier (Gerard Depardieu), who happens to be a comic book fan and a great admirer of Wellman's work. The professor takes Wellman and Elise to the country manor owned by his mother. There Wellman is reconciled with his daughter and finds such a kindred spirit in the professor's mother that he decides to stay in France. His daughter and Lena Apthorp return to the United States. *I Want to Go Home* was reviewed at Club 13 in Paris on August 31, 1989, and competed in the Venice Film Festival. The film did not receive good reviews. The reviewer for *Variety* wrote that "Resnais is at a loss to extract nuance and coordinate his cast as an ensemble" (September 13-19, 1989).

RADIO PROGRAMS PRESENTED BY THE REVUERS

The Revuers had a half-hour, weekly radio show on NBC from March 5, 1940, until November 3, 1940. They wrote the sketches, songs, and music, usually on a different subject each week, though some programs did not have a single subject. The format was an introduction, an opening number, a dialogue, a sketch, a song, another sketch or number, and a closing. Each member of The Revuers played a distinct character throughout the series. Some of the subjects were "Magazines," "Radio," "Newspapers," "Books," "Inventions,", and "Hollywood." For some of the shows there were guest singers who sang popular songs of the day.

NBC gave their files of these shows to the Library of Congress. The shows that the Library of Congress has are listed below.

RA01 *A Program of Music and Fun*   (3/5/40; NBC Radio, the Blue Network; 30 minutes, 9:30-10:00 p.m.)

The Revuers (Betty Comden, Judy Tuvim, Adolph Green, Alvin Hammer, and John Frank) appeared with Hiram Sherman, comedian, Elinor French, singer, Norman Cloutier's orchestra.

RA02 *A Program of Music and Fun* (4/9/40)

The Revuers with Charles Cantor, comedian, as "Randolph Schwee"; Elinor French, singer; Paul Laval's orchestra.

RA03 *A Program of Music and Fun* (4/23/40)

The Revuers with Charles Cantor as "Randolph Schwee;" Paul Laval's orchestra, and Gwen Williams, guest singer.

RA04 *A Program of Music and Fun* (4/30/40)

The Revuers with Charles Cantor, Paul Laval's orchestra, and Elinor French, guest singer.

212 Comden and Green

RA05 *A Program of Music and Fun* (5/14/40)

> The Revuers with Charles Cantor and Gwen Williams.

RA06 *A Program of Music and Fun* (5/21/40)

> The Revuers with Gwen Williams, Kenny Gardner, Paul Laval's orchestra.

RA07 *A Program of Music and Fun* (6/4/40)

> The Revuers with Gwen Williams, Kenny Gardner, Paul Laval's orchestra.

RA08 *A Program of Music and Fun* (6/11/40)

> The Revuers with Elinor French and Kenny Gardner.

RA09 *A Program of Music and Fun* (6/18/40)

> The Revuers with Gwen Williams, Kenny Gardner, Paul Laval's orchestra.

RA10 *A Program of Music and Fun* (7/2/40)

> The Revuers with Dinah Shore and Kenny Gardner.

RA11 *A Program of Music and Fun* (7/25/40)

> The Revuers with Dinah Shore and Kenny Gardner.

RA12 *A Program of Music and Fun* (7/30/40)

> The Revuers with Gwen Williams and Kenny Gardner.

RA13 *The Revuers' Audition for a Promotion for the Blue Network* (8/6/40; 2:40-2:51)

> The Revuers recorded an eleven minute audition for a promotion for the NBC experimental Blue Network.

RA14 *A Program of Music and Fun* (8/6/40)

> The Revuers with Dinah Shore and Kenny Gardner.

RA15 *A Program of Music and Fun* (8/25/40; Sunday, 4:30-5:00 p.m.)

The Revuers with Irving Miller's orchestra, Gwen Williams, and Kenny Gardner.

RA16 *A Program of Music and Fun* (9/22/40; 4:30-5:00)

The Revuers with Gwen Williams.

RA17 *A Program of Music and Fun* (9/29/40; 4:30-5:00)

The Revuers with Gwen Williams and Kenny Gardner. This program was a salute to Station WSFA, Montgomery, Alabama.

RA18 *A Program of Music and Fun* (10/6/40; 4:30-5:00)

The Revuers' program was in salute to Station WSM on its fifteenth anniversary.

RA19 *A Program of Music and Fun* (10/13/40; 4:30-5:00)

The Revuers' program was dedicated to the Auto Show. Kenny Gardner and Betty Randall, guest singers.

RA20 *A Program of Music and Fun* (11/3/40; 1:30-2:00 p.m.)

The Revuers' program for this day only was at 1:30 p.m. and was in celebration of the 20th anniversary of Radio Broadcasting. Gwen Williams and Kenny Gardner, guest singers.

OTHER RADIO APPEARANCES BY COMDEN AND GREEN

RA21 *Maggi McNellis Show* (1/25/45; NBC Radio)

Betty Comden and Adolph Green were guests on the *Maggi McNellis Show*.

RA22 *Mary Margaret McBride Show* (12/28/45; NBC Radio)

Betty Comden was a guest on the *Mary Margaret McBride Show*.

RA23 *Christmas Program*, 1956 (12/25/56; NBC Radio and TV)

214 Comden and Green

A "Special All-Star Show for Hungarian Relief." Betty Comden and Adolph Green were guests. They sang the popular song, "Inspiration," (from *Bonanza Bound!* and *A Party With Betty Comden and Adolph Green*). This show was taped.

TELEVISION APPEARANCES OF COMDEN AND GREEN

T01 *The Revuers* (1939; DuMont Television)

The Revuers (Adolph Green, Betty Comden, Judy Tuvim (Holliday), John Frank, and Alvin Hammer) presented a satirical tour of the World's Fair that was being held in New York City in 1939.

T02 *The Revuers* (6/1/40; NBC Television; 60 minutes)

The Revuers appeared in a full hour television program on NBC.

T03 *The Tonight Show* (10/21/54; NBC Television; 60 minutes)

Betty Comden and Adolph Green were guests on the show, which starred Steve Allen.

T04 *The Tonight Show* (3/9/55; NBC Television; 60 minutes)

Betty Comden and Adolph Green were guests on the show.

T05 *The Tonight Show* (5/30/55; NBC Television; 60 minutes)

Betty Comden and Adolph Green were guests on the show.

T06 *Middle East Crisis and Hungarian Revolt Against Soviet Occupation* (12/25/56; NBC Television)

Betty Comden and Adolph Green performed their well-known song, "Inspiration," (*Bonanza Bound!* and *A Party With Betty Comden and Adolph Green*) on this special Hungarian Refugee Relief Program.

T07 *The Today Show* (sponsor segment) (12/6/57; NBC Television; 60 minutes)

Betty Comden and Adolph Green were interviewed and performed on the occasion of the second anniversary of their play, *Bells Are Ringing*.

T08 *The Jack Parr Show* (6/58; NBC Television; 105 minutes)

Betty Comden and Adolph Green appeared on *The Jack Parr Show* in June 1958. They sang some of their own material. It was this appearance that gave Gus Schirmir the idea for having Comden and Green appear at the Cherry Lane Theatre presenting their own songs. The result was the original production of *A Party With Betty Comden and Adolph Green*. (See P01.)

T09 *The Jack Parr Show* (sponsor segment and co-op) (8/11/58; NBC Television; 60 minutes)

Betty Comden and Adolph Green were guests on the show.

T10 *The Ed Sullivan Show* (l/21/59; CBS Television; 60 minutes)

Betty Comden and Adolph Green appeared on the show. They did some of their songs from *A Party*. Some of Ed Sullivan's other guests were Celeste Holm, Andrew Duggan, Pat Sazuki, Antoinetta Stella, Edith Piaf, Alan Drake, and the columnist Marie Torre.

T11 *Leonard Bernstein and the New York Philharmonic: The Humors of Music* (3/22/59; CBS Television; 60 minutes)

Leonard Bernstein used the subject of humor in music in this his last of the season sessions on musical appreciation. With the help of the New York Philharmonic symphony orchestra, he explored humor in music with illustrations from the classical catalogue. In order to distinguish between parody and satire in music, he presented Betty Comden and Adolph Green in an amusing operatic take-off from the musical, *On the Town*.

T12 *The Jack Parr Show* (sponsor) (5/1/59; NBC Television; 60 minutes)

Betty Comden and Adolph Green were guests on the show.

T13 *Music From Shubert Alley* (11/13/59; NBC Television) color tape

This television special included songs from musical comedies of the past sixty years. Comden and Green sang "Just in Time" with Andy Williams, the

Master of Ceremonies. Comden and Green also sang "I Said Good Morning to the Sun" and "New York, New York."

T14 *The Fabulous Fifties* (1/31/60; CBS Television; 2 hours)

Comden and Green appeared in *The Fabulous Fifties*, a two hour special saluting the decade of the 1950s. The show was produced by Leland Hayward. The director was Norman Jewison. Also appearing on the show were Julie Andrews, Shelly Berman, Henry Fonda, Jackie Gleason, Rex Harrison, Elaine May, Mike Nichols, Suzy Parker, and Eric Severeid. Writers of the show were Max Wolk, A. J. Russell, and Stephen Sondheim. The music was directed by Alfredo Anotonini, Franz Allers, John Lesko, and Jay Blackton. Comden and Green did a parody on "Television."

T15 *The Arthur Murray Party* (alternate sponsor) (4/16/60; NBC Television) color tape

Betty Comden and Adolph Green were guests.

T16 *The Today Show* (sponsor segments) (7/8/60; NBC Television; 60 minutes)

Betty Comden and Adolph Green were guests. Dave Garroway was the host.

T17 *The American Musical Theatre* (1/15/61; WCBS Television, New York; 30 minutes)

Betty Comden, Adolph Green, and Jule Styne appeared on this educational series. The emphasis was upon musical developers rather than the development of musicals. The programs were designed primarily for a teenaged studio audience. The young people were able to ask questions. Comden, Green, and Styne were currently represented on Broadway by *Do Re Mi*. Susan Johnson and Earl Wrightson sang several songs from *Do Re Mi* and other musicals. The host for the show was Jim Morske.

T18 *Academy Awards 1961* (4/16/61; CBS Television; 60 minutes)

Betty Comden and Adolph Green were presenters on the Academy Awards show in 1961. They presented Daniel Mandell an Oscar for his film editing of *The Apartment*, the picture which won the award for Best Picture of the Year.

218 Comden and Green

T19 *PM East/PM West* (9/7/61; WNEW Television and all Westinghouse Stations; 60 minutes)

Betty Comden and Adolph Green and their spouses, along with Jule Styne, appeared on *PM East/PM West*. The host was Mike Wallace. The "East" portion of the program consisted of a kind of "The Life and Times of Betty Comden and Adolph Green." As the critic for *Variety* wrote, they "had a ball" (September 13, 1961). Phyllis Newman assisted Comden and Green in the singing of songs from *On the Town, Bells Are Ringing,* and *Do Re Mi*. *PM West* featured a tribute to Wolfie Gilbert with Buddy DeSilva and Morton DaCosta.

T20 *David Brinkley's Journal* (alternate sponsor) "The Birth of a Broadway Musical" (12/27/61; NBC Television; 30 minutes) color

On the same night that the musical, *Subways Are for Sleeping*, debuted on Broadway, David Brinkley devoted his entire half-hour show to the study of how *Subways* was prepared for its opening night. He showed story conferences by Comden and Green, Jule Styne, and Michael Kidd, the director. He showed some ensemble rehearsals and some musical sessions by the stars of the show. Then he presented scenes from the Boston tryout.

T21 *The Tonight Show* (sponsor segments) (8/24/62; NBC Television)

Betty Comden and Adolph Green were guests on the show.

T22 *That Was the Week That Was* (various sponsors) (12/15/64; NBC Television; 30 minutes) live, color

Betty Comden and Adolph Green were special guest stars.

T23 *The Match Game* (11/2/66; NBC Television; 25 minutes)

Gene Rayburn was the host. Guest panelists included Phyllis Newman, Mark Goodson, Sue Oakland, Richard Adler, Betty Comden, and Adolph Green.

T24 *The Today Show* (12/2/66; NBC Television; 60 minutes) pre-taped

Betty Comden and Adolph Green were guests on a pre-taped special, "A Morning With Comden and Green." Phyllis Newman joined them in presenting a medley of Comden and Green musical hits.

T25 *The Today Show* (3/7/67; NBC Television; 60 minutes)

Betty Comden and Adolph Green were guests who talked about their new musical, *Hallelujah, Baby!*.

T26 *Tony Awards 1968*, presented by Eastern Airlines, Inc. (4/21/68; NBC Television; 110 minutes) live, color

The 1968 Tony Awards program was telecast live from the Sam S. Shubert Theatre, New York City. *Hallelujah, Baby!* was chosen the Best Musical Play. The music was by Jule Styne. Comden and Green did the lyrics, and Arthur Laurents wrote the book. Jule Styne and Betty Comden and Adolph Green also were awarded a Tony as Best Composer and Lyricists. Leslie Uggams, the star of *Hallelujah, Baby!*, won a Tony as Best Actress in a Musical Play. The Awards program included a recreated scene from *Hallelujah, Baby!*. The producer for the television show was Alexander H. Cohen. The writer was Hildy Parks, and the director was Stan Harris. Other recipients were Leonard Bernstein, Carol Burnett, and Sir Laurence Olivier. (For more information about *Hallelujah, Baby!* see S13.)

T27 *Tony Awards 1969* (4/20/69; NBC Television; 127 minutes)

The Tony Awards were presented live from the Mark Hellinger Theatre, New York City. Special awards were presented to Leonard Bernstein, Carol Burnett, and Rex Harrison. Comden and Green were among the presenters. The Tony Awards show was written by Hildy Parks, directed by Clark Jones, and produced by Alexander H. Cohen.

T28 *The Tonight Show Starring Johnny Carson* (10/23/69; NBC Television; 90 minutes)

Betty Comden and Adolph Green were guests on the show.

T29 *The Today Show* (4/10/70; NBC Television; 60 minutes)

Betty Comden and Adolph Green were guests.

T30 *Tony Awards 1970* (4/19/70; NBC Television; 103 minutes)

The 1970 Tony Awards program was telecast live from the Mark Hellinger Theatre. *Applause* was chosen the Best Musical Play. The music was by Charles Strouse and the lyrics by Lee Adams. Betty Comden and Adolph Green wrote the book. Lauren Bacall was presented a Tony for her leading role and Ron Field received Tony Awards for his directing and his choreography. The television show used the title tune from *Applause*. The producer was Alexander H. Cohen. The writer was Hildy Parks, and the director was Clark Jones. (For more information about *Applause* see S15.)

T31 *The Today Show* (10/25/71; NBC Television; 60 minutes)

Betty Comden and Adolph Green were guests on the show.

T32 *Tony Awards 1978* (6/4/78; CBS Television; 97 minutes)

The 1978 Tony Awards program was telecast live from the Sam S. Shubert Theatre. Betty Comden and Adolph Green were presented Tony Awards for their book for *On the Twentieth Century* and also, along with Cy Coleman, for their score for the musical. The musical itself was nominated but did not win a Tony. John Cullum and Kevin Kline both won Tonys for their performances. Robin Wagner won for his Outstanding Scenic Design. (For more information about *On the Twentieth Century* see S07.)

T33 *Bernstein at 60, An Appreciation From Wolf Trap* (8/25/78; PBS Television; 8:30; 150 minutes)

Leonard Bernstein celebrated his sixtieth birthday with fellow conductor Mstislav Rostopovich and other artists including Betty Comden, Adolph Green, Lauren Bacall, Aaron Copland, Lillian Hellman, tenor James King, mezzo-soprano Christa Ludwig, and composer William Schuman. Presented live from Wolf Trap.

T34 *A Party With Betty Comden and Adolph Green* (7/80; Mobil Showcase Network; 2 hours)

Comden and Green's stage show, *A Party With Betty Comden and Adolph Green*, had been videotaped and was shown on the Mobil Showcase Network's *Summershow* in July 1980. (For more information about *A Party With Betty Comden and Adolph Green* see P01.)

T35 *Kennedy Center Honors* (12/27/80; CBS Television; 9:00 p.m., 120 minutes)

Kennedy Center honorees for lifetime achievement were Leonard Bernstein, James Cagney, Agnes de Mille, Lynn Fontanne, and Leontyne Price. In the tribute to Bernstein there was a performance of the overture for his *Candide* and Betty Comden and Adolph Green sang "New York, New York" from *On the Town*.

T36 *Kennedy Center Honors* (12/25/82; CBS Television; 8:00 p.m., 120 minutes)

Tributes were paid to George Abbott, Lillian Gish, Benny Goodman, Gene Kelly, and Eugene Ormandy. In the tribute to Gene Kelly, the famous dance in the rain from the film, *Singin' in the Rain*, was shown. Then Betty Comden Adolph Green, and Cyd Charisse danced and sang a take-off on the *Singin' in the Rain* dance. George Stevens, Jr., was the producer of the television show.

T37 *A Party With Betty Comden and Adolph Green* (4/21/85; Cable Television, Arts and Entertainment Network; 2 hours)

The videotaped version of Comden and Green's stage show, *A Party With Betty Comden and Adolph Green*, was shown on national cable television, the Arts and Entertainment Network. (See P01.)

T38 *American Film Institute Tribute to Gene Kelly* (5/7/85; CBS Television; 9:30 p.m., 90 minutes)

In this tribute to Gene Kelly the complete *Singin' in the Rain* solo sequences by Kelly were shown. Betty Comden and Adolph Green paid tribute to Gene Kelly. Green called him "a torrent of dance, song, and charm." George Stevens, Jr., was the producer of the television show. Don Mischer was the director and Nick Perito was the musical director.

T39 *Great Performances: Follies in Concert* (3/14/86; PBS Television; 9:00 p.m., 120 minutes)

This was a behind-the-scenes look at the all-star cast gathering to perform the concert version of Stephen Sondheim's musical *Follies*. Betty Comden and Adolph Green were in the cast. Filmed at Lincoln Center's Avery Fisher Hall.

T40 *Tony Awards 1991* (6/2/91; CBS Television; 2 hours)

The Tony Awards program for the 1990-1991 season was presented in a live telecast from the Minskoff Theatre on June 2, 1991. *The Will Rogers Follies* was chosen Best Musical Play. The book was by Peter Stone. The music was by Cy Coleman and the lyrics by Betty Comden and Adolph Green. Coleman and Comden and Green also received a Tony Award for the Best Score for a Musical. (For more information about *The Will Rogers Follies* see S14.)

Comden and Green

T41 *Kennedy Center Honors* (12/30/91; CBS Television; 2 hours)

On December 6, 1991, Comden and Green were honored at the Kennedy Center Honors Gala in Washington, D.C., for their Lifetime Achievements in the Performing Arts. The program was telecast on December 30, 1991. Honored along with Comden and Green were Gregory Peck, Fayard and Harold Nicholas, Roy Acuff, and Robert Shaw.

T42 *Kennedy Center Honors* (12/8/92; CBS Television; 2 hours)

Betty Comden paid tribute to Paul Taylor, dancer and choreographer, at the Kennedy Center Honors Gala in Washington, D.C., on December 8, 1992. The program was telecast on December 26, 1992.

COMDEN AND GREEN MUSICALS PRESENTED ON TELEVISION

T43 *Peter Pan* (3/7/55; NBC Television; 2 hours)

In 1955 the first colorcast of *Peter Pan* was presented by the original Broadway cast on *Producers Showcase* on NBC. The New York run of the show had ended only nine days before. Richard Halliday was the Broadway producer and Fred Coe was the producer for the live television version. Jerome Robbins had directed the Broadway show; Clark Jones directed the show for television. The *Variety* reviewer, George Rosin, called the show "a sheer delight" (March 9, 1955). (For more information about *Peter Pan* see S17.)

T44 *Peter Pan* (1/9/56; NBC Television; 2 hours)

In 1956 *Peter Pan* was telecast once again on *Producers Showcase* on NBC. The original cast was also used for this re-staging of the show. The *Variety* reviewer noted that the "score...improved with repeat hearings" (January 11, 1956). (See S17.)

T45 *Wonderful Town* (11/30/58; CBS Television; 2 hours)

Wonderful Town was presented on television after the show had closed on Broadway. Rosalind Russell played Ruth once again, but many of the cast members for the television production were new. Jacquelyn McKeever played Eileen and Sydney Chaplin played Robert Baker. The producers for the telecast were Joseph Fields and Robert Fryer. The director was Mel Ferber. The *Variety* reviewer thought the musical needed updating and he was disappointed in Jacquelyn McKeever's Eileen, calling her "affected" and "kittenish" (December 3, 1958). (For more information about *Wonderful Town* see S10.)

T46 *Peter Pan* (12/8/60; NBC Television; 2 hours)

This third telecast of *Peter Pan* was taped and has become a favorite for showing on television at Christmas time. The video tape is now available for home viewing. Lynn Fontanne did the off-screen narration for the show. Mary Martin, Cyril Ritchard, Sondra Lee (Tiger Lily), and most of the original adult cast members were in this production. However, there was a new Wendy--Maureen Bailey. The child actors who had appeared in earlier versions had by now outgrown their characters. New young actors were cast in these roles. The production was directed by Vincent J. Donehue. The *Variety* reviewer called this version "the best of the *Pans*" (December 14, 1960). (For more information about *Peter Pan* see S17.)

T47   **Scenes from *Do Re Mi* on *The Ed Sullivan Show*** (10/22/61; CBS Television; 60 minutes)

The Ed Sullivan Show presented on October 22, 1961, started off with Chubby Checker and twenty dancers from the *Do Re Mi* cast doing the "Twist." Wayne and Shuster presented a takeoff on *The Twilight Zone*, and Matt Munro sang. During the last half hour of the show, Phil Silvers, Nancy Walker, George Mathews, and 45 members of the cast of *Do Re Mi* presented the first three scenes of the Broadway show. These scenes included four songs with lyrics by Comden and Green--"Waiting, Waiting," "Take a Job," "It's Legitimate," and a sampling of "All You Need Is a Quarter." (For more information about *Do Re Mi* see S12.)

T48   *I'm Getting Married* (3/16/67; ABC Television; 60 minutes)

I'm Getting Married was an original musical written by Comden and Green especially for television. It was presented on ABC's *Stage 67* on March 16, 1967. There were only two characters, the young man and young woman who are getting married. These roles were played by Dick Shawn and Anne Bancroft. Comden and Green tried to write for the intimacy of television and thus used a minimum of plot with the concentration on the actions and reactions of the two people contemplating their marriage. Comden and Green have written about this venture into television writing in "He Says 'I Do,' She Says 'I Do,'" *New York Times*, March 12, 1967.

T49   *Applause* (3/15/73; CBS Television, 2 hours)

In 1973 the stage musical, *Applause*, for which Comden and Green had written the book, was playing in London. Lauren Bacall and Penny Fuller, who had both been in the Broadway production, were continuing in their roles as Margo, the aging actress, and Eve, the young actress out to take Margo's place. The London cast was taped in a production of the show for television. Ron Field, who had directed the show on Broadway, was the director and choreographer. The television director was Bill Foster. John J. O'Connor, the *New York Times* television critic, wrote that "the book ... distills enough of the film and Mary Orr's original short story to provide a narrative structure unusually strong for any Broadway musical." He thought the score by Charles Strouse and Lee Adams "a considerably less impressive matter."

He also thought that Lauren Bacall's "intensity" was occasionally a little "excessive" for television (March 15, 1973). (For more information about *Applause* see S15.)

T50 *The Madwoman of Central Park West* (8/18/80; ABC Television; 60 minutes)

Phyllis Newman's one woman show, *The Madwoman of Central Park West*, had been taped in March of 1980 and was shown on the Mobil Showcase Network's *Summershow* on August 18, 1980. This musical program includes the song, "Up, Up, Up" with music by Leonard Bernstein and lyrics by Comden and Green. (For more information about *The Madwoman of Central Park West* see S21.)

DISCOGRAPHY

The following is a list of recordings made of stage musicals, revues, and films for which Betty Comden and Adolph Green wrote the book or the lyrics or both. Most of the records are original cast recordings with the New York casts. However, there are also some recordings listed that were made by the traveling company, from the television production, or by the original London cast. The records are under the title of the musical and are listed in alphabetical order. At the end, beginning with D42, are listed other recordings which include Comden and Green lyrics. Many of these recordings have been reissued on compact discs or on cassette tapes.

D01 *Applause*　　Broadway Cast　(ABC; 1970) ABC OCS-11
　　　　　　　　　　Reissued: (MCA Records; 1970) MCA 1632

Original Broadway cast recording with Lauren Bacall, Len Cariou, Penny Fuller, and Bonnie Franklin. The book is by Betty Comden and Adolph Green and is based on the film *All About Eve* and the original story by Mary Orr. Music by Charles Strouse. Lyrics by Lee Adams. Orchestrations by Philip J. Lang. Musical direction and vocal arrangements by Donald Pippin. See S15 for more information.

Songs include:
Overture (Orchestra); Back Stage Babble (First Nighters); Think How It's Gonna Be (Len Cariou); But Alive (Lauren Bacall and Boys); The Best Night of My Life (Penny Fuller); Who's That Girl? (Bacall and Fuller); Applause (Bonnie Franklin and the Gypsies); Hurry Back (Bacall); Fasten Your Seat Belt (Bacall, Ann Williams, Cariou, Robert Mandan, Lee Roy Reams, and Guests); Welcome to the Theatre (Bacall); Good Friends (Bacall, Williams, Brandon Maggart); She's No Longer a Gypsy (Franklin, Reams, and the Gypsies); One of a Kind (Bacall and Cariou); One Hallowe'en (Penny Fuller); Something Greater (Bacall and Cariou); Finale (Company).

Note: There are also recordings by the Original Television Cast (CBS, March 215, 1973), by the Original Cast with replacements, including Anne Baxter, and by the Road Company with Eleanor Parker.

D02 *Auntie Mame* Highlights from the Film (Bronislau Kaper; 1958)
Bronislau Kaper WB W1242/WS 1242

The record contains highlights from the score of the film which starred Rosalind Russell. The screenplay is by Betty Comden and Adolph Green and was based on the novel, *Auntie Mame*, by Patrick Dennis and the play, *Auntie Mame*, by Jerome Lawrence and Robert E. Lee. See F08 for more details about the film.

D03 *The Band Wagon* Film (Metro-Goldwyn-Mayer; 1953) E 3051
(soundtrack) mono. Compact Disc: MCA 25015

The original soundtrack recording featuring Fred Astaire, Jack Buchanan, Nanette Fabray, Oscar Levant, and India Adams (for Cyd Charisse). Screenplay by Betty Comden and Adolph Green. Music by Arthur Schwartz and lyrics by Howard Dietz. Orchestrations by Conrad Salinger, Skip Martin, and Alexander Courage. Musical direction by Adolph Deutsch. See F06 for more information.

Songs include:
A Shine on Your Shoes (Fred Astaire); By Myself (Astaire); Dancing in the Dark (Orchestra); Triplets (Astaire, Nanette Fabray, Jack Buchanan); New Sun in the Sky (India Adams); I Guess I'll Have to Change My Plans (Astaire, Buchanan); Louisiana Hayride (Fabray, Chorus); I Love Louisa (Astaire, Chorus); That's Entertainment (Astaire, Fabray, Buchanan, Adams, Oscar Levant, Chorus); The Girl Hunt Ballet (Astaire) spoken (musical adaptation: Roger Edens; narration written by Alan Jay Lerner).

Note: The following selections were not used in the film, but were released on other albums:

Out Takes OTF 1 Gotta Bran' New Suit (Fabray, Astaire)
You Have Everything (Orchestra)

Out Takes OTF 2 Sweet Music to Worry the Wolf Away (Fabray, Levant)

Music from *The Band Wagon* (includes seven songs not on the original album) (Sony Music Special Products; 1990) Compact Disc: AK 46197; Tape: AT-46197

D04 *The Barkleys of Broadway* Film (Metro-Goldwyn-Mayer; 1949)
Metro-Goldwyn-Mayer L-8 (78 rpm soundtrack) mono; Reissued: Metro-Goldwyn-Mayer 2-SES-51 ST

The original soundtrack featuring Fred Astaire and Ginger Rogers. Screenplay by Betty Comden and Adolph Green. Music by Harry Warren.

Lyrics by Ira Gershwin. Orchestrations by Conrad Salinger. Musical direction by Lennie Hayton. See F02 for more information.

Songs include:
Overture (Swing Trot) (Chorus); Sabre Dance (Oscar Levant, piano) music: Khatchaturian; You'd Be Hard to Replace (Fred Astaire); Bouncin' the Blues (Orchestra); My One and Only Highland Fling (Astaire, Ginger Rogers); A Weekend in the Country (Astaire, Rogers, Levant); Shoes with Wings On (Astaire); Piano Concerto (Levant, piano) music: Tchaikovsky; They Can't Take That Away from Me (Astaire); Sarah Bernhardt Audition (Rogers) spoken; Manhattan Downbeat (Astaire, Chorus); Finale (Orchestra).

Note: The following songs were released on other albums:

Metro-Goldwyn-Mayer (78 rpm) 50016	You'd Be Hard to Replace (Fred Astaire); My One and Only Highland Fling (Astaire, Ginger Rogers)
Metro-Goldwyn-Mayer (78 rpm) 50017	Shoes With Wings On (Astaire); They Can't Take That Away from Me, Music and lyrics: George and Ira Gershwin (Astaire)

Soundtrak STK - 116 (soundtrack) mono

D05 *Bells Are Ringing* Broadway Cast (Columbia; 1958) Col. OL 5170 and Col. OS 2006; Compact Disc: CK-2006; Tape: JST2006 mono

Original Broadway cast recording with Judy Holliday, Sydney Chaplin, and Jean Stapleton. Book and lyrics by Betty Comden and Adolph Green. Music by Jule Styne. Orchestrations by Robert Russell Bennett. Musical direction by Milton Rosenstock. See S04 for more information.

Songs include:
Overture (Orchestra); Bells Are Ringing (Girls); It's a Perfect Relationship (Judy Holliday and Boys); On My Own (Sydney Chaplin, Ensemble); It's a Simple Little System (Eddie Lawrence, Ensemble); Is It a Crime? (Holliday); Hello, Hello There! (Holliday, Chaplin, Ensemble); I Met a Girl (Chaplin, Ensemble); Long Before I Knew You (Holliday, Chaplin); Mu-Cha-Cha (Holliday, Peter Gennaro, Ensemble); Just in Time (Holliday, Chaplin, Ensemble); Drop That Name (Holliday, Ensemble); The Party's Over (Holliday); Salzburg (Jean Stapleton, Lawrence); The Midas Touch (Ensemble); I'm Going Back (Holliday).

D06 Bells Are Ringing Film (Metro-Goldwyn-Mayer; 1960) Capitol W/SW 1435 (soundtrack) stereo; Compact Disc: Capitol CDP 792060-2

The original soundtrack for the film featuring Judy Holliday, Dean Martin, and Eddie Foy, Jr. Screenplay and lyrics by Betty Comden and Adolph Green. Music by Jule Styne. Orchestrations by Alexander Courage and Pete King. Musical direction by André Previn. See F09 for more information.

Songs include:
Overture/Bells Are Ringing (Orchestra, Chorus); It's a Perfect Relationship (Judy Holliday); Do It Yourself (Dean Martin); It's a Simple Little System (Eddie Foy, Jr., Chorus); Better Than a Dream (Holliday, Martin); I Met a Girl (Martin, Chorus); Just in Time (Martin, Holliday, Chorus); Drop That Name (Holliday, Chorus); The Party's Over (Holliday, Chorus); The Midas Touch (Hal Linden, Girls); I'm Going Back (Holliday); Finale (Chorus).

Additional soundtrack selections cut from the film:

Out Takes OTF 1   Is It a Crime? (Holliday) LP

SPO (45rpm) 145 B   My Guiding Star (Martin)

Music from *Bells Are Ringing* (Capitol; 1989); Tape: C41F-92060

D07 Billion Dollar Baby Four Songs (Premier; 1991) Compact Disc: PR 1016

There was no original Broadway cast recording of *Billion Dollar Baby*. Four songs from the musical have been recorded with a piano accompaniment on a compact disc called *Broadway Dreams*. This contains some of Morton Gould's songs from *Enter Juliet*, *Billion Dollar Baby*, and *Something To Do*. Also on the disc are some songs by Jerome Moross from *Underworld* and *Parade*. Betty Comden and Adolph Green wrote the book and lyrics for *Billion Dollar Baby*. The music was by Morton Gould. The musical starred Joan McCracken. This compact disc recording features singers Helene Williams, Sheila Wormer, Craig Mason, Robert McCormick, and Aldyn McKean. Leonard Lehrman is at the piano. See S02 for more information about *Billion Dollar Baby*.

Songs include:
I Got a One Track Mind (Aldyn McKean, Helene Williams); Bad Timing (Robert McCormick); I'm Sure of Your Love (Craig Mason); Lovely Girl (McCormick).

Note: The following selections have been released on other recordings:

Heritage H 0057   Broadway Blossom and Bad Timing are sung by
(12" LP)   Betty Comden and Adolph Green.

	RCA LM 2633 (12" LP)	I'm Sure of Your Love was recorded by the Morton Gould Orchestra.
	RCA 60150 (12" LP) Compact Disc Set: 60150-2-RD	The song and dance, Charleston, was included in the and Broadway production of *Jerome Robbins' Broadway* and has been recorded on that album. The song is sung by the ensemble. (See D19.)
D08	*Bonanza Bound!*	One Song Recorded on *A Party With Betty Comden and Adolph Green* (Capitol; 1958 and Stet; 1977) Capitol SWAO 1197 and Stet S2L 5177

Bonanza Bound! never reached Broadway and there was no original cast recording of it released. Betty Comden and Adolph Green have included one song from the musical in two of their versions of *A Party With Betty Comden and Adolph Green*, both of which have been recorded. (See D27 and D28.) Book and lyrics for *Bonanza Bound!* are by Comden and Green. Music is by Saul Chaplin. In the 1958 version of *A Party With Betty Comden and Adolph Green* the pianist was Peter Howard, and in the 1977 version Paul Trueblood was at the piano. See S03 for more information about *Bonanza Bound!* and P01 for information about *A Party*.

The song from *Bonanza Bound!* included in the recordings of *A Party With Betty Comden and Adolph Green* is Inspiration (Comden, Green).

D09	*Bonanza Bound!/The Revuers*	(Boxoffice) Boxoffice JJA 19764 (12"LP)

Songs from *Bonanza Bound!* were recorded by the original cast along with some of the songs that had been used by the Revuers. The original RCA album was never released, but the songs have been released on this record.

Songs include:
Little Fish; Tell Me Why; Fill 'Er Up; Misunderstood; Up in Smoke; Bonanza; True; Spring; Inspiration.

D10	*Do Re Mi*	Broadway Cast (RCA Victor; 1961) RCA Victor LOCD/LSOD 2002 and (RCA Victor; 1965) LOC/LSO 1105

Original Broadway cast recording featuring Phil Silvers, Nancy Walker, John Reardon, and Nancy Dussault. The book is by Garson Kanin. The lyrics are by Betty Comden and Adolph Green. Music by Jule Styne. Orchestrations by Luther Henderson and musical direction by Lehman Engel. See S12 for more information.

Songs include:
Overture (Orchestra); Waiting, Waiting (Nancy Walker); All You Need Is a Quarter (Chorus); Take a Job (Phil Silvers, Walker); It's Legitimate (Silvers, George Mathews, David Burns, George Givot, Chorus); I Know About Love (John Reardon); Cry Like the Wind (Nancy Dussault); Ambition (Silvers, Dussault); Fireworks (Reardon, Dussault); What's New at the Zoo? (Dussault, Chorus); Asking for You (Reardon); The Late, Late Show (Silvers); Adventure (Silvers, Walker); Make Someone Happy (Reardon); All of My Life! (Silvers); Finale (Entire Company).

D11 *Do Re Mi* London Cast (That's Entertainment; 1961) That's Entertainment TER 1075

Original London cast featuring Max Bygraves, Maggi Fitzgibbon, Steve Arlen, and Jan Waters. Same songs as the Broadway recording.

D12 *Do Re Mi, Behind the Scenes with George Marek* Interviews with the producer and the authors of *Do Re Mi* (RCA) RCA SP 33-113

Interviews with David Merrick, Jule Styne, Betty Comden, and Adolph Green. Side 1: An interview with David Merrick. Side 2: Jule Styne, Betty Comden, and Adolph Green discuss the development of the musical.

D13 *A Doll's Life* Broadway Cast (CBS; 1982) CBS OC 8241 Reissued: (CBS in Association with Topaz Entertainment; 1965) CBS P18846; Compact Disc: Bay Cities BCD 3031; Tape: OCC824

The original Broadway Cast featuring Betsy Joslyn, George Hearn, Peter Gallagher, Edmund Lyndeck, and Barbara Lang. Book and lyrics by Betty Comden and Adolph Green. Music by Larry Grossman. Orchestrations by Billy Byers and musical direction by Paul Gemignani. See S08 for more information.

Songs include:
Overture (Orchestra); Prologue: A Woman Alone (Betsy Joslyn, Peter Gallagher, Norman A. Large, Company); Letter to the Children (Joslyn); New Year's Eve (Edmund Lyndeck, George Hearn, David Vosburgh, Large); Stay With Me, Nora (Gallagher, Joslyn); She Thinks That's the Answer (Barbara Lang, Company); The Arrival (Lang, Company); Loki and Baldur (Gallagher, Singers); You Interest Me (Hearn); The Departure (Lang, Company); Letter from Klemnacht (Lang); Learn to Be Lonely (Joslyn); Rats and Mice and Fish (Women); Jailer, Jailer (Joslyn, Women); Rare Wines (Lyndeck, Joslyn); No More Mornings (Joslyn, Company); There She Is (Hearn, Lyndeck, Gallagher); Power (Joslyn); Reprise: Letter to the Children (Joslyn); At Last (Hearn); The Grand Cafe (Company); Finale: Can You Hear Me Now? (Joslyn, Company).

D14 *Fade Out–Fade In* Broadway Cast (ABC Paramount; 1964) ABC/ABCS OC3

Original Broadway cast featuring Carol Burnett, Jack Cassidy, Dick Patterson, Tina Louise, Mitchell Jason, and Lou Jacobi. Book and lyrics by Betty Comden and Adolph Green. Music by Jule Styne. Orchestrations by Ralph Burns and Ray Ellis. Musical direction by John Berkman. See S06 for more information.

Songs include:
Overture (Orchestra); Oh, Those Thirties (Jack Cassidy); It's Good to Be Back Home (Carol Burnett); Fear (Dick Patterson, Mitchell Jason, Cassidy, Nephews); Call Me Savage (Burnett, Patterson); The Usher from the Mezzanine (Burnett); I'm With You (Burnett, Cassidy); My Fortune Is My Face (Cassidy); Lila Tremaine (Burnett); Go Home Train (Burnett); Close Harmony (Cassidy, Lou Jacobi, Tina Louise, Nephews); You Mustn't Be Discouraged (Burnett, Tiger Haynes); The Dangerous Age (Jacobi); L. Z. In Quest of His Youth (Orchestra); My Heart Is Like a Violin (Cassidy); The Fiddler and the Fighter (Cassidy, Ensemble); Fade Out--Fade In (Burnett, Patterson); Finale (Entire Company).

D15 *Good News* Film (Metro-Goldwyn-Mayer; 1947) Metro-Goldwyn-Mayer E 504 (soundtrack) mono; Compact Disc: MCA 39083; (Sony Music Special Products) Compact Disc: AK-47025; Tape: AT-47025

The original soundtrack featuring June Allyson, Peter Lawford, Joan McCracken, Pat Marshall, Mel Tormé. Screenplay by Betty Comden and Adolph Green. Music by Ray Henderson. Lyrics by B. G. DeSylva and Lew Brown. Musical direction by Lennie Hayton. See F01 for more information.

Songs include:
Good News (Tait College) (Joan McCracken, Chorus); Be a Ladies' Man (Peter Lawford, Ray MacDonald, Tom Dugan, Lou Tindall, Mel Tormé); Lucky in Love (Pat Marshall, McCracken, Tormé, June Allyson, Lawford, Chorus); The French Lesson (Lawford, Allyson) music: Roger Edens; lyrics: Betty Comden, Adolph Green; The Best Things in Life Are Free (Allyson, Lawford); Pass That Peace Pipe (McCracken, Chorus) music: Roger Edens; lyrics: Hugh Martin, Ralph Blane; Just Imagine (Allyson); The Varsity Drag (Allyson, Lawford, Chorus).

Good News Film (Metro-Goldwyn-Mayer; 1947) Sunbeam STK 111 (soundtrack) mono
This record includes the same songs. Both recordings include spoken dialogue. The following additional selection was not used in the film but released on another album:

Out Takes OTF 1   An Easier Way (Allyson, Marshall) music: Roger Edens; lyrics: Betty Comden and Adolph Green; LP

234 Comden and Green

  Musicraft (78 rpm) 15118   Studio Recording, The Best Things in Life Are Free (Mel Tormé)

D16 *Hallelujah, Baby!*   Broadway Cast (Columbia; 1967) Columbia KOL 6690/KOS 3090; Compact Disc: Sony Broadway SK 48218; Tape: ST-48218

The original Broadway cast featuring Leslie Uggams, Robert Hooks, Allen Case, and Lillian Hayman. Book by Arthur Laurents. Lyrics by Betty Comden and Adolph Green. Music by Jule Styne. Orchestrations by Peter Matz. Musical direction by Buster Davis. See S13 for more information.

Songs include:
Overture (Orchestra); My Own Morning (Leslie Uggams); The Slice (Robert Hooks, the Provers); Feet Do Yo' Stuff (Uggams, Winston DeWitt Hemsley, Alan Weeks, the Cuties); Watch My Dust (Hooks); Smile, Smile (Uggams, Hooks, Lillian Hayman); Witches' Brew (Uggams, Barbara Sharma, Marilyn Cooper, Chorus); Being Good (Uggams); I Wanted to Change Him (Uggams); Another Day (Hooks, Uggams, Allen Case, Sharma); Talking to Yourself (Uggams, Hooks, Case); Hallelujah, Baby! (Hemsley, Weeks, Uggams); Not Mine (Case); I Don't Know Where She Got It (Hayman, Case, Hooks); Now's the Time (Uggams, Company).

D17 *It's Always Fair Weather*   Film (Metro-Goldwyn-Mayer; 1955) Metro-Goldwyn-Mayer E 3241 (soundtrack) mono Reissued: MCA 25018

The original soundtrack featuring Gene Kelly, Dan Dailey, Michael Kidd, and Dolores Gray. Screenplay and lyrics by Betty Comden and Adolph Green. Music by André Previn and others. Musical direction by André Previn. See F07 for more information.

Songs include:
March, March (Male Chorus); Once Upon a Time (Gene Kelly, Dan Dailey, Michael Kidd); Thanks a Lot But No Thanks (Dolores Gray); The Time for Parting (Kelly, Dailey, Kidd); Blue Danube (Why Are We Here?) (Kelly, Dailey, Kidd) music: Strauss; Music Is Better Than Words (Gray) lyrics: Roger Edens; Situation-Wise (Dailey); I Like Myself (Kelly); Stillman's Gym (Lou Lubin, Chorus); Baby, You Knock Me Out (Chorus).

D18 *It's Always Fair Weather*   Film (Heritage) Heritage H 0058 (10"LP); (Sony Music Special Products) Compact Disc: AK-47026; Tape: AT47026

Betty Comden and Adolph Green perform their own songs from the Metro-Goldwyn-Mayer film.

Songs include:
March, March; Stillman's Gym; The Time for Parting; Thanks a Lot But No Thanks; I Said Good Morning; I Like Myself; Love Is Nothing But a Racket; Once Upon a Time.

D19 *Jerome Robbins' Broadway*   Broadway Cast (RCA Victor; 1989) RCA 2 LP set: 60150-1-RC; Compact Disc set 60150-2-RC; 2 Tapes: 60150-4 and 60150-9 RC (D) (longbox)

Original Broadway cast recording of *Jerome Robbins' Broadway* with book, music, and lyrics by James M. Barrie, Irving Berlin, Leonard Bernstein, Jerry Bock, Sammy Cahn, Mark ("Moose") Charlap, Betty Comden, Larry Gelbart, Morton Gould, Adolph Green, Oscar Hammerstein II, Sheldon Harnick, Arthur Laurents, Carolyn Leigh, Stephen Longstreet, Hugh Martin, Jerome Robbins, Richard Rodgers, Burt Shevelove, Stephen Sondheim, Joseph Stein, and Jule Styne. Production choreographed and directed by Jerome Robbins. Orchestrations by Sid Ramin and William D. Brohn. Musical direction by Paul Gemignani. See R03 for more information.

Songs and dances include:
Disc One: Overture: Gotta Dance from *Look, Ma, I'm Dancin'!* (Michael Lynch, Company); Papa, Won't You Dance with Me? from *High Button Shoes* (Debbie Shapiro, Company); Shall We Dance? from *The King and I* (Company). *On the Town*: New York, New York; Sailors on the Town (Robert LaFosse, Scott Wise, Michael Kubala, David Lowenstein); Ya Got Me (Wise, Kubala, Shapiro, Mary Ellen Stuart). *Billion Dollar Baby*: Charleston (Ensemble). *A Funny Thing Happened on the Way to the Forum*: Comedy Tonight (Jason Alexander, Wise, Joey McKneely, Kubala, Company). *High Button Shoes*: I Still Get Jealous (Jason Alexander, Faith Prince). *West Side Story*: Prologue (Ensemble); The Dance at the Gym (Ensemble); Cool (Wise and the Jets and their Girls); America (Charlotte d'Amboise, Shapiro, Barbara Yeager, Nancy Hess, Elaine Wright, Renee Stork); The Rumble (Ensemble); Somewhere (Dorothy Benham, Christophe Caballero, Ensemble).

Disc Two: *The King and I*: The Small House of Uncle Thomas (Yeager, Dorothy Benham, Donna Marie Elio, Leslie Trayer, Hess, Louise Hickey, Stuart). *Gypsy*: You Gotta Have a Gimmick (Shapiro, Prince, Susann Fletcher). *Peter Pan*: I'm Flying (d'Amboise, Donna Di Meo, Linda Talcott, Steve Ochoa). *High Button Shoes*: On a Sunday by the Sea (Ensemble). *Miss Liberty* and *Call Me Madam*: Mr. Monotony (Shapiro) Mr. Monotony Dance (Orchestra). *Fiddler on the Roof*: Tradition (Alexander, Ensemble); The Dream (Alexander, Fletcher, Barbara Hoon, Troy Myers, Hess, Ensemble); Sunrise, Sunset and Wedding Dance (Fletcher, Alexander, Ensemble). Finale--*On the Town*: Some Other Time; New York, New York (LaFosse, Wise, Kubala, Shapiro, Stuart, Alexia Hess, Caballero, Kelly Patterson, Michael Scott Gregory).

236 Comden and Green

D20 Lorelei   Broadway Cast (Metro-Goldwyn-Mayer Records; 1973)
Metro-Goldwyn-Mayer M3G-55

Broadway cast recording of *Lorelei* based on the original show, *Gentlemen Prefer Blondes*, with book by Anita Loos and Joseph Field and music by Jule Styne and lyrics by Leo Robin. *Lorelei* featured Carol Channing and had a new book by Kenny Solms and Gail Parent and additional music by Jule Styne with lyrics by Betty Comden and Adolph Green. Orchestrations by Philip J. Lang and Don Walker. Musical direction by Milton Rosenstock. See S18 for more information.

Songs include:
Overture (Orchestra); Looking Back (Carol Channing) lyrics: Betty Comden and Adolph Green; Bye Bye Baby (Channing, Peter Palmer, Singers); A Little Girl From Little Rock (Channing); I Love What I'm Doing (Tamara Long); It's Delightful Down in Chile (Channing, Jack Fletcher, Singers); I Won't Let You Get Away (Lee Roy Reams) lyrics: Comden and Green; Keeping Cool With Coolidge (Lee Roy Reams, Singers); Men (Channing) lyrics: Comden and Green; Mamie Is Mimi (Channing, John Mineo, Bob Fitch, Singers); Diamonds Are a Girl's Best Friend (Channing); Lorelei (Palmer, Singers) lyrics: Comden and Green; Homesick Blues (Channing, Palmer, Singers); Looking Back and Diamonds (Channing); Finale (Channing, Singers).

Lorelei   Pre-Broadway Recording (Metro-Goldwyn-Mayer-Verve; 1973) MV 5097

This recording has the following extra songs that are not on the record above:
It's High Time (Long, Singers); I'm A'Tingle, I'm A'Glow (Channing, Brandon Maggart, Dody Goodman, Boy Singers); Paris, Paris (Singers); Just a Kiss Apart (Long, Reams).

D21 On the Town   Selections (Decca; 1950) Decca DL 8030 mono

There was no recording during the original Broadway production of *On the Town*. This first recording was in 1950 and featured Nancy Walker, Betty Comden, and Adolph Green from the original production. They were joined by Mary Martin. The selections from *On the Town* were recorded along with selections from *Lute Song* by Michael Myerberg. *On the Town* had book and lyrics by Betty Comden and Adolph Green and music by Leonard Bernstein. See S01 for more information.

Songs include:
I Feel Like I'm Not Out of Bed Yet and New York, New York (Lyn Murray Chorus and Orchestra); I Get Carried Away (Betty Comden, Adolph Green) Orchestra conductor: Lyn Murray; Lucky To Be Me (Mary Martin) Orchestra directed by Camarata; Lonely Town (Mary Martin) Orchestra directed by Camarata; I Can Cook Too (Nancy Walker) Orchestra directed by Leonard Joy; Ya Got Me (Nancy Walker) Orchestra conductor: Leonard Joy.

D22 *On the Town*   First Full-Length Recording (Columbia; 1961) OL 5540/OS2028 Reissued: (Columbia; 1970) Columbia S 31005 Compact Disc: Columbia CK 2038 and CBS 02028; Tape: JST 2038

This second recording of the musical was made in 1961 and then reissued in 1970. The orchestra was conducted by Leonard Bernstein. The singers included Nancy Walker, Betty Comden, Adolph Green, and Chris Alexander from the original cast. John Reardon sang the role of Gabey.

Songs include:
Opening: New York, New York (Adolph Green, John Reardon, Chris Alexander, Chorus); Dance: Miss Turnstiles' Variations (Orchestra); Taxi Number: Come Up to My Place (Nancy Walker, Alexander); Carried Away (Betty Comden, Green); Lonely Town (Reardon); Dance: Lonely Town (Orchestra); I Can Cook Too (Walker); Lucky To Be Me (Reardon, Chorus); Dance: Times Square (Orchestra); Finale, Act I (Orchestra); Night Club Sequence: So Long, Baby (Chorus), I'm Blue (Nightclub Singer), Ya Got Me (Walker, Comden, Green, Alexander); Ballet: Imaginary Coney Island (Subway Ride, Dance of the Great Lover, Pas de deux) (Orchestra); Some Other Time (Comden, Walker, Green, Alexander); Dance: The Real Coney Island (Orchestra); Finale (Ensemble).

The compact disc CK 2038 includes the song I Understand sung by George Gaynes.

D23 *On the Town*   Original London Cast Recording (CBS; nd) CBS APG 60005

This is the original London cast recording of the stage musical produced by H. M. Tennent Ltd., with Roger L. Stevens and Oliver Smith by arrangement with Bernard Delfont. The record features Elliott Gould, Don McKay, Franklin Kiser, Carol Arthur, and Gillian Lewis. Musical direction by Lawrence Leonard. This record contains the same songs as listed above.

D24 *On the Town*   Film (Metro-Goldwyn-Mayer; 1949) Show Biz Records 5603 (soundtrack) mono

The original film soundtrack features Gene Kelly, Frank Sinatra, Jules Munshin, Betty Garrett, Ann Miller, Vera-Ellen, and Alice Pearce. Screenplay and lyrics by Betty Comden and Adolph Green. Music by Leonard Bernstein and Roger Edens. Musical direction by Lennie Hayton. See F04 for more information.

Songs include:
Overture (Orchestra); Opening: I Feel Like I'm Not Out of Bed Yet (Bern Hoffman); New York, New York (Gene Kelly, Frank Sinatra, Jules Munshin); Prehistoric Man, Music: Roger Edens (Ann Miller, Kelly, Sinatra, Munshin,

Betty Garrett); Come Up to My Place (Garrett, Sinatra); When You Walk Down Mainstreet With Me, Music: Edens (Kelly); You're Awful, Music: Edens (Sinatra, Garrett); Count on Me, Music: Edens (Sinatra, Garrett, Munshin, Miller, Alice Pearce, Kelly); On the Town, Music: Edens (Sinatra, Kelly, Munshin, Miller, Garrett, Vera-Ellen).

D25 *On the Town*   London Studio Cast Recording (Stet; nd) Stet DS 15029

A London cast recreates the music from the film. It features Dennis Lotis, Lionel Blair, Shane Rimmer, Noele Gordon, Stella Tanner, and Rita Williams. Also featured are the Williams Singers and Geoff Love and his Orchestra. The record includes the same songs as are on the soundtrack.

D26 *On the Twentieth Century* Broadway Cast (Columbia; 1978) Columbia PS 35330 Compact Disc: Sony Broadway SK 35330; Tape: ST 35330

The original Broadway cast featuring John Cullum, Madeline Kahn, and Imogene Coca. Book and lyrics by Betty Comden and Adolph Green, based on plays by Ben Hecht, Charles MacArthur, and Bruce Millholland. Music by Cy Coleman. Orchestrations by Hershy Kay. Musical direction by Paul Gemignani. See S07 for more information.

Songs include:
Overture (Orchestra); Stranded Again (Charles Rule, Hal Norman, Singers); On the Twentieth Century (Tom Batten, Stanley Simmonds, Porters, Passengers); I Rise Again (John Cullum, George Coe, Dean Dittman); Veronique (Madeline Kahn, Singers); Together (Cullum, Porters, Passengers); Never (Kahn, Coe, Dittman); Our Private World (Kahn, Cullum); Repent (Imogene Coca); Mine (Cullum, Kevin Kline); I've Got It All (Kahn, Cullum); Five Zeros (Coe, Dittman, Coca, Cullum); Sextet (Coe, Dittman, Cullum, Coca, Kahn, Kline); She's a Nut (Company); Babette (Kahn,Chorus); The Legacy (Cullum); Lily, Oscar (Cullum, Kahn); Life Is Like a Train (Porters).

Note: The 1992 re-release of the original cast recording of *On the Twentieth Century* includes the song, I Have Written a Play, sung by Tom Batten, and reprises of "On the Twentieth Century" that were edited out of the original recording. The sound of the record has also been improved.

D27 *A Party With Betty Comden and Adolph Green*
     Broadway Cast (Capitol; 1958) Capitol WAO 1197

This recording was made during a live performance and featured Betty Comden and Adolph Green performing their own comedy and musical numbers. They were accompanied by Milton Greene at the piano with

Reuben Jamitz on bass and Jules Greenberg on drums. Musical supervision was by Peter Howard. Music was by André Previn, Leonard Bernstein, Roger Edens, Jule Styne, and Saul Chaplin. Both Betty Comden and Adolph Green are the singers unless otherwise indicated. See P01 for more details.

Comedy material and songs include:
I Said Good Morning (written for but not used in the film, *It's Always Fair Weather*); Readers Digest (The Revuers); Baroness Bazooka (The Revuers); New York, New York (*On the Town*); Lonely Town (Green, *On the Town*); Some Other Time (*On the Town*); I Get Carried Away (*On the Town*); The French Lesson (*Good News*); Movie Ads (The Revuers); If You Hadn't, But You Did (Comden, *Two on the Aisle*); Catch Our Act at the Met (*Two on the Aisle*); O! My Mysterious Lady (*Peter Pan*); A Quiet Girl (Green, *Wonderful Town*); Inspiration (*Bonanza Bound!*); Just in Time (*Bells Are Ringing*); The Party's Over (*Bells Are Ringing*).

D28 *A Party With Betty Comden and Adolph Green*
     Broadway Cast (Stet; 1977) Stet S2L 5177; DRG 2 Compact Discs: CD2-5177

This is the complete 1977 Broadway performance of *A Party*, featuring Betty Comden and Adolph Green in their own comedy material and songs. Music by André Previn, Leonard Bernstein, Jule Styne, Roger Edens, Cy Coleman, and Saul Chaplin. Paul Trueblood is at the piano. Singers are both Betty Comden and Adolph Green unless indicated. See P01 for more information.

Comedy material and songs include:
The Reader's Digest (The Revuers); The Screen Writers (The Revuers); The Banshee Sisters (The Revuers); The Baroness Bazooka (The Revuers); New York, New York (*On the Town*); Medley: Lonely Town, Lucky to Be Me, Some Other Time (*On the Town*); Carried Away (*On the Town*); One Hundred Easy Ways (Comden, *Wonderful Town*); Medley: Ohio, The Wrong Note Rag (*Wonderful Town*); Capital Gains (Green, *Subways Are For Sleeping*); If You Hadn't, But You Did (Comden, *Two on the Aisle*); Catch Our Act at the Met (*Two on the Aisle*); The French Lesson (*Good News*); The Lost Word (Comden, *Straws in the Wind*); Captain Hook's Waltz (Green, *Peter Pan*); Never, Never Land (Comden, *Peter Pan*); O! My Mysterious Lady (*Peter Pan*); Simplified Language (*Straws in the Wind*); Inspiration (*Bonanza Bound!*); Medley: Just in Time, Make Someone Happy, The Party's Over (*Bells Are Ringing* and *Subways Are for Sleeping*)

D29 *Peter Pan* Broadway Cast (RCA Victor; 1954) RCA LOC 1019 mono Compact Disc: RCA Victor 3762-2-RG mono; Tape: AYKI-3762E

The Broadway cast recording featuring Mary Martin and Cyril Ritchard. Based on the play by Sir James M. Barrie. Music by Mark ("Moose") Charlap. Lyrics by Carolyn Leigh. Additional music by Jule Styne and

240 Comden and Green

additional lyrics by Betty Comden and Adolph Green. See S17 for more information.

Songs include:
Overture (Orchestra); Prologue (Orchestra); Tender Shepherd (Margalo Gillmore, Robert Harrington, Kathy Nolan, Joseph Stafford); I've Gotta Crow (Mary Martin, Nolan); Never, Never Land (Martin, Nolan); I'm Flying (Martin, Nolan, Harrington, Stafford); Pirate Song (Pirates, Boys); Hook's Tango (Cyril Ritchard, Pirates); Indians (Indians); Wendy (Martin, Harrington, Stafford, Boys); Tarentella (Ritchard, Pirates); I Won't Grow Up (Martin, Harrington, Stafford, Nolan, Boys); O! My Mysterious Lady (Martin, Ritchard); Ugg-a-Wugg (Martin, Sondra Lee, Boys, Indians); Distant Melody (Martin, Nolan); Captain Hook's Waltz (Ritchard, Pirates); I've Gotta Crow (reprise) (Martin, Nolan); Tender Shepherd (reprise) (Gillmore, Harrington, Nolan, Stafford); I Won't Grow Up (reprise) (Ritchard, Harrington, Nolan, Stafford); Never, Never Land (reprise) (Nolan, Martin).

D30   *The Revuers*   (Boxoffice) Boxoffice JJA 19764 (12"LP) with *Bonanza Bound!*, listed above.

This recording contains skits and songs presented by the five young Revuers: Adolph Green, Betty Comden, Judy Tuvim (Holliday), John Frank, and Alvin Hammer. Leonard Bernstein plays the piano. Some of these skits are also on the recordings of *A Party With Betty Comden and Adolph Green*. See D27 and D28. For more information about The Revuers, see the biography.

Songs and skits include:
The Girl With Two Left Feet (a mini-musical); The Joan Crawford Fan Club; The Reader's Digest; The Baroness Bazooka; Movie Ads.

D31   *Say, Darling*   Broadway Cast (RCA Victor; 1958) RCA Victor LOC/LSO 1045

The original Broadway cast recording featuring David Wayne, Vivian Blaine, and Johnny Desmond. Book by Richard Bissell, Abe Burrows, and Marian Bissell. Songs by Betty Comden, Adolph Green, and Jule Styne. Musical direction and orchestrations for the album by Sid Ramin. See S11 for more information.

Songs include:
Overture (Orchestra); Try to Love Me (Vivian Blaine); It's Doom (Johnny Desmond); The Husking Bee (Desmond, Chorus); It's the Second Time You Meet That Matters (Desmond); Let the Lower Lights Be Burning (David Wayne, Jerome Cowan); Chief of Love (Blaine); Say, Darling (Desmond); The Carnival Song (Wayne, Blaine, Steve Condos); Try to Love Me (Blaine); Dance Only With Me (Blaine, Mitchell Gregg); Something's Always

Happening on the River (Wayne, Company); Say, Darling; Finale (Entire Company).

D32 *Singin' in the Rain*   Film (Metro-Goldwyn-Mayer; 1952) Metro-Goldwyn-Mayer E 113 (soundtrack) mono. Reissued: MCA 39044 CD Compact Disc: CBS Special Products AK 45394 mono; Tape: AT-45394 mono

The original soundtrack for the film features Gene Kelly, Donald O'Connor, and Debbie Reynolds. The screenplay is by Betty Comden and Adolph Green. The music is by Nacio Herb Brown and others. Lyrics are by Arthur Freed and others. Musical direction by Lennie Hayton. See F05 for more information.

Songs include:
Singin' in the Rain (Gene Kelly); Make 'em Laugh (Donald O'Connor); You Were Meant For Me (Kelly); All I Do Is Dream of You (Debbie Reynolds, Girly Chorus); Fit As a Fiddle, Music: Al Hoffman, Al Goodhart (Kelly, O'Connor); Moses Supposes, Music: Roger Edens, Lyrics: Betty Comden, Adolph Green (Kelly, O'Connor); All I Do Is Dream of You (Kelly); Good Morning (Kelly, O'Connor, Reynolds); You Are My Lucky Star (Kelly, Reynolds).

Note: An additional soundtrack selection, later included with the above album:
Metro-Goldwyn-Mayer (45 rpm) X1026 Broadway Ballet (The Broadway Melody, Broadway Rhythm) (Kelly, Chorus).

An additional selection, cut from the final film:

Out Takes OTF 1   You Are My Lucky Star (Reynolds) LP

D33 *Singin' in the Rain*   Original London Cast (Safari; 1984) Safari Rain 1

The original London cast recording featuring Tommy Steele, Roy Castle, Sarah Payne, and Danielle Carson. The story and screenplay by Betty Comden and Adolph Green. Music by Nacio Herb Brown and lyrics by Arthur Freed. Additional songs by Betty Comden, Adolph Green, and Roger Edens and also by Dorothy Fields and Jimmy McHugh, George and Ira Gershwin, Johnny Mercer, Richard Whiting, and Cole Porter. Orchestrations by Larry Wilcox. Musical direction by Michael Reed. See S16 for more details.

Songs include:
Overture (Orchestra); Fit as a Fiddle, Music and lyrics: Freed, Al Hoffman, Al Goodhart (Tommy Steele, Roy Castle); Temptation, Music and lyrics: Freed, Brown (Sarah Payne, Steele, Company); I Can't Give You Anything

242 Comden and Green

But Love, Music and lyrics: Fields, McHugh (Danielle Carson, the Valentine Girls); Be a Clown, Music and lyrics: Porter (Roy Castle); Too Marvellous for Words, Music and lyrics: Whiting, Mercer (Company); You Are My Lucky Star, Music and lyrics: Freed, Brown (Steele); Moses Supposes, Music and lyrics: Comden, Green, Edens (Steele, Castle); Good Morning, Music and lyrics: Freed, Brown (Steele, Castle, Carson); Singin' in the Rain, Music and lyrics: Freed, Brown (Steele); Would You?, Music and lyrics: Freed, Brown (Carson); Fascinating Rhythm, Music and lyrics: George and Ira Gershwin (Steele, Company); Finale (Company).

D34 *Subways Are for Sleeping* Broadway Cast (Columbia; 1962) Columbia KOL 5730/KOS 2130; (Columbia; 1973) CSP AKOS 2130

The original Broadway cast recording featuring Sydney Chaplin, Carol Lawrence, Orson Bean, and Phyllis Newman. Book and lyrics by Betty Comden and Adolph Green. Music by Jule Styne. Orchestrations by Philip J. Lang. Musical direction by Milton Rosenstock. See S05 for additional information.

Songs include:
Overture (Orchestra); Subways Are for Sleeping (Gene Varrone, Cy Young, Bob Gorman, John Sharpe); Girls Like Me (Carol Lawrence); Subway Directions: Ride Through the Night (Sydney Chaplin, Lawrence, Chorus); I'm Just Taking My Time (Chaplin, Lawrence, Chorus); I Was a Shoo-In (Phyllis Newman, Orson Bean); Who Knows What Might Have Been (Chaplin, Lawrence); Strange Duet (Bean, Newman); Swing Your Projects (Chaplin); I Said It and I'm Glad (Lawrence); Be a Santa (Chaplin, Chorus); How Can You Describe a Face? (Chaplin); I Just Can't Wait (Bean); Comes Once in a Lifetime (Chaplin, Lawrence); What Is This Feeling in the Air? (Lawrence, Company); Finale (Chaplin, Lawrence, Company).

D35 *Subways Are for Sleeping* The McGuire Sisters (Coral) Coral CRL 57398 (12"LP)

The McGuire Sisters recorded the songs from *Subways Are for Sleeping*, including some songs that were cut from the Broadway production.

Songs include:
Ride Through the Night; Who Knows What Might Have Been?; Comes Once in a Lifetime!; How Can You Describe a Face?; What Is This Feeling in the Air?; Getting Married (cut from the original show); I'm Just Taking My Time; I Said It and I'm Glad; When You Help a Friend Out (cut); Now I Have Someone (cut); Be a Santa.

D36 *Take Me Out to the Ball Game* Film (Metro-Goldwyn-Mayer; 1949) Curtain Calls 100/18 (soundtrack) mono

The original soundtrack recording featuring Gene Kelly, Frank Sinatra, Jules Munshin, Betty Garrett, and Esther Williams. The screenplay is by Harry Tugend, George Wells, and Harry Crane, based on a story by Gene Kelly and Stanley Donen. Music by Roger Edens and others. Lyrics by Betty Comden and Adolph Green and others. Musical direction by Adolph Deutsch. See F03 for more information.

Songs include:
Titles (Orchestra); Take Me Out to the Ball Game, Music: Harry Von Tilzer, Lyrics: Jack Norwood (Gene Kelly, Frank Sinatra); Yes, Indeedy (Kelly, Sinatra, Jules Munshin, Chorus); O'Brien to Ryan to Goldberg (Kelly, Sinatra, Munshin); She's the Right Girl for Me (Sinatra); Boys and Girls Like You and Me, Music: Richard Rodgers, Lyrics: Oscar Hammerstein II (cut from film) (Sinatra); It's Fate, Baby, It's Fate (Sinatra, Betty Garrett); Baby Doll, Music: Harry Warren, Lyrics: Johnny Mercer (cut from film) (Kelly); Strictly U.S.A. (Munshin, Garrett, Sinatra, Williams, Kelly, Chorus); It's the Hat My Dear Old Father Wore Upon St. Patrick's Day, Music and Lyrics: Jean Schwartz, William Jerome (Kelly, Chorus); Strictly U.S.A. (reprise) (cast).

Note: Additional recordings by cast members:

Columbia (78 rpm) 38456; LP: Columbia CL 2913; The Right Girl for Me (Sinatra)

Metro-Goldwyn-Mayer (78 rpm) 30193; LP: Lion L 70089; Stet D5 15010 Take Me Out to the Ball Game (Kelly, Garrett)

Metro-Goldwyn-Mayer (78 rpm) 30190; It's Fate, Baby, It's Fate (Garrett)

Out Takes OTF 2   Boys and Girls Like You and Me (Sinatra) Music and lyrics by Rodgers and Hammerstein

D37 *Two on the Aisle*   Broadway Cast (Decca; 1951) Decca DL 8040 78 RPM Album: DA886 45 RPM Album: 9-275

The original cast recording featuring Bert Lahr and Dolores Gray. Lyrics and sketches by Betty Comden and Adolph Green. Music by Jule Styne. Additional sketch by Nat Hiken and William Friedberg. Orchestrations by Philip Lang. Orchestra directed by Herbert Greene. See S09 for additional information.

Songs include:
Overture (Orchestra); Show Train (Chorus, Orchestra); Hold Me, Hold Me, Hold Me (Hold Me Tight) (Dolores Gray); Here She Comes Now (East River Hoe Down) (Chorus, Orchestra); There Never Was a Baby Like My Baby (Gray); 1. Vaudeville Ain't Dead, 2. Catch Our Act at the Met (Bert Lahr, Gray, Chorus); Give a Little--Get a Little (Gray, Chorus); Everlasting (Kathryne Mylroie, Fred Bryan, Chorus); If You Hadn't, But You Did (Gray); The Clown (Lahr); How Will He Know? (Gray); Finale (Chorus).

244   Comden and Green

D38 *What a Way to Go*   Film Score (20th; 1964) 20th 3143/S4143

The film starred Shirley MacLaine, Dean Martin, Paul Newman, Robert Mitchum, Gene Kelly, and Dick Van Dyke. Screenplay by Betty Comden and Adolph Green, based on a story by Gwen Davis. Music and lyrics for the songs I Think That You and I Should Get Acquainted and Musical Extravaganza, were by Jule Styne and Betty Comden and Adolph Green. Other music for the film was by Nelson Riddle. Orchestration was by Arthur Morton. See F10 for more information.

D39 *The Will Rogers Follies*   Broadway Cast (Columbia; 1991) Columbia; Compact Disc: CK 48606; Tape: CT 48606

The original Broadway cast recording featuring Keith Carradine, Dee Hoty, Dick Latessa, and Cady Huffman. Book by Peter Stone. Lyrics by Betty Comden and Adolph Green; music by Cy Coleman. Orchestrations by Billy Byers and musical direction by Eric Stern. See S14 for more details.

Songs include:
Let's Go Flying (Ensemble); Will-a-Mania (Cady Huffman, Ensemble); Never Met a Man I Didn't Like (short version) (Keith Carradine); Give a Man Enough Rope (Carradine, Four Men); It's a Boy (Dick Latessa, Roxane Barlow, Maria Calabrese, Colleen Dunn, Dana Moore, Wendy Waring, Leigh Zimmerman, Carradine); So Long, Pa (Carradine); My Unknown Someone (Dee Hoty); Wild West Show/Dog Act (Huffman, Orchestra); We're Heading For a Wedding (Carradine, Hoty, Four Men, Four Women); The Big Time (Carradine, Hoty, Rick Faugno, Tammy Minoff, Lance Robinson, Gregory Scott Carter); My Big Mistake (Hoty); The Ziegfeld Follies (Ensemble, Women); Marry Me Now/I Got You/First Act Finale (Hoty, Huffman, Carradine, Four Men); Entre'acte/Give a Man Enough Rope/Rope Act (Four Men); Look Around (Carradine); Our Favorite Son (Carradine, Huffman, Ensemble); No Man Left For Me (Hoty); Presents for Mrs. Rogers (Carradine, Four Men); Will-a-Mania (Reprise); Without You (Carradine, Latessa, Hoty, Paul Ukena, Jr., Ensemble); Never Met a Man I Didn't Like (Carradine, Hoty, Ukena, Jr., Ensemble).

D40 *Wonderful Town*   Broadway Cast (Decca; 1953) Decca DL9010; (Decca; 1964) Decca 79010; (MCA 1973) MCA 2050
Compact Disc: MCA Classics, Broadway Gold series, MCAD l0050; (AAD) mono; Tape: MCAC-10050 mono

The original Broadway cast featuring Rosalind Russell, Edith Adams, and George Gaynes. Book by Joseph Fields and Jerome Chodorov. Lyrics by Betty Comden and Adolph Green. Music by Leonard Bernstein. Orchestrations by Don Walker and musical direction by Lehman Engel. See S10 for more information.

Songs include:
Christopher Street (Warren Galjour, the Villagers Chorus); Ohio (Rosalind Russell, Edith Adams); One Hundred Easy Ways (Russell); What a Waste (George Gaynes, Galjour, Albert Linville); A Little Bit in Love (Adams); Pass the Football (Jordan Bentley); Conversation Piece (Russell, Adams, Gaynes, Dort Clark); A Quiet Girl (Gaynes); Conga! (Russell, the Cadets); My Darlin' Eileen (Adams, Delbert Anderson, the Police); Swing! (Russell, the Villagers Chorus); It's Love (Adams, Gaynes, the Villagers Chorus); Ballet at the Village Vortex (Orchestra); The Wrong Note Rag (Russell, Adams, the Villagers Chorus).

D41 *Wonderful Town*   Television Cast (Columbia; 1958) Columbia OL 5360; (Columbia; 1959) Columbia OS 2008; Compact Disc: Sony Broadway SK 48021; Tape: ST 48021

A full-length version of the musical was presented on television on November 30, 1958. The television version and the record feature Rosalind Russell, Sydney Chaplin, and Jacquelyn McKeever. The music was directed by Lehman Engel.

Songs include:
Overture (Orchestra); Christopher Street (Tourists and Villagers); Ohio (Rosalind Russell, Jacquelyn McKeever); One Hundred Easy Ways (Russell); What a Waste (Sydney Chaplin, Russell); A Little Bit in Love (McKeever); Pass the Football (Jordan Bentley, Chorus); Conversation Piece (Russell, Chaplin, McKeever, Sam Kirkham, Chris Alexander); A Quiet Girl (Chaplin, Chorus); Conga! (Russell, Cadets); My Darlin' Eileen (McKeever, Police); Swing! (Russell, the Villagers); It's Love (McKeever, Chaplin); Ballet at the Village Vortex (Orchestra); The Wrong Note Rag (Russell, McKeever).

Additional records of interest:

D42 *The Addams Family*   Film (Paramount Pictures; 1991) (soundtrack); Compact Disc: Capitol C2-98172; Tape: C41J 98172

This soundtrack for the film includes the full length version of "Mamushka" with lyrics by Comden and Green and music by Marc Shaiman. "Mamushka" is performed by Raoul Julia and Christopher Lloyd.

D43 *American Musical Theatre: Shows, Songs, and Stars*, a Smithsonian Collection of Recordings; 6 LPs 6010, 4 cassettes 6011, and 4 Compact Discs 6012; complete set of compact discs: RD036-I, RD036-II, RD036-III, and RD036-IV

246 *Comden and Green*

The collection includes songs from *Bells Are Ringing*, *Do Re Mi*, *On the Town*, and *Wonderful Town*.

Songs include:
Vol. II: New York, New York (*On the Town*); Vol. III: Ohio (*Wonderful Town*); Vol. IV: Just in Time (*Bells Are Ringing*); Adventure (*Do Re Mi*).

D44 *American Musicals*, (Time Life Records)

Leonard Bernstein, STL-AM15; *Wonderful Town*, a complete recording with original cast; P3-15988, P-15990, AM-15990

Jule Styne, STL-AM05; *Bells Are Ringing*, a complete recording with the original cast; P3-15608, P-15609, AM-15609

D45 *The Bernstein Songbook* (CBS Records) Compact Disc: CBS MK 44760

Songs include:
From *On the Town*: New York, New York (Adolph Green, John Reardon, Chris Alexander, Chorus); Lonely Town (Reardon); Carried Away (Green, Betty Comden); Finale: Some Other Time (Comden, Green, Alexander, Nancy Walker). From *Wonderful Town*: Conga! (Rosalind Russell, Chorus); Ohio (Russell, Jacquelyn McKeever); The Wrong Note Rag (Russell, McKeever).

D46 *Blossom Dearie Sings Comden and Green* (Verve) Verve MGV 2109 (12"LP)

Songs include:
Lucky To Be Me; Just In Time; Some Other Time; Dance Only With Me; I Like Myself; The Party's Over; How Will He Know?; It's Love; Hold Me, Hold Me, Hold Me; Lonely Town.

D47 *Broadway Classics Vol. One* (MCA Records) Compact Disc: MCAD 10051; Tape: MCAC 10051

Songs include: But Alive and Applause from *Applause*.

D48 *Broadway Magic: the 1950s* (CBS Records; 1987) Cassette Tape JST 40660; Compact Disc CK 40660

Song: Just in Time from *Bells Are Ringing*.

D49 *Broadway Magic: the 1960s* (CBS Records; 1987) Cassette Tape JST 40698; Compact Disc CK 40698

Song: The Party's Over from *Bells Are Ringing*.

D50 *Candide* (Deutsche Grammophon; 1991) 2 CD Set; Compact Disc 429 734-2; the complete recording. (Deutsche Grammophon; 1991) 1 CD; Compact Disc 437 328-2 GH; Highlights from the Complete Recording

Called the final revised version of *Candide* based on the book by Voltaire with music by Leonard Bernstein and lyrics by Richard Wilbur and additional lyrics by John Latouche, Dorothy Parker, Lillian Hellman, Leonard Bernstein, and Stephen Sondheim. Orchestrations by Leonard Bernstein and Hershy Kay with the London Symphony Chorus and the London Symphony Orchestra, Leonard Bernstein conducting. Adolph Green sings the roles of Dr. Pangloss and Martin.

Songs sung by Adolph Green include:
The Best of All Possible Worlds (Adolph Green as Pangloss, Jerry Hadley as Candide, June Anderson as Cunegonde, Kurt Ollmann as Maximilian, Della Jones as Paquette); Dear Boy (Green and Chorus); Auto-de-fe (What a Day) (Green and Chorus); Words, Words, Words (Martin's Laughing Song) (Green as Martin); The Kings' Barcarolle (Green as Pangloss and others); The Venice Gavotte (Green as Pangloss, Christa Ludwig as the Old Lady, Jerry Hadley as Candide, and June Anderson as Cunegonde); Make Our Garden Grow (Finale) (Green, Hadley, Anderson, Ludwig, Jones, Ollmann, Nicolai Gedda, and Chorus).

The Highlights version includes: The Best of All Possible Worlds, Auto-de-fe, and Make Our Garden Grow.

D51 *The Comden and Green Songbook* (Sony Broadway); Sony Broadway; Compact Disc SK 48202; Consists of previously released material

The recording features Betty Comden, Adolph Green, Sydney Chaplin, Imogene Coca, John Cullum, Judy Holliday, Madeline Kahn, Rosalind Russell, Leslie Uggams, and Nancy Walker. The material is from original cast albums.

Songs include:
From *On the Town*: New York, New York, Carried Away, I Can Cook Too, Lucky To Be Me, Some Other Time. From *Wonderful Town*: Ohio, One Hundred Easy Ways To Lose a Man, A Quiet Girl, Pass the Football. From *Bells Are Ringing*: It's a Perfect Relationship, Long Before I Knew You, It's a Simple Little System, Drop That Name, Just in Time. From *Hallelujah,*

248 Comden and Green

Baby!: My Own Morning, Talking to Yourself, The Slice, Being Good. From *On the Twentieth Century*: Our Private World, Repent, Five Zeros, The Legacy.

D52 *Follies (The Concert Version)* (RCA; 1985); RCA Red Seal Digital; two record set: HBC2-7128; also on Compact Disc: RCD2-7128; Tape: HBE-2-7128(D)

This concert version of Stephen Sondheim's 1971 musical was recorded live at Avery Fisher Hall, New York City, on September 6 and 7, 1985. In the cast are Licia Albanese, Carol Burnett, Liz Callaway, Betty Comden, Barbara Cook, Adolph Green, André Gregory, George Hearn, Howard McGillin, Erie Mills, Liliane Montevecchi, Phyllis Newman, Mandy Patinkin, Daisy Prince, Lee Remick, Arthur Rubin, Elaine Stritch, and Jim Walton. Music and lyrics by Stephen Sondheim; book and new continuity by James Goldman. Orchestrations by Jonathan Tunick. The New York Philharmonic is under the direction of Paul Gemignani. Directed by Herbert Ross.

Betty Comden and Adolph Green sing the humorous song, Rain on the Roof.

D53 *The Greatest Recordings of the Broadway Musical Theater*
(The Franklin Mint Record Society - Archive Collection)

This 20-volume set contains several songs from some of Comden and Green's musicals:

"A Salute to New York," Vol. II, includes selections from: *On the Town*, FM-BWY-058A; *Wonderful Town*, FM-BWY-058B

"Show Business," Vol. II, includes selections from: *On the Twentieth Century*, FM-BWY-054B

"Spotlight on Youth," includes selections from: *Peter Pan*, FM-BWY-039B

"Stars in Revue," includes selections from: *Two on the Aisle*, FM-BWY-073B

D54 *Jule Styne in The Great American Composers Series*
(Columbia Music Collection, Columbia House Company)
Two Compact Discs: C21-8151 and C22-8151

Songs include:
Cassette 1: Independent (On My Own) from *Bells Are Ringing*, (Rosemary Clooney); Hello, Hello There from *Bells Are Ringing*, (Judy Holliday, Sydney Chaplin, and Ensemble).

Cassette 2: Make Someone Happy from *Do Re Mi*, (Robert Goulet); Comes Once in a Lifetime from *Subways Are for Sleeping*, (Tony Bennett); I Know About Love from *Do Re Mi*, (Polly Bergen); Just in Time from *Bells Are Ringing*, (Tony Bennett); Long Before I Knew You from *Bells Are Ringing*, (Judy Holliday and Sydney Chaplin); Being Good from *Hallelujah, Baby!*, (Leslie Uggams); I'm Just Taking My Time from *Subways Are for Sleeping*, (Robert Goulet); My Own Morning from *Hallelujah, Baby!*, (Leslie Uggams); and The Party's Over from *Bells Are Ringing*, (Judy Holliday).

D55 *Lady in the Dark*   Selections (Columbia 1963); Columbia Records OL 5990, (M); OS 2390 (S)

A 1963 recording of the musical play. The original play starred Gertrude Lawrence and introduced Danny Kaye. The record features Risë Stevens, Adolph Green in the Danny Kaye role, and John Reardon. Book by Moss Hart, music by Kurt Weill, lyrics by Ira Gershwin. Orchestrations by Kurt Weill. Chorus and orchestra directed by Lehman Engel.

In this recording Adolph Green sings the "Tschaikovsky" number which lists the names of some forty-nine Russian composers sung at a dizzying pace.

D56 *Leonard Bernstein in The Great American Composers Series* (Columbia Music Collection, Columbia House Company) Two Compact Discs: C21-8061 and C22-8061

Songs include:
From *On the Town*: Overture (Orchestra conducted by Lehman Engel); New York, New York (The Norman Luboff Choir); Lonely Town (Judy Holliday); Dance of the Great Lover (New York Philharmonic Orchestra, Leonard Bernstein conducting); Lucky To Be Me (John Reardon); Times Square (New York Philharmonic Orchestra, Bernstein conducting); Some Other Time (Betty Comden, Adolph Green, Nancy Walker, Chris Alexander). From *Wonderful Town*: Overture (Orchestra conducted by Lehman Engel); Ohio (Rosalind Russell, Jacquelyn McKeever); A Little Bit in Love (Julie Andrews); It's Love (McKeever, Sydney Chaplin); A Quiet Girl (Leon Bibb); Swing! (Russell); Ballet at the Village Vortex (Orchestra conducted by Lehman Engel); The Wrong Note Rag (Russell, McKeever).

D57 *The Madwoman of Central Park West*   (DRG; 1990) Compact Disc: SL-5212; Tape: SLCS 5212

Written by Phyllis Newman and Arthur Laurents, this record contains the song, Up, Up, Up, lyrics by Betty Comden and Adolph Green. Music by Leonard Bernstein.

D58 *A Musical Spectacular: Songs and Production Numbers from the Classic Metro-Goldwyn-Mayer Musicals*
(Chandros)
Compact Disc: CHA-878(DDD); Tape: CHALB-024(D)

Recorded by the Royal Philharmonic Orchestra with the Ambrosia Singers, Elmer Bernstein conductor, performing the original Conrad Salinger arrangements. (The arrangements have been reconstructed by Christopher Palmer.) Includes selections from *The Band Wagon* and *Singin' in the Rain*.

D59 *Original Cast! 100 Years of the American Musical Theater!*
(Metropolitan Opera Guild)

This ten-volume series of recordings is being compiled from original cast albums. The first volume is "The 50's, Part I. The second volume will be "The 50's, Part II. "The 50's, Part I" includes *Wonderful Town*. (No number has yet been given.)

D60 *Remember These*   (Ava); Ava Records AS-26. (That's Entertainment); That's Entertainment Records TER-1039.

Betty Comden sings songs from *Treasure Girl* with music and lyrics by George and Ira Gershwin and from *Chee-Chee* by Richard Rodgers and Lorenz Hart. Richard Lewine at the piano, George Duvivier playing bass, and Mundell Lowe playing guitar.

Songs include:
From *Treasure Girl*: Don't Think I'll Fall in Love Today; What Are We Here For?; Feeling I'm Falling; Oh, So Nice; Where's the Boy? Where's the Girl? From *Chee-Chee*: Dear, Oh Dear; Moon of My Delight; Singing a Love Song; I Must Love You, Better Be Good to Me.

D61 *Selections from Fancy Free and On the Town*   (MCA Classics) MCAD-10280 Compact Disc

The recording features Mary Martin with Nancy Walker, Betty Comden and Adolph Green from the original cast of *On the Town*. The selections from *Fancy Free* feature the Ballet Theatre Orchestra under the direction of Leonard Bernstein.

Songs from *On the Town* include:
On the Town Opening (Lyn Murray Chorus); I Get Carried Away (Betty Comden and Adolph Green); Lucky To Be Me (Mary Martin); Lonely Town (Mary Martin); I Can Cook Too (Nancy Walker), On the Town Opening Extended Version.

Discography 251

D62 *Show Music At Its Best—Comden and Green Perform Their Own Songs*
(Heritage) Heritage H 0057 (Reissue on DRG MRS 906) (12" LP)

Songs include:
From *On the Town*: New York, New York; Lonely Town; Taxi Song; Some Other Time; Carried Away. From *Billion Dollar Baby*: Bad Timing; Broadway Blossom. From *Good News*: The French Lesson. From *Two on the Aisle*: If You Hand't, But You Did; How Will He Know?, Catch Our Act at the Met. From *Peter Pan*: Distant Melody; Captain Hook's Waltz; Never Never Land; O! My Mysterious Lady. From *Wonderful Town*: Ohio; It's Love; A Quiet Girl; The Wrong Note Rag.

D63 *The Unknown Theatre Songs of Jule Styne*   Studio cast recording (Blue Pear Records; nd); Blue Pear BP 1011

This record contains some songs that were written for Broadway musicals but were not used. Included are songs written for *Two on the Aisle*, *Hallelujah, Baby!*, *Do Re Mi*, and *Subways Are for Sleeping*, all with lyrics by Betty Comden and Adolph Green and music by Jule Styne. The recording does not list the singers.

Songs with lyrics by Comden and Green include:
So Far, So Good from *Two on the Aisle*; Life's Not Simple from *Do Re Mi*; Let's Talk, Getting Married, Now I Have Someone from *Subways Are for Sleeping*; When the Weather's Better, Big Talk, and Ugly, Ugly Gal from *Hallelujah, Baby!*.

D64 *Vamps and Rideouts*   A private tape of the complete show performed at the Hudson Guild Theatre, New York, February 4, 1982.

This show was conceived by Phyllis Newman and adapted by her and by James Pentecost. The original cast included Phyllis Newman, George Lee Andrews, and Paulette Pearson. The music is all by Jule Styne. The lyrics are by Susan Birkenhead, Sammy Cahn, Betty Comden, Adolph Green, E. Y. Harburg, Bob Merrill, Leo Robin, and Stephen Sondheim. The book material is by Betty Comden, Adolph Green, Arthur Laurents, Isobel Lennart, and Anita Loos.

Scenes and lyrics by Comden and Green include:
Scene from *Bells Are Ringing*; It's a Perfect Relationship (from *Bells Are Ringing*); Fireworks (from *Do Re Mi*); Is It a Crime? (from *Bells Are Ringing*); Long Before I Knew You (from *Bells Are Ringing*); Ambition (from *Do Re Mi*); Scene from *Fade Out--Fade In*; You Mustn't Be Discouraged (from *Fade Out--Fade In*); Hallelujah, Baby! (from *Hallelujah, Baby!*); Just in Time (from *Bells Are Ringing*); I Was a Shoo-In (from *Subways Are For Sleeping*); My Fortune Is My Face (from *Fade Out--Fade In*); Scene from *Hallelujah, Baby!*; My Own

Morning (from *Hallelujah, Baby!*); Captain Hook's Waltz (from *Peter Pan*); Comes Once in a Lifetime (from *Subways Are For Sleeping*).

BIBLIOGRAPHY

B01 Astaire, Fred. *Steps in Time*. New York: Harper and Row, 1959; Reprinted, New York: Da Capo Press, 1981.

B02 Aston, Frank. Review of *Do Re Mi*. *World Telegram and Sun*, 12/27/60.

B03 Atkinson, Brooks. Review of *Bells Are Ringing*. *New York Times*, 11/30/56.

B04 Atkinson, Brooks. Review of *A Party With Betty Comden and Adolph Green*. *New York Times*, 12/24/58.

B05 Atkinson, Brooks. Review of *Peter Pan*. *New York Times*, 10/21/54.

B06 Atkinson, Brooks. Review of *Say, Darling*. *New York Times*, 4/4/58.

B07 Atkinson, Brooks. Review of *Say, Darling*. *New York Times*, 4/13/58.

B08 Atkinson, Brooks. Review of *Two on the Aisle*. *New York Times*, 7/20/51.

B09 Atkinson, Brooks. Review of *Two on the Aisle*. *New York Times*, 7/29/51.

B10 Atkinson, Brooks. Review of *Wonderful Town*. *New York Times*, 3/8/53.

B11 *Auntie Mame* film review. *Newsweek*, 12/15/58.

B12 *Auntie Mame* film review. *Variety*, 11/26/58.

B13 Bacall, Lauren. *By Myself*. New York: Alfred A. Knopf, Inc., 1978.

B14 *Band Wagon, The,* film review. *Cue*, 7/11/53.

B15 *Band Wagon, The*, film review. *Fortnight*, 8/17/53.

B16 *Band Wagon, The*, film review. *Newsweek*, 7/6/53.

B17 *Band Wagon, The*, film review. *Saturday Review of Literature*, 7/25/53.

B18 *Band Wagon, The,* film review. *Variety*, 7/8/53.

B19 *Barkleys of Broadway, The*, film review. *Theatre Arts*, 6/49.

B20 *Barkleys of Broadway, The*, film review. *Time*, 4/25/49.

B21 *Barkleys of Broadway, The*, film review. *Variety*, 5/2/49.

B22 Barnes, Clive. Review of *Applause*. *New York Times*, 3/31/70.

B23 Barnes, Clive. Review of *Diamonds*. *New York Post*, 12/17/84.

B24 Barnes, Clive. Review of *Jerome Robbins' Broadway*. *New York Post*, 2/27/89.

B25 Barnes, Clive. Review of *The Madwoman of Central Park West*. *New York Post*, 6/14/79.

B26 Barnes, Clive. Review of *On the Twentieth Century*. *New York Post*, 2/20/78.

B27 Barnes, Clive. Review of *A Party With Betty Comden and Adolph Green*. *New York Times*, 2/11/77.

B28 Barnes, Clive. Review of *Singin' in the Rain*. *New York Post*, 7/3/85.

B29 Barnes, Howard. Review of *Billion Dollar Baby*. *Herald Tribune*, 12/22/45.

B30 Barnes, Howard. Review of *On the Town*. *Herald Tribune*, 12/29/44.

B31 Beaufort, John. Review of *By Bernstein*. *Christian Science Monitor*, 12/28/75.

B32 *Bells Are Ringing* review. *Time*, 2/10/56.

B33 *Bells Are Ringing* film review. *New Yorker*, 7/9/60.

B34 *Bells Are Ringing* film review. *Newsweek*, 6/27/60.

B35 *Bells Are Ringing* film review. *Time*, 6/20/60.

B36 *Bells Are Ringing* film review. *Variety*, 6/8/60.

B37 Berkvist, Robert. "Comden and Green Throw Another Party!" *New York Times*, 2/6/77.

B38 Bernstein, Burton. *Family Matters, Sam, Jennie, and the Kids*. New York: Summit Books, 1982.

B39 Bernstein, Leonard. *Findings*. New York: Simon and Schuster, 1982.

B40 *Best Plays* Annuals. Vols. to date. New York: Dodd Mead and Company, and Applause Theatre Book Publishers, 1894- .

B41 *Bonanza Bound* review. *Variety*, 12/27/47.

B42 Bordman, Gerald. *American Musical Comedy from Adonis to Dreamgirls*. New York: Oxford University Press, 1982.

B43 Bordman, Gerald. *American Musical Revue from The Passing Show to Sugar Babies*. New York: Oxford University Press, 1985.

B44 Briggs, John. *Leonard Bernstein, The Man, His Work, and His World*. New York: The World Publishing Co., 1961.

B45 Buckley, Priscilla L. Review of *Hallelujah, Baby! National Review*, 9/5/67.

B46 Canby, Vincent. Film review of *Funny. New York Times*, 6/28/89.

B47 Canby, Vincent. Film review of *Simon. New York Times*, 3/16/80.

B48 *Candide* record review. *New York*, 9/2/91.

B49 *Candide* record review. *American Record Guide*, November/December 1991, Vol. 54, no. 6.

B50 Carey, Gary. *Judy Holliday, An Intimate Life Story*. New York: Seaview Books, 1982.

B51 Carpozi, Jr., George. *The Carol Burnett Story*. New York: Warner Books, Inc., 1975.

B52 Casper, Joseph Andrew. *Stanley Donen*. Metuchen, N.J., and London: The Scarecrow Press, Inc., 1983.

B53 Chapman, John. Review of *Applause. Daily News*, 3/31/70.

B54 Chapman, John. Review of *Billion Dollar Baby. Daily News*, 12/22/45.

B55 Chapman, John. Review of *Do Re Mi. Daily News*, 12/27/60.

B56 Chapman, John. Review of *Fade Out--Fade In. Daily News*, 5/27/64.

B57 Chapman, John. Review of *Gentlemen Prefer Blondes. Daily News*, 12/9/49.

B58 Chapman, John. Review of *Hallelujah, Baby! Daily News*, 4/27/67.

B59 Chapman, John. Review of *A Party With Betty Comden and Adolph Green. Daily News*, 12/31/58.

B60 Chapman, John. Review of *Subways Are For Sleeping. Daily News*, 12/28/61.

B61 Chapman, John. Review of *Two on the Aisle. Daily News*, 7/20/51.

B62 Chapman, John. Review of *Wonderful Town*. *Daily News*, 2/26/53.

B63 Chase, Anthony. "Playing the Palace Theatre." *Theatre Crafts*, 4/91.

B64 Churcher, Susan. "Still Kicking: Miracle on 51st Street." *New York Magazine*, 10/14/85.
Discusses the attempt by the producers to keep the stage musical, *Singin' in the Rain*, running after the bad reviews.

B65 Clarke, Gerald. Review of *A Party with Betty Comden and Adolph Green*. *Time*, 2/21/77.

B66 Clurman, Harold. Review of *Do Re Mi*. *The Nation*, 1/14/61.

B67 Clurman, Harold. Review of *Wonderful Town*. *The Nation*, 3/14/53.

B68 Coleman, Robert. Review of *Do Re Mi*. *New York Mirror*, 12/27/60.

B69 Coleman, Robert. Review of *Say, Darling*. *Daily Mirror*, 4/4/58.

B70 Coleman, Robert. Review of *Subways Are for Sleeping*. *New York Mirror*, 12/28/61.

B71 Comden, Betty. "Jerome Robbins Gets a Little Help from His Friends." *New York Times*, 12/4/88.

B72 Comden, Betty. "So Eat Your Heart Out, Elizabeth Taylor." *New York Times*, 3/31/85.
Betty Comden writes about her early acting career in grade school.

B73 Comden, Betty and Adolph Green. Personal Interview. March 9, 1993.

B74 Comden, Betty and Adolph Green. *Applause*, with music by Charles Strouse and lyrics by Lee Adams. Based on the film *All About Eve* and the original story by Mary Orr. New York: Random House, 1971.

B75 Comden, Betty and Adolph Green. *Bells Are Ringing*, with music by Jule Styne. New York, Random House, 1957.

B76 Comden, Betty and Adolph Green. *A Doll's Life*, with music by Larry Grossman. New York: Samuel French, Inc., 1983.

B77 Comden, Betty and Adolph Green. *Good Morning, Good Night*. New York: Holt, Rinehart and Winston, 1967.
A children's book based on their song lyric.

B78 Comden, Betty and Adolph Green. "He Says 'I Do,' She Says 'I Do'." *New York Times*, 3/12/67.
An article about their play, *Getting Married*, written for television.

B79 Comden, Betty and Adolph Green. "Head of Steam for the Old Twentieth Century." *New York Times*, 2/19/78.
An article about the writing of their musical, *On the Twentieth Century*.

B80 Comden, Betty and Adolph Green. "I'm Getting Married." *New York Times*, 3/12/67.
Comden and Green talk about their musical for television.

B81 Comden, Betty and Adolph Green. "My Sister Eileen Goes on the Town with Songs." *Theatre Arts*, August 1953.
Comden and Green discuss the writing of the lyrics for *Wonderful Town*.

B82 Comden, Betty and Adolph Green. *On the Twentieth Century*, with music by Cy Coleman. New York: Drama Book Specialists, 1978, 1981.

B83 Comden, Betty and Adolph Green. A Party With Betty Comden and Adolph Green. Capitol WAO 1197, 1958. Record album cover.

B84 Comden, Betty and Adolph Green. *Singin' in the Rain*. New York: The Viking Press, Inc., 1972.
Contains an introduction by Comden and Green about their experiences in writing the screenplay.

B85 Comden, Betty and Adolph Green. "When New York Was a Helluva Town." *New York Times*, 10/31/71.
Comden and Green look back on their first musical, *On the Town*.

B86 "Comden and Green Work at Play." *Theatre Arts*, II/61.
Contains photographs of Comden and Green taken by Roger Prigent and captioned by Comden and Green.

B87 Conrad, Jon Alan. "Are *Candide*'s Adventures at an End?" *New York Times*, August 18, 1991.

B88 *Contemporary Theatre, Film, and Television*, Vol. II. Ed. Monica M. O'Donnell. Detroit, Michigan, and London: Gale Research, Inc., 1986.

B89 "Conversation with Comden and Green and Guare." *Dramatists Guild Quarterly*, Summer 1981.

B90 Cooke, Richard P. Review of *Hallelujah, Baby! Wall Street Journal*, 4/28/67.

B91 Crichton, Kyle, "Musical Express." *Colliers*, 11/25/39.
Crichton discusses The Revuers.

B92 Croce, Arlene. Review of *Singin' in the Rain*. *New Yorker*, 7/22/85.

B93 Crowther, Bosley. Film review of *Auntie Mame*. *New York Times*, 12/5/58.

B94 Crowther, Bosley. Film review of *The Band Wagon*. *New York Times*, 7/9/53.

B95 Crowther, Bosley. Film review of *The Barkleys of Broadway*. *New York Times*, 5/5/49.

B96 Crowther, Bosley. Film review of *Bells Are Ringing*. *New York Times*, 6/24/60.

B97 Crowther, Bosley. Film review of *Good News*. *New York Times*, 12/5/47.

B98 Crowther, Bosley. Film review of *It's Always Fair Weather*. *New York Times*, 9/15/55.

B99 Crowther, Bosley. Film review of *On the Town*. *New York Times*, 12/9/49.

B100 Crowther, Bosley. Film review of *Singin' in the Rain*. *New York Times*, 3/28/52.

B101 Crowther, Bosley. Film review of *Take Me Out to the Ball Game*. *New York Times*, 3/10/49.

B102 Crowther, Bosley. Film review of *What a Way to Go! New York Times*, 5/15/64.

B103 *Current Biography, 1945*. Ed. Anna Rothe. New York: H. W. Wilson Company, 1946.
This contains an early biography of Betty Comden with some information about Adolph Green.

B104 *Dictionary of Literary Biography*, Vol. 44, *American Screenwriters*, Second Series. Ed. Randall Clark. Detroit, Michigan: Gale Research Company, 1986-1990.

B105 *Do Re Mi* review. *New York Times*, 1/8/61.

B106 *Do Re Mi* review. *Newsweek*, 1/9/61.

B107 Dunne, John Gregory. *The Studio*. New York: Farrar, Straus & Giroux, 1969.

B108 Eder, Richard. Review of *On the Twentieth Century*. *New York Times*, 2/20/78.

B109 Eder, Richard. Review of *The Madwoman of Central Park West*. *New York Times*, 6/14/79.

B110 Ewen, David. *Leonard Bernstein*. Philadelphia and New York: Chilton Company, 1960.

B111 *Fade Out--Fade In* review. *Newsweek*, 6/8/64.

B112 *Fade Out--Fade In* review. *Time*, 6/6/64.

B113 Ferguson, Otis. "Vanguard Underground," *The New Republic*, 8/30/39.
A review of The Revuers.

B114 *First Lady* review. *Hampton Star* (East Hampton, N.Y.), 8/11/38.
A review of a play by the Studio Players in East Hampton, New York. The review specifically mentions Betty Comden.

B115 Flatow, Sheryl. "On the Town," *Stagebill* for the Kennedy Center, October, 1992.

B116 Fordin, Hugh. *The World of Entertainment! Hollywood's Greatest Musicals*. Garden City, N.Y.: Doubleday and Company, Inc., 1975.

B117 Freedland, Michael. *Fred Astaire*. London: W. H. Allen, 1976.

B118 Funke, Lewis. Review of *Leonard Bernstein's Theatre Songs*. *New York Times*, 6/29/65.

B119 Gelb, Arthur and Barbara Gelb, "'*On the Town*' with Comden and Green." *New York Times Magazine*, 12/11/60.

B120 Gerard, Jeremy. "Hal Prince and the Poetry of Abstraction," *Los Angeles Times*, 6/13/82.

B121 Gerard, Jeremy. "Will Ibsen's 'Doll' Come to Life on the Musical Stage?" *New York Times*, 9/19/82.

B122 Gibbs, Wolcott. Review of *Billion Dollar Baby*. *New Yorker*, 1/5/46.

B123 Gibbs, Wolcott. Review of *Say, Darling*. *New Yorker*, 4/12/58.

B124 Gibbs, Wolcott. Review of *Wonderful Town*. *New Yorker*, 3/7/53.

B125 Gill, Brendan. Review of *Applause*. *New Yorker*, 4/11/70.

B126 Gill, Brendan. Review of *A Doll's Life*. *New Yorker*, 10/4/82.

B127 Gill, Brendan. Review of *The Madwoman of Central Park West*. *New Yorker*, 6/25/79.

B128 Gill, Brendan. Review of *Singin' in the Rain*. *New Yorker*, 7/15/85.

B129 Gill, Brendan. Film review of *What a Way to Go! New Yorker*, 5/16/64.

B130 Gilman, Richard. Review of *A Doll's Life*. *The Nation*, 10/16/82.

B131 Gilman, Richard. Review of *Hallelujah, Baby! Newsweek*, 5/6/67.

260 Comden and Green

B132 *Good News* film review. *Newsweek*, 12/15/47.

B133 *Good News* film review. *Time*, 12/22/47.

B134 *Good News* film review. *Variety*, 12/3/47.

B135 Gordon, Max. *Live at the Village Vanguard*. New York: St. Martin's Press, 1980.

B136 Gottfried, Martin. "The Last American Musical?" *Theatre Week*, 7/8/91.
Gottfried discusses *The Will Rogers Follies*.

B137 Gottfried, Martin. Review of *Applause*. *Women's Wear Daily*, 3/31/70.

B138 Gottfried, Martin. Review of *Hallelujah, Baby! Women's Wear Daily*, 4/27/67.

B139 Gottfried, Martin. Review of *Lorelei*. *Women's Wear Daily*, 1/28/74.

B140 Gottfried, Martin. Review of *On the Twentieth Century*. *Saturday Review of Literature*, 4/15/78.

B141 Gottfried, Martin. Review of *A Party with Betty Comden and Adolph Green*. *New York Post*, 2/11/77.

B142 Gradenwitz, Peter. *Leonard Bernstein*. Providence: Berg Publishers, 1987.

B143 Green, Adolph. "The Day They Made Music on Mt. Scopus," *New York Times*, 8/6/67.
Green recounts attending a concert conducted by Leonard Bernstein.

B144 Green, Adolph. "A Day with Miss Liberty," *Theatre Arts*, November 1949.

B145 Green, Adolph. "The Magic of Fred Astaire," *American Film*, April 1981.

B146 Green, Adolph. "Spotlight on Opening Nightmares," *New York Times Magazine*, 5/7/61.

B147 Green, Stanley. *The World of Musical Comedy*. New York: A. S. Barnes and Co., and London: Thomas Yoseloff, Ltd., 1960.

B148 Gruen, John. *The Private World of Leonard Bernstein*. New York: Viking Press, 1968.

B149 Guernsey, Jr. Otis L. Review of *Two on the Aisle*. *Herald Tribune*, 7/20/51.

B150 *Hallelujah, Baby!* review. *Christian Century*, 8/30/67.

B151 *Hallelujah, Baby!* review. *Time*, 5/5/67.

Bibliography 261

B152 Harris, Steve, editor. *Film, Television and Stage Musicals on Phonograph Records*. Jefferson, N.C., and London: McFarland and Co., 1988.

B153 Harvey, Stephen. *Fred Astaire*. New York: Pyramid Publications, 1975.

B154 Herman, Carter. Review of *Leonard Bernstein's Theatre Songs*. *Life*, 7/30/65.

B155 Hawkins, William. Review of *Peter Pan*. *World-Telegram and Sun*, 10/21/54.

B156 Hayes, Richard. Review of *Say, Darling*. *Commonweal*, 7/4/58.

B157 Hewes, Henry. Review of *Applause*. *Saturday Review of Literature*, 4/18/70.

B158 Hewes, Henry. Review of *Bells Are Ringing*. *Saturday Review of Literature*, 12/29/56.

B159 Hewes, Henry. Review of *Fade Out--Fade In*. *Saturday Review of Literature*, 6/20/64.

B160 Hewes, Henry. Review of *Say, Darling*. *Saturday Review of Literature*, 4/19/58.

B161 Hewes, Henry. Review of *Wonderful Town*. *Saturday Review of Literature*, 3/14/53.

B162 Hirschhorn, Clive. *Gene Kelly*. New York: St. Martin's Press, 1974 and 1984.

B163 Hodcins, Gordon W. *The Broadway Musical, A Complete Discography*. Metuchen, N.J., and London: Scarecrow Press, 1980.

B164 Holtzman, Will. *Judy Holliday*. New York: Putnam Press, 1982.

B165 *I Want to Go Home* film review. *Variety*, 9/13/89.

B166 Ilson, Carol. *Harold Prince: From Pajama Game to Phantom of the Opera*. Ann Arbor, Michigan: UMI Research Press, 1989.

B167 *International Dictionary of Films and Filmmakers, The*. Vol. IV, *Writers and Production Artists*. Ed. Christopher Lyon. Chicago: St. James Press, 1984. See "Comden and Green" by Mark W. Estrin.

B168 Isaacs, H. R. "Musical Takes Shape: *Bonanza Bound!* in Rehearsal." *Theatre Arts*, 2/48.

B169 *It's Always Fair Weather* film review. *Time*, 9/5/55

B170 *It's Always Fair Weather* film review. *Variety*, 8/24/55.

B171 Kalem, T. E. Review of *On the Twentieth Century*. *Time*, 3/6/78.

B172 Kaplan, Mike, editor. *Variety, Major U.S. Showbusiness Awards*. New York and London: Garland Publishing, Inc., 1982.

B173 Kasha, Al and Joel Hirschhorn. *Notes on Broadway, Intimate Conversations with Broadway's Greatest Songwriters*. New York: Simon and Schuster, Inc., 1985, 1987.
    Contains interviews with Comden and Green, Leonard Bernstein, Cy Coleman, and Jule Styne, among others.

B174 Kauffmann, Stanley. Review of *Applause*. *The New Republic*, 5/23/70.

B175 Kauffmann, Stanley. Review of *On the Twentieth Century*. *The New Republic*, 3/18/78.

B176 Kauffmann, Stanley. Film review of *Auntie Mame*. *The New Republic*, 1/19/59.

B177 Kauffmann, Stanley. Film review of *What a Way to Go!* *The New Republic*, 5/30/64.

B178 Kelley, Kitty. *His Way, The Unauthorized Biography of Frank Sinatra*. New York, London: Bantam Books, 1986.

B179 Kerr, Walter. Review of *Applause*. *New York Times*, 4/5/70.

B180 Kerr, Walter. Review of *Bells Are Ringing*. *New York Herald Tribune*, 11/30/56.

B181 Kerr, Walter. Review of *Do Re Mi*. *New York Herald Tribune*, 12/27/60.

B182 Kerr, Walter. Review of *Fade Out--Fade In*. *New York Herald Tribune*, 5/27/64.

B183 Kerr, Walter. Review of *Hallelujah, Baby!* *New York Times*, 4/27/67.

B184 Kerr, Walter. Review of *Isn't It Romantic?* *New York Times*, 2/26/84.

B185 Kerr, Walter. Review of *Say, Darling*. *New York Herald Tribune*, 4/4/58.

B186 Kerr, Walter. Review of *Subways Are for Sleeping*. *New York Herald Tribune*, 12/28/61.

B187 Kerr, Walter. Review of *Two on the Aisle*. *Commonweal*, 8/3/51.

B188 Kerr, Walter. Review of *Wonderful Town*. *New York Herald Tribune*, 2/26/53.

B189 Kissel, Howard. Review of *By Bernstein*. *Women's Wear Daily*, 11/24/75.

B190   Kissel, Howard. Review of *A Doll's Life*. *Women's Wear Daily*, 10/24/82.

B191   Kissel, Howard. Review of *Jerome Robbins' Broadway*. *New York Daily News*, 2/27/89.

B192   Kissel, Howard. Review of *On the Twentieth Century*. *Women's Wear Daily*, 2/21/78.

B193   Kissel, Howard. Review of *A Party with Betty Comden and Adolph Green*. *Women's Wear Daily*, 2/11/77.

B194   Kissel, Howard. Review of *The Will Rogers Follies*. *New York Daily News*, 5/2/91.

B195   Knight, Arthur. Film review of *Auntie Mame*. *Saturday Review of Literature*, 12/27/58.

B196   Kroll, Jack. Review of *Singin' in the Rain*. *Newsweek*, 7/15/85.

B197   Kroll, Jack. Review of *The Will Rogers Follies*. *Newsweek*, 5/13/91.

B198   Kronenberger, Louis. Review of *Billion Dollar Baby*. *PM*, 12/23/45.

B199   Kronenberger, Louis. Review of *On the Town*. *PM*, 12/29/44.

B200   Kyle, Stephen. Obituary. *New York Times*, 10/18/1979.

B201   Lahr, John. *Astonish Me, Adventures in Contemporary Theatre*. New York: The Viking Press, 1973.

B202   Lauffe, Abe. *Broadway's Greatest Musicals*. New York: Funk and Wagnalls, 1973.

B203   Lawrence, Carol. "Broadway." *New York Times*, 1/6/84.
        Betty Comden talks about appearing in *Isn't It Romantic?*.

B204   Lefferts, Barney. "Two on the Town," *New York Times*, 1/11/59.

B205   Leonard, William Torbert. *Broadway Bound: A Guide to Shows That Died Aborning*. Metuchen, N.J., and London: The Scarecrow Press, Inc., 1983.

B206   Lewis, Theophilus. Review of *Leonard Bernstein's Theatre Songs*. *America*, 7/31/65.

B207   *Lily in Love* film review. *New York Times*, 4/19/85.

B208   Lynch, Richard Chigley. *Movie Musicals on Record, A Directory of Recordings of Motion Picture Musicals, 1927-1987*. Westport, Connecticut: Greenwood Press, Inc., 1989.

B209 Lyon, Peter. "Two Minds That Beat As One." *Holiday*, 12/30/61.
Lyon describes the way Comden and Green work together.

B210 Maclaine, Shirley. *Don't Fall Off the Mountain*. New York: W. W. Norton and Co., 1970.

B211 *Magill's Survey of Cinema. English Language Films*, Second Series, Four Vols. Ed. Frank N. Magill. Englewood Cliffs, New Jersey: Salem Press, 1981.

B212 *Madwoman of Central Park West, The*, review. *New York Magazine*, 7/9/79.

B213 Mallet, Gina. Review of *By Bernstein*. *Time*, 12/15/74.

B214 Mandelbaum, Ken. *Not Since Carrie, 40 Years of Broadway Musical Flops*. New York: St. Martin's Press, 1991.

B215 Maslin, Janet. Film review of *Slaves of New York*. *New York Times*, 3/17/89.

B216 McCarten, John. Review of *Do Re Mi*. *New Yorker*, 1/14/61.

B217 McCarten, John. Review of *Hallelujah, Baby! New Yorker*, 5/6/67.

B218 McClain, John. Review of *Bells Are Ringing*. *New York Journal American*, 11/30/56.

B219 McClain, John. Review of *Do Re Mi*. *New York Journal American*, 12/27/60.

B220 McClain, John. Review of *Fade Out--Fade In*. *New York Journal American*, 5/27/64.

B221 McClain, John. Review of *A Party With Betty Comden and Adolph Green*. *New York Journal American*, 12/29/58.

B222 McClain, John. Review of *Say, Darling*. *New York Journal American*, 4/4/58.

B223 McClain, John. Review of *Subways Are for Sleeping*. *New York Journal American*, 12/28/61.

B224 McClain, John. Review of *Wonderful Town*. *New York Journal American*, 2/26/53.

B225 Mordden, Ethan. *Better Foot Forward*. New York: Grossman Publishers, The Viking Press, 1976.

B226 Morehouse, Ward. Review of *Billion Dollar Baby*. *New York Sun*, 12/22/45.

B227 Morehouse, Ward. Review of *Two on the Aisle*. *New York World Telegram*, 7/20/51.

B228 Morrow, Lee Alan. *The Tony Award Book, Four Decades of Great American Theater*. New York: Abbeville Press, 1987.

B229 Nadel, Norman. Review of *Hallelujah, Baby!* *World Journal Tribune*, 4/27/67.

B230 Nadel, Norman. Review of *Subways Are for Sleeping*. *New York World Telegram*, 12/28/61.

B231 Nash, Jay Robert and Stanley Ralph Ross. *The Motion Picture Guide*. Evanston, Illinois: Cinebooks, Inc., 1987.

B232 *New York Theatre Critics Reviews* Annuals. New York: Critics Theatre Reviews, 1940- .

B233 *New York Times Film Reviews*. New York: The New York Times and Arno Press, 1913-1980, and Times Books and Garland Press, 1981- .

B234 *New York Times Theater Reviews*, 1920-1970. New York: New York Times and Arno Press, 1972- .

B235 Newman, Phyllis. *Just in Time, Notes From My Life*. New York: Simon and Schuster, 1988.

B236 Nichols, Lewis. Review of *Billion Dollar Baby*. *New York Times*, 12/22/45.

B237 Nichols, Lewis. Review of *On the Town*. *New York Times*, 12/29/44.

B238 *Notable Names in the American Theatre*. New York: James T. White and Co., 1976.

B239 O'Connor, John J. Review of *Applause*. *Wall Street Journal*, 4/1/70.

B240 Oliver, Edith. Review of *The Cockeyed Tiger*. *New Yorker*, 1/24/77.

B241 *On the Town* review. *The Nation*, 1/13/45.

B242 *On the Town* review. *Saturday Review of Literature*, 2/17/45.

B243 *On the Town* review. *Time*, 1/8/45.

B244 *On the Town* film review. *The New Republic*, 12/26/49.

B245 *On the Town* film review. *Newsweek*, 12/19/49.

B246 *On the Town* film review. *Time*, 1/2/50.

B247 On the Town film review. *Variety*, 12/7/49.

B248 *Party With Betty Comden and Adolph Green, A*, review. *Theatre Arts*, 3/59.

B249 Peyser, Joan. *Bernstein, A Biography*. New York: Beach Tree Books, William Morrow, 1987.

B250 Prideaux, T. "They're Still Ringing the Bells." *Life*, 7/25/60.

B251 Rich, Frank. Review of *Diamonds*. *New York Times*, 12/17/84.

B252 Rich, Frank. Review of *A Doll's Life*. *New York Times*, 9/24/82.

B253 Rich, Frank. Review of the concert version of *Follies*. *New York Times*, 9/9/85.

B254 Rich, Frank. Review of *Jerome Robbins' Broadway*. *New York Times*, 2/27/89.

B255 Rich, Frank. Review of *Singin' in the Rain*. *New York Times*, 7/3/85.

B256 Rich, Frank. Review of *The Will Rogers Follies*. *New York Times*, 5/2/9l.

B257 Richards, David. "The Tall Truths of a Yarn Spinner," *New York Times*, 5/12/91.

B258 Rogow, Leo. Film review of *It's Always Fair Weather*. *Saturday Review of Literature*, 9/3/55.

B259 Roscoe, Burton. Review of *Billion Dollar Baby*. *New York World Telegram*, 12/22/45.

B260 Rosenberg, Ben. Review of *Billion Dollar Baby*. *New York Post*, 12/26/45.

B261 *Say, Darling* review. *Newsweek*, 4/14/58.

B262 Schloss, Edwin H. Review of the tryout performance of *Bonanza Bound! Philadelphia Evening Bulletin*, 12/27/47.

B263 *Schwann Spectrum* record catalogue, Vol. 4, no. 2. Spring 1993. Santa Fe, New Mexico: Stereophile, Inc., 1993.

B264 Shaw, Irwin. "When You and I Were Young." Review of *Billion Dollar Baby*. *The New Yorker*, 1/5/1946.

B265 Simas, Rick. *The Musicals No One Came to See, 1943-1983*. New York: Garland Publishing, Inc., 1987.

B266 Simon, John. Review of *A Doll's Life*. *New York Magazine*, 10/4/82.

B267 *Singin' in the Rain* film review. *Newsweek*, 4/7/52.

B268 *Singin' in the Rain* film review. *Saturday Review of Literature*, 4/12/52.

B269 *Singin' in the Rain* film review. *Time*, 4/21/52.

B270 *Singin' in the Rain* film review. *Variety*, 3/12/52.

B271 Sinyard, Neil. *Basic Movies*. Salem, N.H.: Salem House, 1985.

B272 Slide, Anthony, ed. *Selected Film Criticism, 1951-1960*, Vol. 5. Metuchen, N.J., and London: The Scarecrow Press, Inc., 1985.

B273 Smith, Cecil and Glenn Litton. *Musical Comedy in America*. New York: Theatre Arts Books, 1981.

B274 Solomon, Aubrey. *Twentieth Century-Fox: A Corporate and Financial History*. Metuchen, N.J., and London: The Scarecrow Press, 1988.

B275 Spindle, Les. *Julie Andrews, A Bio-Bibliography*. Westport, Connecticut: Greenwood Press, 1989.

B276 Stearns, David Patrick. "Will Rogers." *USA Today*, 5/2/91.

B277 Streiker, Lowell D. Review of *Hallelujah, Baby! Christian Century*, 8/30/67.

B278 Stuart, Jan. Review of *The Will Rogers Follies*. *New York Newsday*, 5/2/91.

B279 *Subways Are for Sleeping* review. *Newsweek*, 1/8/62.

B280 *Subways Are for Sleeping* review. *Time*, 1/8/62.

B281 Suskin, Steven. *Opening Night on Broadway*. New York: Schirmer Books, Macmillan, Inc., 1990.

B282 Suskin, Steven. *Show Tunes, 1905-1991*. New York: Limelight Editions, 1991.

B283 Suskin, Steven. *Show Tunes, The Songs, Shows and Careers of Broadway's Major Composers*. New York: Dodd, 1986.

B284 *Take Me Out to the Ball Game* film review. *Time*, 3/28/49.

B285 *Take Me Out to the Ball Game* film review. *Variety*, 3/9/49.

B286 "Talk of the Town, The." *New Yorker*, May 12, 1975.

B287 Tallmer, Jerry. "Comden and Green," *Playbill*, Vol. 11, no. 7, April 30, 1993.

B288 Taubman, Howard. Review of *Do Re Mi*. *New York Times*, 12/27/60.

B289 Taubman, Howard. Review of *Fade Out--Fade In*. *New York Times*, 5/27/64.

B290 Taubman, Howard. Review of *Subways Are for Sleeping*. *New York Times*, 12/28/61.

B291 Taubman, Howard. Review of *Wonderful Town*. *New York Times*, 2/15/63.

B292 Taylor, Theodore. *Jule, The Story of Composer Jule Styne*. New York: Random House, 1979.

B293 *Theatre World* Annuals. 47 Vols. New York: Greenberg Publisher; Philadelphia: Chilton Co.; New York: Crown Publishers, Inc., 1944- .

B294 *Two on the Aisle* review. *The New Yorker*, 7/28/51.

B295 *Two on the Aisle* review. *Time*, 7/30/51.

B296 Valentine, Dean. Review of *On the Twentieth Century*. *New Leader*, 3/27/78.

B297 *Variety Film Reviews*. 19 Vols. New York and London: Garland Publishing, Inc., 1983- .

B298 *Variety Television Reviews*. 15 Vols. New York and London: Garland Publishing, Inc., 1989- .

B299 Vinson, James, ed. *The International Dictionary of Films and Filmmakers*. Vol. IV. *Writers and Production Artists*. Chicago and London: St. James Press, 1987.

B300 Wahls, Robert. "After Five Big Musicals, Adolph and Betty Juke Box Hits." *New York Times*, 6/23/57.

B301 Wallach, Allan. "Harold Prince." *Newsday*, 2/3/80.

B302 Watt, Douglas. Review of *By Bernstein*. *Daily News*, 11/24/75.

B303 Watt, Douglas. Review of *Diamonds*. *Daily News*, 12/17/84.

B304 Watt, Douglas. Review of *A Doll's Life*. *Daily News*, 9/24/82.

B305 Watt, Douglas. Review of *Lorelei*. *Daily News*, 1/28/74.

B306 Watt, Douglas. Review of *On the Twentieth Century*. *Daily News*, 2/20/78.

B307 Watt, Douglas. Review of *Singin' in the Rain*. *Daily News*, 7/3/85.

B308 Watt, Douglas. Review of *The Will Rogers Follies*. *Daily News*, 5/10/91.

B309 Watts, Jr., Richard. Review of *Applause*. New York Post, 3/31/70.

B310 Watts, Jr., Richard. Review of *Bells Are Ringing*. New York Post, 1/30/56.

B311 Watts, Jr., Richard. Review of *Fade Out--Fade In*. New York Post, 5/27/64.

B312 Watts, Jr., Richard. Review of *Hallelujah, Baby!* New York Post, 4/27/67.

B313 Watts, Jr., Richard. Review of *A Party With Betty Comden and Adolph Green*. New York Post, 12/29/58.

B314 Watts, Jr., Richard. Review of *Peter Pan*. New York Post, 10/21/54.

B315 Watts, Jr., Richard. Review of *Say, Darling*. New York Post, 4/4/58.

B316 Watts, Jr., Richard. Review of *Subways Are for Sleeping*. New York Post, 12/28/61.

B317 Watts, Jr., Richard. Review of *Two on the Aisle*. New York Post, 7/20/51.

B318 Watts, Jr., Richard. Review of *Wonderful Town*. New York Post, 2/26/53.

B319 *What a Way to Go!* film review. Newsweek, 5/18/64.

B320 *What a Way to Go!* film review. Time, 5/22/64.

B321 *What a Way to Go!* film review. Variety, 4/1/64.

B322 Wilson, Edwin. Review of *Jerome Robbins' Broadway*. Wall Street Journal, 2/28/89.

B323 Wilson, Edwin. Review of *Lorelei*. Wall Street Journal, 1/31/74.

B324 Wilson, Edwin. Review of *The Madwoman of Central Park West*. Wall Street Journal. 6/22/79.

B325 Wilson, Edwin. Review of *On the Twentieth Century*. Wall Street Journal, 2/22/78.

B326 Wilson, Edwin. Review of *Singin' in the Rain*. Wall Street Journal, 5/10/85.

B327 Wilson, Edwin. Review of *The Will Rogers Follies*. Wall Street Journal, 5/8/91.

B328 *Wonderful Town* review. Theatre Arts, 3/53.

B329 Zolotow, Sam. "*Skin of Our Teeth* Musical Dropped." New York Times, 1/5/65.

B330 Zunser, Jesse. Film review of *The Band Wagon*. Cue 7/11/53.

APPENDIX: AWARDS, NOMINATIONS, AND HONORS

Tony Awards

Wonderful Town (1953 awards; opened 1953)

Best Musical Play:
    Music: Leonard Bernstein
    Lyrics: Betty Comden, Adolph Green
    Book: Joseph Fields, Jerome Chodorov
    Producer: Robert Fryer
Best Musical Actress: Rosalind Russell
Best Scenic Designer: Raoul Pène DuBois
Best Choreographer: Donald Saddler
Best Conductor and Musical Director: Lehman Engel

Bells Are Ringing (1957 awards; opened 1956)

Best Musical Actress: Judy Holliday
Best Supporting or Featured Musical Actor: Sydney Chaplin

Hallelujah, Baby! (1968 awards; opened 1967)

Best Musical Play:
    Music: Jule Styne
    Lyrics: Betty Comden, Adolph Green
    Book: Arthur Laurents
    Producers: Albert Selden, Hal James, Jane C. Nusbaum, Harry Rigby
Best Composer and Lyricist: Jule Styne, Betty Comden, Adolph Green
Best Actress in a Musical Play: Leslie Uggams
Best Supporting Actress in a Musical Play: Lillian Hayman

Applause (1970 awards; opened 1970)

Best Musical Play:
    Music: Charles Strouse
    Lyrics: Lee Adams
    Book: Betty Comden, Adolph Green
    Producers: Joseph Kipness, Lawrence Kasha
Best Actress in a Musical Play: Lauren Bacall
Best Director of a Musical: Ron Field
Best Choreographer: Ron Field

On the Twentieth Century (1978 awards; opened 1978)

Best Score of a Broadway Musical:
    Music: Cy Coleman
    Lyrics: Betty Comden, Adolph Green
Best Book of a Broadway Musical: Betty Comden, Adolph Green
Best Performance by an Actor in a Broadway Musical: John Cullum
Best Performance by an Actor in a Featured Role in a Broadway Play: Kevin Kline
Best Scenic Designer of a Broadway Play: Robin Wagner

The Will Rogers Follies (1991 awards; opened 1991)

Best Musical Play:
    Music: Cy Coleman
    Lyrics: Betty Comden, Adolph Green
    Book: Peter Stone
    Producers: Pierre Cossette, Martin Richards, Sam Crothers, James M. Nederlander, Stewart F. Lane, Max Weitzenhoffer, Japan Satellite Broadcasting, Inc.
Best Score:
    Music: Cy Coleman
    Lyrics: Betty Comden, Adolph Green
Best Costumes: Willa Kim
Best Lighting: Jules Fisher
Best Director: Tommy Tune
Best Choreographer: Tommy Tune

Tony Award Nominations

Bells Are Ringing (1957 awards; opened 1956)

Best Musical Play:
    Music: Jule Styne
    Book and Lyrics: Betty Comden, Adolph Green

Producer: The Theatre Guild
Best Choreographer: Jerome Robbins, Bob Fosse

Do Re Mi (1961 awards; opened 1960)

Best Musical Play:
    Music: Jule Styne
    Lyrics: Betty Comden, Adolph Green
    Book: Garson Kanin
    Producer: David Merrick
    Director, Musical: Garson Kanin
Best Musical Actress: Nancy Walker
Best Musical Actor: Phil Silvers
Best Musical Actress, Supporting or Featured: Nancy Dussault

Hallelujah, Baby! (1968 awards; opened 1967)

Best Actor in a Musical Play: Robert Hooks
Best Director: Burt Shevelove
Best Choreographer: Kevin Carlisle
Best Costume Designer: Irene Sharaff

Applause (1970 awards; opened 1970)

Best Actor in a Musical Play: Len Cariou
Best Supporting Actress: Bonnie Franklin, Penny Fuller
Best Supporting Actor: Brandon Maggart
Best Scenic Designer: Robert Randolph
Best Costume Designer: Ray Aghayan
Best Lighting Designer: Tharon Musser

On the Twentieth Century (1978 awards; opened 1978)

Best Musical Play:
    Music: Cy Coleman
    Lyrics: Betty Comden, Adolph Green
    Book: Betty Comden, Adolph Green
    Producer: Producers Circle 2, Inc.
Best Performance by an Actress in a Broadway Musical: Madeline Kahn
Best Performance by an Actress in a Featured Role: Imogene Coca
Best Director of a Broadway Musical: Harold Prince

A Doll's Life (1983 awards; opened 1982)

Best Musical Play:
  Music: Larry Grossman
  Book and Lyrics: Betty Comden, Adolph Green
  Producers: James M. Nederlander, Sidney L. Shlenker,
    Warner Theatre Productions, Joseph Harris, Mary Lea
    Johnson, Martin Richards, Robert Fryer, Harold Prince
Best Book of a Musical: Betty Comden, Adolph Green
Best Performance by an Actor in a Musical: George Hearn

The Will Rogers Follies (1991 awards; opened 1991)

Best Actor in a Broadway Musical: Keith Carradine
Best Actress in a Broadway Musical: Dee Hoty
Best Featured Actress: Cady Hoffman
Best Book: Peter Stone
Best Scenic Design: Tony Walton

Other Awards for Stage Musicals

Donaldson Award: Best Lyrics for *Wonderful Town* (1953)

New York Drama Critics Award: Best Lyrics for *Wonderful Town* (1953)

Drama Desk Awards: Best Musical, *The Will Rogers Follies* (1991)

Nominations for Stage Musicals

New York Drama Critics Awards Nomination: Best Lyrics for *Hallelujah, Baby!*

Obie (Off Broadway) Award

A Party With Betty Comden and Adolph Green (1958)

Academy Award Nominations

The Band Wagon (1953)
  Best Story and Screenplay

It's Always Fair Weather (1955)
  Best Story and Screenplay

Screenwriters Guild Awards

On the Town (1949)

Singin' in the Rain (1952)

Bells Are Ringing (1960)

Screenwriters Guild Awards Nominations

The Barkleys of Broadway (1949)

It's Always Fair Weather (1955)

Special Film Awards and Honors

Singin' in the Rain (1952)
Ten Best Films List (*Sight and Sound* and other film magazines)

American Film Institute voted it one of the best American films of all time.

A poll of international film critics voted it the third best film ever made.

Grammy Award

The Will Rogers Follies
Best show album, 1991.

Grammy Award Nominations

A Party With Betty Comden and Adolph Green
Nominated for best comedy-musical award, 1959

Bells Are Ringing
Comden and Green nominated, with Jule Styne, for a composer's award for best sound track album, motion picture or television, with original cast, 1960.

"Make Someone Happy" from *Do Re Mi*
Nominated, as best song of the year, 1961.

Do Re Mi
Comden and Green nominated, with Jule Styne, for a composer's award for the best score for an original cast show album, 1961.

Hallelujah, Baby!
Comden and Green nominated, with Jule Styne, for a composer's award for the best score for an original cast show album, 1967.

On the Twentieth Century
Comden and Green nominated, with Jule Styne, for a composer's award for the best score for an original cast show album, 1978.

Personal Awards and Honors

Betty Comden received the Woman of Achievement Award from the Alumni Association of New York University (1978).

Betty Comden and Adolph Green received the Mayor of New York's Certificate of Excellence (1980).

Betty Comden and Adolph Green were installed in the Songwriters' Hall of Fame (March 17, 1980).

Betty Comden and Adolph Green were inducted into the Theatre Hall of Fame (April 5, 1981).

Betty Comden and Adolph Green were presented the Johnny Mercer Award for Lifetime Achievement (May 29, 1991).

Betty Comden and Adolph Green were honored by the Academy of Motion Picture Arts and Sciences (1991).

Betty Comden and Adolph Green were honored by the Vancouver Film Festival (1991).

Betty Comden and Adolph Green were honored at the Kennedy Center for their Lifetime Achievement in the Performing Arts (December 8, 1991).

INDEX

The Index uses both the page numbers and the section entry numbers (S01, F01, R01, P01, RA01, T01, and D01) for reference. In order to distinquish between musicals and films the word (film) has been used after the film name, but nothing is used after the name of the stage musicals. Song titles are in quotation marks.

22 Steps Theatre
  Madwoman of Central Park West, The, 35, 139, 140
"7 1/2 Cents"
  Pajama Game, The, 22, 103
A. and S. Lyons (agents)
  Comden and Green, 151
Abbott, Bud
  Diamonds, 140
Abbott, George, 11, 28, 34, 48, T36 221
  63 years as a Broadway producer, 34
  Billion Dollar Baby, 14, 56
  Comden and Green, *George Abbott ... A Celebration*, 34
  Donaldson Award, *Wonderful Town*, 98
  Fade Out--Fade In, 74, 78
  Kennedy Center Lifetime Achievement Award, 38
  On the Town, 11, 14, 51, 54, 55
  Pajama Game, The, 102

  Singin' in the Rain, 129
  Wonderful Town, 19, 95, 97-99
Abbott, L. B.
  What a Way to Go! (film), 190
Abbott, Pam
  Bells Are Ringing, 65
ABC Records
  Applause, 124
  Fade Out--Fade In, 77
ABC Television
  I'm Getting Married, 47, T48 224
Abrams, Amos
  Madwoman of Central Park West, The, 139
Academy Award
  Fred Astaire, 156
  Judy Holliday, *Born Yesterday* (film), 188
  Lennie Hayton, *On the Town* (film), 164
  Roger Edens, *On the Town* (film), 164

278 Comden and Green

Academy Award (nomination)
  Adolph Green, *It's Always Fair*
    Weather (film), 21, 180
  Band Wagon, The (film), 19, 174
  Betty Comden, *It's Always Fair*
    Weather (film), 21, 180
Academy Awards 1961, T18 217
Academy of Motion Picture Arts
  and Sciences (honors)
  Comden and Green, 276
Ackerman, Loni
  Diamonds, 141
Aco, Lucas
  Billion Dollar Baby, 57
Acuff, Roy T41 222
Adams, Edith, D40 244
  Donaldson Award, *Wonderful*
    Town, 98
  Wonderful Town, 95
Adams, India D03 228
Adams, Lee, D01 227, T30 219,
  T49 224
  Applause, 33, 121, 125
  Tony Award, *Applause,* 34, 124,
    272
Adams, Maude
  Peter Pan, 134
Adams, Trude
  Leonard Bernstein's Theatre
    Songs, 143, 144
Addams Family, The (film) D42
  245
  Paramount Pictures, 41, 49
Adelphi Theatre
  On the Town, 14, 51, 54
Adler, Richard T23 218
"Adventure," D10 232, D42 246,
  D43 246
  Do Re Mi, 107, 109
Aghayan, Ray
  Applause, 121
  Lorelei, 136
  Tony Award (nomination),
    Applause, 273
Ahmanson Theatre (Los Angeles)
  Doll's Life, A, 37, 88
"Ain't Got No Tears Left"
  By Bernstein, 145
Akst, Albert
  Band Wagon, The (film), 171
  Barkleys of Broadway, The (film),
    154
  Good News (film), 149
Albanese, Licia D52 248
Aldredge, Theoni V.
  Madwoman of Central Park West,
    The, 139
Aletter, Frank
  Bells Are Ringing, 65
Alexander, Chris, D22 237, D45
  246, D56 249
  On the Town, 51
  Wonderful Town, 96
Alexander, Jason
  Jerome Robbins' Broadway, 146
Alexander, Jeff
  It's Always Fair Weather (film),
    176
  Singin' in the Rain (film), 165
"Alexander's Ragtime Band," 5
All About Eve, D01 227
  (basis for) *Applause,* 33
  Anne Baxter, 33
  Bette Davis, 33
  Mary Orr, 33, 121
All About Eve (film), 121, 124, 125
All About Eve (musical)
  Bacall, Lauren 33
"All I Do Is Dream of You," D32
  241
  Singin' in the Rain (film), 167
"All of My Life!" D10 232
  Do Re Mi, 106
"All You Need is a Quarter," D10
  231, T47 224
  Do Re Mi, 106
Allen, Clifford
  Hallelujah, Baby!, 110
Allen, John
  Singin' in the Rain, 129
  Two on the Aisle, 91
Allen, Peter
  Madwoman of Central Park West,
    The, 139
Allen, Ralph G.
  Diamonds, 140
Allen, Steve T03 215
Allen, Valerie
  Bells Are Ringing (film), 187

Allen, Virginia
    Fade Out--Fade In, 76
Allers, Franz, T14 217
Allessandrini, Gerard
    Diamonds, 140, 141
Allison, Wana
    Say, Darling, 101
Allsbrook, Bill
    Applause, 121, 122
Allwyn, Marilyn
    Do Re Mi, 105, 106
Allyson, June, D15 233
    Good News (film), 15, 149, 153
Alper, Murray
    Take Me Out to the Ballgame (film), 158
Alton, Robert
    Barkleys of Broadway, The (film), 153
Alumni Association of New York University
    Betty Comden, Woman of Achievement Award, 276
Alvin Theatre
    Billion Dollar Baby, 14, 56, 59
    First Impressions, 26
    Lady in the Dark, 29
Amadeus, 130
Amaro, Richard
    Jerome Robbins' Broadway, 146
"Ambition," D10 232, D64 251
    Do Re Mi, 107
Ambrosia Singers D58 250
Ameche, Don
    Greenwich Village (film), 11
"America," D19 235
    Jerome Robbins' Broadway
America, D19 235
    Leonard Bernstein's Theatre Songs, 144
American Film
    Magic of Fred Astaire, The, 174
American Film Institute
    Singin' in the Rain (film), 169
American Film Institute Tribute to Gene Kelly, T38 221
American in Paris, An, 18, 161
    Arthur Freed, 174
    Gene Kelly, 18, 169
American Musical Theatre, The,
    T17 217
American Musical Theatre: Shows, Songs, and Stars, D43 245
American Musicals, D44 246
American Place Theatre
    Straws in the Wind, 139, 201
American Theatre Festival
    Comden and Green (guest speakers), 39
    On the Town, 39
Americraft
    Steven Kyle, 37
Ames, Preston
    Band Wagon, The (film), 171
    Bells Are Ringing (film), 187
Anania, John
    Applause, 121
Anchors Aweigh, 160, 161
Anderson, David
    Applause, 122
Anderson, Delbert
    Wonderful Town, 95, 96
Anderson, June, D50 247
    Candide, 41
Anderson, Leroy
    Wonderful Town, 19, 97
Anderson, Maxwell, 6
Andrews, Barbara
    Hallelujah, Baby!, 111
Andrews, George Lee, D64 251
    On the Twentieth Century, 80
Andrews, Julie, D56 249, T14 217
    Fabulous Fifties, The, 28
    Les Spindle (biography), 28
    My Fair Lady, 67
Angel, Lou
    Hallelujah, Baby!, 110
Ankrum, Morris
    Good News (film), 150
Annie Get Your Gun
    Dolores Gray, 18
"Anniversary for Susanna Kyle"
    Leonard Bernstein, 10
Annual Theater World Award
    Peter Gallagher, 88
"Another Day," D16 234
    Hallelujah, Baby!, 113
"Another Love"
    By Bernstein, 145
Anotonini, Alfredo, T14 217

280 Comden and Green

ANTA Theatre
  Say, Darling, 22, 100, 102
Apartment, The (Oscar), T18 217
Applause, xiii, 43, 48, 246, D01
  227, D47 246, S15 124, T30 219,
  T49 224
    Comden and Green (book), 33,
      121, 124-126
    Lauren Bacall, xi, 33, 34, 121,
      124-126
    Lee Adams, 33, 121, 124-126
    Palace Theatre, 34, 121
    Charles Strouse, 33
    Tony Award, 34, 124, 272
Aquilina, Jeannett
  Two on the Aisle, 91
Archer, Jeri
  Billion Dollar Baby, 57
Archerd, Army
  What a Way to Go! (film), 191
Arden, Eve
  Auntie Mame (play), 185
Arena Stage (Washington, D.C.)
  On the Town, 55
Arkin, Alan
  My Favorite Year, 38
  Simon, 38, 206
Arlen, Steve, D11 232
Armistead, Diane
  Doll's Life, A, 86
Armstrong, Will Steven
  Subways Are for Sleeping, 69
Arney, Arthur
  Two on the Aisle, 92
Arnold, Anton
  What a Way to Go! (film), 191
Arnold, Diane
  Fade Out--Fade In, 75, 76
Arnold, Edward
  Take Me Out to the Ballgame
    (film), 158
Arnold, Maxine
  On the Town, 51
Arnold, Sydney
  Bonanza Bound!, 62
Aronson, Boris
  Do Re Mi, 105, 109
  Jerome Robbins' Broadway, 146
"Arrival, The" D13 232
Arthur Murray Party, The, T15 217
Arthur, Beatrice
  Tony Award, *Mame* (musical),
    185
Arthur, Carol D23 237
Arthur, Jean
  Peter Pan, 134
Arts and Entertainment Cable
  Network, T37 221
  Party With Betty Comden and
    Adolph Green, A, 202
Ashman, Howard
  Diamonds, 141
"Asking for You" D10 232
Askler, David
  Singin' in the Rain, 127
Astaire Award
  Tommy Tune, *Will Rogers Follies,*
    The, 117
Astaire, Adele, 11, 15, 19
  Band Wagon, The (revue), 155,
    173
Astaire, Fred, D03 228, D04 228
  Band Wagon, The (film), 11, 15,
    19, 171, 174-175
  Band Wagon, The (revue), 173
  Barkleys of Broadway, The (film),
    16, 154-156
  Easter Parade (film), 15, 155,
    173
  Gay Divorce, The, 173
  I Love Louisa, 19
Aston, Fred
  Do Re Mi, 109
"At Home Abroad"
  Schwartz and Dietz, 174
"At Last," D13 232
Atkinson, Brooks
  Bells Are Ringing, 68
  Party With Betty Comden and
    Adolph Green, A, 202
  Peter Pan, 135
  Say, Darling, 103, 104
  Two on the Aisle, 93
  Wonderful Town, 98
Auntie Mame 47, 184, 186, D02
  228
  Broadhurst Theatre, 184
  Patrick Dennis (novel) 22, 184
Auntie Mame (film), 186, F08 182-
  186
  Jerome Lawrence, 22, 182

Index 281

Morton DaCosta, 22, 182, 184-186
Radio City Music Hall, 23, 185
Robert E. Lee, 22, 182
Rosalind Russell, 22, 182, 184-186
Warner Bros., 22, 182, 185
Avedon, Joseph, 28
Ausili, Joseph G.
Jerome Robbins' Broadway, 146
Austen, Jane, 26
"Auto-de-fe (What a Day)," D50 248
Avedon, Richard, 28
Avery Fisher Hall at Lincoln Center, D52 249
Follies (concert version), 39, 208
Avila, Doria
Bells Are Ringing, 65
Do Re Mi, 106
Ayme, Marcel
Moonbirds, 26

"Babette" D26 238
"Baby Doll," D36 243
"Baby, You Knock Me Out," D17 234
It's Always Fair Weather (film), 178, 181
Bacall, Lauren 24, 28, D01 227, T30 219, T33 220, T49 224
All About Eve (musical), 33
Applause, 33, 34, 121, 124-126
By Myself (book), 34
Cactus Flower, 33
Comden and Green, Kennedy Center Honors, xi, 41
Tony Award, *Applause*, 34, 272
"Back Stage Babble," D01 227
"Bad Timing," D07 230, D62 251
Bailey, Maureen, T46 224
Baisley, Helen
Subways Are for Sleeping, 70
Baker, David
Do Re Mi, 105
Baker, Terri
Fade Out--Fade In, 76
Balin, Ed
Wonderful Town, 96
Ball, Diane
Do Re Mi, 105, 106

Subways Are for Sleeping, 70
Ball, Lucille
Mame (film), 185
Ballard, Kay
Wonderful Town, 98
Ballbusch, Peter
Take Me Out to the Ballgame (film), 158
"Ballet at the Village Vortex," D40 245, D41 245, D56 249
Ballet Theatre Company
Fancy Free, 11
Jerome Robbins, 53
Ballet Theatre Orchestra, D61 250
Baltimore
Applause, 124
Banas, Robert
Peter Pan, 134
Bancroft, Anne, T48 224
Garbo Talks (film), 207
I'm Getting Married (television), 31
Band Wagon, The (film), 43, 46, 155, 173-176, 202, D03 228, D58 250, F06 171-176
Academy Award (nomination), 19, 174, 274
Comden and Green, 19, 171, 174-176
Arthur Freed, 19, 171, 174
"By Myself," 19, 172-174
Cyd Charisse, 175
Fred Astaire, 11, 19, 171, 174, 175
"I Love Louisa," 19, 173
Jack Buchanan, 172, 175, 176
Metro-Goldwyn-Mayer, 171
Michael Kidd, 19, 171, 174, 176
Nanette Fabray, 176
Oliver Smith, 19, 174
Radio City Music Hall, 19, 174
Roger Edens, 19, 171, 174
Schwartz and Dietz, 19, 171, 173-175
"Shine on Your Shoes," 176
"That's Entertainment," 172
"Triplets," 173
Vincente Minnelli, 19, 171, 174, 176
Band Wagon, The (play) 173
Band Wagon, The (revue), 15

Adele Astaire, 155
Fred Astaire, 155
Swartz and Deitz, 19
"Banshee Sisters, The," D28 239
   Party With Betty Comden and Adolph Green, A, 200
Barbican Theatre (London)
   On the Town (concert version), 42
Barkleys of Broadway, The (film), 16, 46, 156, 163, D04 228, F02 156, 157
   Arthur Freed, 15, 154, 155
   Charles Walters, 153
   Comden and Green (screenplay), 15, 153, 155
   Fred Astaire, 15, 16, 154, 155, 157
   Ginger Rogers, 16, 154, 155, 157
   Judy Garland, 15, 16, 155, 157
   Metro-Goldwyn-Mayer, 15, 153, 155, 156
   Screenwriters Guild Award (nomination), 16, 156, 275
Barlow, Roxane
   Will Rogers Follies, The, 114, 115
Barnes, Clive
   Applause, 126
   Diamonds, 141
   Jerome Robbins' Broadway, 148
   Madwoman of Central Park West, The, 140
   On the Twentieth Century, 83
   Party With Betty Comden and Adolph Green, A, 202
   Singin' in the Rain, 130
Barnes, Howard
   Billion Dollar Baby, 60
   On the Town, 55
Barnes, Joanna
   Auntie Mame (film), 182
"Baroness Bazooka, The," 9, D27 239, D28 239, D30 240
   Party With Betty Comden and Adolph Green, A, 200
Barrie, James M., D19 235
   Jerome Robbins' Broadway, 146
   Peter Pan, 134
Barrymore, John

   Twentieth Century, 82
Barthelme, Donald
   Straws in the Wind, 138, 139
Barto, Betty Lou
   Bonanza Bound!, 61
Bas, Carlos
   Subways Are for Sleeping, 70
Basile, Frank
   Diamonds, 141
Bates, Florence
   On the Town (film), 162
Batten, Tom
   On the Twentieth Century, 80
Battles, John
   On the Town, 51, 56
Baughman, Renee
   Applause, 122
Bawtree, Michael
   By Bernstein, 144, 145
Baxter, Anne, D01 227
   All About Eve, 33, 124
   Applause, 124
Bay, Howard
   Two on the Aisle, 91
Bayes, Nora
   Ziegfeld Follies, 160
"Be a Clown" D33 242
"Be a Ladies' Man," D15 233
   Good News (film), 150
"Be a Santa," D34 242, D35 242
   Subways Are for Sleeping, 71, 74
Beam, Alvin
   Wonderful Town, 96
Bean, David
   Peter Pan, 134
Bean, Orson, D34 242
   Subways Are For Sleeping, 29, 70, 74
Beaufort, John
   By Bernstein, 145
   Diamonds, 141
   On the Twentieth Century, 83
   Will Rogers Follies, The, 118
"Beautiful Girl"
   Singin' in the Rain (film), 167
Becker, Ray
   Applause, 121
Becket, Marta
   Wonderful Town, 96

Beckham, Willard
Lorelei, 137
Beddow, Margery
Two on the Aisle, 92
"Being Good Isn't Good Enough,"
D16 234, D51 248, D54 249
Hallelujah, Baby!, 111, 113
Bell, Joan
Applause, 122
Bells Are Ringing, 22-24, 43, 46,
200, 203,246-248, D05 229,
D06 230, D27 239, D28 239,
D43 246, D44 246, D64 251,
S04 64-69, T19 218
Comden and Green, 10, 22, 64,
67-69
Jerome Robbins, 22, 64, 68
Judy Holliday, 22, 65-69
Jule Stein, 22, 64, 68, 69
"Just in Time (book), 67, 69
"The Party's Over," 67, 69
Random House (book), 68
Sam S. Shubert Theatre, 22, 64
Theatre Guild, 22, 64, 67
Tony Award 22, 67, 271
Bells Are Ringing (film), 22-24, 43,
46, 200, 203, 246-248, D05
229, D06 230, D27 239, D28
239, D43 246, D44 246, D64
251, F09 186-190, T19 218
André Previn, 186
Arthur Freed, 23, 187, 190
Comden and Green, 23, 24,
186, 188-190
Dean Martin, 187, 188, 190
Grammy Award (nomination),
275
Judy Holliday, xii, 23, 24,
187-190
Jule Styne, 186
Metro-Goldwyn-Mayer, 186
Radio City Music Hall, 24, 189
Screenwriters Guild Award, 189,
275
Vincente Minnelli, 24, 186, 188,
189
Belmonte, Vicki
Subways Are for Sleeping, 70
Benaderet, Bea
On the Town (film), 162
Benham, Dorothy

Jerome Robbins' Broadway, 146
Beniades, Ted
Wonderful Town, 95
Benjamin, Richard
My Favorite Year, 206
Bennett, Constance
Auntie Mame (play), 185
Bennett, Marjorie
What a Way to Go! (film), 191
Bennett, Michael
Follies (concert version), 208
Subways Are for Sleeping, 70
Bennett, Robert Russell, D05 229
Bells Are Ringing, 64
Bennett, Tony, D54 249
Benson, Laura
I Want to Go Home (film), 209
Benson, Ray
Singin' in the Rain, 127
Bentley, Jordan
Wonderful Town, 95
Bergen, Polly, D54 249
Berke, Maxine
Wonderful Town, 96
Berkeley, Busby, 78, 130
Take Me Out to the Ballgame
(film), 157, 160
What a Way to Go! (film), 30
Berkman, Donald, 14, 233
Fade Out--Fade In, 75
Berlin, Irving, D19 235
Jerome Robbins' Broadway, 146
Wonderful Town, 97
Berman, Norman L.
By Bernstein, 144, 145
Berman, Shelly, T14 217
Fabulous Fifties, The, 28
Bernstein, Burton
Family Matters (book), 2, 5
Bernstein, Elmer, D58 250
Peter Pan, 133
Bernstein, Felicia, 24
Bernstein, Jennie, 2
Bernstein, Leonard xi, xiii, 2, 9, 16,
24, 28, 30, 31, 34, 46, 48, 49,
59, 205, D19 235, D21 236,
D22 237, D24 237, D27
239, D28 239, D30 240, D40
244, D44 246, D50 247, D56
249, D57 249, D61 250, T11

284   Comden and Green

216, T26 219, T27 219, T33
   220, T35 220, T50 225
"Anniversary for Susanna Kyle,"
   10
Camp Onata, 2
Candide, 40
Curtis Institute (Philadelphia), 6
Death, 41, 49
Donaldson Award, *Wonderful
   Town*, 98
Drama Critics Circle Award,
   Wonderful Town, 98
Fancy Free, 11, 40, 53
Harvard, 5
Jerome Robbins' Broadway,
   146, 148
*Leonard Bernstein's Theatre
   Songs*, 143
*Madwoman of Central Park West,
   The*, 35, 139, 140
My Sister Eileen (film), 19
Night Life in New York, 8
On the Town, 11, 14, 17, 21, 51,
   54, 56, 161-163
*Party With Betty Comden and
   Adolph Green, A*, 199
Peter Pan, 134
Pianist, The Revuers, 5
Skin of Our Teeth, The, 30
Tony Award, *Wonderful Town*,
   271
West Side Story, 21
Wonderful Town, 19, 95, 97-99,
   200
Bernstein, Sam, 2
*Bernstein at 60, An Appreciation
   From Wolf Trap* T33 220
Bernstein Songbook, The, D45
   246
By Bernstein, 34, 144, 145
Bert, Malcolm
   Auntie Mame (film), 182
Best Foot Forward, 160
"Best Night of My Life, The" D01
   227
"Best of All Possible Worlds, The"
   D50 247
Best Ten List
   Singin' in the Rain (film), 169
"Best Things in Life Are Free, The,"
   D15 233

Good News (musical/film),
   150-153
"Better Be Good to Me," D60 250
"Better Than a Dream," D06 230
Bells Are Ringing (film), 188
"Between the Devil"
   By Myself, 19, 174
   Schwartz and Dietz, 174
Bibb, Leon, D56 249
"Big Talk," D63 251
"Big Time, The," D39 244
Bigelow, Susan
   Diamonds, 141
Billig, Robert
   Singin' in the Rain, 126
Billington, Ken
   Doll's Life, A, 85
   Diamonds, 141
   *Madwoman of Central Park West,
      The*, 139
   On the Twentieth Century, 79
Billion Dollar Baby 14, 15, 40,
   147, 148, 152, D07 230, D19
   235, D62 251, S02 56-61
   Alvin Theatre, 14, 56, 59
   Comden and Green, 14, 56, 59,
      61
   Donaldson Award, 60
   George Abbott, 56, 60
   Irene Sharaff, 56, 60
   Jerome Robbins, 56, 60
   Jerome Robbins' Broadway, 40,
      147
   Joan McCracken, 14, 57, 60
   Morton Gould, 14, 56, 59
   Oliver Smith, 14, 56, 59
   Paul Feigay, 14, 56, 59
Birkenhead, Susan, D64 251
Birks, Joanne
   Bells Are Ringing, 65
Birth of a Broadway Musical, The,
   T20 218
Bishop, Al
   "Blue Prelude," 128
Bissell, George
   Pajama Game, The, 102
Bissell, Marian, D31 240
   Say, Darling, 22, 100, 103, 104
Bissell, Richard, D31 240
   "7 1/2 Cents," 102
   Say, Darling, 22, 100, 102, 104

"Stretch on the River, A," 103
Bittner, Jack
 By Bernstein, 145
"Blackburn Twins, The,"
 Take Me Out to the Ballgame
  (film), 158
Blackstone Hotel (Chicago)
 Revuers, The, 10
Blackton, Jay, T14 217
Blaine, Vivian, D31 240
 Greenwich Village (film), 11
 Say, Darling, 101
Blair, Janet
 My Sister Eileen (film), 97
Blair, Lionel D25 238
Blake, Madge
 Band Wagon, The (film), 172
 Bells Are Ringing (film), 187
 It's Always Fair Weather (film), 177
 Singin' in the Rain (film), 166
Blane, Ralph, D15 233
 Good News (film), 149
 "Pass That Peace Pipe," 152
 Take Me Out to the Ballgame
  (film), 16, 160
Blitzstein, Marc 29, 47
 Cradle Will Rock, The, 29
Block, Chad
 Do Re Mi, 105
 Hallelujah, Baby!, 110
Bloomer Girl, 54
Blossom Dearie Sings Comden and Green D46 246
Blount, Jr., Roy
 Diamonds, 140
Blue Angel 11, 45, 54
 Comden and Green, 46
 Max Gordon, 10
 Revuers, The, xi, 10
"Blue Danube (Why Are We Here?)," D17 234
"Blue Prelude," 128
Bocher, Main
 Wonderful Town, 95
Bock, Jerry, D19 235
 Jerome Robbins' Broadway, 146
 Madwoman of Central Park West, The, 139
Bodenheim, Maxwell (poet)
 Village Vanguard, 3

Bogart, Humphrey, 33
Bolger, Ray, 28
Bolton, Larry
 On the Town, 51
"Bonanza," D09 231
Bonanza Bound!, 15, 23, D08 231, D27 239, D28 239, D30 240, S03 61-64, T06 215
 Comden and Green
  (book/lyrics), 15, 61, 63, 64
 Herman Levin, 15, 61
 "Inspiration," 64, 200, 201
 Oliver Smith, 15, 61
 Paul Feigay, 15, 61
 Sam S. Shubert Theatre
  (Philadelphia), 15, 61
 Saul Chaplin, 15, 61
Bonanza Bound!/The Revuers
 D09 231
Borden, Eugene
 It's Always Fair Weather (film), 177
 On the Town (film), 162
 What a Way to Go! (film), 191
Borden, Lynn
 What a Way to Go! (film), 191
Boris, Ruthanna
 Two on the Aisle, 92
Born Yesterday (film)
 Academy Award, Judy Holliday, 21, 188
 Judy Holliday, 68, 188
 Tony Award, 21
Borstelmann, Jim
 Jerome Robbins' Broadway, 146
Boston
 Do Re Mi, 108
Boston Post
 Revuers, The, 9
Bouchet, Barbara
 What a Way to Go! (film), 191
"Bouncin' the Blues," D04 229
Bovinet, Gordon
 Doll's Life, A, 86
Bower, Brock
 Straws in the Wind, 138
"Boys and Girls Like You and Me,"
 D36 243
Boys from Syracuse, The, 4
Brackney, Bonnie
 Will Rogers Follies, The, 114

Brackney, Tom
  Will Rogers Follies, The, 114
Brandon, Henry
  Auntie Mame (film), 182
Breaux, Marc
  Do Re Mi, 105
  Subways Are for Sleeping, 69
Bregman, Martin
  Simon, 206
Brewster, Carol
  Barkleys of Broadway, The (film), 154
Brickman, Marshall
  Simon, 206
  Straws in the Wind, 138, 139
Briggs, John
  Leonard Bernstein, 2
Brinkley, David, T20 218
Broadbent, Lynne
  Fade Out--Fade In, 76
Broadhurst Theatre, 6, 14, 184
  Auntie Mame (play), 184
  Comden and Green, 22, 182, 185
  Morton DaCosta, 182, 184, 185, 186
  Jerome Robbins' Broadway, 146
  Jerome Lawrence, 28, 182
  Robert E. Lee, 22, 182
  Rosalind Russell, 22, 182, 184-186
  Warner Bros., 22,182, 185
"Broadway Blossom," D07 230, D62 251
Broadway Classics Vol. One, D47 246
"Broadway Dreams," D07 230
Broadway Magic: the 1950s, D48 246
Broadway Magic: the 1960s, D49 247
"Broadway Melody,"
  Singin' in the Rain (film), 17, 168
  Singin' in the Rain (musical), 169
"Broadway Melody, Broadway Rhythm," D32 241
  Singin' in the Rain (film), 170
"Broadway Rhythm," 128
  Singin' in the Rain (film), 168
  Singin' in the Rain (musical), 169
Broadway Theatre
  Candide (revival), 40
Brohn, William D., D19 235
Bronner, Robert
  It's Always Fair Weather (film), 177
Brooklyn Academy of Music
  Singin' in the Rain, 128
Brooklyn Ethical Culture School
  Betty Comden, 1
  Stebbins, Miss Della A., 1
Brooks, Donald
  Fade Out--Fade In, 75
  Party With Betty Comden and Adolph Green, A, 199
Brophy, Sallie
  Peter Pan, 134
Brower, Robert
  Band Wagon, The (film), 171
Brown, Barry M.
  Madwoman of Central Park West, The, 139
Brown, John Mason
  On the Town, 55
Brown, Lew, D15 233
  Good News, 14
Brown, Lew (musical comedy), 149
  Good News (film), 151
Brown, Nacio Herb, D32 241, D33 241
  Good News (film), 151
  Singin' in the Rain, 126
  Singin' in the Rain (film), 17, 165, 169, 171
Browne, Coral
  Auntie Mame (film), 182
Brownlee, Dell
  Fade Out--Fade In, 76
Bruce, Vince
  Will Rogers Follies, The, 114, 115
Bruno, Jean
  Lorelei, 136
Brussels World's Fair
  Wonderful Town, 98
Bryan, Fred
  Two on the Aisle, 91, D37 243
Buchanan, Jack, D03 228

Band Wagon, The (film), 172, 175, 176
Buckley, Priscilla L.
  Hallelujah, Baby!, 113
Buday, Betty
  Two on the Aisle, 92
Bufano, Remo
  On the Town, 52
Burke, Billie
  Barkleys of Broadway, The (film), 154
Burke, James
  Take Me Out to the Ballgame (film), 158
Burke, Michele
  Wonderful Town, 95
Burke, William (Willi)
  Doll's Life, A, 86
  On the Twentieth Century, 80
  Peter Pan, 134
Burnett, Carol, D14 233, D52 248, T26 219, T27 219
  Comden and Green, Kennedy Center Honors, xi, 41
  Fade Out--Fade In, xi, 30, 75, 77, 78
  Follies (concert version), 39, 208
  Garry Moore Show, 30
  Once Upon a Mattress (Princess Winifred), 30
Burns, Bill
  Jerome Robbins' Broadway, 146
Burns, David
  Billion Dollar Baby, 57
  Do Re Mi, 105
  It's Always Fair Weather (film), 177
Burns, Ralph, D14 233
  Fade Out--Fade In, 75
Burrows, Abe, 28, D31 240
  First Impressions, 26
  Say, Darling, 22, 100, 103, 104
  Subways Are for Sleeping, 72
  Two on the Aisle, 91
"But Alive," D01 227, D47 246
Butcher, Cheri
  Singin' in the Rain, 127
Butler, Tracy
  What a Way to Go! (film), 191
"Button Up Your Overcoat,"
  Good News (musical revival), 152
By Bernstein, 34, 48, R02 144
  Adolph Green, 34
  Betty Comden, 34
  Chelsea Theatre Center, 34
  Jerry Leiber, 34
  John Letouche, 34
  Stephen Sondheim, 34
"By Myself," D03 228
  Band Wagon, The (film), 172-174
  Between the Devil, 19, 174
By Myself (book)
  Lauren Bacall, 34
"Bye Bye Baby," D20 236
Bye Bye Birdie, 108, 125
Byers, Bill (Billy), D13 232, D39 244
  Doll's Life, A, 85
  Will Rogers Follies, The, 114
Bygraves, Max, D11 232
  Do Re Mi (London), 108
Byron, Brook
  Auntie Mame (film), 182

Caballero, Christophe
  Jerome Robbins' Broadway, 146
Cactus Flower
  Lauren Bacall, 33
Caesar, Irving
  George White Scandals of 1931, The, 9
  I Want To Be Happy, 9
  My Dear Public, 9
  "My Mammy," 9
  No, No, Nanette, 9
  Pins and Needles of 1922, 9
  "Swanee," 9
  "Tea for Two," 9
Caesar, Sid
  Your Show of Shows, 35
Cafe Society Downtown
  Revuers, The, 10
Cafe Society Uptown
  Revuers, The, 10
Cagney, James, T35 220
Cahn, Sammy, 15, 63, D64 251
  Glad to See You, 93
  High Button Shoes, 93
  Jerome Robbins' Broadway, 146
Calabrese, Maria
  Will Rogers Follies, The, 114, 115

288 Comden and Green

Calhoun, Jeff
  Will Rogers Follies, The, 114
Call Me Madam, D19 235
  Jerome Robbins' Broadway, 40, 147
"Call Me Savage," D14 233
  Fade Out--Fade In, 79
Callaway, Liz D52 248
Camarata, D21 236
Camp Onata
  Adolph Green, *Pirates of Penzance, The,* 2
  Leonard Bernstein, 2
Camp, Richard
  Diamonds, 140
"Can You Hear Me Now?" D13 232
Canby, Vincent
  Funny (film), 208
  Simon, 206
Candide, 40, 49, 220, D50 247
  Leonard Bernstein's Theatre Songs, 144
Cantor, Arthur
  Loeb Theatre Center, 199, 201, 202
Cantor, Charles, RA03 211, RA04 211, RA05 212
  Loeb Theatre Center, Harvard University, 201
  Party With Betty Comden and Adolph Green, A, 199, 202
"Capital Gains," D28 239
  Party With Betty Comden and Adolph Green, A, 200
Capitol Records
  Bells Are Ringing (film), 189
  Party With Betty Comden and Adolph Green, A, 43, 202
Cappy, Ted
  Two on the Aisle, 91
"Captain Hook's Waltz," D28 239, D29 240, D62 251, D64 251
  Party With Betty Comden and Adolph Green, A, 201
  Peter Pan, 21, 135, 201
Carey, Gary
  Judy Holliday, An Intimate Life Story (biography), xiii, 4, 6, 10
Carfagno, Edward
  Barkleys of Broadway, The (film), 153
Good News (film), 149
Cariou, Len, D01 227
  Applause, 121
  Tony Award (nomination), *Applause,* 273
Carlisle, Kevin
  Hallelujah, Baby!, 109
  Tony Award (nomination), *Hallelujah, Baby!,* 273
Carlisle, Kitty, 28
Carnegie Hall, 42
Carnegie Hall Playhouse
  On the Town, 54
Carnelia, Craig
  Diamonds, 140, 141
"Carnival Song, The," D31 241
  Say, Darling, 102, 104
Carol Burnett Story, The
  George Carpozi, Jr., 30
Carousel, 98
Carpenter, Debi
  Applause, 122
Carpozi, Jr., George
  Carol Burnett Story, The, 30
Carradine, Keith, D39 244
  Kennedy Center Honors, Comden and Green, xi
  Tony Award (nomination), *Will Rogers Follies, The,* 117, 274
  Will Rogers Follies, The, xi, 41, 114, 117, 118
"Carried Away," D22 237, D28 239, D45 246, D51 247, D62 251
  On the Town, 52, 56
  Party With Betty Comden and Adolph Green, A, 200
Carson, Danielle, D33 241
Carter, Gregory Scott
  Will Rogers Follies, The, 115
Cartwright, Mindy
  Jerome Robbins' Broadway, 146
Case, Allen, D16 234
  Hallelujah, Baby!, 110, 113
Casey, Sue
  Band Wagon, The (film), 172
Cashman, John
  Applause, 122
Casper, Joseph Andrew
  Stanley Donen (book), 166

Cass, Peggy
   Auntie Mame (film), 182
   Tony Award, *Auntie Mame* (play), 184
Cassard, Frances
   On the Town, 52
Cassidy, Jack, D14 233
   Fade Out--Fade In, 75, 77
Cassmore, Judy
   Fade Out--Fade In, 75
Castelli, Victor
   Jerome Robbins' Broadway, 146
Castle, Roy, D33 241
"Catch Our Act at the Met," D27 239, D28 239, D37 243, D62 251
   Party With Betty Comden and Adolph Green, A, 200
   Two on the Aisle, 92, 200
Cathcart, Daniel B.
   Take Me Out to the Ballgame (film), 157
Cats
   Tony Award, 38, 88
Cavett, Dick
   Funny (film), 40, 208
CBS Special Products
   Doll's Life, A, 88
CBS Television, T10 216, T11 216, T14 217, T18 217, T32 220, T35 220, T36 221, T40 221, T41 222, T45 223, T47 224, T49 224
   Applause, 124
   Comden and Green, Kennedy Center Honors, 41
   Do Re Mi, 108
   Ed Sullivan Show, 28
   Fabulous Fifties, The, 28
   Garry Moore Show, 30
Cella, Susan
   On the Twentieth Century, 80
Chamberlain, Paul B.
   Good News (film) 149
Channing, Carol, D20 236
   Gentlemen Prefer Blondes, 93
   Hello, Dolly, 137
   Lorelei, 34, 136, 137
   Tony Award, *Lorelei*, 138
   Wonderful Town, 98
Chapell and Co., Inc.

Bells Are Ringing, 67
Chaplin, Charlie, 26, 33, 47
Chaplin, Oona 26, 33
Chaplin, Saul, 63, D08 231, D27 239, D28 239
   Bonanza Bound!, 15, 61
   "Inspiration," 200
   On the Town (film), 162
   Party With Betty Comden and Adolph Green, A, 199
Chaplin, Sydney, 26, 28, 47, D05 229, D34 242, D41 245, D51 247, D54 248, D56 249, T45 223
   Bells Are Ringing, 24, 65
   Subways Are for Sleeping, 69
   Tony Award, *Bells Are Ringing*, 67, 271
Chapman, John
   Applause, 125
   Billion Dollar Baby, 60
   Do Re Mi, 108
   Fade Out--Fade In, 77
   Gentlemen Prefer Blondes, 137
   Hallelujah, Baby!, 112
   Party With Betty Comden and Adolph Green, A, 202
   Subways Are for Sleeping, 74
   Two on the Aisle, 93
   Wonderful Town, 98
Chappell Music Company
   Billion Dollar Baby, 59
Charisse, Cyd, 38, T36 221
   Band Wagon, The (film), 171, 175
   It's Always Fair Weather (film), 177, 180, 181
   Singin' in the Rain (film), 166, 168
Charlap, Mark ("Moose"), D17 235, D29 240
   Jerome Robbins' Broadway, 146
   Peter Pan, 21, 133, 134
Charles, Leon
   What a Way To Go (film), 190
"Charleston" D19 235
Charleston (dance)
   Jerome Robbins' Broadway, 147
Charnin, Martin
   Madwoman of Central Park West, The, 139

Chatham, Bill
  Singin' in the Rain (film), 166
Checker, Chubby, T47 224
Chee-Chee, 47, D60 250
Chelsea Theatre (Brooklyn)
  Candide (revival), 40
Chelsea Theatre Center
  By Bernstein, 34, 144, 145
Cherry Lane Theatre
  Gus Schirmer, Jr., 23
  Jack Parr Show, 216
  Monday Nights at Nine, 23
  Obie Award, *Party With Betty Comden and Adolph Green, A*, 23
  Party With Betty Comden and Adolph Green, A, 201
"Chief of Love," D31 240
Say, Darling, 101, 102
Child, Marilyn
  Do Re Mi, 105
Chisholm, Robert
  Billion Dollar Baby, 57
  On the Town, 52
Cho, Irene
  Jerome Robbins' Broadway, 146
Chodorov, Jerome, D40 244
  Donaldson Award, *Wonderful Town*, 98
  My Sister Eileen, 19, 95, 97
  Tony Award, *Wonderful Town*, 271
  Wonderful Town, 95, 97
Christian Century
  Hallelujah, Baby!, 113
Christian Science Monitor, The
  By Bernstein, 145
  Diamonds, 141
  On the Town, 55
  On the Twentieth Century, 83
  Will Rogers Follies, The, 118
Christmas Program, RA23 213
"Christopher Street," D40 245, D41 245
  Leonard Bernstein's Theatre Songs, 144
  Wonderful Town, 100
Churcher, Susan
  New York Magazine, 128, 129
Cinema 1 (New York)
  Slaves of New York (film), 208

Circle in the Square Downtown Theatre
  Diamonds, 38, 141
City Center
  Say, Darling, 102
  Wonderful Town, 98
City of Angels, 117
Clark, Dort
  Bells Are Ringing, 65
  Bells Are Ringing (film), 187, 188
  Wonderful Town, 96
Clark, Fred
  Auntie Mame (film), 182
  Bells Are Ringing (film), 187
Clark, Lyle
  On the Town, 51
Clark, Peggy
  Bells Are Ringing, 64
  Bonanza Bound!, 61
  Peter Pan, 133
  Say, Darling, 100
  Wonderful Town, 95
Clarke, Gerald
  Party With Betty Comden and Adolph Green, A, 203
Clarke, Gordon B.
  Say, Darling, 100
Clarke, Hope
  Hallelujah, Baby!, 110
Classic Movies
  Singin' in the Rain (film), 18, 169
Clay Club
  Betty Comden, 2
  Greenwich Village, 2
Clement, Maris
  On the Twentieth Century, 79, 80
Cleopatra
  Elizabeth Taylor, 194
Clifton, John
  Madwoman of Central Park West, The, 139
Clooney, Rosemary D54 248
"Close Harmony," D14 233
Cloutier, Norman RA01 211
"Clown, The," D37 243
  Two on the Aisle, 92
Club 13 (Paris)
  I Want to Go Home (film), 209
Clurman, Harold
  Bells Are Ringing, 68
  Do Re Mi, 109

Index   291

Fade Out--Fade In, 78
Group Theatre (New York), 5
On the Twentieth Century, 83
Wonderful Town, 99
Clymas, Sari
  Subways Are for Sleeping, 70
Coca, Imogene, 48, D26 238,
    D51 247
  Honored, Fifty Years in Show
    Business, 35
  On the Twentieth Century, 35,
    80, 82, 83, 85, 205
  Tony Award (nomination), *On the
    Twentieth Century,* 273
Coe, Fred, T43 223
Coe, George
  On the Twentieth Century, 79
Coe, Peter
  On the Twentieth Century
    (London), 83
Cohen (Sadvoransky), Rebecca
  Betty Comden's mother, 1
Cohen, Alexander H., T26 219,
    T27 219, T30 220
Cohen, Betty
  Birth, 45
Cohen, Jamie
  Jerome Robbins' Broadway, 146
Cohen, Leo
  Betty Comden's father, 1
Cohen, Margery
  By Bernstein, 145
Cohenour, Patti
  Doll's Life, A, 86
Cohn, Sammy D19 235
Cole, Carol
  Wonderful Town, 96
Cole, Jack
  Bonanza Bound!, 61
Coleman, Cy, D26 238, D28 239,
    D39 244, T32 220, T40 221
  Diamonds, 140
  Garbo Talks (film), 207
  On the Twentieth Century, 35,
    79, 83, 84
  *Party With Betty Comden and
    Adolph Green, A,* 199
  Straws in the Wind, 138, 139,
    201
  Tony Award, *On the Twentieth
    Century,* 35, 272
  Tony Award, *Will Rogers Follies,
    The,* 41, 116, 272
  Tony Award (nomination), *On the
    Twentieth Century,* 273
  Will Rogers Follies, The, 114,
    116-119
Coleman, Robert
  Betty Comden, 19
  Do Re Mi, 108
  Say, Darling, 103
  Subways Are for Sleeping, 73
  Two on the Aisle, 93
  Wonderful Town, 99
Colliers
  Kyle Crichton, Revuers, The, 5
Colonial Theatre (Boston)
  On the Twentieth Century, 82
Colt, Alvin
  Jerome Robbins' Broadway, 146
  Lorelei, 136
  On the Town, 51
  Say, Darling, 100
Colton, Richard
  Singin' in the Rain, 127
Columbia Pictures
  My Sister Eileen, 97, 98
  Twentieth Century (film), 82
Columbia Records
  Fancy Free, 53
  Hallelujah, Baby!, 112
  Lady in the Dark,, 29
  On the Town, 55
  On the Twentieth Century, 83
  Subways Are for Sleeping, 73
  Will Rogers Follies, The, 117
  Wonderful Town, 98
Colyer, Austin
  Singin' in the Rain, 127
Comden, Betty xi, xii, xiii, 10, 42,
    128, 130, 206, D01-D08 227-
    231, D10 231, D12-D22 232-
    237, D24 237, D26-D34 238-
    242, D37-D40 243-245, D45
    246, D51 247, D52 248, D56
    249, D57 249, D60 250, D61
    250, D63 251, D64 251, RA01
    211, RA21-RA23 213-214, T01
    215, T03-T09 215-216, T11-
    T19 216-218, T27 219, T29
    219, T47 224

292 Comden and Green

Academy Award (nomination), *It's Always Fair Weather* (film), 21, 180
All About Eve, 34
Applause (book), 33, 121, 125, 126
Auntie Mame (film), 182, 185
Bachelor of Science Degree, New York University, 45
Band Wagon, The (film), 171, 174-176
Barkleys of Broadway, The (film), 16, 153, 155, 156, 174
Bells Are Ringing (book/lyrics), 22, 64, 67, 68
Bells Are Ringing (film), 23, 24, 186, 188, 189
Billion Dollar Baby (book/lyrics), 14, 56, 59-61
Birth (Betty Cohen), 1, 45
Blue Angel, 46
Bonanza Bound! (book/lyrics), 15, 61, 64
Broken Kneecap, 41
By Bernstein, 34, 144, 145
Corneal Transplant, 37
Cradle Will Rock, The, 30
Diamonds, (lyrics), 38, 141
Do Re Mi (lyrics), 28, 104, 109
Doll's Life, A (book/lyrics), 37-39, 48, 88-90, S08 85
Donaldson Award, *Wonderful Town*, 20, 98
Dramatists Guild Council Member, 33
Education, 1
Fabulous Fifties, The, 28, 47
Fade Out--Fade In (book/lyrics), 30, 74, 77-79
First Performance, 1
Follies (concert version) (Emily Whitman), 39, 49, 208
Garbo Talks (film) (Greta Garbo), 38, 49, 207
George Abbott ... A Celebration, 34
Good News (screenplay/lyrics), 14, 46, 149, 151-153
Greenwich Village (film), 11
Hallelujah, Baby! (lyrics), 31, 109, 112, 113

Having Wonderful Time, 2, 45
I Love Louisa, 19
"I Said Good Morning," 33, T48 224
I'm Getting Married (television), 31
Importance of Being Easnest (Miss Prism), 2
Isn't It Romantic? (Tasha Blumberg), 38, 49, 206
It's Always Fair Weather (film), 134, 176, 179-181
Jerome Robbins' Broadway, 40, 146-148
Johnny Mercer Award, 41, 49
Kennedy Center Award for Lifetime Achievement in the Performing Arts, 41, 49
Leonard Bernstein's Theatre Songs, 31, 143, 144
Lorelei (lyrics), 34, 136, 137
Lyrics and Lyricists, 34, 48, 205
Madwoman of Central Park West, The, (lyrics), 35, 139, 140
New York University, 2
New York University (master classes), 48
On the Town (book/lyrics), 11, 51, 54-56, 205
On the Town (Claire), 205
On the Town (film), 16, 17, 161-164
On the Twentieth Century (book/lyrics), 35, 79, 82-85
On the Twentieth Century (Letitia Primrose), 82
Party With Betty Comden and Adolph Green, A, 35, 47, 48, 199-203
Peter Pan (lyrics), 21, 133, 134
Revuers, The, 45, 205
Say, Darling (lyrics), 22, 100, 103, 104
Screenwriters Guild Award, *Bells Are Ringing* (film), 24, 189
Screenwriters Guild Award, *It's Always Fair Weather* (film), 180
Screenwriters Guild Award, *On the Town*, 17

Screenwriters Guild Award,
  Singin' in the Rain (film), 18,
  169
Screenwriters Guild Award
  (nomination), *It's Always Fair
  Weather*, 21
Sculpture, 2
Siegfried Schutzman (marriage),
  10
Singin' in the Rain (book), 39,
  126, 128, 129
Singin' in the Rain (film), 17, 18,
  165, 168-171
Six and Company, 4
Skin of Our Teeth, The, 30, 31
Slaves of New York (Mrs.
  Wheeler), 40, 49, 208
"So Eat Your Heart Out, Elizabeth
  Taylor," 1
Songwriters Hall of Fame
  (Johnny Mercer Award), 41
Songwriters Hall of Fame, 37, 48
Steven Kyle (marriage), 45
Straws in the Wind (lyrics), 34,
  138, 139, 201
Studio Players, East Hampton,
  NY, 2, 45
Subways Are For Sleeping
  (book/lyrics), 28, 69, 72-74
Take Me Out to the Ball Game
  (film/lyrics), 16, 157, 160, 161
Theatre Hall of Fame, 37
Tisch School of the Arts (master
  classes), 37
Tony Award, *Applause*, 34, 124,
  272
Tony Award, *Hallelujah, Baby!*,
  31, 271
Tony Award, *On the Twentieth
  Century*, 35, 272
Tony Award, *Will Rogers Follies,
  The*, 41, 272
Tony Award, *Wonderful Town*,
  271
Tony Award (nomination), *Bells
  Are Ringing*, 272
Tony Award (nomination), *Do Re
  Mi*, 273
Tony Award (nomination), *Dolls
  Life, A*, 274
Tony Award (nomination), *On the
  Twentieth Century*, 273
Two on the Aisle (sketch/lyrics),
  18, 91, 93, 94
Warner Bros., 22
What a Way to Go! (film), 30,
  190, 195, 196
Will Rogers Follies, The, 41, 114,
  116-119
Wonderful Town, 19, 95, 97-100
*Comden and Green Songbook,
  The* 44, D51 247
"Come Up to My Place," D22 237,
  D24 238
On the Town (film), 56, 162
Comedy Tonight, D19 235
"Comes Once in a Lifetime!," D34
  242, D35 244, D54 249, D64
  251
Subways Are for Sleeping, 72,
  74
Commonweal
  Say, Darling, 104
  Two on the Aisle, 94
Company
  Stephen Sondheim, 126
Condos, Steve
  Say, Darling, 101
"Conga!," D40 245, D41 245,
  D45 246
  Wonderful Town, 99
Conklin, John
  Lorelei, 136
Connell, Gordon
  Subways Are for Sleeping, 70
Connelly, Chris
  What a Way to Go! (film), 191
Conried, Hans
  Barkleys of Broadway, The (film),
    154
  On the Town (film), 162
Consolidated Edison (radio)
  Revuers, The, 8
"Conversation Piece," D40 245,
  D41 245
  *Leonard Bernstein's Theatre
    Songs*, 144
  Wonderful Town, 96, 100
Conway, Tom
  What a Way to Go! (film), 191,
    194
Cook, Barbara, D52 248

294 Comden and Green

Follies (concert version), 39, 208
"Cool" D19 235
Cooper, Darrell
  Hallelujah, Baby!, 110
Cooper, Horace
  Billion Dollar Baby, 58
Cooper, Inez
  Barkleys of Broadway, The (film), 154
Cooper, Marilyn
  Hallelujah, Baby!, 110
Cooper, Peggy
  On the Twentieth Century, 80
Copland, Aaron, T33 220
Corcoran, Billy
  What a Way to Go! (film), 191
Correia, Don
  Singin' in the Rain, 127, 129
Corsaut, John
  Doll's Life, A, 86
Cort Theatre
  Moonbirds, 26
Corti, Jim
  By Bernstein, 145
Cossette, Pierre
  Tony Award, Will Rogers Follies, The, 272
  Will Rogers Follies, The, 114
Costello, Lou
  Diamonds, 140
Coulouris, George
  Bonanza Bound!, 61
Council for the Dramatists Guild, 42
"Count on Me," D24 238
Courage, Alexander, D03 228, D06 230
  Band Wagon, The (film), 171
  Bells Are Ringing (film), 186
Cowan, Jerome
  Say, Darling, 101
Coward, Noel, 6, 16
Cox, Ray
  Lorelei, 136, 137
Coyne, Jeanne
  On the Town, 17
  Singin' in the Rain (film), 165, 166
Cradle Will Rock, The
  Marc Blitzstein, 29
Craig, Joel

Subways Are for Sleeping, 70
Crane, Harry, D36 243
Crawford Music Corporation
  Bonanza Bound!, 63
Crawford, Jerry L.
  Diamonds, 140
Crawford, Joan
  Dancing Lady (film), 173
  Ice Follies of 1939, 6
Crichton, Don
  Fade Out--Fade In, 76
Crichton, Klye
  Revuers, The, 5
Croce, Arlene
  Singin' in the Rain, 130
Crothers, Sam
  Tony Award, Will Rogers Follies, The, 272
  Will Rogers Follies, The, 114
Crowther, Bosley
  Auntie Mame (film), 185
  Band Wagon, The (film), 175
  Barkleys of Broadway, The (film), 156
  Bells Are Ringing (film), 189
  Good News (film), 152
  It's Always Fair Weather (film), 180
  On the Town (film), 164
  Singin' in the Rain (film), 169
  Take Me Out to the Ball Game (film), 160
  What a Way to Go! (film), 194
"Cry Like the Wind," D10 232
Do Re Mi, 107-109
Cryer, David
  Fade Out--Fade In, 75, 76
Cucci, Frank
  Lily in Love (Jatszani Kell), 207
Cuddy, Margaret
  Wonderful Town, 96
Cue
  Band Wagon, The (film), 175
Cullum, John, D26 238, D51 247
  On the Twentieth Century, 80, 84
  Tony Award, On the Twentieth Century, 35, 272
Cummings, Bob
  What a Way to Go! (film), 191, 194

Cunningham, Zamah
  Bonanza Bound!, 61
Curtis Institute (Philadelphia)
  Bernstein, Leonard 6, 9

D'Amboise, Charlotte
  Jerome Robbins' Broadway, 146
D'Arcy, Mary
  Singin' in the Rain, 127
D'Arcy, Richard
  On the Town, 51
D'Beck, Patti
  Applause, 122
D'Honau, Marily
  Applause, 122
D'Orsay, Fifi
  What a Way to Go! (film), 191
DaCosta, Morton, T19 218
  Auntie Mame (film/play), 22, 182, 184-186
Daenen, Jon
  Applause, 122
Dahl, Arlene
  Applause, 124
Dailey, Dan, D17 234
  It's Always Fair Weather (film), 20, 177, 180
Daily Mirror
  Say, Darling, 103
  Two on the Aisle, 93
  Wonderful Town, 99
Daily News
  Applause, 125
  Billion Dollar Baby, 60
  By Bernstein, 145
  Diamonds, 141
  Do Re Mi, 108
  Doll's Life, A, 88
  Fade Out--Fade In, 77
  Hallelujah, Baby!, 112
  Jerome Robbins' Broadway, 148
  Lorelei, 137
  On the Twentieth Century, 83
  Party With Betty Comden and Adolph Green, A, 202
  Singin' in the Rain, 130
  Subways Are for Sleeping, 74
  Two on the Aisle, 93
  Will Rogers Follies, The, 117, 118
  Wonderful Town, 98

Daily Variety
  Doll's Life, A, 88
Dale, Grover
  Jerome Robbins' Broadway, 146
Daley, Bob
  Lorelei, 136, 137
Daly, Tyne
  On the Town (concert version), 42
"Dance at the Gym, The," D19 235
"Dance, Dance Only With Me," D31 241, D46 246
  Say, Darling, 104
"Dance of the Great Lover," D56 249
  Say, Darling, 104
"Dancing in the Dark," D03 228
  Band Wagon, The (film), 173
Dancing Lady
  Joan Crawford and Clark Gable, 173
Dangcil, Linda
  Peter Pan, 134
"Dangerous Age, The," D14 233
Daniels, Danny
  Billion Dollar Baby, 56
Daniels, LeRoy
  Band Wagon, The (film), 172
Dante, Nikolas
  Applause, 122
Danyl, Gloria
  Two on the Aisle, 92
David Brinkley's Journal, T20 218
David, William
  Billion Dollar Baby, 56
Davis, Bette
  All About Eve, 33, 124
Davis, Buster, D16 234
  Bells Are Ringing, 64
  Do Re Mi, 105
  Fade Out--Fade In, 75
  Hallelujah, Baby!, 110
  Lorelei, 136
Davis, George W.
  Bells Are Ringing (film), 187
Davis, Gwen, D38 244
  What a Way to Go! (story/film), 30, 190
Davis, Keith
  On the Twentieth Century, 80

296 Comden and Green

Dawn, Jack
  Barkleys of Broadway, The (film), 153
  On the Town (film), 162
  Take Me Out to the Ball Game (film), 158
"Day in New York, A"
  On the Town (film), 164
"Day They Made Music on Mt. Scopus, The"
  Adolph Green, New York Times, 31
Dayo, Robert
  Singin' in the Rain (film), 166
De Benedictis, Richard
  Fade Out--Fade In, 75
De Chazza, Pepe
  Subways Are for Sleeping, 70
De Leo, Don
  Billion Dollar Baby, 57
de Mille, Agnes, T35 220
  Oklahoma!, 56
De Sylva, B. G. (musical comedy)
  Good News (musical comedy/film), 149, 151
Dean, Jacque
  Singin' in the Rain, 127
Deane, Douglas
  Billion Dollar Baby, 56, 57
DeAnza Theatre
  Singin' in the Rain (film), 169
"Dear Boy," D50 247
"Dear, Oh Dear," D60 250
Decca Records
  On the Town, 55
  Two on the Aisle, 93
  Wonderful Town, 98
DeFelice, Harold
  Diamonds, 141
DeGanon, Camille
  Jerome Robbins' Broadway, 146
Delaney, Geraldine
  Wonderful Town, 96
Delfont, Bernard, D23 237
Denise, Patricia
  Singin' in the Rain (film), 166
Dennis, Patrick, D02 228
  Auntie Mame (novel), 22, 182
Depardieu, Gerard
  I Want to Go Home (film), 209
"Departure, The," D13 232

Derbas, Frank
  Bells Are Ringing, 65
  Do Re Mi, 105, 106
Derleth, Ganine
  Will Rogers Follies, The, 115
DeSilva, Buddy, T19 218
Desmond, John (Johnny), D31 240
  Say, Darling, 101
DeSylva, B. G., D15 233
  Good News, 14
Deutsch, Adolph, D03 228, D36 243
  Band Wagon, The (film), 171
  Take Me Out to the Ball Game (film), 157
Deutsch, Didier C., 44
Deutsche Grammophon
  Candide (revival), 40
Devlin, Sandra
  Do Re Mi, 105, 106
DeWitt Clinton High School
  Adolph Green, 1
Di Meo, Donna
  Jerome Robbins' Broadway, 146
"Dialog Studio, A"
  Lily in Love (Jatszani Kell), 207
Diamonds, 49, D20 236, S21 140
  Circle in the Square Downtown Theatre, 38
  Comden and Green (lyrics), 38
"Diamonds, Are a Girl's Best Friend," D20 236
  Lorelei, 137
Dicker, Dorothy
  Fade Out--Fade In, 75
Dietz, Howard, D03 228
  Band Wagon, The (film), 171
  Loew's, Inc. (vice president), 19, 174
Directors Guild Theatre
  Simon, 206
"Distant Melody," D29 240, D62 251
  Peter Pan, 135
Dittman, Dean
  On the Twentieth Century, 80
Dixon, Ed
  By Bernstein, 145
"Do It Yourself," D06 230

Bells Are Ringing (film), 188
Do Re Mi, 28, 47, 72, 217, 249,
    D10 231, D11 232, D43 246,
    D54 249, D63 251, D64 251,
    S12 104-109, T19 218, T47
    224
  Boston, Philadelphia, 28, 108
  Comden and Green (lyrics), 28,
    104, 108, 109
  Ed Sullivan Show, 28, 108
  Garson Kanin (novella), 28, 104,
    105, 109
  Grammy Award (nomination),
    275
  Jule Styne, 28, 105, 108, 109
  London, 108
  "Make Someone Happy," 28,
    107, 109, 201
  Nancy Walker, 28, 105, 108
  Phil Silvers, 28, 105, 108
  St. James Theatre, 28, 104
  Tony Award (nomination), 273
  "What's New at the Zoo?," 28,
    107, 109
*Do Re Mi, Behind the Scenes with
  George Marek*, D12 232
Dodge, Jacqueline
  Billion Dollar Baby, 57
Dodge, Marcella
  Say, Darling, 101
"Dog Show"
  Two on the Aisle, 92
Doggett, Norma
  Bells Are Ringing, 65
Dolan, Judith
  Diamonds, 141
Doll's House, A
  Henrik Ibsen, 37, 86, 90
Doll's Life, A, 48, D13 232, S08
    85-90
  Ahmanson Theatre (Los
    Angeles), 37, 88
  Comden and Green, 37, 85, 88-
    90
  Harold Prince, 37, 85, 89, 90
  Larry Grossman, 85
  "Learn to Be Lonely," 39
  Mark Hellinger Theatre, 37, 88
  Tony Award (nomination), 38, 88
"Don't Think I'll Fall in Love Today,"
  D60 250

Donaldson Award
  Adolph Green, *Wonderful Town*
    (lyrics), 20, 98
  Betty Comden, *Wonderful Town*
    (lyrics), 20, 98
  Edith Adams, *Wonderful Town*,
    98
  George Abbott, *Billion Dollar
    Baby*, 60
  George Abbott, *Wonderful Town*,
    98
  Jerome Chodorov, *Wonderful
    Town*, 98
  Jerome Robbins, *Billion Dollar
    Baby*, 60
  Joan McCracken, *Billion Dollar
    Baby*, 60
  Joseph Fields, *Wonderful Town*,
    98
  Leonard Bernstein, *Wonderful
    Town*, 98
  Raoul Pène DuBois, *Wonderful
    Town*, 98
  Rosalind Russell, *Wonderful
    Town*, 98
  Wonderful Town, 274
Donaldson, Norma
  Hallelujah, Baby!, 111
Donehue, Vincent J., T46 224
Donen, Stanley, 179, D36 243
  It's Always Fair Weather (film),
    176, 177, 179-182
  Joseph Andrew Casper (book),
    165
  On the Town (film), 17, 162, 164
  Singin' in the Rain, 126, 130
  Singin' in the Rain (film), 18,
    165, 169
  Take Me Out to the Ball Game
    (film), 16, 160, 163
Donovan, King
  Singin' in the Rain (film), 166
"Doom,"
  Say, Darling, 104
Dorian, Ray
  Wonderful Town, 96
Dorne, Phyllis
  Bells Are Ringing, 65
Dorrin, John
  Fade Out--Fade In, 75, 76

Doss, Dean
  Fade Out--Fade In, 75, 76
Downing, Rebecca
  Will Rogers Follies, The, 115
Dr. Doolittle
  Rex Harrison, 194
  Twentieth Century-Fox, 194
Drake, Alan, T10 216
Drama Critics Circle Award
  Lauren Bacall, *Applause,* 124
  Leonard Bernstein, *Wonderful Town*, 98
Drama Desk Award
  Will Rogers Follies, The, 41, 117
  Will Rogers Follies, The, Comden and Green, 274
Drama Desk Award for Special Effects
  Singin' in the Rain, 129
Dramatists Guild Quarterly, The
  "Conversations With Comden and Green and Guare," 135
  On the Town, 55
"Dream With Me," D19 235
  By Bernstein, 145
"Dreams Come True"
  Billion Dollar Baby, 58
"Drink to Me Only With Thine Eyes"
  Party With Betty Comden and Adolph Green, A, 201
"Drop That Name," D05 229, D06 230, D51 247
DuBois, Raoul Pène
  Bells Are Ringing, 64
  Donaldson Award, *Wonderful Town*, 98
  Jerome Robbins' Broadway, 146
  Tony Award, *Wonderful Town*, 271
  Wonderful Town, 95
Duchin, Eddie, 20
Duell, Randall
  Singin' in the Rain (film), 166
Duffy's Tavern
  Revuers, The, 10
Dugan, Tom
  Good News (film), 150
  Take Me Out to the Ball Game (film), 158
Duggan, Andrew, T10 216
DuMont Television
  Revuers, The (television), 215
Dumont, Margaret
  What a Way to Go! (film), 191, 194
Duncan, Diane
  Singin' in the Rain, 127
Duncan, Sandy
  Peter Pan, 135
Dunn, Colleen
  Will Rogers Follies, The, 114, 115
Dunn, Sally Mae
  Will Rogers Follies, The, 115
Dunne, John Gregory
  Studio, The, 194
Duran, Darryl
  Peter Pan, 134
Dussault, Nancy, D10 231
  Do Re Mi, 105
  Tony Award (nomination), *Do Re Mi*, 273
Dutton, Yvonne
  Singin' in the Rain, 127
Duvivier, George, D60 250
Dwelley, Trish
  Fade Out--Fade In, 75, 76

"Easier Way, An," D15 233
Easter Parade (film)
  Fred Astaire, 15, 155, 174
  Harry Warren, 15
  Ira Gershwin, 15
  Judy Garland, 15, 155
  Metro-Goldwyn-Mayer, 174
Eastern Airlines, Inc., T26 219
Ebb, Fred
  Diamonds, (lyrics), 141
  Funny, 40
  Funny (film), 208
  Madwoman of Central Park West, The, 139
Eckart, Jean
  Fade Out--Fade In, 75
  Hallelujah, Baby!, 110
Eckart, William
  Fade Out--Fade In, 75
  Hallelujah, Baby!, 110
Eckhardt, William
  What a Way to Go! (film), 190
Ed Sullivan Show, The, T10 216, T47 224
  CBS Television, 28

Do Re Mi, 28, 108
Eden, Diana
  Fade Out--Fade In, 76
Edens, Roger, 16, D03 228, D15
  233, D17 234, D24 237, D27
  239, D28 239, D33 241, D36
  243
  Band Wagon, The (film), 19, 171,
    174
  Barkleys of Broadway, The (film),
    154, 156
  "French Lesson, The," *Good
    News* (film), 15, 200
  Good News (film), 14, 149
  It's Always Fair Weather (film),
    179
  On the Town (film), 17, 161-163
  *Party With Betty Comden and
    Adolph Green, A,* 199
  "Pass That Peace Pipe," 152
  Singin' in the Rain (film), 165
  Strictly U.S.A., 160
  Take Me Out to the Ball Game
    (film), 16, 154-165, 157-158,
    160, 161
Eder, Richard
  *Madwoman of Central Park West,
    The,* 140
  On the Twentieth Century, 83
Edwards, Ralph
  It's Always Fair Weather (film),
    181
Edwin, Robert
  Billion Dollar Baby, 58
Egelston, Penny
  Fade Out--Fade In, 75
Eichel, Paul
  Fade Out--Fade In, 75, 76
Eiseman, Alvord
  It's Always Fair Weather (film),
    177
Elder, Althea
  Billion Dollar Baby, 57
Elio, Donna Marie
  Jerome Robbins' Broadway, 146
Eliot, Jean
  Wonderful Town, 96
Elliott, Patricia
  By Bernstein, 145
Ellis, Peggy
  Billion Dollar Baby, 57

Ellis, Ray, D14 233
  Fade Out--Fade In, 75
Ellsworth, Hugh
  Bonanza Bound!, 62
Elmore, Steve
  Fade Out--Fade In, 75, 76
Emmett, Bob
  Two on the Aisle, 92
Emmons, Don
  Bells Are Ringing, 65
Emmy Award
  Mary Martin, *Peter Pan,* 135
Engel, Lehman, D10 231, D40
  244, D41 245, D55 249
  Bonanza Bound!, 61
  Do Re Mi, 105
  Tony Award, *Wonderful Town,*
    271
  Wonderful Town, 95
Ensemble Studio Theatre
  New Yorkers, The, 207
Enter Juliet, D07 230
Erasmus Hall High School
  Betty Comden, 1
Esposito, Mark
  Jerome Robbins' Broadway, 146
Etheridge, Dorothy
  Two on the Aisle, 92
Eustrel, Anthony
  What a Way to Go! (film), 191
Evans, David
  Doll's Life, A, 86
Evans, Gregg
  Two on the Aisle, 92
Evans, Robert
  Bonanza Bound!, 62
  Subways Are for Sleeping, 70
Evening Bulletin (Philadelphia)
  Bonanza Bound!, 64
"Everlasting," D37 243
Everybody's Cheering (foreign
    distribution title)
  Take Me Out to the Ball Game
    (film), 160
Ewen, David
  Leonard Bernstein (book), 5

Fabray, Nanette, D03 228
  Band Wagon, The (film), 172,
    176
Fabulous Fifties, The 47, T14 217

CBS Television, 28
Comden and Green, 28
Elaine May, 28
Eric Sevareid, 28
Henry Fonda, 28
Jackie Gleason, 28
Julie Andrews, 28
Leland Hayward, 28
Mike Nichols, 28
Rex Harrison, 28
Shelly Berman, 28
Suzy Parker, 28
Fade Out--Fade In 47, 203, D14
   233, D64 251, S06 74-79
   Betty Hutton, 30
   Carol Burnett, xi, 30, 75, 77-79
   Comden and Green
     (book/lyrics), 30, 74, 78, 79
   George Abbott, 74, 79
   Jack Cassidy, 75, 77
   Jule Styne, 74, 75, 77
   Mark Hellinger Theatre, 30, 74, 77
Fairbanks, Sr., Douglas, 128
"Faithless"
   Billion Dollar Baby, 59
Family Matters (book)
   Burton Bernstein, 2, 5
Fancy Free 11, 40, D61 250
   Ballet Theatre Company, 11, 53
   Jerome Robbins, xi, 11
   Leonard Bernstein, 11
   Metropolitan Opera House, 11
   Oliver Smith, 11
   Paul Feigay, 11
Fancy, Richard
   Singin' in the Rain, 127
Farrell, Aniko
   Lorelei, 137
"Fascinating Rhythm," D33 242
"Fasten Your Seat Belts," D01 227
   Applause, 123
Faugno, Rick
   Will Rogers Follies, The, 114
Fazan, Adrienne
   Bells Are Ringing (film), 187
   It's Always Fair Weather (film), 177
   Singin' in the Rain (film), 166
"Fear," D14 233

Fade Out--Fade In, 79
Federal Theatre Project, 29
Federation for Jewish Charities, 42
"Feeling I'm Falling," D60 250
"Feet Do Yo' Stuff," D16 234
Feiffer, Jules
   I Want to Go Home (film), 209
Feigay, Paul, 11
   Billion Dollar Baby, 14, 56, 59
   Bonanza Bound!, 15, 61
   Fancy Free, 11
   On the Town, 51, 54
Feldman, Jack
   Madwoman of Central Park West, The, 139
Feldshuh, Tovah
   Straws in the Wind, 138
Ferber, Mel, T45 223
Ferdin, Pamelyn
   What a Way to Go! (film), 191
Ferguson, Otis
   New Republic, The, The Revuers, 6
Ferren, Bran
   Funny (film), 40, 208
Ferrer, José
   Band Wagon, The (film) 174
Fiddleback/Bettdolph/Manor Lane/Valendo
   Doll's Life, A, 88
"Fiddler and the Fighter, The," D14 233
Fiddler on the Roof, D19 235
   Jerome Robbins' Broadway, 40, 147
Field, Joseph, D20 236
Field, Ron, T30 219, T49 224
   Applause, 121
   On the Town, 55
   On the Town (revival), 34
   Tony Award, Applause, 272
Fielding, Harold
   Singin' in the Rain, 39, 128
Fields, Dorothy, D33 241
Fields, Joseph, D40 244, T45 223
   Donaldson Award, Wonderful Town, 98
   Lorelei (book), 136, 137
   My Sister Eileen, 19, 95, 97

Tony Award, *Wonderful Town*, 271
Wonderful Town, 95, 100
"Fill 'er Up," D09 231
Bonanza Bound!, 64
Films A2/La Sept
I Want to Go Home (film), 209
"Fireworks," D10 232, D64 251
Do Re Mi, 107, 108
First Impressions
　Abe Burrows, 26
　Alvin Theatre (Philadelphia), 26
　Phyllis Newman, 26
First Lady
　Betty Comden, (Irene Hibbard), 2
Firth, Tazeena
　Doll's Life, A, 85, 90
Fisher, Chester
　Peter Pan, 134
Fisher, Jules
　Leonard Bernstein's Theatre Songs, 143
　Tony Award, *Will Rogers Follies, The*, 41, 117, 272
　Will Rogers Follies, The, 114, 119
Fisher, Nellie
　On the Town, 52
"Fit as a Fiddle," 127, D32 241, D33 241
Fitch, Bob
　Lorelei, 136, 137
Fithian, Jeff
　What a Way to Go! (film), 191
Fitzgerald, Peter
　Will Rogers Follies, The, 114
Fitzgibbon, Maggi, D11 232
Fitzhugh, Ellen
　Diamonds, 141
Fitzpatrick, John
　Party With Betty Comden and Adolph Green, A, 199
"Five Zeros," D26 238, D51 248
　On the Twentieth Century, 81, 85
Flatow, Sheryl
　"On the Town," *Stagebill*, 43
Flatt, Ernest O.
　Fade Out--Fade In, 75
　Lorelei, 136
　Singin' in the Rain (film), 166

Flemming, Carol
　Hallelujah, Baby!, 110, 111
Fletcher, Jack
　Lorelei, 136
Fletcher, Susann
　Jerome Robbins' Broadway, 146
"Flight of the Bumblebee, The"
　Party With Betty Comden and Adolph Green, A, 200
Flippen, Jay C.
　It's Always Fair Weather (film), 177
Flood, Joela
　Lorelei, 137
Flowers, Bess
　Barkleys of Broadway, The (film), 154
Fludd, Quitman, III
　On the Twentieth Century, 80
Flying Colors
　Schwartz and Dietz, 174
Foley, Ken
　Bonanza Bound!, 62
Follies (concert version), D52 248, P12 208, T39 221
　Avery Fisher Hall at Lincoln Center, 39
　Barbara Cook, 39
　Carol Burnett, 39
　Comden and Green, 39, 49
　Elaine Stritch, 39
　George Hearn, 39
　Lee Remick, 39
　Lilianne Montevecchi, 39
　Mandy Patinkin, 39
　New York Times, 208
　Phyllis Newman, 39
　Stephen Sondheim, 39
Follow the Girls, 54
Folsey, George
　Take Me Out to the Ball Game (film), 158
Fonda, Henry, T14 217
　Fabulous Fifties, The, 28
Fontanne, Lynn, T35 220, T46 224
Foote, Gene
　Applause, 122
Ford, Constance
　Say, Darling, 100

Fordin, Hugh
  On the Town (film), 163
  World of Entertainment, The
    (book), 20, 163
Forlow, Ted
  Subways Are for Sleeping, 70
Forrest, Steve
  Band Wagon, The (film), 172
Forrest Theater (Philadelphia)
  Wonderful Town, 98
Fortnight
  Band Wagon, The (film), 175
Forty-Sixth Street Theatre
  Good News (film), 151
Fosse, Bob
  Tony Award (nomination), *Bells Are Ringing,* 273
Foster, Bill, T49 224
Fowler, Marjorie
  What a Way to Go! (film), 190
Fowler, Scott
  Jerome Robbins' Broadway, 146
Fowley, Douglas
  Singin' in the Rain (film), 166
  Take Me Out to the Ball Game (film), 158
Foy, Jr., Eddie, D06 230
  Bells Are Ringing (film), 187
Fraboni, Angelo H.
  Jerome Robbins' Broadway, 146
Frances, Arlene, 28
Francis, Arthur (pseud.)
  Ira Gershwin, 29
Francks, Don
  Leonard Bernstein's Theatre Songs, 143, 144
Francois, Jacques
  Barkleys of Broadway, The (film), 154, 156
Frank, John, D30 240, RA01 211, T01 215
  Peasants' Quartette, 4
  Revuers, The, 4, 45, 205
Franklin, Bonnie, D01 227
  Applause, 122, 124
  Tony Award (nomination), *Applause,* 273
Franks, Laurie
  Applause, 122
Frawley, Craig
  Singin' in the Rain, 127

Frawley, Mark
  Singin' in the Rain, 127
Fred Astaire (book)
  Michael Freedland, 15
Freed Unit
  Barkleys of Broadway, The (film), 155
  Metro-Goldwyn-Mayer, 15, 22
  On the Town (film), 17
  Singin' in the Rain (film), 17
Freed, Arthur 17, 20, 24, 153, 160, 179, 249, D32 241, D33 241
  American in Paris, An (film), 18, 174
  Band Wagon, The (film), 171, 174
  Barkleys of Broadway, The (film), 154, 155
  Bells Are Ringing (film), 23, 187, 188, 190, 201
  Good News (film), 14, 149, 151
  Charles Walters, 149, 152
  Comden and Green, 14, 15, 149, 151, 152
  It's Always Fair Weather (film), 177, 180
  On the Town (film), 16, 162, 163
  Screen Producers Guild (president), 180
  Singin' in the Rain, 126
  Singin' in the Rain (film), 17, 18, 165, 166, 168, 171
  Take Me Out to the Ball Game (film), 16, 158, 160, 161
Freedland, Michael
  Fred Astaire (book), 15
Freeman, Kathleen
  Singin' in the Rain (film), 166
Freericks, Bernard
  What a Way to Go! (film), 190
"French Lesson, The," 15, 23, D15 233, D27 239, D28 239, D62 251
  Good News (film), 150, 152, 153
  Party With Betty Comden and Adolph Green, A, 200
  Roger Edens, 200
French, Elinor RA01 211, RA04 211, RA08 212
Frey, Nathaniel
  Wonderful Town, 95, 96

Friedberg, William, D37 243
   Two on the Aisle, 91, 92
Friedman, Charles
   Bonanza Bound!, 61
Friedman, Leonard
   Party With Betty Comden and Adolph Green, A, 199, 202
Fries, Jerry
   Two on the Aisle, 92
Frings, Ketti
   Subways Are for Sleeping, 72
Frings, Kurt
   Revuers, The, 10
Frisch, Richard
   Fade Out--Fade In, 75, 76
From Here to Eternity (film)
   Academy Award, Frank Sinatra, 20
   Frank Sinatra, 179
"From Sea to Shining Sea"
   Comden and Green (satire), 42
Frome, Milton
   What a Way to Go! (film), 191
Fryer, Robert
   Doll's Life, A, 85
   Tony Award, *Wonderful Town*, 271
   Tony Award (nomination), *Dolls Life, A*, 274
   Tree Grows in Brooklyn, A, 97
   Wonderful Town, 19, 95, T45 223
Full of Life (film)
   Judy Holliday, 22
Fuller, Larry
   Doll's Life, A, 85
   On the Twentieth Century, 79
Fuller, Penny, D01 227, T49 224
   Applause, 121, 124, 126
   Tony Award (nomination), *Applause*, 273
Fullum, Clay
   By Bernstein, 145
Fulton, Future
   Billion Dollar Baby, 57
Funke, Lewis
   Leonard Bernstein's Theatre Songs, 143,, 144
Funny (film), P13 208
   Adolph Green, 40, 49, 208
   Alan King, 40, 208
   Anne Jackson, 40, 208
   Bran Ferren, 40, 208
   Dick Cavett, 40, 208
   Eli Wallach, 40, 208
   Fred Ebb, 40, 208
   John Drew Theatre at Guild Hall, P13 208
   New York Times, 208
   Vincent Canby, 208
Funny Girl
   Jerome Robbins' Broadway, 147
Funny Thing Happened on the Way to the Forum, A, D19 235
   Jerome Robbins' Broadway, 40, 147

"Gabey's Coming"
   By Bernstein, 145
Gable, Clark
   Dancing Lady (film), 173
Gales, Nat
   Hallelujah, Baby!, 111
Galindo, Ramon
   Jerome Robbins' Broadway, 146
Galjour, Warren
   Wonderful Town, 95, 96
Gallagher, Helen
   Billion Dollar Baby, 57
Gallagher, Peter, D13 232
   Annual Theater World Award, 88
   Doll's Life, A, 85
Gallagher, Robert
   Two on the Aisle, 91
Gallery Stage (Los Angeles)
   On the Town, 54
Gammon, Lyn
   Billion Dollar Baby, 57
Ganun, John
   Will Rogers Follies, The, 115
Garbo Talks (film), P10 207
   Adolph Green, 38, 49
   Betty Comden (Greta Garbo), 38, 49
   United Artists, 38
Gardell, Tony
   Billion Dollar Baby, 57, 58
Gardiner, Reginald
   What a Way to Go! (film), 191
Gardner, Ava
   Band Wagon, The (film), 172

304 Comden and Green

Gardner, Kenny RA06-RA12 212, RA14-RA15 213, RA19-RA20 213
Garland, Judy, 16
  Barkleys of Broadway, The (film), 15, 155, 157
  Easter Parade (film), 15, 155
  Take Me Out to the Ball Game (film), 16, 160
Garr, Nicholas
  Jerome Robbins' Broadway, 147
Garrett, Betty, D24 237, D36 243
  On the Town (film), 162
  Take Me Out to the Ball Game (film), 16, 158, 161
  Wonderful Town (film), 98
Garrison, Gregory
  Jerome Robbins' Broadway, 147
Garroway, Dave, T16 217
Garry Moore Show
  Carol Burnett, 30
  CBS Television, 30
Gasman, Ira
  Straws in the Wind, 138, 139
Gay Divorce, The
  Fred Astaire, 173
Gaynes, George, D22 237, D40 244
  Allyn McLerie (marriage), 20
  Wonderful Town, 20, 95
Gedda, Nicolai, D50 247
Gelb, Arthur
  "*On the Town*' With Comden and Green," 43
Gelb, Barbara
  "*On the Town*' With Comden and Green," 43
Gelbart, Larry, D19 235
  Jerome Robbins' Broadway, 146
Gemignani, Paul, D13 232, D19 235, D26 238, D52 248
  Diamonds, 141
  Doll's Life, A, 85
  Follies (concert version), 208
  Jerome Robbins' Broadway, 146
  On the Twentieth Century, 79
Gene Kelly (book)
  Clive Hirschhorn, 16, 17, 38
Gennaro, Peter
  Bells Are Ringing, 65
Gentlemen Prefer Blondes 93, 136, D20 236
  (revised as) *Lorelei*, 34, 137
George Abbott ... A Celebration
  Museum of the City of New York 34
George White Scandals of 1931, The
  Irving Caesar, 9
Georgiana, Toni
  Will Rogers Follies, The, 115
Gerard, Jeremy
  "Hal Prince and the Poetry of Abstraction," 89
Gerry, Alex
  It's Always Fair Weather (film), 177
Gershwin, George, 9, D04 229, D33 241, D60 250
  Shall We Dance? (film), 156
Gershwin, Ira, D04 229, D33 241, D55 249, D60 250
  Barkleys of Broadway, The (film), 153, 155
  Easter Parade (film), 15
  Lady in the Dark,, 29
  Shall We Dance? (film), 156
  "Tschaikovsky" (poem), 29
Gershwin Theatre
  Singin' in the Rain, 39, 126, 128, 130
"Getting Married," D35 242, D63 251
Gibbons, Cedric
  Band Wagon, The (film), 171
  Barkleys of Broadway, The (film), 153
  Good News (film), 149
  It's Always Fair Weather (film), 177
  On the Town (film), 162
  Singin' in the Rain (film), 166
  Take Me Out to the Ball Game (film), 157
Gibbs, Wolcott
  Billion Dollar Baby, 61
  Say, Darling, 103
  Wonderful Town, 99
Gibson, Karen
  On the Twentieth Century, 80
Gilb, Melinda
  Singin' in the Rain, 127

Gilbert, Allan
  Billion Dollar Baby, 57
Gilbert, George
  Say, Darling, 100
Gilbert, John, 18
Gilbert, Wolfie, T19 218
Gilchrist, Connie
  Auntie Mame (film), 182
  Good News (film), 150
Gill, Brendan
  Applause, 125, 126
  Doll's Life, A, 89
  Madwoman of Central Park West, The, 140
  Singin' in the Rain, 130
  What a Way to Go! (film), 195
Gill, Ray
  On the Twentieth Century, 79, 80
Gill, Teri
  Doll's Life, A, 86
Gillespie, A. Arnold
  Bells Are Ringing (film), 187
Gillmore, Margalo
  Peter Pan, 133
Gilman, Richard
  Doll's Life, A, 90
  Hallelujah, Baby!, 113
"Girl Hunt Ballet," D03 228
  Band Wagon, The (film), 173
Girl to Remember, A (original name)
  Fade Out--Fade In, 77
"Girl With the Two Left Feet, The," D30 240
  Revuers, The 5
"Girls Like Me," D34 242
Gish, Lillian, T36 221
  Kennedy Center Lifetime Achievement Award, 38
Gist, Robert
  Band Wagon, The (film), 172
"Give a Little--Get a Little," D37 243
  Two on the Aisle, 92
"Give a Man Enough Rope," D39 244
  Will Rogers Follies, The, 115, 116
Givot, George
  Do Re Mi, 105
Glad to See You, 93

Glasner, Katie
  Singin' in the Rain, 127
Gleason, Jackie, T14 217
  Fabulous Fifties, The, 28
Gleason, John
  Lorelei, 136
Gleason, Keogh
  Band Wagon, The (film), 171
  Bells Are Ringing (film), 187
Glenn, Alice
  Fade Out--Fade In, 75, 76
  "Go Home Train," D14 233
  Fade Out--Fade In, 77
Goberman, Max
  Billion Dollar Baby, 56
  On the Town, 51
Godkin, Paul
  Bonanza Bound!, 62
"Goin' Home"
  Straws in the Wind, 139
Gold, David
  Do Re Mi, 105, 106
Golden Theatre
  Party With Betty Comden and Adolph Green, A, 23
Goldman, James, D52 248
  Follies (concert version), 208
Gooch, James
  On the Town (film), 162
  Singin' in the Rain (film), 166
  Take Me Out to the Ball Game (film), 158
"Good Friends," D01 227
"Good Morning," D32 241, D33 242
Good Morning, Good Night (children's book), 33
  Holt, Reinhart and Winston, 47
Good News (musical), 14, 149, 152
Good News (film), 23, 46, D15 233, D27 239, D28 239, D62 251, F01 149-153
  Arthur Freed, 14, 149, 152
  Charles Walters, 149, 152
  Comden and Green, 14, 15, 149, 151, 152
  "French Lesson, The," 15, 152, 153
  Joan McCracken, 15, 149, 153
  June Allyson, 15, 149, 153

306 Comden and Green

Metro-Goldwyn-Mayer, 14, 149, 151
Radio City Music Hall, 15
Roger Edens, 14, 149, 152
Goodhart, Al D33 242
Goodman, Benny, 20, T36 221
  Kennedy Center Lifetime Achievement Award, 38
Goodman, Dody
  Lorelei, 136
  Wonderful Town, 95, 96
Goodson, Mark, T23 218
Goodwin, Doris
  Two on the Aisle, 92
Goor, Carolyn
  Jerome Robbins' Broadway, 147
Gordon, Jeanne
  On the Town, 52
Gordon, Max, 11
  Blue Angel, 10
  Judy Tuvim, Village Vanguard, 3
  Live at the Village Vanguard, 5
  Village Vanguard, 3
Gordon, Noele, D25 238
Gordon, Ruth, 24
Gorman, Bob
  Subways Are for Sleeping, 69, 70
Gorshin, Frank
  Bells Are Ringing (film), 187
Gorski, Virginia
  Billion Dollar Baby, 57
Gotham, Jerry
  Fade Out--Fade In, 75, 76
"Gotta Bran' New Suit," D03 228
"Gotta Dance," D19 235
Gottfried, Martin
  Applause, 125
  Hallelujah, Baby!, 113
  Lorelei, 138
  On the Twentieth Century, 83
  Party With Betty Comden and Adolph Green, A, 203
Gould, Elliott, D23 237
  Say, Darling, 101
Gould, Morton, D07 230, D19 235
  Billion Dollar Baby, 14, 56, 59
  Jerome Robbins' Broadway, 146
  Party With Betty Comden and Adolph Green, A, 199
Gould, Sid
  What a Way to Go! (film), 191
Goulet, Robert, D54 249
Grace, Edward
  Do Re Mi, 105, 106
Grace, Eileen
  Will Rogers Follies, The, 115
Grace, Henry W.
  Bells Are Ringing (film), 187
  Take Me Out to the Ball Game (film), 157
Graff, Wilton
  Take Me Out to the Ball Game (film), 158
Grammy Award
  Comden and Green, *Will Rogers Follies, The*, 41, 119
"Grand Cafe, The," D13 232
Grant, Faye
  Best Plays, Best Actress in a Secondary Role, *Theatre World* Award, 129
  Singin' in the Rain, 127, 129
Grant, Micki
  Leonard Bernstein's Theatre Songs, 143, 144
Grant, Sean
  Jerome Robbins' Broadway, 147
Gray, Dolores, D17 234, D37 243
  Annie Get Your Gun (Annie Oakley), 18
  It's Always Fair Weather (film), 177, 180, 181
  Two on the Aisle, 18, 91-94
Gray, Mack
  Take Me Out to the Ball Game (film), 158
Gray, Richard
  Two on the Aisle, 91
Gray, Stokely
  Subways Are for Sleeping, 70
Grayson, Kathryn
  Take Me Out to the Ball Game (film), 160
Great American Composers Series, The D54 248, D56 249
Great Performances: Follies in Concert T39 221
Greatest Recordings of the Broadway Musical Theater, The D53 248

Green (Weiss), Helen
  Adolph Green's mother, 1
Green, Adam
  Adolph Green (and Phyllis
  Newman's son), 28, 42, 47
Green, Adolph xi, xii, xiii, 10, 42,
  128, 130, D01-D08 227-231,
  D10 231, D12-D22 232-237,
  D24 237, D26-D34 238-242,
  D37-D40 243-245, D45 246,
  D50-D52 247-248, D55-D57
  249, D61 250, D63 251, D64
  251, RA01 211, RA21 213,
  RA23 213, T01 215, T03-T09
  215-216, T11-T19 216-218,
  T27 219, T29 219
  Academy Award (nomination),
    It's Always Fair Weather (film),
    21, 180, 274
  All About Eve, 34
  Allyn McLerie (divorce), 20
  Allyn McLerie (marriage), 15, 46
  Applause (book), 33, 121, 125,
    126
  Auntie Mame (film), 182, 185
  Band Wagon, The (film), 171,
    174-176
  Barkleys of Broadway, The (film),
    16, 153, 155, 156, 174
  Bells Are Ringing, 23, 24, 64,
    67-69
  Bells Are Ringing (film), 23, 24,
    186, 188, 189
  Billion Dollar Baby (book/lyrics),
    14, 56, 59-61
  Birth, 1, 45
  Blue Angel, 46
  Bonanza Bound! (book/lyrics),
    15, 61, 64
  By Bernstein, 34, 144, 145
  Camp Onata, 2
  Candide, 40, 41
  Cradle Will Rock, The, 30
  "Day They Made Music on Mt.
    Scopus, The," 31, 32
  Diamonds, (lyrics), 38, 141
  Do Re Mi (lyrics), 28, 104, 109
  Doll's Life, A (book/lyrics), 37-
    39, 85, 88-90
  Donaldson Award, *Wonderful
    Town*, 20, 98
  Education, 1
  Elizabeth Reitel (marriage), 9, 45
  Fabulous Fifties, The, 28, 47
  Fade Out--Fade In (book/lyrics),
    30, 74, 77-79
  Follies (concert version)
    (Theodore Whitman), 39, 49,
    208
  Funny (film), 40, 49, 208
  Garbo Talks (film), 38, 49, 207
  George Abbott ... A Celebration,
    34, 48
  Good News (film) 14, 46, 149,
    151-153
  Hallelujah, Baby! (lyrics), 31,
    109, 112, 113
  I Love Louisa, 19
  I Said Good Morning, 33
  I Want To Go Home (Joey
    Wellman) (film), 40, 49, 209
  I'm Getting Married (television),
    31, T48 224
  It's Always Fair Weather (film),
    134, 176, 179-181
  Jerome Robbins' Broadway, 40,
    146-148
  Johnny Mercer Award, 41, 49
  Kennedy Center Award for
    Lifetime Achievement in the
    Performing Arts, 41, 49
  Lady in the Dark,, 29
  *Leonard Bernstein's Theatre
    Songs*, 31, 143, 144
  Lily in Love (Jatszani Kell)
    (film/Jerry Silber), 38, 39, 49,
    207
  Lorelei (lyrics), 34, 136, 137
  Lyrics and Lyricists, 34, 48, 205
  *Madwoman of Central Park West,
    The*, 35, 139, 140
  "Magic of Fred Astaire, The,"
    174
  My Favorite Year (film) (Leo
    Silver), 38, 48, 206
  New York University (master
    classes), 48
  New Yorkers, The, 38, 207
  On the Town (book/lyrics), 11,
    16, 21, 51, 54-56, 205
  On the Town (film), 16, 17, 21,
    161-164

308 Comden and Green

On the Twentieth Century (book/lyrics), 35, 79, 82-84
Party With Betty Comden and Adolph Green, A, 35, 47, 48, 199-203
Peter Pan (lyrics), 21, 133, 134
Phyllis Newman (marriage), 24, 47
Pirate King, *Pirates of Penzance, The*, 2
Poetry, 1
Revuers, The, 45, 205
Say, Darling (lyrics), 22, 100, 103, 104
Screenwriters Guild Award, *Bells Are Ringing* (film), 24, 189
Screenwriters Guild Award, *It's Always Fair Weather* (film), 180
Screenwriters Guild Award, *On the Town*, 17
Screenwriters Guild Award, *Singin' in the Rain* (film), 18, 169
Screenwriters Guild Award (nomination), *It's Always Fair Weather*, 21
Simon, 38, 48, 206
Singin' in the Rain (book), 39, 126, 128, 129
Singin' in the Rain (film), 17, 18, 165, 168-171
Six and Company, 4
Skin of Our Teeth, The, 30, 31
Songwriters Hall of Fame, 37, 48
Songwriters Hall of Fame (Johnny Mercer Award), 41
Straws in the Wind (lyrics), 34, 138, 139, 201
Subways Are For Sleeping (book/lyrics), 28, 69, 73, 74
Take Me Out to the Ball Game (film), 16, 157, 160, 161
Theatre Hall of Fame, 37
Tisch School of the Arts (master classes), 37
Tony Award, *Applause*, 34, 124, 272
Tony Award, *Hallelujah, Baby!*, 31, 271
Tony Award, *On the Twentieth Century*, 35, 272
Tony Award, *Will Rogers Follies, The*, 41, 116, 272
Tony Award, *Wonderful Town*, 271
Tony Award (nomination), *Bells Are Ringing*, 272
Tony Award (nomination), *Do Re Mi*, 273
Tony Award (nomination), *Dolls Life, A*, 274
Tony Award (nomination), *On the Twentieth Century*, 273
Two on the Aisle (sketch/lyrics), 18, 91, 93, 94
Warner Bros., 22
What a Way to Go! (film), 30, 190, 195, 196
Will Rogers Follies, The, 41, 114, 116-119
Wonderful Town, 19, 95, 97-100
Green, Amanda, 42, 47
  Adolph Green (and Phyllis Newman's daughter), 28
  New Yorkers, The, 38, 207
Green, Daniel
  Adolph Green's father, 1
Green, Frank
  Bells Are Ringing, 65
Green, Jame
  Good News (film), 150
Green, Johnny
  On the Town, 16, 17
Green, Mitzi
  Billion Dollar Baby, 57
Green, William
  Adolph Green's brother, 28
Greenberg, Jules, D27 239
Greene, Herbert, D37 243
  Bells Are Ringing, 64
  On the Town, 51, 52
  Two on the Aisle, 91
Greene, Milton, D27 238
Greening, Jack
  What a Way to Go! (film), 191
Greenwich Village (film)
  Don Ameche, 11
  Revuers, The, 11, 46
  Vivian Blaine, 11
Gregg, Mitchell
  Say, Darling, 101
Gregory, André, D52 248

Follies (concert version), 208
Gregory, Michael Scott
   Jerome Robbins' Broadway, 147
Gregus, Luba
   Will Rogers Follies, The, 115
Grimes, Tammy
   Slaves of New York (film), 40
Grose, Andrew
   Jerome Robbins' Broadway, 147
Gross, Saul
   Take Me Out to the Ball Game (film), 158
Gross, Shelly
   Lorelei, 136
Grossman, Larry, D13 232
   Diamonds, 140
   Doll's Life, A, 85
   Tony Award (nomination), *Doll's Life, A*, 274
Group Theatre (New York)
   Clurman, Harold, 5
Groves, Regina
   Do Re Mi, 105, 106
Gruen, John
   Private World of Leonard Bernstein, The, 33
Grusin, Larry
   Garbo Talks (film), 207
Guber, Les
   Lorelei, 136
Guernsey, Jr., Otis L.
   Two on the Aisle, 93
Guilaroff, Sydney
   Band Wagon, The (film), 171
   Barkleys of Broadway, The (film), 153
   Bells Are Ringing (film), 187
   It's Always Fair Weather (film), 177
   On the Town (film), 162
   Singin' in the Rain (film), 166
   Take Me Out to the Ball Game (film), 157
Guild Hall
   Betty Comden, Studio Players, 2
Guiskoff, Michael
   My Favorite Year, 206
Gutierrez, Gerald
   Isn't It Romantic?, 206
Guys and Dolls, 98, 109
Gypsy, D19 235

Jerome Robbins' Broadway, 40, 147

Hackett, Hal
   Bonanza Bound!, 61
Hadley, Jerry, D50 247
   Candide, 41
Hagedon, Charles K.
   Bells Are Ringing (film), 187
Hagen, Jean
   Singin' in the Rain (film), 166, 169
Haggott, Johnny, 6
Hall, Grayson
   Subways Are for Sleeping, 69
Hall, Thurston
   Band Wagon, The (film), 172
Hallelujah, Baby! 48, 203, 247, 249, 250, D16 234, D63 251, D64 251, S13 109-113, T25 219, T26 219
   Arthur Laurents, 31, 109, 112, 113
   Comden and Green (lyrics), 31, 109, 112, 113
   Grammy Award (nomination), 276
   Jule Styne, 31, 109, 112
   Leslie Uggams, 31, 110, 112, 113
   Martin Beck Theatre, 31, 109, 112
   Tony Award, 31, 112, 271
Halliday, Heller
   Peter Pan, 133
Halliday, Richard, T43 223
   Peter Pan, 133
Halton, Marie
   Lorelei, 137
Hamilton, Frank
   Hallelujah, Baby!, 110
Hamilton, Nancy
   One for the Money, 6
Hammer, Alvin 4, 10, 11, D30 240, P02 205, RA01 221, T01 215
   New Theatre School, 4
   Other Performances, 4
   Revuers, The, 45
   Youth Theatre, 4
Hammerstein II, Oscar, D19 235

Jerome Robbins' Broadway, 146
Hampton Star
  Betty Comden in *First Lady*, 2
Handzlik, Jan
  Auntie Mame (film), 182
Haney, Carol
  Singin' in the Rain (film), 165
"Happy All Alone"
  Bonanza Bound!, 63
Haraldson, Marian
  Lorelei, 137
Harburg, E. Y. D64 251
Harlan, Gregg
  Lorelei, 137
Harman, Carter
  Leonard Bernstein's Theatre Songs, 144
Harnick, Sheldon D19 235
  Jerome Robbins' Broadway, 146
  Madwoman of Central Park West, The, 139
Harold Prince (book)
  Carol Ilson, 37, 84, 89
  Newsday, 84
Harper, Sherrill
  Lorelei, 137
Harper, Valerie
  Subways Are for Sleeping, 70
Harrington, Robert
  Peter Pan, 133
Harrington, Wendall K.
  Will Rogers Follies, The, 114
Harris, Charles
  Billion Dollar Baby, 56
Harris, Jed
  Twentieth Century, 82
Harris, Joseph
  Doll's Life, A, 85
  Tony Award (nomination), *Dolls Life, A*, 274
Harris, Stan T26 219
Harrison, Ray
  On the Town, 52
Harrison, Rex, T14 217, T27 219
  Dr. Doolittle, 194
  Fabulous Fifties, The, 28
Harriton, Maria
  Billion Dollar Baby, 56, 57
Harry, Jackee
  Diamonds, 141
Hart, Lorenz, D60 250

Hart, Moss, 28, D55 249
  Lady in the Dark,, 29
Hartford, Dee
  Band Wagon, The (film), 172
Hartford, Eden
  Band Wagon, The (film), 172
Hartly, Neil
  Subways Are for Sleeping, 69
Harvey, Peter
  Straws in the Wind, 138
"Hat My Dear Old Father Wore Upon St. Patrick's Day, The," D36 243
  Take Me Out to the Ball Game (film), 159-161
Having Wonderful Time
  Betty Comden, 2, 45
Hawkins, William
  Peter Pan, 135
Haworth, Ted
  What a Way to Go! (film), 190
Hayes, Helen, 92
Hayes, Richard
  Say, Darling, 104
Hayman, Lillian, D16 234
  Hallelujah, Baby!, 110
  Tony Award, *Hallelujah, Baby!*, 271
Haynes, Tiger
  Fade Out--Fade In, 75
Hayton, Lennie 16, D04 229, D15 233, D24 237, D32 241
  Barkleys of Broadway, The (film), 153
  Good News (film), 149
  On the Town (film), 162
  Singin' in the Rain (film), 165
Hayward, Leland, T14 217
  Fabulous Fifties, The, 28
  Peter Pan, 134
  Skin of Our Teeth, The, 31
Hayworth, Rita
  Applause, 124
"He Says 'I Do,' She Says 'I Do'," T48 224
"He's a V.I.P."
  Do Re Mi, 107
Head, Edith
  What a Way to Go! (film), 190, 194

Hearn, George, D13 232, D52 248
  Doll's Life, A, 85, 88
  Follies (concert version), 39, 208
  Tony Award (nomination), Dolls Life, A, 274
Hearne, Fred
  Billion Dollar Baby, 57
Hecht, Ben, D26 238
  Twentieth Century, 35, 82
  On the Twentieth Century, 79
Heglin, Wally
  Singin' in the Rain (film), 165
Heim, Edward (Eddie)
  Bells Are Ringing, 65
  Wonderful Town, 96
Heindorf, Ray
  Auntie Mame (film) 182
Hellman, Lillian, D50 247, T33 220
  Candide, 40
  Leonard Bernstein's Theatre Songs, 143, 144
  Little Foxes, The, 29
"Hello, Hello There!," D05 229, D54 248
  Bells Are Ringing, 66, 69
  Bells Are Ringing (film), 188
Hemsley, Winston DeWitt
  Hallelujah, Baby!, 110
Henderson, Luther, D10 231
  Do Re Mi, 105
  Hallelujah, Baby!, 110
Henderson, Ray, D15 233
  Good News (musical), 14, 149
  Good News (film), 151
Henie, Sonja, 6
Herald Tribune
  Bells Are Ringing, 68
  Billion Dollar Baby, 60
  Do Re Mi, 108
  Fade Out--Fade In, 78
  On the Town, 55
  Subways Are for Sleeping, 73
  Two on the Aisle, 93
  Wonderful Town, 99
"Here Comes the Sun"
  By Bernstein, 145
"Here She Comes Now"
  Two on the Aisle, 92, D37 243
"Here's What You Said"
  Two on the Aisle, 92
Herman, Jerry
  Mame (musical), 185
Hero, Maria
  Hallelujah, Baby!, 111
Hess, Alexia
  Jerome Robbins' Broadway, 147
Hess, Nancy
  Jerome Robbins' Broadway, 147
Hewes, Henry
  Applause, 125
  Bells Are Ringing, 68
  Fade Out--Fade In, 78
  Say, Darling, 103, 104
  Wonderful Town, 99
Heymann, Edward (lyrics)
  "Takin' Miss Mary to the Ball," 128
Hickey, Louise
  Jerome Robbins' Broadway, 147
High Button Shoes, 93, 108, D19 235
  Jerome Robbins' Broadway, 40, 147
"Highlights from the World of Sports"
  Two on the Aisle, 92
Hiken, Nat, D37 243
  Two on the Aisle, 91, 92
Hill, Joe
  Subways Are for Sleeping, 69, 70
Hillaire, Marcel
  What a Way to Go! (film), 191
Hilliard, Ken
  On the Twentieth Century, 79, 80
Hirschfield, Al
  Party With Betty Comden and Adolph Green, A, 202
Hirschhorn, Clive
  Gene Kelly (book) 8, 9, 16, 17, 38
Hirschhorn, Joel
  Notes on Broadway (book), xii, 21, 43, 44, 94, 134
His Way (book)
  Kitty Kelley, 20
Hodes, Stuart
  Do Re Mi, 105, 106
Hodge, Edward (Eddie)
  Billion Dollar Baby, 56, 58

Hoebec, Mark
  Jerome Robbins' Broadway, 147
Hoffman, Al, D33 241
Hoffman, Cady
  Tony Award (nomination), *Will Rogers Follies, The*, 274
  Will Rogers Follies, The, 117
Hoisington, Eric A.
  Jerome Robbins' Broadway, 147
"Hold Me, Hold Me, Hold Me" D37 243, D46 246
  Two on the Aisle, 92
Holliday, Judy xi, 11, D05 229, D06 230, D51 247, D54 248, D56 249
  (stage name of) Judy Tuvim, 67
  Academy Award, *Born Yesterday* (film), 21, 188
  Bells Are Ringing, xii, 22, 24, 65, 67, 68
  Bells Are Ringing (film), 23, 187-190
  Born Yesterday, 21, 188
  Born Yesterday (film), 188
  Death, 24, 189
  Full of Life (film), 22
  It Should Happen to You (film), 188
  Kiss Them For Me, 21
  Marrying Kind, The (film), 188
  On the Town (film), 162
  Revuers, The, 22 (as Judy Tuvim) 3-11
  Solid Gold Cadillac, The (film), 188
  Tony Award, *Bells Are Ringing*, 271
  Tony Award, *Born Yesterday*, 21
  Wonderful Town (film), 98
Hollingsworth, Doris
  Billion Dollar Baby, 57
Hollywood
  Revuers, The, 46
Holm, Celeste, T10 216
Holmes, Brenda
  Lorelei, 136, 137
Holmes, Rupert
  Mystery of Edwin Drood, The, 129
Holmes, Scott
  Diamonds, 141

Holst, Sven
  Bonanza Bound!, 62
Holt, Fritz
  Madwoman of Central Park West, The, 139
Holt, Rinehart and Winston
  Good Morning, Good Night (children's book), 33, 47
Holt, Will
  Leonard Bernstein's Theatre Songs, 143
Holtzman, Will
  Judy Holliday (biography), xiii, 8
"Homesick Blues," D20 236
Hood, Curtis
  Do Re Mi, 106
Hooks, Robert, D16 234
  Hallelujah, Baby!, 110
  Tony Award (nomination), *Hallelujah, Baby!*, 273
"Hook's Tango," D29 240
Hoon, Barbara
  Jerome Robbins' Broadway, 147
  Singin' in the Rain, 127
Hooper, Lee
  Hallelujah, Baby!, 111
Hoopes, Isabella
  Wonderful Town, 95
Hopkins, George James
  Auntie Mame (film), 182
Horase
  Subways Are for Sleeping, 70
Horne, Lena, 16
Horne, Nat
  Applause, 122
Horne, Pat
  Bonanza Bound!, 62
Horwitt, Arnold
  Wonderful Town, 19, 97
Horwitz, David
  On the Twentieth Century, 80
Hosier, Beverly
  Billion Dollar Baby, 57
Hoty, Dee, D39 244
  Tony Award (nomination), *Will Rogers Follies, The*, 117, 274
  Will Rogers Follies, The, 114, 118
Houseman, John
  Cradle Will Rock, The, 29

"How Can You Describe a Face?,"
D34 242, D35 242
   Subways Are for Sleeping, 72, 74
"How Will He Know?," D37 243, D46 246, D62 251
   Two on the Aisle, 92
Howard, Peter, D08 231, D27 239
   (at the piano) *Party With Betty Comden and Adolph Green, A*, 23, 199
   Say, Darling, 100, 101
   Subways Are for Sleeping, 69
Howard, Robert
   Subways Are for Sleeping, 69, 70
Howells, Reby
   Subways Are for Sleeping, 70
Hoyt, Barbara
   Say, Darling, 101
"Hub Bub"
   Singin' in the Rain, 128
Hudson Guild Theatre (New York), D64 251
   My Mother Was a Fortune Teller, 140
Hudson, Rock
   Oscar, *On the Twentieth Century*, 83
Huffman, Cady, D39 244
   Will Rogers Follies, The, 114
Hughes, Robin
   Auntie Mame (film), 182
Hulbert, Don
   Singin' in the Rain (film), 166
Humphrey, Richard
   What a Way to Go! (film), 190
Hunt, Hugh
   It's Always Fair Weather (film), 177
Hunter, JoAnn M.
   Jerome Robbins' Broadway, 147
"Hurry Back," D01 227
"Husking Bee, The," D31 240
Hutchinson, Ann
   Billion Dollar Baby, 57
Hutton, Betty, 30

"I Can Cook Too," D21 236, D22 237, D51 247, D61 250

On the Town, 56
"I Can't Give You Anything But Love," D33 242
"I Don't Know Where She Got It," D16 234
"I Feel Like I'm Not Out of Bed Yet," D21 236, D24 238
Leonard Bernstein's Theatre Songs, 31, 144
On the Town (film), 162
"I Get Carried Away," D21 236, D27 239, D61 250
Party With Betty Comden and Adolph Green, A, 200
"I Got a One Track Mind," D07 230
"I Got You," D39 244
"I Gotta Crow"
   Peter Pan, 21
"I Guess I'll Have to Change My Plans," D03 228
   Band Wagon, The (film), 173, 176
"I Have Written a Play, D26 238
"I Just Can't Wait," D34 242
   Subways Are for Sleeping, 72, 74
"I Know About Love," D10 232, D54 249
   Do Re Mi, 106, 108
"I Know What a Person's Gonna Do Before He Does It"
   Say, Darling, 102
"I Like Myself," D17 234, D18 235, D46 246
   It's Always Fair Weather (film) 179
I Love Louisa, D03 228
   (title changed to) *Band Wagon, The*, 174
   Band Wagon, The (film), 173, 174
   Band Wagon, The (musical), 173
"I Love What I'm Doing," D20 236
"I Met a Girl," D05 229, D06 230
"I Must Love You," D60 250
"I Rise Again!," D26 238
   On the Twentieth Century, 81
"I Said Good Morning," 216, 217, D18 235, D27 239, T13 217

314 Comden and Green

Party With Betty Comden and Adolph Green, A, 33, 199
Good Morning, Good Night (children's book), 47
"I Said It and I'm Glad," D34 242, D35 242
"I Still Get Jealous," D19 235
"I Think That You and I Should Get Acquainted"
   What a Way to Go! (film), 190
"I Understand," D22 237
I Want To Go Home (film), P15 209
   Adolph Green, 40, 49
   Variety, 209
"I Wanted to Change Him," D16 234
I Was a Shoo-In," D34 242, D64 251
   Subways Are for Sleeping, 29, 71, 74
"I Won't Grow Up," D29 240
   Peter Pan, 21
"I Won't Let You Get Away," D20 236
   Lorelei, 137
"I'm A'Tingle, I'm A'Glow," D20 236
"I'm Afraid It's Love"
   By Bernstein, 145
"I'm Blue," D22 237
"I'm Flying," D19 235, D29 240
   Jerome Robbins' Broadway, 147
   Peter Pan, 147
"I'm Getting Married," T48 224
   ABC Television, *Stage 67*, 31, 47
   Comden and Green (script/lyrics), 31
   Dick Shawn 31
   New York Times, 31
"I'm Goin' Back to the Bonjour Tristesse Brassiere Company," D05 229, D06 230
   Bells Are Ringing, 67, 69
"I'm Just Taking My Time," D34 242, D35 242, D54 249
"I'm Sure of Your Love," D07 230
"I'm With You," D14 233
"I've Got It All," D26 238
"I've Gotta Crow," D29 240
Ibsen, Henrik

   Doll's House, A, 37, 86
Ice Follies of 1939
   Joan Crawford, 6
"If You Hadn't, But You Did," D27 239, D28 239, D37 243, D62 251
   Party With Betty Comden and Adolph Green, A, 200
   Two on the Aisle, 92
Ilson, Carol
   Harold Prince (biography), 37, 84, 89
"Imaginary Coney Island," D22 237
Imperial Theatre
   Jerome Robbins' Broadway, 40, 146, 147
Importance of Being Earnest, The
   Betty Comden (Miss Prism), 2
"Independent" (On My Own), D54 248
"Indians," D29 240
Inside U.S.A., 97
"Inspiration," D08 231, D09 231, D27 239, D28 239, T06 215, RA23 214
   Bonanza Bound!, 64, 200, 201
   Party With Betty Comden and Adolph Green, A, 200, 201
"Intermission's Great, The"
   By Bernstein, 145
Invitation to the Dance (film)
   André Previn, 20, 179
Irene, 152
Irving, George S.
   Bells Are Ringing, 65
"Is It a Crime?," D05 229, D06 230, D64 251
Isenberg, Lee
   Diamonds, 140
Isn't It Romantic?, P08 206
   Betty Comden (Tasha Blumberg), 38, 49
   New York Times, 38, 206
   Playwrights Horizon Theatre, 38
   Wendy Wasserstein, 38
Israel Philharmonic Orchestra
   Leonard Bernstein, 31
It Should Happen to You (film)
   Judy Holliday, 188
"It's a Boy," D39 244

Index 315

Will Rogers Follies, The, 115
"It's a Perfect Relationship," D05 229, D06 230, D51 247, D64 251
"It's a Simple Little System," D05 229, D06 230, D51 247
Bells Are Ringing, 69
It's Always Fair Weather (film), 46, 176-182, D17 234, D18 234, D27 239, F07 176-182, P01 199
   Academy Award (nomination), 21, 180
   André Previn, 176, 179
   Arthur Freed, 20, 177, 179, 180
   Comden and Green, 20, 176, 180, 181
   Dan Dailey, 20, 177, 180
   Dolores Gray, 177, 180
   Gene Kelly, 20, 176, 179-181
   Metro-Goldwyn-Mayer, 176, 180
   Michael Kidd, 20, 177, 179
   Radio City Music Hall, 20, 180
   Screenwriters Guild Award (nomination), 21, 180
   Stanley Donen, 176, 177, 179-182
"It's Delightful Down in Chile," D20 236
Lorelei, 137
"It's Doom," D31 240
"It's Fate, Baby, It's Fate," D36 243
Take Me Out to the Ball Game (film) 16, 159-161
"It's Good to Be Back Home," D14 233
"It's High Time," D20 236
It's Legitimate," D10 231, T47 224
Do Re Mi, 28, 106, 108, 109
"It's Love," D40 245, D41 245, D46 246, D56 249, D62 251
Leonard Bernstein's Theatre Songs, 31, 144
Wonderful Town, 97, 100
"It's the Hat My Dear Old Father Wore upon St. Patrick's Day", D36 243
Take Me Out to the Ball Game (film), 159, 160

"It's the Second Time You Meet That Matters," D31 240
Ivory, James
   Slaves of New York (film), 40, 208

Jack Parr Show, The, T08 216, T09 216, T12 216
Jackson, Anne
   Funny (film), 40, 208
Jackson, Ernestine
   Applause, 122
Jackson, Harry
   Band Wagon, The (film), 171
Jackson, Lonny
   On the Town, 51
Jacob, Abe
   Madwoman of Central Park West, The, 139
Jacobi, Lou, D14 233
   Fade Out--Fade In, 75
Jacobs, Arthur P.
   What a Way to Go! (film), 190, 194
Jaffa, Henri
   Band Wagon, The (film), 171
   Barkleys of Broadway, The (film), 153
   On the Town (film), 162
   Singin' in the Rain (film), 166
"Jailer, Jailer," D13 232
James, Hal
   Hallelujah, Baby!, 110
   Tony Award, *Hallelujah, Baby!*, 271
"Jamitz, Reuben," D27 239
Janowitz, Tama
   Slaves of New York (film), 40, 208
Japan Satellite Broadcasting, Inc.
   Tony Award, *Will Rogers Follies, The*, 272
Will Rogers Follies, The, 114
Jasinski, Daniel
   Do Re Mi, 106
Jason, Mitchell, D14 233
   Fade Out--Fade In, 75
Jasper, Buford
   Two on the Aisle, 91
Jazz Singer, The, 167

316 Comden and Green

"Jealousy"
   New Yorkers, The, 207
Jenkins, Gordon
   "Blue Prelude," (lyrics), 128
Jennings, Al
   It's Always Fair Weather (film), 176
Jerome Robbins Broadway, 40, 49, D19 235, R03 146
   Adolph Green, 40
   Betty Comden, 40
   Billion Dollar Baby, 40
   Call Me Madam, 40
   Fiddler on the Roof, 40
   Gypsy, 40
   High Button Shoes, 40
   Imperial Theatre, 40
   Miss Liberty, 40
   On the Town, 40
   Peter Pan, 40
   Tony Award, 40
   West Side Story, 40
Jerome, William
   Take Me Out to the Ball Game (film), 160
Jewison, Norman, T14 217
Joan Crawford Fan Club, The, D30 240
John Drew Theatre, Guild Hall, East Hampton, NY
   Funny (film), 208
Johnny Mercer Award
   Comden and Green, 41, 49, 276
Johnson, Alan
   Hallelujah, Baby!, 111
Johnson, David Cale
   Doll's Life, A, 86
Johnson, David-Michael
   Singin' in the Rain, 127
Johnson, Jr., Mel
   On the Twentieth Century, 80
Johnson, Mary Lea
   Doll's Life, A, 85
   Tony Award (nomination), *Doll's Life, A*, 274
Johnson, Pat
   Wonderful Town, 96
Johnson, Susan, T17 217
Johnson, Troy Britton
   Will Rogers Follies, The, 115
Johnston, Barney

Fade Out--Fade In, 75, 76
Jones, Clark, T27 219, T30 220, T43 223
Jones, Della, D50 247
Jones, Douglas
   Billion Dollar Baby, 57
Jones, Gordon
   Take Me Out to the Ball Game (film), 158
Jordan, Marc
   Do Re Mi, 105, 106
Josephine Forrestal Productions, Inc.
   Leonard Bernstein's Theatre Songs, 143
Joslyn, Betsy, D13 232
   Doll's Life, A, 85, 89
Journal American
   Bells Are Ringing, 68
   Do Re Mi, 108
   Fade Out--Fade In, 78
   Subways Are for Sleeping, 73
   Wonderful Town, 98
Jovovich, Scott
   Jerome Robbins' Broadway, 147
Joy, Leonard, D21 236
Judy Holliday Biographies
   Judy Holliday, An Intimate Life Story, Gary Carey, xiii, 3, 6, 9, 10
   Judy Holliday, Will Holtzman, xiii, 8
Jule Styne in The Great American Composers Series, D54 248
Julia, Raoul, D42 245
Julliard School of Music
   Party With Betty Comden and Adolph Green, A, 34, 201
Jung, Phillip
   Madwoman of Central Park West, The, 139
"Just a Kiss Apart," D20 236
"Just Imagine," D15 233
"Just in Time," D05 229, D06 230, D27 239, D28 239, D43 246, D46 246, D48 246, D51 247, D54 249, D64 251, T13 216
   Bells Are Ringing, 67, 69, 201
   Party With Betty Comden and Adolph Green, A, 200, 201

Just in Time (autobiography), xiv, 24, 28
  Phyllis Newman, xiii, 24, 26, 28

Kahl, Howard
  Applause, 121
Kahn, Gus (lyrics)
  "Love Is Where You Find It," 128
  "You Stepped Out of a Dream," 128
Kahn, Madeline, D26 238, D51 247
  On the Twentieth Century, 80, 82, 84
  Tony Award (nomination), *On the Twentieth Century*, 273
Kalem, T. E.
  On the Twentieth Century, 84
Kalmus, Natalie
  Barkleys of Broadway, The (film), 153
  Good News (film), 149
  Take Me Out to the Ball Game (film), 158
Kander, John
  Diamonds, 140
  Madwoman of Central Park West, The, 139
Kanin, Garson, 24, D10 231
  Do Re Mi, 28, 104, 105, 108, 109
  Tony Award (nomination), *Do Re Mi*, 273
Kaper, Bronislau
  Auntie Mame (film), 182
  Auntie Mame (film/recordings), 185
Kaplan, Herbert
  Madwoman of Central Park West, The, 139
Karloff, Boris
  Peter Pan, 134
Karmitz, Marin
  I Want to Go Home (film), 209
Karr, Patti
  Bells Are Ringing, 65
  Do Re Mi, 105
Kasday, David
  Singin' in the Rain (film), 166
Kasha, Al
  "Jule Styne," *Notes on Broadway*, 94, 134
  Notes on Broadway, xii, 21, 43
Kasha, Lawrence
  Applause, 121
  Tony Award, *Applause*, 272
Kastner, Burtt Harris
  Garbo Talks (film), 207
Kastner, Elliott
  Garbo Talks (film), 207
Katsaros, Doug
  Diamonds, 140
Kauffmann, Stanley
  Applause, 125
  Auntie Mame (film), 185
  On the Twentieth Century, 84
  What a Way to Go! (film), 195
Kaufman Auditorium
  Party With Betty Comden and Adolph Green, A, 34
Kay, Hershy, D26 238, D50 247
  On the Twentieth Century, 79
Kaye, Danny, 249
  Lady in the Dark, 29, 47
Kaye, Judy
  On the Twentieth Century, 80, 82-84
Kazan, Elia, 54
"Keep Your Sunnyside Up"
  Good News (film) (1974 musical), 152
"Keeping Cool With Coolidge," D20 236
Kelley, Kitty
  His Way (book), 20
Kellogg, Mary Ann
  Singin' in the Rain, 127
Kelly, Betsy, 16
Kelly, Gene 6, 8, 16, 20, 39, 49, 179, D17 234, D24 237, D32 241, D36 243, D38 244, T36 221, T38 221
  American in Paris, An, 18, 169
  Comden and Green, Kennedy Center Honors, xi, 41
  It's Always Fair Weather (film), 176, 180, 181
  Kennedy Center Lifetime Achievement Award, 38
  On the Town, 54
  On the Town (film), 17, 162-164
  One for the Money, 6

318 Comden and Green

Singin' in the Rain, 126, 130
Singin' in the Rain (film), 18, 165, 169, 170
Take Me Out to the Ball Game (film), 16, 158, 160, 161
Westport Country Playhouse, 6
What a Way to Go! (film), 30, 190, 191, 194-196
Kelly, John
   Two on the Aisle, 92
Kelly, Sean
   Diamonds, 140
   Singin' in the Rain, 129
Kelman, Terry
   Auntie Mame (film), 182
Kelton, Gene
   Applause, 122
   Fade Out--Fade In, 75, 76
   Subways Are for Sleeping, 70
Kelvin, Walter
   Two on the Aisle, 91
   Wonderful Town, 95
Kemp, Carolyn
   Fade Out--Fade In, 76
Kennedy Center Award for Lifetime Achievement in the Performing Arts xi, T35 220, T36 221, T41 222
   Carol Burnett, xi
   CBS Television, 41
   Comden and Green, 41, 49, 276
   Gene Kelly, xi
   Lauren Bacall, xi
   Mike Nichols, xi
   Paul Taylor, 42, 50
Kenneth John Productions, Inc.
   Diamonds, 141
Kennett, Karl
   Diamonds, 141
Kent, Betty
   Do Re Mi, 105
Kent, Lenny
   What a Way to Go! (film), 191
Kerr, Walter F.
   Applause, 125
   Bells Are Ringing, 68
   Do Re Mi, 108
   Fade Out--Fade In, 78
   Hallelujah, Baby!, 113
   Isn't It Romantic?, 206
   Say, Darling, 103

Subways Are for Sleeping, 73
Two on the Aisle, 93
Wonderful Town, 99
Khoury, Pamela
   Jerome Robbins' Broadway, 147
Kidd, Michael, D17 234, T20 218
   Band Wagon, The (film), 171, 174, 176
   I Love Louisa, 19
   It's Always Fair Weather (film), 20, 177, 179
   Subways Are for Sleeping, 69, 73
Kikushi, Susan
   Jerome Robbins' Broadway, 147
Kim, Willa
   Tony Award, Will Rogers Follies, The, 41, 117, 272
   Will Rogers Follies, The, 114, 117
King, Alan
   Applause, 121
   Funny (film), 40, 208
King, James, T33 220
King, Lawrence
   By Bernstein, 144, 145
King, Pete, D06 230
   Bells Are Ringing (film), 186
King and I, The, D19 235
   Jerome Robbins' Broadway, 40, 147
"Kings' Barcarolle, The," D50 247
Kipness, Joseph
   Applause, 121
   Tony Award, Applause, 272
Kirchner, Ray
   Do Re Mi, 105, 106
   Wonderful Town, 96
Kiser, Franklin, D23 237
Kiss Them For Me
   Herman Shumlin, 21
Kissel, Howard
   By Bernstein, 145
   Doll's Life, A, 88
   Jerome Robbins' Broadway, 148
   On the Twentieth Century, 83
   "Simplified Language," 139
   Will Rogers Follies, The, 117
Kit Kat Club, 8
Kittelton, Rosemary
   Two on the Aisle, 92

Klavun, Walter
   Say, Darling, 101
Kleban, Ed
   Madwoman of Central Park West, The, 139
Kline, Kevin, T32 220
   On the Twentieth Century, 80, 85
   Tony Award, *On the Twentieth Century*, 35, 272
Klotz, Florence
   Doll's Life, A, 85
   On the Twentieth Century, 79
Knight, Arthur
   Auntie Mame (film), 186
Knowles, Patric
   Auntie Mame (film), 182
Kohler, Marion
   On the Town, 51
Kokich, Kasimir
   Bells Are Ringing, 65
Kole, Robert
   Wonderful Town, 96
Konicki, Joe
   Jerome Robbins' Broadway, 147
Kosa, Jr., Emil
   What a Way to Go! (film), 190
Koussevitzky, Serge 14, 20
Krams, Arthur
   Barkleys of Broadway, The (film), 153
Krasner, Milton
   Bells Are Ringing (film), 187
Kresh, Paul
   Stereo Review, 44
Kroll, Jack
   Singin' in the Rain, 130
   Will Rogers Follies, The, 118
Kronenberger, Louis
   Best Plays of 1960-1961, The, 109
   Billion Dollar Baby, 60
   On the Town, 55
Kubala, Michael
   Jerome Robbins' Broadway, 146
Kurdock, Marybeth
   Applause, 122
Kurshals, Raymond
   Singin' in the Rain, 127
Kyle, Alan, 10
   Betty Comden and Steven Kyle's son
   Birth, 10, 46
   Death, 42, 49
Kyle, Steven 18, 23, 28, 33, 48
   Americraft, 37
   Betty Comden (marriage), 10, 45
   Death, 37, 48
Kyle, Susanna, 42
   Betty Comden and Steven Kyle's daughter
   Birth, 10, 46

"L. Z. In Quest of His Youth," D14 233
La Cage Aux Folles, 116
Lady in the Dark, 47, D55 249
   "Tschaikovsky," Columbia Records, 29
LaFosse, Robert
   Jerome Robbins' Broadway, 146
Lahr, Bert, D37 243
   Two on the Aisle (revue), 18, 91-94, 180
   Wizzard of Oz (Cowardly Lion), 18
Lahr, John
   Diamonds, 140
Lamb, Mary Ann
   Jerome Robbins' Broadway, 146
Lamb, Wayne
   Bonanza Bound!, 62
Landis, Joe
   Billion Dollar Baby, 57
Lane, Georgia
   Good News (film), 150
Lane, Richard
   Take Me Out to the Ball Game (film), 158
Lane, Stewart F.
   Tony Award, *Will Rogers Follies, The*, 272
   Will Rogers Follies, The, 114
Lang, Barbara, D13 232
   Doll's Life, A, 85
   Do Re Mi, 106
Lang, Josephine
   Do Re Mi, 106
Lang, Lisa
   Peter Pan, 134
Lang, Philip J., D01 227, D20 236, D34 242, D37 243
   Applause, 121

320 Comden and Green

Bonanza Bound!, 61
Lorelei, 136
Subways Are for Sleeping, 69
Two on the Aisle, 91
Lange, Bobbi
   Fade Out--Fade In, 76
Langner, Lawrence
   Theatre Guild, 23, 28, 54
Lanier, David
   Jerome Robbins' Broadway, 146
Lanier, Jane
   Jerome Robbins' Broadway, 146
Lansbury, Angela
   Mame (musical), 185
Large, Norman A.
   Doll's Life, A, 85
Larkin, Peter
   Peter Pan, 133
Lascoe, Henry
   Wonderful Town, 95
"Late, Late Show, The," D10 232
   Do Re Mi, 107, 109
Latessa, Dick, D39 244
   Diamonds, 141
   Will Rogers Follies, The, 114
Latouche, John, D50 248
   By Bernstein, 34, 144, 145
   Candide, 40
Lauc, Paula
   What a Way to Go! (film), 191
Lauer, Marion
   Two on the Aisle, 91
Laurence, Larry
   Two on the Aisle, 91
Laurents, Arthur 28, D16 234, D19 235, D57 249, D64 251, T26 219
   Hallelujah, Baby!, 31, 109, 113
   Jerome Robbins' Broadway, 146
   Madwoman of Central Park West, The, 35, 139, 140
   Subways Are for Sleeping, 72
   Tony Award, Hallelujah, Baby!, 271
Lavin, Linda
   I Want to Go Home (film), 209
Lawford, Peter, D15 233
   Good News (film), 15, 16, 149
Lawrence, Carol, D34 242
   "Broadway," New York Times, 38
   Subways Are for Sleeping, 69

Lawrence, Eddie
   Bells Are Ringing, 65
Lawrence, Gertrude, D55 249
   Lady in the Dark,, 29
Lawrence, Jerome, D02 228
   Auntie Mame (film), 22
   Auntie Mame (play), 182, 184
   Mame (musical), 185
Layton, Joe
   On the Town (London), 55
   Wonderful Town, 96
"Learn to Be Lonely," D13 232
   Doll's Life, A, 87
   Party With Betty Comden and Adolph Green, A, 39
LeBlanc, Lee
   Bells Are Ringing (film), 187
Lebowsky, Stanley
   "Hub Bub," 128
Lee, Robert E., D02 228
   Auntie Mame (film), 22
   Auntie Mame (play), 182, 184
   Mame (musical), 185
Lee, Sondra, T46 224
   Peter Pan, 134
Lee, Vera
   Two on the Aisle, 92
Leeds, Peter
   It's Always Fair Weather (film), 177
"Legacy, The," D26 238, D51 248
   On the Twentieth Century, 82, 85
Lehrman, Leonard, D07 230
Leiber, Jerry
   By Bernstein, 34, 144, 145
Leigh, Carolyn, D19 235, D29 239
   "I'm Flying" (lyrics), 147
   Jerome Robbins' Broadway, 146
   Peter Pan, 21, 133, 134
Leigh, Janet
   Wonderful Town (film), 98
Leigh, Kelly
   Say, Darling, 101
Leigh-Smith, Andrea
   Jerome Robbins' Broadway, 146
Lein, Sandra
   Hallelujah, Baby!, 110, 111
Lemmon, Jack
   Wonderful Town (film), 98
Lennart, Isobel, D64 251

Lenters, Howard
   Billion Dollar Baby, 56, 58
Leon, Marc
   Bells Are Ringing, 65
Leonard Bernstein (book)
   John Briggs, 2
Leonard Bernstein and the New York Philharmonic: The Humors of Music, T11 216
Leonard Bernstein in The Great American Composers Series, D56 249
Leonard Bernstein's Theatre Songs, 47, R01 143
   Comden and Green, 31
   Theatre de Lys, 31
Leonard, Howard
   Will Rogers Follies, The, 114
Leonard, Lawrence, D23 237
Leonard, Queenie
   What a Way to Go! (film), 191
Leonardos, Urylee
   Bells Are Ringing, 65
Lerner, Alan Jay, D03 228
LeRoy, Alan
   Two on the Aisle, 91
Lesko, John, T14 217
Lesser, Arthur
   Two on the Aisle, 91, 92
Lester, Edwin
   Peter Pan, 133, 134
"Let the Lower Lights Be Burning," D31 240
   Say, Darling, 104
Let's Go Flying, D39 244
Let's Talk, D63 251
Letchworth, Eileen
   Say, Darling, 101
"Letter from Klemnacht," D13 232
"Letter to the Children," D13 232
   Doll's Life, A, 86
Levant, Oscar, D03 228, D04 229
   Band Wagon, The (film), 172
   Barkleys of Broadway, The (film), 154, 156
Levin, Herman
   Bonanza Bound!, 15, 61
Lewine, Richard, D60 250
Lewis, Al
   Do Re Mi, 105

Lewis, Carol Jean
   Straws in the Wind, 138
Lewis, Gillian, D23 237
Lewis, Morgan
   One for the Money, 6
Lewis, Theophilus
   Leonard Bernstein's Theatre Songs, 144
Library of Congress, The
   What a Way to Go! (film), 195
Lieber, Jerry
   By Bernstein, 144
Life
   Leonard Bernstein's Theatre Songs, 144
"Life Is Just a Bowl of Cherries"
   Good News (1974 musical), 152
"Life Is Like a Train," D26 238
"Life's Not Simple," D63 251
"Lila Tremaine," D14 233
   Fade Out--Fade In, 77
Liliom
   Ferenc Molnar, 2
Lillie, Beatrice
   Auntie Mame (play) (London), 185
   Inside U.S.A., 97
"Lily, Oscar", D26 238
Lily in Love (Jatszani Kell), 38, P11 207
   Adolph Green, 49
   Christopher Plummer, 38
   Maggie Smith, 38
   New York Times, 207
Lincoln Center's Avery Fisher Hall, T39 221
Linden, Hal
   Bells Are Ringing (film), 187, 188
Lindsay, Frank
   Peter Pan, 134
Linhart, Joe
   Hallelujah, Baby!, 110
Linn-Baker, Mark
   My Favorite Year, 206
Linville, Albert
   Do Re Mi, 105
   Wonderful Town, 95, 96
"Little Bit in Love, A," D40 245, D41 245, D56 249
   Wonderful Town, 96, 100
"Little Fish," D09 231

322 Comden and Green

Little Foxes, The
  Lillian Hellman, 29
"Little Girl From Little Rock, A,"
  D20 236
Little Show, The
  Schwartz and Dietz, 174
Little Theatre
  Party With Betty Comden and Adolph Green, A, 202
Litton, Glenn
  Hallelujah, Baby!, 113
Litvinoff, Seymour
  Leonard Bernstein's Theatre Songs, 143
Live at the Village Vanguard
  Max Gordon, The Revuers, 5
Lloyd, Christopher, D42 245
Lober, David
  Wonderful Town, 96
Loeb Theatre Center, Harvard University
  Party With Betty Comden and Adolph Green, A, 201
Loesser, Frank
  Wonderful Town, 97
Loew's State (New York)
  Take Me Out to the Ball Game, 160
Loew's, Inc.
  Barkleys of Broadway, The (film/video), 153
  Howard Dietz, 174
Loews's 72nd Street Theatre (New York)
  Singin' in the Rain (film), 169
"Loki and Baldur," D13 232
Lombard, Carole
  Twentieth Century (film), 82
London
  Do Re Mi, 28
London Palladium
  Singin' in the Rain, 128
London Symphony Chorus, D50 247
London Symphony Orchestra, D50 247
  Candide, 40
  On the Town (concert version), 42
"Lonely Me"
  By Bernstein, 145

"Lonely Town," D21 236, D22 237, D27 239, D28 239, D45 246, D46 246, D56 249, D61 250, D62 251
  On the Town, 56
  Party With Betty Comden and Adolph Green, A, 200
"Lonely Town" (omitted)
  On the Town (film), 162
Lonergan, Arthur
  It's Always Fair Weather (film), 177
"Long Before I Knew You," D05 229, D51 247, D54 249, D64 251
Long Island Stage (benefit)
  Comden and Green, 41
Long Island University
  On the Town (revival), Comden and Green, 49
Long, Tamara
  Lorelei, 136
Longstreet, Stephen, D19 235
  Jerome Robbins' Broadway, 146
"Look Around," D39 244
  Will Rogers Follies, The, 118
Look, Ma, I'm Dancin'!, D19 235
  Jerome Robbins' Broadway, 147
"Looking Back," D20 236
  Lorelei, 137
Loos, Anita, D20 236, D64 251
  Lorelei (book), 136, 137
Loquasto, Santo
  Singin' in the Rain, 126
Lorelei, 48, D20 236, S18 136
  Carol Channing, 34
  Comden and Green (lyrics), 34
  Jule Styne, 34
  Palace Theatre, 34
  (revision of) *Gentlemen Prefer Blondes*, 34
Lorenz, Robert
  On the Town, 52
Los Angeles Times
  "Hal Prince and the Poetry of Abstraction," 89
"Lost Word, The," D28 239
  Party With Betty Comden and Adolph Green, A, 201
  Straws in the Wind, 139
Lotis, Dennis, D25 238

Louise, Tina, D14 233
"Louisiana Hayride," D03 228
Band Wagon, The (film), 173
"Love Is Nothing But a Racket,"
  D18 235
"Love Is Where You Find It," 128
  Singin' in the Rain, 128
Love, Bessie
  Good News (1930 film), 151
Love, Edmund G.
  Subways Are For Sleeping
  (book), 28, 69, 72
Love, Geoff, D25 238
"Lovely Girl," D07 230
Lowe, Mundell, D60 250
Lowenstein, David
  Jerome Robbins' Broadway, 146
Lucas, Craig
  On the Twentieth Century, 80
Lucille Lortel Productions, Inc.
  *Leonard Bernstein's Theatre
  Songs*, 143
Luckey, Suzanne
  Peter Pan, 134
"Lucky in Love," D15 233
  Good News (film), 150, 151, 153
"Lucky to Be Me," D21 236, D22
  237, D28 239, D46 246, D51
  247, D56 249, D61 250
  On the Town, 28, 56
  *Party With Betty Comden and
  Adolph Green, A*, 200
Ludwig, Christa, D50 247, T33
  220
  Candide, 41
Lugenbeal, Carol
  On the Twentieth Century, 80
Lumet, Sidney, 38
  Garbo Talks (film), 207
Lurie, Carol
  Doll's Life, A, 86
  On the Twentieth Century, 79, 80
Lurio, Don
  Peter Pan, 133, 134
"Lute Song," D21 236
Lyday, Paul
  Two on the Aisle, 92
Lyn Murray Chorus, D61 250
Lynch, Michael
  Jerome Robbins' Broadway, 146
Lynde, Janice

Applause, 124
Lyndeck, Edmund, D13 232
  Doll's Life, A, 85
Lynn, Myra
  Bonanza Bound!, 62
Lynn, Tonia
  Will Rogers Follies, The, 115
Lyrics and Lyricists, 34, P04 205
  Comden and Green (performers),
  48, 205

Mabry, Moss
  What a Way to Go! (film), 190
MacArthur, Charles, D26 238
  Twentieth Century (play), 35, 82
MacArthur, Linda Lee
  Lorelei, 137
MacBride, Donald
  Good News (film), 150
MacDermot, Galt
  Straws in the Wind, 138
Mackie, Bob
  Lorelei, 136
MacLaine, Shirley, D38 244
  What a Way to Go! (film), 30,
  191, 194, 196
MacMichael, Florence
  On the Town, 51
Madigan, Thomas
  *Party With Betty Comden and
  Adolph Green, A*, 199
*Madwoman of Central Park West,
The*, 35, 48, D57 249, S20
  139, T50 225
  22 Steps Theatre, 35
  Arthur Laurents, 35
  Mobil Showcase Network,
  Summershow, 35
  Phyllis Newman, 35
Mafilm-Robert Halmi, Inc.
  Lily in Love (Jatszani Kell), 207
"Magazine Page, The"
  Revuers, The, 6
Maggart, Brandon
  Applause, 121
  Lorelei, 136
  Straws in the Wind, 138
  Tony Award (nomination),
  Applause, 273
Maggi McNellis Show, RA21 213

324 Comden and Green

Magic of Fred Astaire, The
  Adolph Green, 174
"Main Street"
  On the Town (film) 163
"Make 'Em Laugh," D32 241
  Singin' in the Rain (film), 167
"Make Our Garden Grow," D50 247
"Make Someone Happy," D10 232, D28 239, D54 249
  Do Re Mi, 28, 107, 109, 201
  Party With Betty Comden and Adolph Green, A, 201
Makk, Koroly
  Lily in Love (Jatszani Kell), 207
Mallet, Gina
  By Bernstein, 145
Malone, Ken
  Do Re Mi, 106
Maloney, William
  New Yorkers, The, 207
Mame (film)
  Lucille Ball, 185
Mame (musical)
  Angela Lansbury, 185
  Jerome Lawrence, 185
  Jerry Herman, 185
  Robert E. Lee, 185
"Mamie Is Mimi," D20 236
"Mamushka," D42 245
  Comden and Green (lyrics) 41, 49
Mandan, Robert
  Applause, 121
Mandell, Daniel, T18 217
  Apartment, The (film)
Mandel, Frank
  Good News (film), 149
"Manhattan Downbeat," D04 229
Manilow, Barry
  Madwoman of Central Park West, The, 139
Mann, Alison
  Singin' in the Rain, 127
Mann, Joan
  Billion Dollar Baby, 57
Manning, Jack
  Say, Darling, 101
Mansfield, Victoria
  Subways Are for Sleeping, 70
Manson, Dick

Revuers, The, 5
Mapes, Jacques
  Singin' in the Rain (film), 166
Marasco, Frank
  Peter Pan, 134
March, Hal
  It's Always Fair Weather (film), 177
"March, March," D17 234, D18 235
  It's Always Fair Weather (film), 181
Marchand, Colette
  Two on the Aisle, 91
Marechal Productions, Inc.
  Leonard Bernstein's Theatre Songs, 143
Mark Hellinger Theatre, T30 219
  Doll's Life, A, 38, 85, 88
  Fade Out--Fade In, 30, 74, 77
  Two on the Aisle, 18, 91, 93
Markee, Dwayne
  Diamonds, 141
Marks, Joe E.
  Peter Pan, 134
Marley, Jim
  Do Re Mi, 106
Marlowe, Julie
  Say, Darling, 101
Marre, Albert
  Singin' in the Rain, 129
"Marry Me Now," D39 244
Marrying Kind, The (film)
  Judy Holliday, 188
Marsac, Maurice
  What a Way to Go! (film), 191
"Marseillaise, The,"
  Party With Betty Comden and Adolph Green, A, 201
Marshall, Armina
  Theatre Guild, 23
Marshall, Patricia (Pat), D15 233
  Good News (film), 149
Marshall, Wendell
  Say, Darling, 101
Martel, Remi
  Bonanza Bound!, 62
Martin, Dean, D06 230, D38 244
  Bells Are Ringing (film), 187-190
  What a Way to Go! (film), 30, 191, 194

Martin, Greta
   Jerome Robbins' Broadway, 146
Martin, Hugh, D15 233, D19 235
   Good News (film), 149
   Jerome Robbins' Broadway, 146
   Lorelei, 136
   "Pass That Peace Pipe," 152
Martin, Leila
   Two on the Aisle, 91
Martin, Mary, D21 236, D29 240, D61 250, T43 223, T44 223, T46 223, 224
   Peter Pan, 21, 133
   Tony Award, *Peter Pan*, 135
Martin, Skip, D03 228
   Band Wagon, The (film), 171
   Singin' in the Rain (film), 165
Martin, Stephen G.
   Diamonds, 141
Martin, Virginia
   Say, Darling, 101
Martin Beck Theatre
   Hallelujah, Baby!, 31, 109, 112
   My Sister Eileen (play), 95, 97
Mary Margaret McBride Show, RA22 213
Masella, Arthur
   Diamonds, 140
Maslin, Janet
   Slaves of New York (film), 208
Mason, Craig, D07 230
Mason, Jane
   Two on the Aisle, 92
Masterson, Jeannine
   Bells Are Ringing, 65
Match Game, The, T23 218
Mathews, George, T47 224
   Do Re Mi, 105
Mathews, Joyce
   Barkleys of Broadway, The (film), 154
Mattox, Jean
   Say, Darling, 101
Mattox, Matt
   Band Wagon, The (film), 172
   Say, Darling, 100, 101
Mattson, Wayne
   Lorelei, 137
Matz, Peter, D16 234
   Hallelujah, Baby!, 110
Maxey, Paul

It's Always Fair Weather (film), 177
May, Elaine, T14 217
   Fabulous Fifties, The, 28
Mayer, Louis B.
   On the Town (film), 16, 163
Mayor of New York's Certificate of Excellence
   Comden and Green, 276
McCarten, John
   Do Re Mi, 109
McClain, John
   Bells Are Ringing, 68
   Do Re Mi, 108
   Fade Out--Fade In, 78
   Party With Betty Comden and Adolph Green, A, 202
   Say, Darling, 103
   Subways Are for Sleeping, 73
   Wonderful Town, 98
McClure, Bob
   Do Re Mi, 105
McClure, Linda
   Lorelei, 137
McComb, Bill
   Diamonds, 141
McCord, J. C.
   Two on the Aisle, 91
McCormick, Robert, D07 230
McCracken, Joan, D07 230, D15 233
   Billion Dollar Baby, 14, 57, 60, 152
   Bloomer Girl, 152
   Good News (film), 15, 149, 152, 153
McDaniel, David
   Bells Are Ringing, 65
McDermot, Galt
   Straws in the Wind, 138, 139
McDonald, Ray
   Good News (film), 149
McDonough, Justin
   Hallelujah, Baby!, 110, 111
McFadden, Beverly
   Two on the Aisle, 91
McGarry, William
   Bells Are Ringing (film), 186
McGillin, Howard, D52 248
McGuire Sisters, The, D35 242
McHugh, Jimmy, D33 241

McKay, Don, D23 237
McKean, Aldyn, D07 230
McKeever, Jacqueline, D41 245,
   D45 246, D56 249, T45 223
  Wonderful Town, 98
McKenney, Ruth
  My Sister Eileen, 19, 95
  Wonderful Town, 97
McKenzie, Julia
  On the Twentieth Century
    (London), 83
McKneely, Joey
  Jerome Robbins' Broadway, 146
McLerie, Allyn
  Adolph Green (divorce), 20, 46
  Adolph Green (marriage), 15, 46
  Bonanza Bound!, 15, 61
  George Gaynes (marriage), 20
  On the Town, 15
McMahon, Horace
  Say, Darling, 101
McPherson, Saundra
  Hallelujah, Baby!, 110, 111
Meader, George
  On the Town (film), 162
Mehl, Charlene
  Fade Out--Fade In, 75, 76
Melton, Sidney
  Bonanza Bound!, 61
"Men," D20 236
  Lorelei, 137
Menken, Alan
  Diamonds, 140
Mercer, Johnny, D33 241
Merrick, David, D12 232
  Do Re Mi, 105
  Subways Are For Sleeping, 29,
    69, 73
  Tony Award (nomination), *Do Re
    Mi*, 273
Merrill, Bob, D64 251
Messager, Lily
  On the Town (film) 163
Metro-Goldwyn-Mayer
  Band Wagon, The (film), 171,
    174
  Barkleys of Broadway, The (film),
    153, 155, 173
  Bells Are Ringing (file) 23, 68,
    186, 201
  Easter Parade (film), 174

  Freed Unit, 15
  Good News (film), 14, 149, 151,
    152
  It's Always Fair Weather (film),
    20, 176, 179, 182
  My Favorite Year, 206
  On the Town, 54
  On the Town (film), 16, 161, 163
  Singin' in the Rain, 17, 126
  Singin' in the Rain (film), 165,
    168
  (soundtrack) *Band Wagon, The*
    (film), 174
  (soundtrack) *It's Always Fair
    Weather* (film), 180
  (soundtrack) *Singin' in the Rain*
    (film), 169
  Take Me Out to the Ball Game
    (film), 157
Metro-Goldwyn-Mayer (record)
  On the Town (film), 164
  Take Me Out to the Ball Game
    (film), 160
Metro-Goldwyn Mayer-United
  Artists
  Band Wagon, The (film), 171
  My Favorite Year, 38
  On the Town (video), 161
  Singin' in the Rain, 39, 128
  Singin' in the Rain (film/video),
    165
Metro-Goldwyn-Mayer-United
  Artists (video)
  Good News (film), 149
  It's Always Fair Weather (film),
    176
Metro-Goldwyn-Mayer/CBS
  Bells Are Ringing (video), 186
Metropolitan Opera House
  Fancy Free, 11
"Mexican Hayride," 54
Meyers, Lenny
  Straws in the Wind, 139
Michael, Jeannine
  Subways Are for Sleeping, 70
Michael, Paul
  Bells Are Ringing, 65
  Fade Out--Fade In, 75
Michaels, Frankie
  Tony Award, *Mame* (musical),
    185

"Midas Touch, The," D05 229,
    D06 230
*Middle East Crisis and Hungarian
    Revolt Against Soviet Occupation*,
    T06 215
Miele, Jonathan
    Lorelei, 137
Mielziner, Jo
    Jerome Robbins' Broadway, 146
Miller, Ann, D24 237
    Mame (musical), 185
    On the Town (film), 162, 163
Miller, Ben
    Bonanza Bound!, 61
Miller, Mitch
    *Party With Betty Comden and
    Adolph Green, A*, 199
Miller, Wesley C.
    It's Always Fair Weather (film),
    177
Millholland, Bruce, D26 238
    Napoleon on Broadway, 35, 82
    On the Twentieth Century, 79
Mills, Erie, D52 248
Milton, Frank
    Bells Are Ringing, 65
    On the Town, 51, 52
Milton, Franklin
    Bells Are Ringing (film), 187
"Mine," D26 238
    On the Twentieth Century, 85
Minnelli, Vincente
    Band Wagon, The, 19
    Band Wagon, The (film), 171,
    174, 176
    Bells Are Ringing (film), 24, 68,
    186, 188, 189
Minoff, Tammy
    Will Rogers Follies, The, 114
Minskoff Theatre, T40 221
"Miracle on 51st Street,"
    New York Magazine, 128
Mischer, Don, T38 221
Misita, Mike
    Applause, 122
Miss Liberty, D19 235
    Jerome Robbins' Broadway, 40,
    147
"Miss Lorelei Lee"
    Lorelei, 137
"Miss Turnstiles' Variations," D22
    237
Mistretta, Sal
    On the Twentieth Century, 80
"Misunderstood," D09 231
    Bonanza Bound!, 64
Mitchell, James
    Band Wagon, The (film), 172
    Billion Dollar Baby, 58
Mitchell, Jerry
    Jerome Robbins' Broadway, 146
    Will Rogers Follies, The, 114,
    115
Mitchell, Jim
    Billion Dollar Baby, 57
Mitchell, Keith
    On the Twentieth Century
    (London), 83
Mitchell, Millard
    Singin' in the Rain (film), 166
Mitchell, Steve
    It's Always Fair Weather (film),
    177
Mitchum, Robert, D38 244
    What a Way to Go! (film), 30,
    191, 194
Mitropoulos, Dimitri, 5
Mobil Showcase Network,
    Summershow, T50 225
    *Madwoman of Central Park West,
    The*, 35, 140
Molnar, Ferenc
    Liliom, 2
Monday Nights at Nine
    Cherry Lane Theatre, 23
    Comden and Green, 23
    Gus Schirmer, Jr., 201
    *Party With Betty Comden and
    Adolph Green, A*, 201
Monge, Julio
    Jerome Robbins' Broadway, 146
Montevecchi, Liliane, D52 248
    Follies (concert version), 39, 208
"Moon of My Delight," D60 250
Moonbirds
    Marcel Ayme, 26
    Cort Theatre, 26
Mooney, John
    Bonanza Bound!, 61
Moore, Dana
    Will Rogers Follies, The, 114,
    115

Moore, Jack D.
  On the Town (film), 162
Moore, James
  Do Re Mi, 106
Moore, Robert
  Lorelei, 136
Moore, Roger
  Barkleys of Broadway, The (film), 154
Moranz, Brad
  Singin' in the Rain, 127
Morehouse, Ward
  Billion Dollar Baby, 60
  Two on the Aisle, 93
Moreno, Rita
  Singin' in the Rain (film), 166
Moreno, Victor
  Wonderful Town, 96
Morgan, Roger
  Straws in the Wind, 138
Morgan, Jane
  Mame (musical), 185
Morley, Ruth
  Straws in the Wind, 138
Morning With Comden and Green, A, T24 218
Morosco Theatre
  Party With Betty Comden and Adolph Green, A, 35, 202
Moross, Jerome, D07 230
Moroz, Barbara
  Singin' in the Rain, 127
Morrell, Charles
  Say, Darling, 101
Morris, Carolyn
  Say, Darling, 101
Morris, Garrett
  Hallelujah, Baby!, 110, 111
Morris, John
  Bells Are Ringing, 64
Morse Center, Manhattan's Trinity School
  New Yorkers, The, 207
Morse, Robert
  Say, Darling, 101, 102, 104
Morse, Tom
  Diamonds, 141
Morske, Jim, T17 217
Morton, Arthur, D38 244
  What a Way to Go! (film), 190
"Moses Supposes," D32 241, D33 242
Singin' in the Rain (film), 18, 169
Most Promising New Broadway Actor
  Allen Case, Hallelujah, Baby!, 112
Most Promising New Broadway Actress
  Leslie Uggams, Hallelujah, Baby!, 112
Mostel, Josh
  Straws in the Wind, 138
Motley
  Peter Pan, 133
"Movie Ads," D27 239, D30 240
"Mr. Monotony"
  Shapiro Orchestra, 236
"Mu-Cha-Cha," D05 229
Mulligan, Gerry
  Bells Are Ringing (film), 187
Munderlok, Otts
  Jerome Robbins' Broadway, 146
Munro, Matt, T47 224
Munshin, Jules 20, 179, D24 237, D36 243
  On the Town (film), 17, 162, 163
  Take Me Out to the Ball Game (film), 17, 158
Murray, Lyn, D21 236
Museum of the City of New York
  Bonanza Bound!, 63
Music From Shubert Alley, T13 216
"Music Hour, The" (poem)
  Lady in the Dark,, 29
"Music Is Better Than Words," D17 234
Musical Comedy in America (book), 77, 113, 126
  Applause, 126
  Fade Out--Fade In, 77
  Hallelujah, Baby!, 113
Musical Extravaganza
  Comden and Green, What a Way To Go! (film), 190
  What a Way to Go! (film), 190
Musical Spectacular, A, D58 250
Musicraft (records)
  Night Life in New York, 8
  Revuers, The, 8

Musser, Tharon
   Applause, 121
   Hallelujah, Baby!, 110
   Tony Award (nomination),
      Applause, 273
Mustin, Burt
   What a Way to Go! (film), 191
"My Big Mistake," D39 244
   Will Rogers Follies, The, 118,
      119
"My Darlin' Eileen," D40 245, D41
   245
   Wonderful Town, 100
My Dear Public, 9
   Irving Caesar, 9
   Philadelphia, 9
   Revuers, The, 45
My Favorite Year (film), P07 206
   Adolph Green (Leo Silver), 38,
      48
   Alan Arkin, 38
   Metro-Goldwyn-Mayer, 206
   Metro-Goldwyn-Mayer-United
      Artists, 38
   Peter O'Toole, 38
"My Fortune Is My Face," D14
   233, D64 251
   Fade Out--Fade In, 79
"My Guiding Star," D06 230
   Comden and Green, 188
"My Heart Is Like a Violin," D14
   233
   Fade Out--Fade In, 79
My Mother Was a Fortune Teller
   (revised as)
   Madwoman of Central Park West,
      The, 140
"My One and Only Highland Fling,"
   D04 229
   Barkleys of Broadway, The (film),
      154
"My Own Morning," D16 234, D51
   248, D54 249, D64 251
   Hallelujah, Baby!, 113
My Sister Eileen, 95, 97, 99
   Columbia Pictures, 98
   (source for) *Wonderful Town*, 19
My Sister Eileen, (film)
   Russell, Rosalind, 19
"My Unknown Someone," D39
   244

Will Rogers Follies, The, 115
Myerberg, Michael, D21 236
Myers, Troy
   Jerome Robbins' Broadway, 146
Mylroie, Kathryne
   Two on the Aisle, 91, D37 243
"Mysterious Lady,"
   Party With Betty Comden and
      Adolph Green, A, 201
   Peter Pan, 21, 201

Nadel, Norman
   Hallelujah, Baby!, 113
   Subways Are for Sleeping, 74
Napoleon on Broadway
   Bruce Millholland, 35, 82
Nation, The
   Bells Are Ringing, 68
   Do Re Mi, 109
   Doll's Life, A, 90
   Fade Out--Fade In, 78
   On the Town, 55
   On the Twentieth Century, 83
   Wonderful Town, 99
National Conference for Christians
   and Jews, 42
National Review
   Hallelujah, Baby!, 113
Naughton, Jack
   Say, Darling, 101
NBC Radio
   Blue Network, RA13 212
NBC Television, T02-T09 215-216,
   T12-T13 216, T15-T16 217,
   T20-T31 218-220, T43-T44
   223, T46 223
   Peter Pan, 135
   Revuers, The, 8, 45
Nederlander Productions
   Applause, 121
Nederlander, James M.
   Doll's Life, A, 85
   Tony Award (nomination), *Doll's*
      Life, A, 274
   Tony Award, *Will Rogers Follies,*
      The, 272
   Will Rogers Follies, The, 114
Neenan, Maria
   Jerome Robbins' Broadway, 146
Nesor, Al
   Do Re Mi, 105

Nettum, Mari
   Fade Out--Fade In, 76
Neukum, Bob
   Fade Out--Fade In, 75
Neuman, David
   Lorelei, 137
"Never Met a Man I Didn't Like," D39 244
   Will Rogers Follies, The, 116, 118, 119
"Never, Never Land," D28 239, D29 240, D62 251
   Peter Pan, 21, 134, 201
New Haven
   Wonderful Town, 98
New Leader
   On the Twentieth Century, 84
New Republic, The
   Applause, 125
   Auntie Mame (film), 185
   On the Town (film), 164
   On the Twentieth Century, 84
   Revuers, The, 6
   What a Way to Go! (film), 195
"New Sun in the Sky," D03 228
   Band Wagon, The (film), 173
New Theatre School
   Alvin Hammer, 4
"New Year's Eve," D13 232
   A Doll's Life
New York
   Madwoman of Central Park West, The, 140
New York City Opera
   Candide (revival), 40
New York Drama Critics Award
   Comden and Green, 274
   Wonderful Town, 98
New York Drama Critics Award (nomination)
   Leslie Uggams, *Hallelujah, Baby!*, 112
   Hallelujah, Baby!, 274
New York Herald Tribune
   Say, Darling, 103
   Subways Are for Sleeping, 73
New York Journal American
   Do Re Mi, 108
   Party With Betty Comden and Adolph Green, A, 202
   Say, Darling, 103

New York Magazine
   Doll's Life, A, 89
   Singin' in the Rain, 128, 129
New York Mirror
   Subways Are for Sleeping, 73
New York Newsday
   Will Rogers Follies, The, 118
New York Philharmonic Orchestra 42, D52 248, D56 249, T11 216
New York Philharmonic Symphony Orchestra
   Follies (concert version), 208
New York Post
   Applause, 125
   Billion Dollar Baby, 60
   Diamonds, 141
   Fade Out--Fade In, 78
   Hallelujah, Baby!, 113
   Jerome Robbins' Broadway, 148
   Madwoman of Central Park West, The, 140
   On the Twentieth Century, 83
   Party With Betty Comden and Adolph Green, A, 202, 203
   Peter Pan, 135
   Revuers, The, 5
   Say, Darling, 103
   Singin' in the Rain, 130
   Subways Are for Sleeping, 73
   Two on the Aisle, 93
   Wonderful Town, 99
New York Public Library for the Performing Arts at Lincoln Center 42
   Hallelujah, Baby! (script), 112
New York Times, T49 224
   Adolph Green, "The Day They Made Music on Mt. Scopus," 33
   Applause, 125, 126
   Auntie Mame (film), 185
   Band Wagon, The (film), 175
   Barkleys of Broadway, The (film), 156
   Bells Are Ringing, 68
   Bells Are Ringing (film), 189
   Billion Dollar Baby, 61
   Diamonds, 141
   Do Re Mi, 108, 109
   Doll's Life, A, 88, 89

Index 331

Fade Out--Fade In, 78
Follies (concert version), 208
Funny (film), 208
Good News (film), 152
Hallelujah, Baby!, 113
I'm Getting Married (television), 31
Isn't It Romantic?, 38, 206
It's Always Fair Weather (film), 180
Jerome Robbins' Broadway, 148
Leonard Bernstein's Theatre Songs, 143, 144
Lily in Love (Jatszani Kell), 207
Madwoman of Central Park West, The, 140
On the Town, 55
On the Town (film), 164
"'On the Town' With Comden and Green," 43
On the Twentieth Century, 83
Party With Betty Comden and Adolph Green, A, 202
Peter Pan, 135
Say, Darling, 103, 104
Simon, 206
Singin' in the Rain, 129
Singin' in the Rain (film), 169
Skin of Our Teeth, The, 31
Slaves of New York (film), 208
"So Eat Your Heart Out, Elizabeth Taylor," 1
Steven Kyle (obituary), 37
Subways Are for Sleeping, 73
Take Me Out to the Ball Game (film), 160
Two on the Aisle, 93
What a Way to Go! (film), 194
Will Rogers Follies, The, 117
Wonderful Town, 98
New York Times Metropolitan Party With Betty Comden and Adolph Green, A, 41
New York University
  Betty Comden, Bachelor of Science degree, 2, 45
  Comden and Green (master classes), 37, 48
New York World Telegram
  Billion Dollar Baby, 60
  Subways Are for Sleeping, 74
  Two on the Aisle, 93
  "New York, New York," D19 235, D21, 236, D22 237, D24 238, D27 239, D28 239, D43 246, D45 246, D51 247, D56 249, D62 251, T13 217, T35 220
Jerome Robbins' Broadway, 147
Leonard Bernstein's Theatre Songs, 144
On the Town, 52, 53, 56
On the Town (film), 162
Party With Betty Comden and Adolph Green, A, 200
New Yorker, The
  Applause, 125, 126
  Bells Are Ringing (film), 189
  Billion Dollar Baby, 61
  Do Re Mi, 109
  Doll's Life, A, 89
  Edmund G. Love, Subways Are for Sleeping, 74
  Madwoman of Central Park West, The, 140
  Say, Darling, 104
  Singin' in the Rain, 130
  Two on the Aisle, 94
  What a Way to Go! (film), 195
  Wonderful Town, 99
New Yorkers, The, P09 207
  Adolph Green, 38
  Amanda Green, 38
  "Jealousy," 207
  Murray Schisgal, 38
  Phyllis Newman, 38
  "Pushcart Peddler," 207
  Trinity School, 38
Newcombe, Warren
  Band Wagon, The (film), 171
  Barkleys of Broadway, The (film), 153
  It's Always Fair Weather (film), 177
  On the Town (film), 162
  Singin' in the Rain (film), 166
  Take Me Out to the Ball Game (film), 158
Newman, Barbara
  Bells Are Ringing, 65
Newman, Judy
  Fade Out--Fade In, 76

Newman, Paul
  What a Way to Go! (film), 30, 191, 194, 196, D38 244
Newman, Phyllis, D34 242, D52 248, D57 249, D64 251, T19 218, T23 218, T24 218, T50 225
  Adolph Green (marriage), 26, 27, 47
  Bells Are Ringing, 24
  First Impressions, 24
  Follies (concert version), 39, 208
  Just in Time (autobiography) xiii, 26, 140
  Kennedy Center Honors, Comden and Green, xi, 41
  Madwoman of Central Park West, The, 35, 139, 140
  New Yorkers, The, 38, 207
  On the Town (revival), 34
  Straws in the Wind, 138, 201
  Subways Are For Sleeping, xi, 29, 70
  Tony Award, *Subways Are For Sleeping*, 29, 73
  Wish You Were Here, 24
Newmar, Julie
  Band Wagon, The (film), 172
Newsday
  Harold Prince, 84
Newsweek
  Auntie Mame (film), 185
  Band Wagon, The (film), 175
  Barkleys of Broadway, The (film), 156
  Bells Are Ringing (film), 189
  Do Re Mi, 109
  Fade Out--Fade In, 78
  Good News (film), 152
  Hallelujah, Baby!, 113
  On the Town (film), 164
  Say, Darling, 103
  Singin' in the Rain, 130
  Singin' in the Rain (film), 170
  Subways Are for Sleeping, 74
  What a Way to Go! (film), 195
  Will Rogers Follies, The, 118
Newton, John
  Peter Pan, 134
Nicholas, Fayard T41 222
Nicholas, Harold T41 222

Nichols, Billy
  Straws in the Wind, 138, 139
Nichols, Lewis
  Billion Dollar Baby, 61
  On the Town, 55
Nichols, Mike, 28, T14 217
  Fabulous Fifties, The, 28
  Kennedy Center Honors, Comden and Green, xi
  Singin' in the Rain, 129
Nickerson, Dawn
  Do Re Mi, 106
Nickerson, Wendy
  Subways Are for Sleeping, 70
Night Life in New York
  Musicraft, 8
Nine Sinatra Songs, 128
  Twyla Tharp, 39
"No Man Left for Me," D39 244
  Will Rogers Follies, The, 116
"No More Mornings," D13 232
  A Doll's Life
No, No, Nanette, 152
  Irving Caesar, 9
Nolan, Kathy
  Peter Pan, 133, 134
Nolfi, Ed
  Applause, 122
Norman Cloutier Orchestra, RA01 211
Norman Luboff Choir, The, D56 249
Norman, Hal
  On the Twentieth Century, 79, 80
Norworth, Jack, D36 243
  Diamonds, 141
  Take Me Out to the Ball Game (film), 160
Noseworthy, Jack
  Jerome Robbins' Broadway, 146
"Not Mine," D16 234
  Hallelujah, Baby!, 113
Notara, Darrell
  Hallelujah, Baby!, 110, 111
Notes on Broadway, xii, 44
  "Jule Styne," *Bells Are Ringing* (film), 22
  "Jule Styne," *Peter Pan*, 21
"Notice Me"
  Fade Out--Fade In, 77

Nova, Lou
  What a Way to Go! (film), 191
"Now I Have Someone," D35 242,
  D63 251
  (cut from *Subways Are For
  Sleeping*)
"Now's the Time," D16 234
  Hallelujah, Baby!
Nurock, Kirk
  *Madwoman of Central Park West,
  The*, 139
Nusbaum, Jane C.
  Hallelujah, Baby!, 110
  Tony Award, *Hallelujah, Baby!*,
  271
Nyack-Tappen Zee Playhouse
  *Party With Betty Comden and
  Adolph Green, A*, 201
Nyberg, Mary Ann
  Band Wagon, The (film), 171
NYC Commission on Human
  Rights
  Will Rogers Follies, The, 117
Nye, Ben
  What a Way to Go! (film), 190
NYPL, Billy Rose Theatre
  Collection
  Doll's Life, A, 88
  *Madwoman of Central Park West,
  The*, 140
NYPL, Performing Arts Research
  Center
  Billion Dollar Baby, 59

"O! My Mysterious Lady," D27-29
  239-240, D62 251
  Peter Pan, 135
  *Party With Betty Comden and
  Adolph Green, A*, 200
"O'Brien to Ryan to Goldberg,"
  D36 243
  Take Me Out to the Ball Game
  (film), 16, 159-161
O'Brien, Timothy
  Doll's Life, A, 85, 90
O'Connor, Donald 38, 130, D32
  241
  Singin' in the Rain (film), 166,
  169
O'Connor, John J., T49 224
  Applause, 125

O'Curran, Charles
  Bells Are Ringing (film), 187
O'Day, Kevin
  Singin' in the Rain, 127
O'Moore, Pat
  What a Way to Go! (film), 191
O'Steen, Tom
  Bells Are Ringing, 65
O'Toole, Peter
  My Favorite Year, 38, 206
Oakland, Sue, T23 218
Obie Award
  *Party With Betty Comden and
  Adolph Green, A*, 23, 201, 274
Ochoa, Steve
  Jerome Robbins' Broadway, 146
Oesterman, Phillip
  Will Rogers Follies, The, 114
"Oh, So Nice," D60 250
"Oh, Those Thirties," D14 233
"Ohio," D28 239, D40 245, D41
  245, D43 246, D45 246, D51
  247, D56 249, D62 251
  *Leonard Bernstein's Theatre
  Songs*, 144
  *Party With Betty Comden and
  Adolph Green, A*, 200
  Wonderful Town, 96, 100
Ohman, Susan
  Lorelei, 137
Oklahoma!, 54-56, 68
Olivier, Sir Laurence, T26 219
Ollmann, Kurt, D50 247
"On a Sunday by the Sea," D19
  235
  Jerome Robbins' Broadway
"On My Own," D05 229
  Bells are Ringing
On the Town (stage and film), xi,
  11-15, 17, 20, 21, 23, 31, 32,
  39, 40, 43, 46, 54, 55, 60, 99,
  161, 144, 147, 148, 200, 203,
  D19 235, D21-D25 236-238,
  D27 239, D28 239, D43 246,
  D45 246, D51 247, D53 248,
  D56 249, D61 250, D62 251,
  S01 51-56, T11 216, T19 218,
  T35 220
On the Town
  Adelphi Theatre, 14, 51, 54

Comden and Green
  (book/lyrics), 11, 51, 54-56
Fancy Free, 11, 53
George Abbott, 11, 51, 54
Jerome Robbins, 11, 51, 53, 56
Leonard Bernstein, 11, 51, 53, 55, 56
Nancy Walker, 51, 56
"New York, New York," 52, 56
Oliver Smith, 11, 51, 54
Paul Feigay, 11, 51, 54
On the Town (concert version)
  Comden and Green, 41, 42, 49
  London Symphony Orchestra, 42
  PBS Television, 42
On The Town (film), 46, F04 161-165
  Academy Award, 164
  Arthur Freed, 16, 17, 162, 163
  Comden and Green, 16, 17, 161, 164
  Frank Sinatra, 17, 162
  Gene Kelly, 17, 162, 164
  Jules Munshin, 17, 161, 164
  Leonard Bernstein, 17, 161, 164
  Louis B. Mayer, 16, 17, 163
  Metro-Goldwyn-Mayer, 16, 17, 161
  Radio City Music Hall, 17
  Roger Edens, 17, 161, 163
  Screenwriters' Guild Award, 17, 164, 275
  Stanley Donen, 17, 162, 164
On the Town (revival) 34
  Bernadette Peters, 34
  Comden and Green, Long Island University, 49
On the Town (songs)
  Leonard Bernstein's Theatre Songs, 144
"On the Town," Opening D61 250
"On the Town," Opening Extended Version D61 250
On the Twentieth Century, 43, 48, D26 238, D53 248, P03 205, S07 79-85, T32 220,
  (based on) *Twentieth Century* (play), 35
  Betty Comden (Letitia Primrose), 35, 205
  Comden and Green
    (book/lyrics), 35, 79-84
  Cy Coleman, 35, 79, 82
  Grammy Award (nomination), 276
  Harold Prince, 35, 82, 84
  Imogene Coca, 35, 82
  John Cullum, 80, 82, 84
  Judy Kaye, 80, 82, 84
  Kevin Kline, 80, 82, 84
  London, 35
  Madeline Kahn, 80, 82, 84
  Robin Wagner, 35, 79, 82, 85
  St. James Theatre, 35, 79
  Tony Awards, 35, 82, 272
Once in a Lifetime, 78
Once Upon a Mattress
  Carol Burnett (Princess Winifred), 30
"Once Upon a Time," D17 234, D18 235
It's Always Fair Weather (film), 181
One for the Money
  Nancy Hamilton, 6
  Gene Kelly, 6
"One Hallowe'en," D01 227
"One Hundred Easy Ways to Lose a Man," D28 239, D40 245, D41 245, D51 247
Party With Betty Comden and Adolph Green, A, 200
Wonderful Town, 96, 99, 100
"One of a Kind," D01 227
Applause
Onrubia, Cynthia
  Jerome Robbins' Broadway, 146
Opsahl, Jason
  Will Rogers Follies, The, 115
Original Cast! 100 Years of the American Musical Theater!, D59 250
Orion
  Simon, 206
Orloff, Penny
  Doll's Life, A, 85
Ormandy, Eugene, T36 221
  Kennedy Center Lifetime Achievement Award, 38
Orr, Mary
  All About Eve, 33
  Applause, 121, 224

Orry-Kelly
  Auntie Mame (film), 182
Osato, Sono
  On the Town, 15, 52
Osterman, Lester
  Fade Out--Fade In, 75
  Say, Darling, 100
"Our Favorite Son," D39 244
  Will Rogers Follies, The
"Our Private World," D26 238,
    D51 248
  On The Twentieth Century
Outer Circle Award for 1966-1967
  Leslie Uggams, *Hallelujah, Baby!*,
    31, 112
Outer Circle Citation
  Betty Franklin, *Applause*, 124

Page, Evelyn
  Wonderful Town, 96
Page, Janis
  Mame (musical), 185
Pajama Game, The
  "7 1/2 Cents," 22
Pal Joey, 55, 60, 160
Palace Theatre
  Applause, 34, 121, 124
  Lorelei, 34, 136, 138
  Will Rogers Follies, The, 41, 114, 116
Palmer, Christopher, D58 250
Palmer, Peter
  Lorelei, 136
Palumbo, Dennis
  My Favorite Year, 206
Pan, Hermes
  Barkleys of Broadway, The (film), 153, 155
"Papa, Won't You Dance with Me?," D19 235
  Jerome Robbins' Broadway
Papell, Lee
  Wonderful Town, 95, 96
Pappas, Theodore
  Diamonds, 141
Parade (ballet), 130
Parade (musical), D07 230
Paramount Pictures
  Addams Family, The (film), 41
  Duffy's Tavern 10
Parent, Gail, D20 236

Lorelei, 136, 137
"Paris, Paris," D20 236
  Lorelei
Parker, Dell
  Two on the Aisle, 92
Parker, Dorothy, D50 247
  Candide, 40
Parker, Eleanor, D01 227
Parker, Patricia
  Doll's Life, A, 86
Parker, Suzy, T14 217
  Fabulous Fifties, The, 28
Parkes, Eddie
  Take Me Out to the Ball Game (film), 158
Parks, Hildy, T26 219, T30 219
Parry, Leslie
  Two on the Aisle, 91
Partington, Arthur
  Billion Dollar Baby, 57
Party With Betty Comden and Adolph Green, A, xi, xii, 23, 26, 41, 42, 47, 94, 188, 190, 205, 206, 216, D08 231, D27 238, D28 239, P01 199-203, RA23 213, T06 215, T10 216, T34 220, T37 221
  Arts and Entertainment Cable Network, 202
  "Banshee Sisters, The," 200
  Cable Television, 38, 49, 202
  "Capital Gains," 200
  Capitol Records, 43, 202
  "Captain Hook's Waltz," 201
  "Carried Away," *On the Town*, 200
  "Catch Our Act at the Met," 200
  "Drink to Me Only With Thine Eyes," 201
  "Flight of the Bumblebee, The," 200
  "French Lesson, The," 200
  Golden Theatre, 23
  Grammy Award (nomination), 275
  "I Said Good Morning," 33, 199, 200
  "If You Hadn't--But You Did," 200
  It's Always Fair Weather, 33
  "Inspiration," 200, 201

336 Comden and Green

Julliard School of Music, 34, 201
"Just in Time," 200, 201
Kaufman Auditorium, 34
Kennedy Center for the Performing Arts, 42
Little Theatre, 202
Loeb Theatre Center, Harvard University, 201
"Lonely Town," 200
"Lost Word, The," 139, 201
"Lucky to Be Me," 200
Monday Nights at Nine, 201
"Make Someone Happy," 201
"Marseillaise, The," 201
Morosco Theatre, 35, 202
"Mysterious Lady," 201
"Never, Never Land," 201
"New York, New York," 200
Nyack-Tappen Zee Playhouse, 201
"Ohio," 200
"One Hundred Easy Ways to Lose a Man," 200
"Party's Over, The," 200, 201
Philadelphia, 202
"Quiet Girl, A," 200
Reader's Digest, The (sketch), 199, 200
Revuers, The, 199, 200
Screenwriters, The (sketch), 200
"Simplified Language," 139
"Some Other Time," 200
"Stars and Stripes Forever," 201
Stet and Out Take Records, 202
Suffolk YM-YWHA (Commack), 39
Toronto, 202
Variety (sketch), 199
Westport Country Playhouse, 201
WNEW Television, *Summershow*, 202
"Wrong Note Rag, The," 200
"Party's Over, The," D05 229, D06 230, D27 239, D28 239, D46 246, D49 247, D54 249
Bells Are Ringing, xii, 67, 69, 201
Party With Betty Comden and Adolph Green, A, 200, 201
"Pass the Football," D40 245, D41 245, D51 247
"Pass That Peace Pipe," D15 234
Good News (film), 150
Patinkin, Mandy, D52 248
Follies (concert version), 39, 208
Patrick, Julian
  Bells Are Ringing, 65
Patrick, Lee
  Auntie Mame (film), 182
Patterson, Dick, D14 233
  Fade Out--Fade In, 75
Patterson, Kelly
  Jerome Robbins' Broadway, 146
Paul Taylor Dance Company, 42
Payne, Sarah, D33 241
Payne, Virginia
  Fade Out--Fade In, 75
Payton, Bruce
  Subways Are for Sleeping, 70
PBS Television T33 220, T39 221
Pearce, Alice D24 237
  On the Town, 52
  On the Town (film), 162
"Pearl of the Persian Sea"
  On the Town (film), 163
Pearson, Paulette, D64 251
"Peasants' Quartette," John Frank, 4
Peck, Gregory, T41 222
  Will Rogers Follies, The, 115
Peck, Steven
  Bells Are Ringing (film), 187
Penn, Robert
  Bonanza Bound!, 61
Pentecost, George
  Straws in the Wind, 138
Pentecost, James, D64 251
Perelman, S. J.
  Party With Betty Comden and Adolph Green, A, 202
Perez, Luis
  Jerome Robbins' Broadway, 146
Performers Against Racism
  Will Rogers Follies, The, 117
Perito, Nick, T38 221
Perkins, John
  Bells Are Ringing, 65
Perkins, Nancy
  Bells Are Ringing, 65

Perry, Frank
  Party With Betty Comden and Adolph Green, A, 199
Perselle, Jodi
  Fade Out--Fade In, 76
Personette, Joan
  Two on the Aisle, 91
Peter Pan, 21, 46, D19 235, D27-D29 239, D53 248, D62 251, D64 251, S17 133-135, T43 223, T44 223, T46 223
  "Captain Hook's Waltz," 21, 135, 201
  Carolyn Leigh, 21, 133, 134
  Cyril Ritchard, 21, 134
  "I Gotta Crow," 21
  "I Won't Grow Up," 21
  Jerome Robbins, 21, 133, 134
  Jerome Robbins' Broadway, 40, 147
  Jule Styne, 21, 133
  Los Angeles, San Francisco, 21
  Mark ("Moose") Charlap, 21, 133, 134
  Mary Martin, 21, 133, 134
  "Never, Never Land," 21, 134, 201, 240
  "O! My Mysterious Lady," 21, 135, 200
  Television, 21, 135
  Video, 21, 135
  Winter Garden Theatre, 21, 135
Peters, Bernadette
  On the Town (revival), 34
  Slaves of New York (film), 40, 208
Peters, Lisa
  Doll's Life, A, 86
Peterson, Alan
  Hallelujah, Baby!, 110
Peterson, Kurt
  By Bernstein, 145
Petri, Carol
  Applause, 122
Pfeiffer, Ed
  Do Re Mi, 106
Philadelphia
  Do Re Mi, 108
Phoenix Theatre
  Isn't It Romantic?, 206
Piaf, Edith, T10 216

"Piano Concerto," D04 229
  Barkleys of Broadway
Pierson, Thomas
  By Bernstein, 145
Pins and Needles of 1922
  Irving Caesar, 9
Piper, Robert
  Peter Pan, 134
Pippin, Donald, D01 227
  Applause, 121
"Pirate Song," D29 240
  Peter Pan
Pirate, The (film)
  Judy Garland, 155
Pirates of Penzance, The
  Adolph Green, Pirate King, 2
Pitot, Genevieve
  Two on the Aisle, 91
Planet of the Apes (film)
  Twentieth Century-Fox, 194
Playwrights Horizon Theatre
  Isn't It Romantic?, 38, 206
Plummer, Christopher
  Lily in Love (Jatszani Kell), 38, 207
Plunkett, Walter
  Bells Are Ringing (film), 187
  Singin' in the Rain (film), 166
PM
  Billion Dollar Baby, 60
  On the Town, 55
PM East/PM West, T19 218
Poe, Aileen
  Fade Out--Fade In, 75
Poe, Virginia
  Billion Dollar Baby, 57
Pool, Lawrence
  Subways Are for Sleeping, 70
Porte, Mrs. Elliott
  Phyllis Newman's sister, 26
Porter, Cole 203, D33 241
Poser, Linda
  On the Twentieth Century, 80
Post
  Bells Are Ringing, 68
"Power," D13 232
  A Doll's Life
Prager, Stanley
  Two on the Aisle, 91
"Prehistoric Man," D24 237
  On the Town (film), 162

Prescott, Tina
  Bonanza Bound!, 61
"Presents for Mrs. Rogers," D39 244
Will Rogers Follies, The
Previn, André 16, 20, D06 230, D17 234, D27 239, D28 239
  Bells Are Ringing (film), 186, 188
  Good Morning, Good Night (children's book), 33
  "I Said Good Morning," 199
  Invitation to the Dance (film), 20, 179
  It's Always Fair Weather (film), 176, 179
  Party With Betty Comden and Adolph Green, A, 199
Price, Leontyne, T35 220
Pride and Prejudice, 26
Prince, Daisy, D52 248
Prince, Faith
  Jerome Robbins' Broadway, 146
Prince, Harold
  Candide (revival), 40
  Diamonds, 140, 141
  Doll's Life, A, 37, 85, 88, 89
  Follies (concert version), 208
  On the Twentieth Century, 35, 79, 84
  Tony Award (nomination), *Dolls Life, A*, 274
  Tony Award (nomination), *On the Twentieth Century*, 273
Prince of Wales Theatre (London)
  On the Town, 54
Private World of Leonard Bernstein, The
  John Gruen, 33
Prizker, Cindy
  Singin' in the Rain, 127
Producers Circle 2, Inc.
  Tony Award (nomination), *On the Twentieth Century*, 273
Producers Guild of America (formerly) Screen Producers Guild, 180
Producers Showcase T43 223, T44 223
Program of Music and Fun, A, RA01-RA23 211-214
Public Broadcasting Service, Great Performances Series
  Follies (concert version), 39, 208
Pushcart Peddler
  Ensemble Studio Theatre, 207
  New Yorkers, The, 207
  Trinity School, Manhattan, 207
"Put a Shine on Your Shoes," *Band Wagon, The* (film), 172

"Quiet Girl, A," D27 239, D40 245, D41 245, D51 247, D56 249, D62 251
  Leonard Bernstein's Theatre Songs, 31, 144
  Party With Betty Comden and Adolph Green, A, 200
  Wonderful Town, 31, 100, 200

Raaf, Vici
  Bonanza Bound!, 61
Raby, Roger Allan
  Fade Out--Fade In, 75, 76
Rachel, Ann
  Hallelujah, Baby!, 110
Rackmil, Gladys
  Madwoman of Central Park West, The, 139
Radford, Robert
  Singin' in the Rain, 127
Radio Broadcasting's 20th Anniversary, RA20 213
Radio City Music Hall
  Auntie Mame (film), 22, 23, 185
  Band Wagon, The (film), 19, 174
  Bells Are Ringing (film), 24, 189
  Good News (film), 15
  It's Always Fair Weather (film), 20, 180
  My Sister Eileen (film), 97
  On the Town (film), 17, 54, 164
  Revuers, The, 8, 45, 205
  Singin' in the Rain (film), 18, 169
Rae, Sheilah
  Applause, 122
Ragaini, Carolyn
  Do Re Mi, 105, 106
Raguse, Elmer
  What a Way to Go! (film), 190
"Rain on the Roof," D52 248
  Follies (concert version), 39, 208

Index   339

Rainbow Room
   Revuers, The, 8, 45
Raley, Wade
   Diamonds, 141
Ramin, Sid, D19 235, D31 240
   Jerome Robbins' Broadway, 146
Ramsel, Gina
   Lorelei, 137
Randall, Betty, RA19 213
Randolph, Robert
   Applause, 121
   Tony Award (nomination),
      Applause, 273
Random House
   Applause, 124
   Bells Are Ringing (libretto), 67, 68
   Fade Out--Fade In, 77
Raposo, Joe
   Madwoman of Central Park West, The, 139
"Rare Wines," D13 233
   A Doll's Life
"Rats and Mice and Fish," D13 233
   A Doll's Life
Rawe, Tom
   Singin' in the Rain, 127
Ray, Ellen
   Bells Are Ringing, 65
Rayburn, Gene, T23 218
Raye, Carol
   Bonanza Bound!, 61
Raye, John
   Two on the Aisle, 91
RCA Red Seal
   Follies (concert version), 39, 208
RCA Victor
   Do Re Mi, 108
   Peter Pan, 135
   Say, Darling, 103
Reader's Digest, The (sketch), D27 239, D28 239, D30 240
   Party With Betty Comden and Adolph Green, A, 199, 200
"Real Coney Island, The," D22 237
Reams, Lee Roy
   Applause, 121
   Lorelei, 136
Reardon, John, D10 231, D22 237, D45 246, D55 249, D56 249
   Do Re Mi, 105
Reed, Anthony
   Billion Dollar Baby, 56, 57
Reed, Michael, D33 241
Reed, Richard
   Bonanza Bound!, 62
Reed, Stephen
   Jerome Robbins' Broadway, 146
Regan, Charles
   Take Me Out to the Ball Game (film), 158
Regan, Joe
   Fade Out--Fade In, 75
Regina, 29
Reid, Elliott
   Two on the Aisle, 91-93
Reiley, Orrin
   Applause, 121
Reilley, Victor
   Two on the Aisle, 92
Reiner, Michelle
   Bells Are Ringing, 65
Reiss, Marvin
   Party With Betty Comden and Adolph Green, A, 199
Reiss, Peggy
   Two on the Aisle, 91
Reiss, Stuart A.
   What a Way to Go! (film), 190
Reitel, Elizabeth
   Adolph Green (marriage), 9, 45
   Remember These, 47, D60 250
Remick, Lee, D52 248
   Follies (concert version), 39, 208
"Repent," D26 238, D51 248
   On the Twentieth Century, 81
Resin, Dan
   Fade Out--Fade In, 75
Resnais, Alain
   I Want to Go Home (film), 209
Revuers, The xi, xiii, 4-11, 43, 63, 64, 67, 170, 205, D27 239, D28 239, D30 240, RA01-RA20 211-213, T01 215, T02 215
   Blackstone Hotel (Chicago), 10
   Blue Angel, 10
   Boston Post, 9
   Comden and Green, 23

340 Comden and Green

Consolidated Edison (radio), 8
"Girl with Two Left Feet," 8
Greenwich Village (film), 11, 46
Hollywood, 46
Judy Holliday, 22
Kurt Frings, 10
My Dear Public, 45
NBC Radio, 45
NBC Television, 8
New Republic, The, 6
New York Post, 5
Party With Betty Comden and Adolph Green, A, 199, 200
Radio City Music Hall, 8, 45
Revuers, The (radio programs) 211
Rainbow Room, 8, 45
Six and Company (new name), 3
Trocadero (Hollywood), 10, 15, 46
Twentieth Century-Fox, 11
Two on the Aisle, 94
Variety, 8, 9
Village Vanguard, 3-6, 9, 45
Westport Country Playhouse, 6
Revuers, The (Musicraft)
"Joan Crawford Fan Club, The," 8
"Night Life in New York," 8
Reynolds, Debbie, 130, D32 241
Singin' in the Rain (film), 166
Reynolds, Frank
Two on the Aisle, 92
Rice, Helen
Wonderful Town, 96
Rich, Frank
Diamonds, 141
Doll's Life, A, 88
Follies (concert version), 208
Jerome Robbins' Broadway, 148
Singin' in the Rain, 129
Will Rogers Follies, The, 117
Richards, Jeff
Lorelei, 137
Richards, Martin
Doll's Life, A, 85
Tony Award, *Will Rogers Follies, The*, 272
Tony Award (nomination), *Dolls Life, A*, 274

Will Rogers Follies, The, 114
Richardson, John
Fade Out--Fade In, 75, 76
Riddle, Nelson, D38 244
What a Way to Go! (film), 190
"Ride Through the Night," D34 242, D35 242
Subways Are For Sleeping
Ries, Irving G.
Barkleys of Broadway, The (film), 153
It's Always Fair Weather (film), 177
Singin' in the Rain (film), 166
Rigby, Cathy
Peter Pan, 135
Rigby, Harry
Hallelujah, Baby!, 110
Tony Award, *Hallelujah, Baby!*, 271
"Right Girl for Me, The," D36 243
Take Me Out to the Ball Game (film), 16, 160, 161
Riker, Robert
Lorelei, 136, 137
Riley, Larry
Diamonds, 141
Rimmer, Shane, D25 238
Ritchard, Cyril, D29 240, T46 224
Captain Hook, *Peter Pan*, 21, 133, 134
Tony Award, *Peter Pan*, 135
Ritter, Thelma
All About Eve, 125
Rittman, Trude
Peter Pan, 133
"River Song, The"
Say, Darling, 102, 104
Rivera, James
Jerome Robbins' Broadway, 147
Rivers, Marsha
Bells Are Ringing, 65
RKO, 157
Robards, Jason, 33
Robbins, Gale
Barkleys of Broadway, The (film), 154
Robbins, Jerome 40, 130, 223, D19 235
Ballet Theatre Company, 11, 40, 53

Bells Are Ringing, 22, 64, 68
Billion Dollar Baby, 14, 56, 60
Fancy Free, xi, 11, 40, 53
Jerome Robbins' Broadway,
  146-148
On the Town, 14, 51, 56
Peter Pan, 21, 133, 134
Singin' in the Rain, 129
Skin of Our Teeth, The, 31
Tony Award, Jerome Robbins'
  Broadway, 40
Tony Award (nomination), Bells
  Are Ringing, 273
West Side Story, 21
Robbins, Tom
  Jerome Robbins' Broadway, 147
Roberts, Ralph
  Bells Are Ringing (film), 187
Robin, Leo, D20 236, D64 251
  Gentlemen Prefer Blondes, 93
  Lorelei (lyrics), 136, 137
Robinson, Chris
  Wonderful Town, 96
Robinson, Lance
  Will Rogers Follies, The, 115
Rodda, Richard
  Peter Pan, 133
  Tony Award, Peter Pan, 135
Rodgers, Mary
  Madwoman of Central Park West,
    The, 139
Rodgers, Richard, D19 235, D60
  250
  Jerome Robbins' Broadway, 146
Rodzinski, Artur, 9
Rogers, Ginger 173, D04 228
  Barkleys of Broadway, The (film),
    16, 154-157
Rogers, Suzanne
  Hallelujah, Baby!, 111
Rogow, Leo
  It's Always Fair Weather (film),
    181
Roland, Steve
  Bells Are Ringing, 65
  Do Re Mi, 105, 106
Roman, Paul Reid
  Hallelujah, Baby!, 111
Romoff, Colin
  Say, Darling, 100
Ronson, Cleo

What a Way to Go! (film), 191
Roosevelt, President Theodore
  Cradle Will Rock, The, 29
Roquemore, Larry
  Subways Are for Sleeping, 70
Roscoe, Burton
  Billion Dollar Baby, 60
Rose, George
  Mystery of Edwin Drood, The,
    129
Rose, Helen
  Good News (film) 149
  It's Always Fair Weather (film),
    177
  On the Town (film), 162
  Take Me Out to the Ball Game
    (film), 157
Rosenberg, Ben
  Billion Dollar Baby, 60
Rosenfield, Lois F.
  Singin' in the Rain, 127, 128
Rosenfield, Maurice
  Singin' in the Rain, 39, 127-129
Rosenstock, Milton, D05 229,
  D20 236, D34 242
  Bells Are Ringing, 64
  Subways Are for Sleeping, 69
Rosenthal, Jean
  Cradle Will Rock, The, 30
Rosin, George, T43 223
Ross, Emily
  Billion Dollar Baby, 56
Ross, Herbert, D52 248
  Follies (concert version), 208
Rosson, Harold
  On the Town (film), 162
  Singin' in the Rain (film), 166
Rostopovich, Mstislav, T33 220
Roth, Ann
  Singin' in the Rain, 126
Roveta, Sandra
  Subways Are for Sleeping, 70
Rowe, Hansford
  Singin' in the Rain, 127
Royal Philharmonic Orchestra,
  D58 250
Rubanoff, Jaye
  Peter Pan, 134
Rubin, Arthur, D52 248
  Two on the Aisle, 91

Rule, Charles
  On the Twentieth Century, 79, 80
"Rumble, The," D19 235
  Jerome Robbins' Broadway
Russell, A. J., T14 217
Russell, George
  Jerome Robbins' Broadway, 147
Russell, Rosalind
  Auntie Mame, 22, 182, 184, D02 228
  Auntie Mame (film), 182, 185, 186
  Donaldson Award, *Wonderful Town*, 98
  My Sister Eileen, 95, 97
  My Sister Eileen (film) 19
  Tony Award, *Wonderful Town*, 20, 271
  Tony Award (nomination) *Auntie Mame* (play), 184
  Wonderful Town, 19, 95, 98, 99, D02 228, D40 244, D41 245, D45 246, D51 247, D56 249, T45 223
Rutherford, Judith
  Leonard Bernstein's Theatre Songs, 143

"Sabre Dance," D04 229
Saddler, Donald
  Tony Award, *Wonderful Town*, 271
  Wonderful Town, 95
Saffran, Christina
  Singin' in the Rain, 127
Sager, Carol Bayer
  Madwoman of Central Park West, The, 139
Sager, Gene
  Singin' in the Rain, 127
"Sailors on the Town," D19 235
  Jerome Robbins' Broadway, 147
Salinger, Conrad, D03 228, D04 229, D58 250
  Band Wagon, The (film), 171
  Barkleys of Broadway, The (film), 153
  On the Town (film), 17, 162
  Singin' in the Rain (film), 165
"Salzburg," D05 229
  Bells Are Ringing
Sam S. Shubert Theatre, T26

219, T32 220
  Bells Are Ringing, 64, 67
  Bells Are Ringing (film), 22
  Bonanza Bound!, 15, 61, 63
Sam S. Shubert Theatre (Boston)
  Wonderful Town, 98
Sameth, Marten
  On the Town, 51
Samuel Bernstein Hair Company, 5
Samuel French
  Doll's Life, A (libretto), 88
Sanders, Donna
  Bells Are Ringing, 65
  Do Re Mi, 105, 106
Sanders, George
  All About Eve, 125
Sanford, Richard
  Billion Dollar Baby, 57, 58
"Sarah Bernhardt Audition," D04 229
  The Barkleys of Broadway
Saturday Review of Literature, The
  Applause, 125
  Auntie Mame (film), 186
  Band Wagon, The (film), 175
  Bells Are Ringing, 68
  Fade Out--Fade In, 78
  It's Always Fair Weather (film), 181
  On the Town, 55
  On the Twentieth Century, 83
  Say, Darling, 103, 104
  Singin' in the Rain (film), 170
  Wonderful Town, 99
Saunders, Betty
  Billion Dollar Baby, 57
Saverino, Anthony
  Subways Are for Sleeping, 70
Sawyer, Carol
  Two on the Aisle, 91
"Say When"
  By Bernstein, 145
Say, Darling, 46, 203, D31 241, S11 100-105
  Abe Burrows, 22, 100, 103
  ANTA Theatre, 22, 100, 102
  Comden and Green (lyrics), 22, 100, 103, 104
  Jule Styne, 22, 100, 103, 104
  Marian Bissell, 22, 100, 103, 104

Richard Bissell, 22, 100, 102-104
"Say, Darling," 102
Sazuki, Pat, T10 216
Schanuel, Greg
  Jerome Robbins' Broadway, 147
Scheeder, Louis W.
  Diamonds, 141
Schirmer, Jr., Gus, T08 216
  Cherry Lane Theatre, 23, 201
Schisgal, Murray
  New Yorkers, The, 38, 207
Schloss, Edwin H.
  Bonanza Bound!, 64
Schneider, Rick
  Lorelei, 137
"Schneider's Miracle"
  Two on the Aisle, 93
Schoenbaum, Charles
  Good News (film), 149
Schuman, William, T33 220
Schutzman, Siegfried (Steven Kyle),
  Betty Comden (marriage), 10
Schwab, Lawrence
  Good News (musical comedy/film), 149, 151
Schwartz, Arthur, 19, D03 228
  Band Wagon, The (film), 171, 174
Schwartz, Jean
  "Hat My Dear Old Father Wore Upon St. Patrick's Day," 160
  Take Me Out to the Ball Game (film), 160
Schwartz, Stephen
  Straws in the Wind, 138, 139
Scott, Kenneth (Ken)
  Hallelujah, Baby!, 110, 111
Scott, Pippa
  Auntie Mame (film), 182
Scott, Walter M.
  What a Way to Go! (film), 190
Scottish Opera
  Candide (revival), 40
Screen Producers Guild
  (renamed) Producers Guild of America, 180
Screen Writers, The (sketch)
  Party With Betty Comden and Adolph Green, A, 200, D28 239

Screenwriters Guild Award
  Comden and Green, *Bells Are Ringing*, 24, 189, 275
  Comden and Green, *Singin' in the Rain* (film), 18, 169, 275
  Comden and Green, *On the Town*, 17, 164, 275
Screenwriters Guild Award (nominations),
  The Barkleys of Broadway, 16, 156
  It's Always Fair Weather, 21, 180, 275
Seaman, David
  Doll's Life, A, 86
Seibert, Jeannette
  Applause, 122
Selden, Albert W.
  Tony Award, *Hallelujah, Baby!*, 271
  Hallelujah, Baby!, 110
  Selections from Fancy Free and On the Town, D61 251
Sell, Janie
  By Bernstein, 145
Sendrey, Albert
  Peter Pan, 133
Seroy, Helena
  Wonderful Town, 96
Serrano, Nestor
  Diamonds, 141
Sessions, Almira
  It's Always Fair Weather (film), 177
Sevareid, Eric, T14 217
  Fabulous Fifties, The, 28, 217
Sewell, Blanche
  Take Me Out to the Ball Game (film), 158
"Sextet," D26 238
  On The Twentieth Century
Shaer, Carolsue
  Fade Out--Fade In, 76
Shaiman, Marc, D42 246
  "Mamushka," 41
Shall We Dance? (film), 156, D19 235
  Jerome Robbins' Broadway
Shamroy, Leon
  What a Way to Go! (film), 190

Shapiro, Debbie
   Jerome Robbins' Broadway, 147
Sharaff, Irene
   Billion Dollar Baby, 56, 60
   Bonanza Bound!, 61
   Do Re Mi, 105
   Hallelujah, Baby!, 110
   Jerome Robbins' Broadway, 146
   Tony Award (nomination),
      Hallelujah, Baby!, 273
Sharma, Barbara
   Hallelujah, Baby!, 110
Sharpe, John
   Subways Are for Sleeping, 69, 70
Shaw, Robert, T41 222
Shaw, Suzanne
   Do Re Mi, 105, 106
Shawn, Dick, T48 224
   Fade Out--Fade In, 77
   I'm Getting Married (television), 31
"She Thinks That's the Answer," D13 232
   A Doll's Life
"She's a Nut," D26 238
   On The Twentieth Century
"She's No Longer a Gypsy," D01 227
   Applause
"She's the Right Girl for Me," D36 243
   Take Me Out to the Ball Game
Shea, Beth
   Billion Dollar Baby, 57
Shearer, Douglas
   Band Wagon, The (film), 171
   Barkleys of Broadway, The (film), 153
   Good News (film) 149
   On the Town (film), 162
   Singin' in the Rain (film), 166
   Take Me Out to the Ball Game (film), 158
Shearer, Norma, 8
Sheffer, Jonathan
   Diamonds, 140
Sheller, Joan
   Subways Are for Sleeping, 70
Shelly, Norman
   Peter Pan, 133, 134

Shepard, Ruth
   Subways Are for Sleeping, 70
Shepard, Thomas Z.
   Follies (concert version), 208
Sherman, Hiram, RA01 211
Shevelove, Burt, D19 235
   Hallelujah, Baby!, 109, 113
   Jerome Robbins' Broadway, 146
   Tony Award (nomination),
      Hallelujah, Baby!, 273
Shimm, Simeon
   Good Morning, Good Night (children's book), 33
Shimoda, Yuki
   Auntie Mame (film), 182
"Shine on Your Shoes, A," D03 228
   Band Wagon, The (film), 172, 176
Shlenker, Sidney L.
   Doll's Life, A, 85
   Tony Award (nomination), *Dolls Life, A*, 274
"Shoes With Wings On," D04 229
   Barkleys of Broadway, The (film), 154, 155, 157
Shore, Dinah, RA10 212, RA11 212, RA14 212
   NBC Television, Revuers, The, 8
Short, Steve
   Lorelei, 136, 137
Show Music At Its Best--Comden and Green Perform Their Own Songs, D62 251
"Show Train," D37 243
   Two on the Aisle
Showtech
   Singin' in the Rain, special effects, 129
Shumlin, Herman
   Kiss Them For Me, 21
Sidney, Sylvia
   Auntie Mame (play), 185
Sight and Sound
   Singin' in the Rain (film), 169
Sigris, Pat
   Fade Out--Fade In, 76
Silver, Johnny
   Bonanza Bound!, 61
Silver, Ron
   Garbo Talks (film), 207

Silvers, Phil 16, 28, D10 231, T47 224
  Do Re Mi, 28, 105, 108, 109
  High Button Shoes, 93
  Tony Award (nomination), *Do Re Mi*, 273
Simmonds, Stanley
  On the Twentieth Century, 80
Simmons, Richard
  It's Always Fair Weather (film), 177
Simon, 38, 48, P06 206
  Adolph Green, 38, 48
  Alan Arkin, 38
  New York Times, 206
Simon, John
  Doll's Life, A, 89
"Simplified Language," D28 239
  Straws in the Wind, 139
Simpson, Fred R.
  What a Way to Go! (film), 190
Sinatra, Frank 16, 20, 179, D24 237, D36 243
  From Here to Eternity (film), 20, 179
  On the Town, 17
  On the Town (film), 162, 163
  Take Me Out to the Ball Game (film), 16, 158, 160, 161
Singer, Reuben
  Fade Out--Fade In, 75
Singin' in the Rain 39, 49, S16 126-131
  Comden and Green (book), 39, 126, 128-130
  Gene Kelly, 126, 130
  Gershwin Theatre, 39, 126, 130
  Harold Fielding, 39, 128
  London, 39, 128
  Maurice Rosenfield, 39, 127, 128
  Tommy Steele, 39, 128
  Tony Award (nomination), 129
  Twyla Tharp, 39, 126, 128, 129
Singin' in the Rain (film), xi, 18, 21, 38, 39, 78, 165, 169, 170, 174-176, 180-182, 202, D32 241, 242, D33 242, D58 250, F05 165-171, T38 221, T38 221
  Arthur Freed, 17, 166, 168, 171
  Best Film Lists, 169

  Comden and Green (screenplay), 17, 18, 165, 168-171
  Donald O'Connor, 166, 169
  Gene Kelly, 18, 165, 166, 169, 170
  Jean Hagen, 166, 169
  Metro-Goldwyn-Mayer, 17, 165
  "Moses Supposes," 169
  Nacio Herb Brown, 17, 165, 171
  Radio City Music Hall, 18, 169
  Screenwriters Guild Award, 18
  "Singin' in the Rain," 168
  Stanley Donen, 18, 165, 169
Sinyard, Neil
  Classic Movies, Singin' in the Rain (film), 18, 169
"Situation Wise and Saturation Wise," D17 234
  It's Always Fair Weather (film), 179, 181
Six and Company 3, 45
  (new name) Revuers, The, 4
  Village Vanguard, 3
Skin of Our Teeth, The
  By Bernstein, 145
  Comden and Green, 30, 31
  Jerome Robbins, 31
  Leland Hayward, 31
  Leonard Bernstein, 30
  New York Times, 31
  Sam Zolotow, 31
  Thornton Wilder, 31
Skipper, Bill
  Billion Dollar Baby, 57
Slaves of New York (film), P14 208
  Bernadette Peters, 40
  Betty Comden, 40, 49
  James Ivory, 40
  New York Times, 208
  Tama Janowitz, 40
  Tammy Grimes, 40
  Tri-Star Pictures, 40
"Slice, The," D16 234, D51 248
  Hallelujah, Baby!
Slutsker, Peter
  Singin' in the Rain, 127
"Small House of Uncle Thomas, The," D19 235
  Jerome Robbins' Broadway

Small, Larry
 Doll's Life, A, 86
"Smile, Smile," D16 234
 Hallelujah, Baby!, 113
Smith, Cecil
 Hallelujah, Baby!, 113
 Musical Comedy in America
  (book), 77, 126
Smith, Jack Martin
 On the Town (film), 162
 What a Way to Go! (film), 190
Smith, Justin
 What a Way to Go! (film), 191
Smith, Maggie
 Lily in Love (Jatszani Kell), 38, 207
Smith, Oliver 11, D23 237
 Band Wagon, The (film), 171, 174
 Billion Dollar Baby, 14, 56, 59
 Bonanza Bound!, 15, 61
 Fancy Free, 11
 I Love Louisa (The Band Wagon), 19
 Jerome Robbins' Broadway, 146
 On the Town, 51, 54
 Say, Darling, 100
Smith, Roger
 Auntie Mame (film), 182
Smith, Rufus
 On the Twentieth Century, 80
Smith, Sheila
 Mame (musical), 185
Snyder, F.
 On the Twentieth Century, 82
"So Eat Your Heart Out, Elizabeth Taylor"
 Betty Comden, 1
"So Far, So Good," D63 251
 Unknown Theatre Songs of Jule Styne
"So Long, Baby," D22 237
 On the Town
"So Long, Pa," D39 244
 Will Rogers Follies, The
Solid Gold Cadillac, The (film)
 Judy Holliday, 188
Solms, Kenny, D20 236
 Lorelei, 136, 137
"Some Other Time," D19 235, D22 237, D27 239, D28 239,
 D45 246, D46 246, D51 247, D56 249, D62 251
 Jerome Robbins' Broadway, 147
 Leonard Bernstein's Theatre Songs, 31, 144
 On the Town, 56
 Party With Betty Comden and Adolph Green, A, 200
"Something Greater," D01 227
 Applause, 124
Something To Do, D07 230
 with songs from *Billion Dollar Baby*
"Something's Always Happening on the River," D31 241
 Say, Darling, 104
"Somewhere," D19 236
Sondheim, Stephen, 49, 84, D19 235, D50 247, D52 248, D64 251, T14 217, T39 221
 By Bernstein, 34, 144, 145
 Company, 126
 Follies (concert version), 39, 208
 Jerome Robbins' Broadway, 146
 Leonard Bernstein's Theatre Songs, 143, 144
 Madwoman of Central Park West, The, 139
 On the Twentieth Century, 83
 West Side Story, 21
Songwriter's Hall of Fame
 Comden and Green, 37, 276
 Comden and Green (Johnny Mercer Award), 41, 48
Soulé, Olan
 Bells Are Ringing (film), 187
Sound Associates
 Singin' in the Rain, 126
Sound of Music, The
 Twentieth Century-Fox, 194
"Space Brigade"
 Two on the Aisle, 92
Spalla, John
 Singin' in the Rain, 127
"Speaking of Pals", 60
 Billion Dollar Baby
Spencer, Amy
 Singin' in the Rain, 127
Spencer, Buddy
 Fade Out--Fade In, 76
Spiller, Joanne
 Two on the Aisle, 91

Spindle, Les
   Julie Andrews (biography), 28
"Spring," D09 231
Bonanza Bound
"Spring Will Come Again"
   By Bernstein, 145
St. Clement's Church
   American Place Theatre, The, 138
St. James Theatre
   Do Re Mi, 28, 104, 108
   On the Twentieth Century, 35, 79, 82
   Subways Are For Sleeping, 29, 69, 72
Stafford, Joseph
   Peter Pan, 133
Stage 67, T48 224
Staiger, Libi
   Wonderful Town, 96
Stapleton, Jean, D05 229
   Bells Are Ringing, 65
   Bells Are Ringing (film), 187, 188
Starr, Bill
   Fade Out--Fade In, 75, 76
"Stars and Stripes Forever"
   Party With Betty Comden and Adolph Green, A, 201
Station WSFA Salute, RA17 213
Station WSM Salute, RA18 213
Statz, Mary
   Bonanza Bound!, 62
"Stay With Me, Nora," D13 232
   A Doll's Life
Stearns, David Patrick
   Will Rogers Follies, The, 118
Stebbins, Miss Della A.
   Brooklyn Ethical Culture School, 1
Steele, Tommy, D33 242
   Singin' in the Rain, 39, 128
Steell, Susan
   On the Town, 52
Stefan, Mira
   Two on the Aisle, 92
Stein, Harry
   Diamonds, 140
Stein, Joseph, D19 235
   Jerome Robbins' Broadway, 146
Steinberg, Norman
   My Favorite Year, 206

Steinbrenner, III, George M.
   Applause, 121
Stella, Antoinetta, T10 216
Stenner, Stanley
   Peter Pan, 134
Stephens, Ray
   On the Twentieth Century, 80
Stereo Review
   Paul Kresh, 44
Stern, Eric, D39 244
   Will Rogers Follies, The, 114
Stern, Isaac, 31
Stern, Kimberly
   Doll's Life, A, 86
Stet and Out Take Records
   Party With Betty Comden and Adolph Green, A, 202
Stevens, Carol
   Do Re Mi, 105, 106
Stevens, Jr., George T36 221, T38 221
Stevens, Risë, D55 249
   Lady in the Dark (recording), 29
Stevens, Roger L., D23 238
Stevens, Thelma
   Billion Dollar Baby, 57
Stevenson, Allan
   Do Re Mi, 105
"Stillman's Gym," D17 235, D18 235
   It's Always Fair Weather (film), 178
Stone, Peter, D39 244, T40 221
   Straws in the Wind, 138, 139
   Tony Award, *Will Rogers Follies, The*, 272
   Tony Award (nomination), *Will Rogers Follies, The*, 117, 274
   Will Rogers Follies, The, 41, 114, 117
Storey, Ruth
   Bells Are Ringing (film), 187
Stork, Renee
   Jerome Robbins' Broadway, 147
Story of Irene and Vernon Castle, The
   Fred Astaire, 16, 155
   Ginger Rogers, 16, 155
"Story of My Life, The"
   By Bernstein, 145

348   Comden and Green

Stradling, Harry
   Auntie Mame (film), 182
   Barkleys of Broadway, The (film), 153
Straiges, Tony
   Diamonds, 141
"Stranded Again," D26 238
   On The Twentieth Century
Straney, Paul
   Doll's Life, A, 86
"Strange Duet," D34 242
   Subways Are For Sleeping
Stratford Music Corporation
   Bells Are Ringing, 67
Stratford Music Corporation/Chappell
   Subways Are for Sleeping, 73
Stratford Music/Chappell and Company
   Fade Out--Fade In, 77
Stratford/Chappell
   Hallelujah, Baby!, 112
Stratton, Ron
   Subways Are for Sleeping, 70
Straws in the Wind, 34, D28 240, S19 138
   American Place Theatre, 201
   "Lost Word, The," 138
Streiker, Lowell D.
   Hallelujah, Baby!, 113
Stretch on the River, A (novel)
   Richard Bissell, 103
Strickland, Robert
   Good News (film), 149
"Strictly U.S.A.," D36 243
   Take Me Out to the Ball Game (film), 159-161
Stritch, Elaine, D52 248
   Follies (concert version), 39, 208
Strouse, Charles, D01 227, T30 219, T49 224
   Applause, 33, 121, 125
   Tony Award, *Applause,* 34, 124, 272
Stuart, Jan
   Will Rogers Follies, The, 118
Stuart, Liza
   Do Re Mi, 106
Stuart, Mary Ellen
   Jerome Robbins' Broadway, 147
Studio, The
   John Gregory Dunne, 194
Styne, Jule 24, 28, 41, 205, D05 229, D06 230, D10 231, D12 232, D14 233, D16 234, D19 235, D20 236, D27-D29 239-240, D31 240, D34 242, D37 243, D38 244, D44 246, D54 249, D63 251, D64 251, T17 217, T19 218, T20 218, T26 219
   Bells Are Ringing, 22, 24, 64, 68, 69, 200
   Bells Are Ringing (film), 186, 188, 189
   Bells Are Ringing, Grammy Award (nomination), 275
   "Capital Gains," *Subways Are For Sleeping,* 200
   "Catch Our Act at the Met," 200
   Do Re Mi, 28, 105, 108, 109
   Fade Out--Fade In, 74, 75, 77
   Hallelujah, Baby!, 31, 109, 112, 113
   Hallelujah, Baby!, Grammy Award (nomination), 276
   I'm Getting Married (television), 31
   "If You Hadn't--But You Did," 200
   It's Always Fair Weather, 134
   Jerome Robbins' Broadway, 146
   "Just in Time," 200
   Lorelei, 34, 136, 137
   "O! My Mysterious Lady," *Peter Pan,* 200
   On the Twentieth Century, Grammy Award (nomination), 276
   Party With Betty Comden and Adolph Green, A, 199
   "Party's Over, The," 200
   Peter Pan, 21, 133-135
   Say, Darling, 22, 100, 103, 104
   Subways Are for Sleeping, 69, 72, 73
   Theatre Hall of Fame, 37
   Tony Award, *Hallelujah, Baby!,* 31, 271
   Tony Award (nomination), *Bells Are Ringing,* 272

Tony Award (nomination), *Do Re Mi*, 273
Two on the Aisle, 18, 91, 93, 94
What a Way to Go! (film), 190
Subways Are for Sleeping, 47, 249, D28 240, D34 243, D35 243, D63 252, D64 252, S05 69-74, T20 218
  Boston, Philadelphia, 29
  "Capital Gains," 200
  Comden and Green (book/lyrics), 28, 69, 73, 74
  David Merrick, 69, 73
  Edmund G. Love, 28, 69, 72
  "I Just Can't Wait", 71, 74
  "I Was a Shoo-In", 71, 74
  Phyllis Newman, xi, 29, 71, 73, 75
  St. James Theatre, 29, 69, 72
Suffolk YM-YWHA
  Party With Betty Comden and Adolph Green, A, 39
Sullivan, Jo
  Wonderful Town, 98
Summer Holiday, 160
Summer, William (Willy)
  Bells Are Ringing, 65
  Peter Pan, 134
Summershow, T34 220, T50 225
Sumner, Bill
  Billion Dollar Baby, 57
Sun
  Billion Dollar Baby, 60
Sundberg, Clinton
  Barkleys of Broadway, The (film), 154
  Good News (film), 150
"Sunrise, Sunset," D19 235
Superman, 125
Sussman, Bruce
  Madwoman of Central Park West, The, 139
Sutherland, Alan
  Peter Pan, 134
Swanson, Don
  Lorelei, 137
"Sweet Music to Worry the Wolf Away," D03 228
  cut from *The Band Wagon*
"Swing Your Projects," D34 243
  Subways Are for Sleeping, 74

"Swing!," D40 245, D41 245, D56 250
Wonderful Town, 97, 99, 100

Tabbert, William
  Billion Dollar Baby, 57
"Take a Job," D10 232, T47 224
  Do Re Mi, 108
Take Me Out to the Ball Game (film), 16, 17, 46, 157, 160, 161, 163, D36 243, F03 157-161
  Arthur Freed, 16, 158, 160
  Betty Garrett, 16, 158
  Comden and Green (lyrics), 16, 157, 160, 161
  Esther Williams, 16, 158
  Frank Sinatra, 16, 158
  Gene Kelly, 16, 157, 160, 161
  George Wells, 16, 157
  Harry Tugend, 16, 157
  Harry Warren, 16, 160
  "It's Fate, Baby, It's Fate," 16, 159, 161
  Metro-Goldwyn-Mayer (record), 160
  "O'Brien to Ryan to Goldberg," 16, 159, 161
  Ralph Blane, 16, 160
  "Right Girl for Me, The," 16
  Roger Edens, 16, 157, 160
  Stanley Donen, 16, 157
  "Yes, Indeedy," 16, 158
"Takin' Miss Mary to the Ball," 128
  Singin' in the Rain
Talcott, Linda
  Jerome Robbins' Broadway, 147
Taliaferro, Dean
  Do Re Mi, 105, 106
  Subways Are for Sleeping, 70
"Talking to Yourself," D16 234, D51 248
  Hallelujah, Baby!, 113
Talyn, Olga
  Doll's Life, A, 86
Tams-Witmark Music Library
  Bells Are Ringing, 68
  Do Re Mi, 108
  Fade Out--Fade In, 77
  On the Twentieth Century, 83
  Say, Darling, 103

350 Comden and Green

Subways Are for Sleeping, 73
Tannen, Julius
  Singin' in the Rain (film), 166
Tanner, Stella, D25 238
"Tarentella," D29 240
  Peter Pan
Tassone, Ron
  Fade Out--Fade In, 76
Taubman, Howard
  Do Re Mi, 108
  Fade Out--Fade In, 78
  Subways Are for Sleeping, 73
  Wonderful Town, 98
Taubman, Milton
  On the Town, 51
"Taxi Number: Come Up to My Place," D22 237, D62 251
Taylor, Elizabeth
  Cleopatra, 194
Taylor, Paul
  Kennedy Center Honors for Lifetime Achievement in the Performing Arts 42, 50
Taylor, Robert, 8
Teijelo, Gerald
  On the Twentieth Century, 80
"Tell Me Why," D09 231
  Bonanza Bound
"Temptation," 128, D33 242
  Singin' in the Rain (London)
"Tender Shepherd," D29 240
  Peter Pan
Tennent Ltd., H. M., D23 237
Tewkesbury, Joan
  Peter Pan, 133, 134
"Thanks a Lot But No Thanks," D17 234, D18 235
  It's Always Fair Weather (film), 179
Tharp, Twyla
  Nine Sinatra Songs, 39, 128
  Singin' in the Rain, 39, 126, 129, 130
That Was the Week That Was, T22 218
"That's Entertainment," D03 228, D11 232
  Band Wagon, The (film), 172
  Schwartz and Dietz, *Band Wagon, The* (revue), 174
Theatre Arts

  Barkleys of Broadway, The (film), 156
  My Sister Eileen Goes on the Town with Songs, 100
  Party With Betty Comden and Adolph Green, A, 202
  Wonderful Town, 99
Theatre De Lys, 143
  Leonard Bernstein's Theatre Songs, 31, 143
Theatre Guild, The 6, 11
  Armina Marshall, 23
  Bells Are Ringing, 22, 67, 186
  Lawrence Langner, 23
  On the Town, 54
  Party With Betty Comden and Adolph Green, A, 199
  Tony Award (nomination), *Bells Are Ringing*, 273
Theatre Hall of Fame
  Comden and Green, 36, 276
  Comden and Green (inducted), 48
  Jule Styne, 36
Theatre World (list of promising new actors)
  Bonnie Franklin, 124
  Len Cariou, 124
Theatre World Award, Outstanding New Talent (1986)
  Faye Grant, 129
Theodore, Paris
  Peter Pan, 134
"There I'd Be"
  Billion Dollar Baby, 58
"There Never Was a Baby Like My Baby," D37 243
  Two on the Aisle, 92
"There She Is," D13 232
  A Doll's Life
"There's Always One Step Further Down You Can Go"
  Fade Out--Fade In, 76
"They Can't Take That Away From Me," D04 229
  Barkleys of Broadway, The (film), 155, 156
  Shall We Dance? (film), 156
"Think How It's Gonna Be," D01 227
  Applause

Index 351

"Thirties, The"
   Fade Out--Fade In, 77
This Is Your Life
   Ralph Edwards, *It's Always Fair Weather* (film), 181
Thole, Cynthia
   Singin' in the Rain, 127
Thomas, David
   Billion Dollar Baby, 57
Thomas, Richard
   Billion Dollar Baby, 57
Thompson, Ed
   Bells Are Ringing, 65
Thompson, Ella
   Hallelujah, Baby!, 111
Thompson, J. Lee
   What a Way to Go! (film), 190, 195
Thompson, Jay
   Lorelei, 136
Thompson, Jimmie
   Band Wagon, The (film), 172
   Singin' in the Rain (film), 166
Thompson, Kay
   Good News (film), 149
   On the Town (film), 17
Thorpe, Jerry
   Band Wagon, The (film), 171
Those Magnificent Men in Their Flying Machines
   Twentieth Century-Fox, 194
Three's a Crowd
   Schwartz and Dietz, 174
Thurston, Ted
   Bonanza Bound!, 61
Time
   Barkleys of Broadway, The (film), 156
   Bells Are Ringing, 68
   Bells Are Ringing (film), 189
   By Bernstein, 145
   Fade Out--Fade In, 78
   Good News (film), 152
   Hallelujah, Baby!, 113
   It's Always Fair Weather (film), 180
   On the Town, 55
   On the Town (film), 164
   On the Twentieth Century, 84
   Party With Betty Comden and Adolph Green, A, 203

Singin' in the Rain (film), 170
Subways Are for Sleeping, 74
Take Me Out to the Ball Game (film), 160
What a Way to Go! (film), 195
"Time for Parting, The," D17 235, D18 235
"Times Square," D22 237, D56 250
Tindall, Lon
   Good News (film), 150
Tipton, Jennifer
   Jerome Robbins' Broadway, 146
   Singin' in the Rain, 126
Tisch School of the Arts
   Comden and Green (master classes), 37
"To Love and to Lose"
   Bells Are Ringing (film), 188
   Comden and Green, 188
Today Show, The, T07 216, T16 217, T24 218, T25 219, T29 219, T31 220
Todd, Lorraine
   Billion Dollar Baby, 57
"Together," D26 239
   On The Twentieth Century
Toles, Michael
   Fade Out--Fade In, 76
Tolson, Pat
   Do Re Mi, 106
Tone, Richard
   Say, Darling, 101
Tonight Show, The, T03-T05 215, T21 218
Tonight Show Starring Johnny Carson, T28 219
Tony Award
   Adolph Green, *Applause*, 34, 124, 272
   Adolph Green, *Hallelujah, Baby!*, 31, 112, 271
   Adolph Green, *On the Twentieth Century*, 35, 82, 272
   Adolph Green, *Will Rogers Follies The*, 41, 272
   "Ain't Misbehavin'," 82
   Angela Lansbury, *Mame* (musical), 185
   Applause, 34, 124, 272

352 Comden and Green

Beatrice Arthur, *Mame* (musical), 185
Betty Comden, *Applause*, 34, 124, 272
Betty Comden, *Hallelujah, Baby!*, 31, 112, 271
Betty Comden, *On the Twentieth Century*, 35, 82, 272
Betty Comden, *Will Rogers Follies, The*, 39, 272
Carol Channing, *Lorelei*, 138
Cats, 88
Charles Strouse, *Applause*, 34, 124, 272
Cy Coleman, *On the Twentieth Century*, 82
Cy Coleman, *Will Rogers Follies, The*, 39
Cyril Ritchard, *Peter Pan*, 135
Donald Saddler, *Wonderful Town*, 98
Frankie Michaels, *Mame* (musical), 185
Hallelujah, Baby!, 31, 112, 271
Hallelujah, Baby!, Best Musical Play, T26 219
Jack Cassidy, *Fade Out--Fade In*, 77
Jerome Chodorov, *Wonderful Town*, 98
Jerome Robbins, *Jerome Robbins' Broadway*, 38, 148
John Cullum, *On the Twentieth Century*, 82
Joseph Fields, *Wonderful Town*, 98
Judy Holliday, *Bells Are Ringing*, 22, 67, 271
Jule Styne, *Hallelujah, Baby!*, 31, 112
Kevin Kline, *On the Twentieth Century*, 35, 82
Lauren Bacall, *Applause*, 34, 124
Lee Adams, *Applause*, 34, 124, 272
Lehman Engel, *Wonderful Town*, 98, 271
Leonard Bernstein, *Wonderful Town*, 98, 271
Lillian Hayman, *Hallelujah, Baby!*, 112, 271
Mary Martin, *Peter Pan*, 135
On the Twentieth Century, 82, 272
Peggy Cass, *Auntie Mame* (play), 184
Phyllis Newman, *Subways Are for Sleeping*, 29, 73
Raoul Pène duBois, *Wonderful Town*, 98, 271
Robert Fryer, *Wonderful Town*, 98, 271
Robin Wagner, *On the Twentieth Century*, 35, 82, 272
Ron Field, *Applause*, 34, 124, 272
Rosalind Russell, *Wonderful Town*, 20, 98, 271
Sydney Chaplin, *Bells Are Ringing*, 67, 271
Tommy Tune, *Will Rogers Follies, The*, 41, 117, 272
Will Rogers Follies, The, 41, 116, 272
Willa Kim, *Will Rogers Follies, The*, 41, 272
Wonderful Town, 20, 98, 271
Tony Award (nomination)
  Adolph Green, *Doll's Life, A*, 88, 274
  Betty Comden, *Doll's Life, A*, 88, 274
  Burt Shevelove, *Hallelujah, Baby!*, 112
  Carol Channing, *Lorelei*, 138
  Do Re Mi, 108, 273
  Doll's Life, A, 38, 274
  Garson Kanin, *Do Re Mi*, 108, 273
  Harold Prince, *On the Twentieth Century*, 82, 273
  Imogene Coca, *On the Twentieth Century*, 82, 273
  Irene Sharaff, *Hallelujah, Baby!*, 112, 273
  Kevin Carlisle, *Hallelujah, Baby!*, 112, 273
  Larry Grossman, *Doll's Life, A*, 88, 274
  Leslie Uggams, *Hallelujah, Baby!*, 112, 271

Madeline Kahn, *On the Twentieth Century*, 82, 273
Nancy Dussault, *Do Re Mi*, 108, 273
Nancy Walker, *Do Re Mi*, 108, 273
On the Twentieth Century, 82, 273
Orson Bean, *Subways Are for Sleeping*, 73
Phil Silvers, *Do Re Mi*, 108, 273
Robert Hooks, *Hallelujah, Baby!*, 112, 273
Rosalind Russell, *Auntie Mame* (play), 184
Singin' in the Rain, 129
Tony Award for Best Featured Performer in a Musical
Newman, Phyllis, *Subways Are For Sleeping*, 29
Tony Awards 1968, T26 219
Tony Awards 1969, T27 219
Tony Awards 1970, T30 219
Tony Awards 1978, T32 220
Tony Awards 1991, T40 221
"Too Marvellous for Words," D33 242
Tookoian, Arthur
 Peter Pan, 134
Tormé, Mel, T15 233
 Good News (film), 149, 153
Torre, Marie, T10 216
Towbin, Beryl
 Bells Are Ringing, 65
Town Productions
 Party With Betty Comden and Adolph Green, A, 199
"Tradition," D19 236
Trayer, Leslie
 Jerome Robbins' Broadway, 147
Treasure Girl, 47, D60 251
Treat, Roger
 On the Town, 52
Tree Grows in Brooklyn, A, 97
Tri-Star Pictures
 Slaves of New York (film), 40, 208
Tribute to Broadway, A
 Comden and Green (Theatre Hall of Fame), 37
 Uris Theatre, 37

Trinity School
 New Yorkers, The, 38
"Triplets," D03 228
 Band Wagon, The (film), 173
Tristan and Isolde
 Revuers, The, 6
Trocadero (Hollywood), 63
 Revuers, The, 10, 15, 46, 205
Trouble in Tahiti
 Leonard Bernstein's Theatre Songs, 144
Troy, Ellen
 Jerome Robbins' Broadway, 147
"True," D09 231
 Bonanza Bound
Trueblood, Paul, 42, D08 231, D28 240
Trueblood, Paul (at the piano)
 Party With Betty Comden and Adolph Green, A, 199
Trujillo, Sergio
 Jerome Robbins' Broadway, 147
Trunell, Dee
 Band Wagon, The (film), 172
"Try to Love Me," D31 240, 241
 Say, Darling, 104
"Tschaikovsky," D55 249
 Lady in the Dark (recording), 29
Tucker, Forest
 Auntie Mame (film), 182
Tucker, Ian
 Lorelei, 136, 137
 Peter Pan, 134
Tucker, Robert
 Barkleys of Broadway, The (film), 153
 It's Always Fair Weather (film), 176
 Peter Pan, 134
 Take Me Out to the Ball Game (film), 157
Tugend, Harry
 Take Me Out to the Ball Game (film), 16, 157, 160, D36 243
Tune, Tommy
 Tony Award, *Will Rogers Follies, The*, 41, 117, 272
 Will Rogers Follies, The, 41, 114, 117, 119
Tunick, Jonathan, D52 248

354 Comden and Green

Turnell, Dee
  Barkleys of Broadway, The (film), 154
Turner, Aimee
  Will Rogers Follies, The, 115
Tuttle, William
  Band Wagon, The (film), 171
  Bells Are Ringing (film), 187
  It's Always Fair Weather (film), 177
  Singin' in the Rain (film), 166
Tuvim (Holliday), Judy, xi, 3, 10, RA01-RA20 211-214, T01 215
  Judy Holliday, 67
  Max Gordon, Village Vanguard, 3
  Revuers, The, 45, 67, 205, 241
  Six and Company, 3
  Trocadero, The Revuers, 10
Tweddell, Frank
  Fade Out--Fade In, 75
Twentieth Century (play)
  Ben Hecht and Charles MacArthur, 35
Twentieth Century-Fox, 174
  Cleopatra, 194
  Dr. Doolittle, 194
  Judy Tuvim, 10
  Planet of the Apes, 194
  Revuers, The, 11
  Sound of Music, The, 194
  Those Magnificent Men in Their Flying Machines, 194
  What a Way to Go! (film), 30, 190, 194
Twilight Zone, The, T47 224
Two on the Aisle, xiii, 23, 46, 94, 200, D27 239, D28 239, D37 243, D53 248, D62 251, D63 251, S09 91-94
  Bert Lahr, 18, 91, 93, 94
  "Catch Our Act at the Met," 92, 200
  Comden and Green, 18, 91, 93, 94
  Dolores Gray, 18, 91, 93, 94
  "If You Hadn't--But You Did," 92, 200
  Jule Styne, 18, 91, 93, 94
  Mark Hellinger Theatre, 18, 91, 93

Tyler, Andi
  Jerome Robbins' Broadway, 147
Tyler, Jeanne
  Two on the Aisle, 92

Udall, Lynn
  Diamonds, 140
"Ugg-A-Wugg," D29 240
  Peter Pan, 135
Uggams, Leslie, 219, D16 234, D51 248, D54 249, D63 252
  Hallelujah, Baby!, 31, 110, 113
  Most Promising New Broadway Actress, *Variety*, 31
  Outer Circle Award, *Hallelujah, Baby!*, 31
  Tony Award, *Hallelujah, Baby!*, 271
"Ugly, Ugly Gal," D63 251
  cut from *Hallelujah, Baby!*
Ukena, Jr., Paul
  Will Rogers Follies, The, 114
"Underworld," D07 230
United Artists
  Garbo Talks (film), 207
Unknown Theatre Songs of Jule Styne, The, D63 251
"Up in Smoke," D09 231
"Up, Up, Up," D57 249, T50 225
  Madwoman of Central Park West, The, 35, 140
Urbina, Jillana
  Will Rogers Follies, The, 114, 115
Urich, Tom
  Applause, 121
Uris Theatre
  Tribute to Broadway, A, 37
USA Today
  Will Rogers Follies, The, 118
"Usher from the Mezzanine, The," D14 233
  Fade Out--Fade In, 79

Valentine, Dean
  On the Twentieth Century, 84
Valles
  Barkleys of Broadway, The (film), 153
  Good News (film), 149

Take Me Out to the Ball Game (film), 157
Valor, Henrietta
　Applause, 122
Vamps and Rideouts, D64 251
Van Dyke, Dick, D38 244
　What a Way to Go! (film), 30, 191, 194
Van Lein, Charlotte
　Two on the Aisle, 92
Van Rhein, Nancy
　Do Re Mi, 105
Van Treuren, Martin
　Singin' in the Rain, 127
Van, Shirley
　Billion Dollar Baby, 56
Vancouver Film Festival (honors)
　Comden and Green, 276
Vanselow, Robert
　Peter Pan, 134
Vargas, Ben
　Bells Are Ringing, 65
Variety, T43-T46 223-224
　Applause, 124
　Auntie Mame (film), 185
　Band Wagon, The (film), 175
　Barkleys of Broadway, The (film), 156
　Bells Are Ringing (film), 189
　Bonanza Bound!, 64
　Good News (film), 152
　Hallelujah, Baby!, 112
　I Want to Go Home (film), 209
　It's Always Fair Weather (film), 180
　Leslie Uggams, Most Promising New Broadway Actress, 31
　On the Town (film), 164
　On the Twentieth Century, 82
　Revuers, The, 8, 9
　Singin' in the Rain (film), 170
　Take Me Out to the Ball Game (film), 160
　What a Way to Go! (film), 195
Variety (sketch)
　Party With Betty Comden and Adolph Green, A, 199
Varrone, Gene
　Fade Out--Fade In, 75, 76
　Subways Are for Sleeping, 69, 70

"Varsity Drag, The," D15 233
　Good News (film), 151, 152
"Vaudeville Ain't Dead," D37 243
　Two on the Aisle
Vaughan, Melanie
　On the Twentieth Century, 80
Veazie, Carol
　Auntie Mame (film), 182
Venice Film Festival
　I Want to Go Home (film), 209
"Venice Gavotte, The," D50 247
　Candide
Venice Theatre
　Cradle Will Rock, The, 30
Vera-Ellen, D24 238
　On the Town (film), 162, 163
Verdun, Gwen
　Bonanza Bound!, 62
Vernon, Wally
　What a Way to Go! (film), 191
"Veronique," D26 238
　On the Twentieth Century, 81
Vest, Bud
　Hallelujah, Baby!, 110, 111
Village Vanguard, 3-5, 21
　Maxwell Bodenheim (poet), 3
　Revuers, The, 4-6, 9, 205
　Six and Company 3
Vita, Michael
　Doll's Life, A, 86
Vogel, David
　On the Twentieth Century, 80
Voltaire
　Candide, 247
Von Reinhold, Calvin
　Say, Darling, 101
Von Tilzer, Harry, D36 243
　Diamonds, 140
　Take Me Out to the Ball Game (film), 160
Vosburgh, David
　Doll's Life, A, 86

Wagg, Jim
　Doll's Life, A, 86
Wagner, Robin, T32 220
　Jerome Robbins' Broadway, 146
　On the Twentieth Century, 35, 79, 83, 85
　Tony Award, On the Twentieth Century, 35, 272

356 Comden and Green

Waine, Allan
  Billion Dollar Baby, 57
"Waiting," D10 231, T47 224
  Do Re Mi, 106, 108
Wald, Jane
  What a Way to Go! (film), 191
Walker, Don, D20 236, D40 244
  Lorelei, 136
  Wonderful Town, 95
Walker, Nancy 16, D10 231, D21 236, D22 237, D45 246, D51 247, D56 249, D61 250, T47 224
  Do Re Mi, 28, 105, 109
  On the Town, 51
  Tony Award (nomination), *Do Re Mi*, 273
  Wonderful Town, 98
Wall Street Journal
  Applause, 125
  Hallelujah, Baby!, 113
  Jerome Robbins' Broadway, 148
  Lorelei, 138
  Madwoman of Central Park West, The, 140
  On the Twentieth Century, 83
  Singin' in the Rain, 129
  Will Rogers Follies, The, 118
Wallace, Anne
  Bells Are Ringing, 65
Wallace, Mike, T19 218
Wallach, Eli
  Funny (film), 40, 208
Walter, Bruno, 9
Walters, Charles
  Barkleys of Broadway, The (film), 153, 156
  Easter Parade (film), 152
  Good News (film), 149, 152
Walton, Jim, D52 248
Walton, Tony
  Jerome Robbins' Broadway, 146
  Tony Award (nomination), *Will Rogers Follies, The*, 117, 274
  Will Rogers Follies, The, 41, 114, 117, 119
Wann, Jim
  Diamonds, 140
Ward, John
  Bonanza Bound!, 62
Waring, Wendy

Will Rogers Follies, The, 114, 115
Warner Bros.
  Auntie Mame (film), 182, 185
  Auntie Mame (video), 182
  Simon, 206
Warner Theatre Productions
  Doll's Life, A, 85
  Tony Award (nomination), *Dolls Life, A*, 274
Warren, Harry, D04 228
  Barkleys of Broadway, The (film), 153, 155
  Easter Parade (film), 15
  Take Me Out to the Ball Game (film), 16, 160
Warrier's Husband, The
  Betty Comden (Pomposia), 2
Washington, Shelley
  Singin' in the Rain, 127
Wasserstein, Wendy
  Isn't It Romantic?, 38, 206
"Watch My Dust," D16 234
  Hallelujah, Baby!
Waterman, Willard
  Auntie Mame (film), 182
Waters, Jan, D11 232
Watt, Douglas
  By Bernstein, 145
  Diamonds, 141
  Doll's Life, A, 89
  Lorelei, 137
  On the Twentieth Century, 83
  Singin' in the Rain, 130
  Will Rogers Follies, The, 118
Watts, Jr., Richard
  Applause, 125
  Bells Are Ringing, 68
  Fade Out--Fade In, 78
  Hallelujah, Baby!, 113
  Party With Betty Comden and Adolph Green, A, 202
  Peter Pan, 135
  Say, Darling, 103
  Subways Are for Sleeping, 73
  Two on the Aisle, 93
  Wonderful Town, 99
Wayne and Shuster, T47 224
Wayne, David, D31 241
  Say, Darling, 101
WCBS Television, T17 217

"We're Goin' on the Town"
   On the Town (film), 163
"We're Heading For a Wedding,"
   D39 244
   Will Rogers Follies, The
"Wedding Dance," D19 235
   Jerome Robbins' Broadway
"Wedding of the Painted Doll," 128
   Singin' in the Rain
"Weekend in the Country, A," D04 229
   Barkleys of Broadway, The
Weeks, Alan
   Hallelujah, Baby!, 110
Weidman, John
   Diamonds, 140
Weill, Kurt, D55 249
   Lady in the Dark, 29, 47
Weiss, Jim
   Subways Are for Sleeping, 70
Weiss, Marc B.
   By Bernstein, 145
Weitzenhoffer, Max
   Tony Award, *Will Rogers Follies, The*, 272
   Will Rogers Follies, The, 114
"Welcome,"
   By Bernstein, 145
"Welcome to the Theatre," D01 227
   Applause
Welles, Orson, 174
   Cradle Will Rock, The, 29
Wells, George, D36 243
   Take Me Out to the Ball Game (film), 16, 157, 160
"Wendy," D29 240
   Peter Pan
Werner, Fred
   Leonard Bernstein's Theatre Songs, 143
Weslow, William
   Wonderful Town, 96
West Side Story, D19 235
   Jerome Robbins, 21
   Jerome Robbins' Broadway, 40, 147
   Leonard Bernstein, 21
   Leonard Bernstein's Theatre Songs, 144
   Stephen Sondheim, 21

West, Bernie
   Bells Are Ringing, 65
   Bells Are Ringing (film), 187, 188
Westbrook, Frank
   On the Town, 51
Weston, Jack
   Bells Are Ringing, 65
Westport Country Playhouse, 6, 16, 26
   Gene Kelly, 6
   Party With Betty Comden and Adolph Green, A, 201
   Revuers, The, 6
Westside Theatre, Chelsea Theatre Center
   By Bernstein, 144, 145
"What a Waste," D40 245, D41 245
   Leonard Bernstein's Theatre Songs, 144
   Wonderful Town
What a Way to Go! (film), 47, 195, D38 244, F10 190-196
   Arthur P. Jacobs, 190, 194
   Busby Berkeley, 30, 195
   Comden and Green, 30, 190, 195, 196
   Dean Martin, 30, 191, 194
   Dick Van Dyke, 30, 191, 194
   Edith Head, 194
   Gene Kelly, 30, 190, 191, 194, 196
   Gwen Davis, 30, 190
   J. Lee Thompson, 190, 195
   Paul Newman, 30, 191, 194, 196
   Robert Mitchum, 30, 191, 194
   Shirley MacLaine, 30, 191, 194, 195, 196
   Twentieth Century-Fox, 30, 190, 194
"What Are We Here For?" D60 250
   Remember These
"What Is This Feeling in the Air?" D34 242, D35 242
   Subways Are For Sleeping, 74
"What's New at the Zoo?," D10 232
   Do Re Mi, 28, 107-109
Wheeler, Hugh
   Candide (revival), 40

"When the Weather's Better," D63 251
Unknown Theatre Songs of Jule Styne
"When You Help a Friend Out," D35 242
  cut from *Subways Are For Sleeping*
"When You Walk Down Mainstreet With Me," D24 238
  On The Town (film)
"Where's the Boy?," D60 250
  Remember These
"Where's the Girl?," D60 250
  Remember These
White, James
  Peter Pan, 134
White, Miles
  Jerome Robbins' Broadway, 146
White, Roxanna
  Lorelei, 137
Whiting, Richard, D33 242
"Who Knows What Might Have Been? D34 242, D35 242
  Subways Are For Sleeping, 74
"Who's That Girl?" D01 227
  Applause
"Why Do I Feel So Good?,"
  It's Always Fair Weather (film), 182
Wilbur, Richard, D50 247
  Candide, 40
  Leonard Bernstein's Theatre Songs, 143, 144
Wilcox, Larry, D33 241
  Singin' in the Rain
"Wild West Show/Dog Act," D39 244
  Will Rogers Follies, The
Wilder, Thornton
  Skin of Our Teeth, The, 31
Wilkes, Patty (Pat)
  Bells Are Ringing, 65
  Wonderful Town, 96
Will Rogers Follies, The 42, 49, D39 245, S14 114-119, T40 221
  Columbia Records, 117
  Comden and Green, 41, 114, 116-118
  Cy Coleman, 41, 114, 116, 117
  Drama Desk Award, 41, 117
  Keith Carradine, xi, 41, 114, 118
  Palace Theatre, 41, 114, 116
  Peter Stone, 41, 114, 117, 118
  Tommy Tune, 41, 114, 117, 119
  Tony Award, 41, 116, 117, 272
  Tony Walton, 41, 114
  Willa Kim, 41, 114, 117, 119
Will Rogers Follies, The (record album)
  Grammy Award, 41, 117
Williams Singers, D25 238
Williams, Andy, T13 216
Williams, Ann
  Applause, 121
Williams, Esther, D36 243
  Take Me Out to the Ball Game (film), 16, 158, 160
Williams, Gwen RA03 211, RA05-RA07 212, RA09 212, RA12 212, RA15-RA17 213, RA20 213
Williams, Helene, D07 230
Williams, Julie
  Two on the Aisle, 91
Williams, Rita, D25 238
Williams, Sammy
  Applause, 122
Williamson, Laurie
  Singin' in the Rain, 127
Willis, Edwin B.
  Band Wagon, The (film), 171
  Barkleys of Broadway, The (film), 153
  Good News (film), 149
  It's Always Fair Weather (film), 177
  On the Town (film), 162
  Singin' in the Rain (film), 166
  Take Me Out to the Ball Game (film), 157
Willis, Gordon
  Singin' in the Rain, 126
Wilson, Andrea
  Party With Betty Comden and Adolph Green, A, 199
Wilson, Billy
  Bells Are Ringing, 65
Wilson, Edwin
  Jerome Robbins' Broadway, 148
  Lorelei, 138

Madwoman of Central Park West, The, 140
On the Twentieth Century, 83
Singin' in the Rain, 129
Will Rogers Follies, The, 118
Winston, Helen F.
   What a Way to Go! (film), 191
Winter Garden Theatre
   Peter Pan, 21, 133, 135
   Wonderful Town, 19, 95, 98
Winter, Richard
   Peter Pan, 134
Winters, Ralph E.
   On the Town (film), 162
Wise, Joseph
   On the Twentieth Century, 80
Wise, Scott
   Jerome Robbins' Broadway, 147
Wish You Were Here
   Phyllis Newman, 24
"Witches' Brew," D16 234
"Without You," D39 244
   Will Rogers Follies, The, 116
Wittop, Freddie
   Subways Are for Sleeping, 69
Wizard of Oz, The
   Bert Lahr (Cowardly Lion), 18
WNEW Television, T19 218
WNEW Television, *Summershow*
   Party With Betty Comden and Adolph Green, A, 202
Wolk, Max, T14 217
Wolsk, Eugene V.
   Singin' in the Rain, 127
"Woman Alone, A," D13 232
A Doll's Life
Women's Wear Daily
   Applause, 125
   By Bernstein, 145
   Doll's Life, A, 88
   Hallelujah, Baby!, 113
   Lorelei, 138
   On the Twentieth Century, 83
   Wonderful Town, 248, 250, 251, 271, D27 239, D28 239, D40 244, D41 245, D43-D45 246-247, D53 248, D62 251, S10 95-100, T45 223
   (based on) *My Sister Eileen*, 19, 95, 97
   Arnold Horwitt, 19, 97
   Boston, New Haven, Philadelphia, 19, 98
   By Bernstein, 145
   City Center, 98
   Comden and Green (lyrics), 19, 95, 97-100
   George Abbott, 19, 95, 97-100
   Leonard Bernstein, 19, 95, 97-99, 200
   Leonard Bernstein's Theatre Songs, 144
   Leroy Anderson, 19
   New York Drama Critics Circle Award, 98
   Party With Betty Comden and Adolph Green, A, 23
   "Quiet Girl, A," 200
   Robert Fryer, 19, 95, 97
   Rosalind Russell, 19, 95, 98, 99
   Tony Award, 20, 98, 271
   Winter Garden Theatre, 19, 95, 98
Wonderful Town (film)
   Betty Garrett, 98
   Jack Lemmon, 98
   Janet Leigh, 98
Wood, Deedee
   Do Re Mi, 105
Wood, Eugene R.
   Subways Are for Sleeping, 70
Wood, Wilson
   Barkleys of Broadway, The (film), 154
   It's Always Fair Weather (film), 177
Woodburn, Gordon
   Bells Are Ringing, 65
"Words, Words, Words," (Martin's Laughing Song), D50 247
Candide
Works Progress Administration, 29
World Journal Tribune
   Hallelujah, Baby!, 113
World of Entertainment, The
   Hugh Fordin, (book), 20, 163
World Telegram and Sun
   Do Re Mi, 109
   Peter Pan, 135
Wormer, Sheila, D07 230
"Would You?," 128, D33 242
   Singin' in the Rain

Wright, Elaine
   Jerome Robbins' Broadway, 147
Wrightson, Earl, T17 217
"Wrong Note Rag, The," D28 239,
   D40 245, D41 245, D45 246,
   D56 249, D62 251
   Leonard Bernstein's Theatre
    Songs, 144
   Party With Betty Comden and
    Adolph Green, A, 200
   Wonderful Town, 97, 99, 200
Wyatt, Jerry
   Applause, 121, 122
Wyatt, Richard
   Peter Pan, 133, 134

"Ya Got Me," D19 235, D21 236,
   D22 237
   Jerome Robbins' Broadway, 147
Yeager, Barbara
   Jerome Robbins' Broadway, 147
Yeargan, Michael H.
   By Bernstein, 144, 145
Yearsley, Alice
   Jerome Robbins' Broadway, 147
"Yes, Indeedy," D36 243
   Take Me Out to the Ball Game
    (film), 16, 158, 160, 161
York Theatre Company
   On the Twentieth Century, 83
"You Are My Lucky Star," 128,
   D32 241, D33 242
   Singin' in the Rain (film), 168
"You Can Count on Me"
   On the Town (film), 163
"You Gotta Have a Gimmick," D19
   235
   Jerome Robbins' Broadway
"You Have Everything," D03 228
   cut from *The Band Wagon*
"You Interest Me," D13 232
   A Doll's Life
"You Mustn't Be Discouraged,"
   D14 233, D64 252
   Fade Out--Fade In
"You Stepped Out of a Dream,"
   128
   Singin' in the Rain
"You Were Meant for Me," 128,
   D32 241
   Singin' in the Rain (film), 17, 167

Singin' in the Rain (musical),
   169
"You'd Be Hard to Replace," D04
   229
   Barkleys of Broadway, The (film),
    154
"You're Awful," D24 238
   On the Town (film), 163
"You're the Cream in My Coffee"
   Good News (1974), 152
Young Men's-Women's Hebrew
   Association
   Lyrics and Lyricists, 205
Young, Cy
   Subways Are for Sleeping, 69,
    70
Young, Richard
   Do Re Mi, 106
Youngman, Christina
   Will Rogers Follies, The, 115
Youth Theatre
   Alvin Hammer, 4

Zanuck, Darryl
   Twentieth Century-Fox, 194
Ziegfeld, Florenz, 41
"Ziegfeld Follies, The," D39 245
   Will Rogers Follies, The
Ziegler, William
   Auntie Mame (film), 182
Zien, Chip
   Diamonds, 141
Zimmerman, Leigh
   Will Rogers Follies, The, 114,
    115
Zippel, David
   Diamonds, 141
Zipprodt, Patricia
   Jerome Robbins' Broadway, 146
Zoe, Nina
   Greta Garbo, *Garbo Talks* (film),
    207
Zolotow, Sam
   Skin of Our Teeth, The, 31
Zucco, George
   Barkleys of Broadway, The (film),
    154
Zunser, Jesse
   Band Wagon, The (film), 175
Zweibel, Alan
   Diamonds, 140

About the Author

ALICE McDONNELL ROBINSON is Associate Professor of Theatre at the Baltimore County Campus of the University of Maryland, where she teaches courses on theatre history, American theatre, speech for the actor, and the oral interpretation of literature. She has published numerous articles, and her books include *Notable Women in the American Theatre* (Greenwood Press, 1989). She is also a play director and an actress, as well as a member of the American Society for Theatre Research, the Association of Theatre in Higher Education, and the East Central Theatre Conference.

**Titles in
Bio-Bibliographies in the Performing Arts**

Milos Forman: A Bio-Bibliography
Thomas J. Slater

Kate Smith: A Bio-Bibliography
Michael R. Pitts

Patty Duke: A Bio-Bibliography
Stephen L. Eberly

Carole Lombard: A Bio-Bibliography
Robert D. Matzen

Eva Le Gallienne: A Bio-Bibliography
Robert A. Schanke

Julie Andrews: A Bio-Bibliography
Les Spindle

Richard Widmark: A Bio-Bibliography
Kim Holston

Orson Welles: A Bio-Bibliography
Bret Wood

Ann Sothern: A Bio-Bibliography
Margie Schultz

Alice Faye: A Bio-Bibliography
Barry Rivadue

Jennifer Jones: A Bio-Bibliography
Jeffrey L. Carrier

Cary Grant: A Bio-Bibliography
Beverley Bare Buehrer

Maureen O'Sullivan: A Bio-Bibliography
Connie J. Billips

Ava Gardner: A Bio-Bibliography
Karin J. Fowler

Jean Arthur: A Bio-Bibliography
Arthur Pierce and Douglas Swarthout

Donna Reed: A Bio-Bibliography
Brenda Scott Royce

Gordon MacRae: A Bio-Bibliography
Bruce R. Leiby

Mary Martin: A Bio-Bibliography
Barry Rivadue

Irene Dunne: A Bio-Bibliography
Margie Schultz

Anne Baxter: A Bio-Bibliography
Karin J. Fowler

Tallulah Bankhead: A Bio-Bibliography
Jeffrey L. Carrier

Jessica Tandy: A Bio-Bibliography
Milly S. Barranger

Janet Gaynor: A Bio-Bibliography
Connie Billips

James Stewart: A Bio-Bibliography
Gerard Molyneaux

Joseph Papp: A Bio-Bibliography
Barbara Lee Horn

Henry Fonda: A Bio-Bibliography
Kevin Sweeney

Edwin Booth: A Bio-Bibliography
L. Terry Oggel

Ethel Merman: A Bio-Bibliography
George B. Bryan

Lauren Bacall: A Bio-Bibliography
Brenda Scott Royce

Joseph Chaikin: A Bio-Bibliography
Alex Gildzen and Dimitris Karageorgiou

Richard Burton: A Bio-Bibliography
Tyrone Steverson

Maureen Stapleton: A Bio-Bibliography
Jeannie M. Woods

David Merrick: A Bio-Bibliography
Barbara Lee Horn

Vivien Leigh: A Bio-Bibliography
Cynthia Marylee Molt

Robert Mitchum: A Bio-Bibliography
Jerry Roberts

Agnes Moorehead: A Bio-Bibliography
Lynn Kear

Colleen Dewhurst: A Bio-Bibliography
Barbara Lee Horn

Helen Hayes: A Bio-Bibliography
Donn B. Murphy and Stephen Moore

Boris Karloff: A Bio-Bibliography
Beverley Bare Buehrer

Betty Grable: A Bio-Bibliography
Larry Billman

Ellen Stewart and La Mama:
A Bio-Bibliography
Barbara Lee Horn

Lucille Lortel: A Bio-Bibliography
Sam McCready

Noël Coward: A Bio-Bibliography
Stephen Cole

Oliver Smith: A Bio-Bibliography
Tom Mikotowicz

Katharine Cornell: A Bio-Bibliography
Lucille M. Pederson